The Asia-Pacific Profile

This book is part of a series produced in association with The Open University.
The list of other books in the series is:

Asia-Pacific in the New World Order,
edited by Anthony McGrew and Christopher Brook

Economic Dynamism in the Asia-Pacific,
edited by Grahame Thompson

Culture and Society in the Asia-Pacific,
edited by Richard Maidment and Colin Mackerras

Governance in the Asia-Pacific,
edited by Richard Maidment, David Goldblatt and Jeremy Mitchell

The books form part of the Open University course DD302 *Pacific Studies*.
Details of this and other Open University courses can be obtained from the
Call Centre, PO Box 724, The Open University, Milton Keynes MK7 6ZS, United Kingdom:
tel. +44 (0)1908 653231, e-mail ces-gen@open.ac.uk

Alternatively, you may visit the Open University website at http://www.open.ac.uk where you can learn
more about the wide range of courses and packs offered at all levels by The Open University.

For availability of other course components, contact Open University Worldwide Ltd,
The Berrill Building, Walton Hall, Milton Keynes MK7 6AA, United Kingdom:
tel. +44 (0)1908 858785; fax +44 (0)1908 858787; e-mail ouwenq@open.ac.uk;
website http://www.ouw.co.uk

The Asia-Pacific Profile

*Edited by Bernard Eccleston, Michael Dawson
and Deborah McNamara*

London and New York

in association with

The Open
University

First published 1998 by Routledge
11 New Fetter Lane, London EC4P 4EE

Simultaneously published in the USA and Canada
by Routledge
29 West 35th Street, New York, NY 10001

© The Open University 1998

Edited, designed and typeset by The Open University

Printed and bound in the United Kingdom by the Alden Group, Oxford

British Library Cataloguing in Publication Data
A catalogue record for this book is available from The British Library

Library of Congress Cataloging in Publication Data
A catalogue record for this book has been requested

ISBN 0-415-17279-9 (hbk)
ISBN 0-415-17280-2 (pbk)

1.1

Contents

PART 1

Maps of the Asia-Pacific

compiled by Bernard Eccleston

PART 2

Country by country digest

edited by Bernard Eccleston with Deborah McNamara

Appendix A: data for figures in Part 2

Demographic indicators

Economic indicators

Social indicators

Appendix B: data for Brunei, Macau, the Russian Far East and the Pacific Islands

Demographic indicators

Economic indicators

Social indicators

Documents

compiled by Michael Dawson

Series preface

The five volumes in this series are part of a new Open University course, *Pacific Studies*, which has been produced within the Faculty of Social Sciences. The appearance of *Pacific Studies* is due to the generous and enthusiastic support the course has received from the University and in particular from colleagues within the Faculty of Social Sciences. The support has been especially remarkable given that this course has ventured into relatively uncharted scholarly waters. The potential risks were readily apparent but the commitment always remained firm. I am very grateful.

There are too many people to thank individually, both within and outside of the Open University, but I must record my appreciation for some of them. Within the University, I would like to acknowledge my colleagues Anthony McGrew and Grahame Thompson. *Pacific Studies* could not have been made without them. Their role was central. They were present when the course was conceived and they lived with it through to the final stages. They also made the experience of making this course both very enjoyable and intellectually stimulating. Christopher Brook and Bernard Eccleston made an enormous contribution to the course far beyond their editorial roles in two of the books in the series. They read the successive drafts of all chapters with great care and their perceptive comments helped to improve these volumes considerably. David Goldblatt and Jeremy Mitchell, because of their other commitments, may have joined the Course Team relatively late in the production process, but their contributions, especially to *Governance in the Asia-Pacific* have been much appreciated. Michael Dawson played an especially important role in the production of *The Asia-Pacific Profile* and his calm and genial presence was valued as always. Jeremy Cooper and Eleanor Morris of the BBC were responsible for the excellent audio-visual component of *Pacific Studies*. Anne Carson, the Course Manager of *Pacific Studies*, was consistently cheerful and helpful. All of the volumes in this series have been greatly improved by the editorial craftsmanship of Stephen Clift, Tom Hunter and Kate Hunter, who have been under great pressure throughout the production of this course, but nevertheless delivered work of real quality. The striking cover designs of Richard Hoyle and Jonathan Davies speak for themselves and the artwork of Ray Munns in all five volumes has been most impressive. Paul Smith, whose recent retirement from the University will leave a very real gap, made his usual remarkable contribution in providing unusual and interesting illustrations. Giles Clark of the Copublishing Department was a constant source of encouragement and in addition his advice was always acute. Our colleagues in Project Control, especially Deborah Bywater, and in the Operations Division of the University, were far more understanding and helpful than I had any right to expect. Anne Hunt and Mary Dicker, who have been responsible for so much of the work in this Faculty over the past several years, performed to their usual exacting standards by preparing the manuscripts in this series for publication with remarkable speed and accuracy. They were very ably assisted by Chris Meeks and Doreen Pendlebury.

Pacific Studies could not have been made without the help of academic colleagues based in the UK as well as in the Asia-Pacific region. This series of books has drawn on their scholarship and their expertise but above all on their generosity. I must record my appreciation to all of them for their participation in this project. The Course Team owes an especially large debt to Dr Gerry Segal, Senior Fellow at the International Institute for Strategic Studies, who was the External Assessor of *Pacific Studies*. He was both an enthusiastic supporter of this project as well as a very shrewd critic. His wise counsel and tough advice have greatly improved the volumes in this series. It has been a pleasure to work with Professor Colin Mackerras, Director of the Key Centre for Asian Studies and Languages at Griffith University in Australia. Griffith University and the Open University have collaborated over the production of *Pacific Studies*; an arrangement that has worked extremely well. The success of this collaboration has been due in no small part to Colin. Over the past three years I have come to appreciate his many qualities particularly his immense knowledge of the Asia-Pacific region as well as his patience and courtesy in dealing with those of us who know far less. I would also like to thank all of those colleagues at Griffith who have helped to make this collaboration so successful and worthwhile, especially Professor Tony Bennett, who played a key role during the initial discussions between the two universities. Frank Gibney, President of the Pacific Basin Institute, was always available with help, advice and encouragement. It was one of the real pleasures of this project to have met and worked with Frank and the PBI. This series has also benefited considerably from the enthusiasm and insight of Victoria Smith at Routledge.

The production of *Pacific Studies* was helped greatly through the assistance of several foundations. The Daiwa Anglo-Japanese Foundation awarded this project two grants and its Director General, Christopher Everett, was a model of generosity and support. He invited the Course Team to use the attractive facilities of the Foundation; an invitation which was accepted with enthusiasm. The grant from The Great Britain Sasakawa Foundation was also greatly appreciated as was the advice, encouragement and the shrewd counsel of Peter Hand, the Administrator of the Foundation. Mr Tomoyuki Sakurai the Director of the Japan Foundation in London was always interested in the development of *Pacific Studies* and I have no doubt that this resulted in a generous grant from the Foundation. Mr Haruhisa Takeuchi, formerly Director of the Japan Information and Cultural Centre, was most supportive during the early stages of this project and his successor at the Centre, Mr Masatoshi Muto has been no less helpful. Finally, I must record my thanks to the British Council in Australia for their assistance which was much appreciated.

Richard Maidment
Chair, *Pacific Studies*
Milton Keynes, November 1997

The Asia-Pacific Profile: preface

When it was proposed that we have a resource book to complement and supplement the other four books in this series two positive models came to mind. Both the *Third World Atlas* and *The United Sates in the Twentieth Century: Key Documents* are widely regarded as key supporting texts by those working with Open University courses U208 and D214 respectively. They also provided a model to follow because of the interest shown in these books by a wider audience.

In addition to presenting maps and documents that reflect many of the main themes affecting Asia-Pacific, I managed to convince the Course Team that we needed to provide statistical resources that would allow readers to develop their own comparative assessment of this key area. It was important though that the statistical data was designed to relieve the monotony of ploughing through large numbers of tables hence the multiplicity of diagrams in Part 2.

Our coverage of Asia-Pacific in this volume is taken literally to include all states around the rim of the Pacific Ocean as well as all the Pacific Islands within. Our cut-off point for information used in all three parts of this *Profile* was based on documentation available up to Spring 1997.

By having such a wide scope the production of *The Asia-Pacific Profile* inevitably meant an extensive reliance on teamwork between contributors, editorial staff, graphic designers, cartographers and other support staff. Three interlocking teams worked on the three parts and each one was to a greater or lesser extent spatially separated within the Open University campus at Milton Keynes, between Milton Keynes and my base in North Yorkshire with another group led by Deborah McNamara operating from Griffith University in Brisbane, Australia.

Holding this dispersed team together would not have been possible without the assistance of Stephen Clift our publishing editor at the Open University. Not only did Stephen display his punctilious skills in checking manuscripts, tables and diagrams but he played a pivotal role in co-ordinating the input of Richard Hoyle, Janis Gilbert and Ray Munns in the Design Studio at the Open University.

The long gestation period during which the Part 1 maps were developed benefited enormously from the efforts of cartographers Ray Munns and John Hunt. Their contribution went way beyond the task of composing maps and in the course of our lengthy discussions they revealed their full range of cartographic and communication skills.

Contributions for the text in Part 2's country by country digest were initiated by a large number of people.

Deborah McNamara very effectively organized a team from Brisbane whose expertise we were fortunate to have. George Lafferty initiated the entry for Australia; Colin Mackerras for China; Yul Kwon for the Koreas; Courtney Hoogen sent entries for Cambodia, Indonesia, Laos, Papua New Guinea, Thailand and Vietnam; Geoff Watson provided entries for Brunei, Hong Kong, Japan, Macau, Burma/Myanmar, New Zealand, the Philippines, Singapore and Taiwan.

From the Open University Michael Dawson and Richard Maidment contributed entries for Canada and the United States of America.

I provided the other entries and prepared the data sets. I also undertook the final editing of the text in Part 2 which involved attempting to produce coherence between entries and reducing contributions down to our prescribed word limits. Whilst acknowledging the initial contributions of all the other authors I have to accept responsibility for the final versions although I hope they are not too displeased with the outcome.

Two contributors to Part 2 were asked to provide not just text but most of the data too. Michael Bradshaw of the University of Birmingham, UK and Anthony van Fossen from Griffith University, Brisbane took charge of the entries for the Russian Far East and the Pacific Islands respectively. Anthony van Fossen deserves a special vote of thanks for supplying entries for such a complex array of states and devoting herculean efforts to collect statistical data for so many Pacific Islands.

Michael Dawson took charge of selecting and organizing the documents in Part 3 and the time he spent collecting information from World Wide Web pages and other sources has certainly brought a fascinating survey. He gratefully acknowledges the advice given by Anthony McGrew and Stephen Clift and the suggestions from Christopher Brook and Grahame Thompson on appropriate documents to include. He even admitted to finding some of my own suggestions very useful. Michael also expressed his thanks to Paul Smith of the Open University Library for his work in obtaining the illustrations used in Part 3.

A good deal of the material for this *Profile* was transmitted to me electronically by other contributors which is, in theory, a convenient medium. But without the talent of Anne Hunt to help me convert the documents into a version I could read the electronic messages would still be somewhere in the ether. Mary Dicker and Anne Hunt were also their usual models of efficiency in processing the manuscripts for Part 3.

By using such a wide variety of sources the job of dealing with copyright permissions and payments was very complex but Anne Carson's laudable determination to complete this work was extremely helpful.

Other colleagues at the Open University contributed in various ways. I am grateful to Alan Thomas who gave me the benefit of his experience producing the *Third World Atlas*. David Humphreys, Maureen Mackintosh and Grahame Thompson all at some stage helped me sort out problems of data analysis and presentation.

One external institution provided a special kind of support which should be acknowledged. When they gave me access to their outstanding Statistical Section the staff of the British Library of Political and Economic Science at the London School of Economics do not know what a relief this was. After spending several months working within the convenient if clumsy and impersonal electronic world of a CD-ROM, the pleasure of using and reading 'real' books was an absolute tonic.

Finally I have to record a vote of thanks to Richard Maidment whose skills of persuasion managed to secure Open University funding for my secondment to the *Pacific Studies* project.

Bernard Eccleston
North Yorkshire, November 1997

Figure 1 The Asia-Pacific Profile *countries*

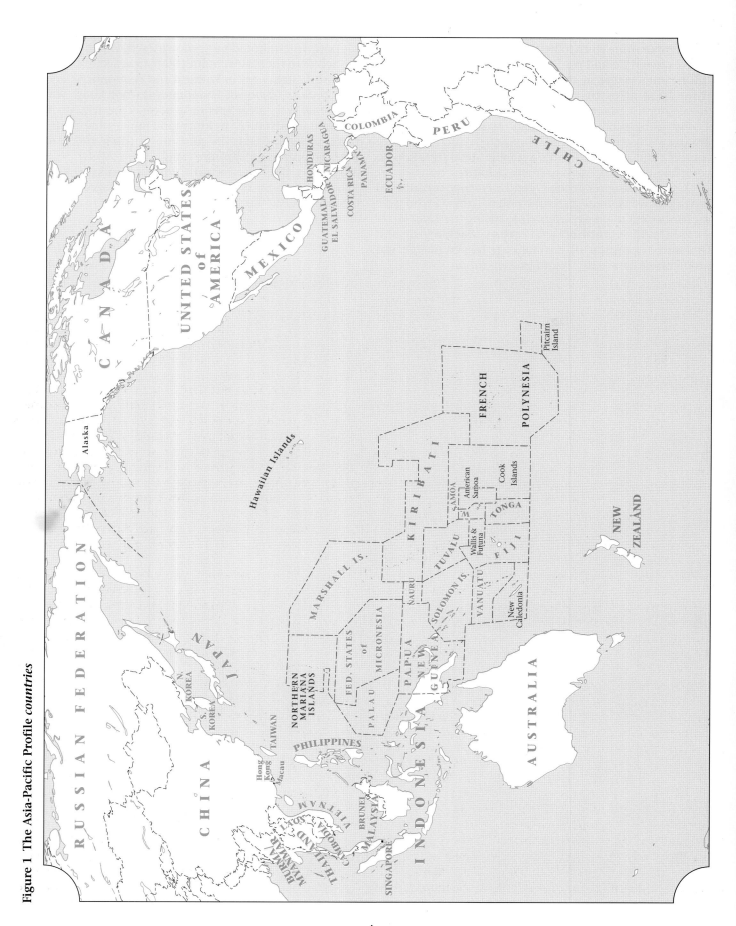

PART 1

Maps of the Asia-Pacific

compiled by Bernard Eccleston

Introduction

All maps are essentially social constructions that reflect the particular kind of representation the compiler wishes to emphasize. This compilation of Asia-Pacific maps is no exception. My overriding objective has been to present a visual representation of flows over time across the Pacific Ocean and within sub-regions of the Asia-Pacific as well as locating key places, events and episodes.

The first and most obvious change from more conventional representations was to 'turn the globe around' and centre the maps on the Pacific rather than the Atlantic Ocean. Then I had to take advice on how to cope with the distortions of space, shape and positions that are inherent in attempts to project the Earth's spherical shape on to the flat surface of the page. Equally problematic for these maps was that the huge size of the Pacific Ocean squeezed land masses to the edges of the page so reducing the space available for locating particular places. A further challenge was that the remit for this book contains a particularly large number of places as the map on the facing page will confirm.

It would have been possible to use projections that in effect expand the land masses but this would have given misleading representations of distances between places and distorted the position and importance of the Pacific Islands. Instead I followed the advice of our cartographer Ray Munns and opted to use the Putnins P4' projection which preserves a broadly global shape, represents regions of equal area on the globe as equal in area on the maps and produces somewhat less spatial distortion than alternative projections.

Even with this particular projection, however, there are some shape distortions as you move away from the map centre and this particularly affected the way polar regions were represented. Given the size of page used in the book it seemed preferable to have better coverage of northern polar regions in the Russian Far East and Alaska rather than underpopulated Antarctica. The centre for the standard Part 1 maps was therefore moved a couple of degrees north of the equator which means that Antarctica virtually disappears from the bottom of the mapped area.

Ultimately all of these decisions about how the Asia-Pacific was to be mapped reflect the functions I wanted the maps to fulfil: to facilitate comparison over time of various flows across and within the Pacific Rim; to capture the place of the Pacific Islands as comprehensively as possible; and to allow sufficient space on land masses to show key locations.

The comparative element in these maps operates on two dimensions, over time and across space. In some cases both of these dimensions are combined on the same map as in the cases, for example, of world trade shares 1913, 1953 and 1993 or foreign direct investment stocks in 1914 and 1994. Certain maps are placed on adjoining pages to allow easier comparison of, say, trade and investment patterns over a similar or sequential period. The adjoining maps for state boundaries 1914 and 1950, and defence expenditure and numbers in armed forces before and after the end of the Cold War are examples of this kind of logic.

While it is advantageous to be able to look across time and space on the same map or on adjoining pages, the longer the time period covered the more problems emerge of data comparability, changing territorial boundaries and interpolating trends between benchmark years. In some ways the recent explosion of data about the Asia-Pacific was encouraging when it came to compiling maps for shorter periods through the last decade. But this then presents problems of how to display such a rich and dense seam of data for nearly 60 countries across a relatively small land mass. Maps may well be a valuable medium for displaying data but their two-dimensional limitations make it difficult to show large amounts of information without complex graphics that can too easily become confusing to 'read'. Because this book has the advantage of using a multitude of graphs and tables in Part 2 I wanted to keep the maps *per se* as simple and as easy to read as possible.

With this in mind several maps combine countries into regional sub-groupings as in the cases, for example, of telecommunications traffic, 1994 trade flows or the movement of tourists. Unfortunately the way data providers like the

World Trade Organization or the International Tele-communication Union categorize their regions does not always coincide with Pacific Rim countries. This makes it impossible, for instance, to separate Rim countries from the rest of Central or Latin America on some maps.

As ever these maps reflect subjective judgements on the significance of, for example, *certain* ancient civiliza-tions, *important* regional organizations, *types* of environ-mental degradation or *major* armed conflicts and anti-colonial struggles. Hopefully the sources identified on each map will provide a sufficient basis for those readers who would want to challenge my judgements or formu-late alternative assessments of significant trends, events and places in the Asia-Pacific.

Figure 2 *Selected civilizations, 16th C. BC to 17th C. AD*

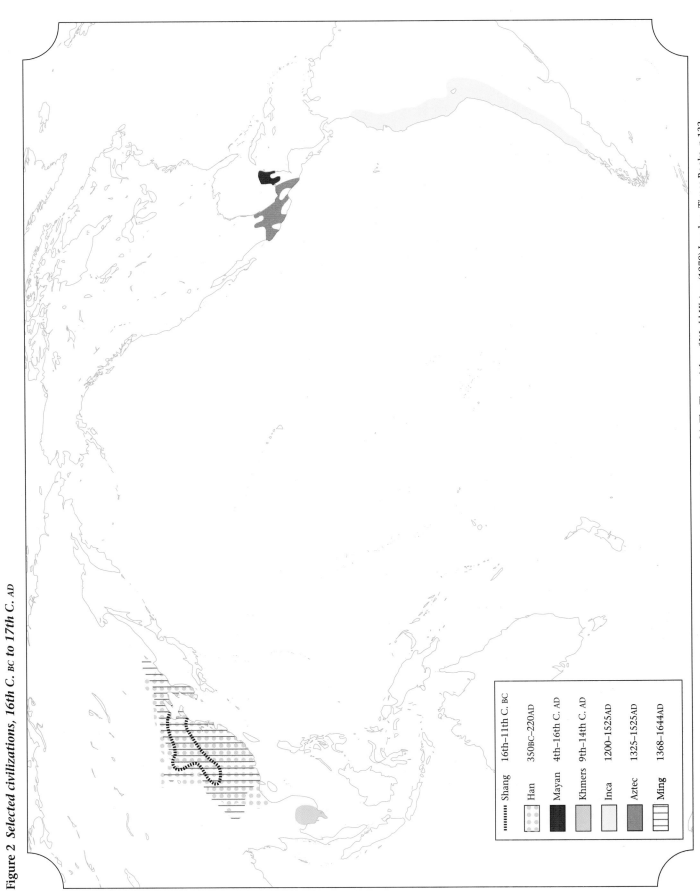

Shang	16th–11th C. BC
Han	350BC–220AD
Mayan	4th–16th C. AD
Khmers	9th–14th C. AD
Inca	1200–1525AD
Aztec	1325–1525AD
Ming	1368–1644AD

Source: Thomas, A. et al. (1994) Third World Atlas, 2nd edn, Buckingham, Open University Press, p.26; The Times Atlas of World History (1978) London, Times Books, p.133.

Figure 3 *Colonization of Latin America, from 16th C. (left) and European expansion into Asia, from 19th C. (right)*

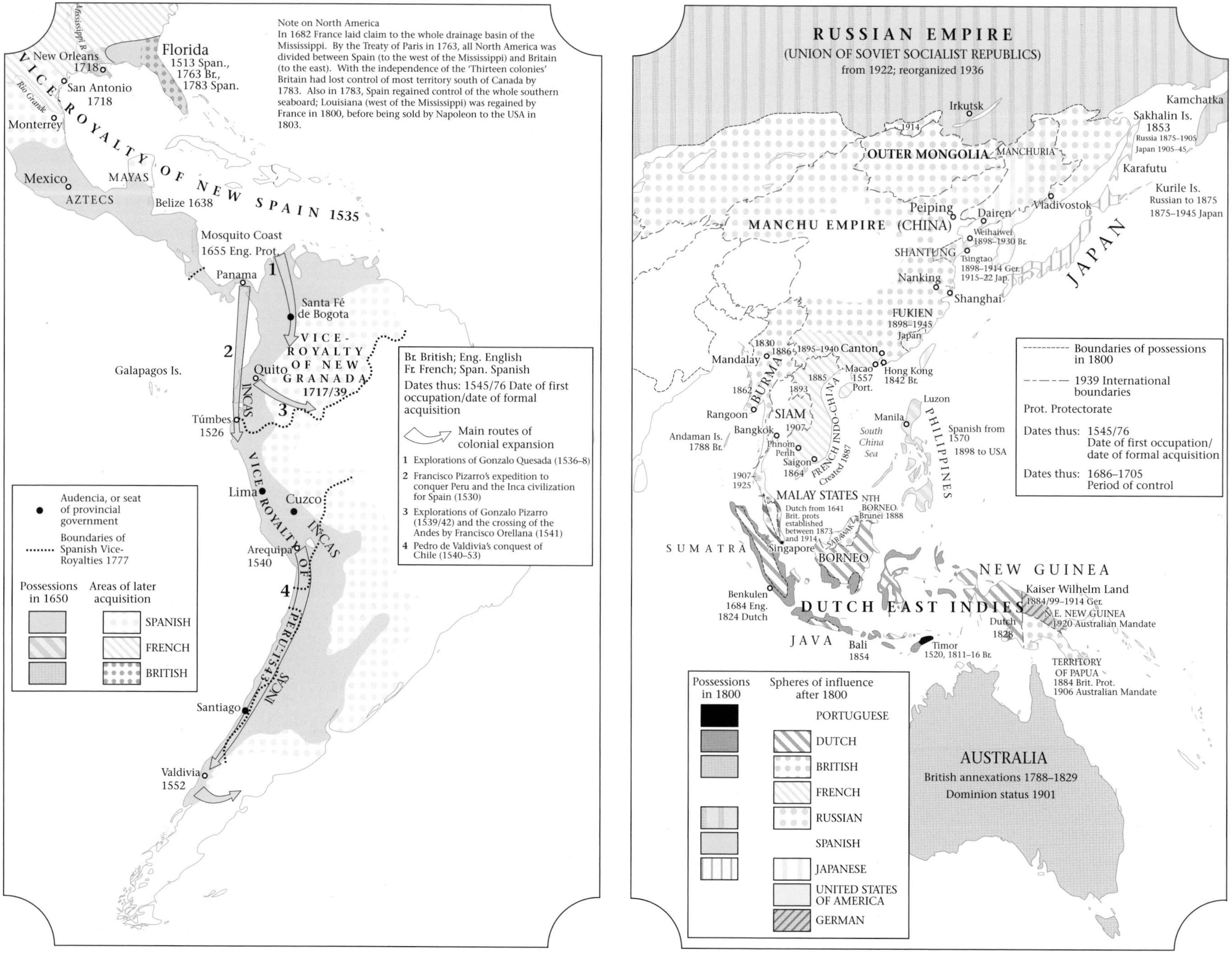

Right map (Asia-Pacific)

Kamchatka

Sakhalin Is.
1853
Russia 1875–1905
Japan 1905–45

Karafutu

Kurile Is.
Russian to 1875
1875–1945 Japan

RUSSIAN EMPIRE
(UNION OF SOVIET SOCIALIST REPUBLICS)
from 1922; reorganized 1936

Irkutsk

Vladivostok

J A P A N

OUTER MONGOLIA

MANCHURIA

Dairen

Weihaiwei
1898–1930 Br.

Tsingtao
1898–1914 Ger.
1915–22 Jap.

Shanghai

MANCHU EMPIRE

Peiping

SHANTUNG

Nanking

FUKIEN
1898–1945
Japan

(CHINA)

Hong Kong
1842 Br.

Canton

Macao
1557
Port.

Luzon

Spanish from
1570
1898 to USA

PHILIPPINES

Manila

*South
China
Sea*

FRENCH INDO-CHINA

BURMA

Mandalay

SIAM

Phnom
Penh

Saigon
1864

Bangkok

Rangoon

Andaman Is.
1788 Eng.

BORNEO
Brunei 1888

NTH
BORNEO

MALAY STATES
Dutch from 1641
Brit. prots.
established
between 1873
and 1914

Singapore

SARAWAK
Created 1887

BORNEO

DUTCH EAST INDIES

Dutch
1854

Bali

J A V A

Benkulen
1684 Eng.
1824 Dutch

S U M A T R A

Timor
1520, 1811–16 Br.

N E W G U I N E A

Kaiser Wilhelm Land
1884/99–1914 Ger.
1920 Australian Mandate

S.E. NEW GUINEA
1884/99–1914 Ger.
1920 Australian Mandate

TERRITORY
OF PAPUA
1884 Brit. Prot.
1906 Australian Mandate

AUSTRALIA
British annexations 1788–1829
Dominion status 1901

Legend (Asia map)

Boundaries of possessions in 1800
1939 International boundaries
Prot. Protectorate
Dates thus: 1545/76 Date of first occupation/ date of formal acquisition
Dates thus: 1686–1705 Period of control

Spheres of influence after 1800
PORTUGUESE
DUTCH
BRITISH
FRENCH
RUSSIAN
SPANISH
JAPANESE
UNITED STATES OF AMERICA
GERMAN

Possessions in 1800

Left map (Latin America)

Note on North America
In 1682 France laid claim to the whole drainage basin of the Mississippi. By the Treaty of Paris in 1763, all North America was divided between Spain (to the west of the Mississippi) and Britain (to the east). With the independence of the 'Thirteen colonies' in 1783, Britain had lost control of most territory south of Canada by 1783. Also in 1783, Spain regained control of the whole southern seaboard; Louisiana (west of the Mississippi) was regained by France in 1800, before being sold by Napoleon to the USA in 1803.

Mississippi R.

New Orleans
1718

San Antonio
1718

Monterrey

Florida
1513 Span.,
1763 Br.,
1783 Span.

Mexico

Rio Grande

V I C E R O Y A L T Y   O F   N E W   S P A I N 1535

AZTECS

MAYAS

Belize 1638

Mosquito Coast
1655 Eng. Prot.

Panama

Galapagos Is.

Santa Fé
de Bogota

Quito

**VICE-
ROYALTY
OF NEW
GRANADA**
1717/39

INCAS

Túmbes
1526

Cuzco

INCAS

Lima

**VICE-ROYALTY OF
PERU** 1543

Arequipa
1540

Santiago

Valdivia
1552

INCAS

Legend (Latin America map)

Br. British; Eng. English
Fr. French; Span. Spanish

Dates thus: 1545/76 Date of first occupation/date of formal acquisition

Main routes of colonial expansion

1 Explorations of Gonzalo Quesada (1536–8)
2 Francisco Pizarro's expedition to conquer Peru and the Inca civilization for Spain (1530)
3 Explorations of Gonzalo Pizarro (1539/42) and the crossing of the Andes by Francisco Orellana (1541)
4 Pedro de Valdivia's conquest of Chile (1540–53)

Audencia, or seat of provincial government
Boundaries of Spanish Vice-Royalties 1777

Areas of later acquisition
SPANISH
FRENCH
BRITISH

Possessions in 1650
SPANISH
FRENCH
BRITISH

Source: Thomas, A. *et al.* (1994) *Third World Atlas*, 2nd edn, Buckingham, Open University Press in association with The Open University, pp.33, 34.

Figure 4 *Expansion of the USA and Japan, 1867–1941*

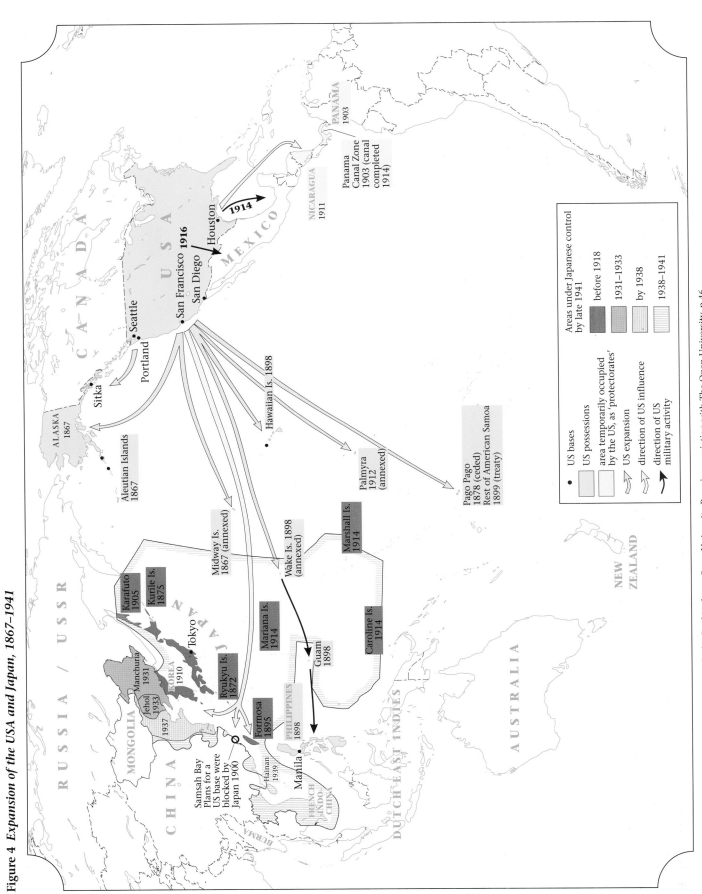

PANAMA 1903

Panama Canal Zone 1903 (canal completed 1914)

NICARAGUA 1911

1914

Houston

MEXICO

San Francisco **1916**

San Diego

Seattle

Portland

Sitka

ALASKA 1867

Aleutian Islands 1867

Hawaiian Is. 1898

Palmyra 1912 (annexed)

Pago Pago 1878 (ceded) Rest of American Samoa 1899 (treaty)

C A N A D A

U S A

Midway Is. 1867 (annexed)

Wake Is. 1898 (annexed)

Marshall Is. 1914

Karafuto 1905

Kurile Is. 1875

Tokyo

J A P A N

Ryukyu Is. 1872

Mariana 1914

Caroline Is. 1914

Guam 1898

Manchuria 1931

Jehol 1933

1937

KOREA 1910

Formosa 1895

PHILIPPINES 1898

Samsah Bay Plans for a US base were blocked by Japan 1900

Hainan 1939

Manila

MONGOLIA

C H I N A

FRENCH INDO-CHINA

BURMA

DUTCH EAST INDIES

R U S S I A / U S S R

NEW ZEALAND

A U S T R A L I A

Areas under Japanese control by late 1941
- before 1918
- 1931–1933
- by 1938
- 1938–1941

- • US bases
- US possessions
- area temporarily occupied by the US, as 'protectorates'
- US expansion
- direction of US influence
- direction of US military activity

Source: Thomas, A. *et al.* (1994) *Third World Atlas*, 2nd edn, Buckingham, Open University Press in association with The Open University, p.46.

Figure 5 *State boundaries, 1914*

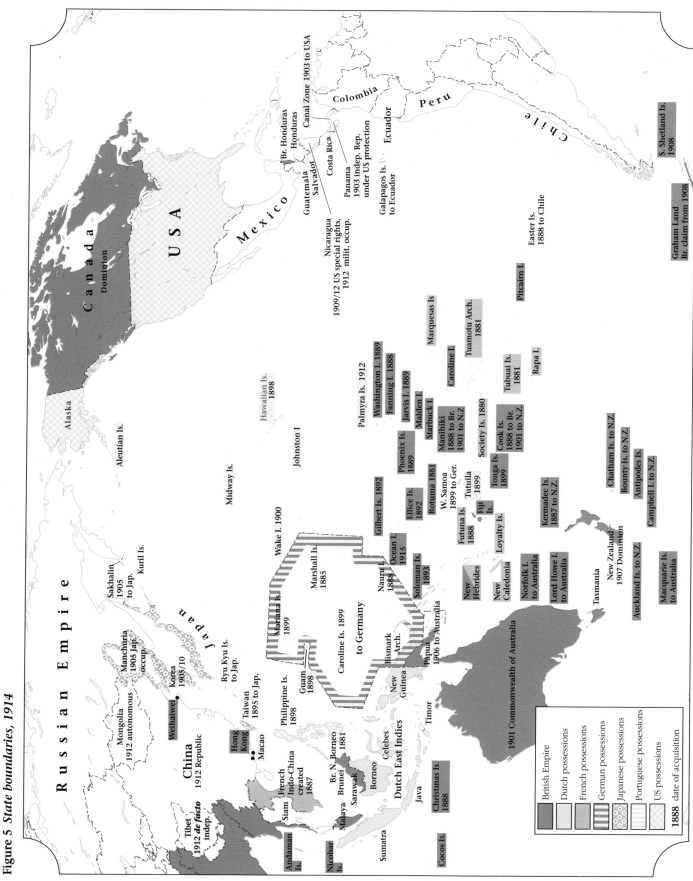

Source: Darby, H.C. and Fullard, H. (eds) (1970) *The New Cambridge Modern History Atlas*, Cambridge, Cambridge University Press, p.17.

Figure 6 *State boundaries, 1950*

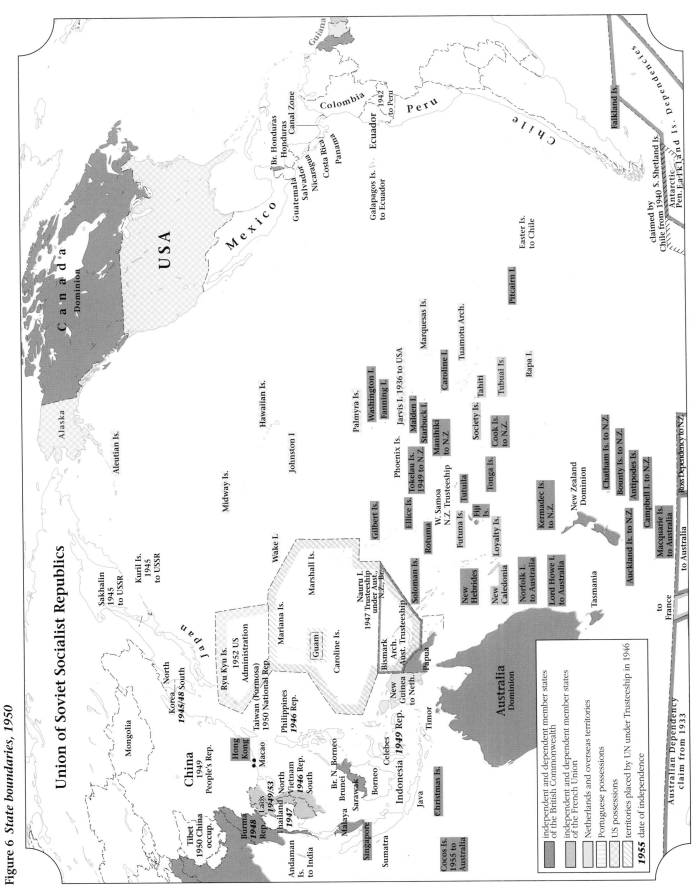

Union of Soviet Socialist Republics

C a n a d a
Dominion

Alaska

USA

Mexico

Br. Honduras
Honduras
Canal Zone
Guatemala
Salvador
Nicaragua
Costa Rica
Panama

Colombia

Ecuador 1942 to Peru

Peru

Chile

Guiana

Falkland Is.

Aleutian Is.

Galapagos Is. to Ecuador

Easter Is. to Chile

claimed by Chile from 1940

S. Shetland Is.

Antarctic Pen. Earkland Is. Dependencies

Sakhalin 1945 to USSR

Kuril Is. 1945 to USSR

Mongolia

Korea North
1945/48 South

J a p a n

Ryu Kyu Is. 1952 US Administration

Taiwan (Formosa) 1950 National Rep.

Midway Is.

Hawaiian Is.

Johnston I

Palmyra Is.

Washington I. Fanning I

Jarvis I. 1936 to USA

Marquesas Is.

Caroline I.

Tuamotu Arch.

Rapa I.

Pitcairn I.

Wake I.

Marshall Is.

Mariana Is.

Guam

Caroline Is.

Nauru I. 1947 Trusteeship under Aust. N.Z., Br.

Phoenix Is.

Tokelau Is. 1949 to N.Z.

Malden I
Starbuck I

Manihiki to N.Z.

Society Is.

Tahiti

Tubuai Is.

Cook Is. to N.Z.

Gilbert Is.

Ellice Is.

W. Samoa N.Z. Trusteeship

Tutuila

Tonga Is.

Kermadec Is. to N.Z.

Chatham Is. to N.Z.
Bounty Is. to N.Z.
Antipodes Is.
Campbell I. to N.Z.

Ross Dependency to N.Z.

China 1949 People's Rep.

Hong Kong
Macao

Tibet 1950 China occup.

Burma 1948 Rep.

Thailand 1947

Laos
1949/53

North Vietnam 1946 Rep. South

Andaman Is. to India

Br. N. Borneo
Brunei
Sarawak

Malaya
Singapore

Sumatra

Borneo

Celebes

Java

Cocos Is. 1955 to Australia

Christmas Is.

Indonesia 1949 Rep.

Timor

New Guinea to Neth.

Papua

Bismark Arch. Aust. Trusteeship

Soloman Is.

New Hebrides

New Caledonia

Rotuma

Futuna Is.

Fiji Is.

Loyalty Is.

Australia Dominion

Tasmania

New Zealand Dominion

Norfolk I. to Australia

Lord Howe I. to Australia

Auckland Is. to N.Z

Macquarie Is. to Australia

Australian Dependency claim from 1933

to France

Philippines 1946 Rep.

independent and dependent member states of the British Commonwealth
independent and dependent member states of the French Union
Netherlands and overseas territories
Portuguese possessions
US possessions
territories placed by UN under Trusteeship in 1946
1955 date of independence

7

Source: Darby, H.C. and Fullard, H. (eds) (1970) *The New Cambridge Modern History Atlas*, Cambridge, Cambridge University Press, p.21.

Figure 7 *The Pacific War, 1941–45*

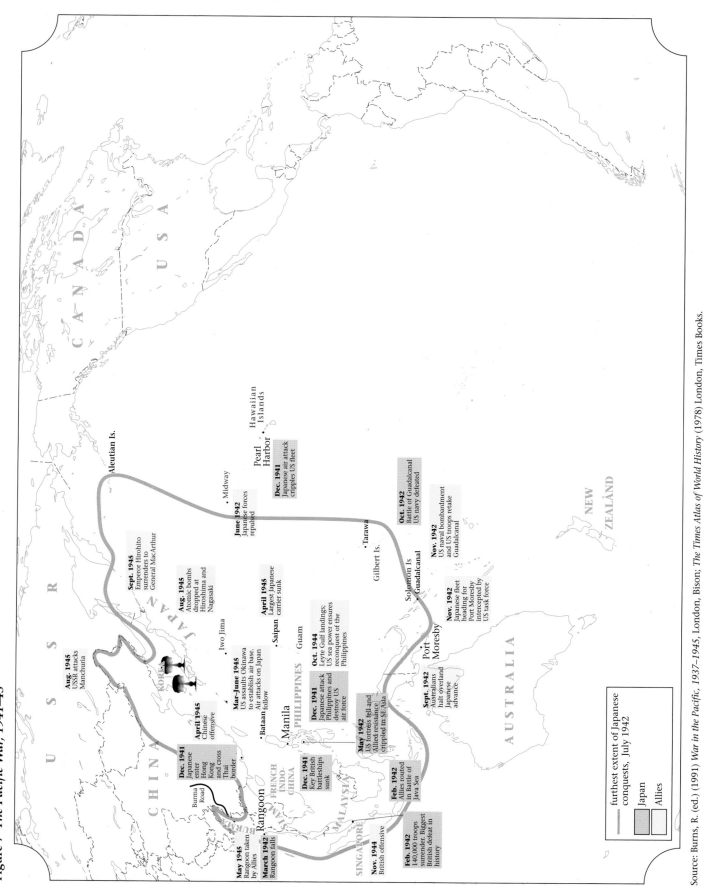

Source: Burns, R. (ed.) (1991) *War in the Pacific, 1937–1945*, London, Bison; *The Times Atlas of World History* (1978) London, Times Books.

Figure 8 *Anti-colonial struggles, from 19th C.*

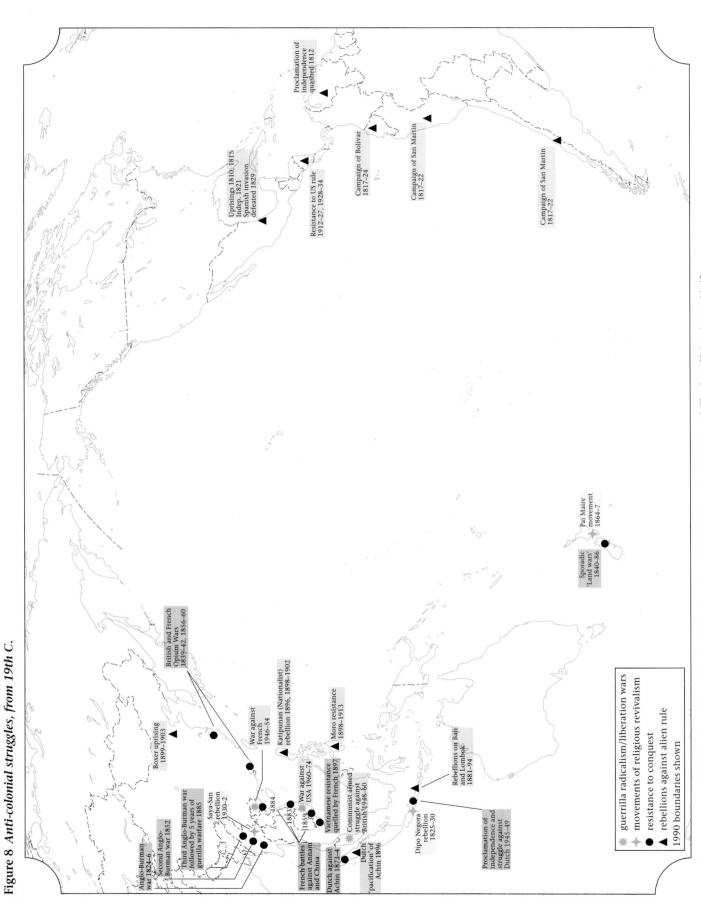

Proclamation of
independence
quashed 1812

Uprisings 1810, 1815
Indep. 1821
Spanish invasion
defeated 1829

Resistance to US rule
1912–27, 1928–34

Campaign of Bolivar
1817–24

Campaign of San Martin
1817–22

Campaign of San Martin
1817–22

British and French
Opium Wars
1839–42, 1856–60

Boxer uprising
1899–1903

War against
French
1946–54

Katipunan (Nationalist)
rebellion 1896, 1898–1902

Moro resistance
1898–1913

Anglo-Burman
war 1824–6

Second Anglo-
Burman war 1852

Third Anglo-Burman war
followed by 5 years of
guerilla warfare 1885

Saya-San
rebellion
1930–2

French battles
against Annam
and China

Dutch against
Achin 1873–4

Dutch
pacification 'of
Achin 1896

War against
USA 1960–74

Vietnamese resistance
quelled by French 1897

Communist armed
struggle against
British 1948–50

Rebellions on Bali
and Lombok
1881–94

Dipo Negora
rebellion
1825–30

Proclamation of
independence and
struggle against
Dutch 1945–49

Pai Maire
movement
1864–7

Sporadic
'Land wars'
1840–86

guerrilla radicalism/liberation wars

movements of religious revivalism

resistance to conquest

rebellions against alien rule

1990 boundaries shown

Source: Thomas, A. *et al.* (1994) *Third World Atlas*, 2nd edn, Buckingham, Open University Press in association with The Open University, pp.44, 45.

Figure 9 *Major armed conflicts since 1950*

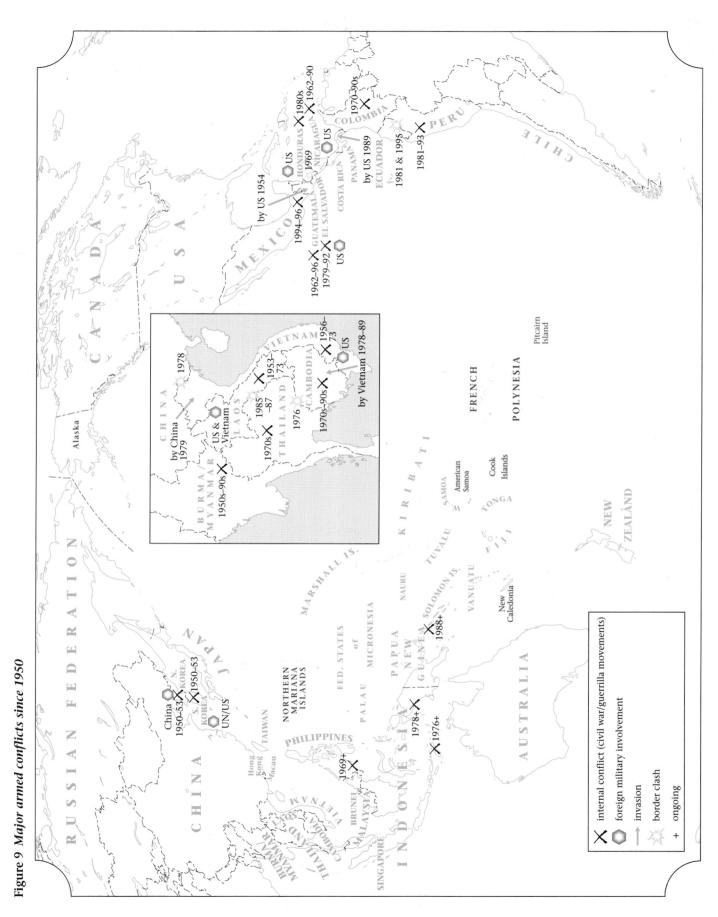

Figure 10 *Membership of regional organizations, 1997*

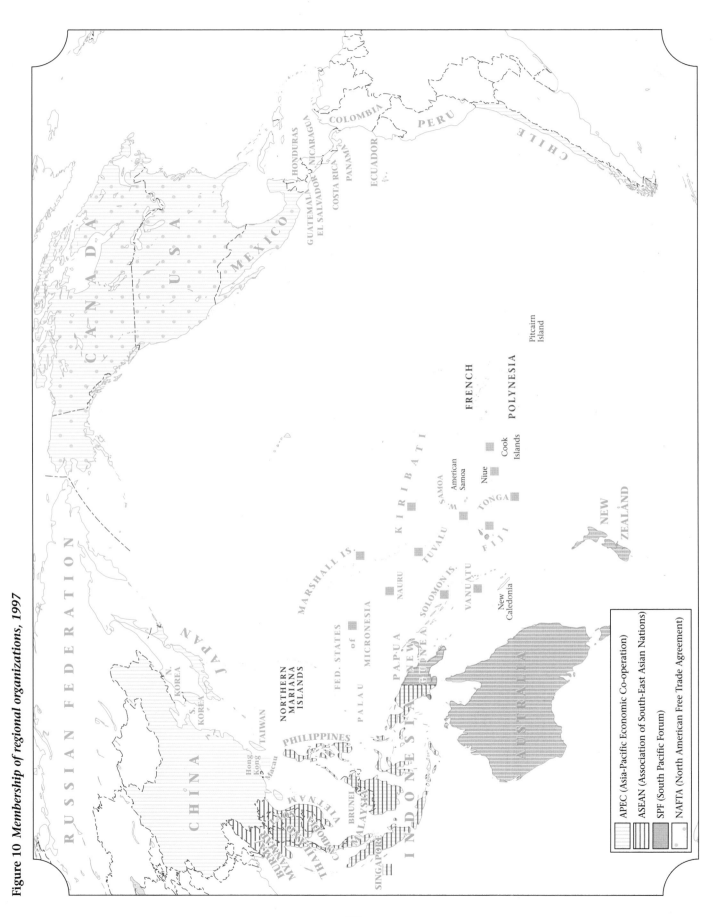

Figure 11 *Defence expenditure, 1985 and 1994*

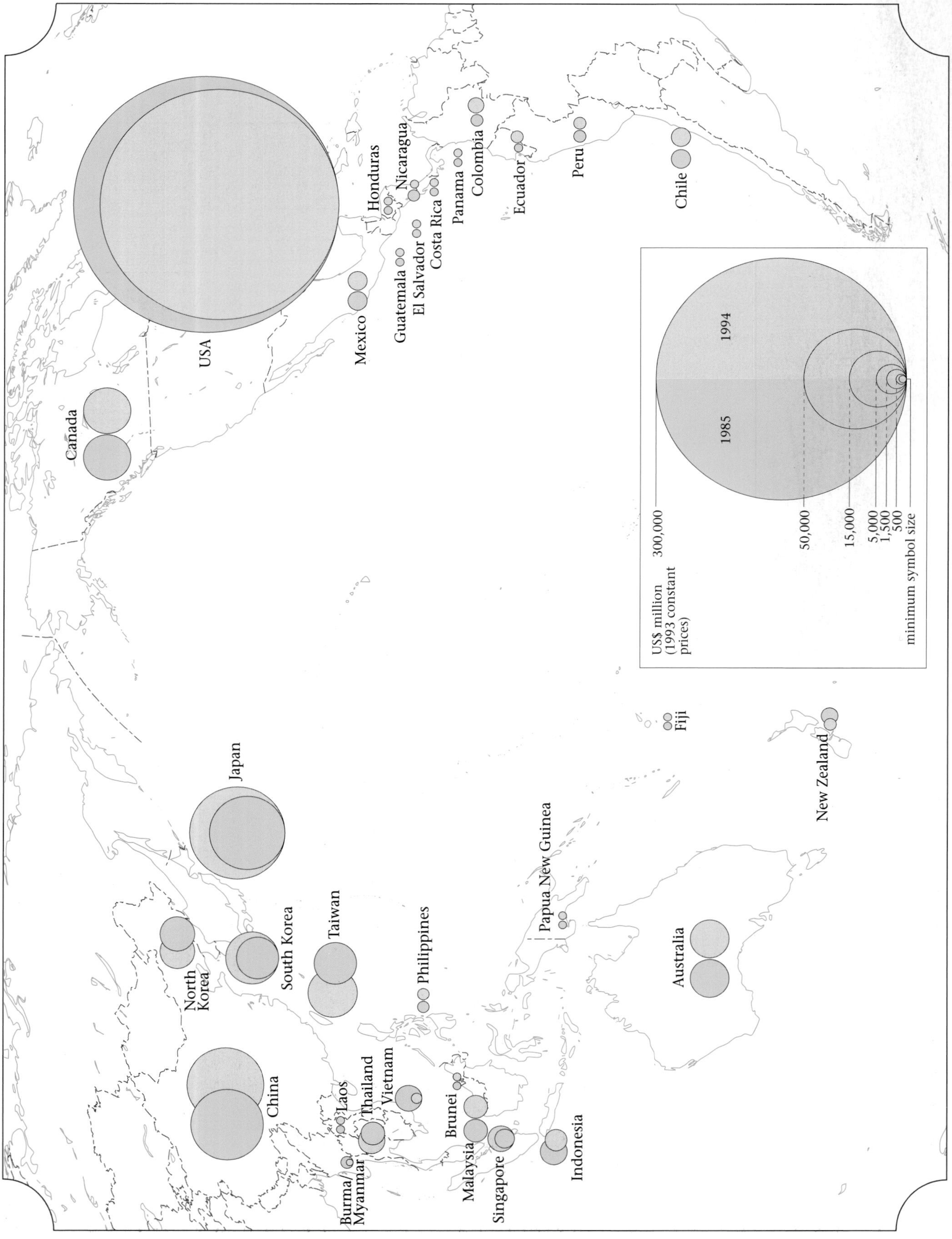

USA

Canada

Mexico

Guatemala
El Salvador
Honduras
Nicaragua
Costa Rica
Panama
Colombia
Ecuador
Peru
Chile

1994
1985

US$ million
(1993 constant
prices)

300,000

50,000

15,000
5,000
1,500
500

minimum symbol size

Fiji

New Zealand

Japan

North
Korea
South Korea
Taiwan
Philippines

Papua New Guinea

Australia

China
Burma/
Myanmar
Laos
Thailand
Vietnam
Brunei
Malaysia
Singapore
Indonesia

Source: *Military Balance* (1996) London, International Institute for Strategic Studies, pp.264–7.

Figure 12 *Numbers in the armed forces, 1985 and 1994*

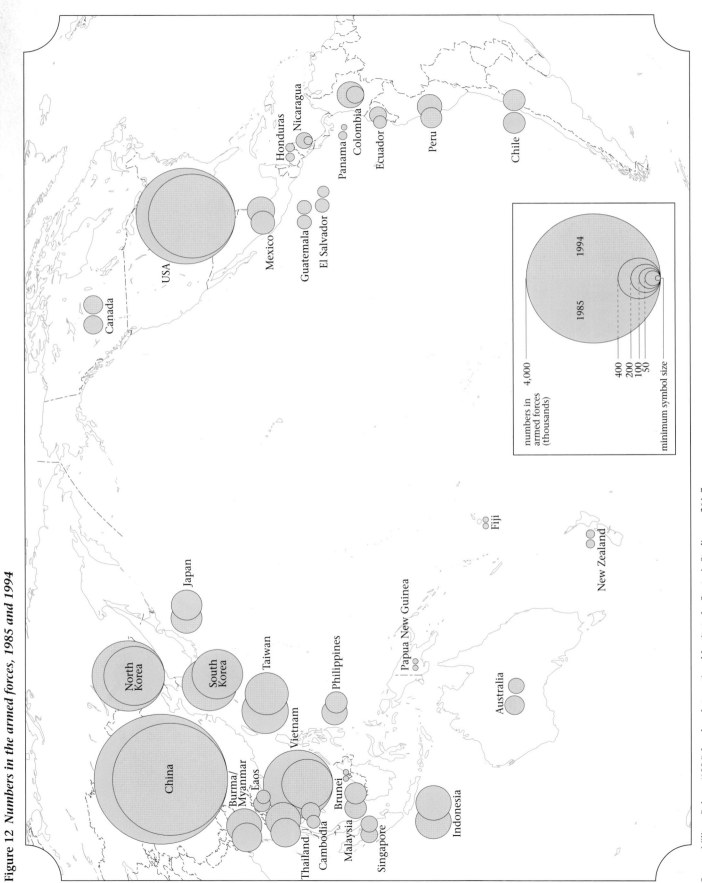

Source: Military Balance (1996) London, International Institute for Strategic Studies, pp.264–7.

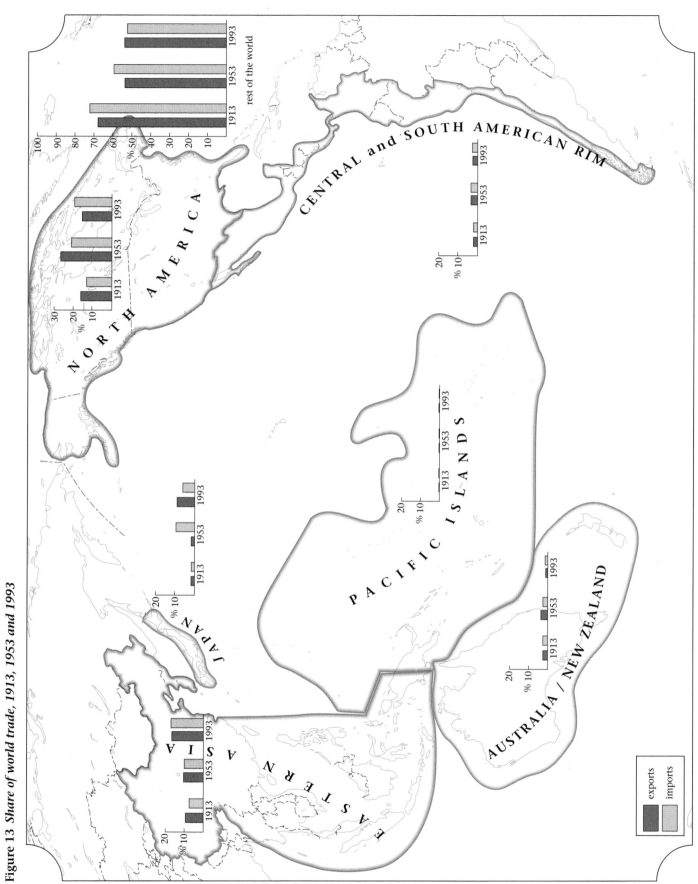

Figure 13 *Share of world trade, 1913, 1953 and 1993*

rest of the world

NORTH AMERICA

CENTRAL and SOUTH AMERICAN RIM

PACIFIC ISLANDS

JAPAN

EASTERN ASIA

AUSTRALIA / NEW ZEALAND

exports

imports

Source: 1913 and 1953, Lamartine Yates, P. (1959) *Forty Years of Foreign Trade*, London, George Allen & Unwin; 1993, *World Data* (1995) CD-ROM Trade Stack, Washington DC, World Bank.

Figure 14 *Foreign direct investment stock, 1914 and 1994*

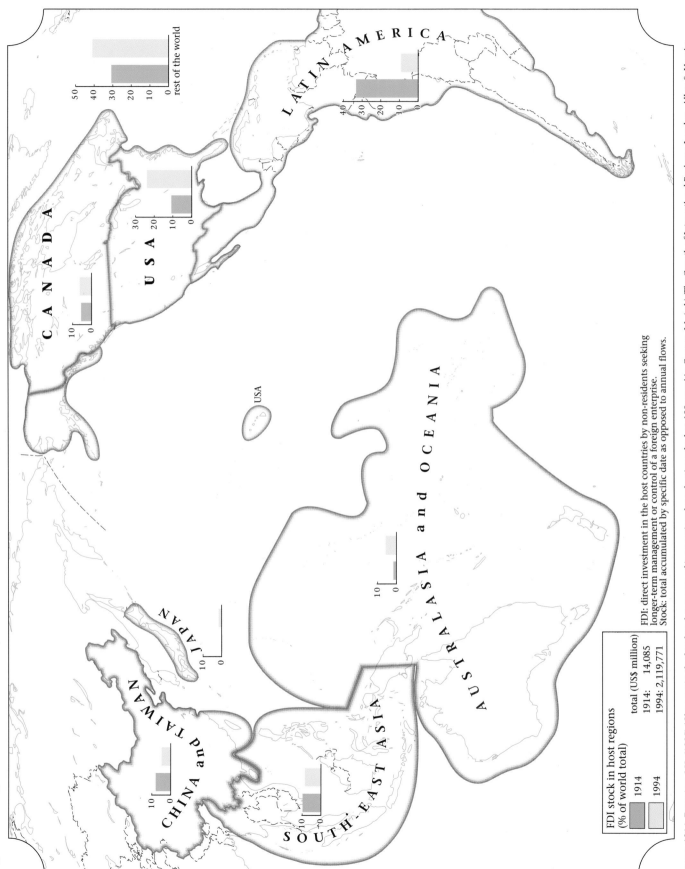

LATIN AMERICA

rest of the world

CANADA

USA

USA

AUSTRALASIA and OCEANIA

JAPAN

CHINA and TAIWAN

SOUTH-EAST ASIA

FDI stock in host regions
(% of world total)

	total (US$ million)
1914	1914: 14,085
1994	1994: 2,119,771

FDI: direct investment in the host countries by non-residents seeking longer-term management or control of a foreign enterprise.
Stock: total accumulated by specific date as opposed to annual flows.

Source: 1914, Dunning, J.H. (1985) 'Changes in the level and structure of international production; the last 100 years' in Casson, M. (ed.) *The Growth of International Business*, London, Allen & Unwin; Svedberg, P. (1978) *Economic Journal*, vol.88, no.1, pp.763–77; 1994, *World Investment Report* (1994) Geneva, UN; *World Data* (1996) CD-ROM, Washington DC, World Bank.

Figure 15 *Trade flows: exports, 1994*

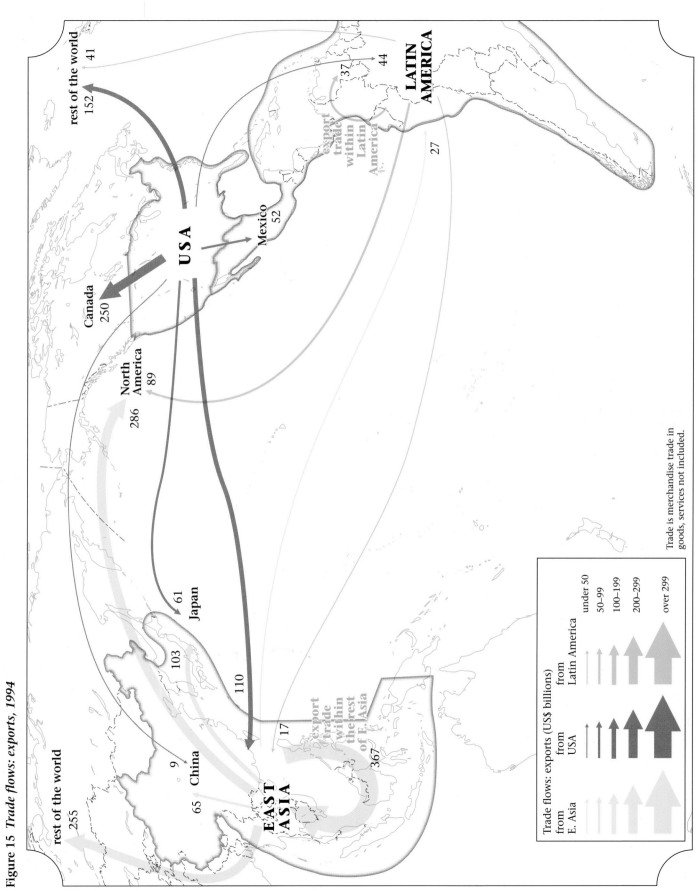

rest of the world
41

37

44

LATIN
AMERICA

27

rest of the world
152

export trade within Latin America

Mexico
52

USA

Canada
250

North
America
89

286

Japan
61

103

China
9

export trade within the rest of E. Asia
17

110

65

EAST
ASIA

367

rest of the world
255

Trade flows: exports (US$ billions)

from E. Asia	from USA	from Latin America	
			under 50
			50–99
			100–199
			200–299
			over 299

Trade is merchandise trade in goods, services not included.

Source: *International Trade: Trends and Statistics* (1996) Geneva, WTO; *Direction of Trade Statistics Yearbook* (1996) Washington DC, IMF.

Figure 16 *Trade flows: imports, 1994*

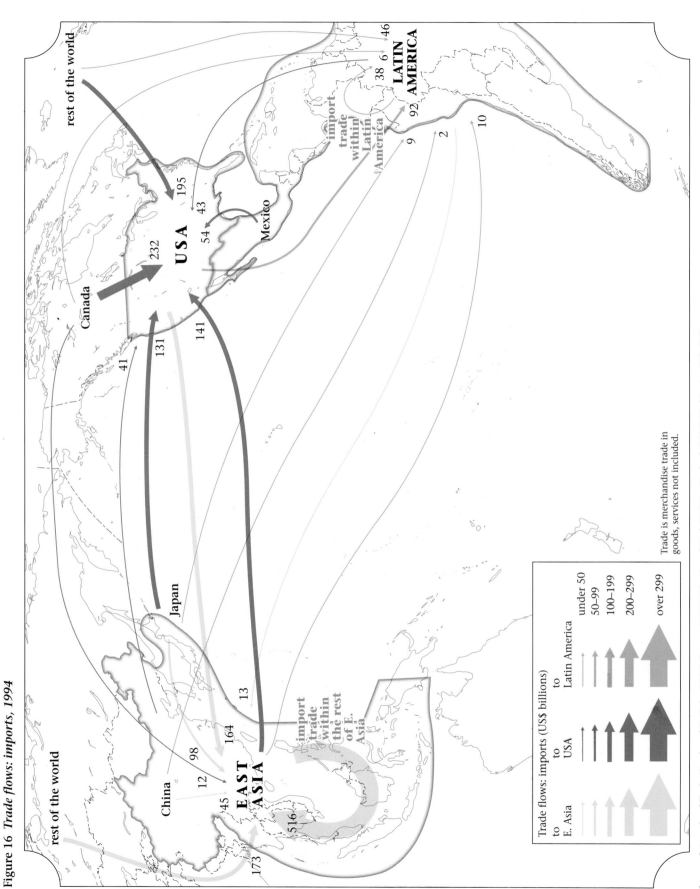

Trade flows: imports (US$ billions)

	to E. Asia	to USA	to Latin America
under 50			
50–99			
100–199			
200–299			
over 299			

Trade is merchandise trade in goods, services not included.

Source: *International Trade: Trends and Statistics* (1996) Geneva, WTO; *Direction of Trade Statistics Yearbook* (1996) Washington DC, IMF.

Figure 17 *Foreign direct investment flows, 1990–94*

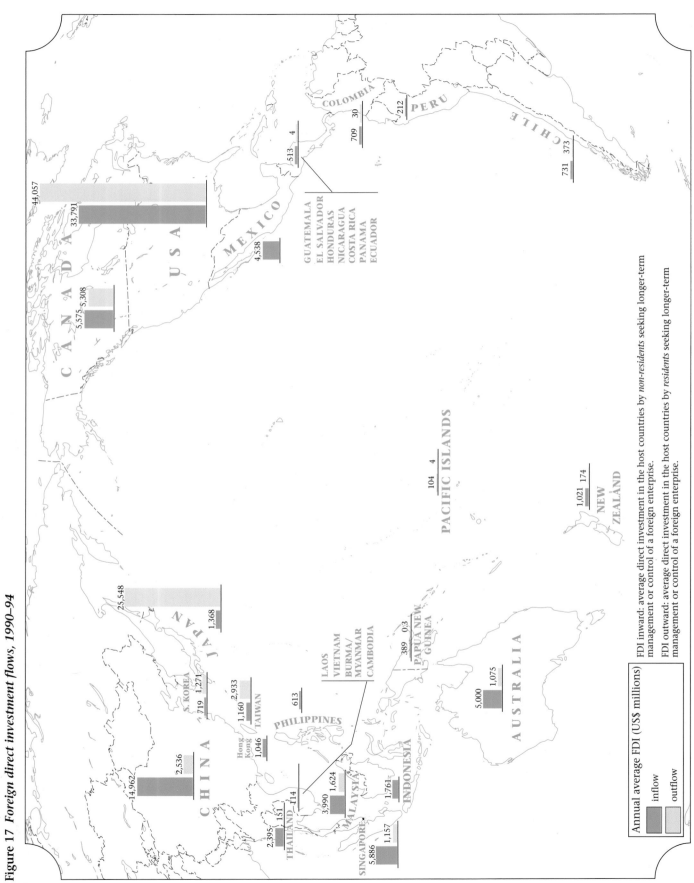

Annual average FDI (US$ millions)	
■ inflow	FDI inward: average direct investment in the host countries by *non-residents* seeking longer-term management or control of a foreign enterprise.
▨ outflow	FDI outward: average direct investment in the host countries by *residents* seeking longer-term management or control of a foreign enterprise.

CANADA 5,575 – 5,308

USA 44,057 / 33,791 / 4,538

MEXICO

COLOMBIA 30

PERU 212 / 709

CHILE 731 / 373

513 / 4

GUATEMALA
EL SALVADOR
HONDURAS
NICARAGUA
COSTA RICA
PANAMA
ECUADOR

JAPAN 25,548 / 1,368

S. KOREA 719 / 1,271

TAIWAN 2,933 / 1,160

Hong Kong 1,046

CHINA 14,962 / 25,36

THAILAND 2,395 / 151 / 14

PHILIPPINES 613

MALAYSIA 3,990 / 1,624 / 4

SINGAPORE 5,886 / 1,157

INDONESIA 1,761

LAOS
VIETNAM
BURMA/
MYANMAR
CAMBODIA

PAPUA NEW
GUINEA 389 / 0.3

PACIFIC ISLANDS 104 / 4

NEW ZEALAND 1,021 / 174

AUSTRALIA 5,000 / 1,075

Source: *World Investment Report* (1994) Geneva, UN; *World Data* (1996) CD-ROM, Washington DC, World Bank.

Figure 18 *Multinational company penetration, 1982–94*

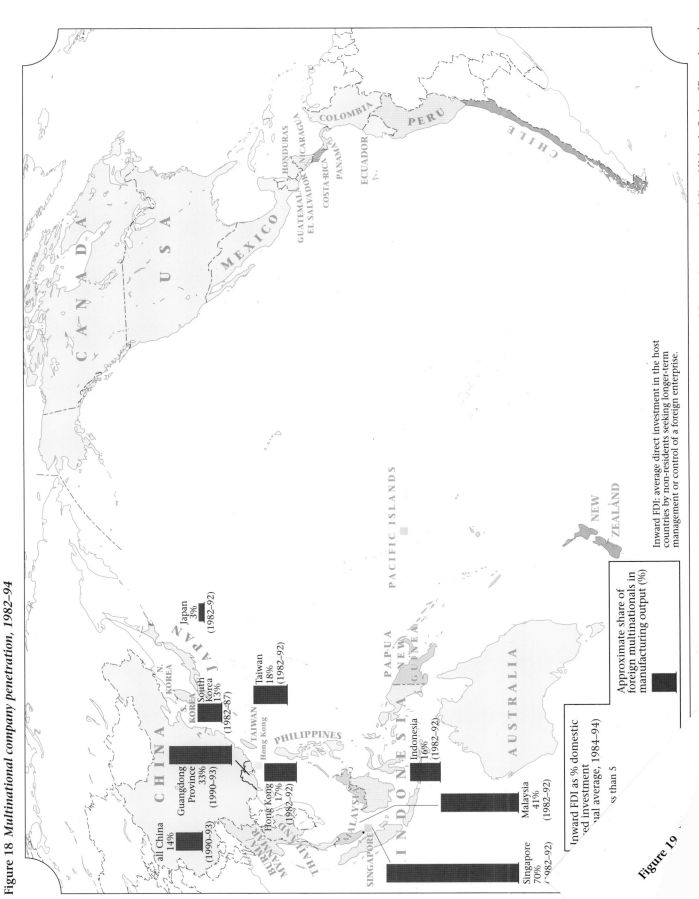

Japan
3%
(1982–92)

S. KOREA
South Korea
13%
(1982–87)

Taiwan
18%
(1982–92)

Guangdong Province 33%
(1990–93)

all China
14%
(1990–93)

Hong Kong
17%
(1982–92)

PHILIPPINES

Indonesia
16%
(1982–92)

Malaysia
41%
(1982–92)

Singapore
70%
(1982–92)

Inward FDI as % domestic
...ed investment
...al average, 1984–94)

...s than 5

Approximate share of
foreign multinationals in
manufacturing output (%)

Inward FDI: average direct investment in the host
countries by non-residents seeking longer-term
management or control of a foreign enterprise.

...e, UN, Annex Table 5; Ramstetter, E.D. (1996) 'Trends in production in foreign multinational firms in Asian economies', *Kansai University Review of Economics and*

Figure 19

International migration, early 20th C.

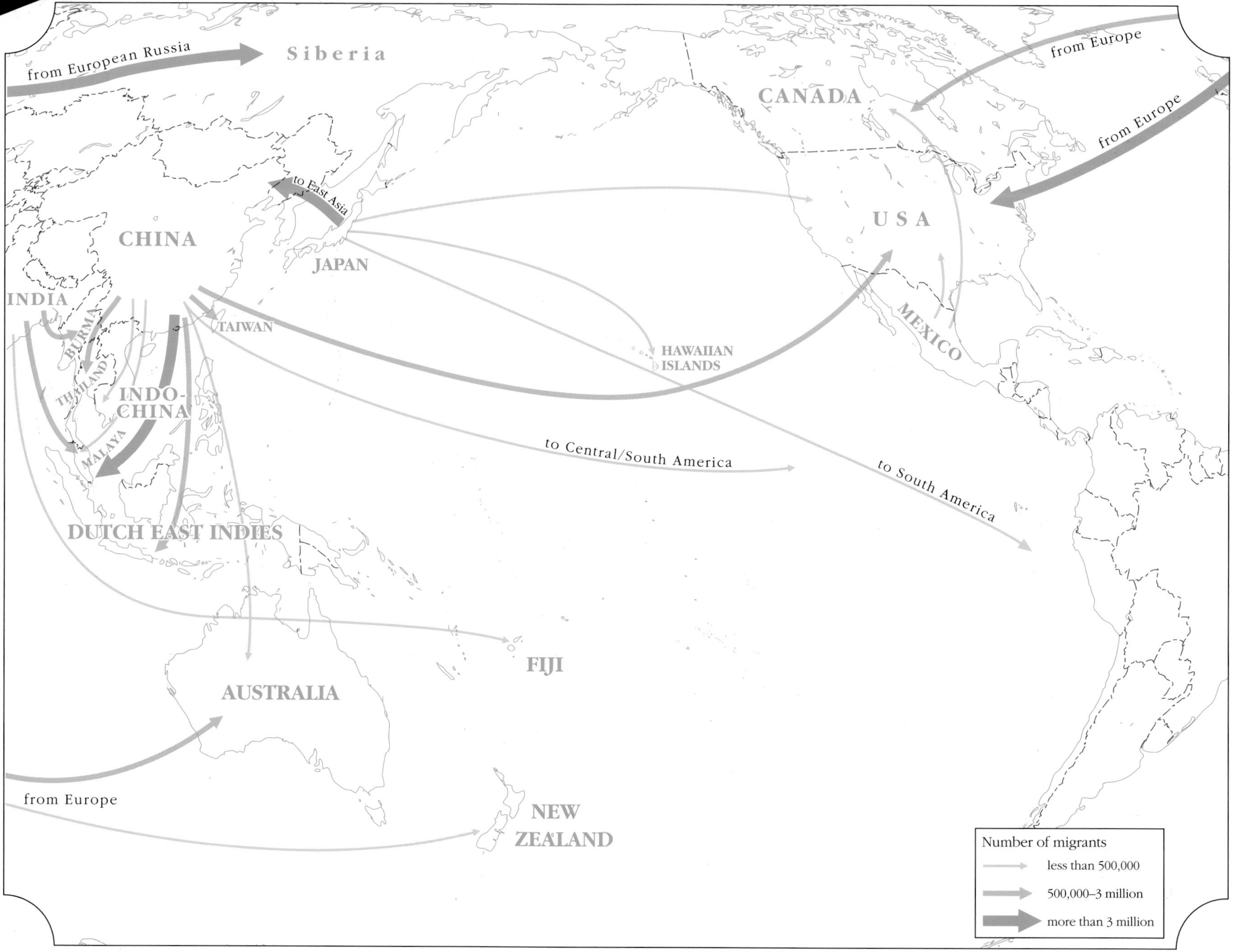
from European Russia
Siberia
CHINA
to East Asia
JAPAN
INDIA
BURMA
THAILAND
INDO-CHINA
MALAYA
TAIWAN
DUTCH EAST INDIES
AUSTRALIA
FIJI
NEW ZEALAND
from Europe
HAWAIIAN ISLANDS
to Central/South America
to South America
CANADA
USA
MEXICO
from Europe
from Europe
Number of migrants
less than 500,000
500,000–3 million
more than 3 million

Source: Segal, A. (1993) *An Atlas of International Migration*, London, Hans Zell; Lewis, W.A. (1978) *Growth and Fluctuations 1870–1913*, London, Allen & Unwin.

Figure 20 *International migration, 1990s*

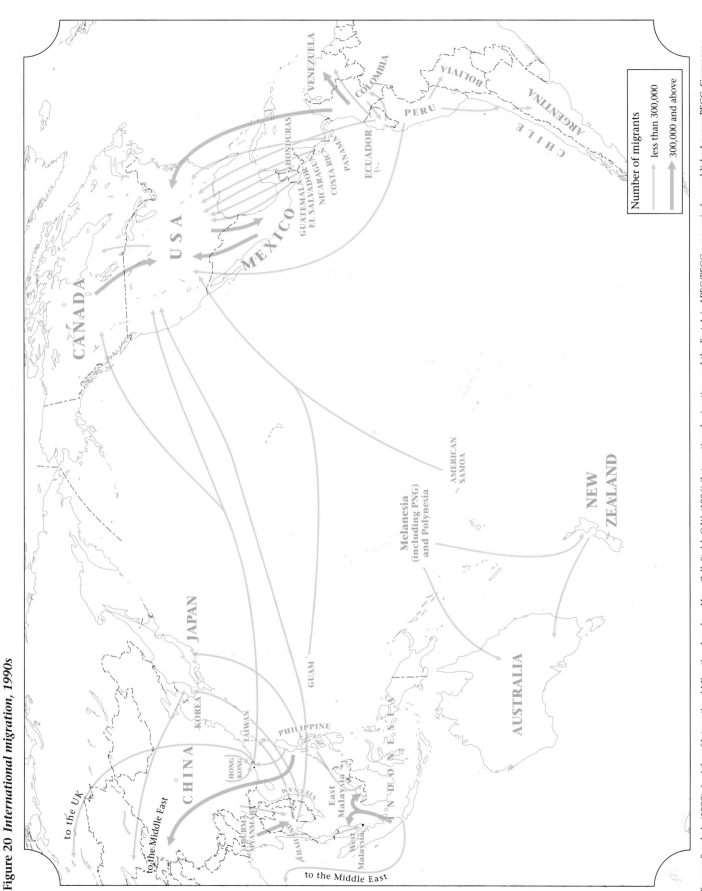

Source: Segal, A. (1993) *An Atlas of International Migration*, London, Hans Zell; Stahl, C.W. (1996) 'International migration and the East Asia APEC/PECC economies', unpublished paper, PECC, Singapore; Silverman, G. (1996) 'Vital and vulnerable', *Far Eastern Economic Review*, 23 May, pp.60–4.

Figure 21 *International telecommunications, 1983–92*

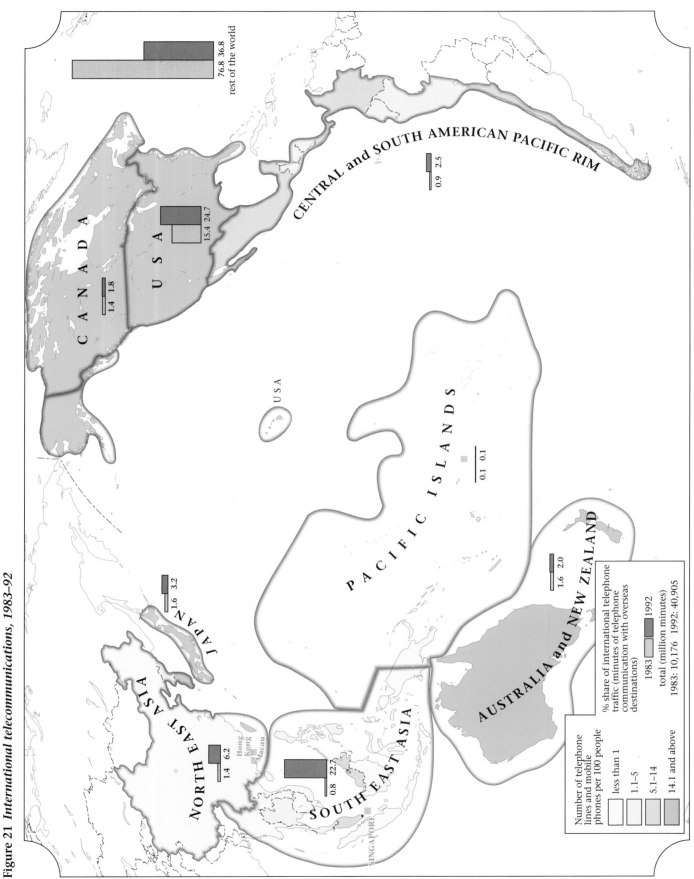

76.8 36.8
rest of the world

CENTRAL and SOUTH AMERICAN PACIFIC RIM

0.9 2.5

15.4 24.7

C A N A D A

1.4 1.8

U S A

U S A

0.1 0.1

P A C I F I C   I S L A N D S

1.6 2.0

AUSTRALIA and NEW ZEALAND

1.6 3.2

JAPAN

NORTH EAST ASIA

1.4 6.2

Hong Kong
Macau

0.8 22.7

SOUTH EAST ASIA

SINGAPORE

% share of international telephone
traffic (minutes of telephone
communication with overseas
destinations)

1983
1992

total (million minutes)
1983: 10,176 1992: 40,905

Number of telephone
lines and mobile
phones per 100 people

less than 1
1.1–5
5.1–14
14.1 and above

Source: *World Telecommunications Development Report* (1994) Geneva, International Telecommunication Union.

Figure 22 *International tourism, 1990–94*

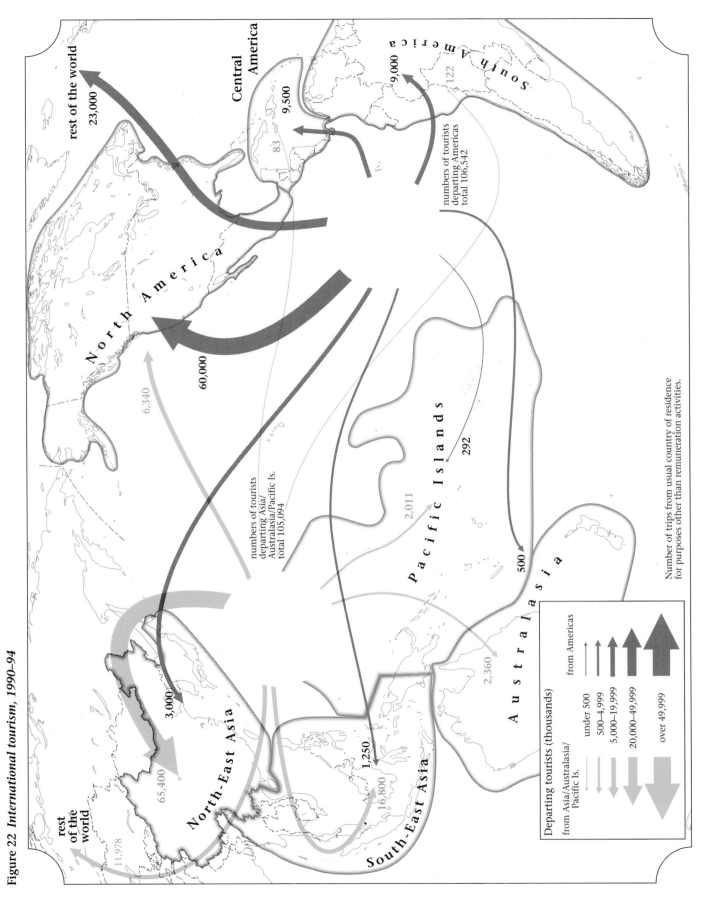

rest of the world

23,000

Central
America

9,500

83

South America

9,000

122

numbers of tourists
departing Americas
total 106,542

North America

60,000

6,340

Pacific Islands

292

2,011

500

numbers of tourists
departing Asia/
Australasia/Pacific Is.
total 105,094

Number of trips from usual country of residence
for purposes other than remuneration activities.

Australasia

2,360

3,000

North-East Asia

65,400

rest
of the
world

11,978

1,250

16,800

South-East Asia

Departing tourists (thousands)

from Asia/Australasia/
Pacific Is.

from Americas

under 500

500–4,999

5,000–19,999

20,000–49,999

over 49,999

Source: Compendium of Tourism Statistics (1996) Madrid, WTO.

Figure 23 *Environmental degradation: CO_2 emissions, rising sea level, and acid rain*

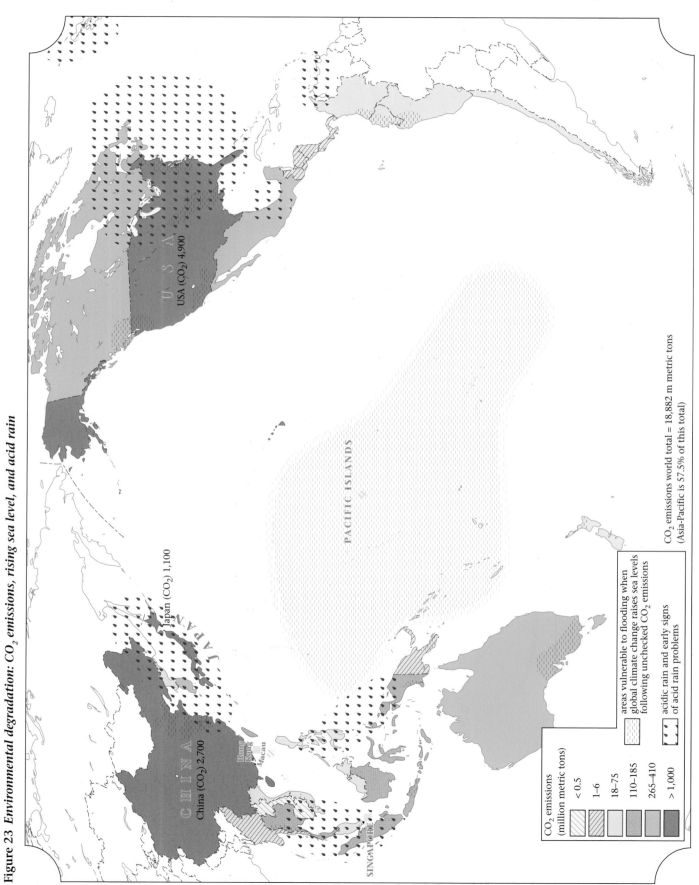

CO₂ emissions
(million metric tons)

< 0.5
1–6
18–75
110–185
265–410
> 1,000

areas vulnerable to flooding when
global climate change raises sea levels
following unchecked CO_2 emissions

acidic rain and early signs
of acid rain problems

CO_2 emissions world total = 18,882 m metric tons
(Asia-Pacific is 57.5% of this total)

USA (CO_2) 4,900

Japan (CO_2) 1,100

China (CO_2) 2,700

Hong Kong
Macau

SINGAPORE

PACIFIC ISLANDS

Source: *World Development Report* (1996) Washington DC, World Bank; *World Statistics Pocketbook* (1995) New York, UN; Seager, J. (1995) *The State of the Environment Atlas*, Harmondsworth, Penguin, pp.48–51.

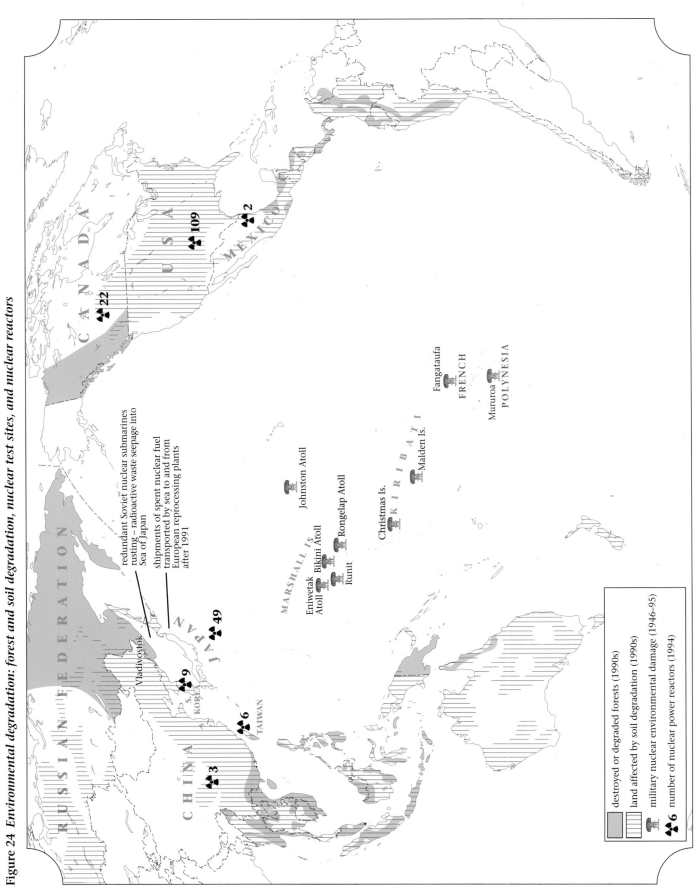

Figure 24 *Environmental degradation: forest and soil degradation, nuclear test sites, and nuclear reactors*

redundant Soviet nuclear submarines
rusting – radioactive waste seepage into
Sea of Japan

shipments of spent nuclear fuel
transported by sea to and from
European reprocessing plants
after 1991

destroyed or degraded forests (1990s)

land affected by soil degradation (1990s)

military nuclear environmental damage (1946–95)

number of nuclear power reactors (1994)

CANADA

U S A

MEXICO

22

109

2

RUSSIAN FEDERATION

Vladivostok

JAPAN

49

9

S. KOREA

CHINA

TAIWAN

6

3

LAOS

MARSHALL IS.

Eniwetak Atoll

Bikini Atoll

Runit

Rongelap Atoll

Johnston Atoll

Christmas Is.

K I R I B A T I

Malden Is.

FRENCH POLYNESIA

Fangataufa

Mururoa

25

Source: Thomas, A. *et al.* (1994) *Third World Atlas*, 2nd edn, Buckingham, Open University Press, p.63; Seager, J. (1995) *The State of the Environment Atlas*, Harmondsworth, Penguin, pp.62–3, 72–5.

Figure 25 *Majority religious affiliation*

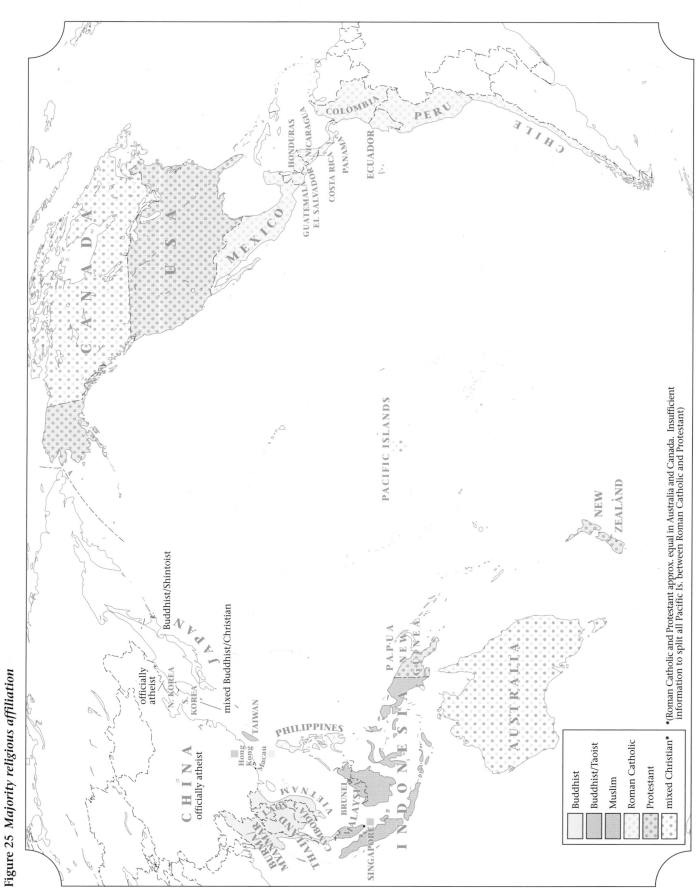

Source: Lye, K. (1995) *Philip's World Factbook*, London, George Philip; Hunter, B. (1995) *Statesman's Yearbook 1995–96*, London, Macmillan.

*(Roman Catholic and Protestant approx. equal in Australia and Canada. Insufficient information to split all Pacific Is. between Roman Catholic and Protestant)

Buddhist
Buddhist/Taoist
Muslim
Roman Catholic
Protestant
mixed Christian*

Figure 26 *Urban centres*

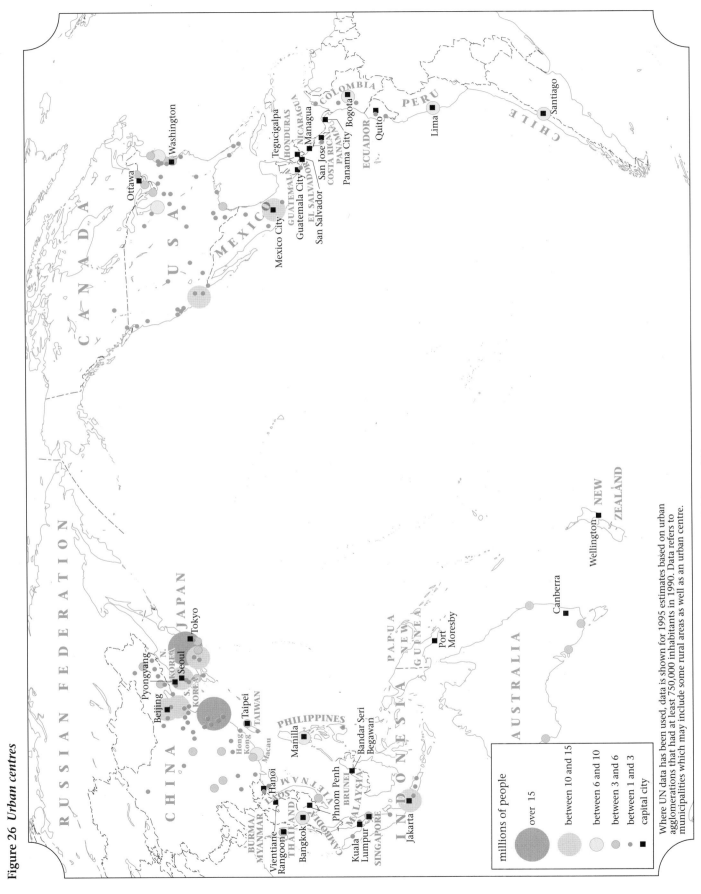

millions of people

over 15
between 10 and 15
between 6 and 10
between 3 and 6
between 1 and 3
capital city

Where UN data has been used, data is shown for 1995 estimates based on urban agglomerations that had at least 750,000 inhabitants in 1990. Data refers to municipalities which may include some rural areas as well as an urban centre.

Source: Europa World Yearbook (1996) London, Europa; World Urbanization Prospect (1994) Geneva, UN.

Figure 27 *GDP per capita at US$ purchasing power parity*

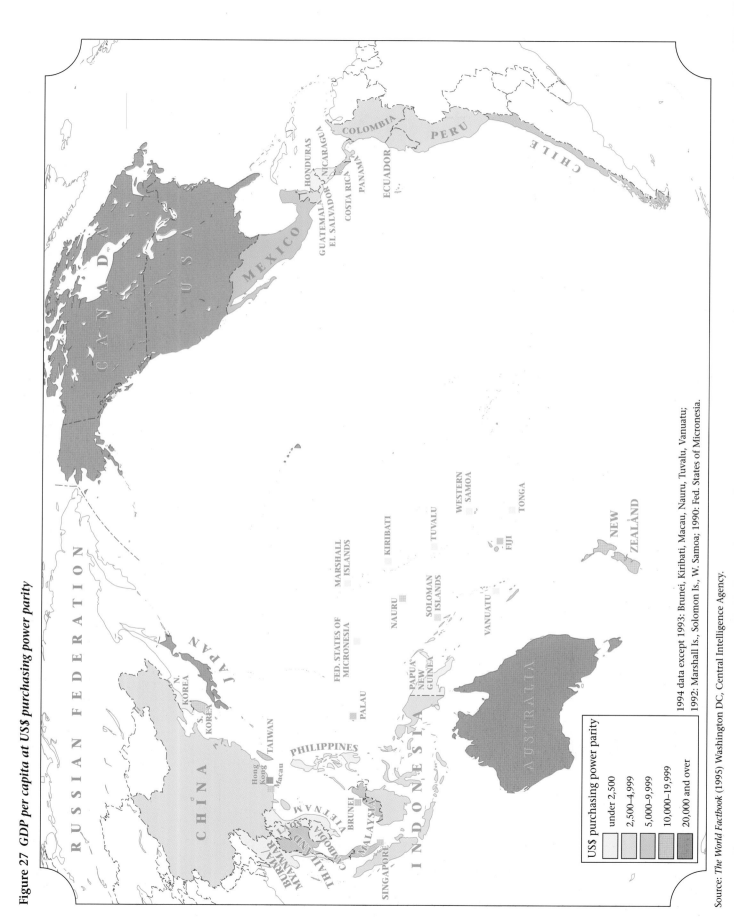

US$ purchasing power parity

- under 2,500
- 2,500–4,999
- 5,000–9,999
- 10,000–19,999
- 20,000 and over

1994 data except 1993: Brunei, Kiribati, Macau, Nauru, Tuvalu, Vanuatu; 1992: Marshall Is., Solomon Is., W. Samoa; 1990: Fed. States of Micronesia.

Source: *The World Factbook* (1995) Washington DC, Central Intelligence Agency.

PART 2

Country by country digest

edited by Bernard Eccleston with Deborah McNamara

Introduction

This part of *The Asia-Pacific Profile* concentrates on individual countries around the Pacific Rim and wherever possible offers a standard presentation with a locator map, bulleted points on background history and current political framework as well as sets of data for key variables.

Individual entries have been grouped into two sections according to whether total population was above or below one million in 1995. The one exception to this rule is the entry for the Russian Far East which is included in the second section largely because it is one administrative province in the Russian Federation and it is difficult to disaggregate local from national data. In general the division between the two sections also tends to reflect the quality of data available in time series that cover the previous quarter century.

Locator maps have been drawn using the Putnins P4' projection that was also used for the maps in Part 1. Each individual map has its own specific centre and scale which allows spatial comparisons to be made whilst attempting to represent the best true shape of individual countries or regions. Scale differences for each of the individual locator maps are shown as a ratio of area on the map to area on the ground.

As noted in the Preface individual bullet point entries were initially compiled by a team of people using their individual expertise culled from a wide variety of sources over many years. While some Further Reading references are given for every entry it is worth pointing readers to other annual digests that we occasionally used to check entries for the bullet points. In addition to their *World Yearbook*, Europa Publications (London) also produce regional volumes for the *Far East and Australasia*, and *Central, South and North America*. Other very useful annual surveys are *The Asia-Australia Survey* (Macmillan Education, Australia), *The SBS World Guide* (Reed Reference, Australia), *Third World Guide* (Third World Institute, Uruguay) and *Asia Yearbook* (Review Publishing, Hong Kong).

Attempting to make the entries for each Political Framework as contemporary as possible meant relying on a wide a range of newspapers and periodicals among which the weekly *Far Eastern Economic Review* was a vital resource.

Data sets

Assembling comprehensive and comparable data across all the places along and within the Pacific Rim since 1970 is not an easy task. Our overall objective was to select key variables that would both support the issues debated in the other four volumes in this series as well as provide useful insights for readers who purchased this volume alone. Once these variables had been selected we then had to ensure as comprehensive coverage as possible which led us to select one central source: *World Data 1995* which is produced in CD-ROM disk format by the World Bank.

It has to be stressed that only a part of the data on the *World Data* CD-ROM is collected and processed by the World Bank itself. Many of the hundreds of series from over 170 countries are actually collated by other international agencies like the UN, UNESCO, UNCTAD, FAO, ILO or the IMF. Ultimately all of these collating agencies are dependent on the ability of statisticians in countries supplying data to collect and process information effectively.

The 1995 edition of *World Data* was the latest available to us in early 1997 and provides information only up to 1994 although Appendix A does have some observations for later years. The *World Data* disk is divided into eight different files which are called 'stacks'. Three of these stacks covering *National Accounts*, *Social Indicators* and *External Debt no.1* provided the basis for thirteen of the eighteen variables used in the entries that follow.

Even this most comprehensive data set did, however, have its problems. First there was very little coverage of Taiwan because international agencies like the UN recognize only the People's Republic of China. Fortunately the Taiwan government produce their own annual *Statistical Data Book* (TSDB) using exactly the same methods of presentation as the World Bank.

Information on North Korea was very scarce on the *World Data* disk especially for economic indicators. Here the problem is partly the veil of secrecy thrown around such data by the government but this is further compounded by the use of an alternative socialist method of calculating national accounts. Only very sketchy economic data is presented for North Korea because access to information is so limited that most figures are little more than guesstimates. Economic data for Vietnam up to the liberalization of the economy in the later 1980s was similarly unavailable.

As the historical background entries for Cambodia and Laos show very clearly their recent history is one bedevilled with conflict and violence which meant the collection of economic data was a less than pressing priority. Hence for these two countries comparable economic data has really only become available within the last decade.

There are occasional gaps in the data for a number of other countries which even searches of alternative sources to the World Bank CD-ROM could not fill but overall the coverage is as complete as we could make it by the end of our data collection period in Spring 1997.

Comparable data for the smaller countries in the second section was exceptionally hard to find from international sources. In order to present similar information to the first it was necessary to use 'country sources' especially in Anthony van Fossen's survey of the Pacific Islands. 'Country sources' is a generic term that covers publications by particular governments, local economic institutions and banks that are not widely available outside the country itself.

Before we look at the sources and relevance of each variable in turn a reminder is in order about data presentation. Data for 31 countries covered in the first section are displayed graphically variable by variable while Appendix A allows comparisons to be made between countries for each of these variables. In some cases there is more contemporary data in the appendix but because this is only partial it has not been displayed graphically. Data for the countries in the second section was too inconsistent to present graphically and is presented only in tabular form in Appendix B.

The source lines for each table in the appendices also allow interested readers to update the information beyond our own 1997 cut-off point.

Demographic indicators

This data comes from the UN Population Division which takes either the returns from the full national census or survey in a particular year or makes projections from the most recent national surveys.

Because the UN represents Taiwan as a province of China demographic data for Taiwan are included under China. But because it is not clear exactly what figures for Taiwan were included we have left the entry for China unchanged. Another problem occurs with data for East Timor because the UN sometimes treats East Timor and Indonesia as two separate states (e.g. *World Statistics Pocketbook*, 1995, New York, UN). In this case also we have similarly not attempted to recalculate the demographic data for Indonesia.

Total population (million) and density (persons per km^2)

The UN defines total population to include all permanent residents regardless of formal citizenship although refugees not permanently resident are excluded.

Density figures – shown on the top of the first and last population columns – use data from the FAO (UN Food and Agriculture Organization) that measure the total surface area of a country comprising land and inland waters.

Infant mortality rate (deaths per 1,000 births) and life expectancy at birth (years)

Infant mortality rate (IMR) records the number of infants who die within their first year of life relative to every thousand born. Life expectancy (LE) estimates the number of years a newly born infant is expected to live if prevailing patterns of mortality remain the same throughout its life.

Because this LE definition is rather static we decided to place both variables on the same graph to capture more dynamic consequences of declining IMR. When comparing different countries one interesting feature is the contrasting sizes of the gap between IMR trends (left-hand scale) and LE trends (right-hand scale) as well as notable differences in the levels of both IMR and LE.

Population distribution

For the pie charts showing the proportion of people living in urban and rural areas the UN does not impose standardized criteria of 'urban' but accepts different national definitions. While this means we should use some caution when making comparisons there are some very significant differences in urbanization levels which highlight the diversity between countries. Also significant are dramatic changes in levels of urbanization such as in South Korea even over a short period of 24 years. An equally important aspect of Asia-Pacific diversity though can be seen in the half-dozen countries where change is notable by its absence.

Economic indicators

To allow comparisons to be made each of these indicators are presented relative to something else. In some cases this means using the benchmark of a common currency where values are computed to their equivalent in US dollars. Other variables covering employment distribution and traded commodities are shown relative to national totals.

Five variables use national accounting measures of gross domestic product and gross national product as a benchmark. Both GDP and GNP record the monetary value of goods and services produced in a particular economy during the course of a given year.

Neither measures are able to capture the value of goods

and services that are not marketed such as food consumed by subsistence producers or unpaid services provided within households. In addition neither GDP nor GNP include any allowance for depreciation in the value of capital equipment or natural, environmental assets as they wear out with use. If measures of depreciation could be properly estimated the totals would be recorded as Net DP or Net NP.

The key difference between *GDP* and *GNP* relates to whether ownership of what is produced is claimed by citizens of a particular country or residents some of whom are citizens of another country. To move from GDP to GNP involves adding labour income paid to citizens working abroad, adding investment income in the form of dividends, rent and profits from the ownership of overseas assets and then subtracting similar payments made to foreign labour and property owners who contribute to domestic economic activity. The technical term for distinguishing between GDP and GNP is called making allowance for 'net factor income from abroad'. (Some interesting examples of the difference between using GDP or GNP can be found in Appendix B, Tables B.3 and B.4 where the data for Brunei, Kiribati, the Solomon Islands, Tonga and Western Samoa uses both measures for some years.)

GNP per capita (US$)

This data shows the total output of a country in a given year valued at prices paid by purchasers and after taking account of net factor income from abroad, the total is divided by the mid-year population.

In converting figures from local currency to their US$ equivalent the World Bank's Atlas method takes the average of the US$ exchange rate in the given year and the two previous years. Adjustments are also made for differences in rates of inflation between particular countries relative to the G5 economies of France, Germany, Japan, the UK and the USA. As a result some fluctuations in prices and exchange rates are smoothed out.

The figures that result give a general measure of how the size of the economy has changed over a quarter century while using per capita figures allows for a more manageable comparison between countries. (In 1994, for example, using GNP totals would mean looking across a range from 1 billion to 7 trillion whereas expressing these as an average reduces the range to 200 to 26,000.) It does have to be emphasized that GNP per capita does not by any means signify anything about living standards or the way total GNP is actually distributed between residents.

Graphing the data as a continuous times series allows readers to compare changes in a country over time while Appendix Table A.4 shows clearly how relative levels and rates of change vary between countries. The contrast between Asian and South American levels and trends since 1980 is particularly striking.

The data for Burma/Myanmar, Cambodia and Vietnam were not supplied by World Bank sources because of problems of data availability, comparability and currency conversion difficulties. Asian Development Bank sources which attempt to overcome these difficulties were used instead. In addition problems in estimating net factor income from abroad made it necessary to use figures for GDP per capita for Cambodia and Vietnam.

GDP distribution

These figures compare the relative contribution of three fairly broad sectors to total value-added in the production of goods and services. (Value-added is derived by subtracting from the value of gross output the cost of intermediate inputs so as to avoid double-counting.)

Agriculture (or what is sometimes called the primary sector) includes forestry, hunting and fishing as well as farming. It is the contribution of this sector that often goes under-recorded in economies with high proportions of subsistence cultivators who consume their own produce.

Industry (the secondary sector) includes mining and quarrying, construction, gas, water and electricity output as well as manufacturing.

Services (the tertiary sector) really represents what is left and covers transport, wholesale and retail trade, finance, insurance, real estate and social services as well as public administration.

Wherever possible the GDP total is calculated to reflect the costs of production and so excludes indirect sales taxes but includes any subsidies paid by governments to keep down prices to consumers. (The technical term is GDP at factor cost as opposed to GDP at market prices or purchasers values.)

Employment distribution

Using exactly the same sector classification as GDP distribution, these figures use International Labour Office (ILO) data derived from national labour force surveys to allocate those in employment to different sectors. Unpaid domestic labour is excluded from what is euphemistically called the 'economically active labour force'.

As well as charting changes over the past quarter century for every country we placed this chart alongside the GDP distribution chart to deliver some rough impressions of labour productivity that can be gained by comparing the proportion of the labour force needed to produce a given proportion of GDP. Appendix Table A.7 reveals a very diverse pattern of levels and trends between countries.

Investment and saving (% of GDP)

Higher rates of saving and investment are frequently offered as reasons why some Asia-Pacific economies grow faster than others. This figure looks at investment and saving as a ratio to GDP estimated at factor cost.

Investment data is based on gross domestic fixed investment and covers public and private outlays on capital goods such as machinery and plant after taking account of any changes in the value of stocks of raw materials or finished goods.

Saving is measured by deducting the total value of public and private consumption from overall GDP to give gross domestic saving. In other words saving is the sum that households, firms and government have left from their incomes after current expenditure on goods and services.

There are some negative saving ratios for Laos and Nicaragua which indicate that households, firms and government collectively were spending more on consumption than they received in income. This gap is most likely to have been filled by accumulating greater foreign debt.

Government expenditure (% of GDP)

It is sometimes argued that the fastest growing Asia-Pacific economies are characterized by lower levels of government intervention and therefore lower current government expenditure. To give a more comprehensive view this figure looks at both current and capital expenditure shown as ratios relative to GDP at factor cost.

Consumption measures the current expenditure of all government bodies whether central, regional or local and includes net purchases of goods and services and payment of salaries to public employees. Capital expenditure on national defence projects are also included.

Investment data covers the gross domestic fixed investment by public enterprises for everything except military projects.

The data available for this variable is more limited because in a number of countries public and private fixed investment is not recorded separately and in the case of Burma/Myanmar public and private consumption expenditure is aggregated together. Some updating of *World Data 1995* has been done from other sources identified in Appendix Table A.9. Updating was easier to do for government consumption so generally the figures were drawn to show the latest available data for the pair of variables.

External debt (US$ million)

The total amount owed by a country to the rest of the world that is repayable in a foreign currency is shown here. This can dramatically increase the burden of debt repayment when the currency of large creditors, like Japan, appreciates dramatically as the yen did in the mid 1980s. For purposes of comparison the World Bank Debtor Reporting System converts foreign debt obligations to a US$ equivalent using the official exchange rate at the end of the year.

Debt totals reflect the obligations of public agencies as well as private entities whether or not their debt repayment is guaranteed by public or governmental agencies.

Country coverage for this data is incomplete for two main reasons. First, the World Bank collects external debt information only for countries it classifies as 'developing' which in 1994 covered those with an annual GNP per capita of less than US$8,900. Other higher income economies (with the apparent exceptions of Japan and Taiwan) are net external debtors but are presumably considered much less problematic in terms of repayment.

Second, the external debt of countries who are not members of the World Bank such as North Korea or Macau are not reported.

Exports and imports (% of GDP)

This figure provides one way of assessing the involvement and dependence of economies on foreign trade relative to their GDP at factor cost.

The data for exports and imports cover both commodity trade in goods (sometimes called visible or merchandise trade) and trade in services (sometimes called invisible trade) such as transport, finance, insurance and tourism as well as government aid and overseas military expenditure.

Exports are valued at the point of departure before the addition of transport charges – known technically as 'free on board'. *Imports* on the other hand are valued at the point of arrival and include transport costs – the technical expression is including cost, insurance and freight or 'c.i.f.'

Comparisons across countries in Appendix Table A.10 reveal some very significant differences ranging from the very low proportions in Burma/Myanmar to what look like absurdly high levels in Singapore and Hong Kong. The important thing about the latter economies is that they are significant examples of entrepôt trading centres so their exports, for instance, will include a high proportion of re-exports. Some sources do separate domestic exports from re-exports but because we are concerned with relative trade dependency we included all trade for this data set. In any case incomes are earned from re-exports as value is added by trans-shipment and re-processing services which thereby provides a local stream of income.

Trading partners and commodity groups

All four of these data sets refer only to visible or merchandise trade because detailed analysis of the trade in services is not available – presumably reflecting the difficulties of collecting comprehensive figures for what are after all 'invisible' items!

Once again exports are valued 'free on board' at the customs frontier of the exporting country and imports valued including cost, insurance and freight.

Trade partners: exports and imports

This data provides a more specific country focus to disaggregate some of the general views of Asia-Pacific trade that were mapped in Figure 13. Of particular interest are the examples of striking trade dependence on just one other country as in the cases of Canada and other states in the Americas.

Most entries name specific countries although data for the sources of Japan's imports uses a group called 'South-

East Asia' which contains almost the same countries who belong to ASEAN. The 1993 expansion of the European Economic Community (EEC) into 15 member states also saw a change in its name to the European Union (EU) and in some cases export markets and import sources are not disaggregated below EEC or EU levels.

Export and import commodities

Wherever possible we have identified particular commodities which in the case of exports was much easier given the significance of items like coffee or bananas in the exports of South American economies or oil, gas and copper exports elsewhere.

The wider variety of import commodities made it necessary to use broader categories which in some cases are also used for exports.

- *Food* products include cultivated crops and animals, plus beverages, tobacco, animal oils and fats. (If agricultural materials like wool or cotton are added this grouping is named *agricultural* products.)
- *Materials* include metals, minerals and fertilizers.
- *Primary products* are food plus materials.
- *Fuels* include oil, gas and other lubricants.
- *Raw materials* are primary products plus fuels.
- *Machinery* is defined broadly to include motor vehicles and transportation equipment.
- *Manufactures* include finished and semi-finished goods.

Social indicators

Main ethnic groups

The complexity of judging the way various categories of ethnicity have been framed by those collecting the data made this variable a particularly difficult one to present.

How far people are free to choose their preferred ethnic affiliation is sometimes questionable as in the case of Indonesia where the government seeks to play down ethnic divisions based on differences between Javanese or Sudanese, for example, and uses a preferred category of 'Indigenous Malay'. Similar comments might be made about Malaysia where surveys incorporate Dayaks from Sarawak or Kadazans from Sabah into an 'Indigenous Malay' ethnic category. Other problems associated with the social construction of ethnicity can be seen in the way people who were once described as White are now encouraged to use Caucasian instead.

Some categories used in the figures may be unfamiliar. A person claiming European and Amerindian ancestry is defined as Mestizo while those with African-Caribbean and European ancestry is defined as Mulatto. The source used for Laos describes Lao Loum as lowland or valley Lao, Lao Theung as Lao of the mountain sides and Lao Soung as Lao of the mountain tops.

Women's labour

This figure shows the proportion of women between the ages of 15 and 65 that are classified as employees, self-employed or employers. These age limits are used to standardize the data and therefore permit better comparisons between countries.

The ILO recently began publishing data that reflects more accurately the ages when women conventionally enter and leave the labour force in different countries. So far the more refined ILO criteria are only available for 1994 but the ILO hope to be able to revise the historical data sometime in the near future.

While it is likely that the data for low-income economies underestimates the numbers of women engaged in the external labour market this is unlikely to radically affect the contrasts the data reveals between South American and most Asian countries.

Population per physician

Changes in the number of physicians give one indication of changes in healthcare over the last quarter century and can offer a partial explanation of the changes in infant mortality rates and life expectancy levels shown in the earlier figure.

The definition of a 'physician' does vary between countries with quite different accreditation given, for example, to practitioners using 'natural', herbal medicines or those who practice acupuncture. In collating the data the World Health Organization (WHO) does not attempt to standardize qualifying criteria. As well as registered medical practitioners, the total number of physicians includes medical assistants who dispense medical services or perform simple operations even though they may have undergone less medical training than qualified physicians.

Government social security expenditure

There are disagreements over the extent to which governments should be responsible for the provision of social security as opposed to individuals, families or employers. This figure attempts to identify comparative trends in the proportion of current government expenditure devoted to social security payments that: (a) compensate people for loss of income due to unemployment, temporary sickness and disability; (b) provide family, maternal and child allowances; and (c) cover the cost of welfare services to children, the elderly and those permanently disabled.

Unfortunately the data collected from countries and presented in the IMF's *Government Financial Statistics Yearbook* is incomplete mainly because social security expenditure is not separated from other spending on, for example, health and housing. However, sufficient data is available to show interesting contrasts between countries in Asia and others in the Americas and Australasia.

Historical background

- Before 1788 Australia populated for at least 60,000 years by peoples described by the English term 'Aboriginal'

- 1788 British fleet arrives Sydney Cove, New South Wales with mission to establish penal colony in *terra nullius* (uninhabited land) – despite the presence of Aboriginal peoples. Separate colonies subsequently established in Victoria, Tasmania, South Australia, Western Australia and Queensland

- 1837 Myall Creek, New South Wales, 28 Aboriginal people massacred. Seven white men later hanged for the murders

- 1854 disputes with the military authorities lead diggers on the Victorian goldfields at Ballarat to set up a fortified headquarters – 'Eureka Stockade'. Rebellion quelled but Eureka Stockade and rebels' flag have played symbolic role in Australian politics

- 1855–58 adult white men enfranchised in South Australia, Victoria and New South Wales

- 1890s economic depression, numerous strikes. Trade unions establish Australian Labour Party (ALP) to promote workers' interests

- 1901 Commonwealth of Australia established as federation of six states. Immigration Restriction Act gives legal status to 'White Australia' policy barring Asian migrants

- 1902 Federal law enfranchises women but Aboriginal and 'non-white' peoples remain excluded

- 1904 Conciliation and Arbitration Act: wages and conditions set centrally through State or Federal industrial courts

- 1907 Harvester Judgement establishes principle of 'living wage' for men, set by 'civilized community' standards – women's wages set at lower levels

- 1908 Pension Act provides universal non-contributory pensions

- 1910 first majority ALP government

- 1914 Australia as part of the British Empire goes to war with Germany and its allies

- 1915 landing at Gallipoli by Australian, New Zealand and French troops, repelled by Turkish defenders – remembered annually on 25 April ANZAC Day

- 1927 Canberra becomes Federal capital replacing Melbourne. Australian Council of Trade Unions formed to co-ordinate trade unions
- 1929 Great Depression leads to widespread unemployment, wage cuts and austerity measures
- 1939 Australia follows Britain into war with Germany
- 1941 Japanese attack Pearl Harbor in Hawaii – as a US ally Australia also at war with Japan
- 1945 massive immigration campaign begins
- 1949 lengthy miners strike, fall of ALP government. Menzies elected PM – 23 years of unbroken conservative rule follows
- 1960s protests by Aboriginal peoples defending traditional land rights – later in decade Aboriginal people enfranchised
- 1964 government commits Australia to military support of USA in Vietnam – increasingly unpopular decision. Australia withdraws in 1972
- 1970s after 25 years support for US/UK role in Asia, Australia increasingly sees its future within the Asia-Pacific region – especially after UK joins EEC

- 1972 ALP government elected – Gough Whitlam PM. Social reforms in health care, women's and Aboriginal rights, and formal abolition of White Australia Policy
- 1975 constitutional crisis over dismissal of Whitlam government by Governor-General: Liberal-Country coalition wins election – Malcolm Fraser PM
- 1976 land rights for Aborigines in Northern Territory established
- 1983 ALP government elected – Bob Hawke PM. Hawke and successor Paul Keating (1991–96) deregulate financial markets, sell off major public corporations and decentralize industrial relations
- 1984 Sex Discrimination Act outlaws sexual harassment and discrimination against women. Two years later Affirmative Action legislation removes barriers to participation of women and disadvantaged groups in employment and education
- 1993 High Court's 'Mabo decision' overturns notion of *terra nullius*, recognizing 'native title' claims to traditional lands
- 1996 Liberal-National coalition wins election – John Howard PM.

Demographic indicators

Total population (million)

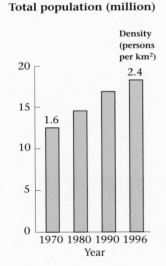

Density (persons per km²)

Infant mortality rate (deaths per 1,000 births)

Life expectancy at birth (years)

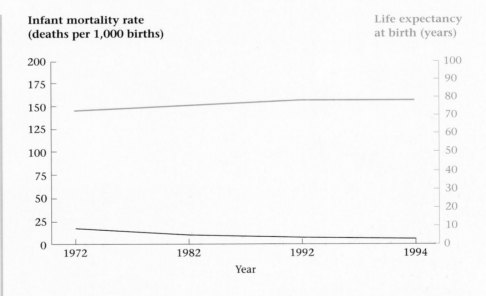

Year

Population distribution

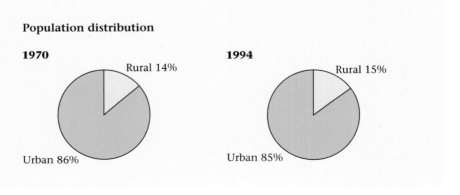

1970
Rural 14%
Urban 86%

1994
Rural 15%
Urban 85%

Australia

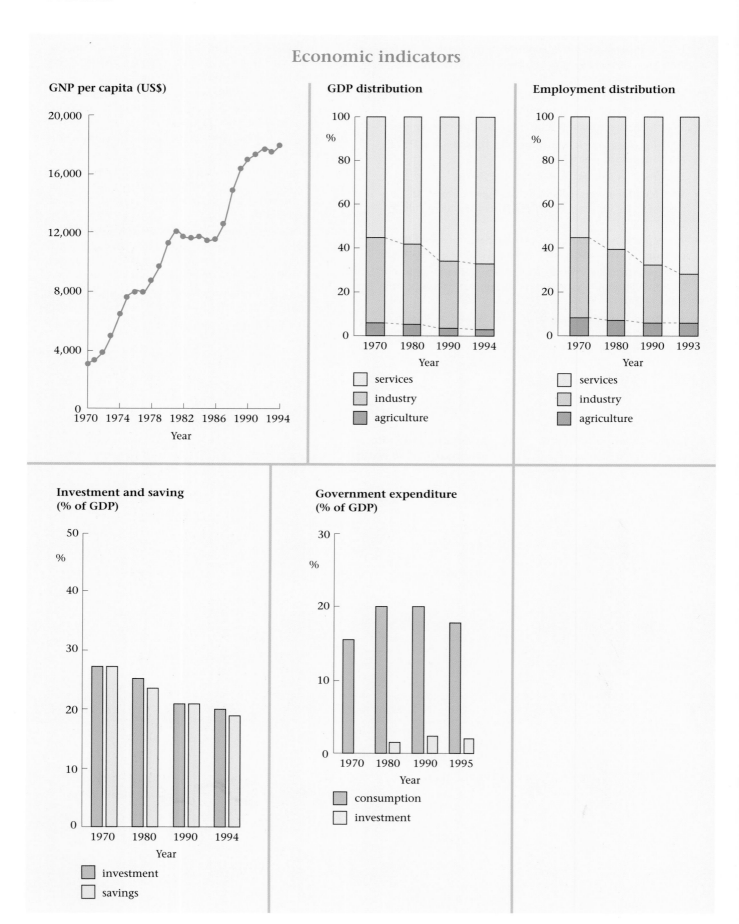

Economic indicators

GNP per capita (US$)

GDP distribution

services
industry
agriculture

Employment distribution

services
industry
agriculture

Investment and saving (% of GDP)

investment
savings

Government expenditure (% of GDP)

consumption
investment

Exports and imports (% of GDP)

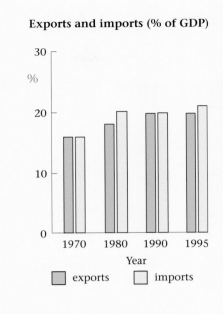

Trade partners: exports

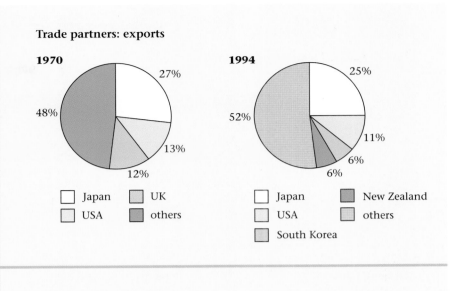

Trade partners: imports

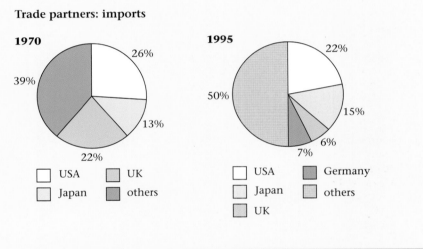

Export commodities

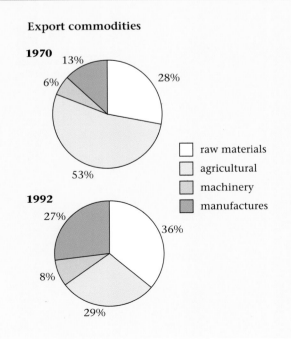

Import commodities

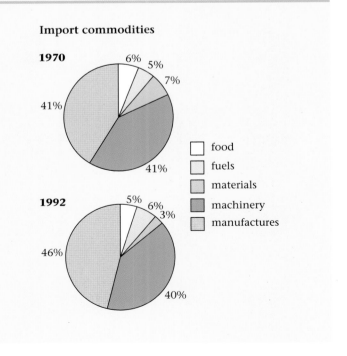

Social indicators

Main ethnic groups

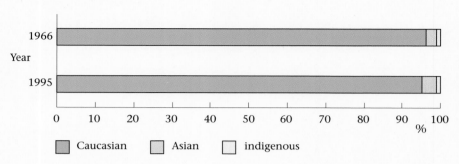

Caucasian Asian indigenous

Women's labour

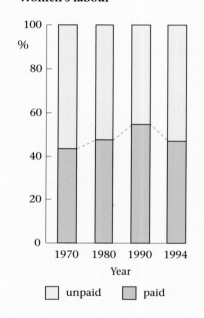

unpaid paid

Population per physician

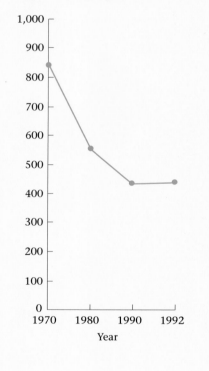

Government social security expenditure

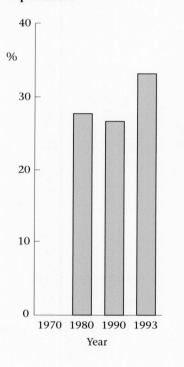

Political framework

- 1901 constitution established federal system (Commonwealth of Australia) with national government in Canberra plus state governments in New South Wales, Victoria, Queensland, South Australia, Western Australia and Tasmania

- State governments with less pervasive powers also established in the Northern Territory (1978) and Australian Capital Territory (1989)

- Two houses of parliament at national level
  - House of Representatives elected by voters in individual constituencies
  - Senate elected by state constituencies

- Separation of powers between Commonwealth and the states but occasional disputes over jurisdiction. Disputes resolved by High Court which has power to make judgements on the interpretation of the constitution

- Australia's main political parties are
  - Australian Labour Party (ALP). Founded as a working-class party but now a 'catch-all', usually left-of-centre party
  - Liberal Party of Australia. Main right-of-centre party dominating Federal government for much of the period since 1945
  - National (formerly Country) Party. Junior partner in coalition with the Liberal Party generally representing rural interests

- House of Representatives' majority determines who governs

- A Senate hostile to the government can block legislation – likely to be the case after 1996 election when Howard government did not have Senate majority

- Howard government aims to reduce public spending, re-establish socially conservative family values especially role of women as paid employees and diminish power of trade unions. Senate could oppose any or all of these policies

- Foreign policy disputes may surround new government's apparent shift from primacy of engagement with Asia to a 'reinvigorated alliance' with USA. Perceptions of government uncertainty over Australia's bridging position between Asian and Anglo states in Asia-Pacific confirmed by publicity given on campaigns to slow or stop Asian immigration

- Remaining issue left on the table by outgoing ALP government – should Australia sever formal links to the British monarchy and become a Republic?

Further reading

Grimshaw, P., Lake, M., McGrath, A. and Quartly, M. (1994) *Creating a Nation*, Ringwood, McPhee Gribble.

Jaensch, D. (1994) *Parliament, Parties and People: Australian Politics Today*, 2nd edn, Melbourne, Longman Cheshire.

Burma/ Myanmar

Historical background

- 5th C. kingdom founded by Pyus above Irrawaddy delta under strong Indian cultural influence
- 11th–13th C. Burmans arrive from north – era regarded as 'Golden Age' of Burmese culture. Disrupted by Kublai Khan's Mongol armies
- 16th C. Toungoo dynasty unites the country for nearly a century
- 18th C. final Burmese dynasty Konbaung emerged – extended to parts of north-eastern India and western Thailand
- 1824–85 Burma annexed in stages by Britain after clashes over disputed territory
- 1937 Burma separated from India – given own constitution and government
- 1942 Japanese occupation – Japanese assisted formation of the Burma Independence Army
- 1945 Anti-Fascist People's Freedom League (AFPFL) headed by Aung San led revolt against Japanese-appointed government and assisted British to regain Burma
- 1947 Burma's independence scheduled within a year during which Aung San and six colleagues were assassinated at a Cabinet meeting. U Nu appointed new leader of the Executive Council
- 1948 Union of Burma declared independent – leaves British Commonwealth
- 1950s AFPFL wins two national elections but splits in 1958 – 'caretaker' government appointed. 1960 U Nu's AFPFL faction elected to government
- 1962 *coup d'état* by armed forces – all members of U Nu government arrested. Ne Win leads Revolutionary Council (RC), suspends constitution, proclaims 'The Burmese Way to Socialism', allows only one political party: Burma Socialist Programme Party (BSPP)
- 1970 Burma restores diplomatic relations with China in attempt to suppress opposition from the Communist Party of Burma
- 1973 election confirms Ne Win President under the new constitution – RC replaced by People's National Congress (PNC)

- 1974 Ne Win introduces martial law as continuing economic problems produce civil unrest
- 1978 second national election – BSPP, the only political party, returned to government
- 1980s protracted unrest – conflict between students and army; universities and schools closed
- 1988 Amnesty International reports human rights abuses by the military against minority groups
- 1988 BSPP announces free elections to be held but military seizes power, led by General Saw Maung – a State Law and Order Restoration Council (SLORC) replaces the PNC
- 1989 SLORC government officially renames Burma as the Union of Myanmar
- 1989 Aung San Suu Kyi (daughter of Aung San, assassinated 1947) and Tin U Chair of the National League of Democracy (NLD) placed under house arrest
- Nomination of Suu Kyi as leader of the NLD for May 1990 election refused. NLD wins 85% of seats in national election but SLORC refuses to cede power until a new constitution ensures unity of Myanmar

- 1990s SLORC replaces socialist system with free market economy to encourage foreign investment
- 1991 Myanmar ratifies Vienna Convention against trafficking of illegal drugs – then given US$1.3 million assistance from UN Development Programme to preventing drug trafficking
- 1991 Aung San Suu Kyi awarded the Nobel Peace Prize. External pressures, emergence of apparently more moderate SLORC leadership – Aung San Suu Kyi released from house arrest 1995.

Demographic indicators

Total population (million)

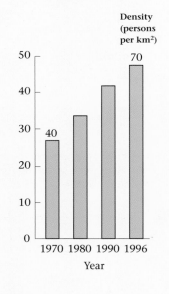

Infant mortality rate (deaths per 1,000 births)

Life expectancy at birth (years)

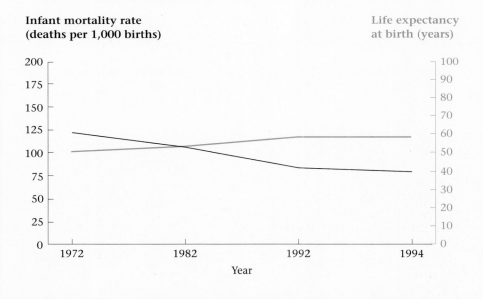

Population distribution

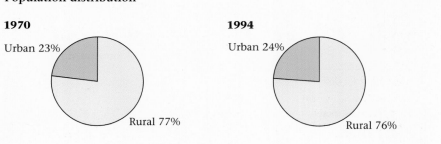

1970
Urban 23%
Rural 77%

1994
Urban 24%
Rural 76%

Burma/Myanmar

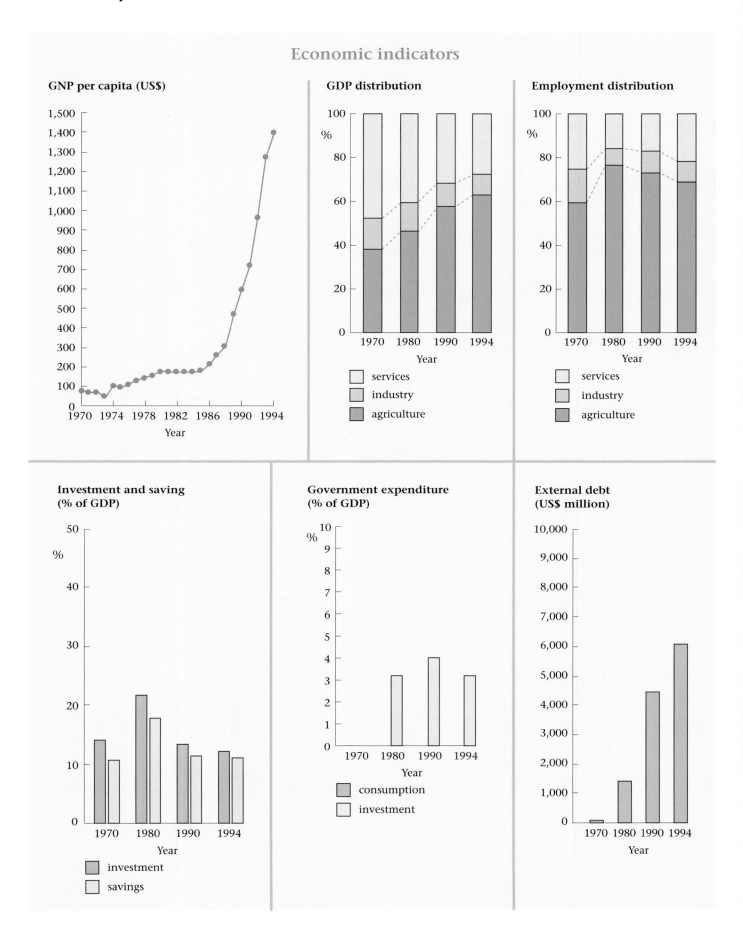

Economic indicators

GNP per capita (US$)

GDP distribution

services
industry
agriculture

Employment distribution

services
industry
agriculture

Investment and saving (% of GDP)

investment
savings

Government expenditure (% of GDP)

consumption
investment

External debt (US$ million)

Exports and imports (% of GDP)

Trade partners: exports

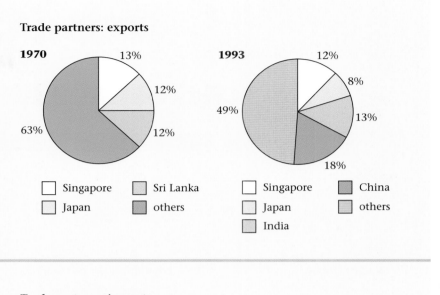

Trade partners: imports

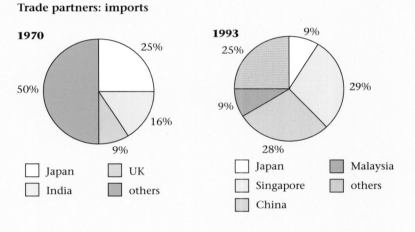

Export commodities

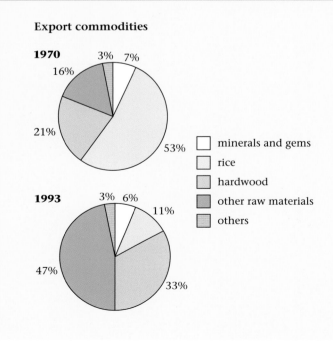

Import commodities

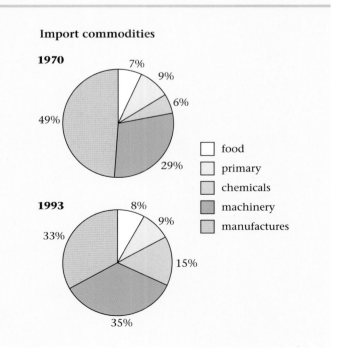

Burma/Myanmar

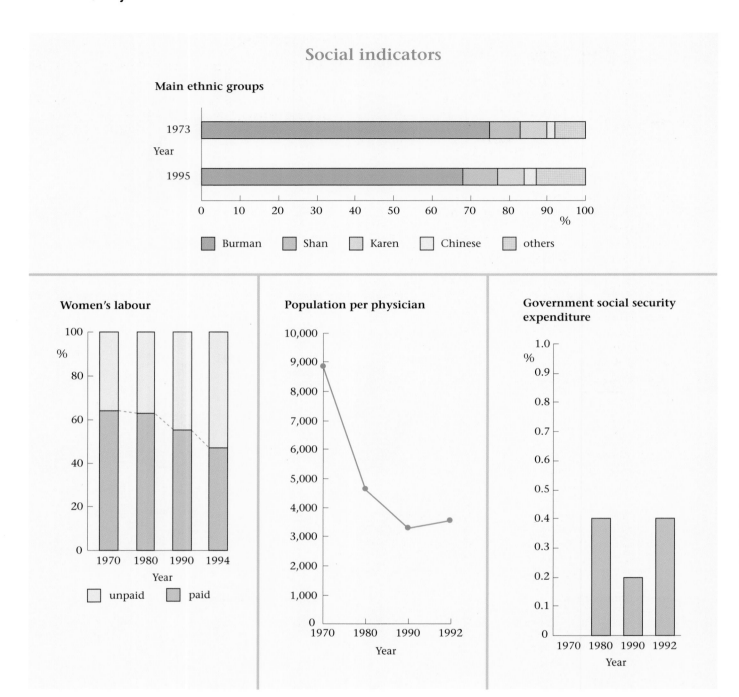

Social indicators

Main ethnic groups

Year: 1973, 1995

0 10 20 30 40 50 60 70 80 90 100 %

Burman   Shan   Karen   Chinese   others

Women's labour

%: 100, 80, 60, 40, 20, 0

Year: 1970, 1980, 1990, 1994

unpaid   paid

Population per physician

10,000, 9,000, 8,000, 7,000, 6,000, 5,000, 4,000, 3,000, 2,000, 1,000, 0

Year: 1970, 1980, 1990, 1992

Government social security expenditure

%: 1.0, 0.9, 0.8, 0.7, 0.6, 0.5, 0.4, 0.3, 0.2, 0.1, 0

Year: 1970, 1980, 1990, 1992

Political framework

- 1988 military coup – State Law and Order Restoration Council assumed government and introduced martial law. SLORC removed all government bodies granted in the 1974 constitution – governs by decree at local, regional and national levels. SLORC currently negotiating a new constitution in a convention – as of March 1997 discussions stalled

- 1996 NLD withdraws from constitutional discussions partly to protest at continued political repression. Also over proposals for the military to retain political role modelled on Indonesia's *Golkar*

- Aung San Suu Kyi's release from house arrest initially thought to indicate more open political scene but public meetings outside her house led throughout 1996 to increasing restrictions on her activities and those of NLD

- SLORC cements its position internally by increasing military spending and mobilizing its own public support base. NLD claims evidence of forced attendance at rallies of SLORC's mass organization – Union Solidarity Development Association

- Western pressures on SLORC for democratization and respect for human rights fitfully led by the US Congress, the UN and the EU backed by some Western companies withdrawing promised foreign investment

- Impact of Western pressure mitigated by countervailing attitudes in ASEAN

- September 1996 ASEAN promises full membership to Burma certainly by 2000 if not sooner – alongside Laos and Cambodia by the end of 1997

- ASEAN political support for SLORC based partly on self-interest – Singapore biggest foreign investor in Burma and key source for arms procurement. Also 'constructive engagement' between ASEAN and Burma helps dilute influence of Burma's most important other ally – China

- ASEAN support for SLORC also seen as way of signalling to the West that political and human rights issues in Asia are internal affairs – closed to outside interference. SLORC therefore justified as only realistic option – 'The one instrument of effective government there is the army' according to Singapore's Lee Kuan Yew, May 1996.

Further reading

Smith, M. (1992) *Burma: Insurgency and Politics of Ethnicity*, London, Zed Books.

Steinberg, D. (1990) *The Future of Burma: Crisis and Choice in Myanmar*, Lanham, University Press of America.

Cambodia

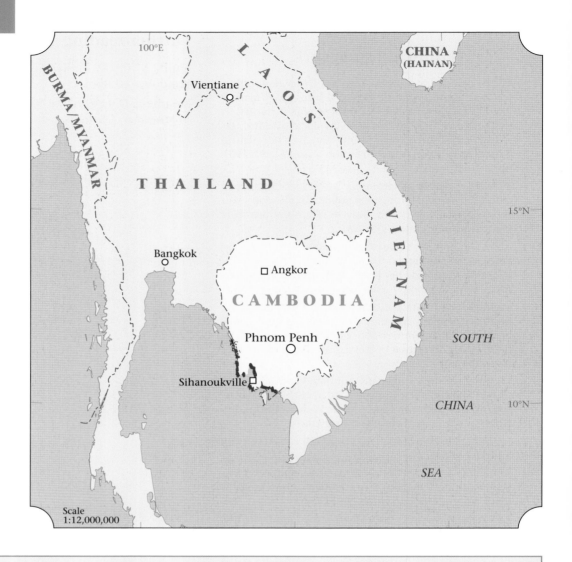

Historical background

- 9th–14th C. Cambodia combined with parts of Thailand and Vietnam in Empire based on Angkor later political centre moves to Phnom Penh

- 16th–19th C. worsening territorial disputes with Thailand and Vietnam eventually encourages King Norodom to opt for French Protectorate status 1863

- 1887 Cambodia formally included in French Indo-Chinese Union

- 1940 occupied by Japan but ruled through authority of Vichy French government

- 1941 King Norodom Sihanouk placed on Cambodian throne by Japanese

- 1945 Japanese grant Cambodia independence but once war ends French colonial rule restored

- 1954 Cambodia becomes independent – ratified by Geneva Conference on Indo-China

- 1955 Sihanouk abdicates in order to enter the political arena – his party Popular Socialist Community (PSC) wins election and he becomes head of state

- 1960s Sihanouk introduces more state controls as economic problems worsen – tries to remain neutral in Vietnam conflict with USA

- 1970 Sihanouk ousted in *coup d'état* led by Lon Nol – country renamed Khmer Republic

- 1972 Lon Nol becomes President and US round-the-clock air bombings temporarily shore up the regime

- Sihanouk establishes government in exile in alliance with Khmer Rouge a radical pro-Chinese guerrilla movement – some initial support from North Vietnam

- 1975 Lon Nol flees to Hawaii and Khmer Rouge occupy Phnom Penh

- Sihanouk returns to Cambodia but his authority superseded by Khmer Rouge led by Pol Pot – country renamed Kampuchea

- 1976–78 country radically restructured as non-monetized agrarian society: population moved to rural areas, famine and disease rampant, suspected opponents eliminated – over 1 million die in the 'killing fields' of Kampuchea

- 1978 after border clashes Vietnam invades Kampuchea and places Kampuchean People's Republic Party (KPRP) in power with support from some Khmer Rouge defectors
- No international recognition for KPRP – coalition government in exile under Sihanouk combining his United National Front for Independent Neutral Peaceful Cooperative Cambodia (FUNCINPEC) and Khmer People's National Front (KPNLF)
- 1980s continued guerrilla war against KPRP – Vietnam later forced to reconsider occupation as USSR reduces financial and military support
- 1988 Vietnam announces withdrawal of military forces within the year – KPRP later changes name to Cambodian People's Party (CPP)
- 1989 France and Indonesia host international conference on Cambodia and momentum builds for broader UN role to facilitate Cambodia's reconstruction
- 1991 UN brokers peace agreements between warring factions and agrees to send peace-keeping force to monitor disarmament and oversee elections

- Exiled political leaders return to find Khmer Rouge refusing to disarm or participate in election also refuse to allow UN into areas still under their control
- 1993 90% of eligible voters participate in national election with FUNCINPEC winning 46% and CPP 38% of votes – leaders of both parties become joint PMs in coalition government with Sihanouk restored to throne as head of state
- 1993–97 fragile period as Cambodia searches for political peace and economic reconstruction after 25 years of chaos.

Demographic indicators

Total population (million)

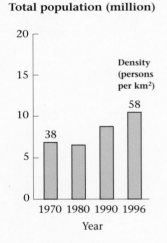

Density (persons per km²)

Infant mortality rate (deaths per 1,000 births)

Life expectancy at birth (years)

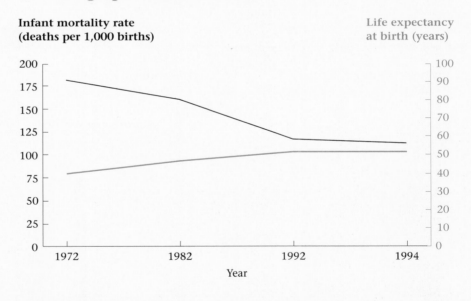

Year

Population distribution

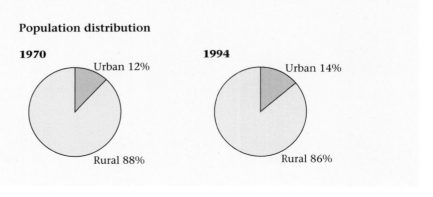

1970
Urban 12%
Rural 88%

1994
Urban 14%
Rural 86%

Cambodia

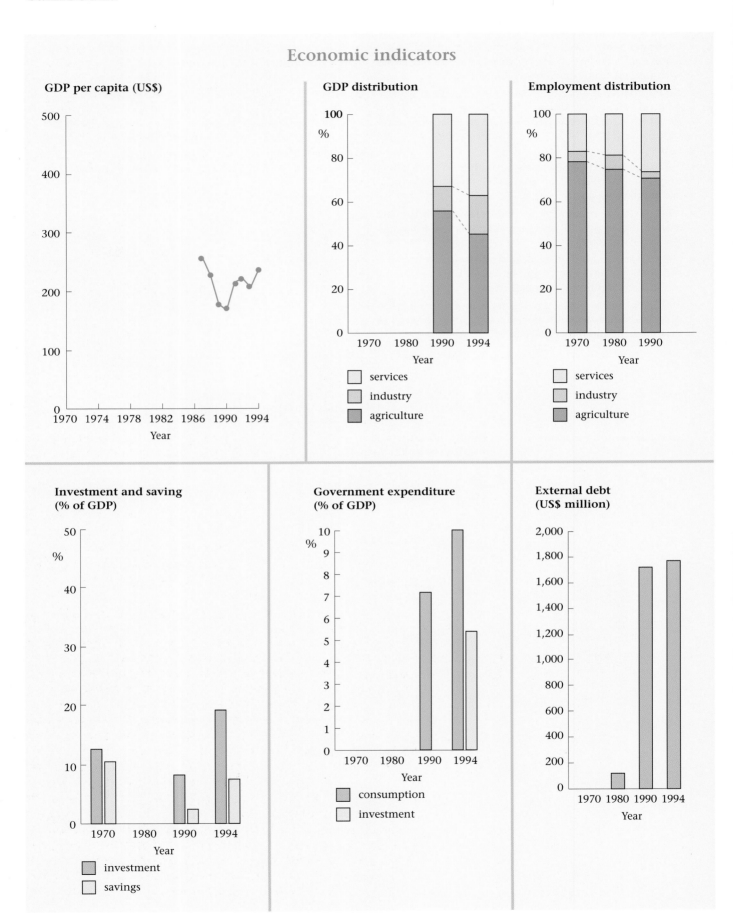

Economic indicators

GDP per capita (US$)

GDP distribution

services
industry
agriculture

Employment distribution

services
industry
agriculture

Investment and saving (% of GDP)

investment
savings

Government expenditure (% of GDP)

consumption
investment

External debt (US$ million)

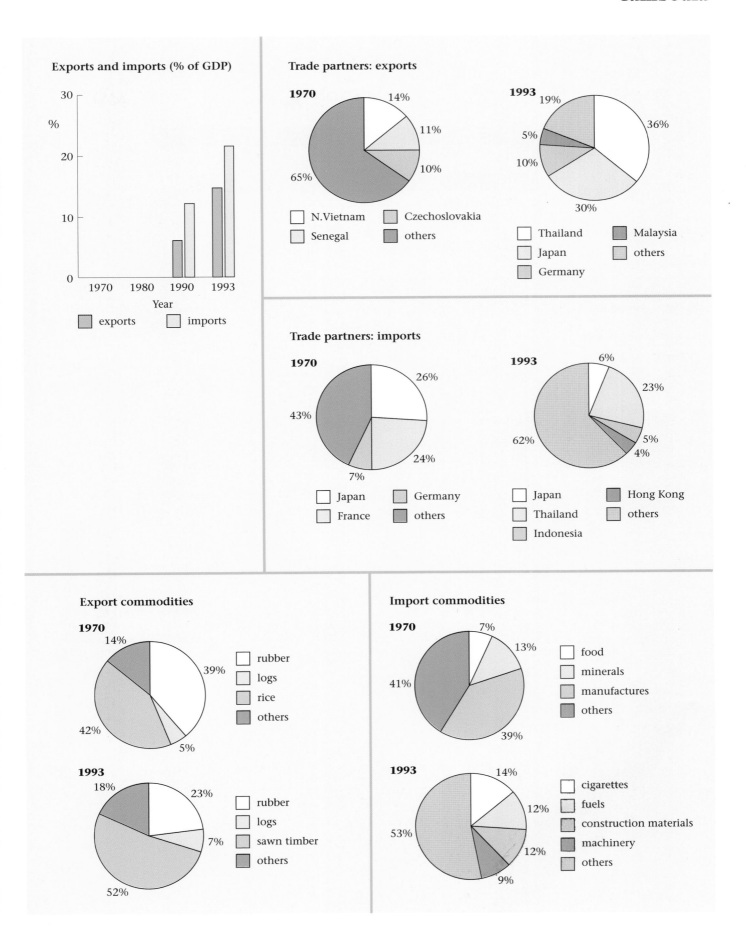

Exports and imports (% of GDP)

Trade partners: exports

1970

- N.Vietnam
- Senegal
- Czechoslovakia
- others

1993

- Thailand
- Japan
- Germany
- Malaysia
- others

Trade partners: imports

1970

- Japan
- France
- Germany
- others

1993

- Japan
- Thailand
- Indonesia
- Hong Kong
- others

Export commodities

1970

- rubber
- logs
- rice
- others

1993

- rubber
- logs
- sawn timber
- others

Import commodities

1970

- food
- minerals
- manufactures
- others

1993

- cigarettes
- fuels
- construction materials
- machinery
- others

Cambodia

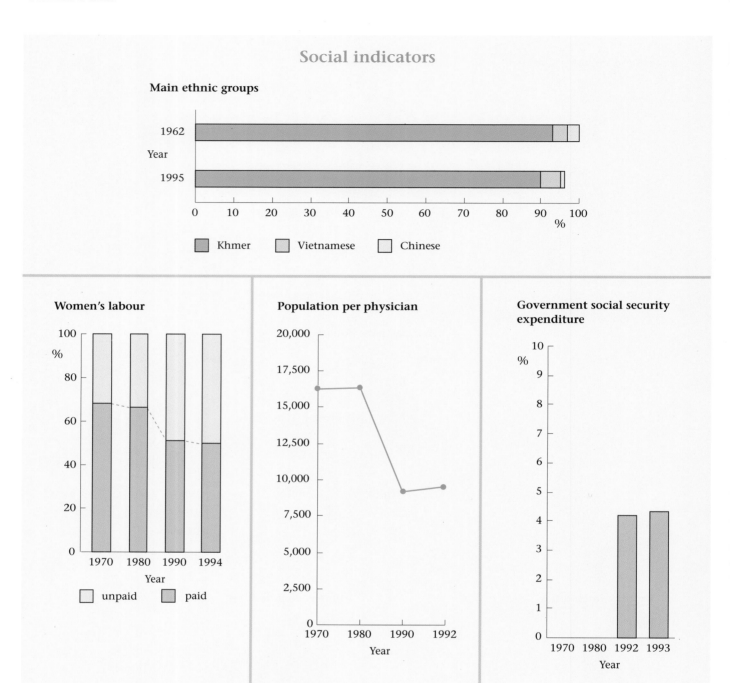

Social indicators

Main ethnic groups

Year

1962

1995

0 10 20 30 40 50 60 70 80 90 100
%

Khmer   Vietnamese   Chinese

Women's labour

%
100
80
60
40
20
0

1970 1980 1990 1994
Year

unpaid   paid

Population per physician

20,000
17,500
15,000
12,500
10,000
7,500
5,000
2,500
0

1970 1980 1990 1992
Year

Government social security expenditure

%
10
9
8
7
6
5
4
3
2
1
0

1970 1980 1992 1993
Year

Political framework

- Political turmoil following 1993 elections continued unabated over next four years

- Divisions within and between FUNCINPEC and CPP coalition partners surface most starkly in political murders on streets of Phnom Penh

- Mid 1996 great hopes for national consolidation and greater control of key trading routes in north-west as remaining Khmer Rouge guerrilla group split apart amidst rumours of Pol Pot's death

- Key Khmer Rouge faction seeks political reconciliation with Phnom Penh government and pledges end to military role. Unexpected bonus for government who could now restore control over areas near Thai border rich in resources of gems and tropical timber

- But FUNCINPEC and CPP badly divided over who takes credit for Khmer Rouge defections and how to accommodate defectors

- Major divisions too over future role of monarchy in light of Sihanouk's serious illness and expected death. Possibility that a FUNCINPEC leader would succeed as King alarms rival CPP

- Late 1996 disputes over role of Khmer Rouge defectors, the monarchy, rash of murders and attacks on foreigners alarms ASEAN states considering application from Cambodia for full membership in 1997

- ASEAN membership seen as key to Cambodia's future – ASEAN states use this in attempt to force governing coalition partners into more effective political co-operation

- ASEAN status becomes even more crucial after IMF cancels loan instalments in 1996 over lax implementation of timber logging policies. Other donors and foreign investors expected to follow IMF lead making Cambodian government desperate for ASEAN partners to fill expected gap.

Further reading

Chandler, D.P. (1991) *The Tragedy of Cambodian History: Politics, War and Revolution since 1945*, New Haven, Yale University Press.

Martin, M.A. (1994) *Cambodia: a Shattered Society*, Berkeley, University of California Press.

Canada

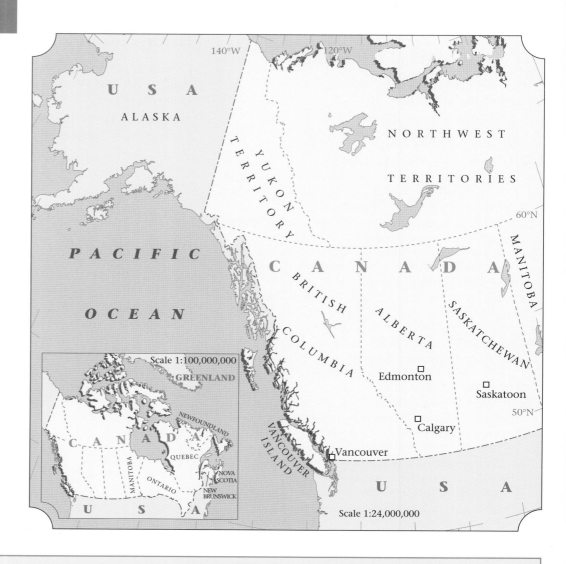

Historical background

- Indigenous peoples including the Inuit arrive from Asia over past 40,000 years
- 1497 first documented European contact
- 1534 after fishing expeditions around Newfoundland French lay claim to Canada
- 1605 first permanent French settlement – Quebec founded 1608
- 17th–18th C. French and British vie for control of North America
- 1713 Treaty of Utrecht cedes Newfoundland, Nova Scotia and Hudson Bay area to Britain
- 1759 British capture Quebec. France gives up all claims to Canada in 1763 but frictions remain with French-speaking communities concentrated in Quebec region
- 1774 Spanish explore Pacific coast followed by Captain Cook. Accounts of fur wealth encourage British and American fur traders to penetrate interior of western Canada
- 1775–83 American War of Independence – migration of British loyalists to Canada

- 1792–94 Captain George Vancouver surveys Pacific coast of North America furthering British interests in the region of what is now Vancouver Island
- 1849 Vancouver Island becomes British Crown Colony
- 1858 gold discovery leads to large-scale immigration into western Canada including some Chinese. Colony of British Columbia proclaimed
- 1867 British North America Act establishes the self governing Dominion of Canada comprising the provinces of Nova Scotia, New Brunswick, Quebec and Ontario
- 1871 Vancouver Island and British Columbia join Canada as the Province of British Columbia
- 1870s and 1880s despite discrimination policies large numbers of Chinese and other Asian workers arrive to build Canadian Pacific railroad. Asian population nears 10% in British Columbia
- 1887 Vancouver City becomes terminal of the Canadian Pacific railroad, the first to cross Canada
- 1891 steamship links from Vancouver to Asia established

and from 1914 British Columbia's prosperity boosted by the construction of the Panama Canal. Journey times from eastern North America and Europe drastically reduced

- 1914–18 Canada as part of the British Empire at war with Germany
- 1923 Chinese Immigration Act responds to anti-Asian sentiments by severely limiting immigration. Discrimination continues and Asian community declines
- 1931 Statute of Westminster – Britain recognizes legislative autonomy for Canada
- 1939–45 Canada joins Britain in war against Germany
- Post-war period sees rapid economic development, industrialization and urbanization across Canada. British Columbia becomes a leading province in terms of population and economic growth
- 1960s separatist movement in Quebec gains momentum
- 1963–79 Liberal Party in government first under Lester Pearson and then Pierre Trudeau from 1968
- 1970s–1980s revival of Asian immigration to British Columbia especially from Hong Kong

- 1979–80 Progressive Conservatives form minority government
- 1980 Liberal Party under Trudeau returned to power. Referendum in Quebec rejects independence
- 1982 Canada Act removes last constitutional and legal ties between Britain and Canada
- 1984–93 Progressive Conservatives in government
- 1985 Meech Lake Accord initiative allowing Quebec recognition as a distinct society within Canada fails when two provinces withhold approval
- 1989 Canada joins APEC and approves plans for NAFTA
- 1993 Liberal Party returns to power after Progressive Conservatives decimated – *Bloc Quebecois* become largest opposition party
- 1994 NAFTA agreement signed with USA and Mexico
- 1995 referendum in Quebec calling for sovereignty and a new partnership with Canada narrowly defeated
- 1997 Liberal Party returned to power with a slim majority – election campaign exposes more regional differences over special cultural and linguistic privileges for Quebec.

Demographic indicators

Total population (million)

Density (persons per km²)

Infant mortality rate (deaths per 1,000 births)

Life expectancy at birth (years)

Population distribution

1970

Rural 24%

Urban 76%

1994

Rural 23%

Urban 77%

Canada

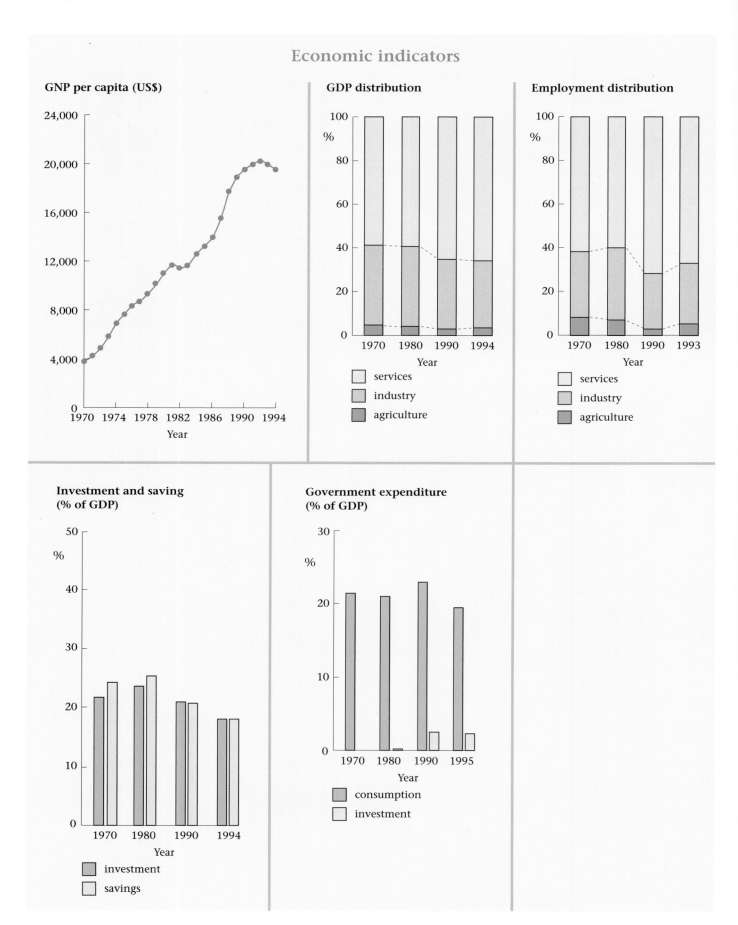

Economic indicators

GNP per capita (US$)

GDP distribution

Employment distribution

Investment and saving (% of GDP)

Government expenditure (% of GDP)

Exports and imports (% of GDP)

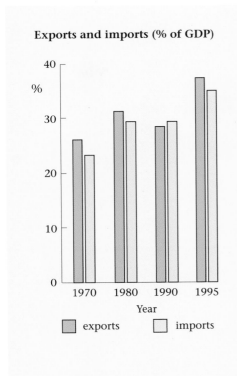

Trade partners: exports

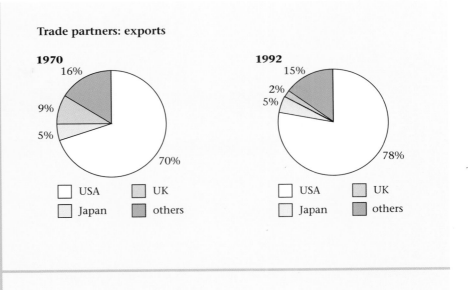

Trade partners: imports

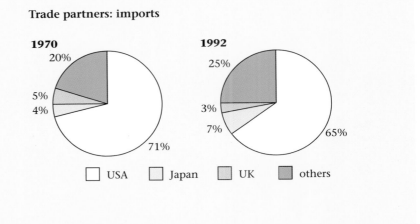

Export commodities

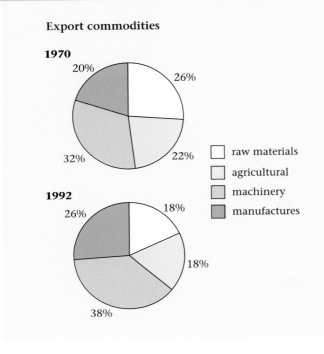

Import commodities

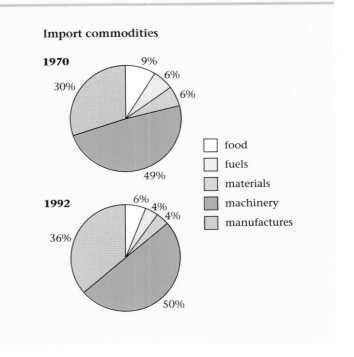

Canada

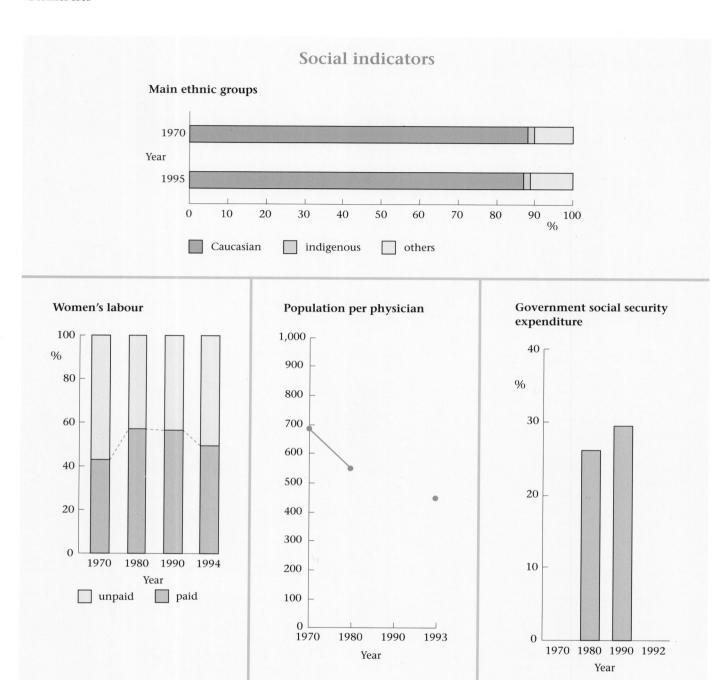

Social indicators

Main ethnic groups

Year

1970

1995

0 10 20 30 40 50 60 70 80 90 100

%

■ Caucasian ▨ indigenous □ others

Women's labour

%

100
80
60
40
20
0

1970 1980 1990 1994

Year

□ unpaid ▨ paid

Population per physician

1,000
900
800
700
600
500
400
300
200
100
0

1970 1980 1990 1993

Year

Government social security expenditure

%

40
30
20
10
0

1970 1980 1990 1992

Year

Political framework

National

- Though British connections were removed in 1982 the British monarch remains symbolic Head of State appointing a Governor General on the advice of Canadian Prime Minister

- The 1867 British North America Act established the constitution and the parliamentary system

- The national parliament has two houses
  - a House of Commons elected by universal adult suffrage
  - a Senate appointed by the Governor General on the advice of the Prime Minister who is leader of the majority party in the House of Commons

- Legislation must pass through both houses but only the House can introduce legislation committing public funds or adjusting taxes

- The main political parties include
  - Liberal Party, left of centre
  - Progressive Conservative Party, right of centre
  - Reform Party
  - New Democratic Party, a social democratic party
  - *Bloc Quebecois*, the Quebec separatist party

- Either the Liberal Party or the Progressive Conservatives have formed the national government since 1945

- Tension between English- and French-speaking communities remains important in Canadian domestic politics. This was a key feature of the 1997 election campaign especially in Alberta and British Columbia where voters returned Reform Party candidates in an apparent backlash against government concessions to separatist sentiments in Quebec.

Provincial

- There is some separation of power between the national parliament and the legislative assemblies of the provinces and territories

- Canada now comprises ten provinces: British Columbia, Nova Scotia, New Brunswick, Quebec, Ontario, Manitoba, Saskatchewan, Alberta, Prince Edward Island and Newfoundland. There are also two territories, the Yukon Territory and the Northwest Territories

- In British Columbia a Lieutenant Governor representing the Crown but appointed by the national government calls on the majority party leader in the Legislative Assembly to form a government

- Two parties have dominated British Columbia's Legislative Assembly in recent times
  - the Social Credit Party, a market oriented conservative provincial party
  - the New Democratic Party, a social democratic party which also contests national elections

- The Social Credit Party has formed the provincial government for most of the period since it first came to power in 1952.

Further reading

Barman, J. (1991) *The West beyond the West: a History of British Columbia*, Toronto, Toronto University Press.

Dunn, C. (1996) *Provinces: Canadian Provincial Politics*, Ontario, Broadview.

Li, P.S. (1996) *Making Postwar Canada*, Ontario, Oxford University Press.

McNaught, K. (1988) *The Penguin History of Canada*, Harmondsworth, Penguin Books.

Chile

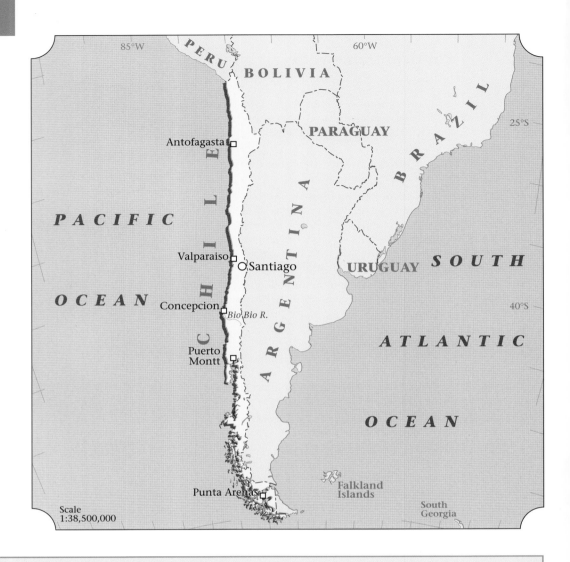

Scale
1:38,500,000

Historical background

- Current territorial boundaries date from late 19th C.
- To 16th C. territory occupied by Inca peoples to the north and Araucanian Indians in south
- 1541 Spain colonizes Chile – most remote Spanish outpost in Latin America
- Vast area south of military frontier along Bio Bio river occupied only by Araucanian Indians
- Society stratified into minority European elite and largely illiterate mestizo masses
- 1810 independence and new constitution lasting from 1833 until 1925
- Territory expands with subjugation of Araucanian Indians and conquest of nitrate- and copper-rich provinces in the north in 1883 at conclusion of wars with Bolivia and Peru
- Extensive presidential powers within embryonic party system dominated by aristocrats – only one revolution, 1891, so some say evolutionary politics embedded
- Independence brings little economic and social change
  - land inequalities: 90% owned by 2% landholders
  - resource inequalities in profits from copper, nitrates and silver exports
- Challenge of labour movement met by state repression
- 1924 divided party politicians allow military coup, new constitution and corporatist government
- From 1929 world depression shatters an economy reliant on raw material exports – taxes on which yield 75% government revenues. Political parties fractured along spectrum from communist to fascist – government attempts to manage economic diversification and import substitution
- 1938–64 middle-class parties dominate fractious governing coalitions but more state intervention fails to relieve dependence on raw materials
- 1964–70 President Frei and Christian Democrats attempt agrarian and social reforms as well as taking 50% stake in US-owned copper mines but upper house opposition dilute impact
- 1970–73 Marxist Allende elected President and promises a 'Chilean Road to Socialism' within democratic regime.

Nationalization of resource industries, banking and commerce provokes fierce reaction from centre-right and the military. Allende's contacts with Cuba's Castro and the takeover of US companies provokes USA to slash foreign aid. 500% inflation in early 1970s as copper prices plunge 50%

- 1973 Allende killed in military coup and new President Pinochet committed to reverse Marxist policies in brutal authoritarian repression

- Pinochet's monetarist experiment to radically restructure economy. State employees drastically cut, industries denationalized, tariff barriers fall to lowest in world, tax laws liberalized to attract foreign companies. Inflation rate falls, some diversification from copper dependence into exports of wine, fruit and wood but overall high social costs as unemployment and bankruptcies rise dramatically

- Despite severe repression through 1980s accelerating bouts of public protest are not subdued – even pressure from within the military and from USA for return to civilian rule

- 1988 plebiscite allowed on whether President should be elected or nominated by Pinochet

- 1988 voters reject Pinochet and civilian Aylwin wins 1989 election though Pinochet still head of armed forces

- Remnants of Pinochet's regime block complete removal of military influence from political scene even after new President Frei elected in 1994 within much more democratized scene

- Economic recovery continues in 1990s with extensive international interest in Latin America's fastest growing economy. Joined APEC 1994 where Chile sells over half its exports – negotiating NAFTA membership arguably seen as permanent anchor for continued growth.

Demographic indicators

Total population (million)

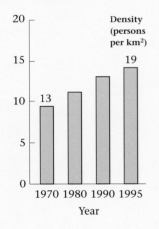

Infant mortality rate (deaths per 1,000 births)

Life expectancy at birth (years)

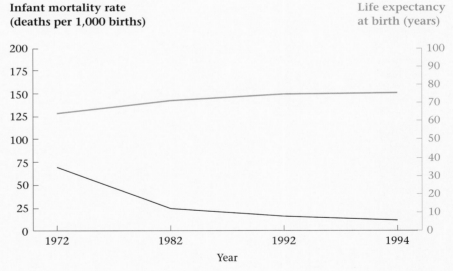

Population distribution

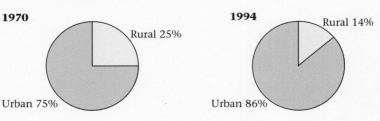

1970
Rural 25%
Urban 75%

1994
Rural 14%
Urban 86%

Chile

Economic indicators

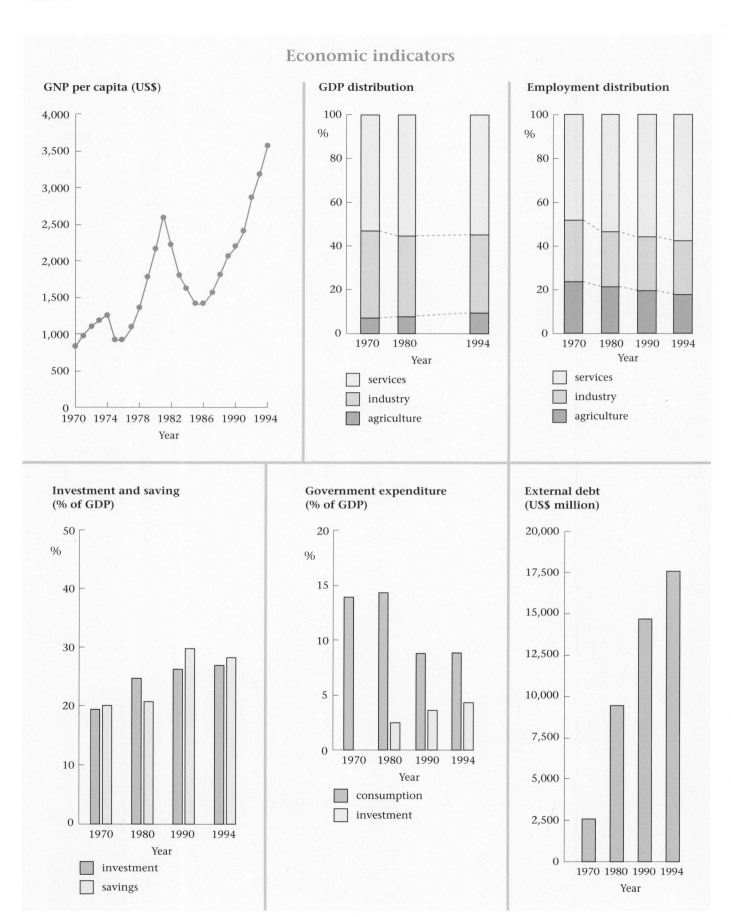

Exports and imports (% of GDP)

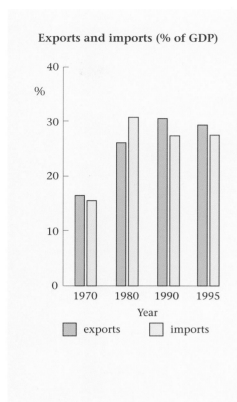

Trade partners: exports

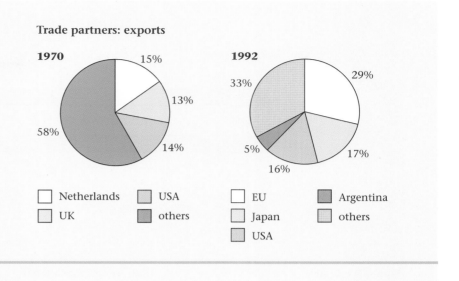

Trade partners: imports

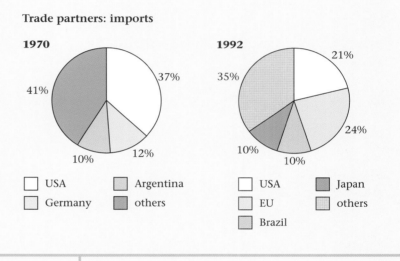

Export commodities

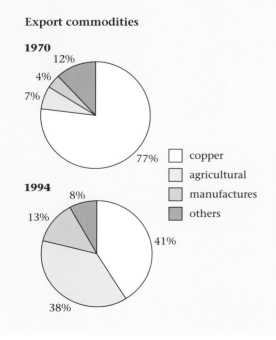

Import commodities

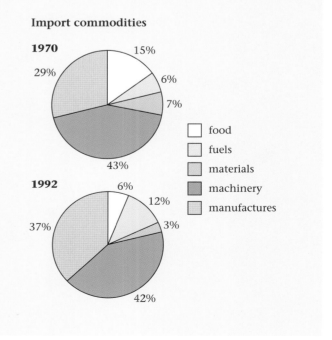

Chile

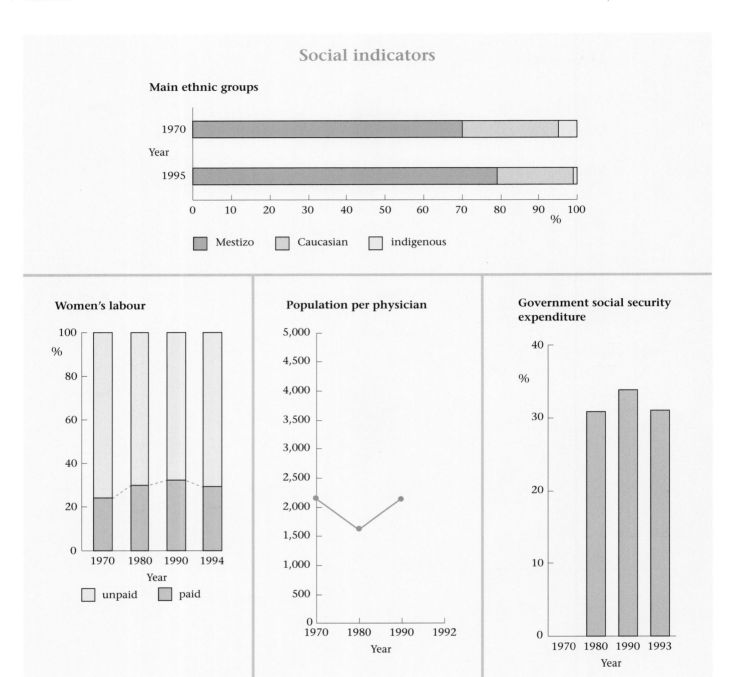

Social indicators

Main ethnic groups

Year
1970
1995

0 10 20 30 40 50 60 70 80 90 100 %

■ Mestizo   ■ Caucasian   □ indigenous

Women's labour

100 %
80
60
40
20
0

1970 1980 1990 1994
Year

□ unpaid   ■ paid

Population per physician

5,000
4,500
4,000
3,500
3,000
2,500
2,000
1,500
1,000
500
0

1970 1980 1990 1992
Year

Government social security expenditure

40 %
30
20
10
0

1970 1980 1990 1993
Year

Political framework

- Post-Pinochet governments dominated by centre-left coalition with twin aims to consolidate democracy and generate economic growth with equity. Implementation of both aims troublesome

- Divisions within ruling coalition over how to deal with those guilty of human rights violations under Pinochet – called 'systematic policy of extermination' by 1991 Commission for Truth and Reconciliation. Spectre of military opposition forces elected government to eschew attention to past crimes and so avoid destabilizing fragile democratic regime

- Pinochet's allies in Supreme Court and upper house of Senate able to block attempts to remove from the constitution the continuing sources of military influence

- 1995 again dissent within governing coalition over preferential treatment for military offenders to be housed in separate prisons from civilian offenders

- Economic policies also open up divisions within government
  - over the 'growth with equity' objective relating to housing, education and social justice reforms designed to reverse inequalities of Pinochet era
  - over the extent of further privatization
  - over the impact of NAFTA's membership requirements to have even more trade liberalization

- Ultimately governing coalition seemed to retain power because the opposition centre-right coalition is even more divided.

Further reading

Bethell, L. (1993) *Chile Since Independence*, Cambridge, Cambridge University Press.

Oppenheim, L.H. (1993) *Politics in Chile: Democracy, Authoritarianism and the Search for Development*, Boulder, Westview.

China

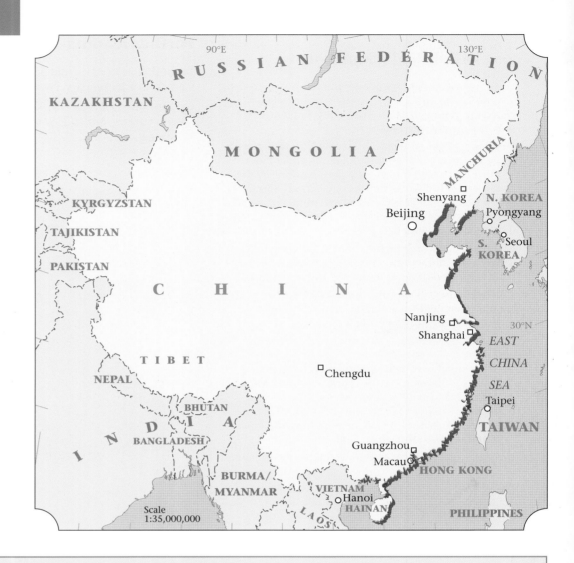

Historical background

- 221 BC First Emperor of Qin unifies China
- 206 BC–AD 220 Han dynasty
- 618–907 Tang dynasty
- 1206–1368 Mongol rule and from 1279 controlling all China – first time foreigners had subjugated whole country
- 1368–1644 Ming dynasty
- 1644–1911 Qing dynasty – ruled by Manchus
- 1842 Sino-British Treaty of Nanjing – first of the unequal treaties
- 1851–66 Taiping rebellion ravages China
- 1898 Hundred Days Reform favours modernizing influences – suppressed by Empress Dowager Cixi
- 1900 Boxer rebellion provokes occupation of Beijing by eight foreign powers
- 1912 Republic of China established – Sun Yat-sen President
- 1921 First Congress of Chinese Communist Party (CCP)
- 1926–28 Chiang Kai-shek's Northern Expedition to reunify China under his Nationalist Party (Kuomintang)

- 1931 Japan seizes control of Manchuria – puppet government established 1932
- 1937–45 China fights its 'War of Resistance' against Japan
- 1946–49 civil war between CCP and Kuomintang
- 1949 Mao Zedong proclaims the People's Republic of China (PRC)
- 1950 Treaty of Friendship with Soviet Union
- 1950–53 Chinese military involvement in Korean War
- 1958 Great Leap Forward launched to hasten economic development
- 1959 rebellion in Tibet fails
- 1960 withdrawal of Soviet experts – drastic deterioration in Sino-Soviet relations
- 1966 Mao launches Great Proletarian Cultural Revolution
- 1976 Mao Zedong dies
- 1976 radical 'gang of four' overthrown in coup – Cultural Revolution reversed
- 1978 Third Plenary Session of the Eleventh Central Com-

mittee of CCP establishes Deng Xiaoping's authority and policies of
- reform
- modernization of industry, agriculture, national defence, science and technology
- opening China to the outside world
- rapid economic development

- 1979 diplomatic relations established with the USA
- 1979 Sino-Vietnamese border war
- 1981 CCP formally negates Cultural Revolution, downgrades Mao Zedong's role in CCP history and appoints Hu Yaobang first as CCP Chairman and later General Secretary
- 1984 agreement with UK – Hong Kong to revert to Chinese sovereignty July 1997
- 1986 large-scale student movement suppressed – leads to Hu Yaobang's dismissal
- 1987 agreement with Portugal – Macau to revert to Chinese sovereignty December 1999
- 1987 and 1989 Tibetan independence demonstrations suppressed

- April–June 1989 student movement for greater freedom and democracy in Beijing and other cities
- May 1989 Soviet leader Gorbachev visits China to normalize Sino-Soviet relations
- 3–4 June 1989 student movement suppressed – considerable bloodshed especially in Beijing's Tiananmen Square
- 24 June 1989 Jiang Zemin CCP General Secretary
- 1992 Deng Xiaoping revives policies of reform, modernization and opening to the outside world
- 1993 failure of China's bid to host Olympic Games in 2000 leads to rise in nationalism and anti-Western feeling
- 1995 Taiwan's President Lee Teng-hui visits USA – strong Chinese pronouncements that both Lee and USA are trying to detach Taiwan from China permanently and split the country
- 1996 Jiang Zemin attempts to use CCP Central Committee Plenary Session to revive Marxist–Leninist ideology and China's 'spiritual revolution' – socialist ethics to go alongside economic development
- 1997 Deng Xiaoping dies.

Demographic indicators

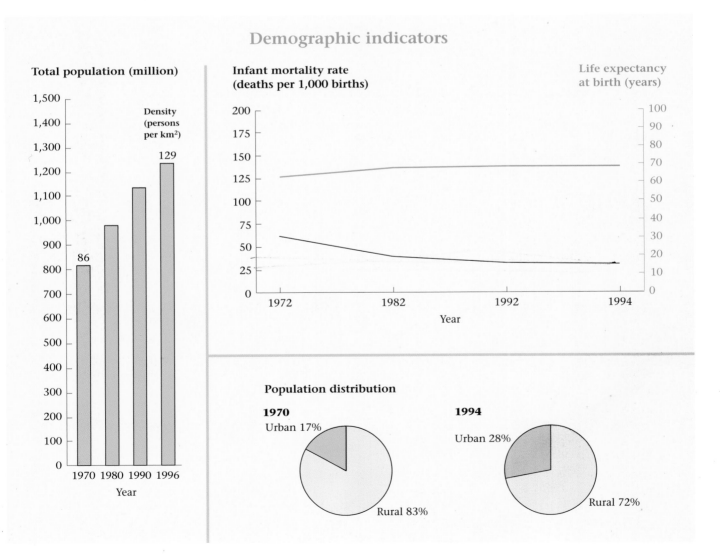

Total population (million)

Density (persons per km²)

129

86

Year
1970 1980 1990 1996

Infant mortality rate (deaths per 1,000 births)

Life expectancy at birth (years)

Year
1972 1982 1992 1994

Population distribution

1970
Urban 17%
Rural 83%

1994
Urban 28%
Rural 72%

China

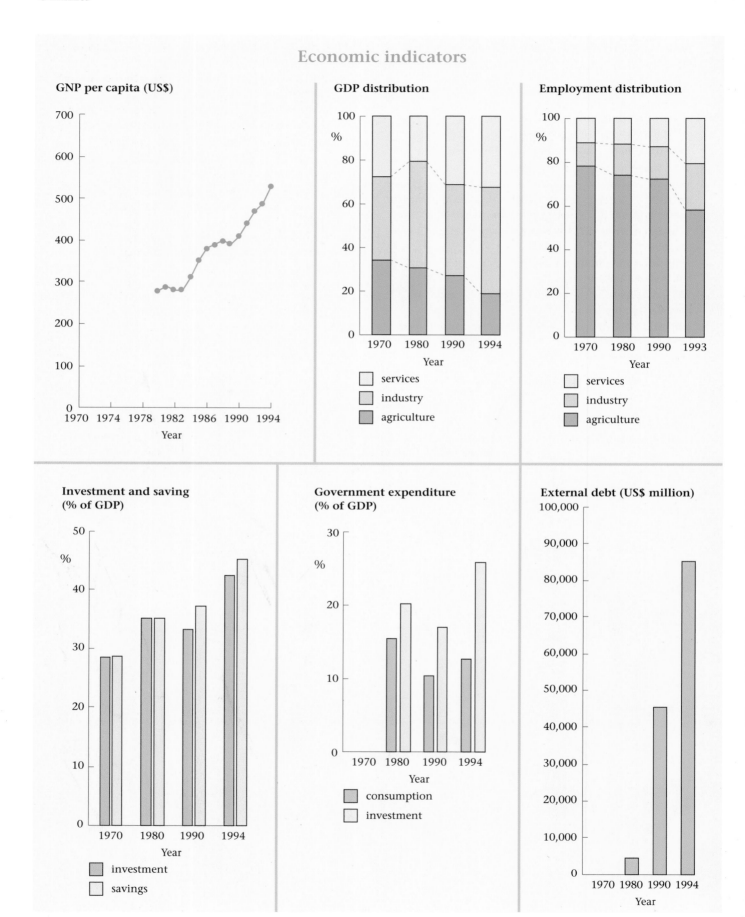

Economic indicators

GNP per capita (US$)

GDP distribution

services
industry
agriculture

Employment distribution

services
industry
agriculture

Investment and saving (% of GDP)

investment
savings

Government expenditure (% of GDP)

consumption
investment

External debt (US$ million)

Exports and imports (% of GDP)

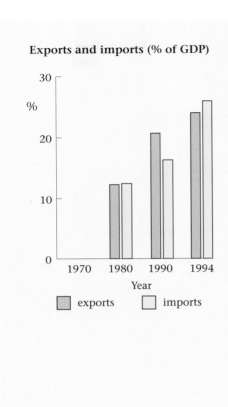

Trade partners: exports

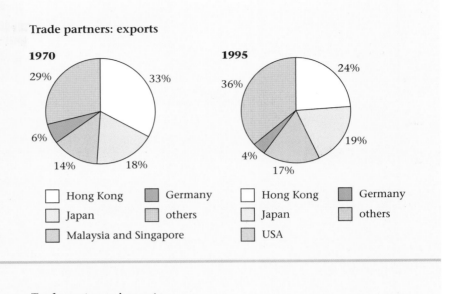

1970

1995

Hong Kong | Germany | Hong Kong | Germany
Japan | others | Japan | others
Malaysia and Singapore | | USA

Trade partners: imports

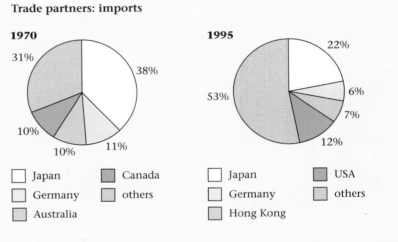

1970

1995

Japan | Canada | Japan | USA
Germany | others | Germany | others
Australia | | Hong Kong

Export commodities

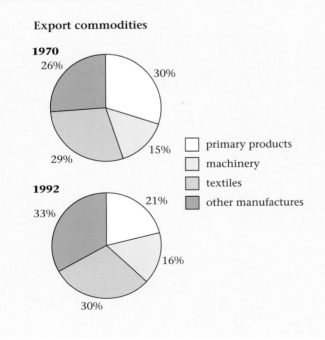

1970

1992

primary products
machinery
textiles
other manufactures

Import commodities

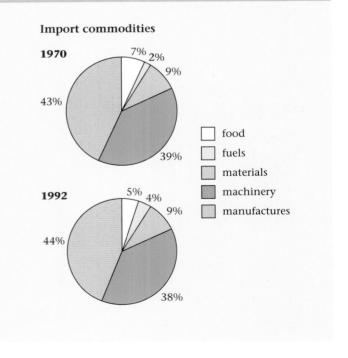

1970

1992

food
fuels
materials
machinery
manufactures

China

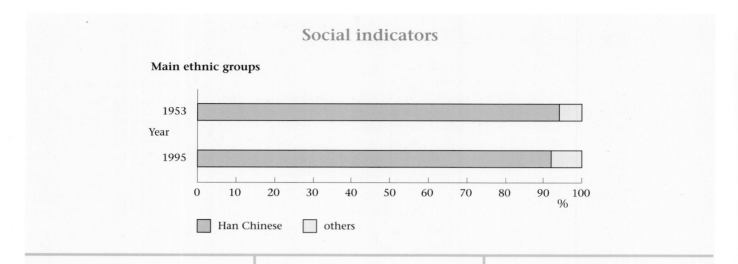

Social indicators

Main ethnic groups

Year

1953
1995

Han Chinese   others

Women's labour

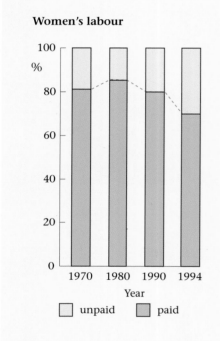

%

unpaid   paid

Year

Population per physician

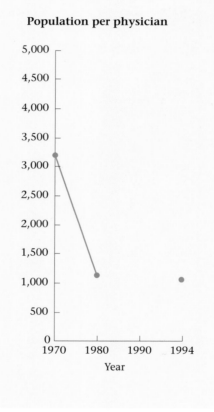

Year

Government social security expenditure

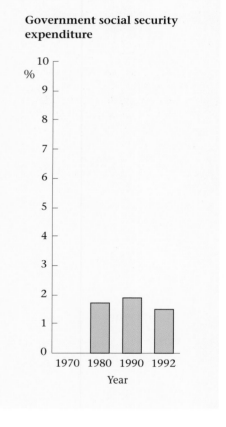

%

Year

Political framework

- The People's Republic of China regards itself as a multi-national, unitary state under the leadership of the Chinese Communist Party (CCP). This means
  - autonomy for ethnic minorities but
  - absolute proscriptions on all attempts at secession or threats to national unity
- The main organs of power in China are
  - the CCP
  - the People's Liberation Army (PLA)
  - the government
- The CCP National Party Congress meets every fifth year. The most important body below the Congress is the Central Committee. Main power is concentrated in a small number of CCP leaders
- Among political parties only the CCP has any real power. The electoral laws – especially the 1987 Villages Law – produced some popular participation in China but pose no threat to CCP power
- The legal system is characterized by
  - the lack of an independent judiciary
  - becoming stronger under reform policies with the legal bureaucracy growing enormously, though remaining very small indeed by Western standards
  - a growing number of laws in economic and social arenas.

Further reading

Benewick, R. and Wingrove, P. (1995) *China in the 1990s*, London, Macmillan.

Brugger, B. and Reglar, S. (1994) *Politics, Economy and Society in Contemporary China*, London, Macmillan.

Dietrich, C. (1994) *People's China: a Brief History*, 2nd edn, Oxford, Oxford University Press.

Dwyer, D. (1994) *China: the Next Decades*, London, Longman.

Colombia

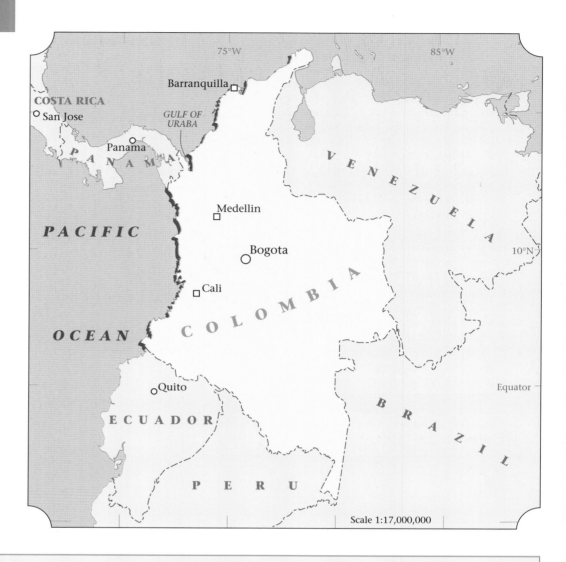

Scale 1:17,000,000

Historical background

- To 16th C. occupied by Amerindian peoples in scattered rural communities
- 1509 first Spanish settlements established around Gulf of Uraba
- 1538 Bogota founded as colonial capital – extensive gold deposits thereafter exploited using slaves from Africa
- 1739 Colombia raised to status of New Granada Viceroyalty as the leading gold producer in Spanish Empire
- 1819 New Granada gains independence from Spain in union with Ecuador, Panama and Venezuela
- 1830 Ecuador and Venezuela leave union
- 1863 country renamed Colombia
- 1903 with US encouragement Panama declares independence
- 19th C. politics dominated by Conservative Party favouring strong central state with close links to Catholic Church; Liberal Party has more reformist federal agenda. Repeated civil wars dispute centralized state authority

- Economy based mainly on poorly developed subsistence agriculture. Coffee replaces gold as main export but badly affected by collapse of primary product prices in 1930s
- 1948 decade of severe civil war begins – 300,000 killed and military in power 1953–57
- 1957 civilian rule restored in National Front where Conservative and Liberal Parties alternate presidency in four-year terms with equal shares of ministerial posts and Congress seats. This highly restrictive polity lasts 20 years
- 1970–75 political groups representing the poorest in society unsuccessfully attempt to break Conservative/Liberal monopoly. Some radicals begin armed revolt and are joined by communist guerrillas
- 1978 bi-partisan presidential rotation ends when Ayala is elected. Major counter-offensive against guerrillas aided by rightist paramilitary groups associated with drug barons
- Early 1980s as part of economic strategy to encourage foreign investment President Betancur seeks peace with guerrillas but fails after major battle in heart of Bogota – over 100 killed

- Betancur also attempts to extradite leading drug traffickers to the USA to increase chances of conviction but Colombian Supreme Court declares extradition treaty illegal

- 1986 Barco Vargas becomes President and rules by emergency decree in effort to eliminate drugs cartels. Little success as violence continues – hundreds killed including three presidential candidates for May 1990 election

- 1990 new President Gaviria seeks peace with guerrillas and restrains drug-cartels offensive in order to secure stable background for neo-liberal economic reforms

- Some drug leaders surrender – given immunity from US extradition and receive reduced prison sentences; some guerrilla leaders surrender and move into mainstream politics

- Neo-liberal agenda includes reduced trade barriers, privatization and promotion of foreign investment. New constitution in 1994 also pledges end to rule by emergency decree, more space for minority parties, safeguards for rights of individuals, judiciary and Congress

- Gaviria also signs free trade agreement with Venezuela and Mexico hoping it will lead to membership of NAFTA

- 1994 new President Samper elected but his administration is undermined because he faces judicial investigation over allegations that his election campaign was funded by drug barons

- March 1996 USA decertifies Colombia from list of countries making acceptable progress against drugs trade which removes eligibility for certain kinds of financial assistance

- June 1996 Samper acquitted of any election funding irregularities

- Early 1997 state of economic emergency declared in attempt to reduce government deficit and prevent further foreign exchange appreciation – widespread labour unrest especially among public sector workers.

Demographic indicators

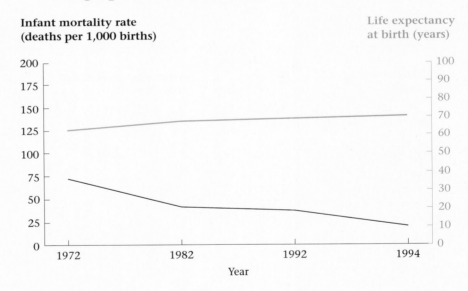

Total population (million)

Density (persons per km²)

Infant mortality rate (deaths per 1,000 births)

Life expectancy at birth (years)

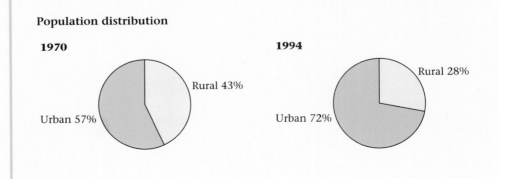

Population distribution

1970

Rural 43%

Urban 57%

1994

Rural 28%

Urban 72%

Colombia

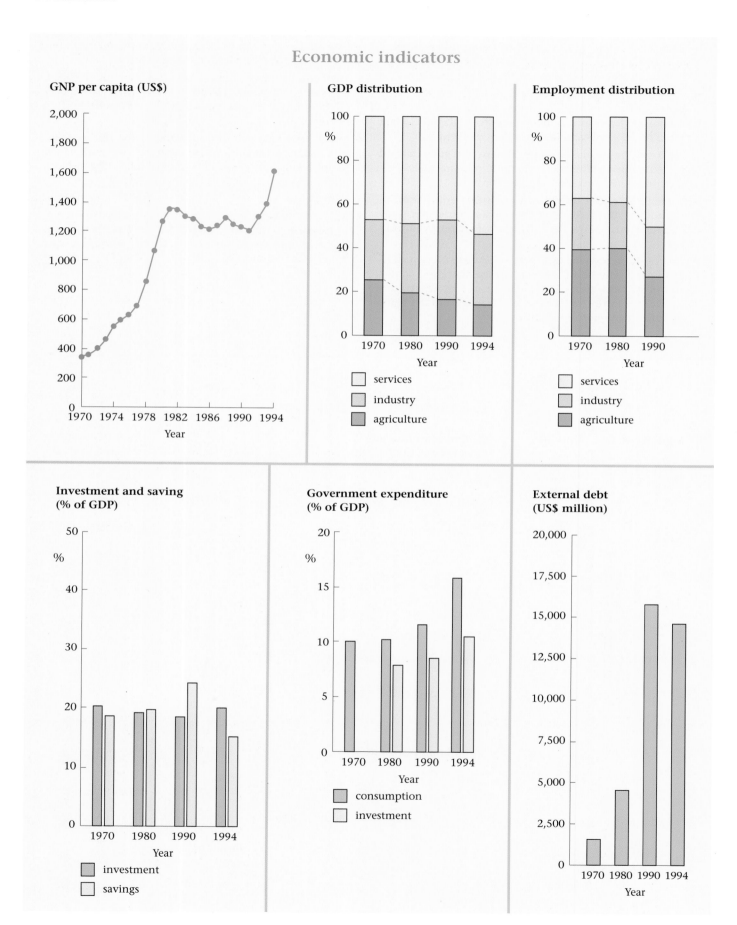

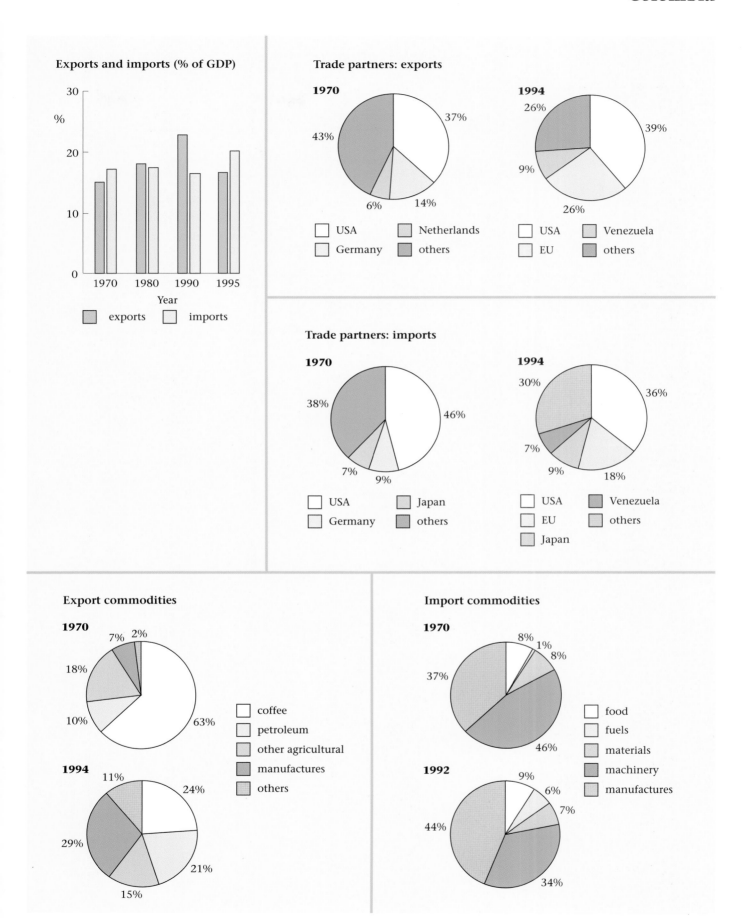

Exports and imports (% of GDP)

Trade partners: exports

1970

USA 37%
others 43%
Netherlands 6%
Germany 14%

1994

USA 39%
others 26%
EU 9%
Venezuela 26%

USA   Netherlands
Germany   others

USA   Venezuela
EU   others

Trade partners: imports

1970

USA 46%
others 38%
Germany 7%
Japan 9%

1994

USA 36%
others 30%
Germany 7%
Japan 9%
EU 18%

USA   Japan
Germany   others

USA   Venezuela
EU   others
Japan

Export commodities

1970

coffee 63%
others 18%
petroleum 10%
other agricultural 7%
manufactures 2%

1994

coffee 24%
others 11%
manufactures 29%
other agricultural 15%
petroleum 21%

coffee
petroleum
other agricultural
manufactures
others

Import commodities

1970

food 8%
fuels 1%
materials 8%
manufactures 37%
machinery 46%

1992

food 9%
fuels 6%
materials 7%
manufactures 44%
machinery 34%

food
fuels
materials
machinery
manufactures

Colombia

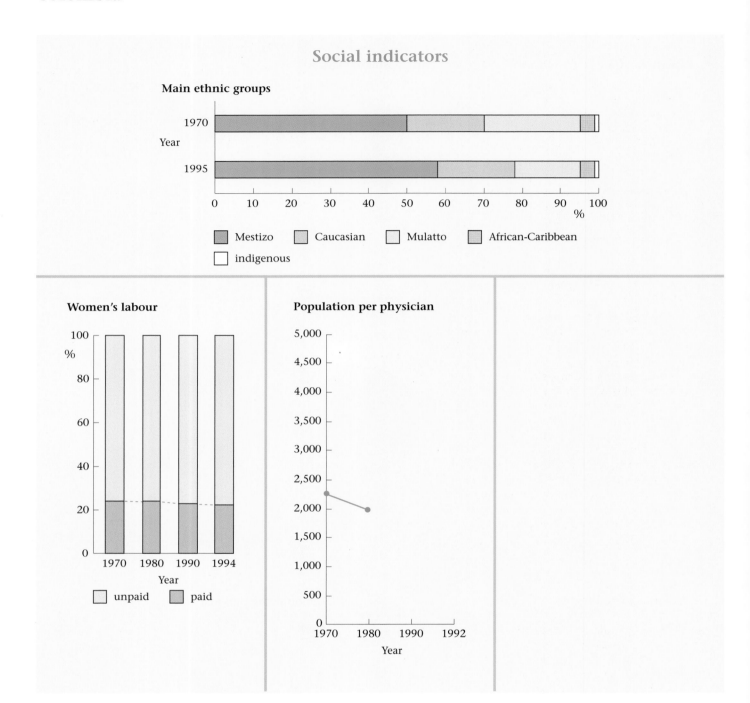

Social indicators

Main ethnic groups

Year
1970
1995

0 10 20 30 40 50 60 70 80 90 100
%

■ Mestizo   ■ Caucasian   ☐ Mulatto   ■ African-Caribbean
☐ indigenous

Women's labour

%
100
80
60
40
20
0

1970 1980 1990 1994
Year

☐ unpaid   ■ paid

Population per physician

5,000
4,500
4,000
3,500
3,000
2,500
2,000
1,500
1,000
500
0

1970 1980 1990 1992
Year

Political framework

- The problems of the Samper Administration since 1994 highlight three key political issues confronting Colombia: guerrilla violence, the drugs trade and the impact of neo-liberal economic policies

- Some small but active guerrilla groups refuse to surrender without major economic and political concessions

- Violence worsens in the mid 1990s during the political hiatus over the possible impeachment of President Samper – over 30,000 people killed annually

- New wave of kidnapping and extortion see guerrillas target foreign companies in the petroleum sector which threatens activity in this key economic area

- Despite using less confrontational tactics drug traders continue to operate fairly freely bringing domestic and external pressures

- Government contacts with drug cartels over plea bargaining and lighter sentences for convicted traffickers means political corruption remains a vibrant issue

- Though the Colombian Congress did acquit Samper of using funds from the drugs mafia in his 1994 election campaign this was interpreted as self-interest. A presidential impeachment would inevitably implicate many other elected legislators

- Externally, Colombia faces the ever present threat of US sanctions designed to force more action to curb the drugs trade. Sanctions could undermine foreign investment from US companies and trigger similar reactions from other international financial institutions

- Relations with USA deteriorate dramatically in 1996 when Samper's entry visa was withdrawn. Heroin later found on Samper's personal aircraft about to depart for the UN where he was to address anti-drugs session of the General Assembly

- The USA would only apparently be satisfied by Colombia's agreement to extradite all serious drug offenders for trial in the USA

- Despite nationalist sentiment opposed to US intervention in Colombian affairs government commitment to neo-liberal economic policies continues to produce internal political unrest

- Even with improved economic growth based on the petroleum sector in particular, wealth distribution remains grossly unequal – over 40% of Colombians live in dire poverty

- Relieving basic poverty was supposed to have been a key element of government policy since 1994 but public spending reductions and tax increases associated with neo-liberal reforms inevitably worsen the plight of the poor

- The privatization programme also generates intense opposition from public sector unions. Nation-wide strikes aimed at slowing the pace of neo-liberal reforms dominate Colombia through the early months of 1997.

Further reading

Bushnell, D. (1993) *The Making of Modern Colombia: a Nation Inspite of Itself*, Berkeley, University of California Press.

Giraldo, J. (1996) *Colombia: the Genocidal Democracy*, Maine, Common Courage Press.

Costa Rica

Scale 1:8,000,000

Historical background

- To 16th C. occupied by indigenous Amerindian peoples
- 1502 Christopher Columbus lands on Caribbean coast – Spanish settlement follows from 1522
- Indigenous peoples decimated by diseases brought with Spanish
- Expected gold deposits never found and Spanish settlers remain subsistence farmers with little expansion until 18th C. – San Jose founded 1739
- 1821 independence as part of Mexican Empire
- 1823 break with Mexico to join Guatemala, Honduras and Nicaragua as United Provinces of Central America
- 1838 Costa Rica becomes independent republic
- 1889 long democratized tradition begins with franchise extension. Land allocation for coffee and later banana cultivation establishes substantial number of smaller farmers with weaker landowning elite. More stable polity especially in absence of politicized military

- Later 19th–20th C. only two short periods of political upheaval
  - 1917 Tinoco's revolutionary government ousts elected President but after a counter-revolution democratic government restored in 1919
  - 1948 Jose Figueres leads revolt when government presidential candidate refuses to accept election defeat – military junta headed by Figueres cedes power following year and new constitution abolishes armed forces
- 1953 Figueres elected President as leader of Partido de Liberacion Nacional (PLN) initiating social welfare programme and nationalization policies
- 1953–82 alternating PLN and Conservative Party governments successively increasing then decreasing state intervention in economic and social spheres
- Early 1980s onwards Costa Rican politics dominated by problems of Central American military conflicts and escalating economic crisis
- Governments attempt to remain neutral especially in Nicaraguan war despite US pressure to allow 'Contra' bases

to be established on Costa Rican territory to attack Nicaragua's Sandinista government

- 1986 PLN President Arias plays major role in brokering peace agreement to end Central American conflict. Agreement signed in 1987 between Presidents of Costa Rica, El Salvador, Guatemala, Honduras and Nicaragua pledging ceasefires, end to external military involvement and programme of democratization. Arias awarded Nobel Peace Prize

- Worsening economic crisis triggered by falling world primary product prices in economy where coffee and banana exports dominate. Falling export earnings with higher public spending on education and social welfare forces government to seek further loans from IMF/World Bank

- Later 1980s IMF/World Bank agree loans to cover external debt repayments but conditional on continuing with neoliberal policies and implementation of a Structural Adjustment Programme

- Privatization of public sector prioritized with substantial reductions in government expenditure especially on education and public health provision

- 1994 domestic political opposition to Structural Adjustment Programme results in election of new PLN President Jose Maria Figueres. PLN pledged to protect Costa Rica's high literacy levels and low incidence of poverty

- Figueres also tries to follow export promotion strategy developed under previous government that joined GATT in 1991

- 1995 free trade agreement with Mexico comes into effect with aim of eventually cementing trade links with Canada and the USA into membership of NAFTA

- 1996 Figueres government accepts need to follow more neoliberal economic policies in order to secure IMF credits and therefore be able to repay outstanding foreign debt.

Demographic indicators

Total population (million)

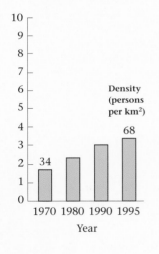

Infant mortality rate (deaths per 1,000 births)

Life expectancy at birth (years)

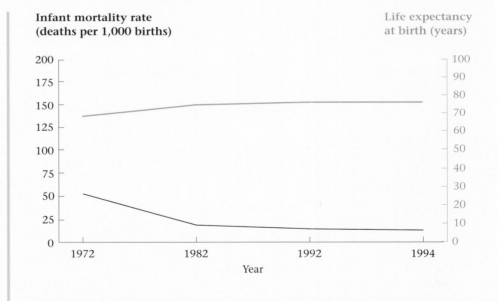

Population distribution

1970

Urban 41%

Rural 59%

1994

Urban 49%

Rural 51%

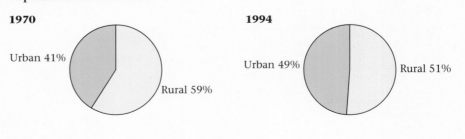

Costa Rica

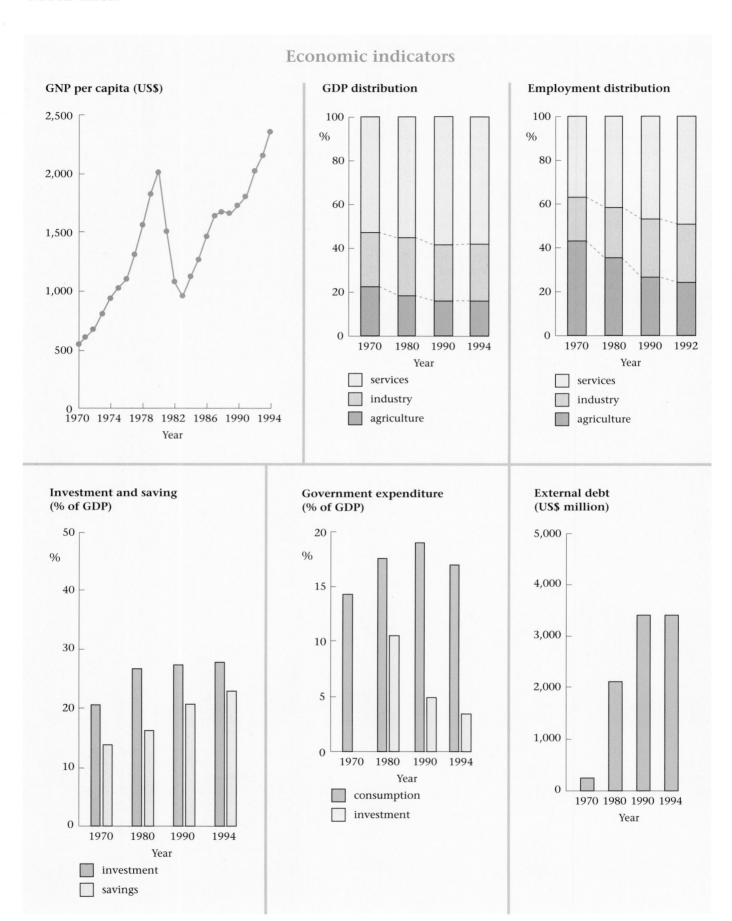

Economic indicators

GNP per capita (US$)

GDP distribution

- services
- industry
- agriculture

Employment distribution

- services
- industry
- agriculture

Investment and saving (% of GDP)

- investment
- savings

Government expenditure (% of GDP)

- consumption
- investment

External debt (US$ million)

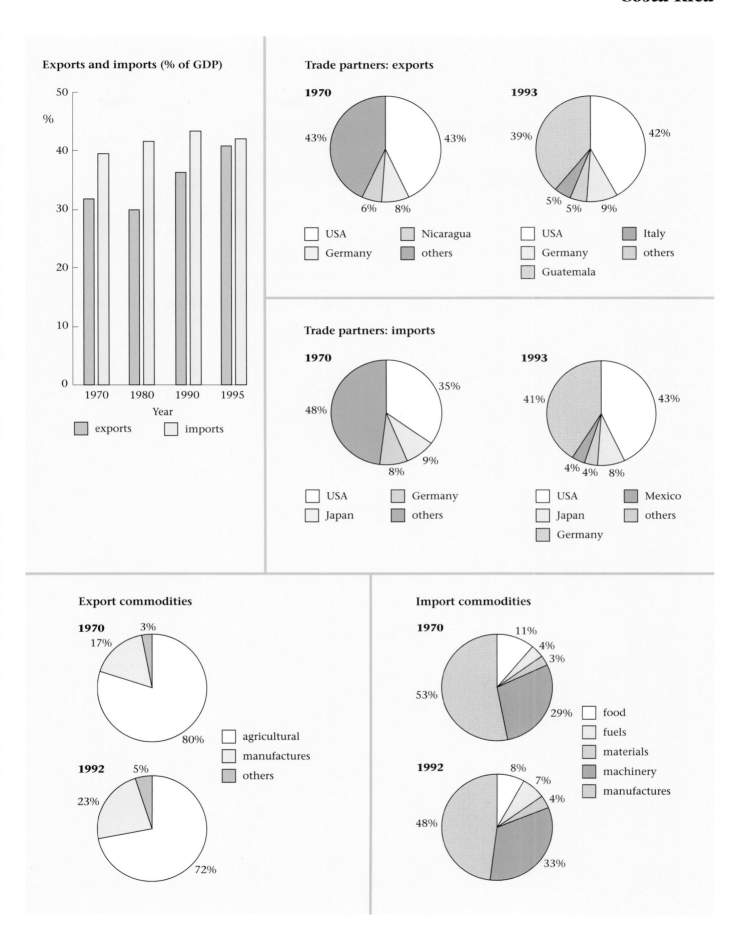

Exports and imports (% of GDP)

Trade partners: exports

1970
USA 43%
others 43%
6%
8%

1993
USA 42%
39%
5% 5%
9%

USA · Nicaragua
Germany · others

USA · Italy
Germany · others
Guatemala

Trade partners: imports

1970
USA 35%
48%
8% 9%

1993
USA 43%
41%
4% 4% 8%

USA · Germany
Japan · others

USA · Mexico
Japan · others
Germany

Export commodities

1970
3%
17%
80%

agricultural
manufactures
others

1992
5%
23%
72%

Import commodities

1970
11%
4%
3%
53%
29%

food
fuels
materials
machinery
manufactures

1992
8%
7%
4%
48%
33%

Costa Rica

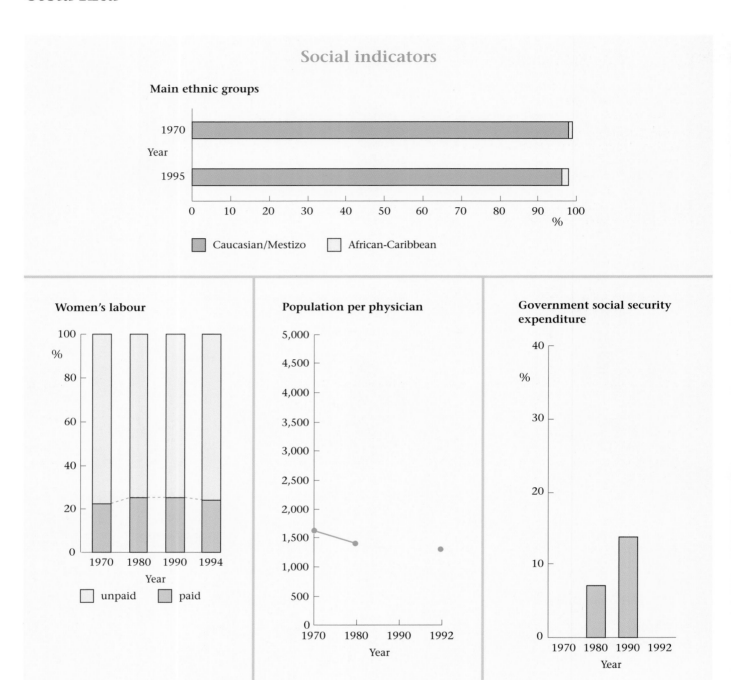

Social indicators

Main ethnic groups

Caucasian/Mestizo   African-Caribbean

Women's labour

unpaid   paid

Population per physician

Government social security expenditure

Political framework

- Economic problems continue to dominate Costa Rican politics especially over the consequences of international pressure to follow more neo-liberal policies

- Notwithstanding 1994 election promises the Figueres PLN government only one year later accepted conditions imposed by the IMF that would ensure sufficient finance to allow Costa Rica to repay part of her foreign debt

- IMF loan conditionality addressed the public-sector fiscal deficit by encouraging increased taxation, reduced public expenditure, accelerating the programme of privatization designed to reduce public-sector employment and placing strict controls on salaries as well as the pensions of public employees

- A significant political divide therefore opens over the threat to Costa Rica's longstanding public commitment to equity and social welfare

- June 1996 Figueres agrees to statutory limits on government fiscal deficits as proposed by IMF and his popularity falls dramatically

- Successive neo-liberal economic policies since the 1980s in Costa Rica had already begun to lower some of Latin America's highest literacy rates and raise poverty levels

- The 25% of the population classified as poor in Costa Rica doubled in the decade after 1980 as did the numbers living in extreme poverty. State education spending fell by over one-third in real terms threatening to reduce Costa Rica's 95% literacy rates

- From 1996 the Figueres government seemed trapped between international pressure backed by local businesses for even more neo-liberal policies and political opposition to such policies led by public-sector unions

- The government's other economic strategy of export promotion through closer links with NAFTA countries was also threatened in trade disputes with the USA that led to an official complaint from Costa Rica to WTO in 1996

- US companies alleged discrimination in the allocation of trade licences for banana exports to the EU. In retaliation the USA threatens to withdraw duty free status for Costa Rican exports to the USA and imposed a quota on textile imports

- Costa Rica attains higher international political prominence leading the G77 group of developing countries at the UN Security Council. But the domestic political dilemma remains of how to accommodate the structural economic change demanded by international financial institutions with a longstanding political commitment to social equity.

Further reading

Bird, L. (1984) *Costa Rica: Unarmed Democracy*, London, Sheppard Press.

Lara, S. (1995) *Inside Costa Rica*, Albuquerque, Interhemispheric Resource Centre.

Ecuador

Historical background

- Later 15th C. Ecuador incorporated into Inca Empire centred on Peru – indigenous Amerindian peoples subjugated

- 1534 Spanish begin colonization after Quito captured from Incas – Ecuador becomes a peripheral outpost administered from Lima and later Bogota

- 1822 Spanish defeated and Ecuador federated with Colombia and Venezuela

- 1830 Ecuador becomes independent republic incorporating Galapagos Islands – over next century 60% of territory lost in wars with neighbouring countries

- 19th C. long period of political instability and economic stagnation – average duration of governments less than two years

- 1920s collapse of cocoa export prices heralds more instability

- 1931–72 27 different governments including five terms for demagogic populist President Velasco

- 1942 after war with Peru coastal province and large tract of Oriente region conceded by Ecuador under Rio Protocol

- though sovereignty claims retained

- 1972 military seize power triggered by discovery of oil in upper reaches of Amazon, Oriente region. After joining OPEC government leads national development programme based on petroleum export revenues

- Later 1970s military regime becomes increasingly unpopular and internally divided over its political role – eventually elections are allowed

- 1979 return to civilian government but bitter opposition between President and Congress generates legislative paralysis – social unrest too as oil prices collapse and IMF/World Bank make loan renewal conditional on public expenditure cuts

- 1981 border clashes with Peru in areas lost under Rio Protocol

- 1984 populist Febres elected President promising neo-liberal economic revival. State economic intervention reduced and foreign investment encouraged but high social costs of austerity policies required to repay foreign debt

- Febres government becomes increasingly authoritarian with

widespread allegations of human rights abuse – major constitutional conflicts with Congress and economy stagnates after oil prices collapse

- 1987 earthquake hits Napo province – hundreds killed and trans-Amazonian oil pipeline destroyed

- 1988 Borja elected President promising to reverse neo-liberalism and lead a social-democratic consensus between government, business and labour

- 1990 Borja loses Congress majority and administration undermined by Legislature's censure motions. Widespread social unrest as inflation and labour reform proposals threaten to cut real wages. Amerindian peoples become more vociferous defenders of their land rights and critics of pollution associated with petroleum industry

- 1992 Duran Ballen elected President – heads Cabinet of prominent business leaders. New government restores neo-liberal privatization policies, reduces public sector employment, renegotiates IMF loans and tries to entice foreign investment by joining Andean free trade area

- 1993 major divisions emerge within Cabinet – congressional

opposition to neo-liberalism signals wider public unrest in strikes, demonstrations and guerrilla bombings

- 1994 further politicization of indigenous Amerindian peoples protesting against government proposals to commercialize their traditional lands for farming and resource extraction. Widespread unrest paralyses country and closes many highways leading to some modification of land legislation

- 1994 congressional elections produce humiliating defeat for government and disputes over Duran Ballen's demand for constitutional reform

- 1995 one month war with Peru diverts national attention from internal political disputes but thereafter corruption scandals get closer to President himself as Vice-President flees country over bribery charges

- July 1996 populist Bucaram elected President – voters apparently disillusioned with established parties

- February 1997 Bucaram deposed by Congress on grounds of corruption and mental incompetence – Alarcon becomes interim President until 1998 election.

Demographic indicators

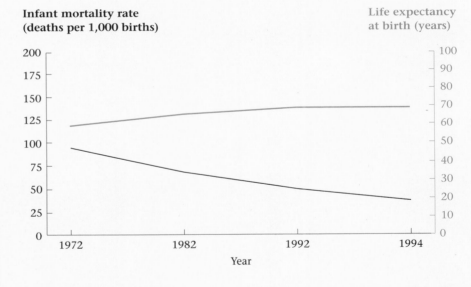

Total population (million)

Infant mortality rate (deaths per 1,000 births)

Life expectancy at birth (years)

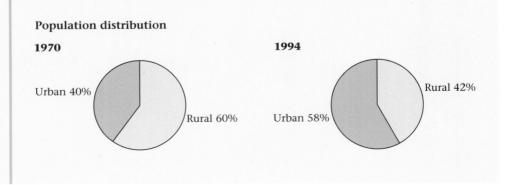

Population distribution

1970

Urban 40%

Rural 60%

1994

Rural 42%

Urban 58%

Ecuador

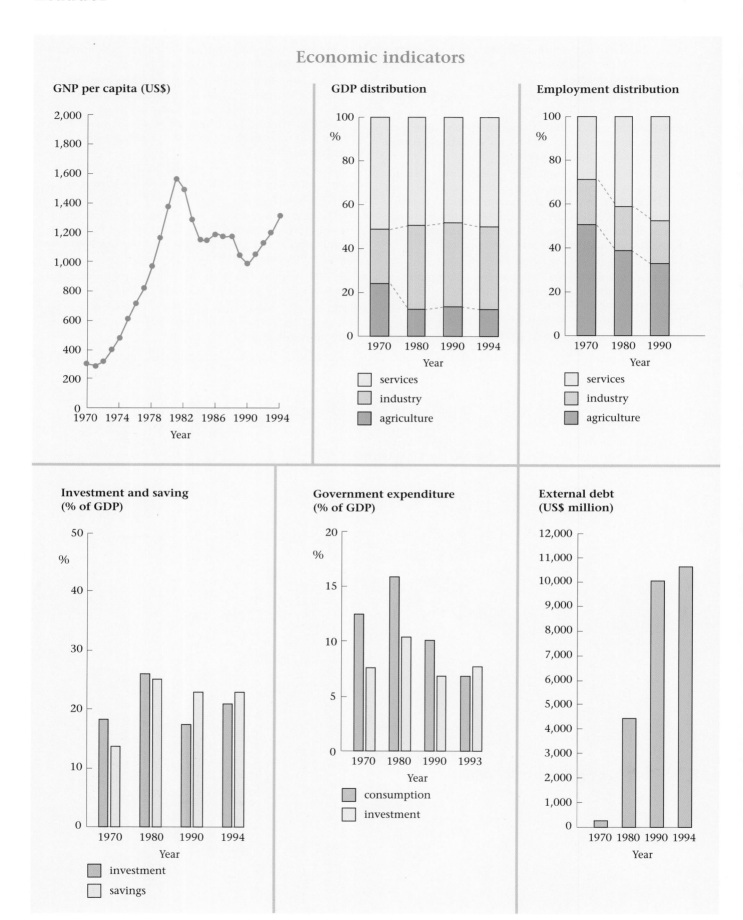

Economic indicators

GNP per capita (US$)

GDP distribution

Employment distribution

Investment and saving (% of GDP)

Government expenditure (% of GDP)

External debt (US$ million)

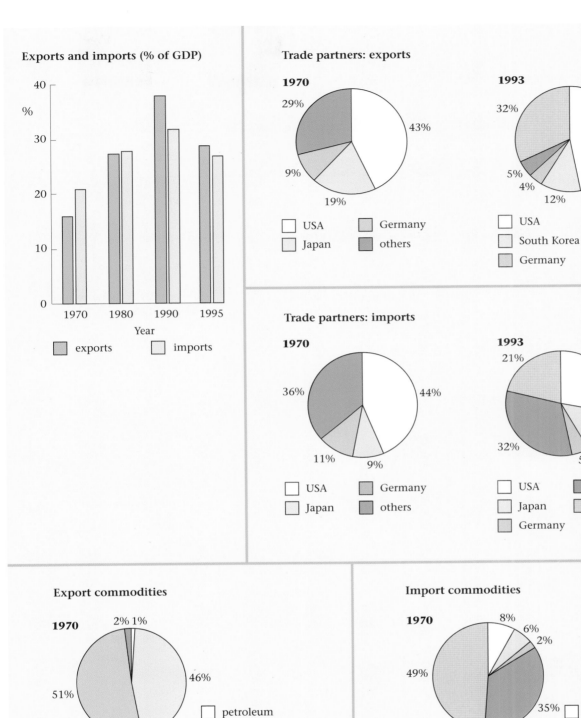

Exports and imports (% of GDP)

Trade partners: exports

1970
29%
43%
9%
19%

- USA
- Japan
- Germany
- others

1993
32%
5%
4%
12%
47%

- USA
- South Korea
- Germany
- Chile
- others

Trade partners: imports

1970
36%
44%
11%
9%

- USA
- Japan
- Germany
- others

1993
21%
28%
32%
14%
5%

- USA
- Japan
- Germany
- Trinidad and Tobago
- others

Export commodities

1970
2% 1%
46%
51%

1994
12%
39%
32%
17%

- petroleum
- bananas
- other agricultural
- others

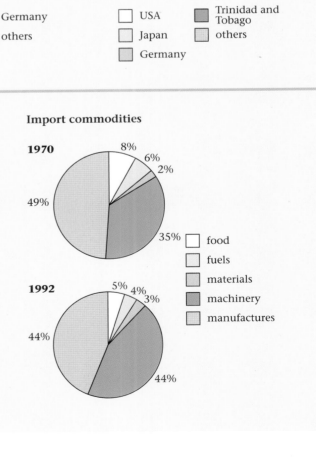

Import commodities

1970
8%
6%
2%
49%
35%

1992
5% 4%
3%
44%
44%

- food
- fuels
- materials
- machinery
- manufactures

Ecuador

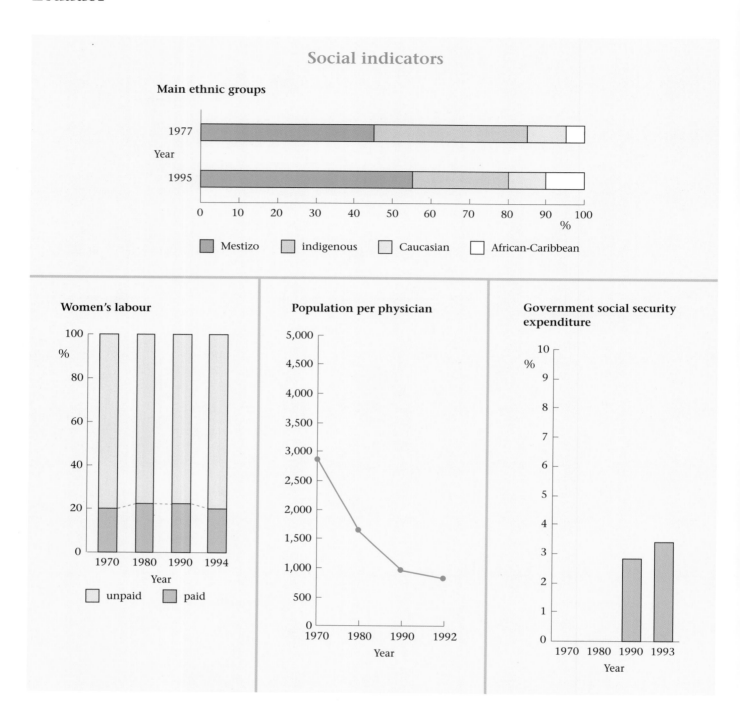

Social indicators

Main ethnic groups

Year

1977

1995

0 10 20 30 40 50 60 70 80 90 100
%

Mestizo   indigenous   Caucasian   African-Caribbean

Women's labour

%

100
80
60
40
20
0

1970 1980 1990 1994

Year

unpaid   paid

Population per physician

5,000
4,500
4,000
3,500
3,000
2,500
2,000
1,500
1,000
500
0

1970 1980 1990 1992

Year

Government social security expenditure

%

10
9
8
7
6
5
4
3
2
1
0

1970 1980 1990 1993

Year

Political framework

- Since the 1979 return to civilian rule perennial power disputes evident between Presidents, the Judiciary and Congress as the single chamber Legislature
- Disputes emerge regularly when elections to Congress in mid-presidential term produce Legislatures dominated by opposition parties and political paralysis ensues
- Typical crisis of political deadlock 1994–96 sees President attempt constitutional reform to reduce power of Congress
- Referendum to judge proposals removing from Congress the right to manage public funds, reducing congressional control over public finance and an end to the election of the Judiciary by legislators from a list provided by the President
- Referendum proposals also embody additional neo-liberal policies to curb trade union rights to withdraw labour especially in the public sector and to privatize public utilities and the social security system
- 1994–95 two referendums approve constitutional changes by narrow majorities. But bitter political disputes follow between President, Congress and the Judiciary that necessitate Organization of American States (OAS) mediation amid rumours of a military coup
- November 1995 OAS brokers another referendum which this time rejects all constitutional reforms in an apparent protest against neo-liberalism and presidential corruption
- Amidst the consequent political turmoil and the aftermath of another border war with Peru little attention paid to Ecuador's underlying social problems
- Massive wealth and income inequalities become ever wider as large numbers of poor subsistence farmers in rural areas fail to share the economic benefits of resource development
- Amerindian peoples in particular lose access to tropical forests and suffer negative environmental consequences of oil and gas exploration
- 1996 populist Bucaram elected President promising a 'government for the poor' with food subsidies, better housing, a reversal of privatization, public sector pay increases and the establishment of Amerindian land rights
- In office Bucaram mixed highly eccentric personal behaviour (becoming popularly known as *El Loco*) with nepotism as key Cabinet posts allocated to family and friends
- More significantly Bucaram's economic policies did not increase public subsidies but reduced them and proposals to increase public utility prices generate massive public demonstrations and a wave of industrial unrest
- Political stability and attention to Ecuador's social problems seemed as far away as ever when in February 1997 Congress voted to eject Bucaram from office. In this political vacuum the shadow of the military was evident when the Army Commander voiced 'a terrible sense of unease in the more democratic-minded armed forces'.

Further reading

Corkill, D. and Cubbitt, D. (1988) *Ecuador: a Fragile Democracy*, London, Latin America Bureau.

Isaacs, A. (1993) *Military Rule and Transition in Ecuador*, Basingstoke, Macmillan.

El Salvador

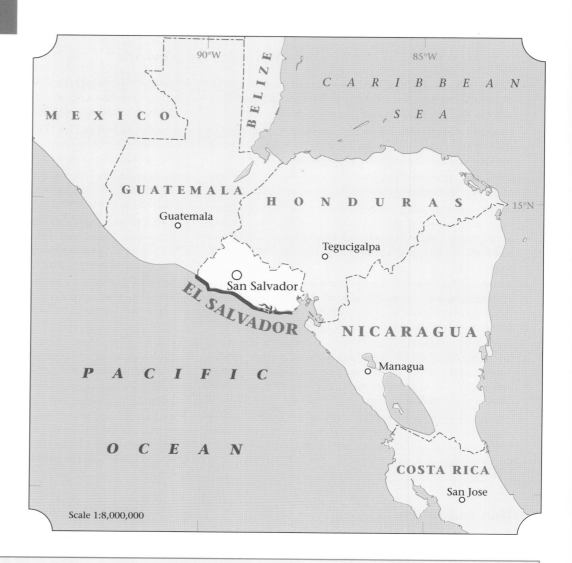

Scale 1:8,000,000

Historical background

- Up to 16th C. densely settled by indigenous Amerindian peoples
- 1524 Spanish force moves south from Mexico to begin colonization
- 1821 end of Spanish rule – El Salvador federated in United Provinces of Central America but rivalries and civil wars see federation disbanded 1839
- 1841 El Salvador becomes independent republic
- 1860s crucial exports of indigo undermined by development of colouring substitute – coffee becomes dominant export crop
- Increasing population density worsens competition for land – cash crop plantations means expropriating land used for subsistence food production
- 1882 common lands abolished leaving 2% of population confirmed as landowning elite and peasantry as mainly seasonal labour
- Elite oligarchy ignore constitutional process and appoint governments that will confirm the economic power of land-

owners and merchants
- 1931 military coup against background of escalating rural protest about land distribution, collapse of world coffee and cocoa prices that induce widespread starvation and formation of Communist Party
- 1932 large-scale peasant rebellion brutally repressed – 30,000 killed
- 1932–79 military governments predominant as landowning elite abdicates power to ensure their continued economic pre-eminence
- Periodic coups and counter-coups 1944, 1960 and 1979 as governments swing between limited political reformism and military dictatorships
- 1960s military try to institutionalize their political role in Party of National Conciliation – opposition parties tolerated but electoral manipulation ensures military governments continue
- 1970s parties opposed to military rule unite around Christian Democratic Party (PDC) led by Duarte but refused access to political power. Many become convinced that

- armed insurrection is only alternative especially after right-wing paramilitaries extend campaign of violence
- March 1980 Archbishop of El Salvador outspoken defender of human rights assassinated while celebrating mass
- October 1980 armed opposition unites around Farabundo Marti Liberation Front (FMLN) – civil war lasts 12 years
- Early 1980s civilians like Duarte enticed into government as military pressed by their US allies to terminate their overtly political role
- 1984 Duarte elected President committed to accelerate land reform and negotiate end to civil war
- 1984–89 abortive peace negotiations with FMLN founder on government's inability to control military and therefore allow the removal of conservative army commanders, reduce the size of the army and end the assassinations campaign. Other obstacle was government demand that FMLN return to mainstream politics and contest elections which FMLN consider fraudulent
- 1989 Cristiani elected President from Nationalist Republican Alliance Party (ARENA) apparently committed to mili-tary solution. More bitter fighting – FMLN attack and occupy parts of the capital and in revenge their supporters, trade unionists and catholic priests are assassinated
- 1990 UN intervenes in peace process after Soviet aid to FMLN drastically reduced and the USA presses for more progress in El Salvador to cement wider Central American peace agreements facilitated by Costa Rica in 1987
- February 1992 despite worsening violence Peace Accords eventually signed in Mexico – demilitarization to be supervised by UN Observer Mission
- 15 December 1992 National Reconciliation Day formally ends civil war and FMLN recognized as legitimate political party
- 1994 ARENA's Calderon Sol elected President with 62% votes against 32% for FMLN candidates
- 1995–96 implementing Peace Accords remains problematic but UN decides sufficient progress made to allow Observer Mission to be scaled down.

Demographic indicators

Total population (million)

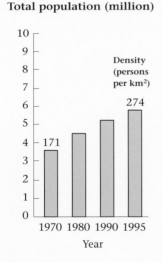

Density (persons per km²)

Infant mortality rate (deaths per 1,000 births)

Life expectancy at birth (years)

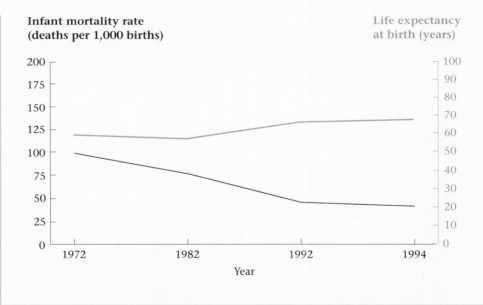

Population distribution

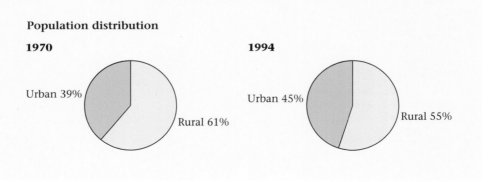

1970

Urban 39%
Rural 61%

1994

Urban 45%
Rural 55%

El Salvador

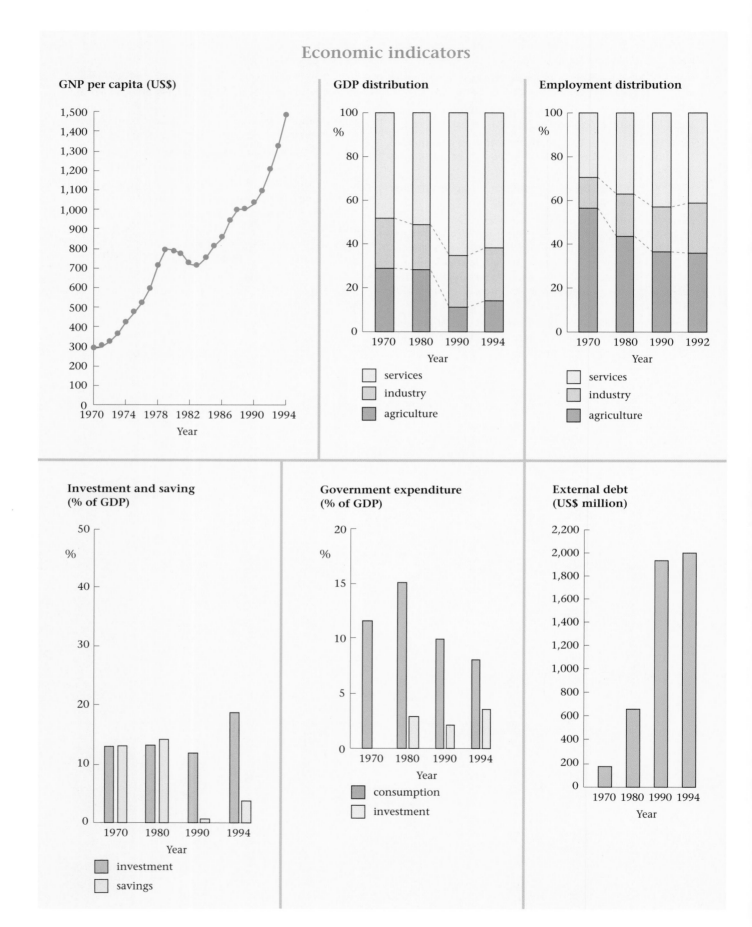

Economic indicators

GNP per capita (US$)

GDP distribution

Employment distribution

Investment and saving (% of GDP)

Government expenditure (% of GDP)

External debt (US$ million)

Exports and imports (% of GDP)

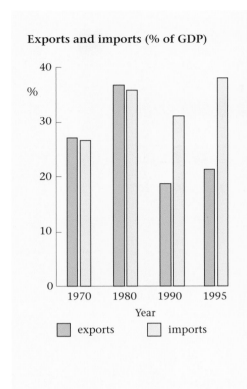

Trade partners: exports

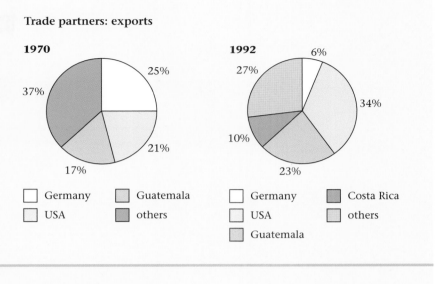

Trade partners: imports

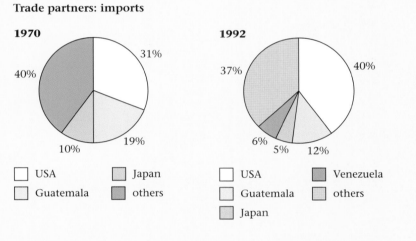

Export commodities

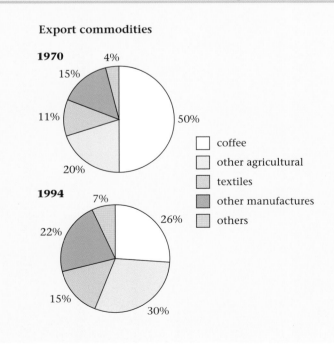

Import commodities

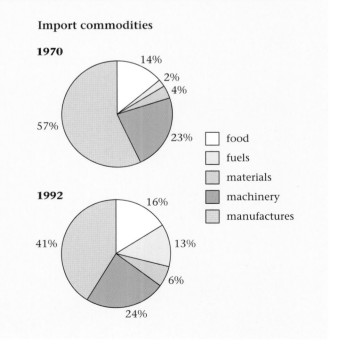

El Salvador

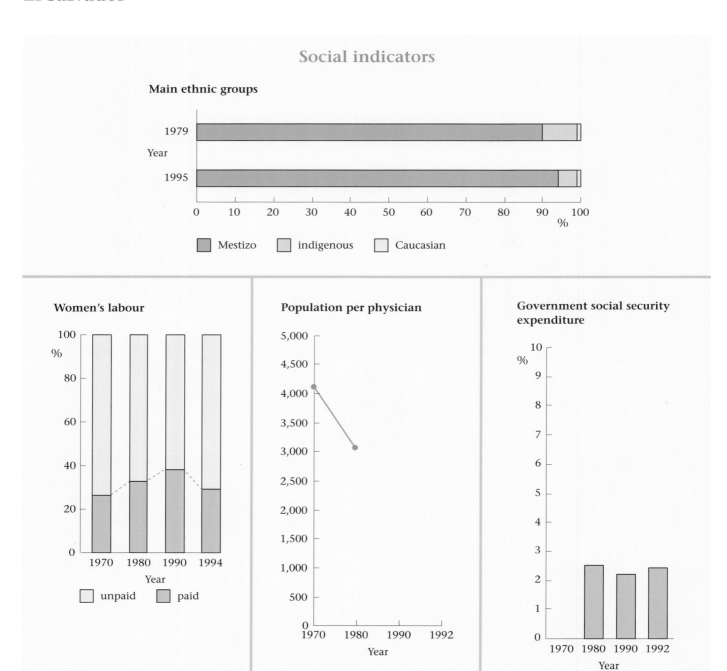

Social indicators

Main ethnic groups

Year

1979

1995

0 10 20 30 40 50 60 70 80 90 100 %

☐ Mestizo ☐ indigenous ☐ Caucasian

Women's labour

%
100
80
60
40
20
0

1970 1980 1990 1994
Year

☐ unpaid ☐ paid

Population per physician

5,000
4,500
4,000
3,500
3,000
2,500
2,000
1,500
1,000
500
0

1970 1980 1990 1992
Year

Government social security expenditure

%
10
9
8
7
6
5
4
3
2
1
0

1970 1980 1990 1992
Year

Political framework

- Severe problems of economic and social reconstruction after the civil war continues to dominate the political scene in El Salvador

- During the war over 80,000 people were killed, 20% of the population were displaced from their homes half of whom fled overseas

- War damage and an inevitable process of neglect also badly undermines the basic infrastructure of the economy

- Financing government expenditure on defence meant a threefold increase in foreign debt between 1980 and 1992 leaving serious burdens of debt repayment – by the mid 1990s foreign debt interest charges equivalent to 20% of export earnings

- Securing further IMF loans to sustain debt repayment gives the Calderon government little choice but to continue with the neo-liberal economic policies recommended by international financial institutions

- Such policies, however, conflict with the need to increase government expenditure on health, education and welfare if the social infrastructure is to be reconstructed

- Meeting IMF demands to increase taxation and reduce government expenditure means conceding any substantial increase in social spending and leads to sharp divisions within opposition coalition led by FMLN

- With basic economic and social problems unresolved more immediate reconciliation issues remain in the slow process of implementing 1992 Accords

- Government armed forces have been reduced and the FMLN demilitarized but delayed compensation payments for former soldiers saw the National Assembly occupied by protesters three times in the mid 1990s

- A new civilian police force including FMLN supporters was established but lack of resources and consequent underpolicing unable to slow the pace of civilian crime

- Human rights institutions have followed Accords' principles and investigated civil war crimes, but hesitant prosecution levels raise questions about the independence of the judiciary

- Accords' agreement to transfer at least 10% of land to demobilized combatants and displaced civilians has progressed only slowly as have wider land reform policies

- By 1997 it appears that the government of Calderon Sol sees the solution to reconstruction problems at all levels in galvanizing faster economic growth through neo-liberal policies of trade liberalization and the privatization of public utilities.

Further reading

McLintock, M. (1988) *The American Connection: State Terror and Popular Resistance in El Salvador*, London, Zed Books.

Murray, K. (1995) *Inside El Salvador*, Albuquerque, Inter-hemispheric Resource Centre.

Guatemala

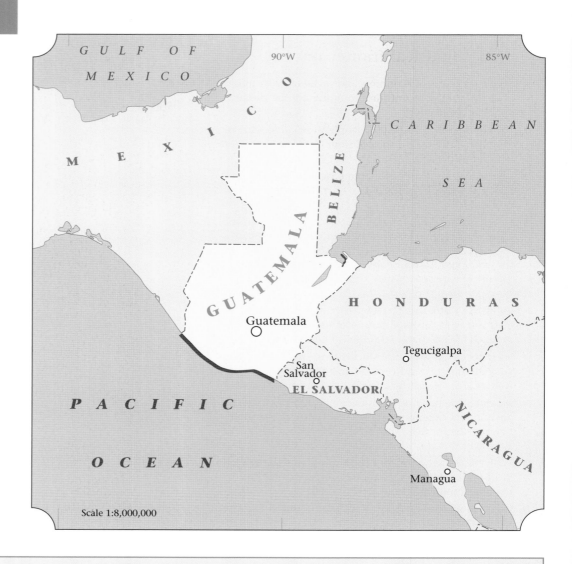

Scale 1:8,000,000

Historical background

- AD 300–900 zenith of Mayan civilization originating from highlands of Guatemala
- 10th–16th C. Amerindian population ruled by a Mexican people
- 1524 Spanish begin colonization
- 1821 Spanish rule ends – Guatemala federated in United Provinces of Central America
- 1831 territory on eastern coast yielded to British – sovereignty over British Honduras (later Belize) disputed until 1991
- 1839 Guatemala becomes independent republic after Central American federation disintegrates
- 1839–1944 oligarchic power of landowning elite confirmed in series of dictatorships interspersed with some constitutional governments
- 1871 large landowners expropriate many common lands for coffee and later banana plantations after synthetic dyes undermine exports of vegetable dyes
- Late 1890s–1920s US companies take control of transport infrastructure, hydro-electric generation and banana plantations
- 1944–54 popular uprisings see military rule replaced by reformist Presidents – large estates returned to peasantry to intense opposition of US companies and US government
- 1954 CIA organize armed invasion confirming US government drive against communism in Central America – three decades of military government follows and peasant lands expropriated by plantation owners
- 1962 start of armed insurgency against abuses of military rule involving assassination campaigns against regime opponents and widespread violations of human rights
- February 1982 diverse groups of insurgents in urban and rural areas unite around Unidad Revolucionaria Nacional Guatemalteca (URNG)
- March 1982 military coup closes Congress, suspends constitution and political parties. War against URNG intensifies including emergence of right-wing 'death squads' – 15,000 killed; 500,000 flee to mountains; 70,000 refugees go abroad

- 1983 another military coup but this time promising return to democratic rule
- 1986 Cerezo elected first civilian President since 1954 promising to curb military excesses and reach peace agreement with URNG – both prove impossible
- Late 1980s very real threat of another military coup constrains power of civilian politicians – 'death squads' continue torture, kidnapping and assassination campaigns against regime opponents
- International attempts to halt the civil war founder on major divisions between US Congress and President Reagan over suspending aid to Guatemala until human rights abuse ends
- 1990 Serrano elected President with only 20% of the popular vote as over two-thirds of electors abstain
- 1990–93 violence continues remorselessly but USA and EU appear more united in making further aid conditional on end to extra-judicial killings and installation of human rights regime
- May 1993 Serrano adopts dictatorial powers – dismisses Congress and Supreme Court but is removed by the military after overwhelming show of domestic opposition
- June 1993 Congress elects De Leon interim President but his constitutional reform proposals divert attention from attempts to end killings and human rights abuses by military
- 1994–95 UN mission established to supervise implementation of human rights agreement – reports persisting abuses by government militia. USA suspends military aid in protest at refusals to investigate abuses – URNG peace talks stall over same issue
- January 1996 Alvaro Arzu elected President with primary task of negotiating peace with URNG – promises subordination of military to elected officials and agrarian reform
- December 1996 peace agreement signed by government and URNG designed to end over 30 years of war in which an estimated 150,000 killed or missing.

Demographic indicators

Total population (million)

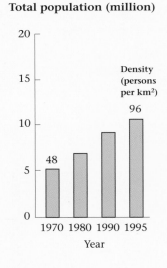

Infant mortality rate (deaths per 1,000 births)

Life expectancy at birth (years)

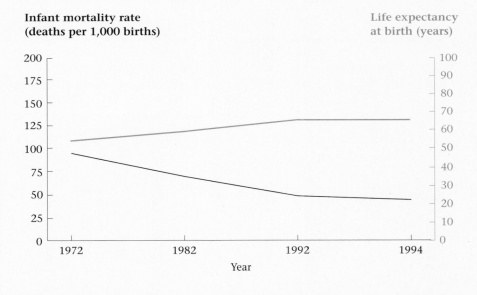

Population distribution

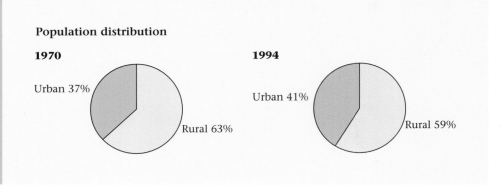

Guatemala

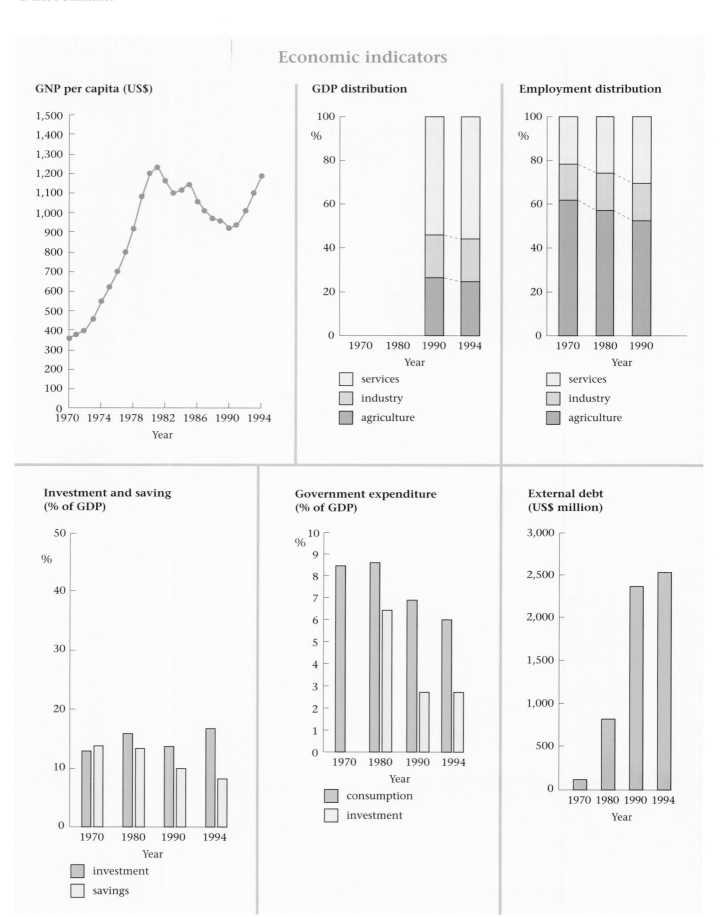

GNP per capita (US$)

GDP distribution

Employment distribution

Investment and saving (% of GDP)

Government expenditure (% of GDP)

External debt (US$ million)

96

Exports and imports (% of GDP)

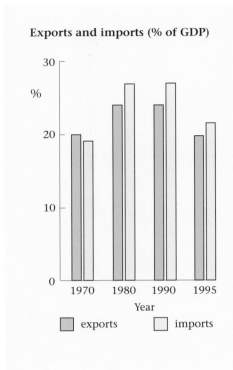

Trade partners: exports

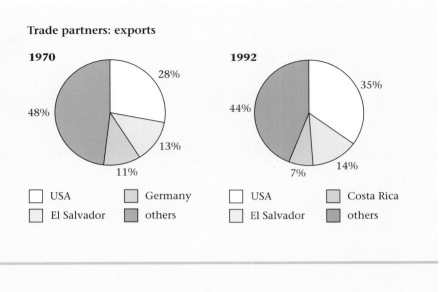

Trade partners: imports

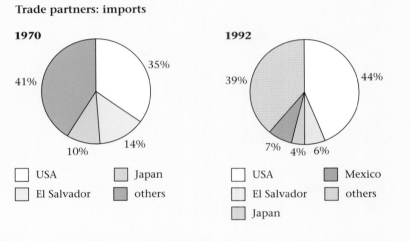

Export commodities

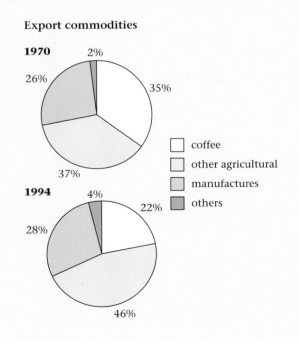

Import commodities

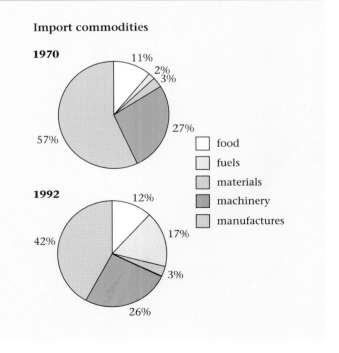

Guatemala

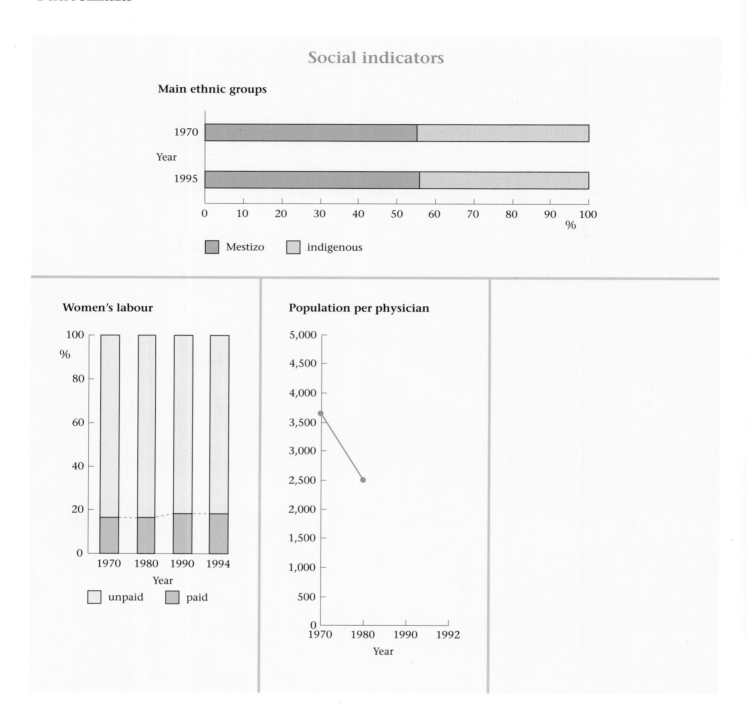

Social indicators

Main ethnic groups

Year

■ Mestizo □ indigenous

Women's labour

□ unpaid ■ paid

Population per physician

Political framework

- Reconciliation and reconstruction problems inevitably dominate political life after the 1996 peace agreement ended over three decades of civil war

- The terrible scale of killings, torture and gross abuse of human rights is so recent and with the military presence still evident any attempt by civilian politicians to forge a programme of reconciliation is bound to be fraught with difficulty

- Finally ending the climate of terror by itself not easy but as in other Latin American countries the crucial test for politicians will be how they organize the investigation and prosecution of the worst offenders, especially those with military connections

- Long delays in confirming an internationally-recognized human rights regime held up peace negotiations for nearly ten years leaving many people pessimistic about future prosecutions for those guilty of murder and grossly violating human rights

- At least as important for post-war reconstruction will be government attempts to address deeper social and economic problems

- In an already poor country the 1980s saw the poverty rate increase by a third to 90% while the number in extreme poverty and unable to meet the most basic nutritional requirements rose from 31% to 67%

- Gross inequalities in wealth inherently connected to inequalities in the distribution of land but implementing agrarian reform inevitably require large landowners, business and the military to make concessions if peace over the longer term is to be safeguarded

- Many years of high military expenditure also leave huge foreign debts which have to be repaid at the same time as further loans secured to rebuild Guatemala's shattered economy

- 1997 sees promises by international financial institutions of nearly US$1 billion of additional foreign aid but attached conditions difficult to square with broader social equity objectives

- The 1997 aid package was made dependent on the Guatemalan government contributing another US$700 million by raising taxation to 50% more than 1995 levels. Implementation of neo-liberal policies such as the privatization of public utilities also expected

- The Guatemalan government continues to look for a more secure economic future through export promotion and trade liberalization first within a free trade zone in Central America as, they hope, a first step to joining NAFTA

- Apart from probably contradicting post-war social equity objectives the government has to confront continuing threats that the USA will undermine this trade strategy. Unless human rights abuses offenders are punished and the trade in drugs controlled the USA appears ready to block progress for Guatemala even within the Central America free trade area let alone eventual NAFTA membership

- The implementation of an effective human rights regime and attempting to end the drugs trade clearly impinges on military interests which of necessity makes for a contentious political scenario.

Further reading

Black, G.G. (1984) *Guatemala*, London, Zed Books.

Trudeau, R.H. (1993) *Guatemalan Politics: the Popular Struggle for Democracy*, Boulder, Co., Lynne Rienner.

Honduras

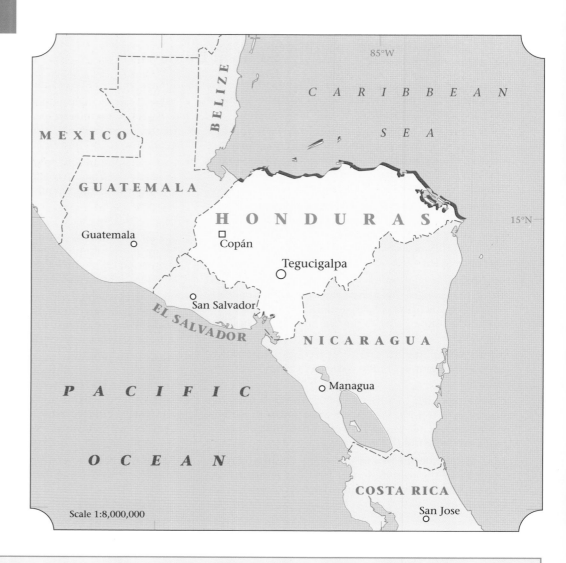

Scale 1:8,000,000

Historical background

- AD 300–900 Honduras part of Mayan Empire centred locally on Copan

- Early 16th C. indigenous Amerindians unable to resist Spanish colonization

- 1821 Spanish rule ends – Honduras federated in United Provinces of Central America

- 1838 full independence when federation disintegrates

- 19th C. internal political divisions over restoration of a federal Central America spill over into persistent interference in affairs of neighbouring states – develops into border wars 1906, 1930 and 1969

- Domestic weakness allows political leverage for foreign interests in mining and later coffee and banana plantations. Mutual support as Honduran leaders grant land and US companies confirm the power of local political elite

- Early 20th C. United Fruit Company from USA monopolizes production and trade in bananas then extends control to wider transport network

- 1924 US Marines invade to establish democratic rule – but power later handed over for Carias Andino's authoritarian rule, 1933–48

- 1948–71 despite sporadic attempts to initiate moderate social reforms coups and counter-coups see military governments predominate

- Early 1970s turmoil after defeat in border conflict with El Salvador – party politicians sign Unity Pact and elections allowed but military coups still a regular occurrence

- 1975 land reform promises redistribution of 600,000 hectares to peasant families by 1980 – intense opposition from landowners and US companies backed by allies in the military. Only 200,000 hectares transferred by 1990 and two years later programme effectively abandoned

- 1981 despite strict controls over political parties Cordova elected President promising new constitution to consolidate democratic rule. Military subverts political change in amendments making head of armed forces national Commander-in-Chief and role of President becomes ceremonial

- 1980s major divisions emerge in military with more coup attempts against background of repressive legislation against labour unions and political opponents. 'Death squads' operate with impunity and opposition supporters tortured, killed or disappear
- Despite relatively small and inactive armed guerrilla groups the armed forces succeed in becoming one of the best equipped in Central America thanks to US military aid
- Honduras drawn into Central American war by allowing right-wing Contra guerrillas and US troops opposed to Sandinista regime in Nicaragua to operate from her territory
- In return USA re-equips Honduran armed forces as well as using Honduras as conduit for aid to Contras
- 1990 defeat of Sandinista regime in Nicaragua terminates flow of US aid to Honduras. Thereafter USA becomes severe critic of previous allies in Honduran military for gross human rights violations and involvement in drugs trade. Economic crisis follows as Honduras unable to repay foreign debt and World Bank declines further credits

- 1990–93 some restrictions on political and union activity lifted and some exiled party leaders return but social unrest over World Bank/IMF economic policy prescriptions to increase taxes and reduce government expenditure. Attempted coups by military in response to attempts to reduce their political power and prosecute human rights offenders
- 1993 Reina, former head of the Inter-American Court of Human Rights, elected President promising judicial reform and an end to the military's political power
- 1994–96 continuing attempts to reduce military influence and try senior officers for human rights abuse produces tense period of attempted coups.

Demographic indicators

Total population (million)

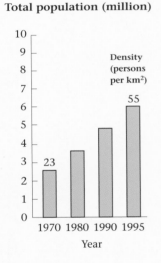

Infant mortality rate (deaths per 1,000 births)

Life expectancy at birth (years)

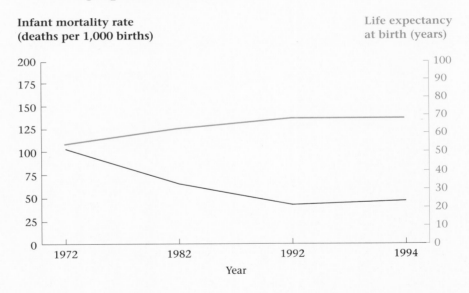

Population distribution

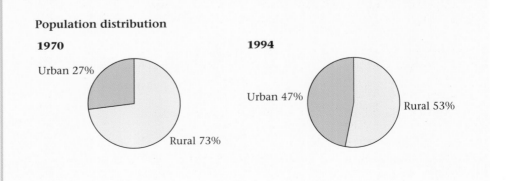

Honduras

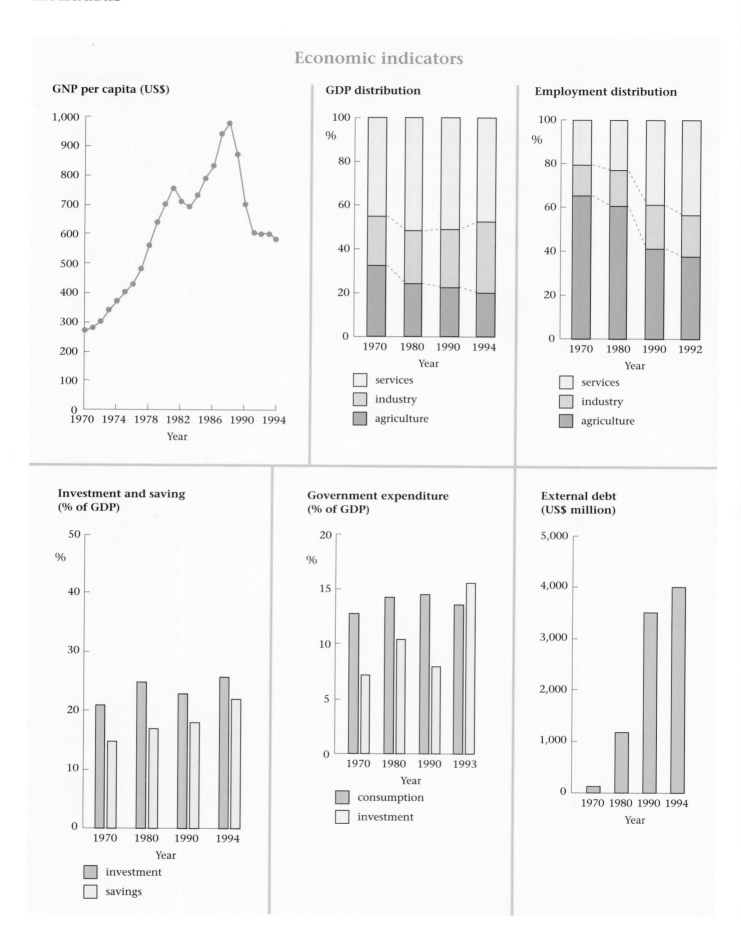

Economic indicators

GNP per capita (US$)

GDP distribution

Employment distribution

services
industry
agriculture

services
industry
agriculture

Investment and saving (% of GDP)

investment
savings

Government expenditure (% of GDP)

consumption
investment

External debt (US$ million)

Exports and imports (% of GDP)

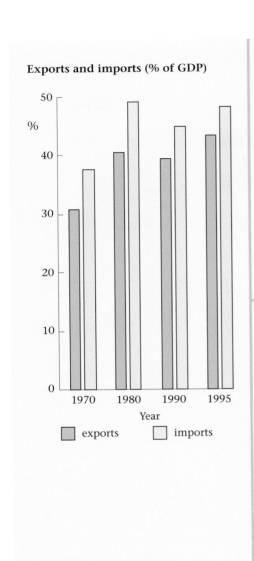

Trade partners: exports

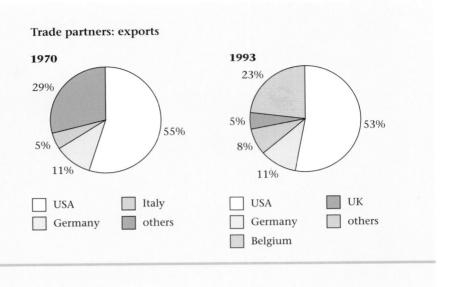

Trade partners: imports

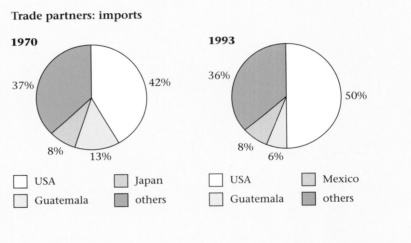

Export commodities

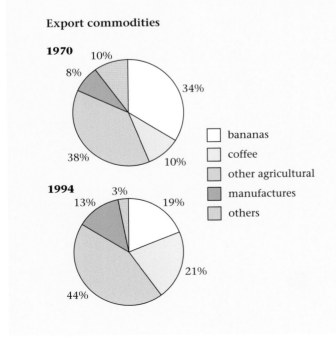

Import commodities

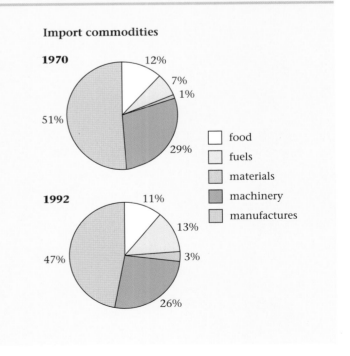

Honduras

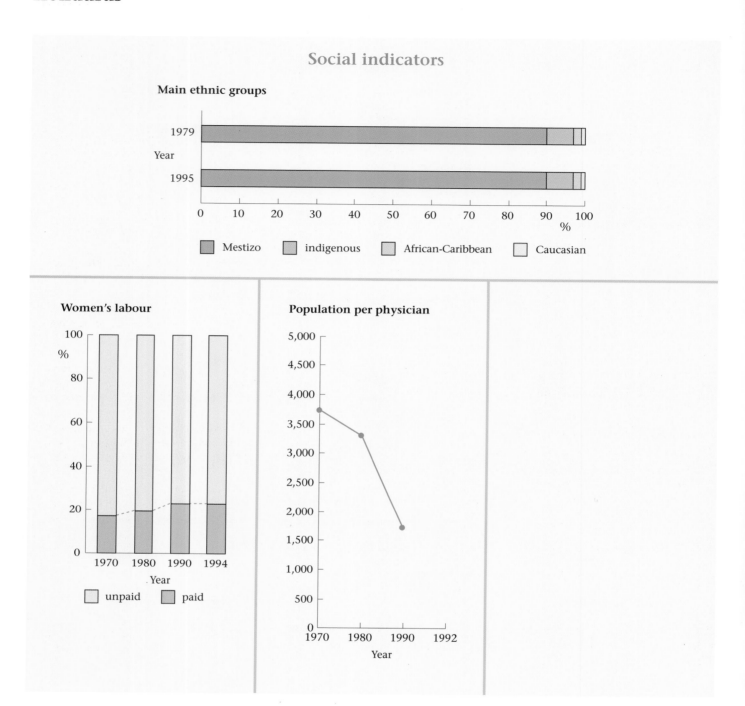

Social indicators

Main ethnic groups

Year
- 1979
- 1995

%

■ Mestizo   ■ indigenous   ■ African-Caribbean   □ Caucasian

Women's labour

%

Year

□ unpaid   ■ paid

Population per physician

Year

Political framework

- The long process of consolidating a more democratic polity by reducing both the influence of the military and defence expenditure remains a central political focus in the 1990s

- Military resistance to cuts in their budget at first meant limited real reductions as their leaders suggested merely a shift in role towards internal policing of drugs trafficking and assisting environmental protection programmes within the forestry sector

- More progress apparent by 1997 not just in reducing military spending but recovering key defence administration posts for elected civilians

- President Reina also continues the slow process of eradicating extra-judicial violence by military groups – new criminal investigation body replaced counter-intelligence unit in 1995

- Prosecutions of military offenders for human rights violations, corruption and drugs trade involvement crystallizes resentment against the whole package of measures to limit the power of the armed forces

- October 1995 Supreme Court denies the validity of claims by senior officers to indemnity from prosecution under previous amnesties – sets off a series of highly visible troop movements amid rumours of impending military coup

- March 1996 bomb explodes at presidential palace

- Without the active support of the USA that was so apparent in the 1980s the role of the military in politics is being eroded but unease remains about reactionary elements in the armed forces

- Serious economic problems compound tensions about military influence

- Recent short-term economic policies increasing sales taxes, reducing government expenditure and privatizing key public-sector organizations apparently satisfied international financial institutions and more loans are promised

- Even so only a minimal level of foreign debt was restructured such that one-third of the 1997 government budget has to be allocated to foreign debt interest payments

- The social costs of implementing neo-liberal policies, however, serve to accentuate the deeper problems in one of the poorest countries in Central America

- Chronic shortage of productive land magnifies the problems of securing adequate food supplies for a rapidly growing population

- The land reform programme begun in 1975 was effectively suspended by 1992 at the same time as IMF recommendations to modernize agriculture meant even more concentration on large-scale plantations

- Gross over dependence on just one or two export crops to generate foreign exchange places severe pressure on better quality land available for basic subsistence food production

- On top of long-term structural problems come neo-liberal policies raising consumption taxation and reducing necessary government expenditure on education, health and social welfare

- As a result the 1990s saw increasing incidence of unauthorized occupation of under used land in rural areas as part of a wider protest against the absence of fundamental social and agrarian reform.

Further reading

Anderson, T.D. (1988) 'Politics and the military in Honduras', *Current History*, vol.87, December.

Peckenham, N. and Street, A. (eds) (1985) *Honduras: Portrait of a Captive Nation*, New York, Praeger.

Hong Kong

Historical background

- Originally part of Guangdong Province, China – settled from the 2nd C. BC by Cantonese
- 1277 child-emperor Duan Zong (Sung dynasty) spends year in Kowloon whilst fleeing Mongols
- 1842 Island of Hong Kong ceded by China to Britain under Treaty of Nanking following First Opium War (1840–42)
- 1843 Hong Kong formally proclaimed British Colony – administered by a Governor advised by an Executive Council and a Legislative Council. Key economic role begins as entrepôt trade connection between Asia and Europe
- 1850 first 'unofficial' members (i.e. not government officials) appointed to Legislative Council
- 1860 Kowloon peninsula annexed by British under Convention of Beijing
- 1865 Hong Kong and Shanghai Bank founded
- 1880 first unofficial Chinese member of the Legislative Council appointed
- 1896 first unofficial member of the Executive Council appointed
- 1898 Britain obtains 99-year lease for mainland north of Kowloon plus adjoining islands
- 1899 Chinese magistrates in the old walled city of Kowloon expelled – pretext was encouraging resistance to British occupation
- 1912 University of Hong Kong opened
- 1925–26 strikes and trade boycotts in Hong Kong follow anti-foreign protests in China. 100,000 Chinese workers leave Hong Kong – remainder refuse to work
- 1926 first Chinese unofficial member of the Executive Council appointed
- 1941 Japanese invade Hong Kong – occupied until 1945
- 1946 civil government restored in traditional colonial pattern
- 1949 Mao declares People's Republic of China
- 1950 Hong Kong government ends free access across Chinese border
- 1953 government commences resettlement programme to relieve housing shortage

Hong Kong

- 1962 border restrictions briefly relaxed – 120,000 refugees enter Hong Kong
- 1966 three nights rioting after ferry charges increased
- 1972 government announces 10-year housing project to accommodate 1.5 million people
- 1972 cross-harbour tunnel opens
- 1974 anti-corruption commission established
- 1980 government says all illegal immigrants discovered are to be repatriated – sharp decline in illegal immigration
- 1984 Sino-British agreement signed – Britain to cede sovereignty over Hong Kong in July 1997. China says Hong Kong will be Special Administrative Region (SAR) ruled for 50 years by own inhabitants with own legal system – except in foreign affairs and defence
- 1985 committee established in Beijing to devise new constitution for Hong Kong
- 1985 British announce changes to Legislative Council – 24 to be elected, 22 appointed plus 10 government officials
- 1989 Tiananmen Square massacre in China – property market and stock exchange fall, emigration increases
- 1990 Hong Kong Legislative Council objects to Beijing proposals giving China the right after 1997 to suspend Hong Kong constitution by declaring state of emergency – and the right to station troops there
- 1992 Chris Patten loses seat in UK general election – becomes Governor of Hong Kong
- 1994 legislation passed altering Legislative Council – 30 members elected by functional constituencies, 20 directly elected by geographical constituencies, 10 by electoral college. China objects and threatens to annul legislation after 1997
- 1995 most open elections yet for Legislative Council
- 1996 shipping magnate Tung Chee Hwa becomes first Chief Executive of Hong Kong SAR
- July 1997 Hong Kong reverts to China.

Demographic indicators

Total population (million)

Infant mortality rate (deaths per 1,000 births)

Life expectancy at birth (years)

Population distribution

1970 Rural 10% Urban 90%

1994 Rural 5% Urban 95%

107

Hong Kong

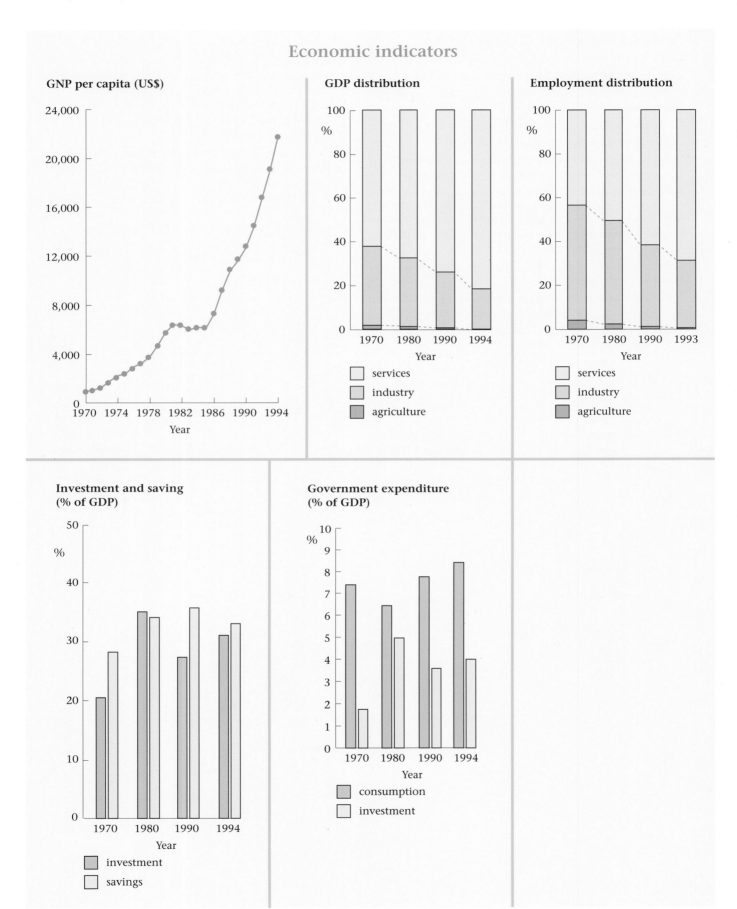

Economic indicators

GNP per capita (US$)

GDP distribution

Employment distribution

Investment and saving (% of GDP)

Government expenditure (% of GDP)

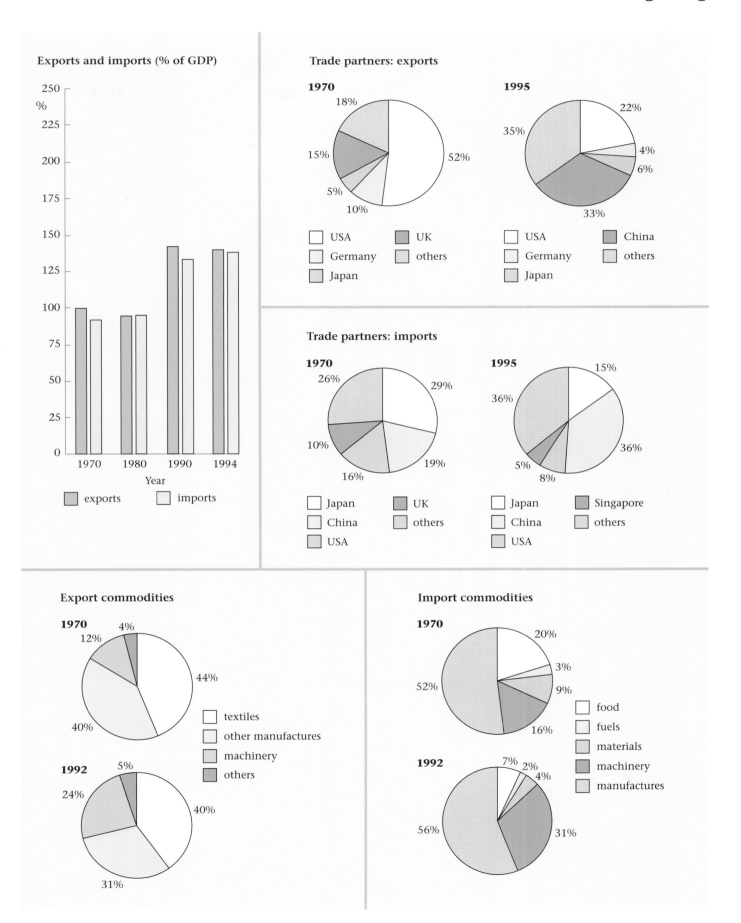

Exports and imports (% of GDP)

Trade partners: exports

1970

- USA
- Germany
- Japan
- UK
- others

1995

- USA
- Germany
- Japan
- China
- others

Trade partners: imports

1970

- Japan
- China
- USA
- UK
- others

1995

- Japan
- China
- USA
- Singapore
- others

Export commodities

1970

1992

- textiles
- other manufactures
- machinery
- others

Import commodities

1970

1992

- food
- fuels
- materials
- machinery
- manufactures

Hong Kong

Social indicators

Main ethnic groups

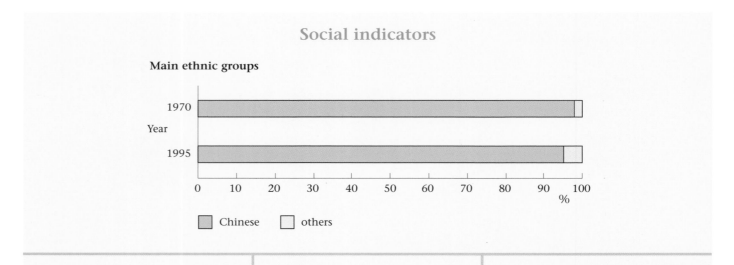

Women's labour

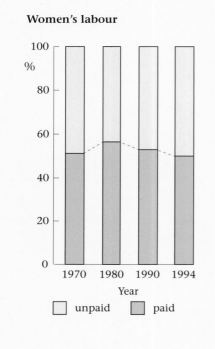

Population per physician

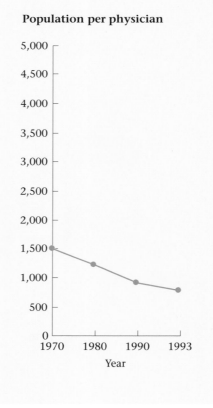

Government social security expenditure

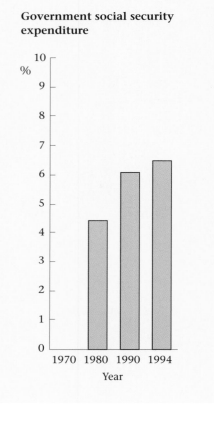

Political framework

- Four years bitter Sino-British disputes peter out in final few months before Hong Kong hand over. Residents uncertain over how much local autonomy will remain in China's commitment to 'one country: two systems'

- Fears
  - Beijing's key role in selection of Tung as new Chief Executive: is he a docile servant?
  - Beijing's key role in appointment of Provisional Legislators – are they an unrepresentative pro-China lobby designed to exclude others previously critical of Beijing's human rights record?
  - Beijing pledges to reverse recent improvements in civil freedoms that were rushed through by the British after 1989 Tiananmen Square massacre
  - press and media worry that only the freedoms of those with past pro-China record will be respected
  - 1998 elections promised but candidate eligibility expected to include patriotic credentials and commitment to prosperity with 'social stability'
  - Hong Kong to garrison People's Liberation Army troops – what will be their internal role?

- Hopes
  - apparently high status in Beijing for Tung; not just an ordinary Provincial Governor of China but close enough to leadership to defend Hong Kong's special position
  - Tung allowed in 1997 to continue high-level international contacts – may mean preserving Hong Kong's special entrepôt role in trade and finance
  - vast majority of top colonial civil servants to retain positions after 1997 to ensure some continuity
  - even civil servants who publicly criticized China's pledge to revoke human rights reforms are retained
  - Beijing's view of 'one country: two systems' interpreted by China's Foreign Minister to include political participation of those holding 'different opinions about the course and pace of democratic development'.

Further reading

McMillen, D.H. and DeGolyer, M.E. (1993) *One Culture, Many Systems?: Politics in the Reunification of China*, Hong Kong, Chinese University Press.

Miners, N. (1991) *The Government and Politics of Hong Kong*, 5th edn, Hong Kong, Oxford University Press.

Indonesia

Historical background

- 8th–13th C. Srivijaya's Buddhist empire rules Sumatra coast

- 13th C. Islam spread through Indian trade routes and over following centuries dominates all royal courts

- 14th–15th C. Majapahit's Hindu–Buddhist empire dominates central Java

- 1602 Dutch East India Company establishes trade base at Batavia (now Jakarta) to dominate region's European trade

- 1702 Portugal colonizes East Timor

- Late 18th C. Dutch East India Company bankrupt – Dutch government takes over administration

- 1811–16 brief British occupation

- By early 20th C. Dutch control entire archipelago but preserve position of traditional rulers

- 1920 Partai Kommunis Indonesia (PKI) formed

- 1927 Partia Nasional Indonesia (PNI) formed led by Sukarno

- 1942–45 Japanese occupation then Sukarno leads claims for independence from Dutch

- 1949 Dutch grudgingly concede independence except for West New Guinea

- 1955 first national elections increased power of Java-based political parties – leads to conflict in Sumatra 1956–57

- 1957 Sukarno declares martial law – replaces parliamentary system with authoritarian system of 'Guided Democracy'

- 1963 West New Guinea (later named Irian Jaya) recovered from Dutch

- 1963–66 conflict (konfrontasi) with Malaysia

- 1965 attempted army coup suppressed by General Suharto who later establishes opposition coalition calling for political and economic reforms. PKI lose essential Sukarno protection – members persecuted and killed

- 1967 Sukarno ousted, replaced as President by Suharto

- Suharto's New Order government reverses 'Guided Democracy', revitalizes national symbol of pancasila – non-ideological government. Dwifungsi (dual function) gives military greater role in government beyond security issues and army able to contest elections through Golkar (Functional Groups) organization

- 1971 Suharto introduces 'monoloyalty' policy – government officials able to support only the government during elections. Then with military backing, government able to win parliamentary elections
- August 1975 Revolutionary Front for Independent East Timor (Fretelin) claims independence from Portugal
- December 1975 Indonesia invades East Timor – incorporated as province in Republic of Indonesia
- 1980 *pancasila* redesigned to become state ideology – placed above social position of religion
- 1975–88 constant political repression – PKI and Muslim-based opposition groups targeted
- 1991 Indonesia security forces kill estimated 180 demonstrators at funeral in East Timor
- 1992 Indonesia elected to the Presidency of the Non-Aligned Movement
- 1994 Indonesia hosts APEC meeting
- 1995 State Administrative Court declares government's ban on three national newspapers in breach of 1982 Press Law

- 1995 Indonesia chairs ASEAN
- 1995 Indonesia signed first defence treaty with Australia
- 1996 government stunned when Nobel Peace Prize awarded to East Timorese activists Bishop Carlos Felipe Ximines Belo and Jose Ramos-Horta (residing in Australia).

Demographic indicators

Total population (million)

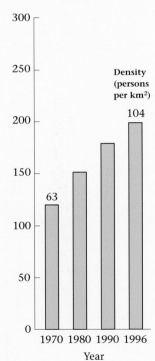

Density (persons per km²)

Infant mortality rate (deaths per 1,000 births)

Life expectancy at birth (years)

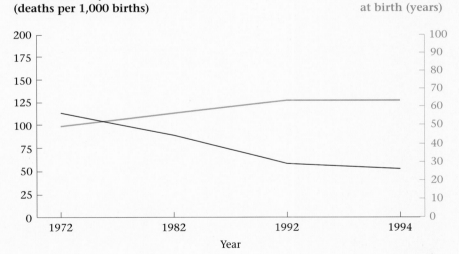

Population distribution

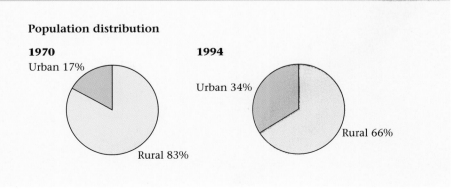

1970
Urban 17%
Rural 83%

1994
Urban 34%
Rural 66%

Indonesia

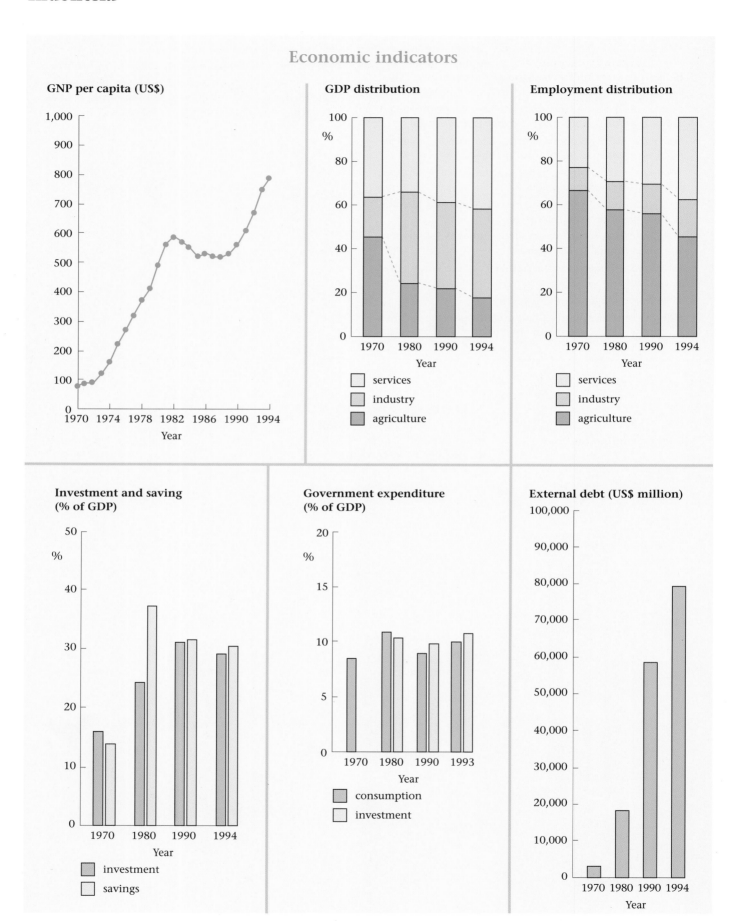

Economic indicators

GNP per capita (US$)

GDP distribution

services
industry
agriculture

Employment distribution

services
industry
agriculture

Investment and saving (% of GDP)

investment
savings

Government expenditure (% of GDP)

consumption
investment

External debt (US$ million)

Exports and imports (% of GDP)

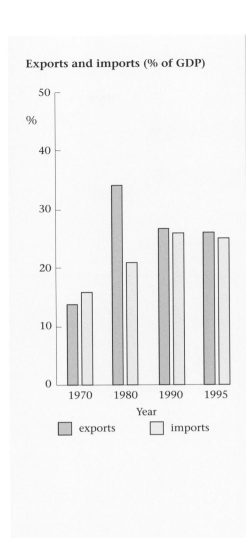

Trade partners: exports

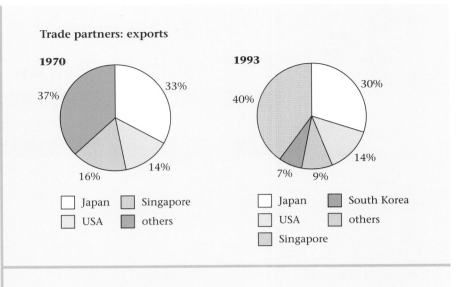

Trade partners: imports

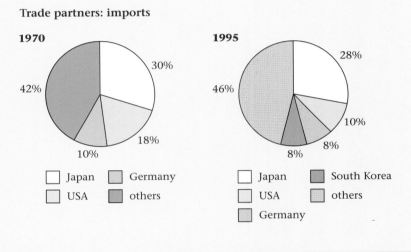

Export commodities

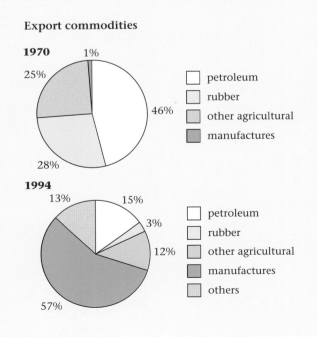

Import commodities

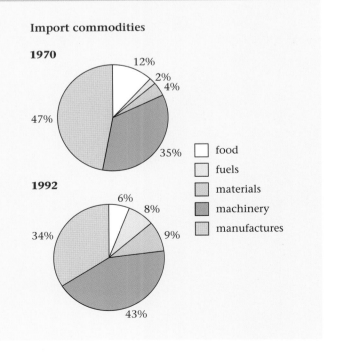

Indonesia

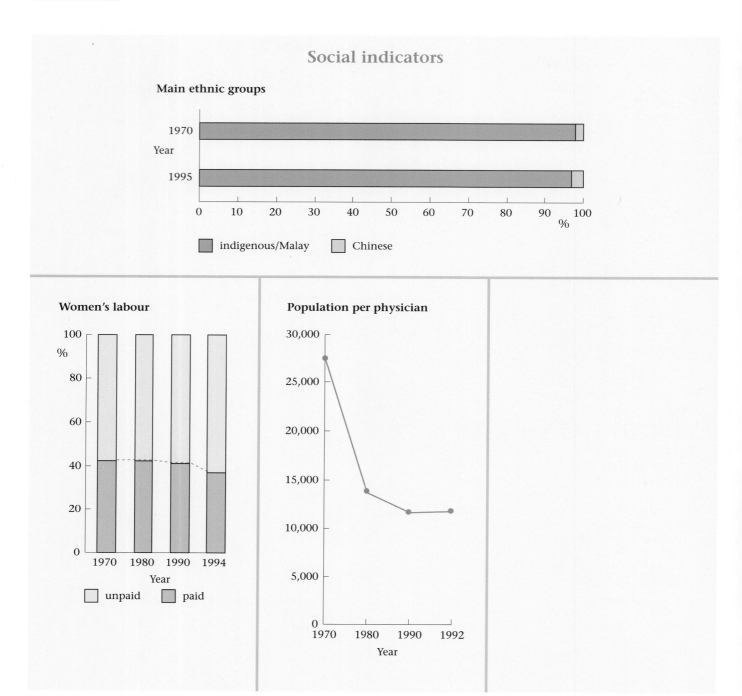

Social indicators

Main ethnic groups

Year

1970

1995

0 10 20 30 40 50 60 70 80 90 100 %

■ indigenous/Malay ▢ Chinese

Women's labour

%

100

80

60

40

20

0

1970 1980 1990 1994

Year

▢ unpaid ■ paid

Population per physician

30,000

25,000

20,000

15,000

10,000

5,000

0

1970 1980 1990 1992

Year

<table>
<tr><td colspan="1">

Political framework

- 1996 saw worst political violence for over a decade in numerous parts of Indonesia against background of doubts about President Suharto's health and longer term questions about what kind of regime will follow his demise

- Riots in Jakarta after government/military machinations engineer removal of Sukarno's daughter as leader of 'opposition' Indonesian Democratic Party (PDI)

- Rioting used as pretext to suppress wide range of political activists, trade union and NGO leaders demanding political reform

- Other violent disputes over land rights in Java, influence of Chinese in Sumatra then in Irian Jaya over distribution of benefits from world's biggest copper and gold mines

- Evidence of some reservations even within military about their role in fomenting then suppressing social unrest

- Alongside violence go longer term concerns over what kind of regime will follow one so dependent on Suharto's personal authority

- Currently under *pancasila* a People's Consultative Assembly is the highest authority that elects the President but only 40% of members are elected – remainder appointed from a network significantly influenced by presidential cronies. Even elected members are subject to approval and control of President through Golkar – not really the ruling party rather the party of civilian and military rulers

- Underlying *pancasila* is belief that an ethnically diverse and multi-religious society needs centrally imposed order to avoid social disintegration. Growing pressures for more open political participation have to confront such an ideology supported by military interests

- Younger army officers said to be contemplating possibility of post-Suharto reforms but political influence of senior officers and fears of social disintegration seem to rule out any removal of the military from centres of power

- Continued military partnership in government not civilian dominance of politics remains top of the agenda in debates about Suharto succession.

</td></tr>
</table>

Further reading

Cribb, R. and Brown, C. (1995) *Modern Indonesia. A History Since 1945*, London, Longman Cheshire.

Hal Hil (1994) *Indonesia's New Order. The Dynamics of Socio-Economic Transformation*, St. Leonards, Allen & Unwin.

Japan

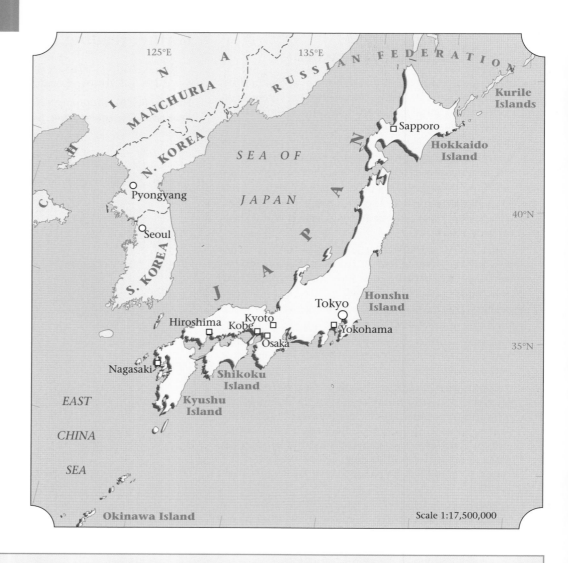

Historical background

- 660 BC Emperor Jimmu accedes to throne beginning unbroken line of 125 Emperors
- 5th C. AD Yamato period – Chinese script imported, Buddhism introduced *c*. AD 600
- *c*. 14th C. start of period where a shogun rules in Emperor's name
- 16th C. internal disorder – civil wars between rival clans
- 1600–1868 Tokugawa shogunate leads policy of seclusion – Chinese and Dutch traders only allowed in Nagasaki plus some Christian missionaries
- 1853–54 Commodore Perry's naval squadron arrives – secures agreement to open some trading ports and accept US Consul
- 1868 full governing powers restored to Emperor Meiji
- 1894–95 Japan defeats China, colonizes Taiwan and gains recognition for her 'special interests' in Korea
- 1904–5 Japan defeats Russia
- 1910 Korea annexed

- 1923 half of Tokyo and all of Yokohama destroyed after series of earthquakes
- 1930s militant nationalism at home and imperialism abroad
- 1931 Japan colonizes Manchuria – creates puppet-state of Manchukuo
- 1937–45 Sino-Japanese War
- 1941 Japan attacks Pearl Harbor to enter Second World War
- 1945 atomic bombs dropped on Hiroshima and Nagasaki – Japan surrenders
- 1945–52 US occupation under General MacArthur who orchestrates new constitution renouncing war and external use of armed forces. MacArthur also attempts to reconstruct Japan along US lines
- 1950–53 Japanese industry boosted by military demand in Korean War
- 1955 Liberal Democratic Party (LDP) formed from merger of Liberal Party and Democratic Party – holds unbroken power for next 38 years

- 1960s rapid economic growth – 'income-doubling era'
- 1971 'Nixon shock' – USA restores relations with China (PRC) without consultation
- 1972 Japan recognizes PRC
- 1973 'oil shock' – massive petroleum price increase hits import-dependent Japan
- 1976 PM Tanaka forced to resign in first of many publicized financial scandals involving senior politicians
- 1985 Plaza Accord forces revaluation of yen – in 8 months yen appreciates 40% against US$. Higher export prices encourage Japanese companies to locate more production overseas where wages lower
- 1989 Recruit affair – leading LDP politicians implicated in share-trading irregularities. Three ministers including the Finance Minister forced to resign. PM Takeshita subsequently resigns when implicated
- 1990 government promises troops for Gulf War but meets intense domestic criticism – instead US$4 billion contributed to UN war funds

- 1992 legislation passed allowing Japanese troops to serve overseas on UN peace-keeping missions. Further financial scandals within LDP – party Vice-President forced to resign
- 1993 coalition government elected – LDP loses power for first time since 1955
- 1994 legislation to reform electoral system promises an end to the unequal constituency distribution that kept LDP in power so long
- 1994 new coalition government led by minority Socialist Party but with long-term opponents LDP back in key Cabinet posts
- 1995 Kobe earthquake – worst natural disaster since 1927
- 1995 PM Murayama gives first apology for Japanese wartime atrocities
- 1996 general election – LDP minority government.

Demographic indicators

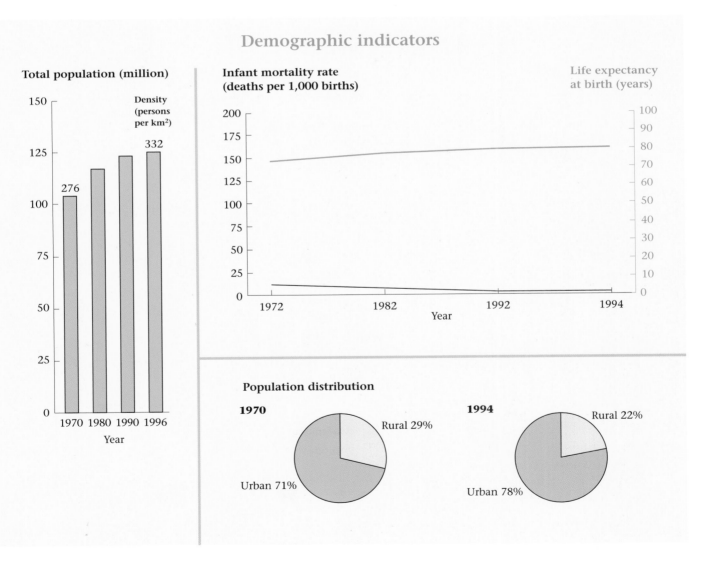

Total population (million)

Density (persons per km²)

332

276

Infant mortality rate (deaths per 1,000 births)

Life expectancy at birth (years)

Population distribution

1970

Rural 29%

Urban 71%

1994

Rural 22%

Urban 78%

Japan

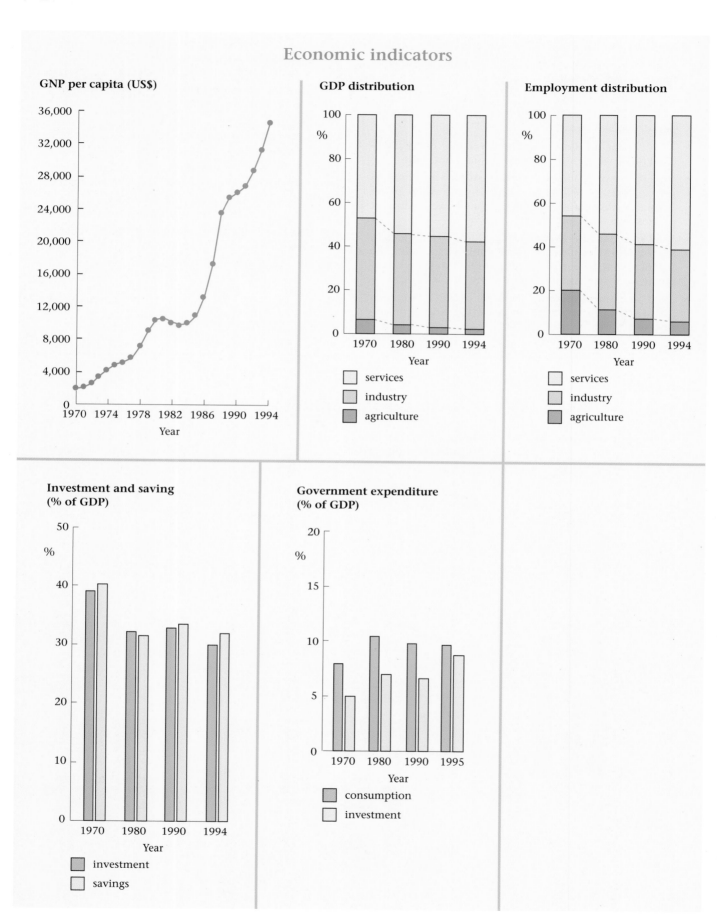

Economic indicators

GNP per capita (US$)

GDP distribution

Employment distribution

Investment and saving (% of GDP)

Government expenditure (% of GDP)

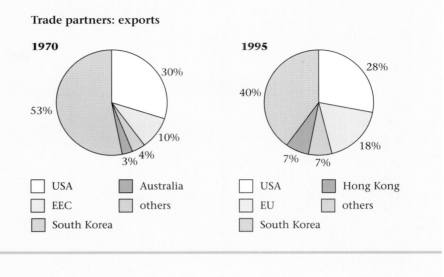

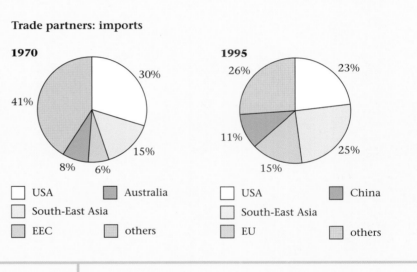

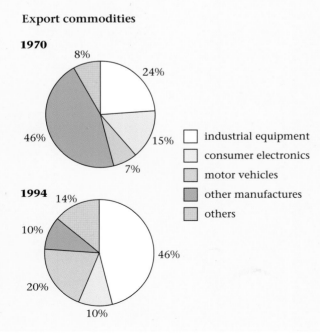

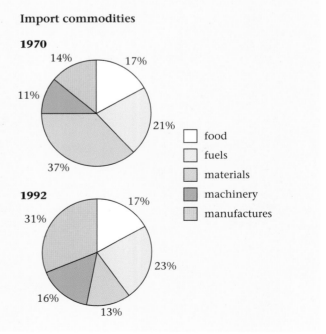

Japan

Exports and imports (% of GDP)

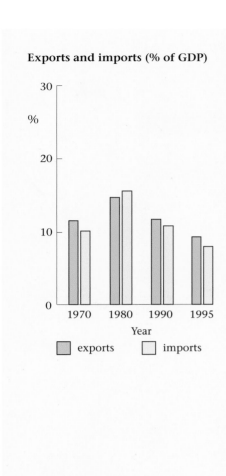

Trade partners: exports

1970

30% USA
10% EEC
4% South Korea
3% Australia
53% others

1995

28% USA
18% EU
7% South Korea
7% Hong Kong
40% others

Trade partners: imports

1970

30% USA
15% South-East Asia
6% EEC
8% Australia
41% others

1995

23% USA
25% South-East Asia
15% EU
11% China
26% others

Export commodities

1970

24% industrial equipment
15% consumer electronics
7% motor vehicles
46% other manufactures
8% others

1994

46%
10%
20%
10%
14%

- industrial equipment
- consumer electronics
- motor vehicles
- other manufactures
- others

Import commodities

1970

17% food
21% fuels
37% materials
11% machinery
14% manufactures

1992

17%
23%
13%
16%
31%

- food
- fuels
- materials
- machinery
- manufactures

Japan

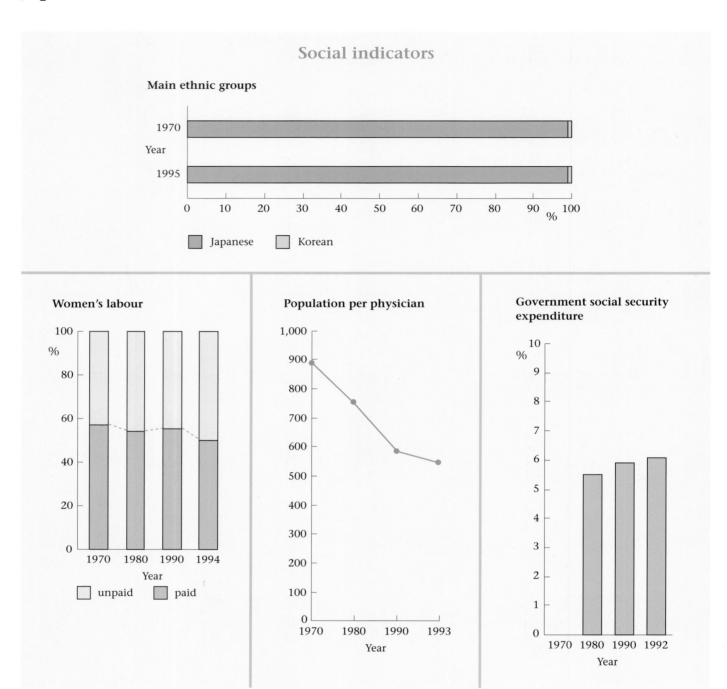

Social indicators

Main ethnic groups

Year

1970

1995

0 10 20 30 40 50 60 70 80 90 100 %

Japanese   Korean

Women's labour

%

100

80

60

40

20

0

1970 1980 1990 1994

Year

unpaid   paid

Population per physician

1,000

900

800

700

600

500

400

300

200

100

0

1970 1980 1990 1993

Year

Government social security expenditure

%

10

9

8

7

6

5

4

3

2

1

0

1970 1980 1990 1992

Year

Political framework

- 1996 elections confirm public mood of apathy and disillusionment with political leadership as only 60% of voters participate – record low

- In the three years after LDP dominance ended politicians rearrange four different coalition governments forging *ad hoc* alliances with long time enemies and apparently ignoring policy commitments – whole process appears to ignore electorate

- LDP biggest party again in 1996 but with only 48% seats has to rely once more on smaller parties. Despite more promises to reform government Cabinet filled with ageing power-brokers from pre-1993 era of LDP dominance

- Main source of public disillusionment with elected politicians is their failure to deliver policies to curb power of unelected bureaucrats

- High levels of respect for bureaucracy disappears in 1990s

- Even all-powerful Finance Ministry apparently unable to slow upward spiral of speculative property boom in late 1980s – 'bubble economy'

- As speculative bubble bursts in early 1990s Finance bureaucrats again unable to manage Japan out of worst recession since 1945

- Citizen taxpayers even told they have to pay for these mistakes – massive debts accumulated by mortgage companies (*jusen*) who had switched lending from home buyers to property speculators. Taxpayers expected to contribute US$18 billion to avert liquidity crisis in whole financial system

- Similar episodes of bureaucratic incompetence revealed elsewhere – health officials ignore warnings about haemophiliacs being given blood infected with HIV and later seem helpless when confronting *E. coli* food poisoning outbreak

- Foreign policy achievements – like new security pact for USA to offer unlimited protection under their nuclear umbrella – are claimed but cannot compensate for failure to deliver domestic political reform.

Further reading

Eccleston, B. (1995) *State and Society in Post-War Japan*, Cambridge, Polity Press.

Johnson, C. (1995) *Japan: Who Governs? The Rise of the Developmental State*, New York, W.W. Norton.

Korea

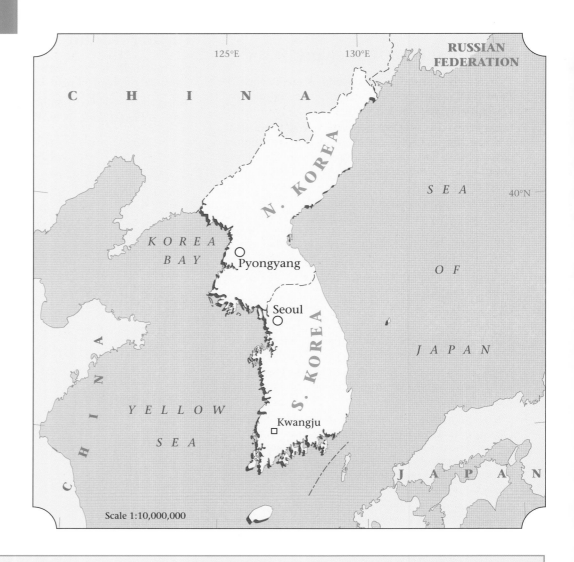

Historical background

- 180 BC Wiman Choson kingdom founded
- 108 BC China invades – four colonial outposts established
- AD 668 three kingdoms of Koguryo, Paekche and Shilla unified under Shilla
- 936–1392 Koryo dynasty
- 1231 Mongol invasion
- 1392 founding of Yi dynasty
- 1866 *USS General Sherman* arrives – first contact between USA and Korea
- 1875 first Japanese incursion into Korea in modern times
- 1894 peasant uprising against government corruption and 'modernization' policies
- 1895–1905 Japanese victories against China and Russia allows Japan to establish protectorate over Korea
- 1910 Japanese colonial government formally established
- 1919 uprising against colonial rule rocks Korea – brutally suppressed
- 1919 provisional government in exile formed in Shanghai
- 1934–41 forced assimilation into Japan's war effort throughout Korea
- 1941–45 Korean soldiers conscripted into Japanese battles throughout Pacific
- 1945 Korea becomes independent after Japan's defeat
- 1945 under trusteeship plan Soviet and US armies move into northern and southern Korea respectively
- 1947 USA takes 'Korea question' to UN as agreement breaks down on the form of an interim government.

North Korea: Historical background

- 1945 North Korean Communist Party formed under Kim Il Sung
- 1948 general elections bring Kim Il Sung to power and formalize split between South and North Korea
- 1950 backed by China's People's Liberation Army North Korean army invades South Korea and Korean War begins
- 1953 Panmujon truce signed after 500,000 die
- 1955 Kim Il Sung idolizes *juche* – mix of self-reliant nationalism, socialism and personality cult
- 1956 Khrushchev denounces Stalin and encourages criticism of Kim Il Sung which is quickly suppressed
- 1967–69 subversive operations against South Korea staged including seizure of *USS Pueblo* and shooting down US aircraft
- 1974 Kim Jong-Il, the son of Kim Il Sung emerges as a possible successor
- 1980 Kim Jong-Il confirmed as successor

- 1991 Kim Jong-Il installed as supreme commander of Korean People's Army
- 1992 CIA reveals North Korea may have potential to build nuclear weapons
- 1994 Kim Il Sung dies and Kim Jong-Il takes over as army head though not as President or Party General Secretary
- 1994 USA brokers halt to North Korea's nuclear weapons programme in return for oil imports and South Korean assistance with civil nuclear programme
- 1995 disastrous floods devastate rice harvest and undermine planting for following seasons
- 1996 widespread starvation and famine reported
- 1996 North Korean submarine spying mission goes aground in South Korea
- 1997 architect of *juche* and most senior leader yet to defect seeks asylum in South Korea to discuss how to save North from war and famine.

Demographic indicators

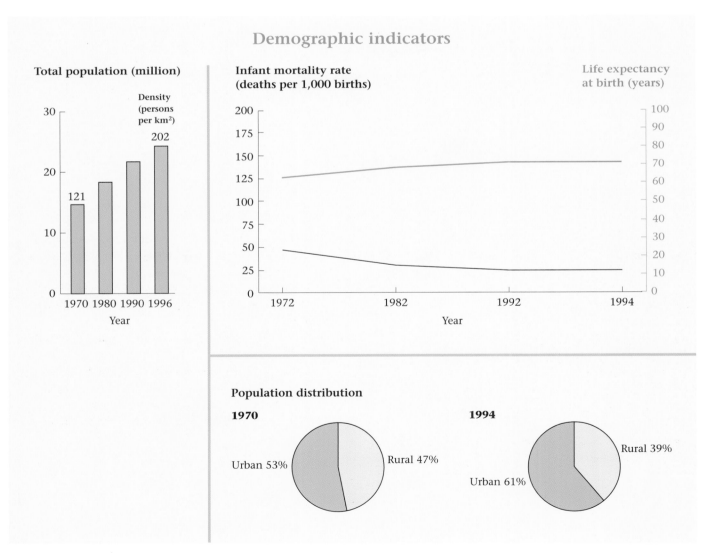

Total population (million)

Density (persons per km²)

Infant mortality rate (deaths per 1,000 births)

Life expectancy at birth (years)

Population distribution

1970

Urban 53% Rural 47%

1994

Rural 39% Urban 61%

Democratic People's Republic of Korea (North)

Economic indicators

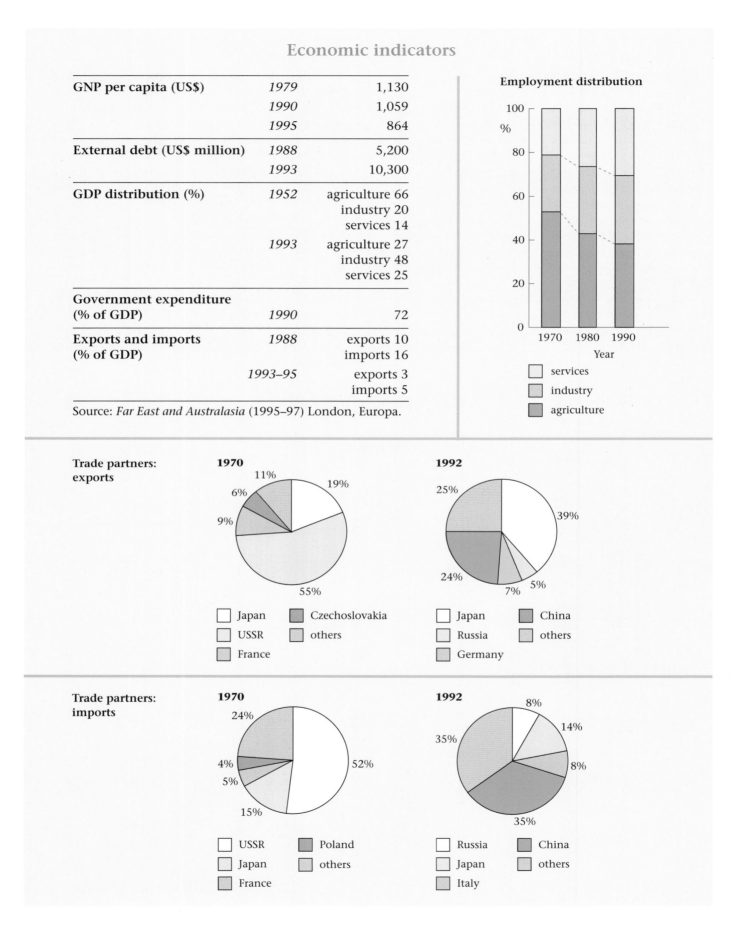

GNP per capita (US$)	1979	1,130
	1990	1,059
	1995	864
External debt (US$ million)	1988	5,200
	1993	10,300
GDP distribution (%)	1952	agriculture 66 industry 20 services 14
	1993	agriculture 27 industry 48 services 25
Government expenditure (% of GDP)	1990	72
Exports and imports (% of GDP)	1988	exports 10 imports 16
	1993–95	exports 3 imports 5

Source: *Far East and Australasia* (1995–97) London, Europa.

Employment distribution

services
industry
agriculture

Trade partners: exports

1970

- Japan 19%
- USSR 55%
- France 9%
- Czechoslovakia 6%
- others 11%

1992

- Japan 39%
- Russia
- Germany
- China 24%
- others 25%, 7%, 5%

Trade partners: imports

1970

- USSR 52%
- Japan 15%
- France 5%
- Poland 4%
- others 24%

1992

- Russia 8%
- Japan 14%
- Italy 8%
- China 35%
- others 35%

126

Export commodities

1965

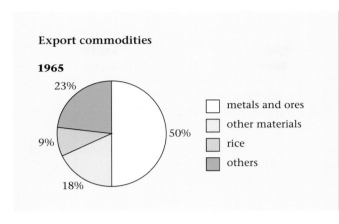

- metals and ores
- other materials
- rice
- others

Import commodities

1965

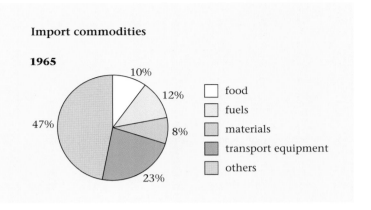

- food
- fuels
- materials
- transport equipment
- others

Social indicators

Main ethnic groups

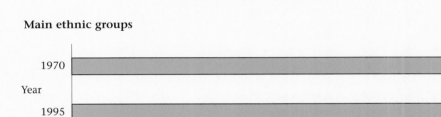

Korean

Women's labour

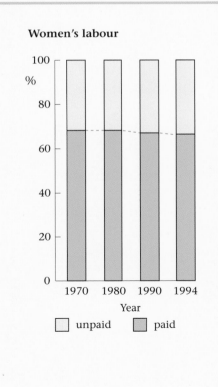

unpaid paid

Population per physician

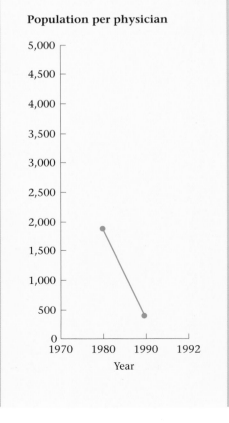

Democratic People's Republic of Korea (North)

Political framework

- In world's most secretive state with most reclusive leadership political developments emerge piecemeal – absences noted from official events like funerals or in reports from defectors

- Kim Jong-Il by 1997 still not President nor Party General Secretary but signs of him consolidating military power base by promoting those loyal to him to replace those that remain from his father's generation

- Chronic food shortage since 1995 means even tighter internal security and desperate search for foreign currency to acquire food imports – North Korea agrees (1997) to store Taiwan's nuclear waste and recycle Germany's plastic garbage

- Without old socialist allies in Europe diplomatic missions from this near-autarchic state now target Japan and USA for aid and loans – China tries to keep equidistant from North and South Korea not least to protect its US$20 billion trade ties to South Korea

- Continued uncertain and tense relations with South Korea especially as North prefers direct negotiations with USA who then mediates South Korean reaction. USA for instance tries to push South Korea into faster progress on assisting North's civil nuclear reactor programme

- Defectors consistently report evidence of economic dislocation but say even tighter political control makes regime collapse unlikely.

Further reading

Chong, Yong-ki (1995) *North Korea: the Land that Never Changes*, Seoul, Naewoe Press.

Foster-Carter, A. (1992) *Korea's Coming Reunification*, London, Economist Intelligence Unit.

Howard, K. (1996) *Korea: People, Country and Culture*, London, School of Oriental and African Studies.

Lone, S. and McCormak, G. (1993) *Korea Since 1985*, New York, St. Martin's Press.

South Korea: Historical background

- 1948 general election held – Syngman Rhee elected President of First Republic
- 1950 North Korea attacks South
- 1950–53 with UN mandate USA leads fifteen other states in military support of South Korea
- 1953 Panmujon truce signed after 500,000 die
- 1960 Syngman Rhee re-elected amidst widespread allegations of vote rigging – student uprising forces government to resign and fresh elections called
- 1960 Democratic Party wins new elections – Chang Myon PM in Second Republic's revised parliamentary system
- 1961 military coup – power shifts to army and General Park Chung Hee
- 1963 Park Chung Hee elected President of Third Republic under presidential system
- 1972 Park proclaims martial law and dissolves National Assembly. He is now able to appoint one-third of the National Assembly – becomes virtual dictator

- 1974 Park's wife killed in North Korean assassination attempt on the President
- 1979 Park assassinated
- 1980 military coup and Chun Doo Hwan seizes power to become President of the Fifth Republic
- 1980 military forces quell violent demonstrations centred on Kwangju
- 1987 Roh Tae Woo declared Chun's successor in the midst of civil unrest – promises democratic reforms
- 1988 Roh Tae Woo directly elected President of the Sixth Republic
- 1993 Kim Young Sam elected as first civilian head of state for 30 years
- 1996 two ex-Presidents, thirteen retired generals and numerous businessmen tried for bribery, corruption and treason
- Early 1997 widespread industrial unrest following attempts to revise labour laws.

Demographic indicators

Total population (million)

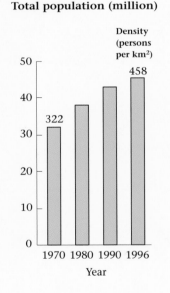

Infant mortality rate (deaths per 1,000 births)

Life expectancy at birth (years)

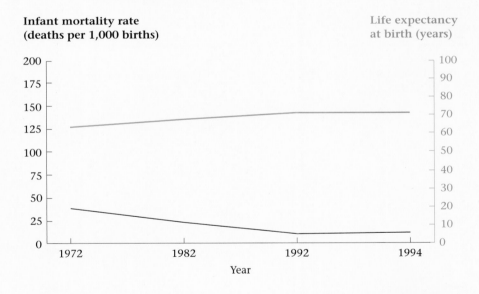

Population distribution

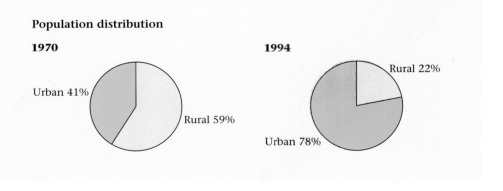

1970 — Urban 41%, Rural 59%

1994 — Rural 22%, Urban 78%

Republic of Korea (South)

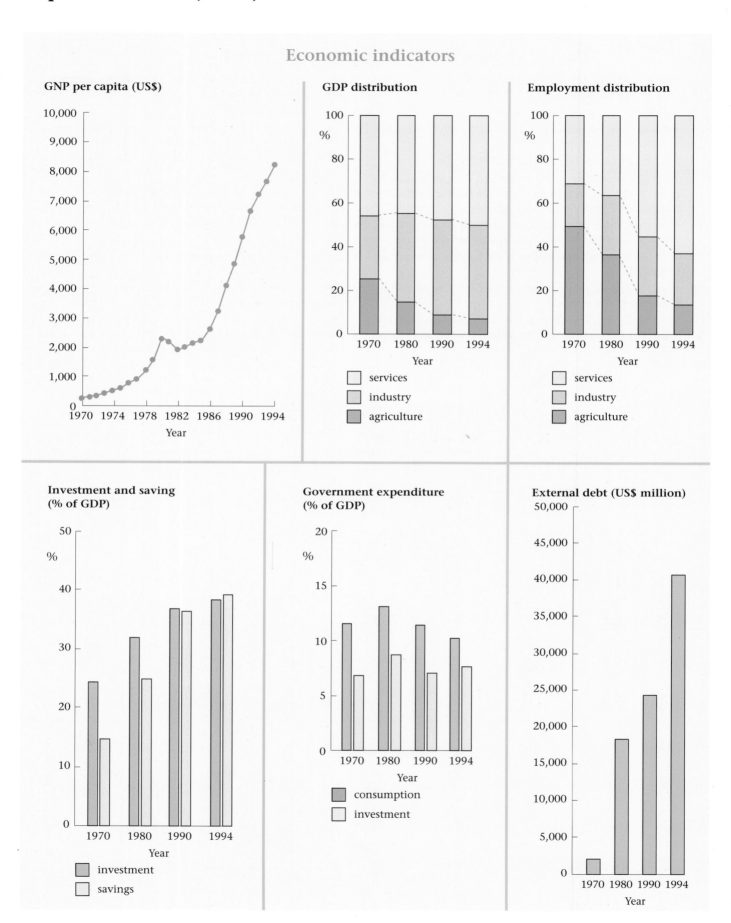

Economic indicators

GNP per capita (US$)

GDP distribution

Employment distribution

Investment and saving (% of GDP)

Government expenditure (% of GDP)

External debt (US$ million)

Exports and imports (% of GDP)

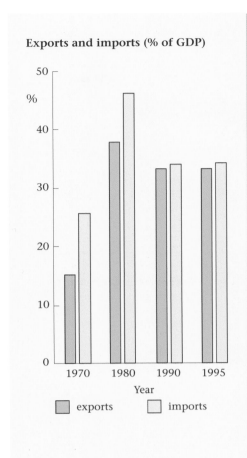

Trade partners: exports

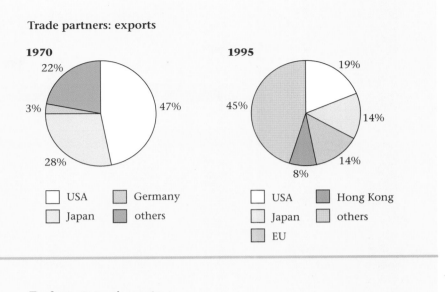

Trade partners: imports

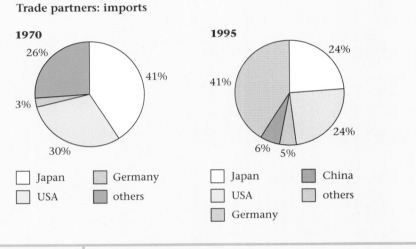

Export commodities

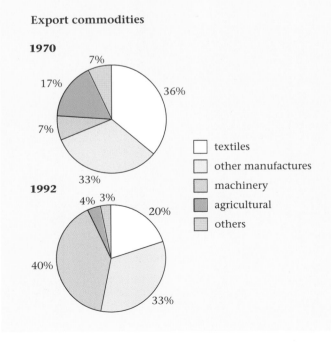

Import commodities

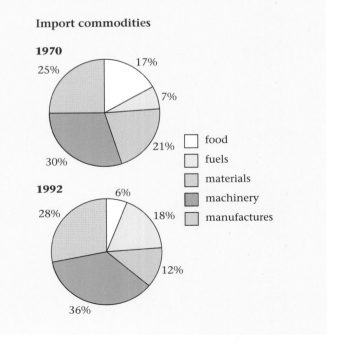

Republic of Korea (South)

Social indicators

Main ethnic groups

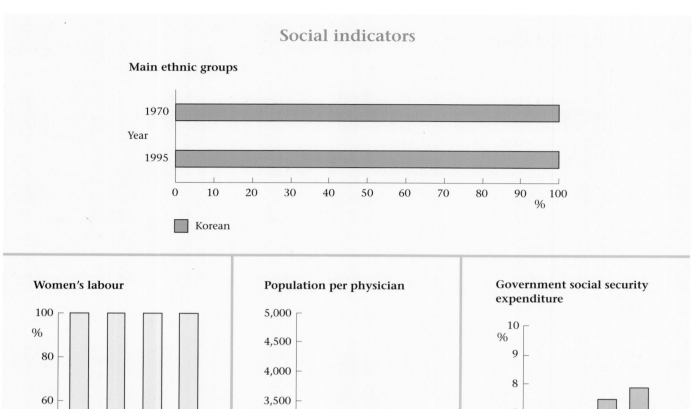

Women's labour

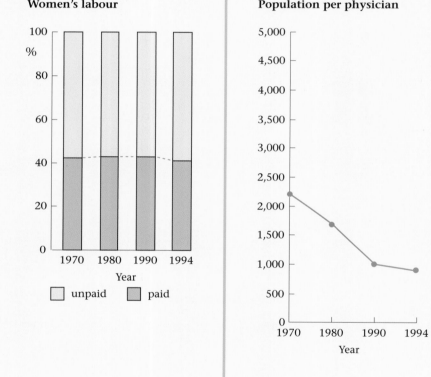

Population per physician

Government social security expenditure

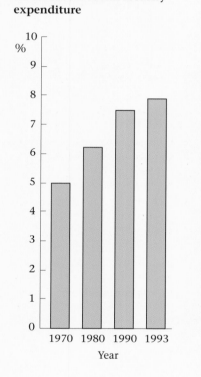

Political framework

- Following four years of civilian government President Kim Young Sam faces major political problems

- Kim elected with pledge to exorcize past misrule and root out political corruption. Apparently being implemented with 1996 conviction of ex-President Chun Doo Hwan for illegally mobilizing troops and bribery – ex-President Roh Tae Woo also convicted of bribery and conspiring with Chun

- Concerns though when no businessmen convicted of corruption are imprisoned – Kim's government accused of not tackling structural corruption but seeking personal political retribution from predecessors

- Deeper problems apparently confirmed over role of Kim's family and leading politicians when Hanbo Iron & Steel company collapses in 1997 – one of South Korea's biggest failures

- Kim apologizes to nation but questions remain over how Hanbo was able to secure US$6 billion preferential loans with assets of just US$0.4 billion

- Widespread public disillusionment with Kim's anti-corruption pledges

- Deepening economic problems – slower growth rates, huge trade deficit and escalating external debt – used by Kim to justify deregulation of labour markets

- Legislation to introduce flexible working hours, allow short-term employment reduction and replace striking workers passed in 6 a.m. parliamentary session when no opposition members present

- Both reforms and method of implementation galvanize political and union opposition in strikes and demonstrations in early 1997 – Kim later agrees to take legislation back to parliament for reconsideration

- As next election looms opposition parties voice ideas about switching to parliamentary government from current presidential system that is thought to encourage old authoritarian political style.

Further reading

Khoo, H. (ed.) (1993) *State and Society in Contemporary Korea*, Ithaca, Cornell University Press.

Lone, S. and McCormak, G. (1993) *Korea Since 1985*, New York, St. Martin's Press.

Ogle, G. (1990) *South Korea: Dissent within the Economic Miracle*, London, Zed Books.

Laos

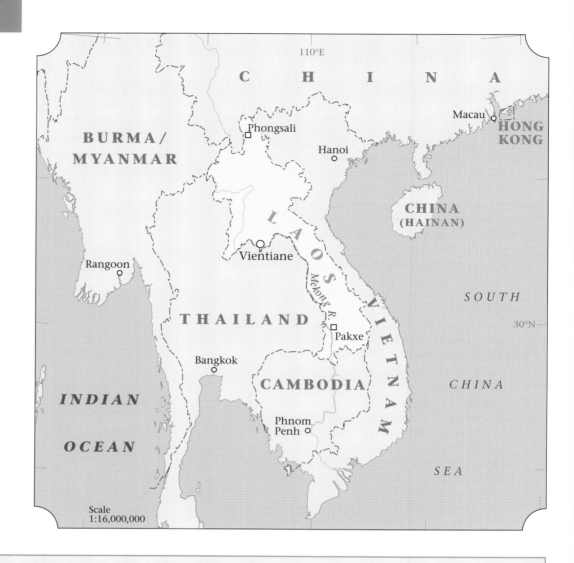

Scale
1:16,000,000

Historical background

- 1353 Laos first unified as Kingdom of Lan Xang – 'a million elephants'

- 17th–18th C. Lao territory divided by rival princes and exposed to expansionist influence of Vietnam and Siam (Thailand)

- 19th C. Laos virtually collection of Thai vassal principalities

- 1885 France colonizes Vietnam and gains Lao territory

- 1893 French protectorate established – incorporates Laos into Union of Indo-China once Siam accepts French authority over all Lao territory east of Mekong River

- 1940–45 Japanese occupation of Laos under administration of Vichy French government

- April 1945 King Sisavang Vong declares Laos independent under Japanese protection

- September 1945 Lao Issarak movement (Free Laos) declares independence from Japan and France

- 1946 France regains Laos, restores monarchy and establishes Laos a free state within the French Union

- 1951 Royal Lao Government formed by Souvanna Phouma

- 1953 Laos granted full independence against background of conflict between pro-communist Pathet Lao (Land of the Lao) and US-backed Royal Lao Government in Vientiane

- 1954 conflict addressed by Geneva Agreement – allows Pathet Lao to dominate the north and royalists the south

- 1955 national elections boycotted by the Pathet Lao – Laos admitted to UN

- 1957 agreement between Vientiane and Pathet Lao to form coalition government – collapses following year

- 1957–73 protracted military conflict between Royal Lao Government and Pathet Lao with USA supporting former and North Vietnamese latter – attempts to keep Laos neutral in Vietnam War are thwarted as USA and North Vietnam treat Laos as war theatre

- 1973 cease fire agreed between Royal Lao Government and Pathet Lao – coalition government established following year

- 1975 communist victories in Cambodia and Vietnam

allows Lao People's Revolutionary Party to seize control of government, abolishes monarchy within renamed Lao People's Democratic Republic

- 1980 UN High Commissioner for Refugees initiates programme to repatriate Lao refugees from Thailand
- 1985 border clashes between Laos and Thai armed forces
- Late 1980s economy on verge of collapse and aid from USSR cut – government initiates liberal market reforms
- 1989 USA removes eligibility for aid accusing Lao government officials of active involvement in drug trafficking
- 1991 new constitution adopted confirming dominant hold of Lao People's Revolutionary Party on political power. Kaysone Phomvihane appointed President – continues pledge to develop market economy
- 1992 Laos signs ASEAN Treaty of Amity and Co-operation
- 1992 Kaysone dies – Nouhak Phoumsavanh re-elected President by the National Assembly the next year
- 1994 opening of the symbolic Thai–Lao Friendship Bridge across Mekong River

- 1994 Laos attends ASEAN as observer – promised full membership by 2000 but possibly as early as 1997.

Demographic indicators

Total population (million)

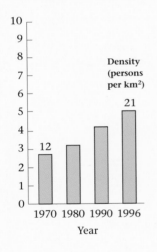

Density (persons per km²)

Infant mortality rate (deaths per 1,000 births)

Life expectancy at birth (years)

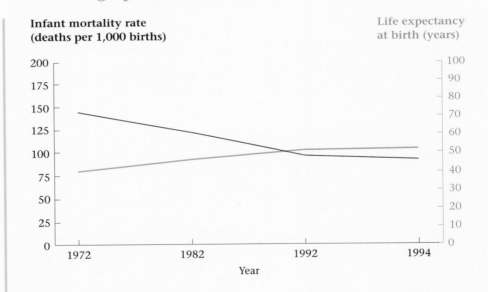

Population distribution

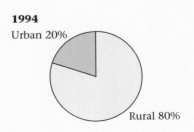

1970
Urban 11%
Rural 89%

1994
Urban 20%
Rural 80%

Laos

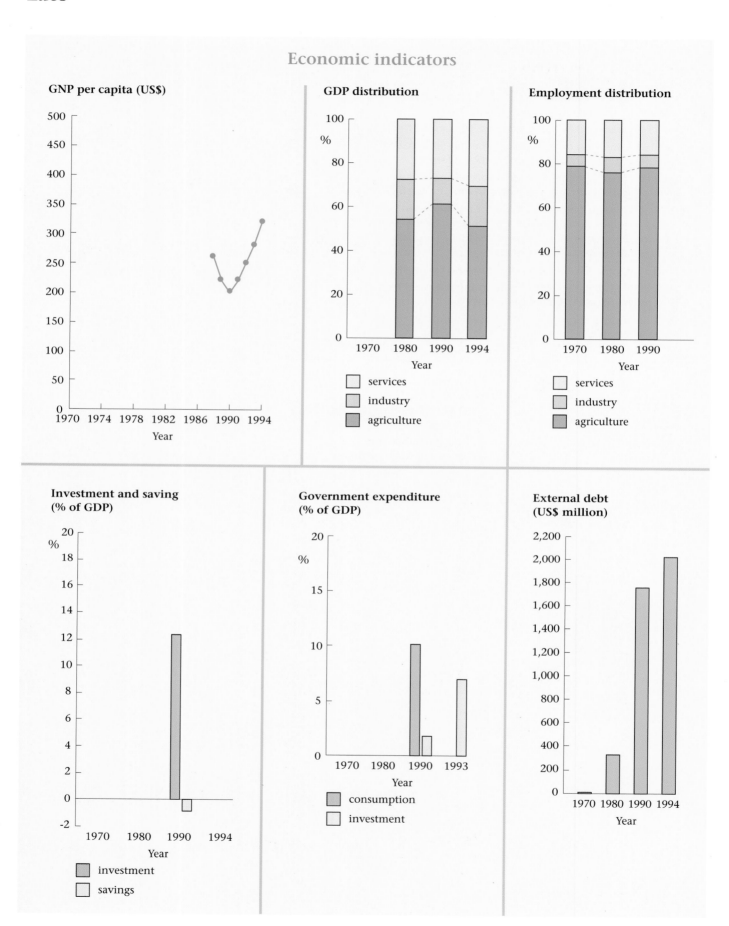

Economic indicators

GNP per capita (US$)

GDP distribution

Employment distribution

Investment and saving (% of GDP)

Government expenditure (% of GDP)

External debt (US$ million)

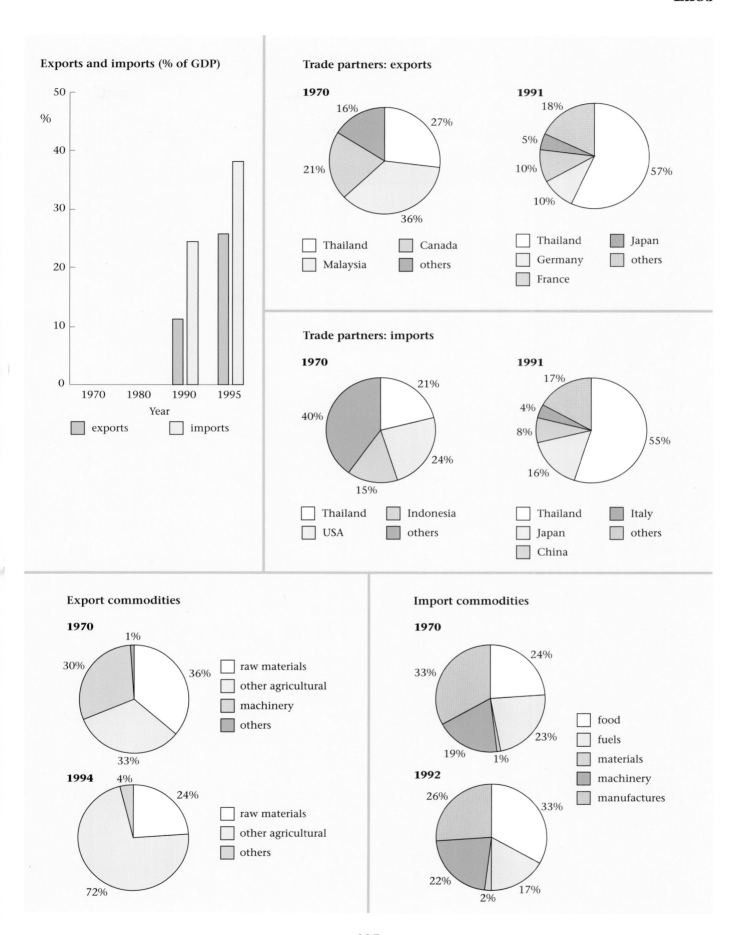

Laos

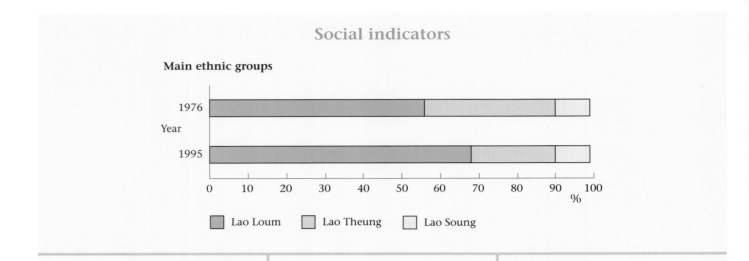

Social indicators

Main ethnic groups

Lao Loum   Lao Theung   Lao Soung

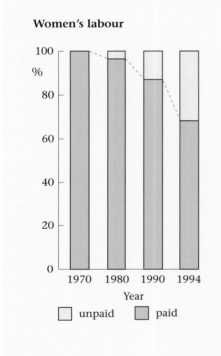

Women's labour

unpaid   paid

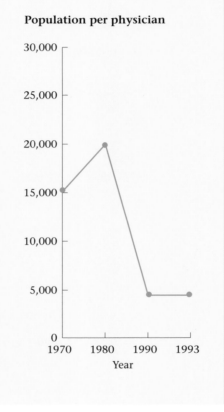

Population per physician

Political framework

- 1996 congress of ruling Lao People's Revolutionary Party sees notable increase in role of military in political leadership

- To secure an even more prominent place in government military interests join civilian leaders building mass political organizations to legitimize their blend of authoritarian nationalism

- Close similarities noted with SLORC in Burma/Myanmar and Indonesia's Golkar – not only in ideology but in military combining political power with more obvious economic role – especially in exploitation of natural resources

- Also similarities in curbing opposition voices who argue for a more democratic system with freedom for multi-party political activity

- Laos government pressing for accelerated ASEAN membership in 1997 partly it appears to follow Burma/Myanmar's lead using ASEAN's collective assistance to resist pressures from Western donor countries for more political reform and secure civil rights

- Additional benefits from full ASEAN status would be to dilute dependence on Thai foreign investors who currently supply nearly one half of all foreign investment

- Alongside historical roots to animosity go fears that Laos might become merely an expendable offshore site for Thai textile firms attracted temporarily to a low-wage country

- ASEAN membership might offer other foreign investment sources and allow government to diversify from Thailand's dominant role

- Hydro-electric power projects seen as key to self-sustained economic growth especially as neighbouring countries have insatiable demand for power. But World Bank funding has too many conditions covering environmental protection and position of villagers to be resettled after dams built

- Spreading inward foreign investment among ASEAN partners might give Laos government more control and also allow more attention to maldistribution of economic growth benefits

- Current concerns that potentially dissident minorities in Highlands need to be given greater share of prosperity. Also need to keep tighter control of negative aspects of transition to market economy seen in social dislocation caused by spread of AIDS, crime and corruption.

Further reading

Cordell, H. (1991) *Laos*, Santa Barbara, Clio Press.

Stuart-Fox, M. (1996) *Buddhist Kingdom, Marxist State: the Making of Modern Laos*, Bangkok, White Lotus Press.

Malaysia

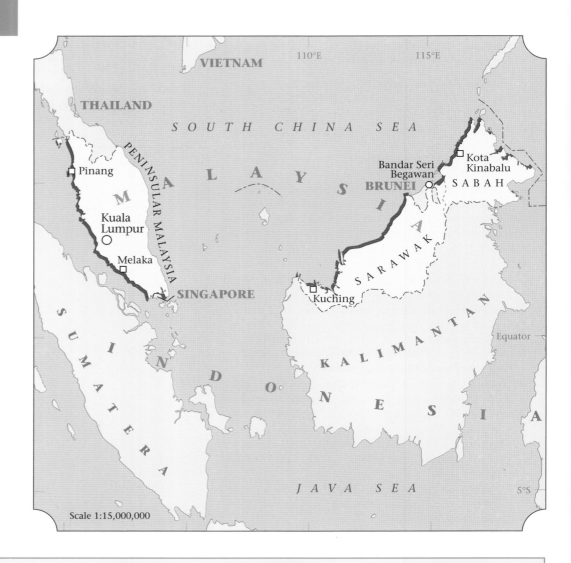

Historical background

- Territorial boundaries influenced by late 19th C. British colonialism but formalized only in 1965

- Key geographical position of Malacca Straits at confluence of Arab, Indian, Chinese trade and navigation routes bequeathing varying layers to cultural heritage over 40,000 years

- AD 900 Indian Empire locally centred on Sumatra but influences Malay Peninsula

- 14th C. Islamic influence especially Muslim Trading Empire with Malacca as entrepôt centre for exotic trade – China to/from Arab world via Straits

- Portuguese take over Malacca Empire 16th C.

- Dutch naval and commercial power replaces Portuguese mid 17th C. – Java now becomes trading centre but Malacca still important for its strategic location

- British influence from late 18th C. mainly in key ports Penang/Pinang, Malacca/Melaka and Singapore – colonized as 'Straits Settlements' from 1820s

- Vital entrepôt functions within British Imperial economic system especially Singapore

- Later 19th C. 'informal' British Imperialism outside Straits Settlements – protection for local state Sultanates through colonial 'advisors' especially in mineral-rich states of West Peninsula but later padi states in the east too. North Borneo similar 'protection' for Sabah and Sarawak

- Network of protected states on Peninsula – 1895 Federated Malay States

- Parallel development of twin resource pillars: (a) tin and Chinese migrant labour from 1870s – 0.5 m 'permanent' settlers by 1900; (b) rubber and South Indian labour from 1900s – 4 m 'temporary' settlers though 1.2 m stay

- 1941–48 Japanese and later British military occupation sees first centralized administration for Peninsular Malaya

- 1946 British propose formal colony as Malaya Union to widespread local opposition

- 1948 Federation of Malaya (excluding Singapore) established on Peninsula as colonial regime

- 1948–60 'Emergency' era against communist insurgents

- 1957 Federation becomes independent

- 1963 Malaysia formed: Federation on Peninsula plus Singapore plus North Borneo states Sarawak and Sabah – not Brunei
- 1965 Singapore departs to become independent city state
- 1963–68 anti-communist *konfrontasi* with Sukarno's Indonesia especially along Borneo (Kalimantan) border; recedes when ASEAN formed 1967
- May 1969 key watershed for Malaysia – intercommunal violence around misplaced if powerful notion of 'politics for Malays but economy for Chinese' – military rule to 1971
- Thereafter
  - political management of ethnically divided political parties in expanded *Barisan Nasional* (National Front) coalition
  - social engineering to create and reproduce a Malay middle class through positive discrimination in employment, education, share holding, etc.
  - state economic direction to eradicate poverty
- From 1970s rapid economic growth via export promotion, diversification from primary product exports replacing previous import-substitution strategy

- Mid 1980s growth hiccup presages new era of Malaysian-style privatization as economy rebounds to real 8% growth per annum 1986–96
- Mahathir emerges as *the* political force after being expelled from dominant Malay party UMNO; becomes Deputy Prime Minister 1976 and PM 1981
  - intellectual claims as theorist of Malay and later Asian values especially looking East to Japan thereby attacking 'Western' influence from UK, USA and Australia
  - uses economic self-confidence to raise geopolitical role among southern states via Islam connections, in G77 especially around UNCED at Rio and GATT/WTO
  - deeply ambivalent over APEC, would prefer an East Asian Economic Caucus (EAEC) under leadership of Japan not USA.

Demographic indicators

Total population (million)

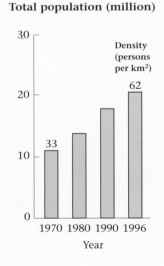

Infant mortality rate (deaths per 1,000 births)

Life expectancy at birth (years)

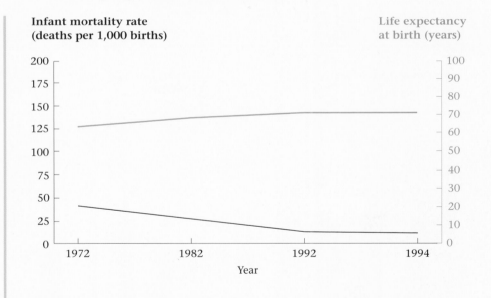

Population distribution

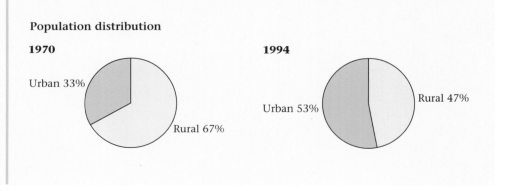

1970

Urban 33%

Rural 67%

1994

Urban 53%

Rural 47%

Malaysia

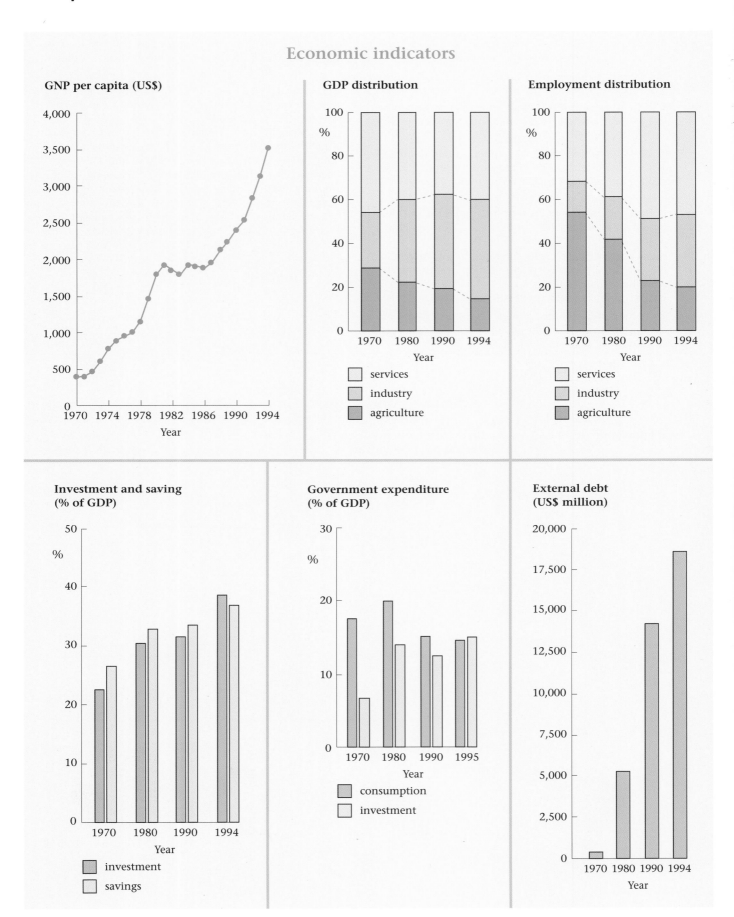

Economic indicators

GNP per capita (US$)

GDP distribution

services
industry
agriculture

Employment distribution

services
industry
agriculture

Investment and saving (% of GDP)

investment
savings

Government expenditure (% of GDP)

consumption
investment

External debt (US$ million)

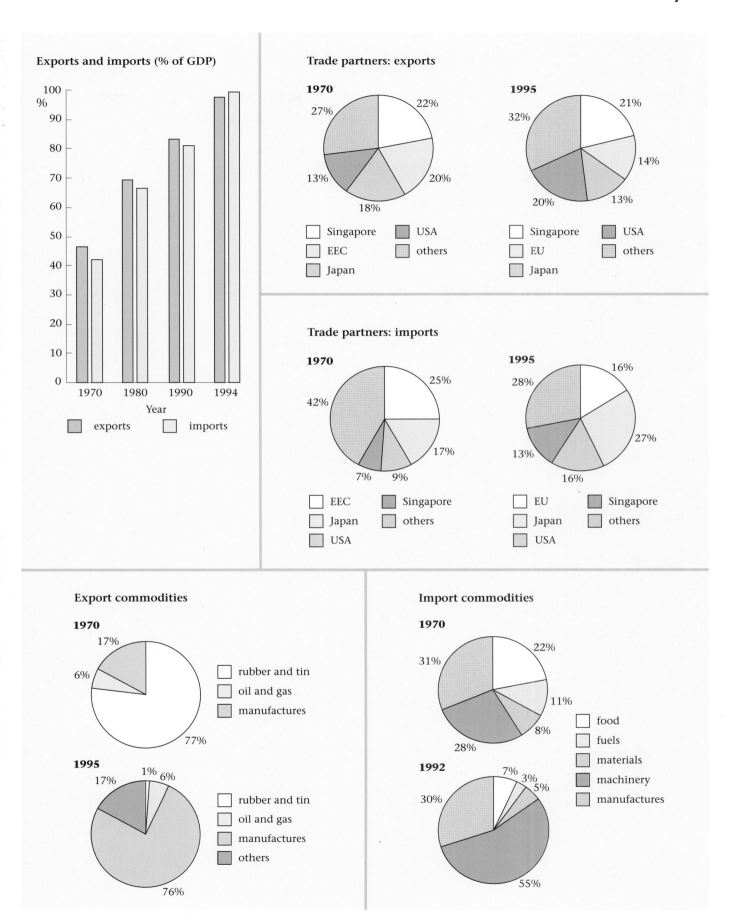

Malaysia

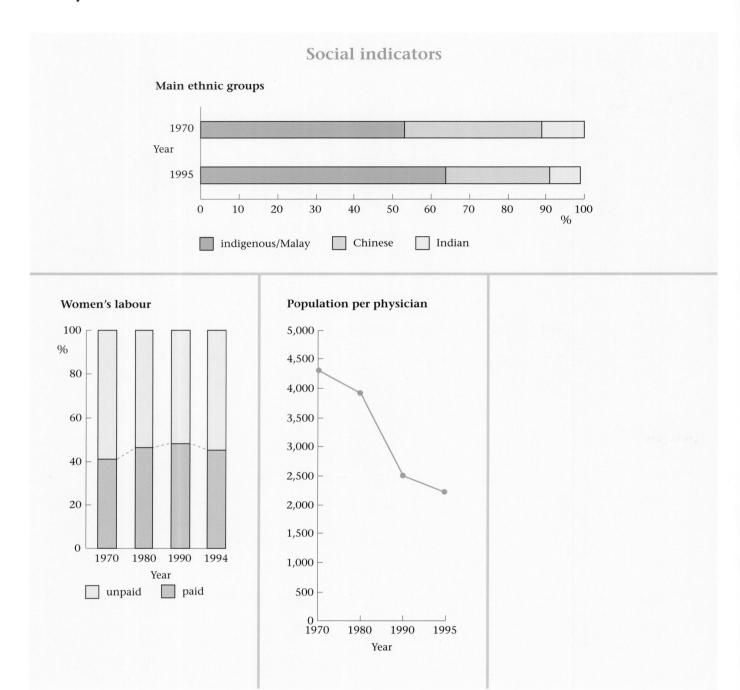

Social indicators

Main ethnic groups

Year

1970

1995

0 10 20 30 40 50 60 70 80 90 100 %

☐ indigenous/Malay   ☐ Chinese   ☐ Indian

Women's labour

%
100
80
60
40
20
0

1970 1980 1990 1994
Year

☐ unpaid   ☐ paid

Population per physician

5,000
4,500
4,000
3,500
3,000
2,500
2,000
1,500
1,000
500
0

1970 1980 1990 1995
Year

Political framework

- Formally a federal system with clear divisions of power but Federal Government in Kuala Lumpur deeply involved in economies and polities of local states. National Front (*Barisan Nasional*) political co-ordination extends to local leadership selection
- Constitutionally modelled on British parliamentary system though 30 years experience leads many analysts to label the outcome as 'semi' or 'pseudo' democratic
  - ethnic peace objective used to justify restrictions on parties labelled as 'opposition' with bouts of strict social control of 'political' activities throughout civil society
  - interpenetration of BN politics and economic elites surfaces clearly in media control that limits the voices of 'opposition'
  - strong and overt political control by BN coalition; for example, in federal elections since 1959 the ruling Alliance/BN averaged 80% parliamentary seats from only 57% popular vote leading to accusations of constituency gerrymandering
  - regular challenges to the independence of the judiciary by political elites
- But not simply unilateral authoritarian domination from above
  - generally deep supportive roots within Malay majority for UMNO leadership of BN
  - Malays and non-Malays apparently share the fruits of rapid economic growth giving the regime some legitimacy by results
  - frictions *within* BN member parties forces some responsiveness to pressures from citizens
- In sum, a political framework with a complex mix of democratic and repressive potential.

Further reading

Crouch, H. (1996) *Government and Society in Malaysia*, New York, Cornell University Press.

Jomo, Kwame Sundaram (ed.) (1995) *Privatizing Malaysia*, Colorado, Westview Press.

Wee, Chong Hui (1995) *Sabah and Sarawak in the Malaysian Economy*, Kuala Lumpur, INSAN.

Mexico

Scale 1:21,000,000

Historical background

- To 16th C. series of highly developed Amerindian civilizations: Olmec 800–400 BC; Mayan AD 300–900; Toltec 900–1200; Aztec 1325–1521

- 1521 Spanish colonization – Aztec capital rebuilt as Mexico City

- Precious metals and minerals plundered – sent to Spain with treasures shipped to Acapulco from Philippines

- 1810 revolution against Spanish crushed and former army commander rules until full independence 1823

- 1833–55 Santa Ana's dictatorial rule and Mexico loses half of its territory
  - Texas rebels 1835; annexed by USA 1845
  - military defeat by USA in 1847; New Mexico ceded along with other areas

- 1863 civil war and Mexico cancels foreign debt – France, Spain, UK and USA sponsor invasion, occupy Mexico City and install Habsburg Maximillian as Emperor

- 1867 uprising – Maximillian executed

- 1876–1910 Diaz dictatorship re-opens Mexico to UK and US foreign investment in railways, mining and plantations – landless peasantry remain in dire poverty

- 1910–11 bloody revolution led by Madero begins over 20 years of violence and anarchy

- 1914 US intervention leads to Madero's assassination followed by rural uprising led by Zapata and Pancho Villa but bitter conflict between revolutionary factions

- 1934 Cardenas restores stability after factions unite in what becomes Partido Revolucionario Institucional (PRI) – PRI monopolizes politics through to 1990s winning eleven consecutive presidential elections

- Cardenas consolidates reforms promulgated in 1917 constitution
  - large *haciendas* divided into smallholdings
  - transport system and petroleum sector nationalized
  - organized labour incorporated within PRI

- 1950–80 PRI centralizes power becoming the party of the state but loses socialist principles rooted in 1910 revolution. Largely authoritarian regime promotes industrialization through trade protection and Mexico becomes fastest growing Latin American economy, but benefits of economic growth favour urban middle classes

- 1980s decade of interconnected economic, political and social problems

- Accumulating foreign debt becomes unsustainable after oil prices fall. IMF/World Bank make further loans conditional on neo-liberal structural adjustment

- Cuts in food subsidies and increased taxation generates social unrest also protesting lack of effective democracy

- Despite electoral fraud PRI confronted for first time in 50 years with elected opposition at local, state and federal levels

- 1986 earthquake kills over 15,000 – government officials appropriate foreign relief aid in inept reconstruction programme. PRI forced to open political space for opposition in electoral reforms

- 1990s opposition consolidate political support but PRI retains power

- 1993 Mexico joins APEC and following year NAFTA and OECD – but more instability in 1994

- Zapatistas in Chiapas state declare war on government demanding end to marginalization of indigenous peoples – cease-fire only after government agrees to accelerate poor relief, introduce land reform and allow political representation

- PRI presidential candidate assassinated allegedly by party colleagues – turbulent election campaign follows

- 'Peso crisis' – unpaid foreign debt, dramatic capital outflow, gravely depleted foreign exchange reserves and banking system on verge of collapse

- International monetary system so threatened that USA organizes US$50 billion rescue package – biggest since Marshall Plan reconstructed post-war Europe

- 1997 after stringent neo-liberal economic policies implemented and a severe recession Mexico repays emergency loans and financial credibility restored.

Demographic indicators

Total population (million)

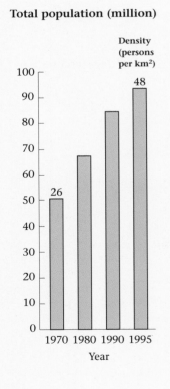

Infant mortality rate (deaths per 1,000 births)

Life expectancy at birth (years)

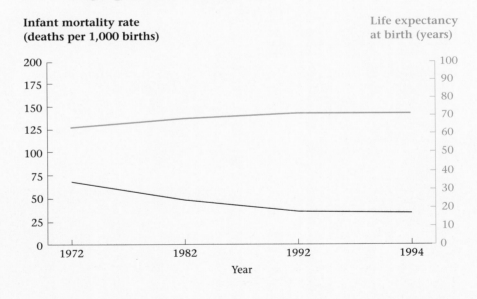

Population distribution

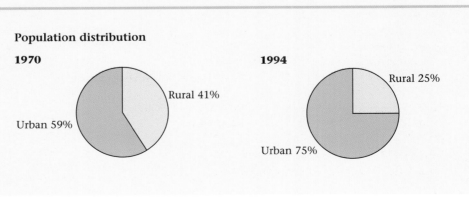

1970

Rural 41%

Urban 59%

1994

Rural 25%

Urban 75%

Mexico

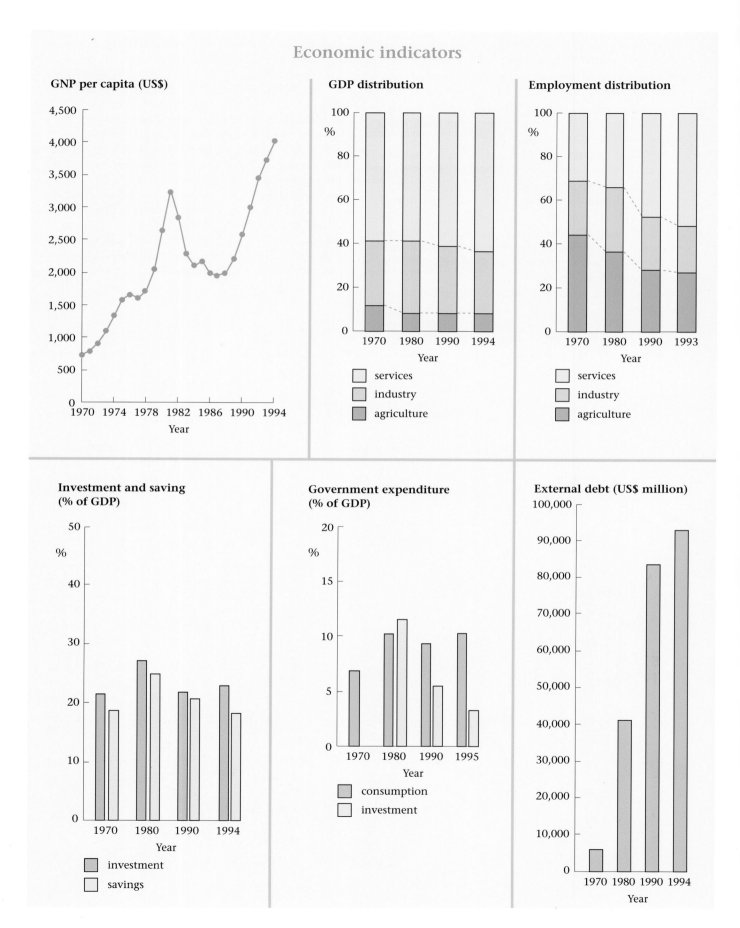

Economic indicators

GNP per capita (US$)

GDP distribution

Employment distribution

services
industry
agriculture

services
industry
agriculture

Investment and saving (% of GDP)

investment
savings

Government expenditure (% of GDP)

consumption
investment

External debt (US$ million)

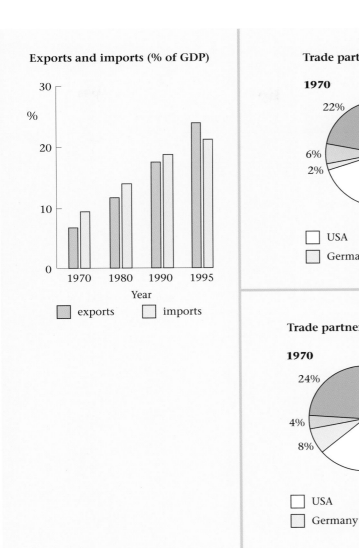

Exports and imports (% of GDP)

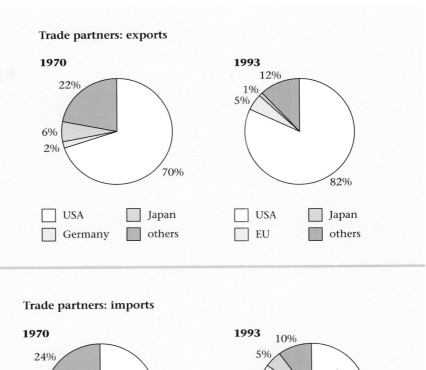

Trade partners: exports

Trade partners: imports

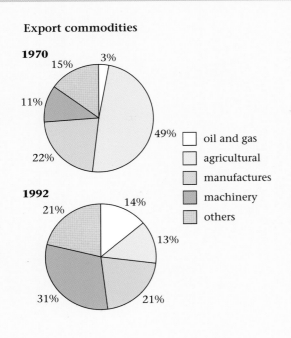

Export commodities

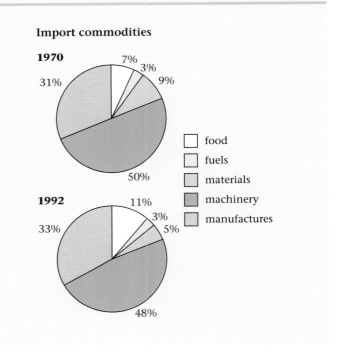

Import commodities

Mexico

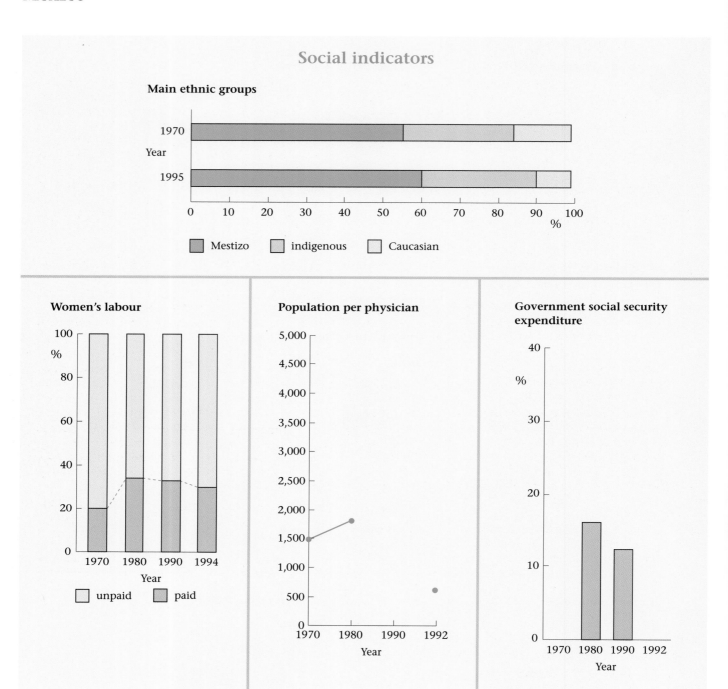

Social indicators

Main ethnic groups

Mestizo indigenous Caucasian

Women's labour

unpaid paid

Population per physician

Government social security expenditure

Political framework

- Political scene still dominated by slow process of dismantling one-party rule of PRI, accommodating shift from state economic guidance to neo-liberalism and presence of armed groups in southern states opposed to government

- Series of political reforms increase opposition government in several large states and numerous municipalities

- At national level limited proportional representation allowed 40% opposition membership of Lower House and 25% of Senate by 1997. PRI continues as majority party not least because their long-term supremacy guarantees extensive media influence and superior financial resources

- PRI continues process of moving from the party of the state towards a dedicated party machine but internecine strife is common. Murder of PRI presidential candidate in 1994 followed by murder of party Secretary General in which previous President Salinas and his family implicated. Other unexplained disappearances, allegations of drugs trade connections and corruption accusations highlight strife within PRI

- More pluralist political contestation also sees PRI attempt to assert its independence from the presidency to consolidate legislative over executive power

- 1997 against wishes of President Zedillo PRI majority in Congress allocate US$43 million of public funds to finance election campaigns. Opposition parties refuse their share claiming whole programme is designed to preserve PRI domination, will provide another source of corruption and is immoral use of public expenditure in period of general austerity

- Opposition appears united on this issue though not on proposals to form united front to defeat PRI in 1997 congressional elections. Main opposition party argues that fragile democratic process needs clearly demarcated parties

- Zapatista rebels continue campaign on behalf of indigenous cultural, linguistic and social rights in protracted and thus far abortive negotiations with government. Sporadic violence because armed struggle not formally ended – Zapatistas become a more organized political force but refuse to participate in electoral process which they claim is corrupt and fraudulent

- Insurgent force in Guerrero state also remains active

- Both rebel groups symptomatic of wider social discontent in face of widening maldistribution of wealth and income that follow stringent neo-liberal economic policies before and after 1994 'peso crisis'

- Rising unemployment, increased rates of taxation on a wider tax base, reduction in food subsidies and declining government social spending add immediate pressure to more deep-seated structural problems

- More than 20% live in extreme poverty in southern states where land fragmentation is very common

- Land reforms from 1930s did permit some re-allocation of land to smallholders but the land remains communal property. Distributing land between descendants is allowed with result that individual holdings become ever smaller undermining food production for subsistence

- NAFTA membership coincided with substantial industrial growth along US border particularly in electronics and car assembly. Foreign investment increases threefold between 1985 and 1995 allowing this *maquiladora* sector to supply over 40% of Mexico's exports

- Disputes abound though over the extent to which local people benefit directly in the northern states or more indirectly throughout Mexico.

Further reading

Bartra, R. (1993) *Agrarian Structure and Political Power in Mexico*, Baltimore, Johns Hopkins University Press.

Bethell, L. (ed.) (1992) *Mexico Since Independence*, Cambridge, Cambridge University Press.

Camp, R.A. (1996) *Politics in Mexico*, Oxford, Oxford University Press.

New Zealand

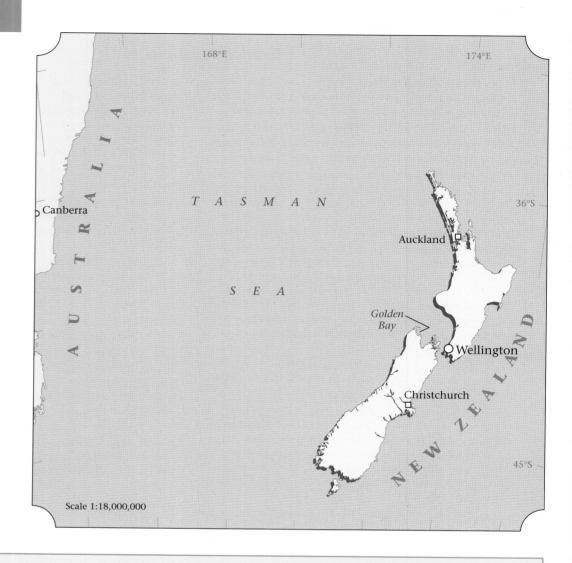

Scale 1:18,000,000

Historical background

- 9th–10th C. settlement by Polynesian Maoris
- 1642 first recorded contact between Maoris and Europeans – Dutch ships under Abel Tasman anchor in Golden Bay
- 1769 Captain Cook leads first European landing
- 1840 controversial Treaty of Waitangi signed. Many Maori Chiefs concede sovereignty to British in return for continued possession of their land and Taonga (treasures). Differences in English and Maori versions of treaty
- 1845–72 wars result in Maori population losing most of their land
- 1882 first shipment of frozen meat departs for England
- 1893 women enfranchised 26 years after men
- 1914–18 New Zealand troops join British fighting First World War
- 1935 first Labour government – introduces guaranteed price scheme for farmers, compulsory unionism, large-scale public works and 40-hour working week
- 1938 Social Security Act provides free medical treatment, family allowances and increased superannuation

- 1939–45 New Zealand troops join Allies fighting Second World War
- 1947 Statute of Westminster gives New Zealand full autonomy in international affairs
- 1949 National Party defeats Labour to end their fourteen-year term of office
- 1951 ANZUS agreement signed between Australia, New Zealand and USA
- 1951 Waterfront industrial dispute – government declares state of emergency and wins snap election
- 1954 New Zealand becomes member of SEATO
- 1957 Labour wins election with one-seat majority
- 1958 'black budget' – first imposition of taxes on cigarettes, petrol and tobacco
- 1960 National Party regains office starting twelve-year term
- 1960 protest over exclusion of Maoris from All Blacks Rugby Union team to South Africa – 'no Maoris, no tour' becomes popular slogan

- 1970s as Britain joins EEC New Zealand forced to search for different export markets
- 1972 Labour Party wins landslide election victory
- 1975 National Party re-elected in landslide victory Muldoon begins nine-year term as PM
- 1975 Maori land march led by Dame Whina Cooper demands no further alienation of Maori land
- 1976 All Blacks Rugby Union tour of South Africa – 29 African countries boycott Montreal Olympic games
- 1978 Maori land rights dispute – protesters evicted by police
- 1981 South African Rugby Union Tour of New Zealand divides nation – fierce clashes between protesters and police. National government re-elected by a one-seat margin
- 1982–84 wage/price freeze imposed
- 1983 extensive free trade agreement signed with Australia
- 1984 Labour Party wins election Lange new PM. Finance Minister Douglas leads dramatic economic deregulation –

farm price subsidies removed, state assets sold, currency floated
- 1985 anti-nuclear policy enforced – US warship denied entry
- 1989 Lange resigns after protracted dispute with Douglas. Palmer becomes PM
- 1990 National Party elected in a landslide victory, Jim Bolger PM
- 1990 Finance Minister Richardson announces cuts to welfare benefits
- 1991 Employment Contracts Act heralds significant labour-market changes
- 1993 last election held under the first past the post system – Bolger retains power by one-seat majority. Referendum chooses new electoral system moving towards more proportional representation
- 1996 first election under new system. National Party under Bolger retain power in coalition with New Zealand First Party led by Winston Peters after lengthy negotiations.

Demographic indicators

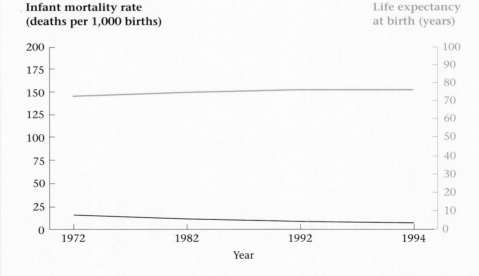

Total population (million)

Density (persons per km²)

Infant mortality rate (deaths per 1,000 births)

Life expectancy at birth (years)

Population distribution

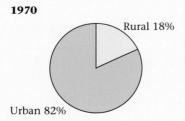

1970

Rural 18%

Urban 82%

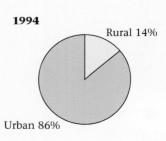

1994

Rural 14%

Urban 86%

New Zealand

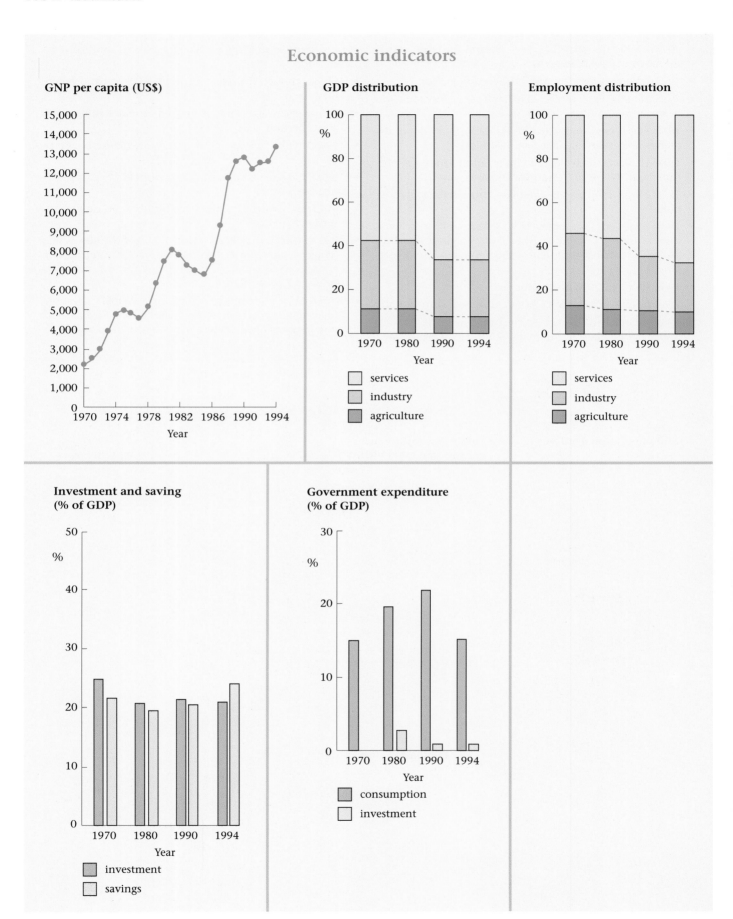

Economic indicators

GNP per capita (US$)

GDP distribution

Employment distribution

Investment and saving (% of GDP)

Government expenditure (% of GDP)

Exports and imports (% of GDP)

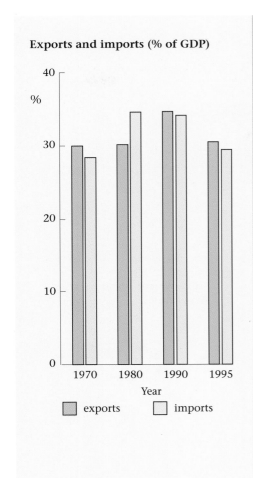

Trade partners: exports

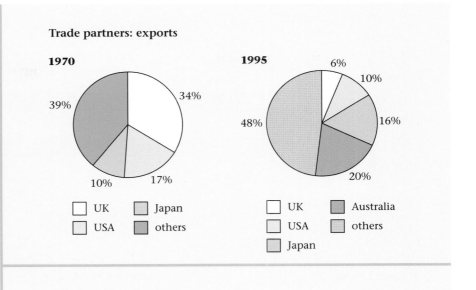

Trade partners: imports

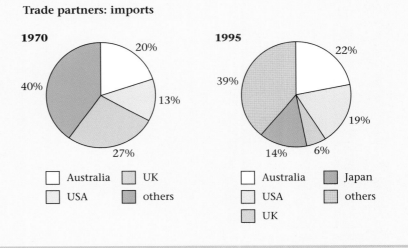

Export commodities

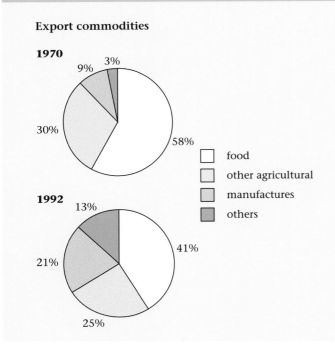

Import commodities

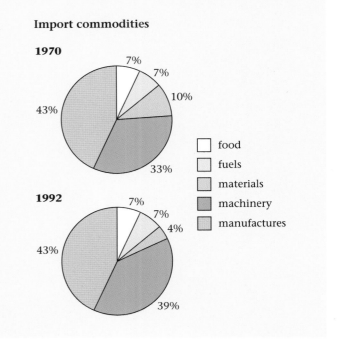

New Zealand

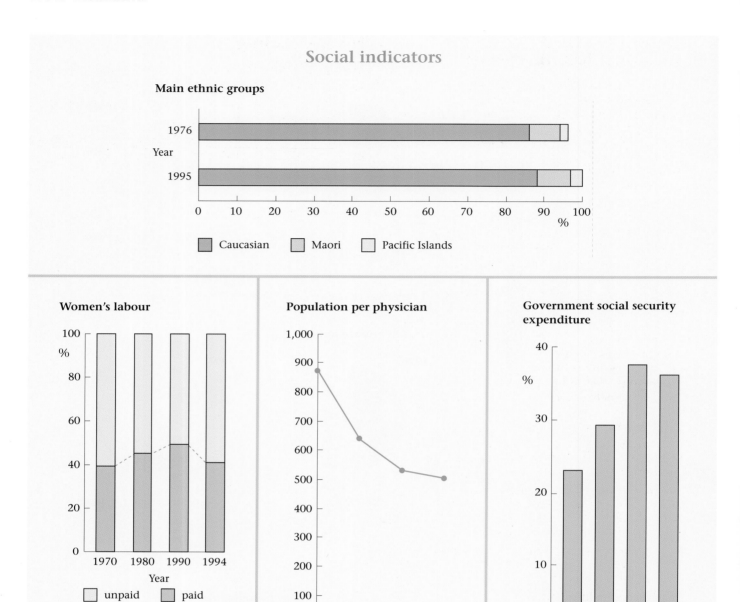

Social indicators

Main ethnic groups

Year

1976

1995

0 10 20 30 40 50 60 70 80 90 100
%

■ Caucasian ■ Maori □ Pacific Islands

Women's labour

100
%
80
60
40
20
0

1970 1980 1990 1994
Year

□ unpaid ■ paid

Population per physician

1,000
900
800
700
600
500
400
300
200
100
0

1970 1980 1990 1993
Year

Government social security expenditure

40

%

30

20

10

0

1970 1980 1990 1994
Year

Political framework

- 1996 witnesses first use of new Mixed Member Proportional electoral system: 65 members elected from geographical constituencies and 55 members elected according to their ranking on a party list. Number of seats each party awarded is calculated on the percentage of votes each party receives. A party must exceed 5% of the vote if it is to be awarded any seats from the party list of 55

- As elsewhere more proportional representation meant a proliferation of political parties and with no single majority party protracted negotiations followed about the formation of a government

- Contrary to expectations Winston Peters led New Zealand First Party into a National Party Cabinet led by the person who had sacked him five years earlier

- The New Zealand First Party sought populist appeal opposing foreign ownership of the economy and uncontrolled immigration – the party gains all five seats reserved for voters of Maori descent previously the preserve of the Labour Party

- National Party itself lost ground after three years of policies to reduce public expenditure on welfare which their new coalition partner pledged to reverse

- Despite the immigration stance of Peters new government tries to quieten anger from Asian states that their migrants were being singled out in moves towards more control of immigration

- Government tries to balance immigration policy with obvious need to recognize role of Asian export markets in a foreign policy looking more to an established position for New Zealand in Asia-Pacific

- More emphasis too on developing economic links with Chile and South America. Government's 'Focus Latin America' initiative stresses trade and investment links especially for dairy and forest products. Free trade agreement expected with Mercosur common market group – Argentina, Brazil, Paraguay, Uruguay as well as Chile.

Further reading

McLeay, E. (1995) *The Cabinet and Political Power in New Zealand*, Oxford, Oxford University Press.

Rice, G.R. (1992) *The Oxford History of New Zealand*, Auckland, Oxford University Press.

Roper, B. and Rudd, C. (1995) *State and Economy in New Zealand*, Oxford, Oxford University Press.

Nicaragua

Historical background

- To 16th C. populated by scattered Amerindian peoples
- 1502 Columbus lands on Caribbean coast – colonization from 1524
- 1524–1821 neglected colonial outpost without territorial cohesion – British control eastern 'mosquito coast' from 1768
- 1838 independent republic after federation of United Provinces of Central America disintegrates
- 1838–55 internal civil wars between elite landowners and merchants based on Granada and artisans and smaller landowners based on Leon
- 1858 in one brief period of peace Managua chosen as compromise capital city
- USA and Britain vie for control – possible site for trans-isthmus canal
- USA gains predominance despite abortive attempt to install US mercenary as President 1855–57
- British cede claim to 'mosquito coast' 1860
- 1863–93 socially repressive Conservative rule

- 1893 rebellion leads to Zelaya dictatorship – US influence repulsed
- 1909–27 USA supports Zelaya overthrow then from 1912 US Marines supervise customs collection and US management of central bank and railways. More land expropriated for coffee and sugar plantations – peasantry become migratory seasonal labour
- 1927–33 Sandino leads guerrilla war against US forces who organize local National Guard headed by Samoza
- 1936 Samoza takes power founding family dynasty of dictators that rule until 1979
- Samoza dynasty ruthlessly suppresses all opponents appropriates one-sixth of all agricultural land and controls 60% of national economy
- US support vital in height of Cold War especially after Cuban revolution in 1959
- 1962 very broad based popular insurrection begins after opposition left unites around Frente Sandinista de Liberacion Nacional (FSLN) in partnership with centrist political groups

- 1972 earthquake kills 20,000 and destroys Managua – foreign relief aid misappropriated by Samoza regime which brutally represses consequent unrest
- 1979 FSLN commander Ortega leads Junta for National Reconstruction and Samoza regime eventually collapses
- Sandinista People's Army replaces National Guard, Samozan property expropriated, state farms and co-operatives reconstruct landholding
- 1981 Samoza supporters begin border raids from Honduras – CIA finances this 'Contra' force and other guerrillas operating from Costa Rican border area
- US President Reagan leads anti-communist crusade against Nicaragua – 1981 all US loans stopped and international agencies follow suit
- 1984–85 Ortega elected President – US trade embargo removes Nicaragua's main export market and source of imports. Reagan circumvents opposition in US Congress by secretly financing 'Contras' from illegal arms sales to Iran
- Late 1980s perilous economy – inflation 36,000%, no foreign exchange, dire food and electricity supplies and aid from Eastern Europe ended with break-up of Soviet bloc
- 1989 after international attempts to end regional conflict 'Contras' agree partial demobilization. Nicaraguan government proclaims cease-fire, grants amnesty to some 'Contra' leaders and agrees to elections supervised by UN and OAS
- 1990 opposition alliance candidate Chamorros elected President – Sandinistas agree to UN demobilization programme and to facilitate peaceful transition
- 1990–96 political instability though cease-fire generally holds
  - rural discontent over threats to reverse Sandinista land reforms
  - political strife within and between parties over post-war reconciliation bargaining
  - relative power disputes between President and National Assembly legislature
  - widespread strikes over social consequences of the neo-liberal policies demanded by international donors
- 1996 Aleman elected President promising poverty alleviation and 100,000 new jobs within the year.

Demographic indicators

Total population (million)

Infant mortality rate (deaths per 1,000 births)

Life expectancy at birth (years)

Density (persons per km²)

Population distribution

1970

Urban 48% Rural 52%

1994

Rural 38% Urban 62%

159

Nicaragua

GNP per capita (US$)

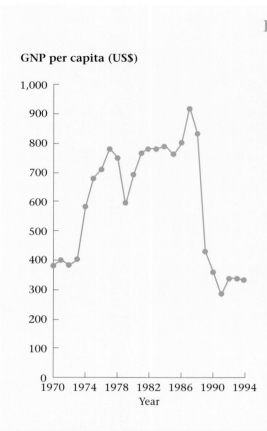

GDP distribution

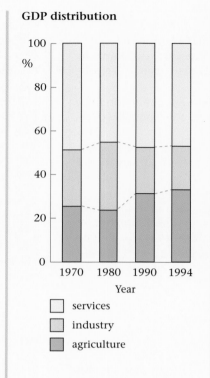

- services
- industry
- agriculture

Employment distribution

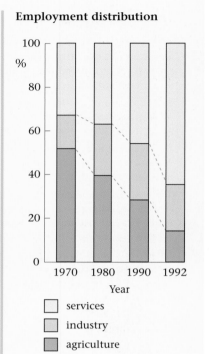

- services
- industry
- agriculture

Investment and saving (% of GDP)

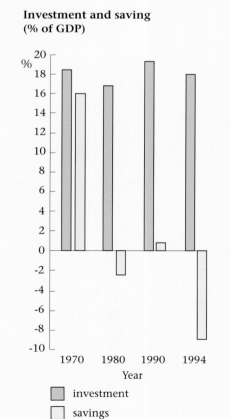

- investment
- savings

Government expenditure (% of GDP)

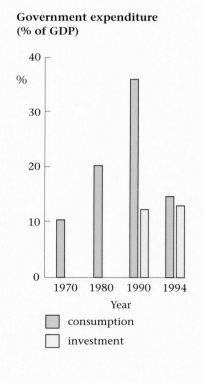

- consumption
- investment

External debt (US$ million)

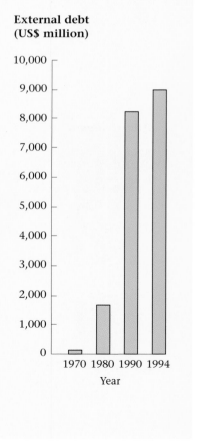

Exports and imports (% of GDP)

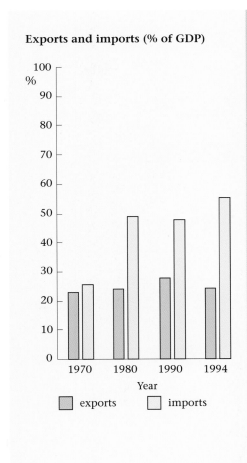

Trade partners: exports

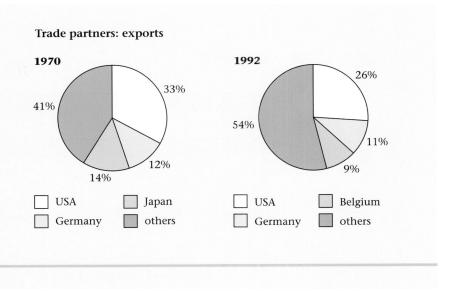

Trade partners: imports

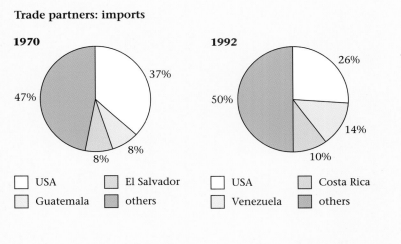

Export commodities

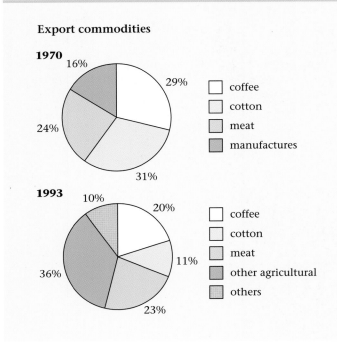

Import commodities

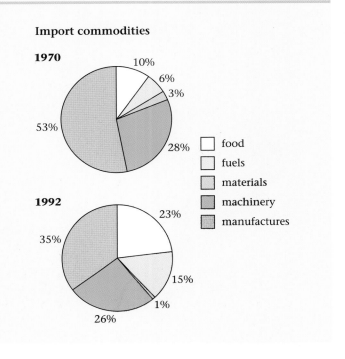

Nicaragua

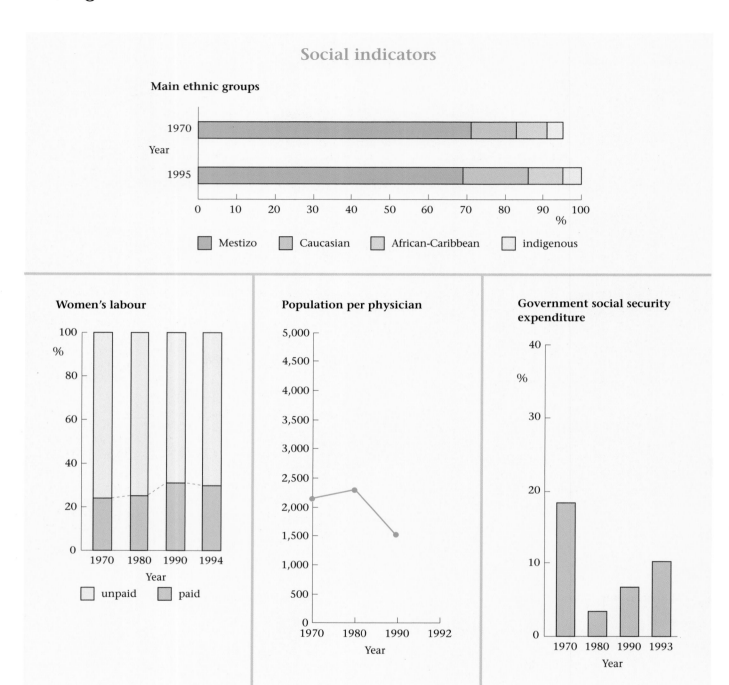

Social indicators

Main ethnic groups

Year

1970
1995

0 10 20 30 40 50 60 70 80 90 100
%

■ Mestizo   ■ Caucasian   ■ African-Caribbean   □ indigenous

Women's labour

%
100
80
60
40
20
0

1970 1980 1990 1994
Year

□ unpaid   ■ paid

Population per physician

5,000
4,500
4,000
3,500
3,000
2,500
2,000
1,500
1,000
500
0

1970 1980 1990 1992
Year

Government social security expenditure

40
%
30
20
10
0

1970 1980 1990 1993
Year

Political framework

- Post-war reconstruction problems dominate Nicaraguan politics. Attempts to reconcile divisions after over 30 years of continuous conflict not at all helped by intractable economic weakness

- Consolidating elements of a more democratic polity is inevitably contentious. Former Sandinistas press for the retention of some elements of their reform programme while their opponents press for the complete reverse

- Amidst the fractious process of forming independent parties the National Assembly legislature argues that more democracy should mean less executive power for the presidency which in turn presses for a judiciary more independent from the National Assembly

- An overarching obstacle to political stability remains the desperate consequences of war on an already weak economy

- Wartime economic devastation saw Nicaragua fall to fourteenth poorest in the world. Per capita incomes in the mid 1990s were but one-third of their level in 1980 while exports were barely one-half of the 1980 total in real terms

- Dependence on exports of coffee and sugar magnify perennial problems of land distribution. 1991 promises to recognize Sandinista land reforms later confused by further promises to allocate state land to demobilized soldiers

- By 1996 large tracts of land lay under-utilized in state hands leaving neither the peasantry nor demobilized soldiers from either side satisfied – illegal occupation of land a source of instability

- 1995 rural workers occupy the National Assembly demanding legal title to land they had farmed since the Sandinista reforms

- More cash-crop cultivation to earn vital foreign exchange undermines subsistence food production. Food supply problems exacerbated by accelerated urban drift of people initially escaping rural areas worst affected by the war – Managua now houses approximately half the total population

- Longer-term structural reform to alleviate 75% poverty level and raise literacy rates require additional government expenditure. But international financial support is conditional on implementing neo-liberal policies that work in the opposite direction

- The 1991 restoration of borrowing rights saw foreign debt burden increase rapidly as virtually all new loans used to repay interest on older commitments. By 1994 Nicaragua had one of the highest per capita levels of foreign debt in the world

- 1995 brought some relief when foreign debt was halved as creditors agreed to write-off or reschedule debt

- However, consequent neo-liberal economic policies sharply reduce living standards and generate social unrest. Increases in petrol taxation and a privatization programme cutting public employment levels inevitably unpopular in an economy already suffering high unemployment and severe seasonal underemployment in agriculture

- The inauguration speech of President Aleman in January 1997 pledged a commitment to increase employment, reduce poverty and resolve land distribution problems as well as securing an independent judiciary to fight political corruption

- However, the allocation of Cabinet posts to previous members of the Chamorro Administration governing within a neo-liberal policy framework makes it difficult to believe that resolving deeper economic and social problems will be the number one priority in the next few years.

Further reading

Close, B. (1988) *Nicaragua: Politics, Economics and Society*, London, Pinter.

Massey, D. (1987) *Nicaragua*, Milton Keynes, Open University Press.

Prevot, G. and Vanden, H.E. (1997) *The Undermining of the Sandinista Revolution*, Basingstoke, Macmillan.

Panama

Scale 1:8,000,000

Historical background

- To 16th C. Amerindian population influenced from south by Colombian cultures

- 1502 Spanish colonization of crucial geo-political isthmus linking Pacific to Caribbean

- 1821 independence from Spain as province of Colombia along with Ecuador and Venezuela

- 1850–55 US companies complete rail link across Panama – regular US intervention to protect railway

- 1879–1914 Panama Canal finished by US companies after French project bankrupted. Sea journey from New York to San Francisco cut by 40%

- 1903 USA encourages Panama to declare independence from Colombia to expedite negotiations over Canal Zone Treaty. USA pays $10 million for 100-year lease on sovereign bases along canal and right to military intervention if canal traffic disrupted

- Conflict over this sovereignty transfer becomes endemic as 20th C. progresses

- 1918–41 less overt US political role within period of relatively stable government

- 1941–55 political turmoil marked by coups and ending with presidential assassination

- 1955–68 stable elected governments but conflict with USA over discrimination against Panamanian workers in Canal Zone – frequent anti-American riots

- 1968–81 Torrijos leads military junta – limited social reforms but political freedoms suspended to concentrate nationalist sentiment on re-negotiating canal treaty

- 1979 US government concedes sovereignty in favour of lease on 40% of Canal Zone until 1999. Some US bases relinquished, Canal Zone neutrality to be guaranteed by both parties and limited local participation agreed in canal administration

- To secure US Congress ratification clauses added to allow US military intervention if canal transport threatened and to leave options for US presence beyond 1999

- 1981 after preparing a return to elected governments Torrijos dies in air crash – allegations of CIA involvement.

National Guard and civilian leadership at odds – army supports closer US ties which politicians reject

- 1983–84 Legislative Assembly attempts to keep military out of politics – especially critical of General Noriega the new head of the National Guard
- 1985 President Barletta resigns amidst allegations that murder charge against Noriega being suppressed. USA targets removal of their former protégé Noriega after his failure to collaborate in Nicaraguan war
- 1986–87 USA withdraws aid and imposes economic sanctions crippling the Panamanian economy – banking operations suspended and $16 billion of foreign capital withdrawn. Political instability follows with anti-American riots and demonstrations calling for the dismissal of Noriega
- 1988 Noriega indicted in USA on drugs trafficking charges – President Delvalle seeks his dismissal but is deposed by Noriega
- 1989 Noriega annuls elections when victory for his opponents looks certain
- US-backed coup fails, Noriega declares war on USA and

26,000 US troops invade to overthrow Noriega. Short but bloody conflict – over 1,000 die and damage estimated at US$2 billion

- Noriega sentenced to 40 years imprisonment by US court in 1992
- 1990 restoration of US aid conditional on political reform and dissolution of National Guard
- 1992–94 political unrest over government corruption, encroachment on to Amerindian land and chronic poverty affecting over 50% of population
- 1994–96 new President Perez pledges to fight corruption but has to admit election funding from Colombian drugs cartel. Widespread strikes follow attempts to incorporate dilution of labour rights into privatization programme. Legislature refuses to support presidential amnesty that would release over 1,000 former Noriega supporters convicted of corruption, torture and murder.

Demographic indicators

Total population (million)

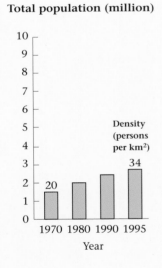

Infant mortality rate (deaths per 1,000 births)

Life expectancy at birth (years)

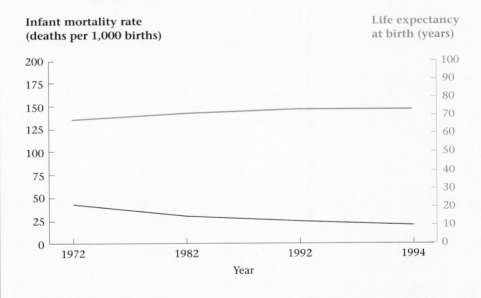

Population distribution

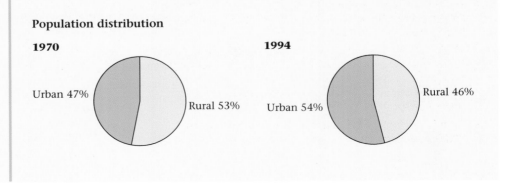

1970

Urban 47% Rural 53%

1994

Urban 54% Rural 46%

Panama

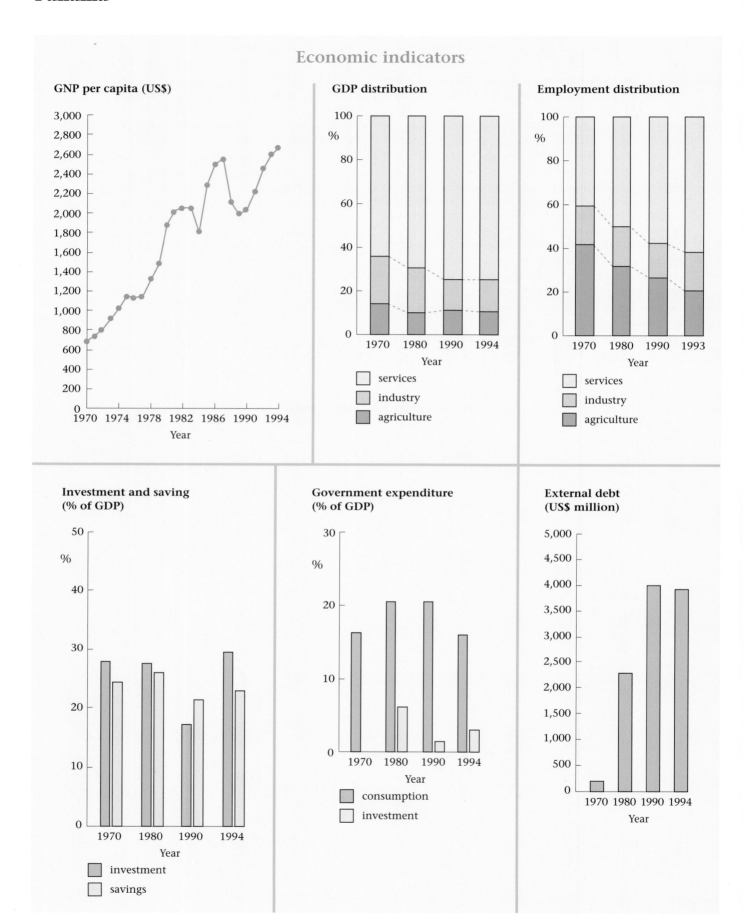

Economic indicators

GNP per capita (US$)

GDP distribution

services
industry
agriculture

Employment distribution

services
industry
agriculture

Investment and saving (% of GDP)

investment
savings

Government expenditure (% of GDP)

consumption
investment

External debt (US$ million)

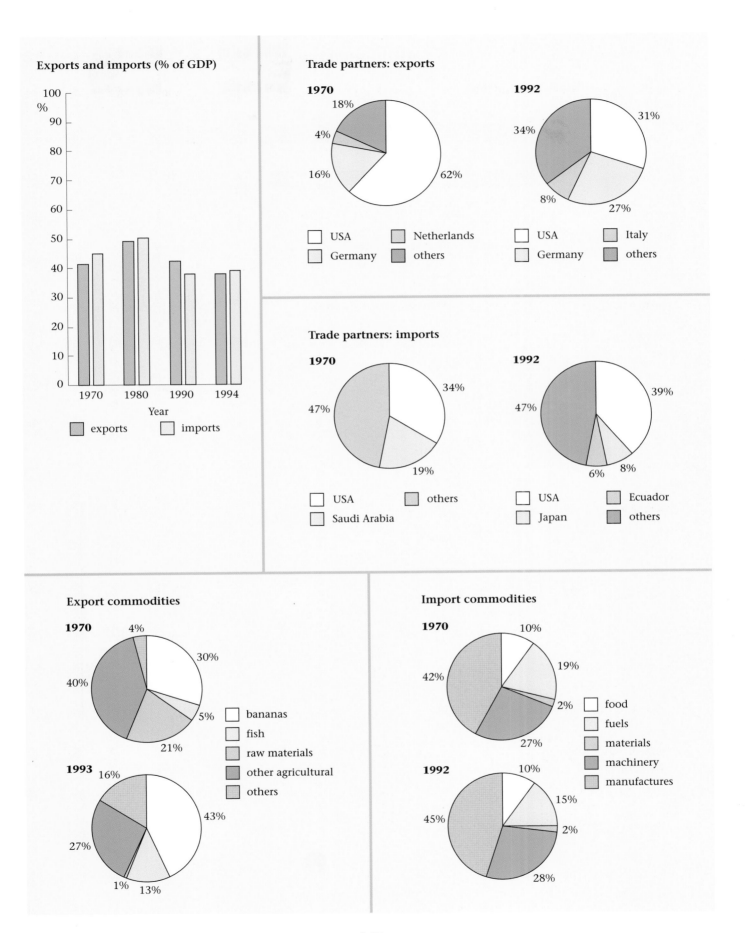

Exports and imports (% of GDP)

Trade partners: exports

1970

18%
4%
16%
62%

□ USA   ▨ Netherlands
□ Germany   ▨ others

1992

34%
8%
27%
31%

□ USA   ▨ Italy
□ Germany   ▨ others

Trade partners: imports

1970

47%
34%
19%

□ USA   ▨ others
□ Saudi Arabia

1992

47%
6%
8%
39%

□ USA   ▨ Ecuador
□ Japan   ▨ others

Export commodities

1970

4%
30%
40%
5%
21%

□ bananas
□ fish
□ raw materials
▨ other agricultural
▨ others

1993

16%
43%
27%
1%
13%

Import commodities

1970

10%
19%
42%
2%
27%

□ food
□ fuels
□ materials
▨ machinery
▨ manufactures

1992

10%
15%
45%
2%
28%

Panama

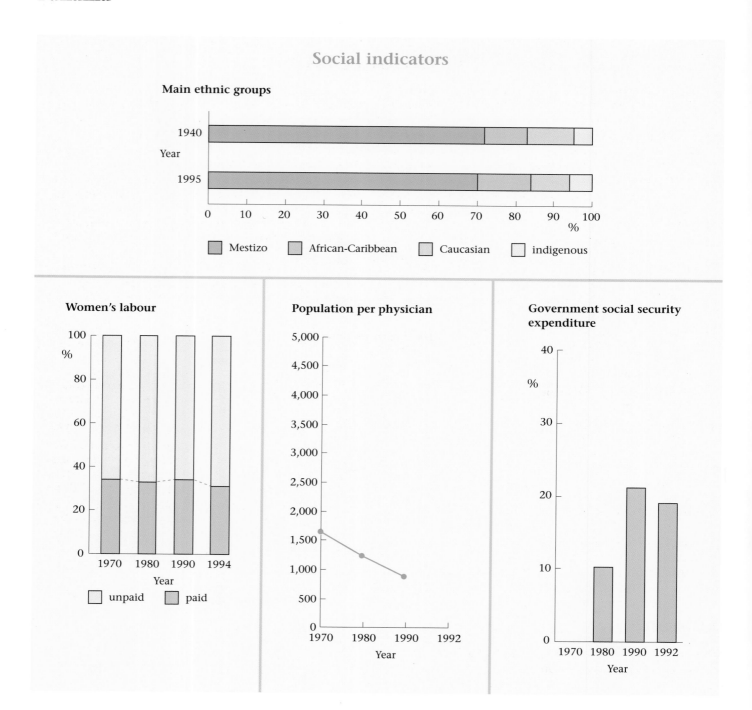

Social indicators

Main ethnic groups

Year
1940
1995

0 10 20 30 40 50 60 70 80 90 100
%

- Mestizo
- African-Caribbean
- Caucasian
- indigenous

Women's labour

%
100
80
60
40
20
0

1970 1980 1990 1994
Year

- unpaid
- paid

Population per physician

5,000
4,500
4,000
3,500
3,000
2,500
2,000
1,500
1,000
500
0

1970 1980 1990 1992
Year

Government social security expenditure

%
40
30
20
10
0

1970 1980 1990 1992
Year

Political framework

- The consequences of the US economic blockade and later invasion in 1989 continues to exert a profound influence on the political scene in Panama

- After failing to secure Legislative Assembly approval for an amnesty that would free former Noriega officials from prison President Perez appeared from 1996 to put aside his association with the military

- In a programme of *concertacion* opposition representatives were included in government allowing Perez to claim broad political support

- Perez recovered from admitting that unbeknown to him his 1994 election campaign received funding from a Colombian arrested on suspicion of drugs trafficking offences. Other politicians were unwilling to press for a formal investigation when it emerged that they too might have received funding from the same source

- A less overt political role for the military has been substituted by a more substantial presence within a security force which, following US pressure, will police the production and export of narcotics

- Beyond the sphere of national politics economic problems remain significant

- Over-concentration on the expected benefits of recovering more control over the canal in 1999 masks underlying economic weaknesses that surface in social protest over high levels of poverty and unemployment

- The presence of the canal and the associated offshore financial sector has produced an economic structure grossly over dependent on the services sector which employs two-thirds of the labour force and accounts for 75% of GDP

- Many fear that the canal will become less and less significant as a source of income given the dominance of super-tankers and bulk cargo carriers that are too large to use it

- Prospects for the offshore banking sector were badly undermined by political instability and one-year suspension of banking operations in 1987. Competition from other sites has grown at the same time as Panama lost the advantage of strict secrecy when the USA forced more transparency to uncover the financial operations of drug cartels

- Diversification from dependence on services was a key component in World Bank/IMF strategies that were followed from the mid 1980s. However, as a condition of international financial support diversification was to be preceded by the implementation of neo-liberal policies that imposed high social costs

- Social unrest has been common following successive attempts to cut subsidies, reduce public employment, raise taxation levels, speed the process of privatization and reduce labour rights

- A substantial package of foreign debt re-scheduling in 1995 did reduce the burden of using 40% of public revenue collection to pay the interest on overseas debt. But the accompanying conditions included labour market de-regulation to remove mandatory collective bargaining, cut redundancy payments and end state supervision of wages. Labour unrest and a national strike in protest at these attempts to revise the 1972 labour code dominated the summer of 1995

- Managing a political recovery from the Noriega era and the consequences of structural economic problems were not helped by signs that the USA wanted to explore the possibility of extending its military presence beyond 1999

- Not only would such a possibility produce another source of political conflict but Panama would be expected to pay fees to the USA for military assistance in eliminating the trade in drugs.

Further reading

Johns, C.J. and Ward, J.P. (1994) *State Crime, the Media and the Invasion of Panama*, London, Praeger.

Major, J. (1994) *Prize Possession: the United States and the Panama Canal*, Cambridge, Cambridge University Press.

Mann, G.C. (1996) *Panamanian Militarism*, Ohio, Ohio University Press.

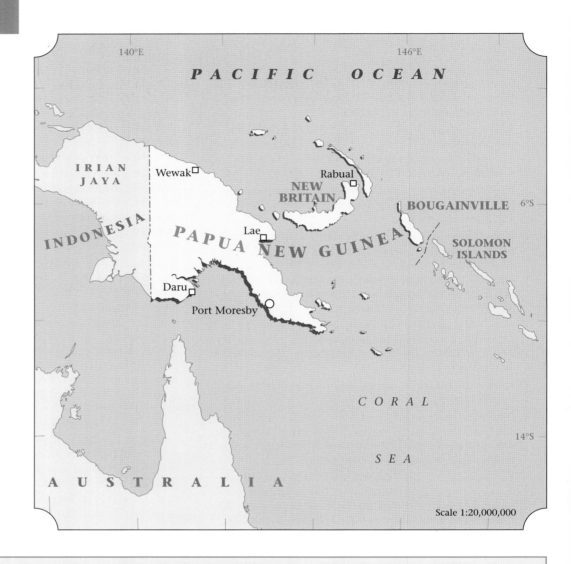

Scale 1:20,000,000

Historical background

- 16th C. European contacts but New Guinea not formally settled until mid 19th C.

- 1828 Netherlands grant Dutch East India Company authority over western New Guinea

- 1884 Germany claims northern region – Britain establishes protectorate in southern New Guinea

- 1906 British transfer authority to Australia – during First World War Australia takes formal control of German New Guinea

- 1920 League of Nations places New Guinea under Australian trusteeship

- 1942 Japanese occupy entire island

- 1945 UN reverts control to Australian trusteeship

- 1963 Indonesia takes over Dutch New Guinea as Indonesian province of Irian Jaya

- 1964 House of Assembly established – enlarged and given greater autonomy in domestic policy 1968–72

- 1975 Papua New Guinea (PNG) becomes independent state

- 1976 Bougainville separatists threaten to secede from PNG – temporarily satisfied when parliament decentralizes government and in 1978 grants all provinces internal self-government

- 1980–89 successive PMs ousted or re-elected through parliamentary motions of 'no-confidence' by opposition coalitions and/or disenchanted members of government

- 1984 Irian Jayan refugees enter PNG – conflict between Indonesian and Free Papua Movement (OPM) extends into PNG

- Late 1988 Bougainville Revolutionary Army (BRA) disrupt operations of island's huge copper mine in dispute over compensation. Continued violence leads to curfew enforced by PNG security forces

- 1989 Treaty of Amity and Co-operation with ASEAN – PNG gets observer status

- January 1990 Australian government assists removal of Australian nationals remaining on Bougainville island

- March 1990 PNG forces removed from Bougainville and PNG introduces trade sanctions on the island

- May 1990 BRA proclaims the island's independence as Republic of Bougainville
- July 1990 PNG and BRA agree to 'Endeavour Accord' delaying independence until further discussions held
- January 1991 discussions fail to resolve dispute and conflict between government security forces and BRA continues through to 1993
- May 1991 PNG parliament passes severe criminal legislation introducing death penalty and tattooing foreheads of criminals
- July 1991 amendments to constitution – a PM needs to be in power 18 months before facing motions of 'no confidence' or attempts to force dissolution. If incumbent PM survives either motion they are not then required to face or use a similar motion for another 18 months
- 1992–94 parliamentary members face numerous accusations of corruption – continued electorate unrest leads to conflict among political factions
- April 1993 BRA propose cease-fire on Bougainville – following year a peace-keeping force from Fiji, Vanuatu and Tonga deployed under supervision of Australian and New Zealand governments
- September 1993 PM Wingti announces resignation then re-elected unopposed
- August 1994 Supreme Court decides Wingti's re-election was illegal. In new election Julius Chan defeats Wingti to become PM
- 1994 State of Emergency declared after volcanic eruptions and earthquakes near Rabaul in East New Britain
- 1996 after two years litigation Australian High Court rules against BHP mining company – BHP to pay A$100 million compensation, A$7.6 million legal costs to land owners and A$300–400 million in reparation for environmental damage inflicted at Ok Tedi copper mine
- 1997 PM Chan steps down after PNG army opposes use of foreign mercenaries to end Bougainville rebellion.

Demographic indicators

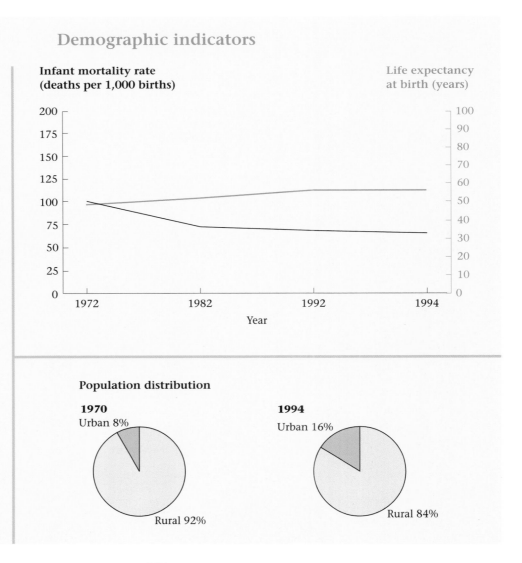

Total population (million)

Density (persons per km²)

Year

Infant mortality rate (deaths per 1,000 births)

Life expectancy at birth (years)

Year

Population distribution

1970
Urban 8%
Rural 92%

1994
Urban 16%
Rural 84%

Papua New Guinea

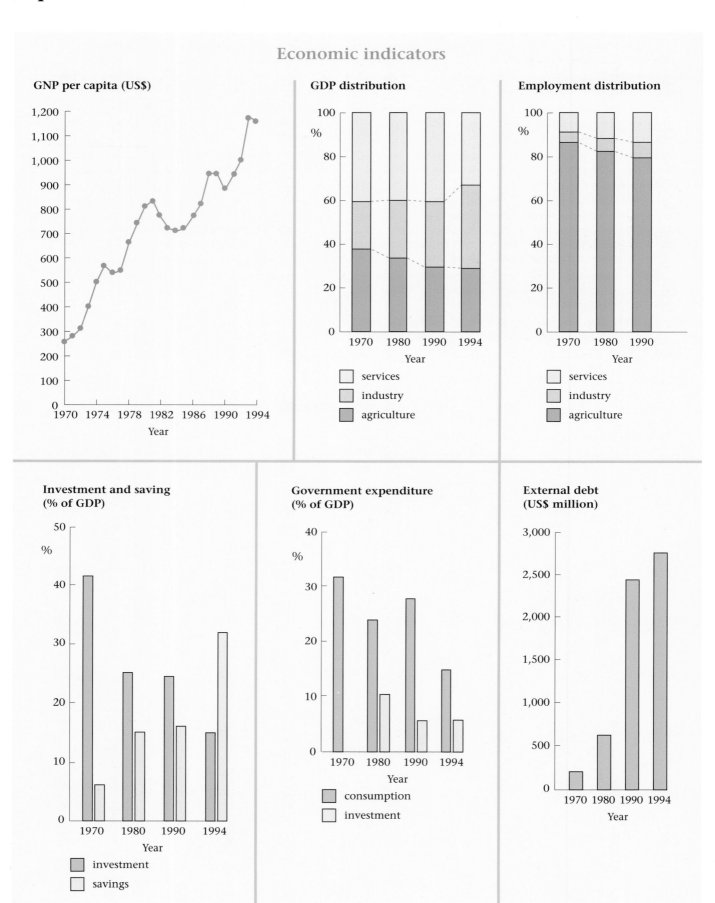

Economic indicators

GNP per capita (US$)

GDP distribution

Employment distribution

Investment and saving (% of GDP)

Government expenditure (% of GDP)

External debt (US$ million)

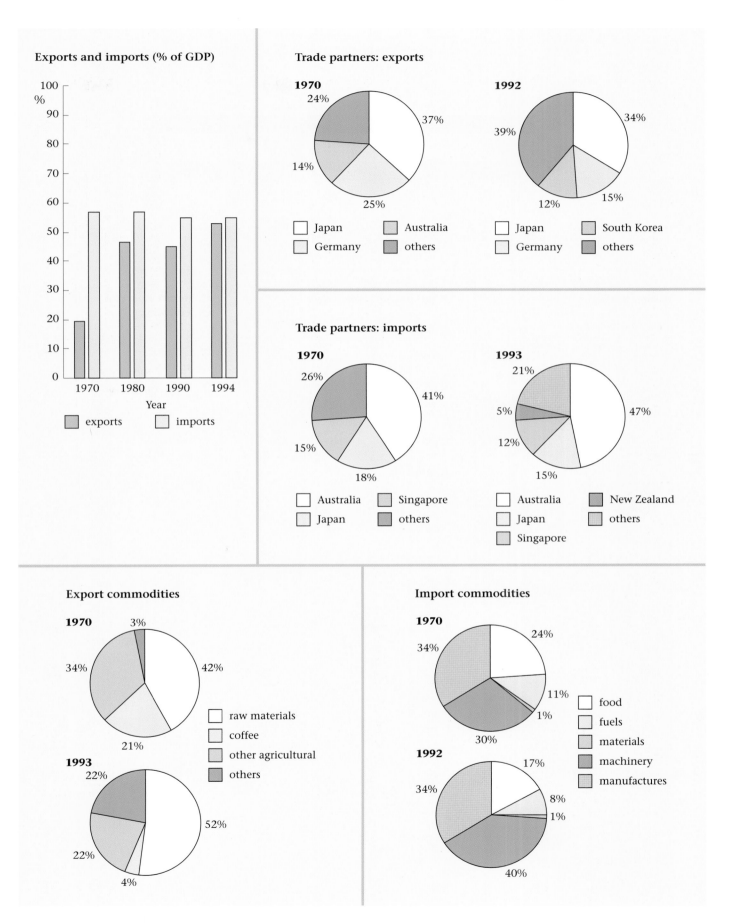

Exports and imports (% of GDP)

Trade partners: exports

1970

37% Japan
24%
14%
25%

1992

34% Japan
39%
12%
15%

Japan Australia
Germany others

Japan South Korea
Germany others

Trade partners: imports

1970

41%
26%
15%
18%

1993

47%
21%
5%
12%
15%

Australia Singapore
Japan others

Australia New Zealand
Japan others
Singapore

Export commodities

1970

42%
34%
21%
3%

raw materials
coffee
other agricultural
others

1993

52%
22%
22%
4%

Import commodities

1970

24%
34%
11%
1%
30%

food
fuels
materials
machinery
manufactures

1992

17%
34%
8%
1%
40%

Papua New Guinea

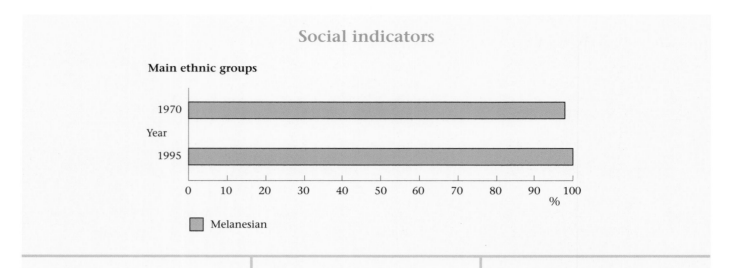

Social indicators

Main ethnic groups

Melanesian

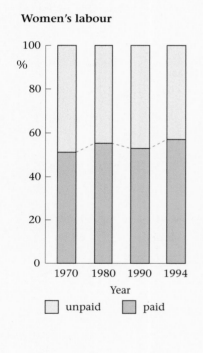

Women's labour

unpaid   paid

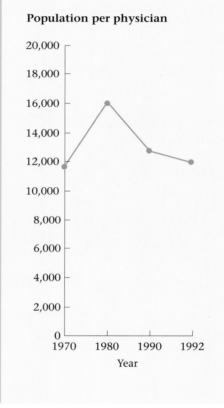

Population per physician

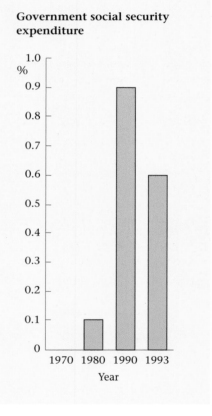

Government social security expenditure

Political framework

- In the run up to the 1997 elections a host of problems beset the PNG government
- Bitter civil war on Bougainville continues
  - rebel leaders returning from talks in Australia attacked by PNG forces
  - four PNG soldiers killed close to Bougainville island
  - in a retaliatory attack PNG forces suffer ignominious defeat
  - Bougainville Premier Miriung assassinated in his own house
- External criticism for PNG government's actions on Bougainville crystallizes in report from Amnesty International which recounts extensive human rights abuses
- Economic policies disrupted as proposed budget increases in personal and corporate taxation withdrawn after public outcry – gaming machines taxed instead
- World Bank threatens to suspend structural adjustment loan package for failure to implement recommended policies or boost bureaucratic administrative capacity or tackle political corruption issues
- Government image on corruption control not helped by appointment to new Committee on Integrity of Political Parties of an ex-Deputy PM removed from office in 1991 on 83 counts of corruption
- Neither does government seem willing to close the loophole allowing politicians to avoid corruption charges if they resign before formally charged
- Government generally seems to be shifting in search for international investment partners towards greater ASEAN involvement – especially to Malaysian companies who increasingly dominate PNG's tropical logging operations.

Further reading

Dorney, S. (1990) *Papua New Guinea: People, Politics and History Since 1975*, Sydney, Random House.

Waiko, J.D. (1993) *A Short History of Papua New Guinea*, Melbourne, Oxford University Press.

Peru

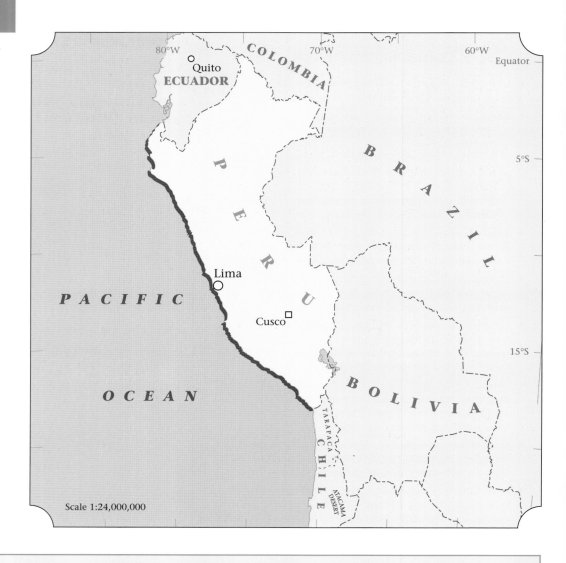

Scale 1:24,000,000

Historical background

- Amerindian settlement for over 10,000 years
- 1200–1520 Inca Empire centred on Cusco but stretching from Chile to Colombia
- 1533 Spanish take advantage of Inca civil war to colonize Peru
- 1820–26 after liberation armies defeat Spanish independence declared
- 19th C. weak central state – prolonged internal conflict between regional military leaders backed by local landowners
- Mid 19th C. economy dominated by exports of guano fertilizer – revenues dissipated on unproductive consumption. Synthetic fertilizers and nitrates undermine guano trade
- 1879–83 war with Chile over nitrate deposits in Atacama desert – Lima occupied and Peru forced to cede Tarapaca province
- 1883–1930 oligarchic rule of landowners and merchants controlling key exports of copper, cotton, sugar and oil. Very limited democratic participation with only 3% enfranchised – social divisions widen

- 1930 collapse of export markets, economic depression and pressure for social reform produces military coup
- 1930–68 unstable era – old oligarchy use military to preserve their economic dominance over middle class and radical opposition
- 1968–80 leftist military regime strives to remove foreign control of economy and reform society. Banks, public utilities, oil and fishing industries nationalized and tariff protection used to promote industrialization. Land reform splits *haciendas* into agricultural co-operatives
- 1980 new constitution enfranchises all adults and in principle consolidates power of legislative Congress against military and presidential authority
- 1980–85 severe foreign debt problems force governments to implement IMF/World Bank austerity programme – sparks social unrest including operations of armed revolutionaries
- Maoist *Sendero Luminoso* (Shining Path) attempt to mobilize peasant revolution drawing on traditional Amerindian resentment of Lima elite and failure to sustain land reform

programme. Separate *Tupac Amaru* group targets foreign companies especially from USA

- Brutal violence and intimidation of rural people throughout 1980s both by revolutionaries and government forces
- 1985–90 Garcia presidency attempts to limit influence of international financial institutions – IMF make Peru ineligible for further loans. Increasing guerrilla conflict and economic chaos – inflation rises to over 5,000%
- 1990 surprise election of President Fujimori. Widespread disillusionment with traditional political leaders over economy and internal violence – Fujimori's political inexperience discounted by his appeal as populist national saviour
- Fujimori cultivates military support – increases their capacity to defeat guerrillas and incorporates senior officers in government. Fujimori also tries to recover international financial credentials in neo-liberal austerity programme of public expenditure reductions and privatization
- 1992 Fujimori dissolves legislature, suspends constitution and rules by decree

- 1992–93 many *Sendero Luminoso* and *Tupac Amaru* leaders captured. Guerrillas isolated – some seek peace, others continue armed struggle but generally no longer serious threat to internal stability
- 1993 in deference to international pressure Fujimori allows Congress just sufficient power to secure flows of foreign financial support
- 1994–95 Fujimori retains military support with amnesty on human rights crimes during their counter insurgency operations – national security given precedence over constitutional rights
- 1995 benefiting from reduced guerrilla conflict and economic recovery Fujimori re-elected
- 1996 Fujimori's personal autocratic rule confirmed as Congress waives constitutional impediments and allows him to stand for re-election in 2000.

Demographic indicators

Total population (million)

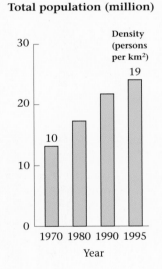

Infant mortality rate (deaths per 1,000 births)

Life expectancy at birth (years)

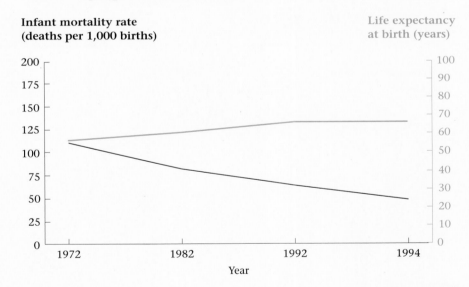

Population distribution

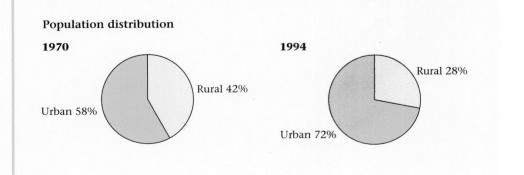

1970

1994

Peru

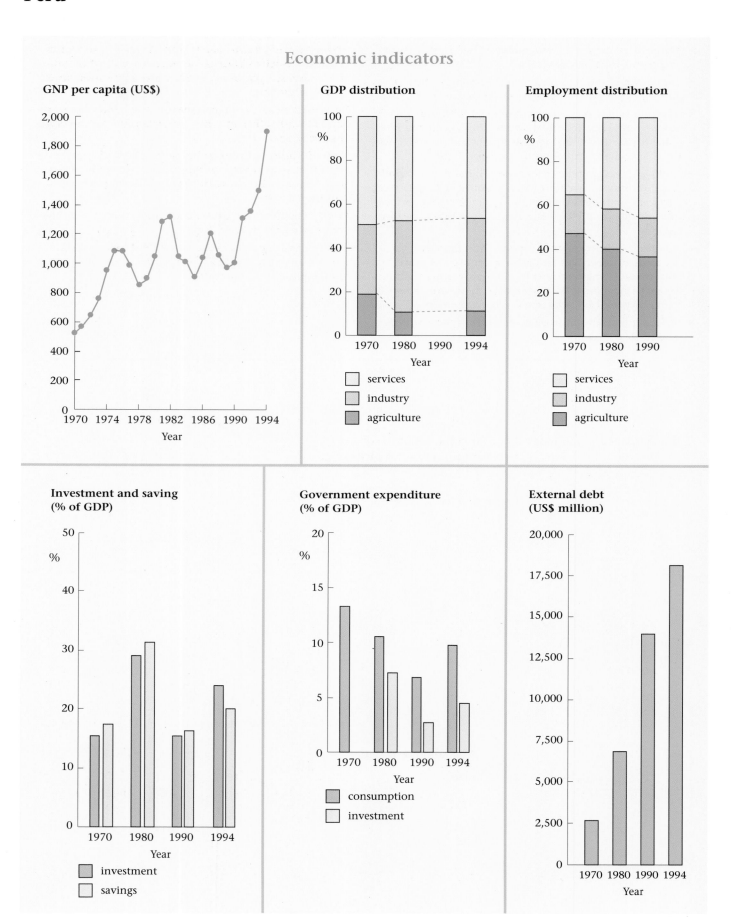

Economic indicators

GNP per capita (US$)

GDP distribution

Employment distribution

services
industry
agriculture

services
industry
agriculture

Investment and saving (% of GDP)

investment
savings

Government expenditure (% of GDP)

consumption
investment

External debt (US$ million)

Exports and imports (% of GDP)

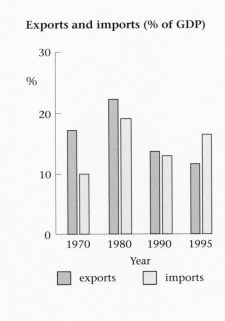

Trade partners: exports

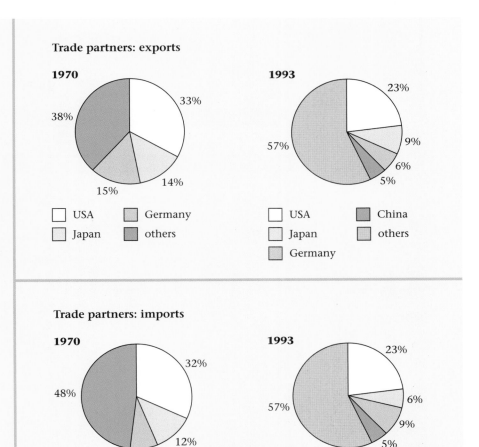

1970

33%
38%
15%   14%

- USA
- Japan
- Germany
- others

1993

23%
9%
6%
5%
57%

- USA
- Japan
- Germany
- China
- others

Trade partners: imports

1970

32%
48%
8%   12%

- USA
- Germany
- Japan
- others

1993

23%
6%
9%
5%
57%

- USA
- Germany
- Japan
- China
- others

Export commodities

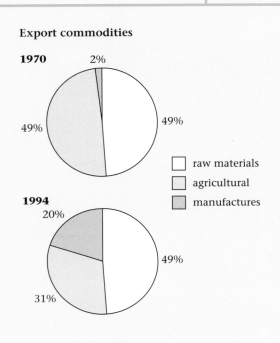

1970

2%
49%   49%

- raw materials
- agricultural
- manufactures

1994

20%
31%   49%

Import commodities

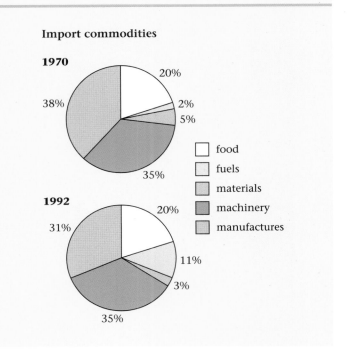

1970

20%
2%
5%
38%   35%

- food
- fuels
- materials
- machinery
- manufactures

1992

20%
11%
3%
31%   35%

Peru

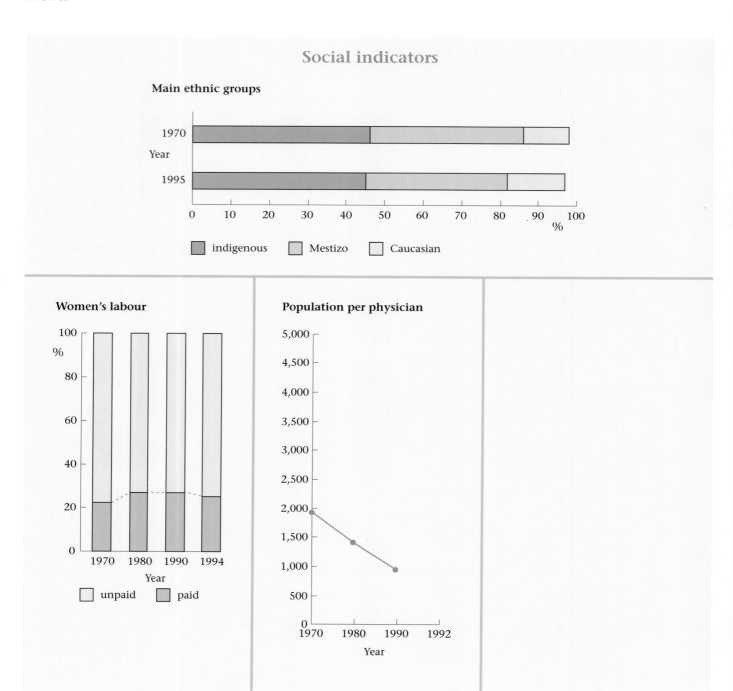

Social indicators

Main ethnic groups

Year

1970

1995

0 10 20 30 40 50 60 70 80 90 100
%

■ indigenous   ■ Mestizo   □ Caucasian

Women's labour

%
100
80
60
40
20
0

1970 1980 1990 1994
Year

□ unpaid   ■ paid

Population per physician

5,000
4,500
4,000
3,500
3,000
2,500
2,000
1,500
1,000
500
0

1970 1980 1990 1992
Year

Political framework

- Peru's polity is currently dominated by the personal power of President Fujimori with subservient civilian politicians inside and outside Congress and a judiciary discredited by corruption. Only the military remain as an alternative power centre

- Fujimori labels his regime as directly democratic and that his weekly visits throughout Peru supplemented by extensive opinion polling allows him to heed the popular will

- Bureaucrats and elected politicians are trained to manage the implementation of Fujimori's policies rather than participate in their formulation. Political contestation has all but disappeared except from leaders of the armed forces

- The symbiotic alliance of convenience between Fujimori and the military saw the armed forces accept the 1992 suspension of the constitution. Without an organized political base of his own Fujimori relies on the military as his key support network to safeguard his vision of direct democracy

- The 1995 amnesty given to military personnel accused of human rights crimes gave Fujimori leverage to take more control over armed forces promotions. An equally important source of strength lies in the revamped intelligence service reporting directly to Fujimori especially about signs of military discontent

- In 1997 despite reduced guerrilla conflict the army still retained emergency control of a quarter of the country where among other activities it is deeply involved in the illegal production of materials used to produce cocaine. Estimates suggest that Peru supplies over half of the world's cocaine raw material with military and guerrilla groups key organizers of coca production

- Fujimori's military allies are not, however, docile servants especially when neo-liberal cuts in public expenditure lead to reduced defence spending. Equally significant has been military opposition to the privatization of strategic industries like oil and electricity generation. Bitterness remains among some military echelons who realize their importance to Fujimori but also fear they are progressively being disarmed

- Armed guerrilla activity has declined drastically but still has not ceased. Even *Tupac Amaru*, thought to have been totally defeated, managed to penetrate Lima's diplomatic quarter in 1996. A four-month hostage crisis was ended in April 1997 when commandos freed the captives and killed the guerrillas

- The underlying reasons for armed insurrection remain evident in gross social inequalities which have worsened with neo-liberal cuts in subsidies and social spending at the same time as taxes increased

- Even official figures show more than half the population living in poverty and over 20% unable to meet basic nutritional needs. However, very marked regional differences mean that in Andean areas 90% poverty is common with infant mortality rates four times the national average

- This bleak picture of inequality was supposed to have been addressed in programmes funded by the US$5 billion proceeds of Fujimori's privatization projects, but little had been forthcoming by 1997

- Fujimori's claim to legitimacy by results makes his position contingent on economic recovery to meet high expectations and on careful management of the military.

Further reading

Cameron, M.A. (1994) *Democracy and Authoritarianism in Peru: Political Coalitions and Social Change*, Basingstoke, Macmillan.

Durand, F. (1994) *Business and Politics in Peru*, Oxford, Westview Press.

Strong, S. (1993) *Shining Path: the World's Revolutionary Deadliest Force*, London, Fontana.

Philippines

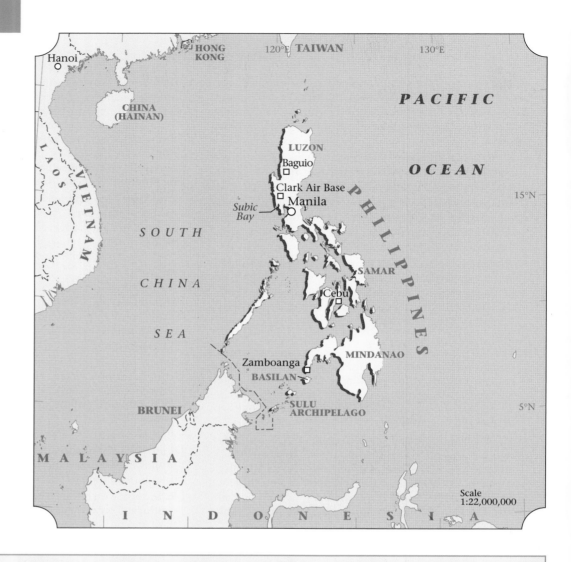

Historical background

- AD 900–1200 Chinese establish coastal trading posts
- *c.* 1380 Muslim clergy from Malaya introduce Islam
- 1521 Spanish expedition led by Magellan lands in Samar
- 1565 first Spanish settlement established in Cebu
- 1834 Spain allows foreign investment and trade in Manila
- 1896 Philippine Revolution – *Katipunan* secret society begins uprising but Spain suppresses rebellion
- 1898 Spanish–American war – US navy destroys Spanish Fleet in Manila
- 1898 Spain cedes Philippines to USA for US$20 million
- 1899 Philippine Republic inaugurated – Aguinaldo President. Conflict follows between Philippine Republican Army and US occupying forces
- 1901 resistance ends – Aguinaldo swears allegiance to USA
- 1920s–1930s peasant unrest but USA supports landowners
- 1934 USA promise independence by 1946
- 1935 Sakdalista peasant uprising around Manila
- 1935 Philippine Commonwealth inaugurated under President Quezon. Legislation to improve conditions of peasants effectively resisted by landowners
- 1941–45 Japanese occupation
- 1946 Philippine independence – Roxas President
- 1947 25-year leases granted for US military bases
- 1948 Roxas dies – Liberal Party's Quirino elected President
- 1953 new Nacionalista President Magsaysay attempts land reform
- 1957 Magsaysay dies – succeeded by Garcia
- 1961 Liberal candidate Macapagal elected President – negotiates loans with IMF and removes import controls
- 1965 Nacionalista candidate Ferdinand Marcos elected President. Increases overseas borrowing to develop infrastructure
- 1969 Marcos re-elected against background of dire financial crisis due to foreign debts and election spending. Many student demonstrations; Muslim secessionist movement (MNLF) active in Southern Islands of Mindanao and Sulu; communist National Democratic Front (NDF) formed

- 1972 Marcos declares martial law on pretext of conspiracy between right-wing and Maoist forces – decade of authoritarian rule follows
- 1976 Marcos pledges autonomy for Muslim areas
- 1981 martial law ends
- 1983 Benigno Aquino, main political rival of Marcos, assassinated on return from exile – major political crisis and massive anti-government demonstrations
- January 1986 Marcos re-elected but Roman Catholic Church and US observers claim electoral fraud
- 21 February 1986 military leaders Enrile and Ramos desert Marcos – they receive support and backing from USA
- 25 February 1986 Corazon Aquino becomes President – restores civil freedoms and seeks peace with MNLF and NDF. Marcos exiled to USA. First of seven attempted coups put down by Enrile
- 1987 'the Mendiola massacre': large demonstration demanding land reform in Manila attacked by security forces – 20 killed
- 1987 new constitution on US model approved in referendum

- 1987 Aquino's Lagas ng Bayan alliance win decisive majorities in elections to House of Representatives and Senate
- 1988 Ramos appointed Secretary of National Defence despite involvement in earlier attempted coups
- 1988 Comprehensive Agrarian Reform Plan attempts land redistribution
- 1989 Mindanao becomes autonomous region after referendum
- 1990 earthquake in Baguio City in northern Luzon kills 1600
- 1991 Philippine Senate votes to terminate leases on US military facilities at Subic Bay and Clark air base – USA withdraws following year
- 1992 Ramos elected President – pledges law and order but despite repeated attempts NDF peace talks collapse
- 1993 Ramos launches 'Philippines 2000' – aiming for newly-industrialized country (NIC) status by 2000
- 1995 ruling coalition win around 70% of seats in House of Representatives and 9 out of 12 contested seats in Senate.

Demographic indicators

Total population (million)

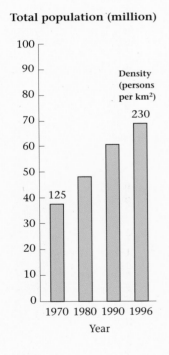

Density (persons per km²)
230
125

Infant mortality rate (deaths per 1,000 births)

Life expectancy at birth (years)

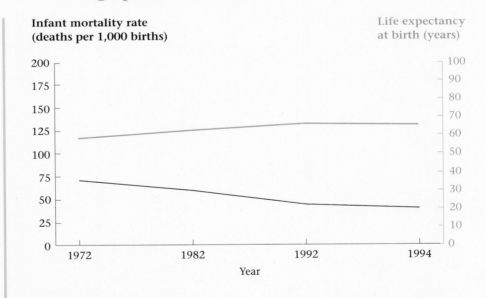

Population distribution

1970

Urban 33%

Rural 67%

1994

Urban 53%

Rural 47%

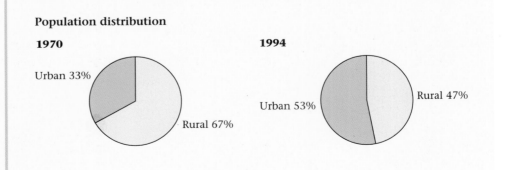

Philippines

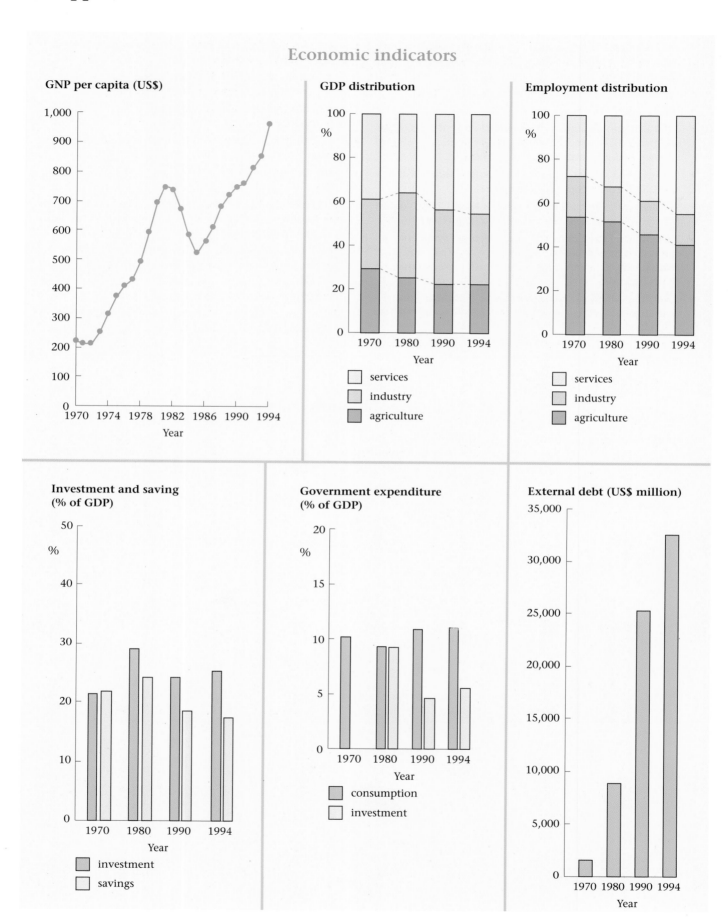

Economic indicators

GNP per capita (US$)

GDP distribution

services
industry
agriculture

Employment distribution

services
industry
agriculture

Investment and saving (% of GDP)

investment
savings

Government expenditure (% of GDP)

consumption
investment

External debt (US$ million)

Exports and imports (% of GDP)

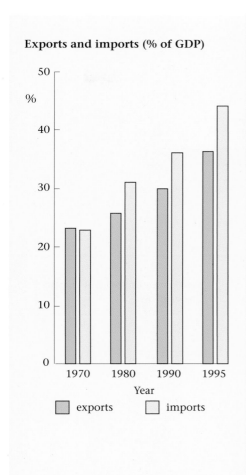

Trade partners: exports

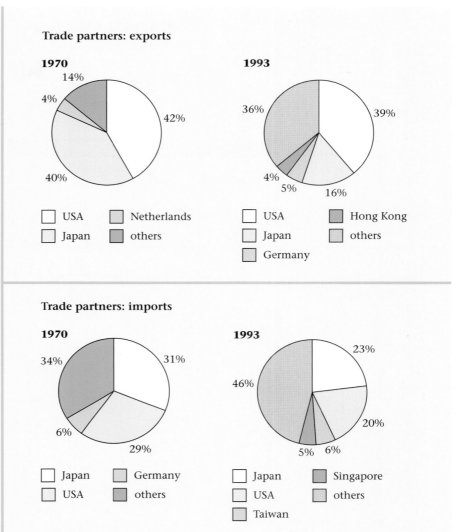

1970

14%
4%
42%
40%

USA   Netherlands
Japan   others

1993

36%
39%
4%
5%
16%

USA   Hong Kong
Japan   others
Germany

Trade partners: imports

1970

34%
31%
6%
29%

Japan   Germany
USA   others

1993

46%
23%
20%
5%   6%

Japan   Singapore
USA   others
Taiwan

Export commodities

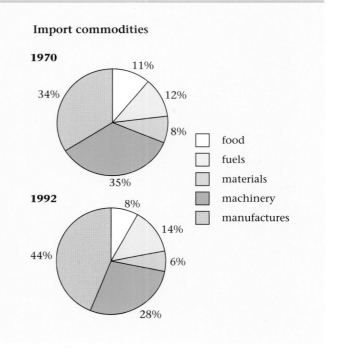

1970

1%   8%
21%
70%

copper
agricultural
machinery
manufactures

1992

6%   2%
19%
17%
56%

copper
agricultural
machinery
manufactures
others

Import commodities

1970

11%
34%
12%
8%
35%

food
fuels
materials
machinery
manufactures

1992

8%
14%
44%
6%
28%

food
fuels
materials
machinery
manufactures

Philippines

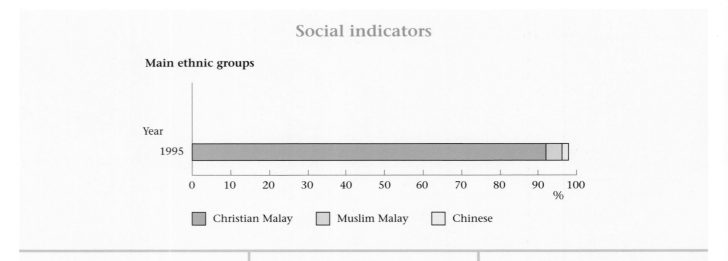

Social indicators

Main ethnic groups

Year
1995

0 10 20 30 40 50 60 70 80 90 100
%

■ Christian Malay ■ Muslim Malay □ Chinese

Women's labour

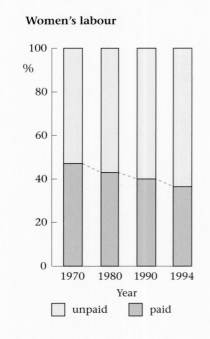

□ unpaid ■ paid

Population per physician

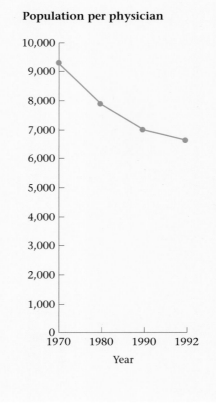

Government social security expenditure

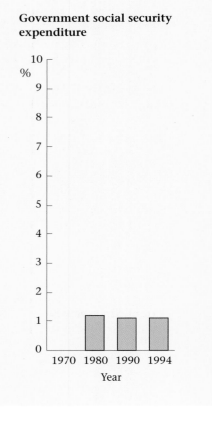

Political framework

- In the final year of his Presidency Ramos uses his position as host to 1996 APEC summit to draw world attention to his economic and political achievements since taking office in 1992

- Some public controversy though over Manila's decision to refuse entry to Nobel Peace Prize winner Ramos-Horta exiled leader of East Timor's independence movement

- Fear of offending Indonesia – an APEC and ASEAN partner – said to justify excluding Ramos-Horta and some other speakers at the unofficial anti-APEC forum

- APEC summit follows closely on significant achievement of peace pact with one rebel Muslim group MNLF who in honourable surrender commit to integration into peaceful mainstream politics

- MNLF leader becomes Governor of Autonomous Region in Muslim Mindanao

- Still no peaceful settlement with Moro Islamic Liberation Front (MILF) who are better armed – major battles (November 1996) on Basilan island off Mindanao's Zamboanga peninsula

- Peace agreement with MILF apparently less likely given their demand for an independent Islamic state

- Domestic politics increasingly dominated by question of who will follow Ramos and contest presidential elections due in 1998

- Some indication that allies of Ramos in Congress may press for constitutional amendment to allow him to run for a second term but with recent Ramos health problems this appears less likely

- Ramos said now to be happier to support close subordinate de Villa who has similar military background and is backed by members of the older business establishment

- Rumours that Ramos may be looking for continuing political role along lines of Lee Kuan Yew's flexible brief as Singapore's Senior Minister.

Further reading

Putzel, J. (1992) *A Captive Land: the Politics of Agrarian Reform in the Philippines*, London, New York and Manila, Catholic Institute for International Relations, Monthly Review Press and Ateneo University Press.

Rivera, T.C. (1995) *Landlords and Capitalists: Class, Family and State in Philippine Manufacturing*, Quezon City, University of Philippines Press.

Timberman, D.G. (1991) *A Changeless Land. Continuity and Change in Philippine Politics*, New York/Singapore, M.E. Sharpe/Institute of South-East Asian Studies.

Singapore

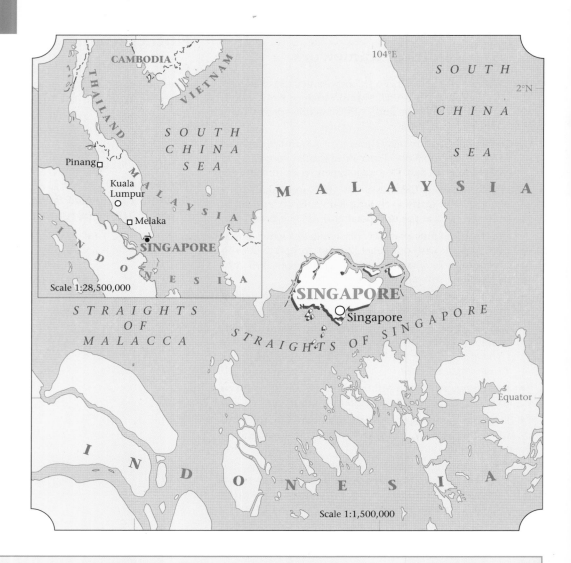

Historical background

- 1160 Sang Nila Utama reputed to have founded city of Singapura

- 12th–13th C. city described as prosperous trading centre by *Malay Annals* written in 14th C.

- 1252 Javanese invade Singapura – inhabitants dispersed over Malay Peninsula

- *c.* 1400 original city destroyed and deserted for next 400 years

- 1819 Stamford Raffles from British East India Company obtains permission from Sultan of Riau-Johore to establish trading post at mouth of Singapore river

- 1826 East India Company merges Singapore with Penang and Malacca as Straits Settlements

- 1867 Straits Settlements become British Crown Colony

- Later 19th C. Singapore becomes major international trading centre after Suez Canal opens and Malaya's rubber and tin resources developed

- 1942 despite massive naval base and extensive fortification,

Singapore falls to Japanese invasion – permanently undermines British Imperial credibility

- 1946 British split Straits Settlements into the Malayan Union and Singapore Crown Colony

- 1948 Malayan anti-communist emergency – radical politics in Singapore repressed and Communist Party barred

- 1955 new constitution establishes legislative assembly and David Marshall leader of the Labour Front forms minority government

- 1957 major reforms – Education Ordinance gives parity to four main languages and citizenship to nearly all residents

- 1959 People's Action Party (PAP) win 43 out of 51 seats in election – remains in power ever since. PM Lee Kuan Yew committed to rapid industrialization and social reform

- 1961 proposal to join Federation of Malaya divides PAP – socialist members form Barisan Sosialis

- 1962 referendum endorses Singapore's entry to Federation of Malaya which was re-named Malaysia the following year

- 1965 tensions between PAP and United Malay National Or-

- ganization in Kuala Lumpur – Singapore departs to become independent city state
- 1967 Singapore becomes a founding member of ASEAN
- 1968 after re-election of PAP, labour laws passed restricting trade union activity to attract foreign investment. Rapid industrialization follows with GDP growth rates averaging 10% a year 1970–96
- 1971 British troops withdraw
- 1979 'Speak Mandarin' campaign discourages use of regional Chinese dialects
- 1980 PAP win election with 76% of the vote
- 1987 new population policy – early marriage encouraged and three-child families
- 1987 new press laws restrict availability of foreign publications critical of government
- 1987 English becomes language of instruction in secondary schools
- 1988 parliament enlarged and PAP re-elected with 63% of popular vote

- 1990 legislation allows government to nominate six MPs for a two-year term to provide non-partisan criticism
- 1990 Lee Kuan Yew steps down as PM but remains in Cabinet as Senior Minister. Succeeded by Goh Chok Tong who promises relaxation of censorship laws
- 1991 PAP wins snap election but share of the vote drops to 61%
- 1992 'Speak Mandarin' campaign revived
- 1993 a state President is elected directly by citizens – empowered to protect financial reserves and has right to veto civil service and judicial appointments
- 1994 nominated MPs experiment retained
- 1995 Barings Bank of London collapses – Nick Leeson, their employee in Singapore, incurs massive US$1.3 billion loss in options trading. Stiff fines for new Barings owners and prison sentence for Leeson protects Singapore's reputation as financial centre
- Singapore hosts first ever meeting of the World Trade Organization.

Demographic indicators

Total population (million)

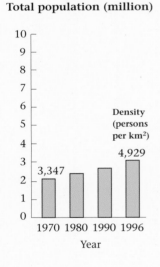

Infant mortality rate (deaths per 1,000 births)

Life expectancy at birth (years)

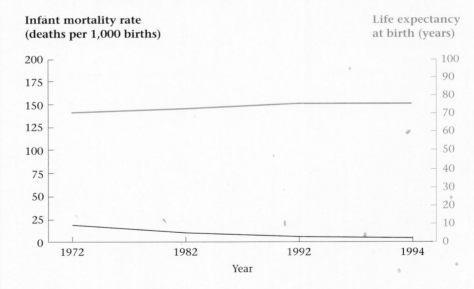

Population distribution

1970   **1994**

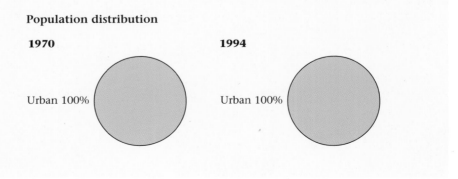

Urban 100%   Urban 100%

Singapore

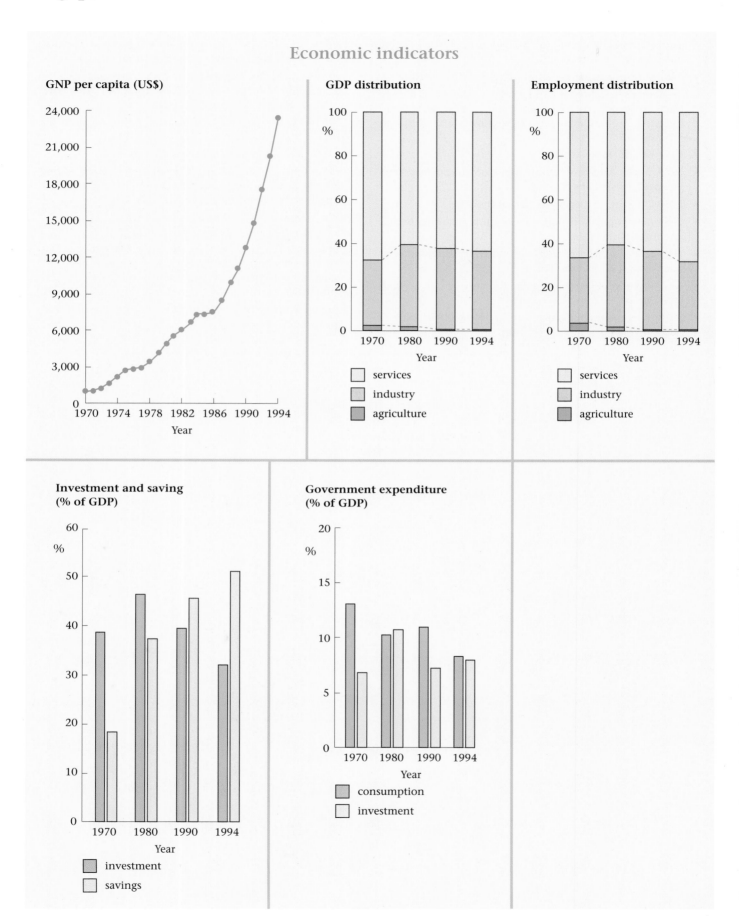

Economic indicators

GNP per capita (US$)

GDP distribution

Employment distribution

Investment and saving
(% of GDP)

Government expenditure
(% of GDP)

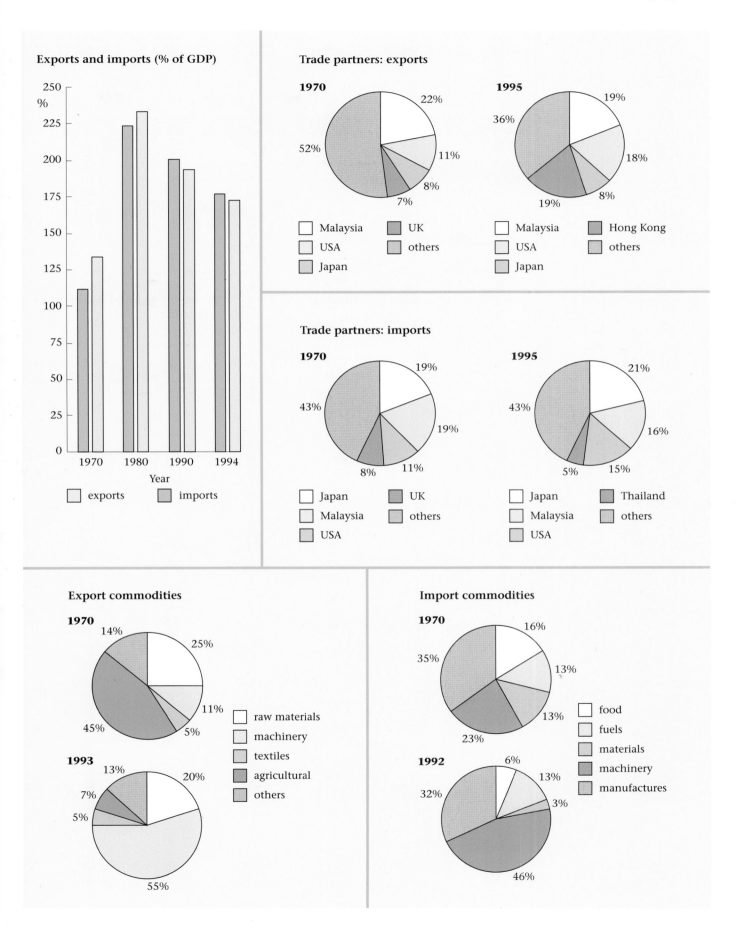

Exports and imports (% of GDP)

Trade partners: exports

1970

22%
11%
8%
7%
52%

☐ Malaysia   ■ UK
☐ USA   ■ others
☐ Japan

1995

19%
18%
8%
19%
36%

☐ Malaysia   ■ Hong Kong
☐ USA   ■ others
☐ Japan

Trade partners: imports

1970

19%
19%
11%
8%
43%

☐ Japan   ■ UK
☐ Malaysia   ■ others
☐ USA

1995

21%
16%
15%
5%
43%

☐ Japan   ■ Thailand
☐ Malaysia   ■ others
☐ USA

Export commodities

1970

14%
25%
11%
5%
45%

1993

13%
20%
7%
5%
55%

☐ raw materials
☐ machinery
☐ textiles
■ agricultural
☐ others

Import commodities

1970

16%
13%
13%
23%
35%

1992

6%
13%
3%
46%
32%

☐ food
☐ fuels
☐ materials
■ machinery
☐ manufactures

Singapore

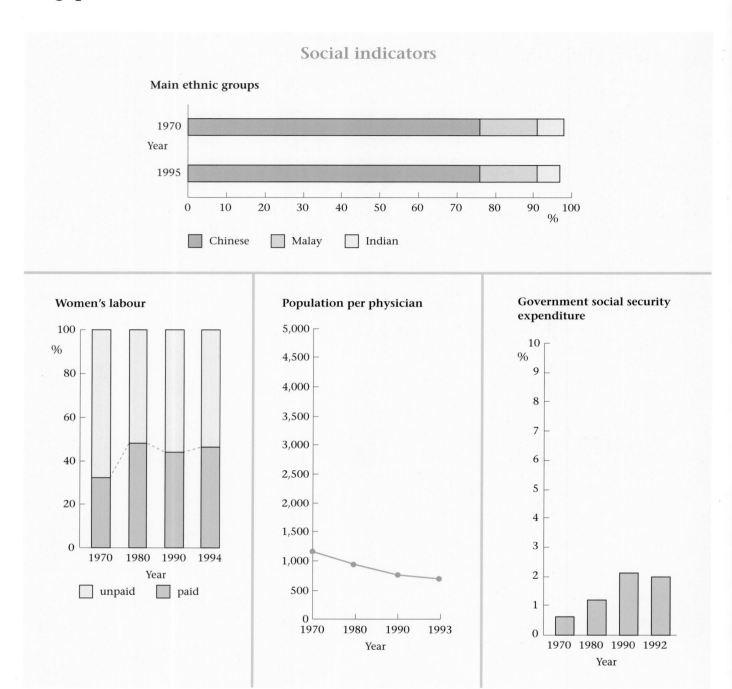

Social indicators

Main ethnic groups

Year

1970

1995

0 10 20 30 40 50 60 70 80 90 100

%

☐ Chinese ☐ Malay ☐ Indian

Women's labour

%

100

80

60

40

20

0

1970 1980 1990 1994

Year

☐ unpaid ☐ paid

Population per physician

5,000

4,500

4,000

3,500

3,000

2,500

2,000

1,500

1,000

500

0

1970 1980 1990 1993

Year

Government social security expenditure

%

10

9

8

7

6

5

4

3

2

1

0

1970 1980 1990 1992

Year

Political framework

- In the strange world of Singaporean politics Goh Chok Tong's government approaches the 1997 elections in a nervous but aggressive mood anxious to halt the long-term decline in its share of the popular vote – this had fallen to 'only' 61% in 1991

- Government nervousness shaped partly by public anxiety over soaring living costs made worse by a recent award of large increases in ministerial salaries

- Government concerns too over how their changes to constituency boundaries – said to favour the PAP – would be received

- Aggressive government campaigning involved promising districts voting for the opposition that their housing estates would be at the end of the queue for upgrading – a crucial tactic in a country where 86% are publicly housed

- Despite well-attended public election rallies opposition parties introduce another twist to Singapore-style politics when they fail to contest over half the available seats

- The electorate can be assured, the opposition say, that there is no threat to unseat the PAP government so citizens are free to record their feelings without worrying about the consequences of a change of government

- Unsurprisingly the outcome was an increase in the PAP popular vote to 65% yielding 96% of parliamentary seats – opposition MPs drop from four to two

- Maintaining the Singapore government's stance on the supremacy of Asian over Western values PM Goh Chok Tong concluded that voters had rejected adversarial Western-style liberal democracy. Confirming the dominance of a single ruling party apparently also rejects the Western preference for 'putting individual rights over that of society'.

Further reading

Chua Beng-Huat (1997) *Communitarian Ideology and Democracy in Singapore*, London, Routledge.

Rodan, G. (ed.) (1993) *Singapore Changes Guard: Social, Political and Economic Directions in the 1990s*, Melbourne, Longman Cheshire.

Taiwan

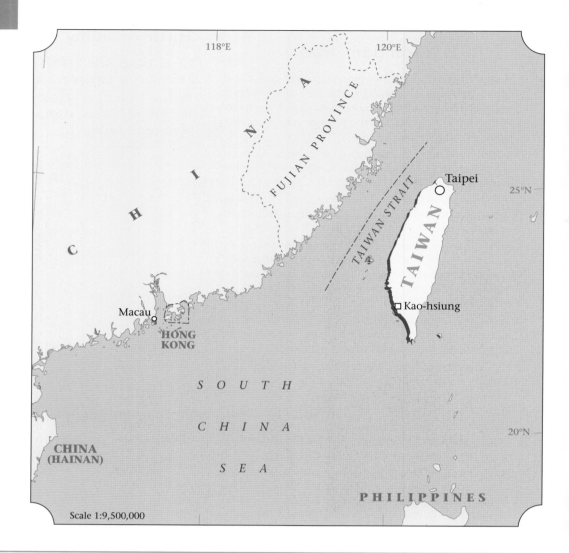

Scale 1:9,500,000

Historical background

- Original inhabitants of Malay origin
- 13th C. first significant Chinese settlements established by people escaping mainland persecution
- 1624 Dutch use island as Far East trading post
- 1661 Dutch expelled by Koxinga after his abortive rebellion against Qing dynasty
- 1663 Qing Emperor Kang Xi invades and conquers Taiwan – substantial immigration from the mainland follows
- 17th–19th C. nominal Qing rule under Fujian provincial governor but Taiwan regarded as effectively beyond control
- 1870s French and Japanese military allowed to prevent Taiwanese from harassing shipping and foreign merchants
- 1895 Taiwan ceded to Japan after Sino-Japanese war – administered directly from Tokyo
- 1945 Taiwan reverts to Chinese control ruled by Chiang Kai-shek's Nationalist Party Kuomintang (KMT)
- 1947 'February 28 Incident' an uprising against abuses of KMT rule brutally suppressed – over 20,000 killed
- 1949 KMT defeated by communists in China's civil war. Chiang and one million followers take refuge in Taiwan establishing government in Taipei
- 1954 Taiwan signs mutual security treaty with USA
- 1971 People's Republic of China (PRC) admitted to UN in place of Taiwan
- 1975 Chiang Kai-shek dies – succeeded later by his son Chiang Ching-kuo
- 1978 USA withdraw diplomatic recognition of Taiwan
- 1980 Taiwan loses IMF/World Bank status as independent economy
- 1986 martial law ends – 135 opposition politicians form Democratic Progressive Party (DPP)
- 1986 KMT wins limited election but DPP receive a quarter of the votes
- 1987 38-year ban on travel to mainland removed – following year mainland Chinese allowed to visit Taiwan
- January 1988 Chiang Ching-kuo dies and is succeeded by Vice-President Lee Teng-hui – first native Taiwanese President

- May 1988 riots in Taipei over the structure of parliament
- 1989 partial elections held for legislature and Provincial Assembly. KMT win 72% of seats and DPP 21%
- 1989 President Lee visits Singapore – first official overseas visit by a Taiwanese President in twelve years
- 1990 demonstrations at the opening of National Assembly that has power to amend constitution and approve judicial as well as executive appointments. Protests over dominance of ageing KMT politicians elected in 1940s and exclusion of DPP
- 1991 Taiwan admitted to APEC as 'Chinese Taipei' but problems over official delegations attending summits
- 1991 two senior Chinese Red Cross envoys allowed to enter Taiwan – first ever visit by official PRC representatives
- December 1991 new National Assembly elected – most open of only two elections since 1946 – KMT win 79% seats
- 1992 Taiwan granted observer status at GATT
- 1992 first full national elections to Legislative Yuan. KMT win 63% seats and DPP win 31%

- February 1995 President Lee formally apologizes for 'February 28 Incident' – legislation grants compensation to relatives of victims
- June 1995 President Lee makes four-day unofficial visit to USA – PRC recalls Chinese ambassador to USA in protest
- 1996 China conducts military exercises during Taiwanese elections – USA pledges support for Taiwan in event of Chinese attack
- 1996 in first direct presidential election Lee Teng-hui becomes President again with 54% of popular vote.

Demographic indicators

Total population (million)

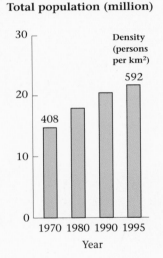

Infant mortality rate (deaths per 1,000 births)

Life expectancy at birth (years)

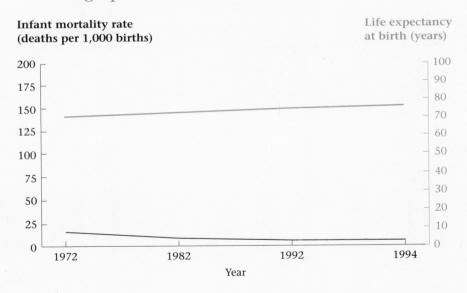

Population distribution

1970

1994

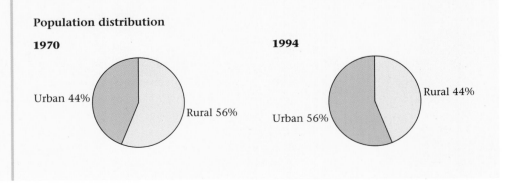

195

Taiwan

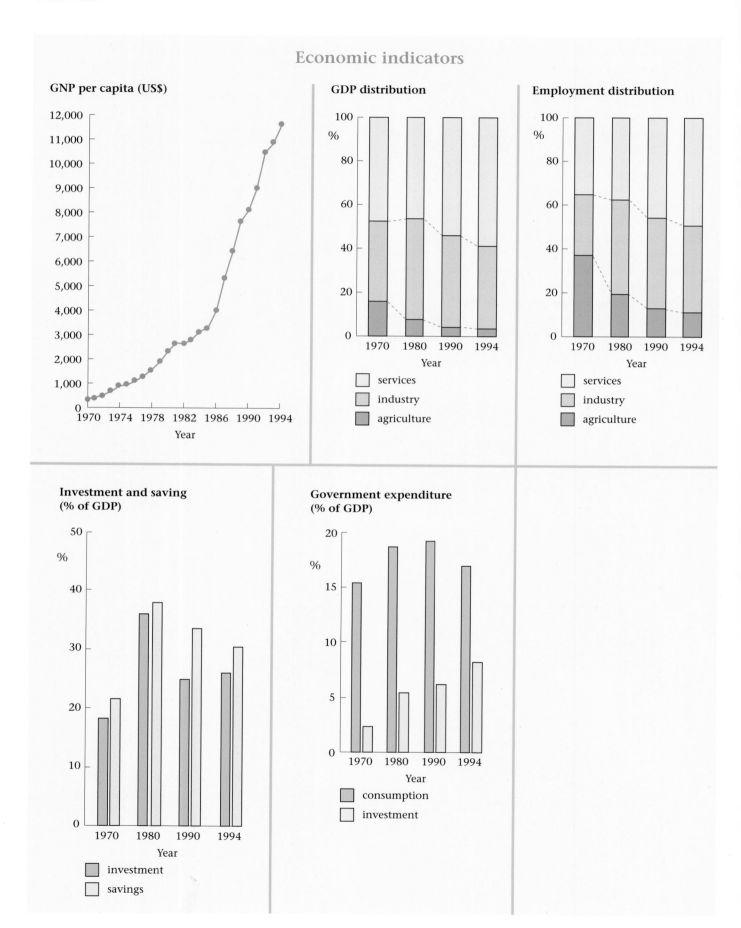

Economic indicators

GNP per capita (US$)

GDP distribution

Employment distribution

Investment and saving (% of GDP)

Government expenditure (% of GDP)

Exports and imports (% of GDP)

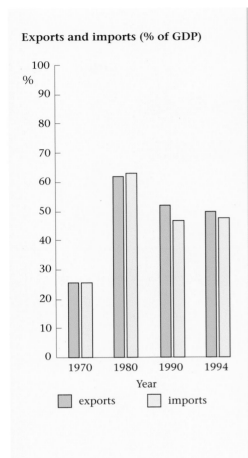

Trade partners: exports

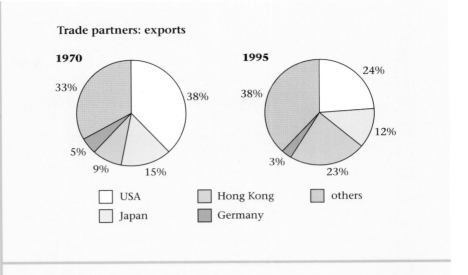

Trade partners: imports

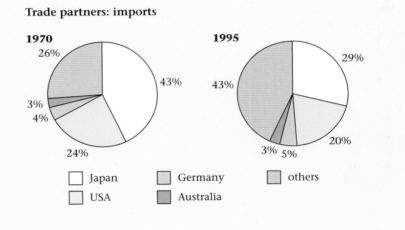

Export commodities

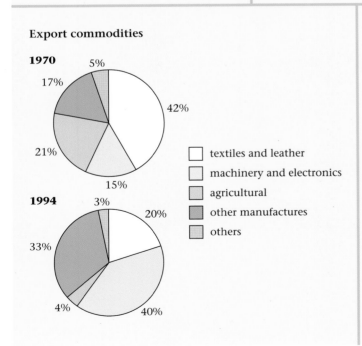

Import commodities

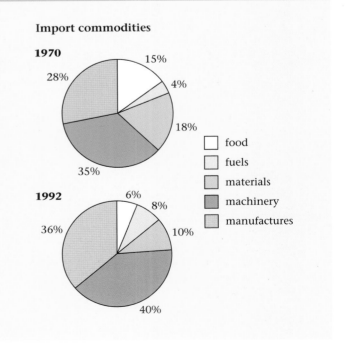

Taiwan

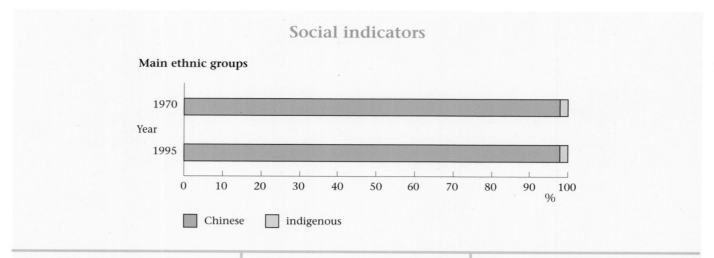

Social indicators

Main ethnic groups

Chinese   indigenous

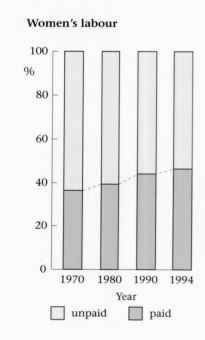

Women's labour

unpaid   paid

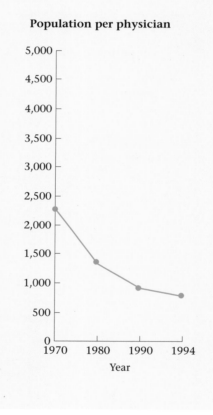

Population per physician

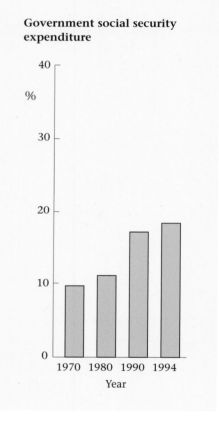

Government social security expenditure

Political framework

- Uniquely intertwined domestic and foreign political scenarios dominated by PRC claims to sovereignty over Taiwan

- Epitomized by Chinese war games in Taiwan Straits during 1996 presidential election

- PRC calls on Taiwan's voters to reject President Lee for stressing an independent Taiwanese identity but only 20% vote for parties seeking reconciliation with PRC

- Lee attempts to use Chinese intimidation to recover international recognition – USA pledges political support and deploys aircraft carriers

- Muted support though from Asian neighbours – Japan and Singapore urge caution on Beijing but others maintain public silence

- Neither is international recognition enhanced – Lee not allowed to attend APEC summit and WTO application still stalled at time of delicate negotiations over PRC membership

- Taiwan's official name – Republic of China on Taiwan – symbolizes the international dilemma and divides political parties in Taiwan

- At either end of Taiwan's political spectrum are parties vehemently opposing or supporting declarations of *de jure* independence. In between KMT and DPP appear pragmatically content with current *de facto* status

- Broader uncertainty too over policies of post-Deng regime in PRC – recovery of Hong Kong and Macau may mean more aggressive campaign to re-absorb Taiwan

- After Lee's re-election internal attention focused on deregulating government and shifting power from unelected bureaucrats to elected legislators

- KMT proposes more presidential power with just one elected legislature

- Controversy though over proposed abolition of provincial government layer that emerged in 1940s when KMT regarded itself as government of China in exile

- PRC says proposal shows re-emergence of KMT authoritarian tendencies and will turn citizens of a province of China into citizens of an independent Taiwan

- Critics within Taiwan argue Lee is using proposals to divert attention from KMT patronage politics and structural corruption that show shallowness of democratization process.

Further reading

Klintworth, G. (1995) *New Taiwan, New China*, Melbourne, Longman Cheshire.

Tien, H. (1989) *The Great Transition: Political and Social Change in the Republic of China*, Stanford, Hoover Institution Press.

Wachman, A. (1994) *Taiwan: National Identity and Democratization*, London, M.E. Sharpe.

Thailand

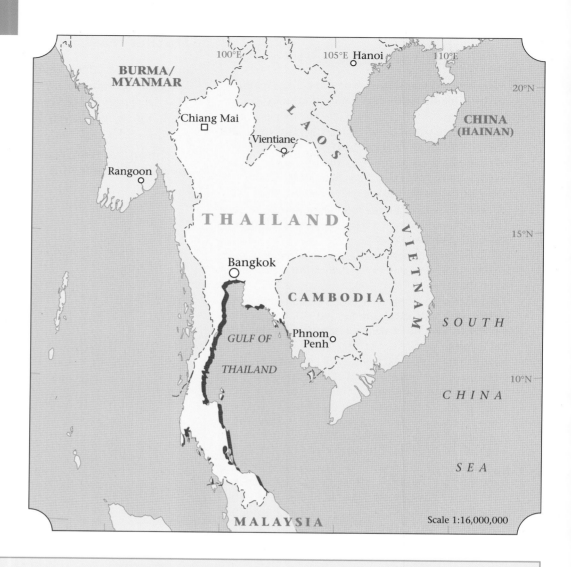

Scale 1:16,000,000

Historical background

- 1238 Kingdom of Sukothai

- Mid 14th C. Kingdom of Ayudhya – conquers Angkor dynasty of Cambodia in 1368

- 1767 Ayudhya falls – replaced by Chinese war-lord Taskin who forms new Thai state centred at Thonburi

- 1782 House of Chakri (King Rama I) replaces Taskin – capital moves to Bangkok

- 1855 treaty with British removes King's foreign trade monopoly

- 1912 failed military coup leads to some changes in Monarchy's role and push toward a Thai form of nationalism – 'Nation, Religion, King'

- 1932 non-violent military coup displaces King – communism made illegal, political parties banned and media censored

- 1938 Phibun heads anti-Chinese and anti-European government modelled on fascism

- 1939 country's name changed from Siam to Thailand

- 1941 Phibun declares war on USA and Britain as Japan launches conquest of Malayan peninsula from Thailand

- 1944 Phibun removed by National Assembly

- 1947 military coup led on behalf of Phibun who recovers power following year

- 1951 Phibun establishes anti-communist dictatorship with US backing

- 1954 Thailand becomes a founding member of SEATO

- 1957 Phibun re-introduces elections in attempt to prevent growing power of military leader Sarit Thanarat. Government discredited by rigged election – Sarit becomes PM following year

- 1958–63 Sarit reforms economy, encourages foreign investment, restores Monarchy as symbolic leader and allows USA to use Thailand as military base for their war in Indo-China

- 1963–71 after Sarit dies Generals Thanom and Praphat gain power

- 1971 martial law declared

- 1973 after protracted civil unrest government collapses when military refuse to disperse a student rally

- 1973–76 political upheaval as student groups and pro-democracy parties attempt to form coalition governments
- 1976 new military-dominated government abolishes National Assembly and bans political parties
- 1980–88 General Prem becomes PM and attempts political reform to limit military role in government – survives attempted coups in 1981 and 1985
- 1988 Chatichai becomes PM as first elected leader of the government since 1976 – introduces social security legislation, resolves border dispute with Laos and bans logging of Thai rain forests but later becomes discredited by corruption
- 1991 non-violent military coup declares martial law, suspends constitution and dissolves National Assembly
- Anand Panyarachun named PM and rules through National Legislative Assembly – temporary body until new constitution framed and general election organized
- 1991–92 new constitution followed by National Assembly elections lead to unstable coalition government with non-elected General Suchinda as PM

- May 1992 extensive civil protest against an unelected PM – more than 50 people killed and Suchinda resigns
- June 1992 Anand restored as PM after King refuses to accept nomination of governing coalition parties – National Democratic Front (NDF) formed by political parties opposed to government led by military
- September 1992 general election – Democratic Party wins most seats and its leader Leekpai heads coalition government with other NDF parties
- 1995 Leekpai government brought down over land reform scandal – after election Banharn Silpa-archa heads new coalition government
- 1996 Banharn government falls apart amid accusations of corruption and inefficiency – after another election Chavalit heads new coalition government.

Demographic indicators

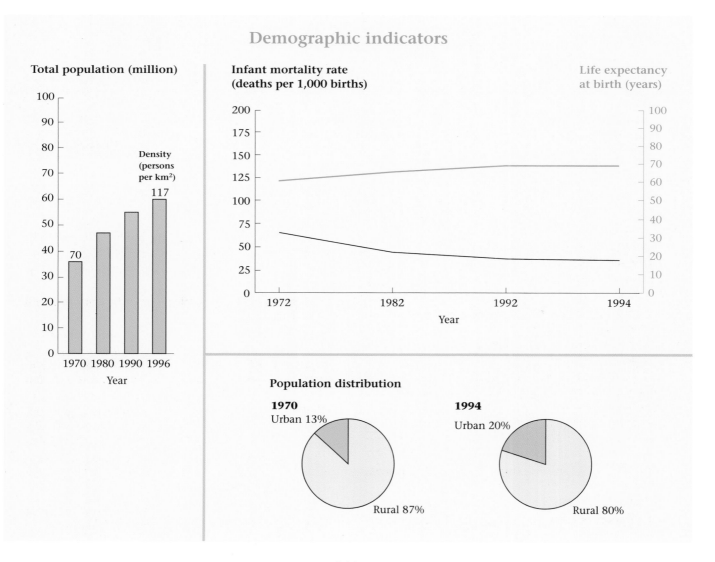

Total population (million)

Density (persons per km²)

117

70

1970 1980 1990 1996
Year

Infant mortality rate (deaths per 1,000 births)

Life expectancy at birth (years)

1972 1982 1992 1994
Year

Population distribution

1970
Urban 13%
Rural 87%

1994
Urban 20%
Rural 80%

Thailand

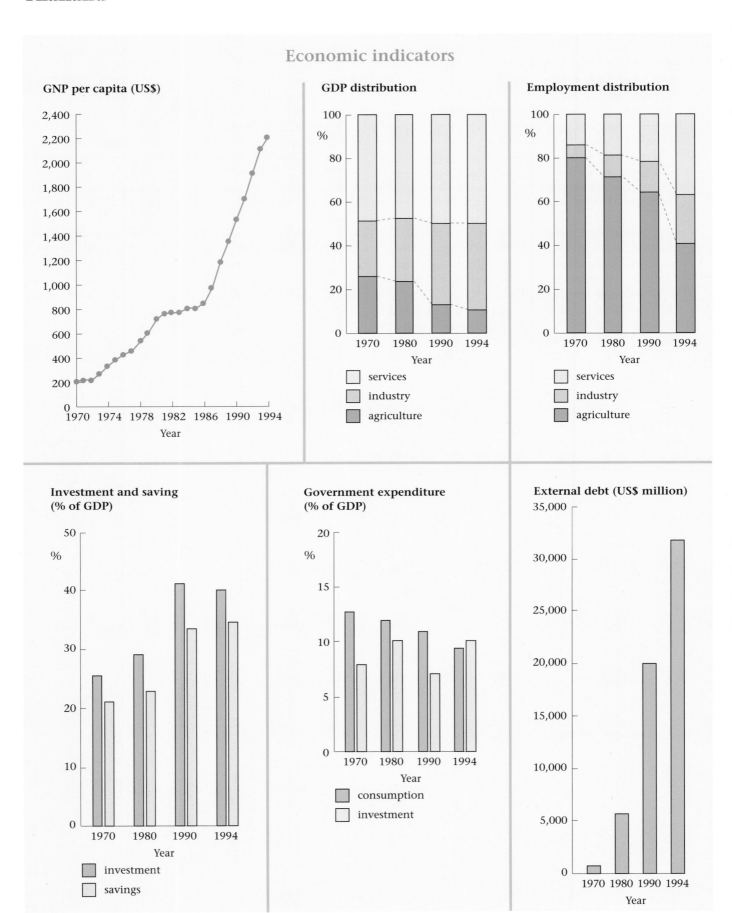

Economic indicators

GNP per capita (US$)

GDP distribution

Employment distribution

Investment and saving (% of GDP)

Government expenditure (% of GDP)

External debt (US$ million)

Exports and imports (% of GDP)

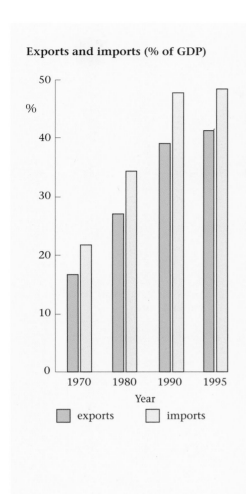

Trade partners: exports

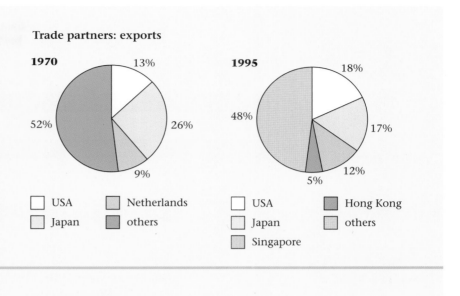

1970

- USA
- Japan
- Netherlands
- others

1995

- USA
- Japan
- Singapore
- Hong Kong
- others

Trade partners: imports

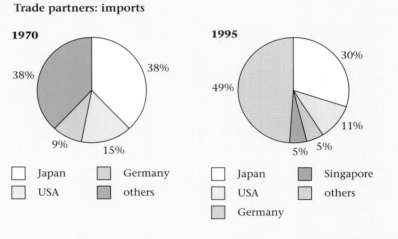

1970

- Japan
- USA
- Germany
- others

1995

- Japan
- USA
- Germany
- Singapore
- others

Export commodities

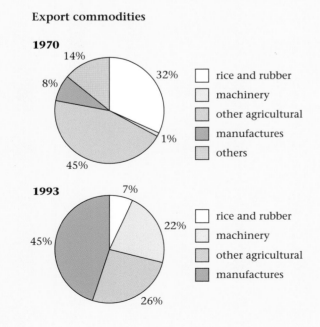

1970

- rice and rubber
- machinery
- other agricultural
- manufactures
- others

1993

- rice and rubber
- machinery
- other agricultural
- manufactures

Import commodities

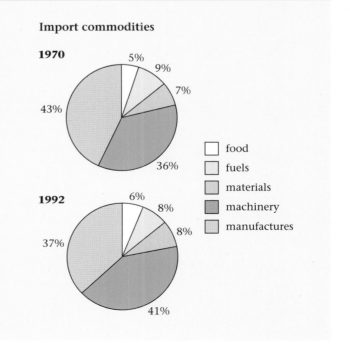

1970

1992

- food
- fuels
- materials
- machinery
- manufactures

Thailand

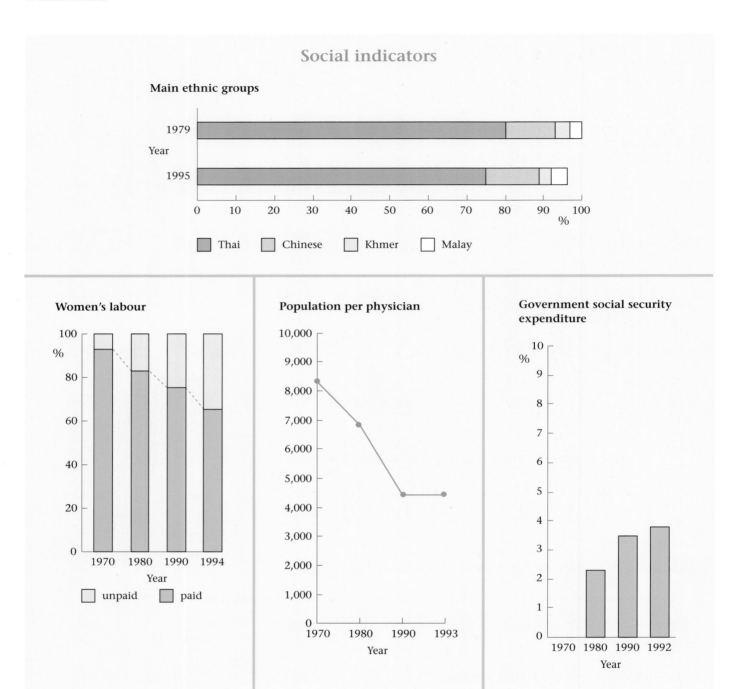

Social indicators

Main ethnic groups

1979

Year

1995

0   10   20   30   40   50   60   70   80   90   100
%

■ Thai   ■ Chinese   □ Khmer   □ Malay

Women's labour

100
%
80
60
40
20
0
1970   1980   1990   1994
Year

□ unpaid   ■ paid

Population per physician

10,000
9,000
8,000
7,000
6,000
5,000
4,000
3,000
2,000
1,000
0
1970   1980   1990   1993
Year

Government social security expenditure

10
%
9
8
7
6
5
4
3
2
1
0
1970   1980   1990   1992
Year

Political framework

- Despite escaping Western colonization political scene dominated by unelected military governments since the country was renamed Thailand in 1939
- 1991 constitution aimed to stabilize a more democratic polity in a National Assembly divided into
  - House of Representatives with 360 elected members
  - 270 member Senate appointed by the King on the PM's recommendation
  - Council of Ministers (Cabinet) led by the PM
- But inconclusive elections and numerous corruption scandals leave citizens weary and disillusioned with politics
- Voter apathy may explain why 1996 election was reported as the most corrupt ever with extensive evidence of candidates bribing voters
- New PM Chavalit achieved a majority of only two seats over ex-PM Banharn and is forced into a complex coalition with five other parties
- Uncertainty over the reaction of the military to the constant flux in civilian politics mitigated by Chavalit's background
- As a former army commander and later Defence Minister with a record of supporting defence expenditure he consolidates allies among those whose promotion he guided
- Chavalit surprisingly gets muted military response to defence cuts in 1997 public expenditure plans
- Chavalit pledges of strong leadership mixing his military and civilian political experience may even confirm that direct military involvement in politics less likely
- Chavalit's leadership style seen when army supreme commander becomes head of Mass Communication Authority and in aggressive campaigns against drug traders
- But this governing style fuels concern over civil rights guarantees that Thailand gained only recently
- Chavalit's military credentials also likely to lead to less friction with neighbouring states of Burma/Myanmar, Laos and Cambodia
- Bangkok hosted 1995 ASEAN summit to consider application of these states for full membership but previous Thai government questioned their commitment to human rights – especially of SLORC regime in Burma/Myanmar
- Chavalit unlikely to follow this line which may also mitigate concern among neighbouring states that Thai companies dominate too much of their economies
- Chavalit's call for political stability through strong leadership in Thailand involves proposals for guaranteed four-year government terms in 1999 constitutional revision. Opposition parties therefore express concern that price of stability may be less accountability.

Further reading

Keyes, C.F. (1994) *Thailand: Buddhist Kingdom to Modern Nation State*, Honolulu, University of Hawaii Press.

Pasuk Phongpaichit and Baker, C. (1995) *Thailand. Economy and Politics*, Kuala Lumpur, Oxford University Press.

Stove, J.A. (1991) *Siam Becomes Thailand*, London, Hurst & Co.

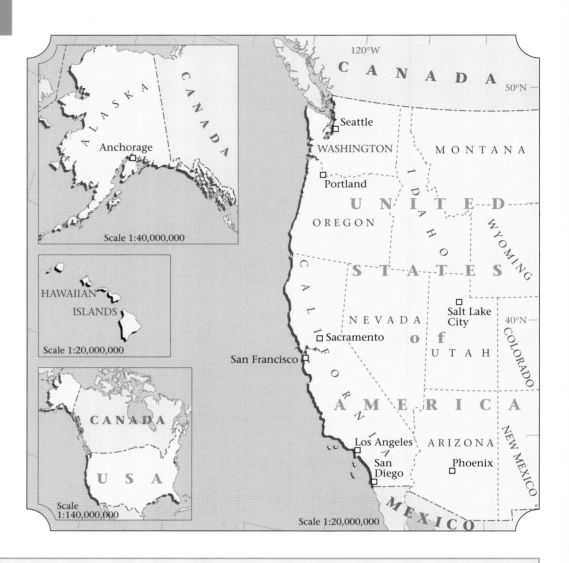

Historical background

- Native Americans arrive most probably between 30,000–40,000 years ago by way of the Bering Strait into present-day Alaska

- 15th C. Native American population estimated at 1.5 million

- 1492 after the 'discovery' of the New World by Christopher Columbus Spanish colonies established in Florida and New Mexico

- 1607 first British settlement in North America established at Jamestown in Virginia

- 1763 the end of the Seven Year War with France establishes British dominance in North America. Thirteen British colonies created by that date

- 1776 American colonists issue Declaration of Independence from Britain

- 1783 War of Independence successfully concluded against Britain

- 1787 American constitution drafted in Philadelphia

- 1789 George Washington elected first President

- 1803 President Thomas Jefferson decisively encourages the westward expansion of the nation through the purchase of the Louisiana Territories from France

- 1823 President James Monroe announces that the USA will oppose the creation of any further European colonization of the western hemisphere. This 'Monroe Doctrine' thereafter becomes basis for regular US intervention in Central and South American affairs

- 1845 doctrine of 'Manifest Destiny' used to provide a rationale for the westward expansion of the USA to the Pacific Ocean

- 1848 Mexico cedes California and other territories to the USA at the end of a two-year war – California joins the Union as a state in 1860

- 1853 US naval force under Commodore Perry arrives in Japan to develop a new relationship between the two countries

- 1861–65 American Civil War ends slavery and any doubts over the supremacy of the federal government in Washington

- 1867 Alaska purchased from Russia
- 1882 US Congress bans Chinese immigration
- 1898 Hawaii annexed
- 1898 Spanish–American War results in Spain ceding the Philippines to the USA
- 1900 US troops sent to suppress Boxer Rebellion in China
- 1917 USA enters the First World War
- 1920 US Senate rejects the League of Nations. Over the next two decades the USA adopts a more isolationist stance in the conduct of foreign policy
- 1941 America enters Second World War after Japan attacks the US naval base at Pearl Harbor, Hawaii
- 1945 USA becomes a founder member of the United Nations
- 1945 uses the 'atom bomb' to destroy the Japanese cities of Hiroshima and Nagasaki. Japan surrenders and a seven-year US occupation begins
- 1949 the USA helps to found the North Atlantic Treaty Organization (NATO)

- 1950 Korean War begins bringing the USA and China into direct military conflict
- 1954 USA creates the South-East Asia Treaty Organization (SEATO) to resist the 'spread of communism' in Asia
- 1961 American military 'advisers' sent to South Vietnam
- 1965 US ground troops are committed to the Vietnam War
- 1972 US government recognizes China
- 1975 war in Vietnam ends in victory for North Vietnam
- 1989 USA joins APEC
- 1994 NAFTA is formed linking Canada, Mexico and the USA in a free trading area – expectations raised in South America of wider membership within a decade.

Demographic indicators

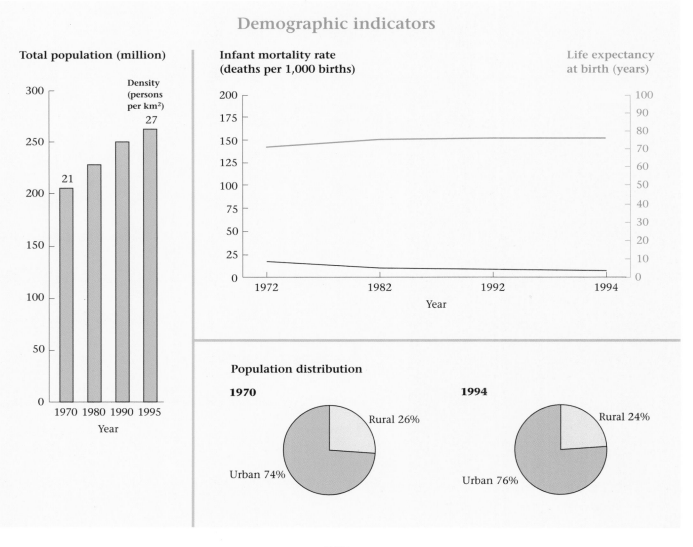

Total population (million)

Density (persons per km²)

Infant mortality rate (deaths per 1,000 births)

Life expectancy at birth (years)

Population distribution

1970
Rural 26%
Urban 74%

1994
Rural 24%
Urban 76%

United States of America

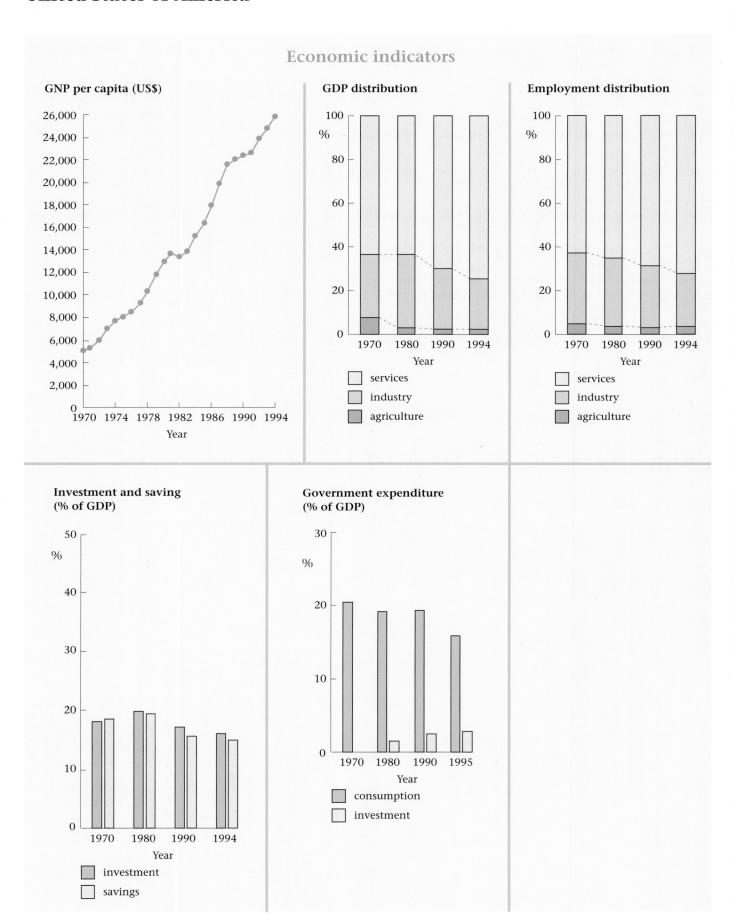

Economic indicators

GNP per capita (US$)

GDP distribution

services
industry
agriculture

Employment distribution

services
industry
agriculture

Investment and saving (% of GDP)

investment
savings

Government expenditure (% of GDP)

consumption
investment

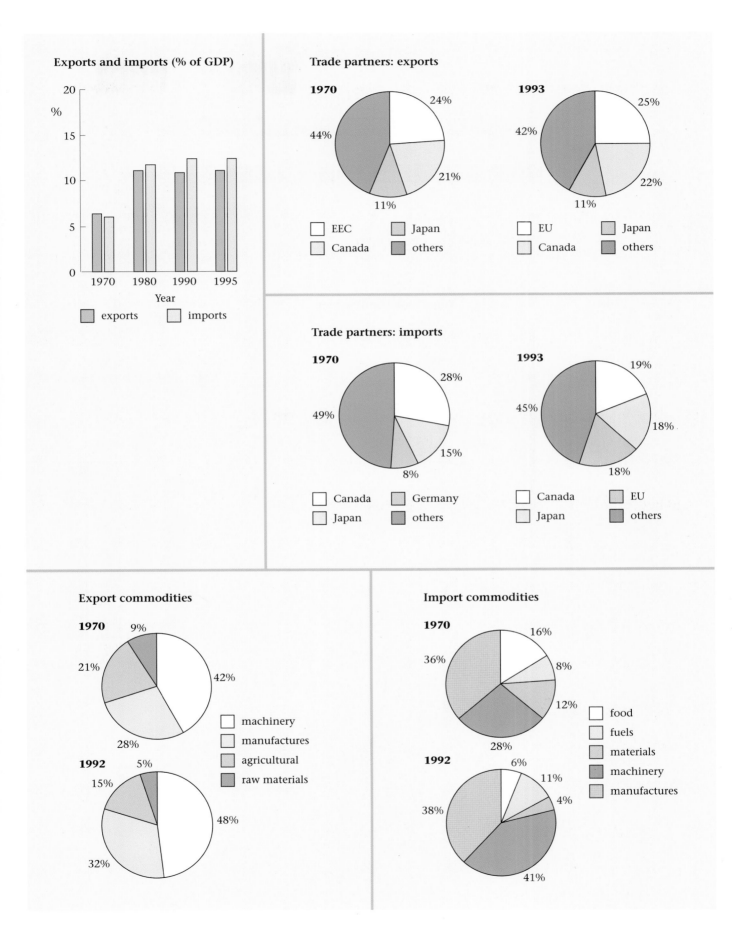

Exports and imports (% of GDP)

Trade partners: exports

1970
- 24% EEC
- 21% Japan
- 11% Canada
- 44% others

1993
- 25% EU
- 22% Japan
- 11% Canada
- 42% others

Trade partners: imports

1970
- 28% Canada
- 15% Japan
- 8% Germany
- 49% others

1993
- 19% Canada
- 18% Japan
- 18% EU
- 45% others

Export commodities

1970
- 42% machinery
- 28% manufactures
- 21% agricultural
- 9% raw materials

1992
- 48% machinery
- 32% manufactures
- 15% agricultural
- 5% raw materials

Import commodities

1970
- 16% food
- 8% fuels
- 12% materials
- 28% machinery
- 36% manufactures

1992
- 6% food
- 11% fuels
- 4% materials
- 41% machinery
- 38% manufactures

United States of America

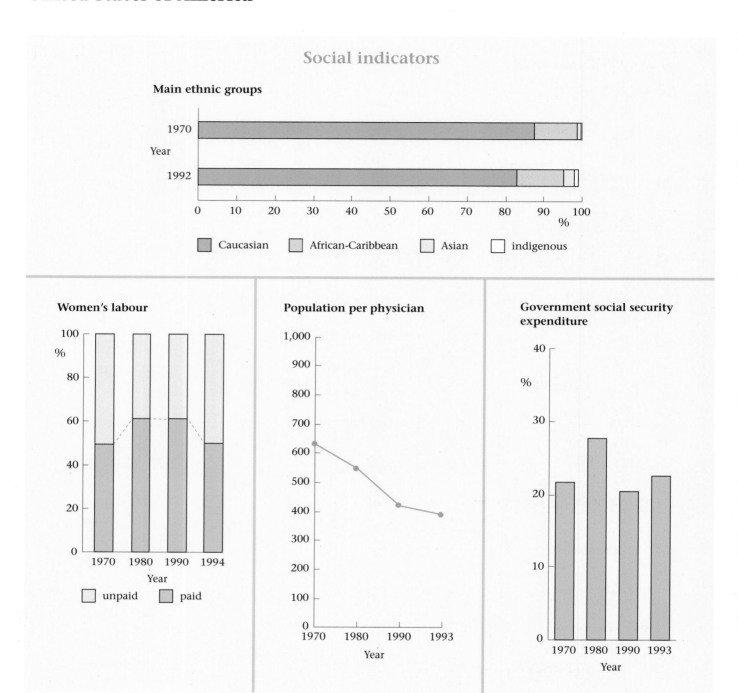

Social indicators

Main ethnic groups

Year

1970

1992

0 10 20 30 40 50 60 70 80 90 100
%

■ Caucasian ■ African-Caribbean □ Asian □ indigenous

Women's labour

%

100

80

60

40

20

0

1970 1980 1990 1994
Year

□ unpaid ■ paid

Population per physician

1,000

900

800

700

600

500

400

300

200

100

0

1970 1980 1990 1993
Year

Government social security expenditure

%

40

30

20

10

0

1970 1980 1990 1993
Year

Political framework

- The United States of America has one of the most distinctive, complex and enduring political systems. It is a model that has been widely emulated and admired although in recent years its advantages are not quite so apparent

- The American constitution was written in 1787 but only 26 amendments have been adopted over the past 200 years. As a result the USA will have to deal with the problems of the early twenty-first century through a set of political institutions that continues to display many of the concerns and philosophical beliefs of the eighteenth century

- The American constitutional structure was designed to prevent government from acting decisively and quickly and in this respect it has been a success

- The combination of federalism, separation of powers plus checks and balances has produced a political process that is frequently characterized by 'gridlock', or an apparent inability to deal with some of the most pressing economic and social problems that confront the nation

- In recent years the conflict between the two major parties, Democrats and Republicans, and between the President and Congress has seen a number of issues, including the federal budget deficit, urban decay and welfare being the subject of continuous and increasingly bitter partisan debate but without achieving a consensual resolution

- The American electorate are increasingly disenchanted with politicians, the institutions of government and the very activity of politics

- After the end of the Cold War, the focus of the polity has shifted from international to domestic affairs. Security and defence issues have been replaced by economic concerns at the top of the political agenda

- Trade, trade deficits and economic competitiveness are matters that worry voters

- The Asia-Pacific is both a source of concern, as the site of America's principal competitors, as well as a potential source of the nation's future prosperity because this region is the most dynamic component of the global economy.

Further reading

Destler, I.M. (1995) *American Trade Politics*, Washington, International Institute of Economics.

Shafer, B. (ed.) (1990) *Is America Different?*, Oxford, Clarendon Press.

Vallado, A.G.A. (1996) *The Twenty First Century Will Be American*, London, Verso.

Vietnam

Historical background

- Chinese rule for several centuries to AD 937
- 1009–1225 Viet Nam (Dai Viet) dynasty of Ly
- 1225–1400 Tran dynasty
- 1427 two further decades of Chinese rule ended by Le dynasty
- 17th C. country divided into rival clan dynasties: Trinh in the north and Nguyen in central Vietnam
- 1802 country reunified under Nguyen dynasty
- 1858-83 French progressively colonize country
- 1887 France places Vietnam and Cambodia into Union of Indo-China
- 1930 Ho Chi Minh founds Communist Party of Indo-China
- 1941–45 Japanese occupation – Vietnam administered by Vichy French
- August 1945 Ho Chi Minh declares independence and becomes President
- August 1945 Potsdam Conference divides country between China in north and Britain in south
- Early 1946 French take over British part of Vietnam and Chinese agree to hand over the north
- January 1946 National Assembly elections in the north – Ho's Viet Minh party dominate coalition government
- 1947–49 Viet Minh fail to remove French – forced to take anti-colonial struggle into rural areas
- 1949 Associated State of Vietnam formed by anti-communist parties with French support
- Early 1950s Cold War divisions: Democratic Republic of Vietnam in the north supported by USSR and PRC; Associated State of Vietnam supported by France and USA
- 1954 Geneva Conference on Indo-China begins – eventually divides country north and south into Democratic Republic and the State of Vietnam
- May 1954 French defeated at Dien Bien Phu – independence conceded
- 1955 Diem proclaims himself President of the Republic of Vietnam in the south
- 1960 National Front for the Liberation of South Vietnam

212

(NLF) unites communists against Diem

- 1961–62 US troops sent to assist Diem government
- 1963 Diem killed in military coup – communists continue to battle with the South Vietnamese government and USA pledges further support to the south
- 1965–75 General Thieu's military government rules in the south – but even with 500,000 US troops backed by protracted US air bombing communists undefeated
- 1969 Ho Chi Minh dies
- 1973 Paris cease-fire agreement leads to complete US withdrawal and eventual defeat of South Vietnamese government
- 1976 country reunified as Socialist Republic of Vietnam
- 1978 Vietnam invades Cambodia
- Early 1979 border clashes in Cambodia between Vietnam and PRC – flight of ethnic Chinese refugees
- July 1979 UN organizes refugee programme for so-called 'boat people' travelling mainly to Hong Kong and ASEAN countries

- 1985 Vietnam announces withdrawal from Cambodia by 1990
- 1986–87 agreements signed to return US Missing in Action soldiers (MIAs)
- 1987–88 government begin reform programme of political liberalization and shift towards more market-oriented economy
- 1989 UN brokers agreement for repatriation of 100,000 refugees
- April 1992 new constitution increases powers of National Assembly but Communist Party remains dominant – Vo Van Kiet confirmed PM
- July 1992 Vietnam granted ASEAN observer status
- 1993 USA ceases opposition to Vietnam receiving loans from IMF, World Bank and Asian Development Bank
- 1994 USA lifts trade embargo
- 1995 Vietnam becomes full member of ASEAN.

Demographic indicators

Total population (million)

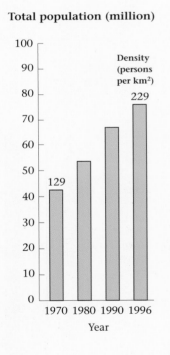

Infant mortality rate (deaths per 1,000 births)

Life expectancy at birth (years)

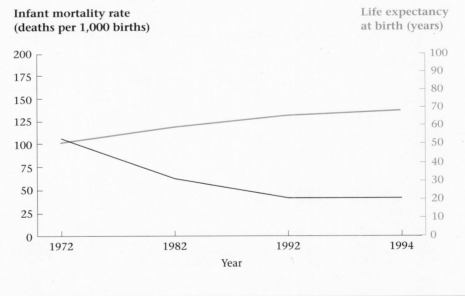

Population distribution

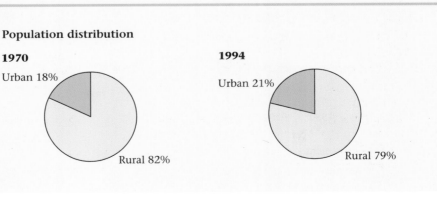

Vietnam

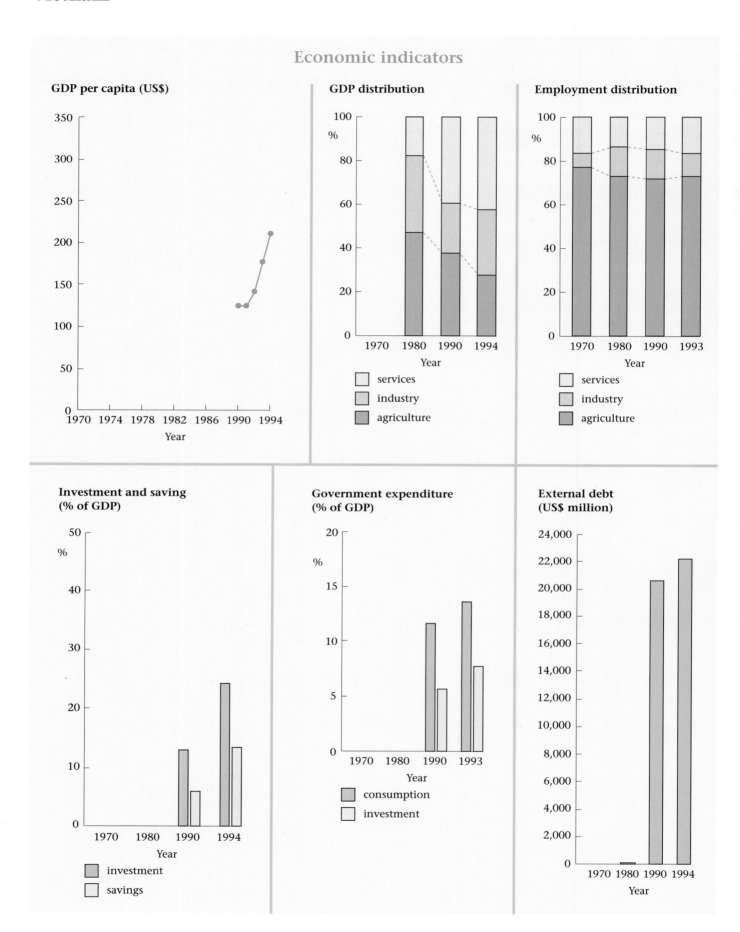

Economic indicators

GDP per capita (US$)

GDP distribution

services
industry
agriculture

Employment distribution

services
industry
agriculture

Investment and saving (% of GDP)

investment
savings

Government expenditure (% of GDP)

consumption
investment

External debt (US$ million)

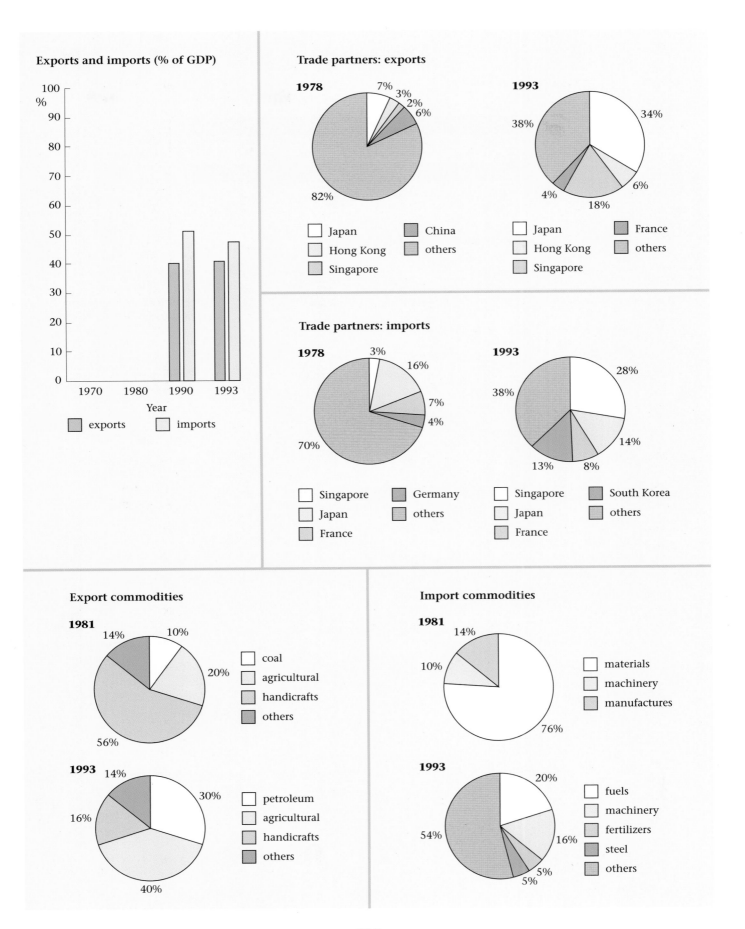

Exports and imports (% of GDP)

Trade partners: exports

1978
- 7%
- 3%
- 2%
- 6%
- 82%

1993
- 34%
- 6%
- 18%
- 4%
- 38%

Japan · China
Hong Kong · others
Singapore

Japan · France
Hong Kong · others
Singapore

exports · imports

Trade partners: imports

1978
- 3%
- 16%
- 7%
- 4%
- 70%

1993
- 28%
- 14%
- 8%
- 13%
- 38%

Singapore · Germany
Japan · others
France

Singapore · South Korea
Japan · others
France

Export commodities

1981
- 14%
- 10%
- 20%
- 56%

coal
agricultural
handicrafts
others

1993
- 14%
- 30%
- 16%
- 40%

petroleum
agricultural
handicrafts
others

Import commodities

1981
- 14%
- 10%
- 76%

materials
machinery
manufactures

1993
- 20%
- 16%
- 5%
- 5%
- 54%

fuels
machinery
fertilizers
steel
others

Vietnam

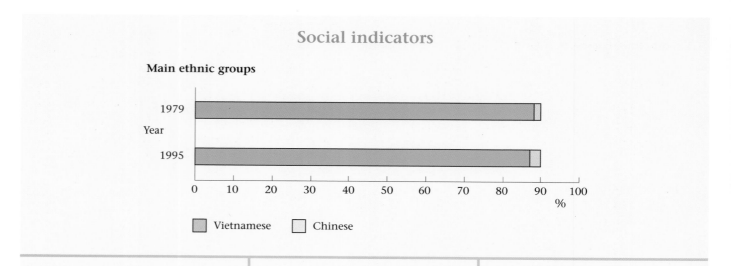

Social indicators

Main ethnic groups

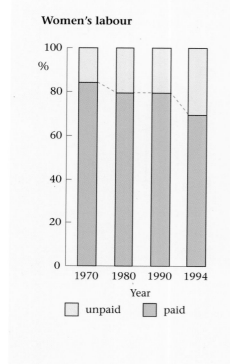

Women's labour

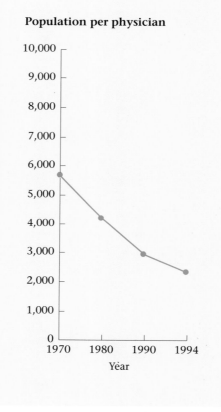

Population per physician

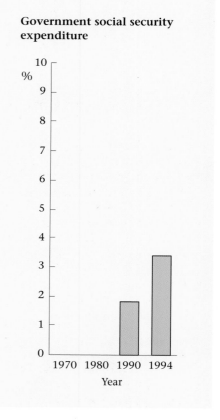

Government social security expenditure

Political framework

- 1992 constitution confirms dominance of Communist Party of Vietnam (CPV) at same time as attempting to increase power of an elected National Assembly that ratifies appointment of PM and government

- Political liberalization since later 1980s continues to emphasize CPV primacy in setting policy goals but government to have clearer responsibility for policy implementation subject to National Assembly scrutiny

- Liberalization excludes acceptance of political organizations independent of CPV – rather liberalization seen as an attempt by political elite to increase internal democracy within state institutions

- Political leadership steer liberalization from the top as response to dire economic performance, reconstruction problems following 40 years of war, loss of aid from USSR and continuing US economic blockade

- In parallel goes shift from centrally planned economy in *doi moi* reforms that dismantle price and foreign exchange controls and allow legal recognition of private business

- Despite significant role remaining for state companies that control nearly half of national output, international organizations like IMF/World Bank generally impressed by anti-inflationary economic policies. IMF and ASEAN partners lead substantial foreign investment despite complex government regulations

- Internal political divisions remain, however, on the extent of Vietnam's political and economic liberalization

- Before, during and after the 1996 8th CPV Congress continuing struggles highlighted between CPV factions, the military, government bureaucrats and reform economists over policy options

- Divisions centre on
  - impact of reform policies on future of less efficient state companies
  - whether increased foreign investment is really benefiting Vietnam
  - dangers of market economy for the social fabric as sex industries grow rapidly alongside more revelations of corruption

- Although position of reformist PM Kiet confirmed by the 1996 CPV Congress, he has to pledge continuation of careful foreign investment screening and address worries over social evils associated with market reforms.

Further reading

Porter, G. (1993) *Vietnam – the Politics of Bureaucratic Socialism*, Ithaca, Cornell University Press.

Turley, W.S. and Selden, M. (eds) (1993) *Reinventing Vietnamese Socialism: Doi Moi in Comparative Perspective*, Boulder, Westview Press.

Vu Tuan Anh (1994) *Development in Vietnam: Policy Reforms and Economic Growth*, Singapore, Institute of South-East Asian Studies.

Appendix A: data for figures in Part 2

Demographic indicators

Table A.1 *Total population and population density*

| | Total population (millions) | | | | | Population density (people per km²) | | |
	1970	1980	1990	1995	1996	1970	1995	1996
Australia	12.5	14.6	16.9		18.3	1.6		2.4
Burma/Myanmar	27.1	33.8	41.8		47.5	40		70
Cambodia	6.9	6.5	8.8		10.5	38		58
Canada	21.3	24.6	27.8	29.6		2.1	2.9	
Chile	9.5	11.1	13.2	14.2		13	19	
China	818.3	981.2	1,135.2		1,234.0	86		129
Colombia	21.4	26.5	33.3	35.1		19	31	
Costa Rica	1.7	2.3	3.0	3.4		34	68	
Ecuador	6.0	8.0	10.3	11.8		21	42	
El Salvador	3.6	4.5	5.2	5.8		171	274	
Guatemala	5.2	6.9	9.2	10.6		48	96	
Honduras	2.6	3.6	4.9	6.0		23	55	
Hong Kong	3.9	5.0	5.7		6.3	3,790		5,905
Indonesia	120.3	151.0	178.1		198.6	63		104
Japan	104.3	116.8	123.5		125.4	276		332
Korea, N.	14.6	18.3	21.8		24.3	121		202
Korea, S.	31.9	38.1	42.9		45.3	322		458
Laos	2.7	3.2	4.2		5.0	12		21
Malaysia	10.9	13.8	17.7		20.6	33		62
Mexico	50.5	67.1	84.5	93.7		26	48	
New Zealand	2.8	3.1	3.4		3.6	10		13
Nicaragua	2.1	2.8	3.7	4.4		16	34	
Panama	1.5	2.0	2.4	2.7		20	34	
PNG	2.4	3.1	3.8		4.4	5		10
Peru	13.2	17.3	21.6	23.9		10	19	
Philippines	37.5	48.3	60.8		68.9	125		230
Singapore	2.1	2.4	2.7		3.1	3,347		4,929
Taiwan	14.7	17.8	20.4	21.7		408	592	
Thailand	35.7	46.7	55.2		60.0	70		117
USA	205.1	227.8	249.9	263.1		21	27	
Vietnam	42.7	53.7	66.7		76.0	129		229

Source: *World Data* (1995) CD-ROM Social Indicators Stack, Washington DC, World Bank; *Taiwan Statistical Data Book* (1996) Taipei, Council for Economic Planning and Development; *Asia-Pacific Population Data Sheet* (1996) Bangkok, UN.

Table A.2 *Infant mortality and life expectancy*

	Infant mortality rate per 1,000 live births				Life expectancy at birth (years)			
	1972	*1982*	*1992*	*1994*	*1972*	*1982*	*1992*	*1994*
Australia	17	10	7	6	72	75	78	78
Burma/Myanmar	122	106	84	80	50	53	58	58
Cambodia	181	160	116	112	40	47	52	52
Canada	16	9	7	6	73	76	77	78
Chile	69	24	16	12	64	71	74	75
China	61	39	31	30	63	68	69	69
Colombia	73	41	37	20	62	67	69	70
Costa Rica	53	19	14	13	68	74	76	76
Ecuador	95	68	50	37	59	65	69	69
El Salvador	99	77	46	42	59	57	66	67
Guatemala	95	70	48	44	54	59	65	65
Honduras	104	65	43	47	54	62	68	68
Hong Kong	17	10	7	5	72	75	79	79
Indonesia	114	90	58	53	49	56	63	63
Japan	12	7	4	4	73	77	79	80
Korea, N.	47	30	24	24	62	68	71	71
Korea, S.	38	23	11	12	63	67	71	71
Laos	145	122	97	92	40	46	51	52
Malaysia	42	28	13	12	63	68	71	71
Mexico	68	49	36	35	63	68	71	71
New Zealand	16	12	9	7	72	74	76	76
Nicaragua	100	86	52	51	55	59	67	67
Panama	43	30	25	20	67	71	73	73
PNG	100	72	68	65	48	52	56	56
Peru	110	82	64	48	56	60	66	66
Philippines	71	60	44	40	58	62	66	65
Singapore	19	10	6	5	70	72	75	75
Taiwan	16	9	6	6	70	72	74	76
Thailand	65	44	37	36	60	65	69	69
USA	18	11	9	8	71	75	76	76
Vietnam	106	63	42	42	50	59	65	68

Source: *World Data* (1995) CD-ROM Social Indicators Stack, Washington DC, World Bank; *Taiwan Statistical Data Book* (1996) Taipei, Council for Economic Planning and Development.

Table A.3 *Population distribution (%)*

	1970		1994	
	Rural	Urban	Rural	Urban
Australia	14	86	15	85
Burma/Myanmar	77	23	76	24
Cambodia	88	12	86	14
Canada	24	76	23	77
Chile	25	75	14	86
China	83	17	72	28
Colombia	43	57	28	72
Costa Rica	59	41	51	49
Ecuador	60	40	42	58
El Salvador	61	39	55	45
Guatemala	63	37	59	41
Honduras	73	27	53	47
Hong Kong	10	90	5	95
Indonesia	83	17	66	34
Japan	29	71	22	78
Korea, N.	47	53	39	61
Korea, S.	59	41	22	78
Laos	89	11	80	20
Malaysia	67	33	47	53
Mexico	41	59	25	75
New Zealand	18	82	14	86
Nicaragua	52	48	38	62
Panama	53	47	46	54
PNG	92	8	84	16
Peru	42	58	28	72
Philippines	67	33	47	53
Singapore	0	100	0	100
Taiwan	56	44	44	56
Thailand	87	13	80	20
USA	26	74	24	76
Vietnam	82	18	79	21

Source: *World Data* (1995) CD-ROM Social Indicators Stack, Washington DC, World Bank; *Taiwan Statistical Data Book* (1996) Taipei, Council for Economic Planning and Development.

Economic indicators

Table A.4 Gross national product per capita (US$)

	1970	1971	1972	1973	1974	1975	1976	1977	1978	1979	1980	1981	1982	1983	1984	1985	1986	1987	1988	1989	1990	1991	1992	1993	1994
Australia	3,100	3,380	3,850	4,970	6,420	7,770	8,080	7,940	8,760	9,710	11,290	12,190	11,670	11,620	11,740	11,380	11,570	12,620	14,840	16,340	17,050	17,340	17,790	17,490	18,000
Burma/Myanmar	79	69	71	41	104	96	113	133	144	160	176	173	173	171	174	176	212	264	302	464	591	712	960	1,267	1,392
Cambodia (GDP)																		256	227	177	167	216	221	207	237
Canada	3,850	4,270	4,880	5,850	6,930	7,720	8,450	8,750	9,360	10,140	11,040	11,850	11,400	11,700	12,610	13,260	13,870	15,470	17,700	18,970	19,630	19,990	20,290	19,960	19,510
Chile	830	980	1,110	1,180	1,260	920	910	1,080	1,350	1,760	2,160	2,610	2,200	1,790	1,600	1,410	1,410	1,550	1,800	2,060	2,180	2,390	2,850	3,170	3,560
China											280	290	280	280	310	350	380	390	400	390	410	440	470	490	530
Colombia	340	360	400	460	550	600	630	700	860	1,070	1,270	1,360	1,350	1,300	1,290	1,230	1,220	1,240	1,300	1,250	1,230	1,210	1,300	1,390	1,620
Costa Rica	550	610	680	810	940	1,030	1,100	1,310	1,560	1,830	2,030	1,510	1,080	950	1,120	1,270	1,470	1,650	1,680	1,660	1,730	1,810	2,020	2,160	2,380
Ecuador	300	290	320	400	480	610	720	820	970	1,160	1,370	1,570	1,490	1,280	1,140	1,150	1,190	1,170	1,180	1,040	980	1,050	1,130	1,200	1,310
El Salvador	290	300	320	360	420	470	520	590	710	800	790	770	720	710	750	810	850	940	1,000	1,000	1,030	1,090	1,200	1,320	1,480
Guatemala	360	380	400	460	550	620	700	800	920	1,080	1,200	1,240	1,160	1,100	1,120	1,150	1,060	1,010	970	960	920	940	1,010	1,100	1,190
Honduras	270	280	300	340	370	400	430	480	560	640	700	760	710	690	730	790	830	940	980	870	700	600	600	600	580
Hong Kong	940	1,070	1,310	1,770	2,190	2,480	2,910	3,310	3,850	4,740	5,790	6,470	6,370	5,980	6,210	6,080	7,260	9,120	10,760	11,610	12,670	14,350	16,670	19,010	21,650
Indonesia	80	90	90	120	160	220	270	320	370	410	490	560	590	570	550	520	530	520	520	530	560	610	670	750	790
Japan	1,940	2,130	2,610	3,470	4,260	4,950	5,190	5,720	7,140	9,050	10,440	10,630	10,070	9,760	10,010	10,950	13,210	17,270	23,550	25,450	26,090	26,940	28,770	31,360	34,630
Korea, N.																									
Korea, S.	270	320	340	430	530	640	780	920	1,210	1,580	2,330	2,160	1,890	2,020	2,160	2,260	2,620	3,230	4,110	4,850	5,770	6,670	7,220	7,660	8,220
Laos																			260	220	200	220	250	280	320
Malaysia	390	410	460	600	780	890	950	1,010	1,160	1,470	1,800	1,940	1,860	1,800	1,940	1,910	1,880	1,960	2,130	2,240	2,400	2,530	2,830	3,140	3,520
Mexico	730	790	910	1,090	1,330	1,590	1,670	1,600	1,710	2,040	2,640	3,250	2,840	2,280	2,100	2,180	1,980	1,950	1,990	2,210	2,570	2,990	3,440	3,730	4,010
New Zealand	2,180	2,460	2,930	3,840	4,790	5,020	4,820	4,550	5,080	6,260	7,410	8,070	7,760	7,250	6,990	6,740	7,490	9,220	11,670	12,610	12,870	12,230	12,530	12,600	13,350
Nicaragua	380	400	380	400	580	680	710	780	750	590	690	770	780	790	760	760	800	920	830	430	360	280	340	340	330
Panama	680	740	800	910	1,020	1,140	1,130	1,140	1,320	1,480	1,880	2,030	2,060	2,050	1,800	2,290	2,500	2,560	2,110	1,990	2,040	2,220	2,450	2,600	2,670
PNG	260	280	310	400	500	570	540	550	660	740	810	840	770	720	710	720	770	820	950	950	880	940	1,000	1,180	1,160
Peru	520	570	640	750	940	1,090	1,080	980	850	890	1,040	1,290	1,320	1,040	1,010	900	1,030	1,210	1,050	970	1,000	1,310	1,350	1,490	1,890
Philippines	220	210	210	250	310	370	410	430	490	590	690	750	740	670	580	520	560	610	680	720	750	760	810	850	960
Singapore	940	1,070	1,300	1,710	2,240	2,770	2,860	2,970	3,370	4,060	4,850	5,600	6,010	6,540	7,330	7,350	7,480	8,420	9,820	11,010	12,740	14,730	17,440	20,130	23,360
Taiwan	389	443	522	695	920	964	1,132	1,301	1,577	1,920	2,344	2,669	2,653	2,823	3,167	3,297	3,993	5,298	6,379	7,626	8,111	8,982	10,470	10,852	11,604
Thailand	210	220	220	270	340	390	430	460	540	610	720	770	770	780	810	810	850	980	1,190	1,350	1,530	1,700	1,910	2,110	2,210
USA	4,980	5,340	5,930	6,950	7,630	8,060	8,490	9,180	10,270	11,680	12,820	13,720	13,410	13,780	15,160	16,260	17,850	19,800	21,610	22,050	22,390	22,620	23,850	24,780	25,880
Vietnam (GDP)																					126	125	142	177	212

Source: *World Data* (1995) CD-ROM National Accounts Stack, Washington DC, World Bank; *Taiwan Statistical Data Book* (1996) Taipei, Council for Economic Planning and Development; *Key Indicators of Developing Asian and Pacific Countries* (1995) Manila, Asian Development Bank.

Table A.5 *External debt (US$ million)*

	1970	1980	1990	1994
Burma/Myanmar	106	1,390	4,444	6,099
Cambodia		112	1,721	1,774
Chile	2,568	9,399	14,689	17,618
China		4,504	45,397	85,137
Colombia	1,580	4,604	15,793	14,615
Costa Rica	246	2,112	3,380	3,383
Ecuador	243	4,422	10,030	10,608
El Salvador	176	659	1,938	2,002
Guatemala	120	831	2,367	2,529
Honduras	111	1,166	3,483	3,984
Indonesia	2,958	18,169	58,326	79,391
Korea, S.	1,991	18,236	24,187	40,652
Laos	8	333	1,758	2,022
Malaysia	440	5,256	14,173	18,578
Mexico	5,966	41,215	83,393	92,843
Nicaragua	147	1,671	8,245	9,006
Panama	194	2,271	3,988	3,923
PNG	209	624	2,440	2,764
Peru	2,655	6,828	13,964	18,149
Philippines	1,544	8,817	25,274	32,522
Thailand	726	5,646	19,941	31,812
Vietnam		6	20,600	22,226

Source: *World Data* (1995) CD-ROM External Debt no.1 Stack, Washington DC, World Bank; *World Development Report* (1996) Washington DC, World Bank; *World Debt Tables* (1996) Washington DC, World Bank.

Table A.6 *Gross domestic product distribution (%). Ag: agriculture; Ind: industry; Ser: ser*

	1970			1980			1990			1994		
	Ag	Ind	Ser	Ag	Ind	Ser	Ag	Ind	Ser	Ag	Ind	Ser
Australia	5.8	39.0	55.2	5.3	36.5	58.2	3.4	30.8	65.8	3.0	30.0	67.0
Burma/Myanmar	38.0	14.2	47.8	46.5	12.7	40.8	57.3	10.5	32.2	62.9	9.1	28.0
Cambodia							55.6	11.2	33.2	45.0	18.0	37.0
Canada	4.4	36.3	59.3	4.2	36.2	59.6	2.5	31.8	65.7	3.1	30.7	66.2
Chile	6.6	40.2	53.2	7.2	37.3	55.5				9.0	36.2	54.8
China	34.1	38.3	27.6	30.4	49.0	20.6	27.0	41.6	31.4	18.8	48.5	32.7
Colombia	25.1	27.6	47.3	19.4	31.6	49.0	16.2	36.7	47.1	14.0	32.0	54.0
Costa Rica	22.5	24.2	53.3	17.8	27.0	55.2	15.8	25.7	58.5	16.0	25.6	58.4
Ecuador	24.0	24.6	51.4	12.1	38.1	49.8	13.4	38.0	48.6	12.0	38.0	50.0
El Salvador	28.4	23.3	48.3	27.8	20.7	51.5	11.2	23.3	65.5	14.0	24.0	62.0
Guatemala							26.1	19.5	54.4	24.6	19.2	56.2
Honduras	32.4	22.2	45.4	23.7	24.3	52.0	22.4	26.4	51.2	20.0	32.0	48.0
Hong Kong	1.7	35.6	62.7	0.8	31.4	67.8	0.3	25.6	74.1	0.1	18.1	81.8
Indonesia	44.9	18.7	36.4	24.0	41.7	34.3	21.6	39.4	39.0	17.4	40.7	41.9
Japan	6.1	46.7	47.2	3.7	41.9	54.4	2.5	42.0	55.5	2.0	40.0	58.0
Korea, N.												
Korea, S.	25.4	28.7	45.9	14.5	40.4	45.1	8.7	43.4	47.9	7.0	43.0	50.0
Laos				54.0	18.0	28.0	61.0	12.0	27.0	51.0	18.0	31.0
Malaysia	28.5	25.2	46.3	21.9	37.8	40.3	19.0	43.0	38.0	14.4	45.3	40.3
Mexico	11.6	29.4	59.0	8.2	32.7	59.1	8.0	30.7	61.3	8.0	28.0	64.0
New Zealand	11.0	31.0	58.0	10.8	31.3	57.9	7.4	26.0	66.6	7.3	25.9	66.8
Nicaragua	25.3	25.6	49.1	23.2	31.4	45.4	31.1	21.2	47.7	33.0	20.0	47.0
Panama	14.2	21.6	64.2	9.9	20.5	69.6	11.0	14.4	74.6	10.3	14.8	74.9
PNG	37.2	22.1	40.7	33.1	26.8	40.1	29.0	30.4	40.6	28.5	38.3	33.2
Peru	18.7	31.6	49.7	10.2	42.0	47.8				10.8	42.4	46.8
Philippines	29.5	31.6	38.9	25.1	38.8	36.1	21.9	34.5	43.6	22.0	32.7	45.3
Singapore	2.3	29.7	68.0	1.3	38.1	60.6	0.3	37.0	62.7	0.2	36.1	63.7
Taiwan	15.5	36.8	47.7	7.7	45.7	46.6	4.2	41.2	54.6	3.6	37.3	59.1
Thailand	25.9	25.3	48.8	23.2	28.7	48.1	12.7	37.0	50.3	10.4	39.4	50.2
USA	7.3	28.7	64.0	2.5	33.5	64.0	2.1	28.0	69.9	1.9	23.4	74.7
Vietnam				47.0	35.0	18.0	37.5	22.7	39.8	27.7	29.6	42.7

Source: *World Data* (1995) CD-ROM National Accounts Stack, Washington DC, World Bank; *Taiwan Statistical Data Book* (1996) Taipei, Council for Economic Planning and Development; *Key Indicators of Developing Asian and Pacific Countries* (1995) Manila, Asian Development Bank.

Table A.7 *Employment distribution (%). Ag: agriculture; Ind: industry; Ser: services*

	1970			1980			1990			1992			1993			1994		
	Ag	Ind	Ser	Ag	Ind	Ser	Ag	Ind	Ser	Ag	Ind	Ser	Ag	Ind	Ser	Ag	Ind	Ser
Australia	8.1	36.5	55.4	6.9	32.1	61.0	6.0	26.0	68.0				6.0	22.0	72.0			
Burma/Myanmar	59.1	15.6	25.3	76.0	8.0	16.0	73.0	10.0	17.0							69.2	9.3	21.5
Cambodia	78.3	4.2	17.5	74.4	6.7	18.9	70.4	3.0	26.6									
Canada	7.8	30.5	61.7	7.0	33.0	60.0	3.0	25.0	72.0				5.0	28.0	67.0			
Chile	23.2	28.6	48.2	21.0	25.1	53.9	19.0	25.0	56.0							17.5	24.9	57.6
China	78.3	10.1	11.6	74.2	14.0	11.8	72.0	15.0	13.0				58.0	21.0	21.0			
Colombia	39.3	23.3	37.4	40.0	21.0	39.0	27.0	23.0	50.0									
Costa Rica	42.6	20.0	37.4	35.0	23.2	41.8	26.0	27.0	47.0	24.1	26.2	49.7						
Ecuador	50.6	20.5	28.9	38.6	19.9	41.5	33.0	19.0	48.0									
El Salvador	56.0	14.4	29.6	43.2	19.4	37.4	36.0	21.0	43.0	35.8	22.7	41.5						
Guatemala	61.3	17.0	21.7	56.8	17.0	26.2	52.0	17.0	31.0									
Honduras	64.9	14.1	21.0	60.5	16.2	23.3	41.0	20.0	39.0	37.4	19.1	43.5						
Hong Kong	4.2	51.8	44.0	1.9	47.6	50.5	0.9	37.0	62.1				0.6	30.1	69.3			
Indonesia	66.3	10.3	23.4	57.2	13.1	29.7	55.4	14.0	30.6							45.0	17.0	38.0
Japan	19.6	34.5	45.9	11.2	34.3	54.5	7.1	34.0	58.9							5.7	32.9	61.4
Korea, N.	52.8	25.7	21.5	42.8	30.3	26.9	38.0	31.0	31.0									
Korea, S.	49.1	19.8	31.1	36.4	26.8	36.8	17.5	26.9	55.6							13.3	23.3	63.4
Laos	78.9	5.2	15.9	75.7	7.1	17.2	78.0	6.0	16.0									
Malaysia	53.8	14.3	31.9	41.6	19.1	39.3	23.0	28.0	49.0							19.9	32.9	47.2
Mexico	44.1	24.3	31.6	36.5	29.0	34.5	28.0	24.0	48.0				26.7	21.1	52.2			
New Zealand	12.9	32.7	54.4	11.1	32.2	56.7	10.3	25.0	64.7							9.8	22.5	67.7
Nicaragua	51.5	15.5	33.0	39.0	24.0	37.0	28.0	26.0	46.0	13.7	21.5	64.8						
Panama	41.6	17.5	40.9	31.7	18.1	50.2	26.0	16.0	58.0				20.6	17.2	62.2			
PNG	86.0	5.0	9.0	82.0	6.0	12.0	79.0	7.0	14.0									
Peru	47.1	17.6	35.3	40.0	18.2	41.8	36.0	18.0	46.0									
Philippines	54.8	16.5	28.7	51.8	15.7	32.5	46.0	15.0	39.0							41.3	14.1	44.6
Singapore	3.4	30.2	66.4	1.6	37.7	60.7	0.3	36.0	63.7							0.2	31.6	68.2
Taiwan	36.7	28.0	35.3	19.5	42.5	38.0	12.9	40.8	46.3							10.9	39.2	49.9
Thailand	79.8	6.0	14.2	70.9	10.3	18.8	64.0	14.0	22.0							40.2	22.6	37.2
USA	4.3	32.5	63.2	3.5	31.0	65.5	3.0	28.0	69.0							3.6	23.8	72.6
Vietnam	76.6	6.5	16.9	73.0	13.0	14.0	71.3	14.0	14.7				72.5	10.7	16.8			

Source: *World Data* (1995) CD-ROM Social Indicators Stack, Washington DC, World Bank; *Taiwan Statistical Data Book* (1996) Taipei, Council for Economic Planning and Development; *Yearbook of Labour Statistics* (1996) Geneva, International Labour Office.

Table A.8 *Investment (I) and saving (S) (% GDP)*

	1970		1980		1990		1994		1995		1996	
	I	S	I	S	I	S	I	S	I	S	I	S
Australia	27.2	27.2	25.4	23.6	21.0	21.0	20.0	19.0	20.4		20.3	
Burma/Myanmar	14.2	10.6	21.5	17.6	13.4	11.2	12.0	11.0	13.2			
Cambodia	12.5	10.5			8.2	2.3	19.2	7.4				
Canada	21.8	24.3	23.6	25.4	20.9	20.6	18.0	18.0	17.3		17.4	
Chile	19.2	19.8	24.6	20.5	26.3	29.7	26.8	28.2	23.2			
China	28.5	28.7	35.0	35.0	33.2	37.3	42.6	45.3				
Colombia	20.2	18.4	19.1	19.7	18.6	24.3	20.1	15.3	20.0			
Costa Rica	20.5	13.8	26.6	16.2	27.3	20.6	27.7	22.9	18.3			
Ecuador	18.2	13.6	26.1	25.9	17.5	22.9	21.0	23.0	18.6			
El Salvador	12.9	13.2	13.3	14.2	11.8	0.7	18.8	3.8	18.8			
Guatemala	12.8	13.6	15.9	13.1	13.6	9.9	16.7	8.1	12.3			
Honduras	20.9	14.7	24.8	17.0	23.0	18.1	25.8	22.1	26.0	14.0	24.3	
Hong Kong	20.5	28.2	35.1	34.1	27.4	35.8	31.1	33.0	31.4			
Indonesia	15.8	13.9	24.3	37.2	31.0	31.5	29.1	30.3	33.3			
Japan	39.0	40.3	32.2	31.4	32.8	33.5	30.0	32.0	28.4		29.9	
Korea, N.												
Korea, S.	24.4	14.8	32.0	24.8	36.9	36.4	38.4	39.2	36.6			
Laos					12.3	−0.8						
Malaysia	22.4	26.6	30.4	32.9	31.5	33.4	38.5	36.9	38.2			
Mexico	21.3	18.7	27.2	24.9	21.9	20.7	22.8	18.2	16.3			
New Zealand	24.6	21.6	20.8	19.6	21.3	20.4	21.0	24.0	21.0		21.8	
Nicaragua	18.4	16.0	16.8	−2.3	19.3	0.8	18.0	−9.0	26.5			
Panama	28.0	24.4	27.5	26.1	17.2	21.3	29.6	22.8				
PNG	41.6	6.1	25.2	15.1	24.4	16.1	15.0	32.0				
Peru	15.5	17.4	29.0	31.4	15.5	16.2	24.0	20.0	23.4		24.1	
Philippines	21.3	21.9	29.1	24.2	24.2	18.4	25.3	17.4	22.3		23.8	
Singapore	38.7	18.4	46.3	37.5	39.5	45.7	32.2	51.1	33.0			
Taiwan	18.2	21.5	36.0	37.9	25.0	33.5	26.1	30.3				
Thailand	25.6	21.2	29.1	22.9	41.1	33.6	40.1	34.5	42.7			
USA	18.1	18.4	19.9	19.3	17.2	15.7	16.0	15.0	17.0		17.3	
Vietnam					13.0	6.0	24.2	13.5				

Source: *World Data* (1995) CD-ROM National Accounts Stack, Washington DC, World Bank; *Taiwan Statistical Data Book* (1996) Taipei, Council for Economic Planning and Development; *Key Indicators of Developing Asian and Pacific Countries* (1995) Manila, Asian Development Bank; *World Development Report* (1996) Washington DC, World Bank; *International Financial Statistics* (Dec. 1996) Washington DC, IMF.

Table A.9 *Government expenditure: consumption (C) and investment (I) (% GDP)*

	1970		1980		1990		1993		1994		1995		1996	
	C	I	C	I	C	I	C	I	C	I	C	I	C	I
Australia	15.4		20.0	1.7	19.9	2.3					17.5	1.9	17.2	
Burma/Myanmar				3.2		4.0				3.2				
Cambodia					7.2				10.0	5.4				
Canada	21.3		21.1	0.3	23.0	2.5					19.4	2.3	19.2	
Chile	13.9		14.2	2.4	8.7	3.6			8.7	4.2	8.8			
China			15.4	20.2	10.3	17.0			12.8	25.8				
Colombia	10.0		10.2	7.8	11.4	8.5			15.8	10.5	12.6			
Costa Rica	14.2		17.6	10.5	19.1	4.9			17.0	3.4	16.8			
Ecuador	12.4	7.5	15.8	10.4	10.0	6.9	6.8	7.7	12.6					
El Salvador	11.6		15.1	2.9	9.9	2.2			8.0	3.5	7.8			
Guatemala	8.5		8.6	6.4	6.9	2.7			6.0	2.7	5.9			
Honduras	12.7	7.2	14.2	10.4	14.5	7.9	13.5	15.6	13.0		9.5			
Hong Kong	7.4	1.8	6.4	5.0	7.8	3.6			8.4	4.0				
Indonesia	8.4		10.9	10.3	9.0	9.9	10.0	10.7	8.0		8.1			
Japan	7.9	5.0	10.4	7.0	9.8	6.6					9.7	8.7	9.6	
Korea, N.														
Korea, S.	11.5	6.8	13.1	8.7	11.4	7.1			10.2	7.7	10.4			
Laos					10.1	1.8	7.0							
Malaysia	17.4	6.7	19.9	14.0	15.2	12.4					14.6	15.1		
Mexico	6.9		10.3	11.6	9.3	5.4					10.4	3.3		
New Zealand	14.8		19.6	2.6	21.8	0.9			15.0	0.9	14.7		15.0	
Nicaragua	10.2		20.1		35.8	12.1			14.4	12.8	13.1			
Panama	16.2		20.5	6.1	20.5	1.4			16.0	3.0	15.4			
PNG	31.6		23.7	10.2	27.8	5.7			15.0	5.6				
Peru	13.3		10.6	7.3	6.8	2.7			9.8	4.5	6.3			
Philippines	10.1		9.3	9.2	11.0	4.6			11.1	5.5	11.2			
Singapore	13.0	6.9	10.3	10.7	11.0	7.2			8.3	8.0	8.5			
Taiwan	15.3	2.4	18.7	5.4	19.2	6.2			16.9	8.3				
Thailand	12.7	7.9	11.9	10.0	10.9	7.1			9.3	10.0	9.7			
USA	20.5		19.1	1.5	19.3	2.5					15.9	2.8	15.9	
Vietnam					11.5	5.6	13.6	7.7	9.0					

Source: *World Data* (1995) CD-ROM National Accounts Stack, Washington DC, World Bank; *Taiwan Statistical Data Book* (1996) Taipei, Council for Economic Planning and Development; *World Development Report* (1996) Washington DC, World Bank; *Key Indicators of Developing Asian and Pacific Countries* (1995) Manila, Asian Development Bank; *Quarterly National Accounts* (March 1996) Paris, OECD; *International Financial Statistics* (Dec. 1996) Washington DC, IMF; *Government Financial Statistics Yearbook* (1996) Washington DC, IMF.

Table A.10 *Exports (X) and imports (M) (% GDP)*

	1970		1980		1990		1993		1994		1995		1996	
	X	M	X	M	X	M	X	M	X	M	X	M	X	M
Australia	15.9	16.0	18.0	20.0	19.8	19.8	21.9	22.4	19.0	20.0	19.6	21.1	20.2	20.5
Burma/Myanmar	5.3	8.8	9.1	12.9	2.6	4.8	2.4	3.2	2.0	3.2	1.2	1.8		
Cambodia					6.1	12.1	14.6	21.5						
Canada	26.1	23.1	31.2	29.2	28.3	29.2	33.8	34.5	30.0		37.4	34.9	38.6	35.4
Chile	16.5	15.4	26.0	30.7	30.5	27.5	23.2	25.2	27.6	23.3	29.3	27.4		
China			12.2	12.4	20.7	16.3	26.2	27.4	24.0	26.0				
Colombia	15.1	17.1	18.0	17.3	22.8	16.4	19.7	24.2	15.2	24.3	16.7	20.2		
Costa Rica	31.7	39.4	30.0	41.7	36.3	43.4			40.0	44.2	40.9	42.1		
Ecuador	15.7	20.8	27.4	27.7	38.0	31.8	29.7	29.0	29.0	26.9	28.8	26.8		
El Salvador	27.0	26.7	36.8	35.8	18.6	31.2	16.4	30.9	20.0	35.2	21.4	37.8		
Guatemala	20.0	19.1	24.0	27.0	22.4	26.2	19.0	27.9	20.4	29.5	19.8	21.6		
Honduras	30.9	37.7	40.5	49.2	39.5	45.0	37.7	47.3	36.0		43.5	48.2		
Hong Kong	99.1	91.1	93.8	94.8	141.5	132.5	149.7	142.4	139.0	137.0				
Indonesia	13.7	15.8	34.2	20.9	26.6	26.0	28.6	26.3	25.0	24.0	26.0	25.2		
Japan	11.5	10.1	14.6	15.5	11.6	10.8	10.3	7.8	9.3	7.2	9.4	8.0	9.6	9.1
Korea, N.														
Korea, S.	15.3	25.8	38.0	46.2	33.6	34.2	33.1	32.6	36.0		33.2	34.2		
Laos					11.3	24.5	21.5	31.2	25.1	40.7	25.7	38.4		
Malaysia	46.6	41.9	69.5	66.4	83.2	81.0	87.9	86.9	97.7	99.4				
Mexico	6.8	9.4	11.6	14.0	17.5	18.8	15.6	16.7	12.7	20.6	24.0	21.2		
New Zealand	29.9	28.3	30.2	34.5	34.7	34.0	35.9	32.5	31.0	28.6	30.5	29.4	30.5	30.5
Nicaragua	23.1	25.6	23.9	48.9	27.6	47.9	24.4	54.3	24.4	55.3	33.8	55.9		
Panama	41.2	45.0	48.9	50.4	42.3	37.8	40.6	41.7	38.0	38.6				
PNG	19.3	56.8	46.2	57.0	45.5	54.8	54.8	43.3	53.0	54.9				
Peru	17.1	10.0	22.3	19.1	13.7	12.9	11.4	14.8	11.1	12.4	11.6	16.5	12.8	16.6
Philippines	23.4	22.9	25.7	31.0	30.0	36.2	34.9	44.7	33.6	47.3	36.3	44.0	41.2	52.2
Singapore	111.4	133.6	223.4	233.0	200.7	194.0	182.9	172.7	177.0	172.8				
Taiwan	25.5	25.5	61.7	63.1	52.2	46.6	49.6	47.5	49.7	47.5				
Thailand	16.8	21.8	27.2	34.3	39.2	47.9	41.4	46.1	39.3	52.0	41.5	48.4		
USA	6.4	6.0	11.1	11.8	10.8	12.4	11.2	12.5	10.0		11.1	12.4	11.2	12.6
Vietnam					40.3	51.0	40.5	47.0	23.0					

Source: *World Data* (1995) CD-ROM National Accounts Stack, Washington DC, World Bank; *Taiwan Statistical Data Book* (1996) Taipei, Council for Economic Planning and Development; *World Development Report* (1996) Washington DC, World Bank; *International Financial Statistics* (Dec. 1996) Washington DC, IMF; Muller, G.P. (1988) *Comparative World Data*, Baltimore, Johns Hopkins University Press.

Table A.11 *Major trading partners: exports (% total)*

Australia	1970	Japan 27	USA 13	UK 12		others 48
	1994	Japan 25	USA 11	S. Korea 6	New Zealand 6	others 52
Burma/Myanmar	1970	Singapore 13	Japan 12	Sri Lanka 12		others 63
	1993	Singapore 12	Japan 8	India 13	China 18	others 49
Cambodia	1970	N. Vietnam 14	Senegal 11	Czechoslovakia 10		others 65
	1993	Thailand 36	Japan 30	Germany 10	Malaysia 5	others 19
Canada	1970	USA 70	Japan 5	UK 9		others 16
	1992	USA 78	Japan 5	UK 2		others 15
Chile	1970	Netherlands 15	UK 13	USA 14		others 58
	1992	EU 29	Japan 17	USA 16	Argentina 5	others 33
China	1970	Hong Kong 33	Japan 18	Malaysia and Singapore 14	Germany 6	others 29
	1995	Hong Kong 24	Japan 19	USA 17	Germany 4	others 36
Colombia	1970	USA 37	Germany 14	Netherlands 6		others 43
	1994	USA 39	EU 26	Venezuela 9		others 26
Costa Rica	1970	USA 43	Germany 8	Nicaragua 6		others 43
	1993	USA 42	Germany 9	Guatemala 5	Italy 5	others 39
Ecuador	1970	USA 43	Japan 19	Germany 9		others 29
	1993	USA 47	S. Korea 12	Germany 4	Chile 5	others 32
El Salvador	1970	Germany 25	USA 21	Guatemala 17		others 37
	1992	Germany 6	USA 34	Guatemala 23	Costa Rica 10	others 27
Guatemala	1970	USA 28	El Salvador 13	Germany 11		others 48
	1992	USA 35	El Salvador 14	Costa Rica 7		others 44
Honduras	1970	USA 55	Germany 11	Italy 5		others 29
	1993	USA 53	Germany 11	Belgium 8	UK 5	others 23
Hong Kong	1970	USA 52	Germany 10	Japan 5	UK 15	others 18
	1995	USA 22	Germany 4	Japan 6	China 33	others 35
Indonesia	1970	Japan 33	USA 14	Singapore 16		others 37
	1993	Japan 30	USA 14	Singapore 9	S. Korea 7	others 40
Japan	1970	USA 30	EEC 10	S. Korea 4	Australia 3	others 53
	1995	USA 28	EU 18	S. Korea 7	Hong Kong 7	others 40
Korea, N.	1970	Japan 19	USSR 55	France 9	Czechoslovakia 6	others 11
	1992	Japan 39	Russia 5	Germany 7	China 24	others 25
Korea, S.	1970	USA 47	Japan 28	Germany 3		others 22
	1995	USA 19	Japan 14	EU 14	Hong Kong 8	others 45

Table A.11 *Major trading partners: exports (% total) (continued)*

Laos	1970	Thailand 27	Malaysia 36	Canada 21		others 16
	1991	Thailand 57	Germany 10	France 10	Japan 5	others 18
Malaysia	1970	Singapore 22	EEC 20	Japan 18	USA 13	others 27
	1995	Singapore 21	EU 14	Japan 13	USA 20	others 32
Mexico	1970	USA 70	Germany 2	Japan 6		others 22
	1993	USA 82	EU 5	Japan 1		others 12
New Zealand	1970	UK 34	USA 17	Japan 10		others 39
	1995	UK 6	USA 10	Japan 16	Australia 20	others 48
Nicaragua	1970	USA 33	Germany 12	Japan 14		others 41
	1992	USA 26	Germany 11	Belgium 9		others 54
Panama	1970	USA 62	Germany 16	Netherlands 4		others 18
	1992	USA 31	Germany 27	Italy 8		others 36
PNG	1970	Japan 37	Germany 25	Australia 14		others 24
	1992	Japan 34	Germany 15	S. Korea 12		others 39
Peru	1970	USA 33	Japan 14	Germany 15		others 38
	1993	USA 23	Japan 9	Germany 6	China 5	others 57
Philippines	1970	USA 42	Japan 40	Netherlands 4		others 14
	1993	USA 39	Japan 16	Germany 5	Hong Kong 4	others 36
Singapore	1970	Malaysia 22	USA 11	Japan 8	UK 7	others 52
	1995	Malaysia 19	USA 18	Japan 8	Hong Kong 19	others 36
Taiwan	1970	USA 38	Japan 15	Hong Kong 9	Germany 5	others 33
	1995	USA 24	Japan 12	Hong Kong 23	Germany 3	others 38
Thailand	1970	USA 13	Japan 26	Netherlands 9		others 52
	1995	USA 18	Japan 17	Singapore 12	Hong Kong 5	others 48
USA	1970	EEC 24	Canada 21	Japan 11		others 44
	1993	EU 25	Canada 22	Japan 11		others 42
Vietnam	1978	Japan 7	Hong Kong 3	Singapore 2	China 6	others 82
	1993	Japan 34	Hong Kong 6	Singapore 18	France 4	others 38

Source: *Taiwan Statistical Data Book* (1996) Taipei, Council for Economic Planning and Development; *Direction of Trade Statistics* (1996) Washington DC, IMF; Muller, G.P. (1988) *Comparative World Data*, Baltimore, Johns Hopkins University Press; *The World Factbook* (1995) Washington DC, Central Intelligence Agency.

Table A.12 *Major trading partners: imports (% total)*

Australia	1970	USA 26	Japan 13	UK 22		others 39
	1995	USA 22	Japan 15	UK 6	Germany 7	others 50
Burma/Myanmar	1970	Japan 25	India 16	UK 9		others 50
	1993	Japan 9	Singapore 29	China 28	Malaysia 9	others 25
Cambodia	1970	Japan 26	France 24	Germany 7		others 43
	1993	Japan 6	Thailand 23	Indonesia 5	Hong Kong 4	others 62
Canada	1970	USA 71	Japan 4	UK 5		others 20
	1992	USA 65	Japan 7	UK 3		others 25
Chile	1970	USA 37	Germany 12	Argentina 10		others 41
	1992	USA 21	EU 24	Brazil 10	Japan 10	others 35
China	1970	Japan 38	Germany 11	Australia 10	Canada 10	others 31
	1995	Japan 22	Germany 6	Hong Kong 7	USA 12	others 53
Colombia	1970	USA 46	Germany 9	Japan 7		others 38
	1994	USA 36	EU 18	Japan 9	Venezuela 7	others 30
Costa Rica	1970	USA 35	Japan 9	Germany 8		others 48
	1993	USA 43	Japan 8	Germany 4	Mexico 4	others 41
Ecuador	1970	USA 44	Japan 9	Germany 11		others 36
	1993	USA 28	Japan 14	Germany 5	Trinidad and Tobago 32	others 21
El Salvador	1970	USA 31	Guatemala 19	Japan 10		others 40
	1992	USA 40	Guatemala 12	Japan 5	Venezuela 6	others 37
Guatemala	1970	USA 35	El Salvador 14	Japan 10		others 41
	1992	USA 44	El Salvador 6	Japan 4	Mexico 7	others 39
Honduras	1970	USA 42	Guatemala 13	Japan 8		others 37
	1993	USA 50	Guatemala 6	Mexico 8		others 36
Hong Kong	1970	Japan 29	China 19	USA 16	UK 10	others 26
	1995	Japan 15	China 36	USA 8	Singapore 5	others 36
Indonesia	1970	Japan 30	USA 18	Germany 10		others 42
	1995	Japan 28	USA 10	Germany 8	S. Korea 8	others 46
Japan	1970	USA 30	S.-E. Asia 15	EEC 6	Australia 8	others 41
	1995	USA 23	S.-E. Asia 25	EU 15	China 11	others 26
Korea, N.	1970	USSR 52	Japan 15	France 5	Poland 4	others 24
	1992	Russia 8	Japan 14	Italy 8	China 35	others 35
Korea, S.	1970	Japan 41	USA 30	Germany 3		others 26
	1995	Japan 24	USA 24	Germany 5	China 6	others 41

Table A.12 *Major trading partners: imports (% total) (continued)*

Laos	1970	Thailand 21	USA 24	Indonesia 15		others 40
	1991	Thailand 55	Japan 16	China 8	Italy 4	others 17
Malaysia	1970	EEC 25	Japan 17	USA 9	Singapore 7	others 42
	1995	EU 16	Japan 27	USA 16	Singapore 13	others 28
Mexico	1970	USA 64	Germany 8	France 4		others 24
	1993	USA 74	EU 11	Japan 5		others 10
New Zealand	1970	Australia 20	USA 13	UK 27		others 40
	1995	Australia 22	USA 19	UK 6	Japan 14	others 39
Nicaragua	1970	USA 37	Guatemala 8	El Salvador 8		others 47
	1992	USA 26	Venezuela 14	Costa Rica 10		others 50
Panama	1970	USA 34	Saudi Arabia 19			others 47
	1992	USA 39	Japan 8	Ecuador 6		others 47
PNG	1970	Australia 41	Japan 18	Singapore 15		others 26
	1993	Australia 47	Japan 15	Singapore 12	New Zealand 5	others 21
Peru	1970	USA 32	Germany 12	Japan 8		others 48
	1993	USA 23	Germany 6	Japan 9	China 5	others 57
Philippines	1970	Japan 31	USA 29	Germany 6		others 34
	1993	Japan 23	USA 20	Taiwan 6	Singapore 5	others 46
Singapore	1970	Japan 19	Malaysia 19	USA 11	UK 8	others 43
	1995	Japan 21	Malaysia 16	USA 15	Thailand 5	others 43
Taiwan	1970	Japan 43	USA 24	Germany 4	Australia 3	others 26
	1995	Japan 29	USA 20	Germany 5	Australia 3	others 43
Thailand	1970	Japan 38	USA 15	Germany 9		others 38
	1995	Japan 30	USA 11	Germany 5	Singapore 5	others 49
USA	1970	Canada 28	Japan 15	Germany 8		others 49
	1993	Canada 19	Japan 18	EU 18		others 45
Vietnam	1978	Singapore 3	Japan 16	France 7	Germany 4	others 70
	1993	Singapore 28	Japan 14	France 8	S. Korea 13	others 38

Source: *Taiwan Statistical Data Book* (1996) Taipei, Council for Economic Planning and Development; *Direction of Trade Statistics* (1996) Washington DC, IMF; Muller, G.P. (1988) *Comparative World Data*, Baltimore, Johns Hopkins University Press; *The World Factbook* (1995) Washington DC, Central Intelligence Agency.

Table A.13 *Major export commodities (% total)*

Australia	1970	raw materials 28	agricultural 53	machinery 6	manufactures 13	
	1992	raw materials 36	agricultural 29	machinery 8	manufactures 27	
Burma/ Myanmar	1970	minerals and gems 7	rice 53	hardwood 21	other raw materials 16	others 3
	1993	minerals and gems 6	rice 11	hardwood 33	other raw materials 47	others 3
Cambodia	1970	rubber 39	logs 5	rice 42		others 14
	1993	rubber 23	logs 7	sawn timber 52		others 18
Canada	1970	raw materials 26	agricultural 22	machinery 32	manufactures 20	
	1992	raw materials 18	agricultural 18	machinery 38	manufactures 26	
Chile	1970	copper 77	agricultural 7	manufactures 4		others 12
	1994	copper 41	agricultural 38	manufactures 13		others 8
China	1970	primary products 30	machinery 15	textiles 29	other manufactures 26	
	1992	primary products 21	machinery 16	textiles 30	other manufactures 33	
Colombia	1970	coffee 63	petroleum 10	other agricultural 18	manufactures 7	others 2
	1994	coffee 24	petroleum 21	other agricultural 15	manufactures 29	others 11
Costa Rica	1970	agricultural 80	manufactures 17			others 3
	1992	agricultural 72	manufactures 23			others 5
Ecuador	1970	petroleum 1	bananas 46	other agricultural 51		others 2
	1994	petroleum 39	bananas 17	other agricultural 32		others 12
El Salvador	1970	coffee 50	other agricultural 20	textiles 11	other manufactures 15	others 4
	1994	coffee 26	other agricultural 30	textiles 15	other manufactures 22	others 7
Guatemala	1970	coffee 35	other agricultural 37	manufactures 26		others 2
	1994	coffee 22	other agricultural 46	manufactures 28		others 4
Honduras	1970	bananas 34	coffee 10	other agricultural 38	manufactures 8	others 10
	1994	bananas 19	coffee 21	other agricultural 44	manufactures 13	others 3
Hong Kong	1970	textiles 44	other manufactures 40	machinery 12		others 4
	1992	textiles 40	other manufactures 31	machinery 24		others 5
Indonesia	1970	petroleum 46	rubber 28	other agricultural 25	manufactures 1	
	1994	petroleum 15	rubber 3	other agricultural 12	manufactures 57	others 13
Japan	1970	industrial equipment 24	consumer electronics 15	motor vehicles 7	other manufactures 46	others 8
	1994	industrial equipment 46	consumer electronics 10	motor vehicles 20	other manufactures 10	others 14
Korea, N.	1965	metals and ores 50	other materials 18	rice 9		others 23
Korea, S.	1970	textiles 36	other manufactures 33	machinery 7	agricultural 17	others 7
	1992	textiles 20	other manufactures 33	machinery 40	agricultural 4	others 3
Laos	1970	raw materials 36	other agricultural 33	machinery 30		others 1
	1994	raw materials 24	other agricultural 72			others 4

Table A.13 *Major export commodities (% total) (continued)*

Malaysia	1970	rubber and tin 77	oil and gas 6	manufactures 17		
	1995	rubber and tin 1	oil and gas 6	manufactures 76		others 17
Mexico	1970	oil and gas 3	agricultural 49	manufactures 22	machinery 11	others 15
	1992	oil and gas 14	agricultural 13	manufactures 21	machinery 31	others 21
New Zealand	1970	food 58	other agricultural 30	manufactures 9		others 3
	1992	food 41	other agricultural 25	manufactures 21		others 13
Nicaragua	1970	coffee 29	cotton 31	meat 24	manufactures 16	
	1993	coffee 20	cotton 11	meat 23	other agricultural 36	others 10
Panama	1970	bananas 30	fish 5	raw materials 21	other agricultural 40	others 4
	1993	bananas 43	fish 13	raw materials 1	other agricultural 27	others 16
PNG	1970	raw materials 42	coffee 21	other agricultural 34		others 3
	1993	raw materials 52	coffee 4	other agricultural 22		others 22
Peru	1970	raw materials 49	agricultural 49	manufactures 2		
	1994	raw materials 49	agricultural 31	manufactures 20		
Philippines	1970	copper 21	agricultural 70	machinery 1	manufactures 8	
	1992	copper 2	agricultural 19	machinery 17	manufactures 56	others 6
Singapore	1970	raw materials 25	machinery 11	textiles 5	agricultural 45	others 14
	1993	raw materials 20	machinery 55	textiles 5	agricultural 7	others 13
Taiwan	1970	textiles and leather 42	machinery and electronics 15	agricultural 21	other manufactures 17	others 5
	1994	textiles and leather 20	machinery and electronics 40	agricultural 4	other manufactures 33	others 3
Thailand	1970	rice and rubber 32	machinery 1	other agricultural 45	manufactures 8	others 14
	1993	rice and rubber 7	machinery 22	other agricultural 26	manufactures 45	
USA	1970	machinery 42	manufactures 28	agricultural 21	raw materials 9	
	1992	machinery 48	manufactures 32	agricultural 15	raw materials 5	
Vietnam	1981	coal 10	agricultural 20	handicrafts 56		others 14
	1993	petroleum 30	agricultural 40	handicrafts 16		others 14

Source: *Taiwan Statistical Data Book* (1996) Taipei, Council for Economic Planning and Development; *Key Indicators of Developing Asian and Pacific Countries* (1995) Manila, Asian Development Bank; *World Development Report* (1996) Washington DC, World Bank; *The Europa World Yearbook* (1970–96) London, Europa.

Table A.14 *Major import commodities (% total)*

Australia	1970	food 6	fuels 5	materials 7	machinery 41	manufactures 41
	1992	food 5	fuels 6	materials 3	machinery 40	manufactures 46
Burma/ Myanmar	1970	food 7	primary 9	chemicals 6	machinery 29	manufactures 49
	1993	food 8	primary 9	chemicals 15	machinery 35	manufactures 33
Cambodia	1970	food 7	minerals 13	manufactures 39		others 41
	1993	cigarettes 14	fuels 12	construction materials 12	machinery 9	others 53
Canada	1970	food 9	fuels 6	materials 6	machinery 49	manufactures 30
	1992	food 6	fuels 4	materials 4	machinery 50	manufactures 36
Chile	1970	food 15	fuels 6	materials 7	machinery 43	manufactures 29
	1992	food 6	fuels 12	materials 3	machinery 42	manufactures 37
China	1970	food 7	fuels 2	materials 9	machinery 39	manufactures 43
	1992	food 5	fuels 4	materials 9	machinery 38	manufactures 44
Colombia	1970	food 8	fuels 1	materials 8	machinery 46	manufactures 37
	1992	food 9	fuels 6	materials 7	machinery 34	manufactures 44
Costa Rica	1970	food 11	fuels 4	materials 3	machinery 29	manufactures 53
	1992	food 8	fuels 7	materials 4	machinery 33	manufactures 48
Ecuador	1970	food 8	fuels 6	materials 2	machinery 35	manufactures 49
	1992	food 5	fuels 4	materials 3	machinery 44	manufactures 44
El Salvador	1970	food 14	fuels 2	materials 4	machinery 23	manufactures 57
	1992	food 16	fuels 13	materials 6	machinery 24	manufactures 41
Guatemala	1970	food 11	fuels 2	materials 3	machinery 27	manufactures 57
	1992	food 12	fuels 17	materials 3	machinery 26	manufactures 42
Honduras	1970	food 12	fuels 7	materials 1	machinery 29	manufactures 51
	1992	food 11	fuels 13	materials 3	machinery 26	manufactures 47
Hong Kong	1970	food 20	fuels 3	materials 9	machinery 16	manufactures 52
	1992	food 7	fuels 2	materials 4	machinery 31	manufactures 56
Indonesia	1970	food 12	fuels 2	materials 4	machinery 35	manufactures 47
	1992	food 6	fuels 8	materials 9	machinery 43	manufactures 34
Japan	1970	food 17	fuels 21	materials 37	machinery 11	manufactures 14
	1992	food 17	fuels 23	materials 13	machinery 16	manufactures 31
Korea, N.	1965	food 10	fuels 12	materials 8	transport equipment 23	others 47
Korea, S.	1970	food 17	fuels 7	materials 21	machinery 30	manufactures 25
	1992	food 6	fuels 18	materials 12	machinery 36	manufactures 28

Table A.14 *Major import commodities (% total) (continued)*

Laos	1970	food 24	fuels 23	materials 1	machinery 19	manufactures 33
	1992	food 33	fuels 17	materials 2	machinery 22	manufactures 26
Malaysia	1970	food 22	fuels 11	materials 8	machinery 28	manufactures 31
	1992	food 7	fuels 3	materials 5	machinery 55	manufactures 30
Mexico	1970	food 7	fuels 3	materials 9	machinery 50	manufactures 31
	1992	food 11	fuels 3	materials 5	machinery 48	manufactures 33
New Zealand	1970	food 7	fuels 7	materials 10	machinery 33	manufactures 43
	1992	food 7	fuels 7	materials 4	machinery 39	manufactures 43
Nicaragua	1970	food 10	fuels 6	materials 3	machinery 28	manufactures 53
	1992	food 23	fuels 15	materials 1	machinery 26	manufactures 35
Panama	1970	food 10	fuels 19	materials 2	machinery 27	manufactures 42
	1992	food 10	fuels 15	materials 2	machinery 28	manufactures 45
PNG	1970	food 24	fuels 11	materials 1	machinery 30	manufactures 34
	1992	food 17	fuels 8	materials 1	machinery 40	manufactures 34
Peru	1970	food 20	fuels 2	materials 5	machinery 35	manufactures 38
	1992	food 20	fuels 11	materials 3	machinery 35	manufactures 31
Philippines	1970	food 11	fuels 12	materials 8	machinery 35	manufactures 34
	1992	food 8	fuels 14	materials 6	machinery 28	manufactures 44
Singapore	1970	food 16	fuels 13	materials 13	machinery 23	manufactures 35
	1992	food 6	fuels 13	materials 3	machinery 46	manufactures 32
Taiwan	1970	food 15	fuels 4	materials 18	machinery 35	manufactures 28
	1992	food 6	fuels 8	materials 10	machinery 40	manufactures 36
Thailand	1970	food 5	fuels 9	materials 7	machinery 36	manufactures 43
	1992	food 6	fuels 8	materials 8	machinery 41	manufactures 37
USA	1970	food 16	fuels 8	materials 12	machinery 28	manufactures 36
	1992	food 6	fuels 11	materials 4	machinery 41	manufactures 38
Vietnam	1981	materials 76	machinery 10	manufactures 14		
	1993	fuels 20	machinery 16	fertilizers 5	steel 5	others 54

Source: *Taiwan Statistical Data Book* (1996) Taipei, Council for Economic Planning and Development; *Key Indicators of Developing Asian and Pacific Countries* (1995) Manila, Asian Development Bank; *World Development Report* (1996) Washington DC, World Bank; *The Europa World Yearbook* (1970–96) London, Europa.

Social indicators

Table A.15 *Main ethnic groups (% total population)*

		Caucasian	Asian	Indigenous		
Australia	1966	96	3	1		
	1995	95	4	1		
		Burman	Shan	Karen	Chinese	Others
Burma/Myanmar	1973	75	8	7	2	8
	1995	68	9	7	3	13
		Khmer	Vietnamese	Chinese		
Cambodia	1962	93	4	3		
	1995	90	5	1		
		Caucasian	Indigenous	Others		
Canada	1970	88	2	10		
	1995	87	2	11		
		Mestizo	Caucasian	Indigenous		
Chile	1970	70	25	5		
	1995	79	20	1		
		Han Chinese	Others			
China	1953	94	6			
	1995	92	8			
		Mestizo	Caucasian	Mulatto	African-Caribbean	Indigenous
Colombia	1970	50	20	25	4	1
	1995	58	20	17	4	1
		Caucasian/Mestizo	African-Caribbean			
Costa Rica	1970	98	1			
	1995	96	2			
		Mestizo	Indigenous	Caucasian	African-Caribbean	
Ecuador	1977	45	40	10	5	
	1995	55	25	10	10	
		Mestizo	Indigenous	Caucasian		
El Salvador	1979	90	9	1		
	1995	94	5	1		
		Mestizo	Indigenous			
Guatemala	1970	55	45			
	1995	56	44			
		Mestizo	Indigenous	African-Caribbean	Caucasian	
Honduras	1979	90	7	2	1	
	1995	90	7	2	1	
		Chinese	Others			
Hong Kong	1970	98	2			
	1995	95	5			
		Indigenous/Malay	Chinese			
Indonesia	1970	98	2			
	1995	97	3			
		Japanese	Korean			
Japan	1970	99	1			
	1995	99	1			
		Korean				
Korea, N.	1970	99.8				
	1995	99.8				

Table A.15 *Main ethnic groups (% total population) (continued)*

		Korean			
Korea, S.	*1970*	99.9			
	1995	99.9			
		Lao Loum	Lao Theung	Lao Soung	
Laos	*1976*	56	34	9	
	1995	68	22	9	
		Indigenous/Malay	Chinese	Indian	
Malaysia	*1970*	53	36	11	
	1995	64	27	8	
		Mestizo	Indigenous	Caucasian	
Mexico	*1970*	55	29	15	
	1995	60	30	9	
		Caucasian	Maori	Pacific Islands	
New Zealand	*1976*	86	8	2	
	1995	88	9	3	
		Mestizo	Caucasian	African-Caribbean	Indigenous
Nicaragua	*1970*	71	12	8	4
	1995	69	17	9	5
		Mestizo	African-Caribbean	Caucasian	Indigenous
Panama	*1940*	72	11	12	5
	1995	70	14	10	6
		Melanesian			
PNG	*1970*	98			
	1995	99.9			
		Indigenous	Mestizo	Caucasian	
Peru	*1970*	46	40	12	
	1995	45	37	15	
		Christian Malay	Muslim Malay	Chinese	
Philippines					
	1995	92	4	2	
		Chinese	Malay	Indian	
Singapore	*1970*	76	15	7	
	1995	76	15	6	
		Chinese	Indigenous		
Taiwan	*1970*	98	2		
	1995	98	2		
		Thai	Chinese	Khmer	Malay
Thailand	*1979*	80	13	4	3
	1995	75	14	3	4
		Caucasian	African-Caribbean	Asian	Indigenous
USA	*1970*	88	11	1	0.4
	1992	83	12	3	0.8
		Vietnamese	Chinese		
Vietnam	*1979*	88	2		
	1995	87	3		

Source: *The World Factbook* (1995) Washington DC, Central Intelligence Agency; *Statesman's Yearbook* (1970, 1996) London, Macmillan.

Table A.16 *Women's labour (%)*

	1970		1980		1990		1994	
	Paid	*Unpaid*	*Paid*	*Unpaid*	*Paid*	*Unpaid*	*Paid*	*Unpaid*
Australia	43	57	48	52	54	46	47	53
Burma/Myanmar	64	36	63	37	55	45	47	53
Cambodia	68	32	66	34	51	49	50	50
Canada	43	57	57	43	56	44	49	51
Chile	24	76	30	70	32	68	29	71
China	81	19	85	15	80	20	70	30
Colombia	24	76	24	76	23	77	22	78
Costa Rica	22	78	25	75	25	75	24	76
Ecuador	20	80	22	78	22	78	20	80
El Salvador	26	74	33	67	38	62	29	71
Guatemala	16	84	16	84	18	82	18	82
Honduras	17	83	19	81	23	77	23	77
Hong Kong	51	49	56	44	53	47	50	50
Indonesia	42	58	42	58	41	59	37	63
Japan	57	43	54	46	55	45	50	50
Korea, N.	68	32	68	32	67	33	66	34
Korea, S.	42	58	43	57	43	57	41	59
Laos	100	0	96	4	87	13	68	32
Malaysia	41	59	46	54	48	52	45	55
Mexico	20	80	34	66	33	67	30	70
New Zealand	39	61	45	55	49	51	41	59
Nicaragua	24	76	25	75	31	69	30	70
Panama	34	66	33	67	34	66	31	69
PNG	51	49	55	45	53	47	57	43
Peru	22	78	27	73	27	73	25	75
Philippines	47	53	43	57	40	60	36	64
Singapore	32	68	48	52	44	56	46	54
Taiwan	36	64	39	61	44	56	46	54
Thailand	93	7	83	17	75	25	65	35
USA	49	51	61	39	61	39	50	50
Vietnam	84	16	79	21	79	21	69	31

Source: *World Data* (1995) CD-ROM Social Indicators Stack, Washington DC, World Bank; *The World's Women* (1995) New York, UN; *Bulletin of Labour Statistics* (1996) Geneva, International Labour Office.

Table A.17 *Population per physician*

	1970	1980	1990	1992	1993	1994	1995
Australia	836	554	434	438			
Burma/Myanmar	8,819	4,595	3,282	3,565			
Cambodia	16,248	16,365	9,192	9,523			
Canada	684	548		501	446		
Chile	2,157	1,620	2,149				
China	3,184	1,100			1,063	1,034	
Colombia	2,256	1,970					
Costa Rica	1,622	1,390		1,270			
Ecuador	2,870	1,620	957	825			
El Salvador	4,101	3,031					
Guatemala	3,656	2,490					
Honduras	3,724	3,290	1,690				
Hong Kong	1,509	1,211	919	866	789		
Indonesia	27,442	13,640	11,598	11,641			
Japan	890	748	584	566	545		
Korea, N.		1,853	370				
Korea, S.	2,216	1,690	1,007	902	950	855	
Laos	15,156	20,060	4,447	4,380	4,450		
Malaysia	4,310	3,917	2,502	2,410			2,207
Mexico	1,485	1,820		600			
New Zealand	873	638	530	512	506		
Nicaragua	2,147	2,308	1,492				
Panama	1,630	1,220	869				
PNG	11,644	16,073	12,754	11,900			
Peru	1,920	1,397	943				
Philippines	9,267	7,847	7,000	6,648			
Singapore	1,155	944	757	711	693		
Taiwan	2,270	1,335	915	830	800	774	
Thailand	8,288	6,803	4,411	4,361	4,420		
USA	634	549	420	420	391		
Vietnam	5,668	4,152	2,918	2,535	2,300	2,298	

Source: *World Data* (1995) CD-ROM Social Indicators Stack, Washington DC, World Bank; *Taiwan Statistical Data Book* (1996) Taipei, Council for Economic Planning and Development; *World Development Report* (1982) Washington DC, World Bank; *Asia-Pacific in Figures* (1994) New York, UN.

Table A.18 *Government social security expenditure (% total)*

	1970	1980	1990	1992	1993	1994
Australia		27.7	26.6	32.5	33.2	
Burma/Myanmar		0.4	0.2	0.4		
Cambodia				4.2	4.3	
Canada		26.1	29.4			
Chile		30.8	33.8	31.2	31.1	
China		1.7	1.9	1.5		
Colombia						
Costa Rica		7.1	13.8			
Ecuador			2.8	3.4	3.4	
El Salvador		2.5	2.2	2.4		
Guatemala						
Honduras						
Hong Kong		4.4	6.1	6.4	6.3	6.5
Indonesia						
Japan		5.5	5.9	6.1		
Korea, N.						
Korea, S.	5.0	6.2	7.5	8.1	7.9	
Laos						
Malaysia						
Mexico		16.0	12.4			
New Zealand	23.1	29.2	37.6	36.2	37.3	36.1
Nicaragua	18.4	3.3	6.7	14.4	10.3	
Panama		10.2	21.1	19.0		
PNG		0.1	0.9	0.6	0.6	
Peru						
Philippines		1.2	1.1	1.8	1.8	1.1
Singapore	0.6	1.2	2.1	2.0		
Taiwan	9.6	11.1	17.1	16.9	16.7	18.3
Thailand		2.3	3.5	3.8		
USA	21.6	27.7	20.5	22.2	22.5	
Vietnam			1.8	3.4	3.3	3.4

Source: *World Data* (1995) CD-ROM Social Indicators Stack, Washington DC, World Bank; *Taiwan Statistical Data Book* (1996) Taipei, Council for Economic Planning and Development; *Government Financial Statistics Yearbook* (1995) Washington DC, IMF.

Russian Far East

by Michael J. Bradshaw

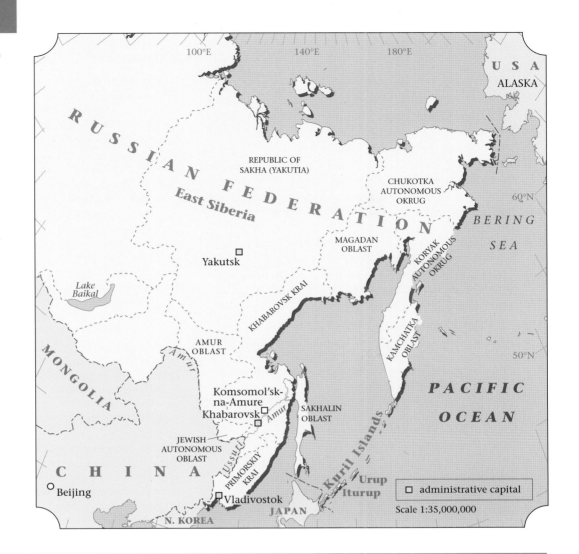

Overview

- The history of the Russian Far East can been seen as a gradual process of expansion and consolidation. The relative position and territorial extent of the region being a measure of the strength of Russia in North-East Asia

- The relationship between Moscow and the Far East has experienced flux: when Moscow is weak the Far East seizes its autonomy. Thus there have been periods when the region has 'gone its own way' and the contemporary position can be characterized as such a period

- Until the 1917 revolution the emphasis was on the demarcation of borders with China and Japan while during the Soviet period the effective occupation of the Far East's territory was of primary concern

- A territorial dispute with Japan over the Kuril Islands remains a major problem in relations between Russia and Japan

- Russia and China are currently demarcating their border in the Far East.

Historical background

- 1581 Yermak's expedition to Siberia and the Far East
- 1632 Fort established at Yakutsk
- 1637 Siberian office established in Moscow to administer Siberia
- 1805 Siberian Governorship-General created
- 1855 Russo-Japanese frontier in Kuril Islands drawn between Iturup and Urup islands – Sakhalin remains unpartitioned
- 1858 China recognizes Russian acquisition of Amur left bank – right bank below Ussuri junction designated a joint possession
- 1860 China recognizes Russian acquisition of the Primorye (Maritime) region and Vladivostok founded
- 1861 the emancipation of Russian serfs results in substantial migration into Siberia and to a lesser extent the Far East
- 1867 Alaska sold to the USA
- 1875 Russia acquires full possession of Sakhalin
- 1890s construction of the trans-Siberian railway linking the Far East with the rest of Siberian and European Russia. The Chinese Eastern Railway constructed across Manchuria and arrived in Vladivostok in 1904
- 1904–5 Japan inflicts humiliating defeat on the Russian Empire. As a consequence Russia cedes southern half of Sakhalin Island and Kuril Islands to Japan – remain under Japanese control until 1945
- 1917 Russian Revolution
- 1918 Admiral Kolchak declared himself to be 'Supreme Ruler' of the Far East but is executed in 1920
- 1920 Far Eastern Republic created. Two years of autonomy now seen as the basis for contemporary demands for the recreation of a Far Eastern Republic
- 1922 Vladivostok captured by the Red Army and Far Eastern Republic absorbed into Soviet Russia
- 1923 Far Eastern District created – administered from Khabarovsk
- 1926–38 Far Eastern territory enjoys a degree of autonomy until dissolved by Stalin whereupon Moscow exerts greater control over the region
- 1931 creation of *Dalstroi* (Far Eastern Construction Trust) – 90% of its work-force was prison labour
- 1932 creation of the city of Komsomol'sk-na-Amure, an ideological steeltown built to create a 'proletarian bastion of socialism' in the Soviet Far East
- 1945 in the final days of the Second World War the Soviet army invades Kuril Islands and southern Sakhalin – they remain part of the Russian Federation. Japan still lays claim to the southern Kuril Islands or the 'Northern Territories' as they are known in Japan
- 1953 Stalin dies
- 1957 *Dalstroi* dissolved symbolizing the end of the Stalin period
- 1953–64 Khrushchev period – USSR divided into 105 regional economic councils with greater decision-making

responsibility. But old problems of competing ministerial interests replaced by new ones as the councils pursue regional self interest. Re-centralization from 1962 sees councils merged into bigger units and eventually replaced by economic planning regions with no administrative status

- 1963 Soviet Far East Economic Planning Region created. Includes: Khabarovsk and Primorskiy Krais; Amur, Sakhalin, Kamchatka, and Magadan Oblasts; and the Yakut Autonomous Soviet Socialist Republic
- 1964–82 Brezhnev period of re-centralization during which the industrial ministries control the Soviet economy. Strategic importance of the Russian Far East ensures a high degree of central control in key sectors such as mining. Unable to pursue local economic development strategies the Far East becomes dependent upon the European regions of the USSR for the supply of most products. Central control of foreign trade also means the region is isolated from the economies of North-East Asia
- 1974 The Baikal–Amur mainline (BAM) rail project restored as Brezhnev's 'Project of the Century'. The railway was to open up the resource-rich hinterland of the Soviet Far East to markets in the Pacific and provide an alternative route to the strategically vulnerable trans-Siberian railway. Officially 'completed' in 1984 the railway is still not fully operational
- 1985–91 Gorbachev's policies of *perestroika* and *glasnost* give hope of increased autonomy but the realities of 'cost accounting' meant the Russian Far East was starved of central investment and economic crisis resulted. During his conflict with Gorbachev, Yeltsin promises Russia's regions greater autonomy. Many regions make the most of the opportunity to gain greater autonomy – particularly the Republic of Sakha (Yakutia) in the case of the Far East
- 1986 Gorbachev's Vladivostok speech declaring that the Soviet Union wished to open its window on the East
- 1987 major government programme for the development of the Soviet Far East announced – shelved two years later due to a lack of funds
- 1991 Vladivostok declared an 'Open City' to symbolize the opening-up of the USSR and Russia
- 1991 failed military coup in Moscow leads to collapse of the USSR which was officially dissolved 31 December. Russian Far East now part of an independent Russian Federation
- 1991 Yeltsin elected President of Russia and soon regrets encouraging greater regional autonomy – Russia's regions have continued to assert their authority, usually at the cost of the central government. At the same time conflict emerges within regions as local politicians seek to promote their own self interest
- 1993 after protracted conflict between President Yeltsin and Moscow legislature Yeltsin orders attack on the parliament building to overthrow the conservative parliament resisting his reforms. New elections and a plebiscite on the government of the Russian Federation – Yeltsin, by a slim margin, gains a mandate to continue his reforms

- 1995 decree allows the election of regional governors. Previously regional governors had been appointed by President Yeltsin and often dismissed if they opposed Moscow. Now governors are to be elected to represent regional interests. Elections still taking place in early 1997 and are likely to start off a new round of centre–region conflict
- 1996 Yeltsin re-elected President of Russia. But with a newly elected Federation Council (the upper house composed of the presidents of republics and regional governors) the fractious relationship between the federal government and Russia's regions remains unresolved
- In the Russian Far East the local leadership is fast realizing that it should turn to its neighbours in North-East Asia rather than Moscow for economic opportunity
- In a very real sense the Russian Far East is further away from Moscow than it has been for a long time.

Political framework

- The Russian Far East currently has official administrative status within the Russian Federation
- In 1997 it comprised the following administrative regions: Republic of Sakha (Yakutia); Jewish Autonomous Oblast; Chukotka and Koryak Autonomous Okrugs; Khabarovsk and Primorskiy (Maritime) Krais; and Amur, Kamchatka, Magadan, and Sakhalin Oblasts
- The region's electorate are represented by elected officials in the Russian Duma (parliament); the region's governors and the President of Sakha are members of Russia's upper house the Federation Council as are the chairs of each local parliament
- The collapse of the USSR and the emergence of a more market-oriented and democratic Russian Federation has created both problems and opportunities for the Russian Far East
- Russia is still in the process of re-negotiating its federal structure and relations between the centre and the regions remain a source of conflict and instability
- At the same time the introduction of market reforms and the withdrawal of the state from the economy has resulted in economic hardship in the Russian Far East
- In addition to political problems in Moscow there is growing dissent in the Far East and rumblings of separatism
- As Moscow's political and economic power declines so the region's politicians are consolidating their own power bases and attempting to secure better economic opportunities by looking towards their neighbours in North-East Asia.

Further reading

Akaha, T. (ed.) (1997) *Politics and Economics in the Russian Far East: Changing Ties with Asia-Pacific*, London, Routledge.

Clay Moltz, J. (1996) 'Core and periphery in the evolving Russian economy: integration or isolation of the Russian Far East', *Post-Soviet Geography and Economics,* vol.37, no.3, pp.175–94.

De Souza, P. (1997) 'The Russian Far East: Russia's gateway to the Pacific' in Bradshaw, M.J. (ed.) *Geography and Transition in the Post-Soviet Republics*, Chichester, Wiley.

Rodgers, A. (ed.) (1990) *The Soviet Far East: Geographical Perspectives on Development*, London, Routledge.

Stephan, J. (1994) *The Russian Far East: a History*, Stanford, Stanford University Press.

Brunei

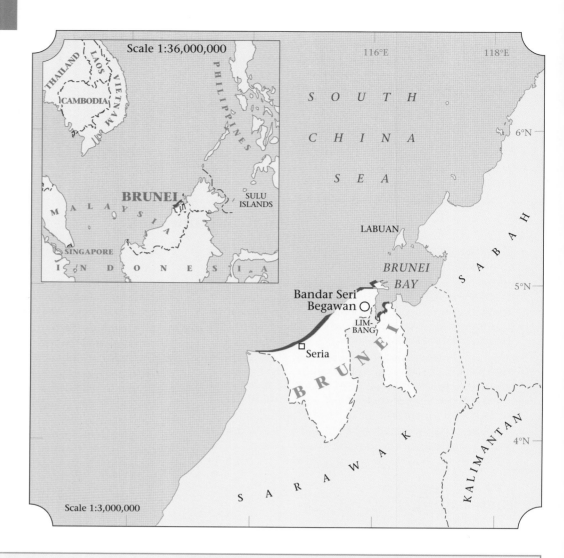

Scale 1:36,000,000

Scale 1:3,000,000

Historical background

- *c.* 680 King of Funan expelled by Khmers and founds new Kingdom in Borneo

- *c.* 1000–1350 Brunei part of what Chinese records called the Kingdom of Po-ni based in Brunei bay – after 13th C. Islamic influence spreads alongside Arab trading connections

- 1473–1521 Bolkiah's Sultanate represents high point of territorial authority over whole of Borneo and Sulu Islands in Philippines

- 16th–19th C. decline and disintegration of Borneo Empire as piracy, internal warfare and European colonizers overwhelm Sultan's control. Portuguese, Spanish, Dutch and British successively attempt to secure territory

- 1841 after helping to quell a rebellion Sultan cedes Sarawak to James Brooke an English adventurer who was appointed Rajah of the Sarawak court. Brooke family dynasty exerts idiosyncratic influence over North Borneo affairs for the next century

- 1846 Brunei cedes strategic island of Labuan to Britain

- 1847 Treaty of Friendship with British to promote trading links and combat piracy

- 1888 Brunei becomes a British Protectorate

- 1890 Sultan cedes the Limbang district to Charles Brooke splitting the country in two – border disputes with Malaysia over this split especially significant from 1960s

- 1905 Sultan Hashim agrees to appoint a British 'Resident' who will exercise executive power

- 1929 onshore oil field discovered at Seria – later jointly exploited by Royal Family and Dutch Shell. Sultan transformed from penury to one of the richest people in the world and national debt repaid by 1936

- 1941–45 occupied by Japan

- 1950–67 reign of Sultan Omar Ali Saifuddin III widely regarded as the architect of modern Brunei

- 1956 Brunei's first political party formed: PRB (Brunei People's Party) led by Shaikh Ahmad Azahari

- 1959 British Residency ended and the first written constitution ratified

- 1962 election victories see PRB claim role in government to pursue their total opposition to interest of Sultan in federating with Malaysia. After being rebuffed Azahari leads a mass rebellion with promises of support from Indonesia and Singapore. Sultan bans PRB, introduces emergency laws, rules by decree and suppresses rebellion with British military assistance
- 1962–97 State of Emergency continues in place
- 1963 Sultan decides against federation with Malaysia – fearful of losing control of oil revenues
- 1968 Sultan Hassanal Bolkiah the present ruler crowned after his father abdicates
- 1971 Sultan takes over internal affairs but Britain retains control of foreign affairs

- 1984 Sultan agrees to full independence for Brunei and immediately joins ASEAN
- 1988–90 political detainees from the former PRB released in a general amnesty
- 1992 Brunei joins Non-Aligned Movement and establishes diplomatic ties with Russia and China
- 1994 agreement signed with Malaysia establishing joint commission to promote co-operation especially over border demarcation
- 1995 Brunei hosts meeting of ASEAN ministers at which Vietnam accepted as full member.

Political framework

- Brunei remains one of a small handful of absolute monarchies similar to some Gulf states
- The Sultan is Head of State, Prime Minister and Defence Minister as well as secular head of the Islamic faith in Brunei
- 1990 political system framed as *Melayu Islam Beraja* (Malay Muslim Monarchy) – an ideology grafting Islamic values on elements of Malay cultural traditions within monarchic rule
- Other key political offices are held by members of the Royal Family and their nominees
- Within such a tightly enclosed system political opponents are easily represented as trouble-making forces prompting unnecessary confrontation between government and people
- One tiny opposition group does exist: the Brunei Solidarity National Party. But as of 1996 it effectively ceased to function when its elected leader – a former PRB detainee – withdrew after failing to secure government permission to take an active part in politics
- There have been recent signs that the State of Emergency may be lifted as a draft of a new constitution was circulating within government circles. Political change though remains a low priority compared to economic initiatives
- Offshore oil and gas fields remain crucial to the Brunei economy enabling high levels of public expenditure on education and welfare without recourse to any collection of revenue by personal taxation
- Awareness of being overly dependent on natural resources has encouraged restrictions on production to conserve stocks and efforts to diversify the economy. The contribu-

tion of oil and gas to GDP fell in the two decades after 1974 from over 90% to 60% but still accounts for nearly 95% of export earnings
- Diversification plans from the late 1980s have as yet produced little impact. Foreign investors have been courted but are discouraged by a limited supply of labour reflecting a strong preference for employment in the public sector that currently accounts for over two-thirds of the national labour force
- Meagre developments in clothing, soft drink canning, plastics and steel roofing still rely heavily on imported materials which means less value-added in Brunei
- Otherwise Brunei continues to rely on foreign labour from Thailand, India and the Philippines which together with expatriate oil and gas workers make up over a third of Brunei's total work-force
- Overall, import-substitution measures have failed to relieve a massive dependence on imported materials, consumer goods and food – domestic agriculture supplies less than 20% of consumption
- Externally, unsolved territorial issues with Malaysia remain important
- There are demarcation problems over maritime resource exploration and fishing rights in Brunei Bay as well as disputes over the Limbang enclave where Sarawak logging companies regularly intrude on Brunei's stricter forest conservation regime
- Recent bi-lateral negotiations with Malaysia have produced only limited progress in resolving outstanding border demarcation issues.

Further reading

Cleary, M. and Wong, S.Y. (1994) *Oil, Economic Development and Diversification in Brunei*, London, Macmillan.

Gunn, G.C. (1993) 'Rentier capitalism in Negara Brunei Darussalam' in Hewison, K., Robison, R. and Rodan, G.

(eds) *Southeast Asia in the 1990s: Authoritarianism, Democracy and Capitalism*, St. Leonards, NSW, Allen & Unwin.

Saunders, G. (1995) *A History of Brunei*, Kuala Lumpur, Oxford University Press.

Macau

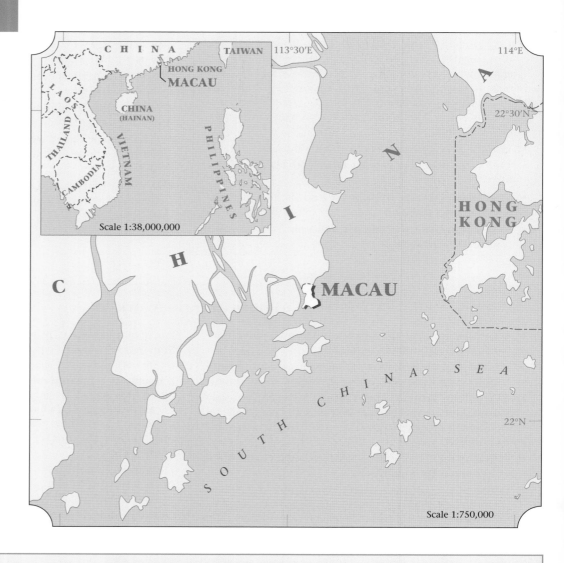

Scale 1:38,000,000

Scale 1:750,000

Historical background

- Early 16th C. Portuguese establish trading contacts

- 1557 Macau colonized by Portugal

- Later 16th and 17th C. Macau prospers as the capital of the East Asian sector of a Portuguese trading empire linking Europe, Africa, India with Asia

- 1602–3 Dutch attacks repelled – Portuguese fortify Macau

- 1667–70 first diplomatic mission from Macau to the Chinese Court

- 1849 Portugal declare Macau independent from China

- 1862 China concedes the occupation of Macau

- 1951 Portugal declares Macau an Overseas Province

- 1966–67 anti-Portuguese riots in Macau during China's cultural revolution – Governor reported to have offered to abandon this colonial outpost

- 1974 after the military coup in Portugal, the new government in Lisbon offers to return Macau to Chinese control. China declines the offer fearing it would unsettle relations with Hong Kong and Taiwan in an uncoordinated attempt to reunify China

- 1976 Portugal grants Macau greater autonomy with a partially elected Legislative Assembly. Conservative political grouping wins 55% of the popular vote

- 1978 Governor Leandro visits Beijing – first visit since 1949 and diplomatic relations established with PRC. Thereafter China's influence expands within little more than façade of Portuguese colonial power

- 1984 elections held for new Legislative Assembly and for first time resident Chinese majority allowed to vote. Two of the six seats won by Chinese candidates; six indirectly elected seats were won unopposed by Chinese candidates; four government officials and a Chinese businessman also appointed

- 1987 Portugal agrees to return Macau to Chinese sovereignty in 1999 – Macau to become a Special Autonomous Region (SAR) with Legislative Assembly retained

- 1989 protests in Macau over the suppression of the pro-democracy movement in China

- 1989–90 Portuguese passports issued to over 100,000 Chinese born in Macau before 1981

- 1990 4,200 Chinese residents granted permanent registration – public disorder follows attempts of other illegal immigrants to seek similar status
- 1990 Governor Melancia resigns over allegations of involvement in a financial scandal – said to be symptomatic of the corruption among officials trying to make quick profits before 1999 handover
- 1990 Legislative Assembly increased from seventeen to 23 members but still only eight elected compared to fifteen appointed

- 1991 General Vieira appointed Governor
- 1993 legislation in Beijing confirms SAR for Macau – Chief Executive to be selected by an electoral college
- 1994 group of local journalists protest to the Portuguese President over press censorship
- 1996 business groupings win half of elected seats in Legislative Assembly
- 20 December 1999 Macau to return to PRC.

Political framework

- Portuguese spend over 30 years attempting to return this tiny 16 km² enclave to China. Beijing's informal influence gets ever stronger as the key source of food, energy and water for Macau
- With an unenthusiastic colonial administration merely serving out time a smoother process of transition to Chinese rule more evident than in Hong Kong
- Strong voice of business in local politics linked to their favourable contacts in Beijing
- Business and civic associations rather than political parties *per se* are present in Legislative Assembly where largest representation from 1996 is for Macau Economic Promotion Association
- Some 1996–97 friction with Beijing over slow pace of removing expatriates in top administrative posts, incorporating Chinese legislation and language in official documents as well as guarantees of labour and religious freedoms. But few of the acrimonious public disputes seen in Hong Kong
- Portuguese passport ownership issue is delicate but Beijing acknowledges their role as travel documents while insisting they preclude Portuguese consular protection after 1999 for ethnic Chinese
- Conciliatory attitude of Governor Vieira generally appeases

Beijing especially as Lisbon government's less confrontational views over human rights in China contrast markedly with their more aggressive stance towards Indonesia over East Timor
- Pro-China business leaders especially keen to continue their role in gambling industry which accounts for 25% GDP. Government also takes one third of casino takings which make up 60% government revenue
- Political connections between business leaders and Beijing expected to leave their control unchanged
- Gambling is closely associated with tourism the other key economic sector. Fifteen times as many people visit Macau than are resident there coming to the casinos mainly from Hong Kong but increasingly from China itself
- Limited attempts to diversify from dependence on tourism and gambling revenues have seen the development of electronics and textiles which account for most merchandise exports
- Mid 1990s saw US trade pressure accusing Macau of being simply a transhipment centre for Chinese exports which therefore circumvented US trade restrictions
- Towards 1999 such pressures may increase as Macau's economic future becomes intertwined with the Free Trade Zone established just across the border in China.

Further reading

Coates, A. (1987) *A Macau Narrative*, Hong Kong, Oxford University Press.

Cremer, R.D. (ed.) (1987) *Macau, City of Commerce and Culture*, Hong Kong, UEA Press.

Leong, K.T. and Davies, S. (1986) *Macau*, Singapore, Times Editions.

Pacific Islands

by Anthony van Fossen

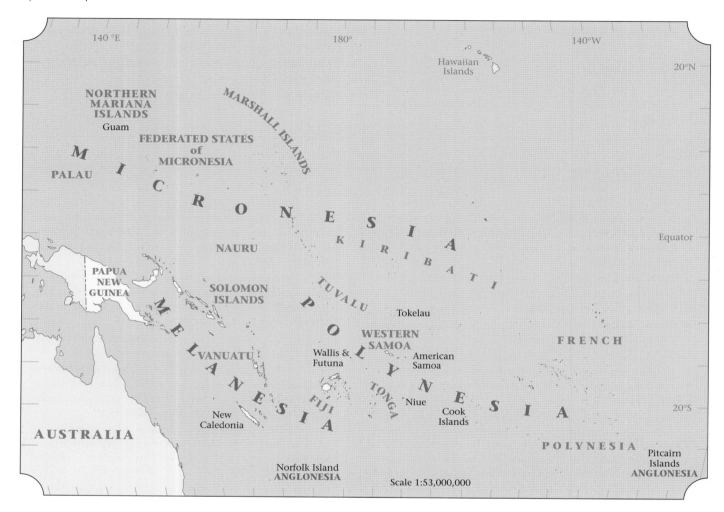

Melanesia	Polynesia
Fiji	American Samoa
New Caledonia	Cook Islands
Papua New Guinea	French Polynesia
Solomon Islands	Niue
Vanuatu	Tokelau
	Tonga
Micronesia	Tuvalu
Federated States of	Wallis and Futuna
Micronesia	Western Samoa
Guam	
Kiribati	**Anglonesia**
Marshall Islands	Norfolk Island
Nauru	Pitcairn Islands
Northern Mariana Islands	
Palau	

- The Pacific Ocean covers one-third of the world's surface and contains over 25,000 islands but the term 'Pacific Islands' usually refers to the 7,500 islands in tropical and subtropical areas removed from the Pacific Rim
- Little more than 10% of these islands are populated – 341 in Melanesia, 287 in Polynesia, 161 in Micronesia and 2 in Anglonesia
- Of the 6.3 million people currently living in the region 83.9% live in Melanesia, 8.9% in Polynesia, 7.1% in Micronesia and less than 0.1% in Anglonesia.

Melanesia

- Melanesia [from the Greek *melas* (black) and *nesos* (islands)] as a category derives from the physical appearance of the indigenous inhabitants of Papua New Guinea (PNG), Vanuatu, New Caledonia, Fiji and the Solomon Islands
- Compared with Polynesia and Micronesia, Melanesia tends (with notable exceptions like Fiji) to have societies which are more egalitarian among men although there are more pronounced gender inequalities.

Polynesia

- Polynesia [from *poly* (many) and *nesos*] extends from Hawaii in the north to Aotearoa/New Zealand in the south-west to Rapanui/Easter Island in the south-east

- This unique triangle is the largest area in the pre-capitalist world over which a single culture takes hold but is eroded by intrusive colonialism. All three of these points on the triangle become fully absorbed into European-dominated settler states of the USA, New Zealand and Chile
- These outlying points to the Polynesian triangle are not considered separately here. Coverage is confined to existing polities where indigenous Polynesians have some degree of effective sovereignty.

Micronesia

- Micronesia [from *micros* (small) and *nesos*] extends from the Northern Marianas in the north, to Palau in the west to Kiribati in the south-east
- These generally smaller islands tend to be more like Polynesian societies emphasizing rule by indigenous hereditary aristocracies both before and after contact with colonial powers.

Anglonesia

- Anglonesia is made up of Norfolk Island and the Pitcairns that were uninhabited at the time when the British arrived in the late 18th C.
- Pitcairn Island was settled from 1790 by mutineers from the *Bounty* and their Tahitian families. Their descendants moved *en masse* to Norfolk Island a former prison colony in 1856.

Early settlement

- Melanesia is settled first – parts of PNG some 50,000 years ago
- More distant parts of Melanesia, all of Polynesia and all of Micronesia settled much later by seafaring speakers of Austronesian languages believed to have a common origin in the Fujian province of southern China
- Austronesians spread to Taiwan around 4000 BC then on to the Philippines, Indonesia and nearby areas of the south-east Asian mainland. They entered Melanesia and Micronesia in about 2000 BC, arrived in Tonga around 1100 BC and from there went to other parts of Polynesia
- The influence of seafaring Austronesians is still apparent today in some coastal areas of Melanesia. It is far clearer in Micronesia and Polynesia where in past centuries Austronesians formed a relatively homogenous political economy, society, culture, and linguistic community on these previously uninhabited islands.

European contact

- European explorers of the Pacific Islands mainly come from the hegemonic core powers of particular eras. Spanish and Portuguese from 1521 (when Magellan visited Guam during the first circumnavigation of the globe) to 1606; Dutch 1615–1722; and British 1765–98

- Spanish galleons made up the vast majority of ships crossing the Pacific before 1769 travelling the Acapulco–Manila route trading Mexican silver for Philippine spices, silk and tea
- While the Spanish pass through Micronesia they have a major impact only in the Northern Marianas and Guam where they stop regularly from 1668 to 1815
- Outside Micronesia Europeans pass hundreds of islands east of New Guinea but land on only about 30 outside Micronesia
- The sheer size of the region severely taxes European marine technology and capacities until the 1770s
- Captain Cook enters the Pacific in 1769 taking advantage of the dramatic improvements in British vessels, techniques of navigation and systems of provisioning which accompanied the hegemonic rivalry with France
- Cook's explorations launch an unprecedented era of rapid political, economic, social, cultural and environmental change for the entire region – equivalent to the transformation set off in the Americas by the 1492 voyage of Columbus
- Cook's explorations accurately map much of Melanesia and Polynesia making them accessible to traders in sandalwood, *bêche-de-mer* (sea-cucumber/sea-slug), whales, Christianity and labour
- Trading networks are established from 1790 connecting Polynesia, Melanesia, China, Europe, North America and Australia
- Many aristocrats in the hierarchical societies of Fiji, Polynesia and Micronesia use trade to consolidate their power through

organizing commoners' labour in exchange for guns. But most islanders are incapable of taking advantage of the new commodity chains to gain much more than alcohol and cheap trade items.

Informal imperialism, 1790s–1870s

- To the 1870s the most significant commercial enterprises are very risky and oriented toward gaining the quickest and largest profits from the rapid extraction of immediately accessible resources

- Sandalwood (used in Chinese ornamental boxes, furniture, incense, perfumes and medicines) is the first significant Pacific Islands commodity to enter the new trading network. Europeans, North Americans and Australians exchange sandalwood for silk, porcelain and tea from China

- Sandalwood vanishes quickly from Fiji 1804–16, the Marquesas in French Polynesia 1815–20, then Hawaii 1811–31 and finally the New Hebrides (Vanuatu) 1841–65

- In places where sandalwood is exhausted it is often replaced by *bêche-de-mer* as the primary export, for example Fiji from 1828 to 1850. Again China is the key market with strong demand for this slug among seafood connoisseurs and those who believe it has aphrodisiac powers

- Whaling flourishes between 1835 and 1860 to meet the demand for whale oil (used in heating and lighting) and bones (for hard structural material) from US and European consumers

- Numerous seafarers desert from American and British whaling ships to become beachcombers or advisers to chiefs and traders. Their rivals for influence over Fijian, Polynesian and eastern Micronesian societies are Christian missionaries who begin arriving in large numbers at about the same time

- Serious depopulation (sometimes up to 95%) follows the arrival of outsiders bringing with them Eurasian disease vectors of influenza, measles, dysentery, tuberculosis, smallpox, typhus, typhoid, whooping cough and venereal diseases. Islanders who have never encountered such diseases have no immunity heightening mortality and sterility

- Indigenous population size generally stabilizes 120–150 years after initial contact (about 1890–1920 in Polynesia and Fiji) and then begins to increase

- The untreated scourges of the 16th to 19th centuries contrast with the quick introduction of medicines and sanitary measures in the last colonial frontiers of the 20th C. The Australian colonial administration, for example, acts to stop epidemics among more than a million New Guinea highlanders when they make first contact with Europeans and the Eurasian disease pool in the 1930s and 1940s

- During the later 19th C. depopulation is accelerated in Melanesia (especially the Solomon Islands and Vanuatu) with forced labour recruitment ('blackbirding') and migration to the plantations of Queensland (Australia), Fiji, and Samoa

- Coercion is less important in explaining Polynesian depopulation and migration which is mostly voluntary despite occasional instances of enslavement by Peruvians for work in the mines and plantations of South America

- In Micronesia migration is relatively limited during this period

- In Anglonesia all the inhabitants of the small and overpopulated Pitcairn Island leave to become free settlers on Norfolk Island

- By 1880 there is a crisis in the system – supplies of sandalwood, *bêche-de-mer*, whales and Melanesian labour are seriously depleted

- There is also a crucial change in patterns of demand. Whale oil and bone are increasingly being substituted by petroleum and steel while the British East India Company converts large areas of Bengal to opium production to unlock the China trade and marginalize Pacific Islands products

- The exhaustion of easily accessible resources exploited in a hunting and gathering labour process ends the initial stage of Pacific Islands capitalism.

Formal incorporation into a global political economy

- France anticipates the next stage of capitalism becoming the first to annex Pacific Island countries in a bid to secure new markets, raw materials and spheres of influence. Tahiti becomes protectorate in 1842 and New Caledonia in 1853

- For the other core powers imperial expansion comes later

- The long economic depression from 1873 to 1896 makes all core countries insecure especially as it is accompanied by accelerating globalization of commodity chains and a 'second industrial revolution'. New industrial processes most evident in the USA and Germany destabilize the existing economic balance of power between core countries. Britain and France are particularly threatened, explaining their intense enthusiasm for imperialism, new colonies, protected markets and new sources of raw materials

- Supplies of copra, sugar, pineapples, margarine, coffee, vanilla, cacao and fruit; the discovery of huge nickel deposits in New Caledonia; demand for guano and phosphate fertilizers to support the burgeoning agricultural industries of Australia, New Zealand and Japan intensify interest in the Pacific Islands

- Some European business people in the Pacific Islands call on their governments to annex the countries where they reside so that their capital investment can flourish

- More general erosion of confidence in *laissez-faire* means state intervention to advance the interests of capital is increasingly accepted. New imperialistic initiatives are reactions to intensified competition between the principal core powers and an attempt to secure a new share of the global market

- In the short period 1870–1900 almost all Pacific Island countries fall under the control of Britain, British New Zealand and Australia, France, Germany, the USA and Chile

- Spain, the original regional imperialist, loses out as Germany and the USA take over its Micronesian colonies

- Initially this new imperialism results in protecting settlers and their small enterprises already in the region, securing sea lanes and building coaling stations. But it soon leads to the development of much larger and far more highly capitalized enterprises characteristic of the new stage of Pacific Islands capitalism

- Monopolistic or oligopolistic enterprises enjoying state support develop plantations, mining, food processing, shipping and retail merchandising

- Plantation agriculture becomes extensive and heavily concentrated in a few companies which in some areas lobby for large-scale labour migration either from hinterlands or from overseas. The Australian Colonial Sugar Refining Co. (CSR), for example, encourages the immigration of large numbers of indentured labourers from India to work on its sugar plantations in Fiji
- The plantation is especially significant as an institution which reorganizes the environment and subordinates the labour force to export-oriented commodity production
- New more highly capitalized export economies are mediated through port cities which develop as centres where disproportionately large numbers of the colonial elite reside in a monetized environment which increasingly takes hold in the countryside
- Germany's defeat in the 1914–18 war leads to the loss of its large Pacific Islands empire – Australia and New Zealand take over New Guinea, Western Samoa, Kiribati, and Nauru
- Most of Micronesia becomes a string of Japanese settler colonies also with economies significantly controlled by large companies which are created for that purpose
- The inter-war period accelerates the concentration of control over export agriculture in a few large firms and smaller plantations virtually disappear either taken over by large firms or replaced by small-scale indigenous producers as dependent suppliers on highly unequal terms
- By 1941 apart from a few American and British outposts Micronesia is predominantly Japanese while Melanesia and Polynesia are increasingly tied to Australia and New Zealand with some French, British and American influence.

Pacific War and the aftermath

- The Second World War has a deeper effect on the Pacific Islands than any other single event in modern history
- The Japanese objective of expanding beyond their Micronesian colonies leads to the occupation of Guam and the bombing of Pearl Harbor in Hawaii in 1941 in an attempt to remove US naval power
- Dramatic battles follow particularly in Micronesia with widespread militarization and infrastructure development in the region
- The war itself ends with the dropping of atomic bombs on Hiroshima and Nagasaki by aeroplanes taking off from the island of Tinian in the Northern Marianas
- Wartime prosperity, the more egalitarian ideas, manners and interracial fellowship among American troops and the expulsion of large numbers of Japanese troops and settlers from Micronesia heightens indigenous expectations and makes colonial rule seem more oppressive
- Strikes, increased political agitation and, in Melanesia, radical religious movements ('cargo cults') follow the war
- Military involvement in all corners of the Pacific Islands creates a much sharper sense of the importance of the islands and their collective identity as a region
- At a most pragmatic and immediate level airfields, harbours and roads are built which provide links with other Pacific Islands and the world outside. Still in use today they are the basis for increasing travel within the region

- Recognition by the governments of Australia and New Zealand of this increasing regionalization and their desire to become its post-war leaders are obvious in their Canberra Pact of 1944 when they propose the creation of the first intergovernmental regional organization
- South Pacific Commission (SPC) is established in 1947 with headquarters in Nouméa, the capital of the French territory of New Caledonia. But SPC, and most other important regional agencies, continue to reflect an Australian and New Zealand definition of the region which also mirrors the interests of the USA
- Within SPC the interests and policies of other metropolitan members (the Netherlands until the absorption of West Papua by Indonesia in 1962, Britain until its recent withdrawal and France) are noted but also questioned
- This definition of the region and the roles of metropolitan powers continues to reflect the implications of post-war geopolitics
- Melanesia–Polynesia–Anglonesia is represented as an Australian–New Zealand 'lake' with the French, British and formerly the Dutch being on the periphery
- Micronesia, after the departure of the Japanese, enters the American sphere of influence once the UN allows the USA to create a unique 'strategic trust' permitting the continuation of military bases and nuclear testing
- SPC starts as an organization co-ordinating the economic, health, and social policies of the colonial powers who are its founding members. Mostly at the insistence of the French it does not engage in what is deemed to be 'political' activities
- SPC makes no criticism of the fact that the largest number of nuclear tests in any area of the world (over 250) take place in the Pacific Islands (see Figure 24): the USA, from 1946 in the Marshall Islands; Britain, starting in the Gilbert Islands (Kiribati) in 1957; and France, from 1962 shifts all its nuclear testing to Polynesia
- SPC does attempt to bring island people together for the first time and constructs a viable regional identity but its caveat on 'politics' does not allow it to be a vehicle for decolonization
- Britain, Australia and New Zealand are more inclined to grant full political independence to their Pacific Island colonies or territories than are the USA or France.

Decolonization and the South Pacific Forum

- Decolonization from the 1960s creates a large number of microstates
- Independence greatly strengthens regionalism as growing numbers of regional organizations become responsible for tasks formerly done by the colonial powers but which the new states are not large enough to perform
- The commitment of metropolitan states to conserve a system of small island sovereignty is expressed in their willingness to fund regional organizations which permit Pacific Island states to meet the obligations of statehood by sharing regional facilities in education, training, research, communications and transportation. Articulating an agreed regional position also gives the islands a stronger voice in international forums

- But substantial growth in bilateral foreign aid from different sources at the same time subverts the development of regional co-operation in many areas

- Increasing dissatisfaction with the SPC's colonial character leads in 1965 to the first indigenous intergovernmental organization – the Pacific Producers Association designed to pursue higher prices for agricultural exports

- 1970 Fijian independence galvanizes wider changes after SPC, under French influence, refuses to reform itself and grant indigenous leaders more power

- 1971 the independent or self-governing island states joined by Australia and New Zealand form and become members of the South Pacific Forum (SPF) (see document in Part 3, Section 2.5)

- SPF quickly becomes the foremost regional organization. Meetings attended by senior government representatives make its proclamations powerful expressions of the policies of member governments

- Australia and New Zealand are the only metropolitan governments holding full membership and contribute the bulk of SPF funding

- Although funding levels for regional intergovernmental organizations are low in absolute terms this does not provide an accurate measure of their more significant role in defining the region's identity, policies and objectives

- SPF sets a pattern by establishing its secretariat in Suva, Fiji's capital, which then becomes the centre of the many new regional organizations created with the advent of independence and self-government

- The location of all but a few in Suva is justified in terms of centralizing interaction and achieving economies of scale although PNG, in particular, having most of the people and land in the Pacific Islands, attacks the centrality of Fiji

- Conflicts within regional organizations between Melanesia, on one hand, and Polynesia and Micronesia, on the other hand, reflect basic geographical, political, economic, social, cultural, and linguistic differences. Anglonesia has little influence in regional organizations

- Melanesia's larger islands which are often rich in natural resources generate a more self-sufficient foundation for nationalist, anti-colonial and Third Worldist aspirations. Reservations are expressed about the roles of Australia, New Zealand, and other metropolitan powers in regional organizations and support given for the independence of Kanaky (New Caledonia)

- Melanesian governments at times portray regionalism itself as an obstacle to national policies

- In 1986 PNG, Vanuatu and the Solomon Islands form the Melanesian Spearhead Group to the concerns and irritation of Polynesians and Micronesians who claim it cracks the collective voice of the region. Fiji later overcomes its reluctance and also joins the Melanesian Spearhead Group

- More radical and volatile politics in the other three Melanesian states stems from the fact that when their independence comes (1975–80) their leaders are far more influenced by the radical ideas of the New Left combined with their countries' tendencies toward egalitarianism

- In contrast traditional aristocratic ideologies are still prevalent in Fiji and most Polynesian states which generally achieve self-government earlier in a more conservative atmosphere

- Polynesia and Micronesia consist of small states which depend more heavily on metropolitan patrons and regional organizations in which they have a majority in a one member–one vote system

- Many Polynesian and Micronesian states (particularly the smaller, less well-endowed ones) want to continue to be associated states of metropolitan countries and fear that any Melanesia-inspired anti-colonial regional agenda may endanger aid flows

- Most of the states of Polynesia have economies characterized by MIRAB – migration, remittance, aid and bureaucracy. They receive the world's highest per capita level of foreign aid and serve as labour reserves for metropolitan countries. In some cases a majority of citizens of these microstates are immigrant labourers in New Zealand, Australia, the USA and French New Caledonia where substantial Polynesian migration began in the 1960s and 1970s

- The same process is more recent in Micronesia as citizens of the freely associated states (the Marshall Islands, the Federated States of Micronesia, and Palau) migrate to Guam, the Northern Marianas, Hawaii and mainland USA

- Few Melanesians today are immigrant workers

- Polynesians and Micronesians tend to favour regional organizations that admit non-independent territories (most of which are in Polynesia and Micronesia), while Melanesians historically insist on independent or at least self-government as necessary for admission

- If Melanesians become too critical of their small influence in regional organizations Polynesians and Micronesians tend to draw more closely to metropolitan states such as Australia, New Zealand and the USA

- In the post-Cold War era and with the admission of new Micronesian states in free association with the USA to even the most restrictive regional organizations, this Polynesian–Micronesian strategy is ever more effective. Melanesians are becoming increasingly resigned to a regional structure which they formerly attacked as conservative and neo-colonial but which provides a more comprehensive coverage of the entire scope of the region

- Melanesians operate as a minority voting bloc in an ever larger number of regional organizations rather than forming separate ones for each of the three major sub-regions within it. In any case the Melanesian Spearhead Group is itself fractured by conflicts between PNG and the Solomon Islands over the mineral-rich secessionist island of Bougainville.

Regionalism: outcomes and prospects

- Regional organizations, particularly those associated with the SPF have some successes in
  - 1980 agreement with Australia and New Zealand allowing non-reciprocal preferential access to their markets for SPF members. This agreement becomes crucial to textiles exports from Fiji and exports of automobile parts from Western Samoa
  - creating the Pacific Forum Line shipping company which provides regular, permanent and dependable liner services to many countries for the first time

- creating an offshore exploration body for the manganese, cobalt, nickel and copper which exists on Pacific Islands seabeds, particularly in Polynesia, but cannot yet be exploited profitably with existing technologies and prices
- developing the South Pacific Nuclear-Free Zone Treaty of 1985 that is ratified quickly by the USSR and China and eleven years later by the USA, UK, and France
- negotiating far less unsatisfactory licensing and royalty arrangements for the Asian and US deep-water fleets which take more than US$1.5 billion of tuna annually from waters within the exclusive economic zones of Pacific Islands – placing pressure on Japanese, South Korean, and Taiwanese vessels operating in Pacific Islands waters to end drift-net fishing by 1992
- with other members of the Association of Small Island States publicizing the threat represented by global warming to islands that lie barely above sea level (see Figure 23)
- providing a vehicle for informal pressure on governments in PNG and the Solomon Islands whose citizens are gaining minimal returns from lucrative logging operations which yield hundreds of millions of dollars a year in profit for foreign companies but are devastating the environment

- Despite some obvious tensions South Pacific regional relations are generally more co-operative than in many other areas of the world not least because of the greater distances between countries. Relative to their size regional intergovernmental organizations in the Pacific Islands are considerably stronger and more effective than they are in South-East Asia or the Caribbean
- However, there is no significant evidence yet that political leaders are seriously interested in compromising sovereignty to form stronger more encompassing regional organizations on the EU model
- Proposals to establish a regional airline from the many national flag carriers or a regional development bank or an economic union have foundered
- There is, nevertheless, considerable attenuation of sovereignty to maintain strong bilateral links with metropolitan countries which provide aid or other assistance
- One unusual feature of regional organizations in the Pacific Islands is the membership and active participation of First World countries particularly Australia and New Zealand
- Although regionalism is primarily oriented toward issues which are not immediately related to security Pacific Island countries expect Australia, New Zealand and the USA to protect their sovereignty in an emergency. Yet they also express some discomfort about their dependency desiring a wider range of trade investment and aid partners especially from Asia
- Indeed the islands are increasingly merged with Asia in the term 'Asia-Pacific' which gains common currency from the 1970s and enters into the titles of numerous intergovernmental organizations
- Despite the post-war suspension of Japanese influence in its former Micronesian colonies Japan has become increasingly important to the economies of these American territories
- Japanese demand for timber, minerals and other natural resources similarly strengthens ties with countries in Melanesia

- A major policy shift in 1987 saw Japan's aid to the region grow at almost three times the rate of its general foreign assistance budget allowing Japan to quickly displace New Zealand as the third largest donor after Australia and the USA. By 1990 Japan indicates a desire to become a member of the SPC but the application has been deferred into the future
- Concerns remain about environmental impact of Japanese operations and ill-feeling lingers over Japanese behaviour during the Pacific War. More fundamentally there are fears that this will be the first of a series of requests for membership in regional organizations from Asian countries with significant implications for the identity and future of the region
- As well as Japan, China, Taiwan and Malaysia are currently the most significant Asian players
- Diplomatic rivalry between Beijing and Taipei surfaced in the region from the 1970s and continues to produce rival offers of economic involvement
- Malaysia's role is far more recent. 1987 coups in Fiji produced a regime to which the Malaysian government is sympathetic and this paved the way for a Malaysian company to acquire Fiji's largest conglomerate from its Australian owners. Malaysian companies also operate rapacious logging projects in PNG and the Solomon Islands to meet demand from Japan that can no longer be satisfied from logged-out areas of South-East Asia
- India's interest is largely limited to concern about the situation of the considerable number of people of Indian descent in Fiji especially after the coups in 1987
- Indonesia has a record of encouraging closer ties between Pacific Island countries and ASEAN. But it is regarded with suspicion after annexing West Papua in 1962, its subsequent creation there of a settler colony subordinating indigenous people and its future intentions toward PNG
- Relations with other Asian countries tend to be almost exclusively commercial
- While the principal links for Pacific Islands are likely to be with each other and their present or former colonial powers into the foreseeable future, expanding links with Asia is seen as a matter of urgency. This is especially the case as regionalism becomes increasingly important in the post-Cold War period when geopolitics are no longer defined in bi-polar terms
- A major question is how this Asia-Pacific regionalism is to be approached
- One direction put forward most often by Melanesian states is that the Pacific Island nations should attempt to become members of Asia-Pacific groupings. PNG has in fact been attending ASEAN meetings as an observer since 1976
- Polynesian and Micronesian states are most likely to propose another strategy. Pacific Island states should consolidate around existing organizations to negotiate collectively with one voice as a unified region with special needs for particular economic programmes which cater to its unique character
- This debate on regionalism is crucial for the new generation of Pacific Islands leaders who emerge almost as a cohort in the 1990s to replace the previous generation. Nothing less than the identity of the Asia-Pacific region and its periphery is involved.

Pacific Islands

Further reading

Crocombe, R. (1989) *The South Pacific: an Introduction*, Suva, University of the South Pacific.

Crocombe, R. (1995) *The Pacific Islands and the USA*, Honolulu, East–West Center.

Douglas, N. and Douglas, N. (eds) (1994) *Pacific Islands Yearbook*, 17th edn, Suva, Fiji Times.

Finney, B. (1994) 'The other one-third of the globe', *Journal of World History,* vol.5, no.2, pp.273–97.

Howe, K.R., Kiste, R.C. and Lal, B.V. (eds) (1994) *Tides of History: the Pacific Islands in the Twentieth Century*, Honolulu, University of Hawaii Press.

McNeill, J.R. (1994) 'Of rats and men: a synoptic environmental history of the island Pacific', *Journal of World History*, vol.5, no.2, pp.299–349.

Stanley, D. (1992) *Micronesia Handbook*, Chico, Calif., Moon Publications.

Stanley, D. (1996) *South Pacific Handbook*, Chico, Calif., Moon Publications.

by Anthony van Fossen

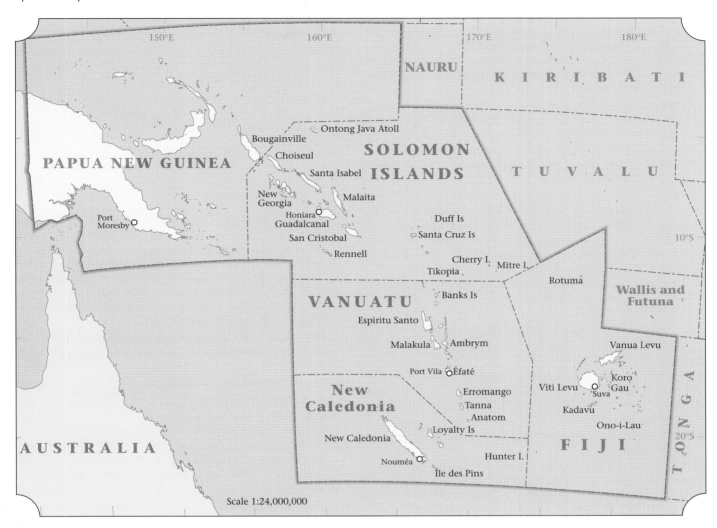

Scale 1:24,000,000

Fiji

Historical background

- Fiji has general linguistic unity for many centuries before European contact but is politically consolidated by King Thakombau with British assistance from 1874 to the 1890s

- Fiji is at the cusp of Polynesia and Melanesia and was regional centre for British imperial administration from 1877 to 1952. Later becomes regional political, economic and educational centre for all the Pacific Islands within the Anglo sphere of influence

- Evidence of human settlement from 1290 BC suggests a hierarchical society particularly in the eastern, Polynesian regions – western areas more Melanesian and egalitarian. Fijians are generally classified as Melanesian because of their appearance not their more Polynesian social system

- Trade, military and aristocratic marriage alliances with Tongans and Samoans for centuries before European contact make Fiji one of the most diversified material cultures in the Pacific Islands

- 17th and 18th C. navigators from Holland (Abel Tasman) and Britain (including Captains Cook and Bligh) visit Fiji

- Capitalist penetration comes only in 1804 through the China trade in sandalwood which collapses with deforestation in 1814. More labour- and capital-intensive trade in *bêche-de-mer* with China 1827–50

Melanesia

- Ratu (Lord) Seru Thakombau becomes the most powerful indigenous aristocrat through monopolizing the China trade in the 1840s when he proclaims himself King of Fiji

- 1851–67 American gunboats visit Thakombau demanding debt repayment. This is eventually paid by the Australian-owned Polynesian Company in exchange for 800 km² of prime land which is converted into freehold and sold to investors and settlers. 3,000 white settlers start arriving in large numbers to establish plantations

- 1874 Fiji becomes a British colony – Thakombau cedes territory but thereby acquires support to subjugate the Tongan domains in eastern Fiji and rebellious western groups

- Government eventually validates settlers claims to 170,000 hectares of prime land which remain freehold to this day – about 9% of Fiji's total area

- Eastern indigenous aristocrats become indirect rulers and builders of a Methodist theocracy. Their power and financial demands on indigenous commoners secured with assurances that no more indigenous land can be sold only leased. Fijians to remain villagers subject to their chiefs and not large-scale plantation workers or town-dwellers

- 1875 Thakombau and two sons return from Australia introducing a measles epidemic which kills 40,000 – 20% of all Fijians

- 1877–1911 23,000 Melanesians from the Solomon Islands and Vanuatu are introduced as indentured labourers mostly gathering copra on white plantations

- 'Free' Fijian labour is scarce and prohibited by chiefs from participating in the large-scale sugar plantation development envisaged by the British government and the Colonial Sugar Refining Co. (CSR) of Australia

- 60,000 indentured labourers immigrate from India – 40,000 settle in Fiji

- Sugar becomes the country's primary industry increasingly monopolized by CSR which swallows up small sugar plantations and begins to encourage Indo-Fijians to become small-scale tenant producers on 10–12 acre blocks from 1924

- Chiefs and their indigenous followers set a pattern of breaking strikes and frustrating unionism often associated with the large numbers of poor, struggling and deeply indebted Indo-Fijian cane farmers

- Australian companies Burns Philp and W.R. Carpenter increasingly diversify from their initial trading in copra

- 1920s–1930s the Messianic indigenous commoner Apolosi Nawai forms popular movements and business enterprises to challenge the collaboration between indigenous chiefs and the Anglo political and economic elite. He is exiled and his movements banned, particularly at the instigation of his nemesis Ratu (Lord) Sir Lala Sukuna

- Sukuna is the foremost synthesizer of indigenous aristocratic ideology and the leading indigenous ally of the Anglo rulers until his death in 1958 when he is replaced in this role by Ratu (Lord) Sir Kamesese Mara

- 1946 Indo-Fijians outnumber indigenous Fijians for the first time

- 1960s tourism begins to develop as a major industry – eventually surpasses fisheries, copra and gold, and equalling sugar in importance. This allows Fiji to remain the least aid-dependent Pacific Island country except Nauru

- 1970 independence is followed by considerable development of infrastructure in electrification, road building and water provision

- 1973 CSR, which controlled the sugar industry for 90 years, sells its operations to the Fiji government

- 1980 plummeting sugar prices end virtually uninterrupted post-war growth and foreshadow relative economic sluggishness and uncertainty thereafter

- April 1987 Fiji Labour Party wins elections but is overthrown a month later by a coup. Second coup in September also directed by Colonel Rabuka prevents the creation of a compromise Government of National Unity and precipitates further devaluation, inflation, Indian emigration and crisis in the tourism industry

- October 1987 Fiji becomes a republic and is expelled from the British Commonwealth

- 1989 indigenous Fijians outnumber Indians for the first time in 43 years

- Later 1980s New Right economic policies pursued and regressive taxation system instituted. Multi-racial labour unions repressed and the regime advocates separate racial unions or no unions at all. Numerous tax-free, low-wage, non-unionized factories established to export garments and other goods to Australia, New Zealand and the USA

- 1990 new constitution promulgated discriminating against Indo-Fijians, westerners, city-dwellers and indigenous commoners

- 1992 and 1994 elections – Rabuka re-appointed Prime Minister

- 1994 W.R. Carpenter conglomerate, which accounts for 25% of Fiji's GDP, is sold by its Australian owners to MBf, a company closely associated with the Malaysian government

- 1995–96 state-owned National Bank of Fiji becomes insolvent with US$100 million in bad loans in many cases to indigenous and Rotuman supporters of Rabuka. Rescue package initiated with public funds

- Tens of thousands of marginal Indo-Fijian sugar farmers have land leases which begin to expire in 1997. Indigenous nationalists are threatening not to renew them contributing to uncertainty about the future of the key sugar industry.

Political framework

- **Federal/local system.** A well-developed system of local government for indigenous people at village, district, provincial, and divisional levels. The Fijian Administration, represented most clearly in the Native Land Trust Board which administers 83% of the country's land, is often called 'a government within a government'. All decisions of the Native Lands Commission are final with no possibility of appeal or recourse to courts. City and town councils also function and only at this level could a person vote for someone of a different race after 1990

- **Constitution – how democratic?** 1990 constitution promulgated without the operation of any democratic processes. It gives the Great Council of Chiefs the power to appoint the President, who must be an indigenous Fijian, and the 24 indigenous Senators in the chamber of 34 members. The President in turn appoints nine Senators to represent the other races with the final Senator being appointed by the council of the Polynesian island of Rotuma. President appoints the Prime Minister who must also be indigenous and the leader of the opposition from the 70-member House of Representatives. House elected directly by racially segregated voters who are not able to vote for anyone who is not a member of their race as defined by the government. Indigenous Fijians elect 37 members with conservative rural and eastern aristocratic areas being heavily over-represented; Indians get 27 seats; Rotumans one; and the other races (Europeans, part-Europeans, Chinese) five. There is uncertainty about the future of the 1990 constitution as a government-funded Commission of Review in 1996 calls for abandoning its key features and increasing the sphere of multi-racial democracy

- **Which party controls?** SVT, often called the Fijian Political Party or 'the Chiefs party', is the largest. Headed by Rabuka the leader of the two military coups and the current Prime Minister, but the real power behind SVT is the Great Council of Chiefs. SVT holds 31 seats in the House, the National Federation Party (NFP) 20 seats and the Labour Party 7 seats

- **Ethnic politics?** Politics are highly racialized and ethnicized despite one brief attempt to overcome this. The formation of the Fiji Labour Party in 1985 represents the first serious attempt to replace ethnic politics with a politics oriented around class in an extensive programme of multi-racial social democratic reform. The government formed by the Labour Party in coalition with the Indian-dominated NFP was overthrown in a 1987 military coup which, with a second coup that year, explicitly re-racialized politics. The 1990 constitution, even more than its 1970 predecessor, encourages ethnic polarization and racially-based parties

- **Political control of the media?** Since the military coups the publication of newspapers is at times suspended – the Fiji *Sun* is shut down permanently and the largest, the Fiji *Times*, practices self-censorship but is still threatened on occasion. The Ministry of Information exercises very tight control over the government-owned company which runs four of six radio stations and 65% of the only television station

- **How independent is the judiciary?** The 1990 constitution guarantees the independence of the judiciary but requires that no less than 50% of those employed in the judiciary be indigenous Fijians or Polynesian inhabitants of Rotuma

- **Legislative and bureaucratic power?** Since the 1987 coups the power and unity of political parties declined especially among indigenous Fijians. The bureaucracy is under increasing pressure from the wider indigenous political movement.

Further reading

Europa World Year Book (1996) London, Europa.

Lal, B. (1992) *Broken Waves: a History of the Fiji Islands in the Twentieth Century*, Honolulu, University of Hawaii Press.

Sutherland, W. (1992) *Beyond the Politics of Race: an Alternative History of Fiji to 1992*, Canberra, Australian National University.

New Caledonia

Historical background

- New Caledonia holds 30% of the world's reserves of nickel – indispensable for nuclear technologies and armaments. Used by France to justify limiting foreign participation in mining ventures which are said to compromise national security

- Pottery dated at earlier than 1000 BC suggests indigenous Kanaks probably come from New Guinea

- Indigenous Kanak society was generally more hierarchical than other Melanesian societies. Chiefs preside over taro gardens and yam cultivation oriented around complicated irrigation systems and terraces. As in other parts of Melanesia there is high linguistic density with 30 indigenous languages

- Polynesians arrive in Loyalty Islands a few hundred years before Europeans

- 1774 Captain Cook first European to explore and name New Caledonia. Succeeded by French navigators and British and American whalers before Europeans settle and trade sandalwood and *bêche-de-mer* for the China market

- 1853 French annex New Caledonia and transport 22,000 convicts between 1864–97. France annexes the Loyalty Islands in 1866 but few settlers move there

- 1878–1917 extensive land expropriation by settlers who defeat indigenous warriors – further expropriation leaves Kanaks with only 10% of the territory

- 1863 high grade nickel discovered and later becomes the major export industry – Rothschilds become key investors and promoters. Falling indigenous Kanak population (60,000 in 1770s to 17,000 in 1921) leads to importation of labour from Asia – initially Japan then Indo-China and Java

- Pacific War sees hundreds of thousands of American soldiers pass through the Allied base in the capital of Nouméa which handles more cargo during the Second World War than any Pacific port except San Francisco. Unprecedented employment opportunities created for Kanaks

- 1951 Kanaks given full French citizenship and enfranchised

- Strong pro-independence movement thwarted by the rise of General de Gaulle in 1958 who establishes the subsequent anti-independence stance of French governments

- 1969–73 nickel boom leads to European population rising by a third and the Polynesian population doubling – indigenous Kanak nationalism grows. Tourism becomes an important industry

Melanesia

- 1984–88 pro-independence Kanak supporters killed and nickel mines are blown up – police killed and captured in retaliation
- 1986 UN General Assembly declares that France should decolonize despite strong French objections – 1980s generally characterized by confrontation and unrest that hurt tourism
- 1988 the Matignon Accords call for a ten-year truce which would end with independence plebiscite but the two most powerful indigenous leaders who signed the Accord killed by Kanak militant
- 1990s increasing labour union militancy, strike activity and social tensions especially among unemployed Kanaks who feel excluded from the benefits of the Matignon Accords. But the overall focus of party political activity shifts from the confrontation of the 1980s to negotiation.

Political framework

- **Federal/local system.** New Caledonia is administered by a High Commissioner (a political appointee of the French President) with very extensive direct powers and can intervene in the legislative process at any time to rule by decree. Kanak political movements seek to reduce the powers of the High Commissioner and Paris. They have had limited success although 1988 Matignon Accords result in more power being devolved to a local and regional level
- **Constitution – how democratic?** The constitutional arrangement is defined by the Fifth French Republic's constitution and special laws which give a very restricted democratic polity. Only deputies of the French National Assembly and members of provincial assemblies are elected by universal suffrage. Provincial and territorial assemblies may be overruled and disempowered by the High Commissioner
- **Which party controls?** The conservative and loyalist Rassemblement pour la Calédonie dans la République (RPCR) has been dominant particularly as its principal rival the liberationist Front de Libération Nationale Kanak et Socialiste

(FLNKS) has had a policy of boycotting national elections. One of the ten richest men in France, Jacques Lafleur, a local mine and land owner, leads the RPCR

- **Ethnic politics?** Although both major parties have multi-racial support RPCR is backed by most French settlers while FLNKS represents more in the indigenous Kanak minority than any other party. FLNKS does best in the two principally rural provinces with overwhelming Melanesian majorities. RPCR gets solid support from the settler-dominated and Nouméa-based South Province
- **Political control of the media?** The government owns the television network and all but one minor radio station. All programmes are in French mostly coming from metropolitan France. The only daily newspaper is conservative and party political periodicals are less important than in the 1980s
- **How independent is the judiciary?** The French metropolitan state controls the judiciary with New Caledonia having limited influence. France supplies the laws although these are supplemented by New Caledonia's subsidiary legislation and the High Commissioner's decrees. The French Minister of Justice appoints the principal officers of the court
- **Legislative and bureaucratic power?** As in metropolitan France the bureaucracy rather than the numerous and schismatic political parties controls the country. Few New Caledonians are prominent in the public service which is drawn almost exclusively from metropolitan France – the top levels often constituting an intellectual and technocratic elite from the most prestigious French universities.

Further reading

Aldrich, R. (1993) *France and the South Pacific since 1940*, Honolulu, University of Hawaii Press.

Henningham, S. (1991) *France and the South Pacific: a Contemporary History*, Honolulu, University of Hawaii Press.

Solomon Islands

Historical background

- Current boundaries established in 1900 by the British colonial government
- 1300 BC earliest material evidence of human habitation
- Migrations from Tuvalu, Wallis and Futuna after AD 500 establish the Polynesian populations which exist today on outer islands. High linguistic density – 87 mutually unintelligible languages
- Repeated Tongan incursions in the centuries before the first European contact
- 16th C. Spanish, French and British explore the Solomons

- 1820s–1860s whalers and traders in sandalwood, turtle, pearl shell, and *bêche-de-mer*
- 1870s labour recruiters for overseas sugar plantations active
- Despite a declining Melanesian population (mostly from introduced disease) 19,000 leave for Queensland and 10,000 for Fiji – only half return before the indentured labour system ends in 1911. Christian missions not very successful until the labour trade ends
- 1893–99 British colonial control develops over the entire archipelago to end the threat of colonization by Germany
- Lever Brothers and Burns Philp develop extensive copra plantations after 1905

- 1942 Japanese conquer the Solomons. Successful US counter-attack over next year results in some of the bloodiest battles in the Pacific War – Guadalcanal 80,000 die including 40,000 islanders (see Figure 7)

- US soldiers and island labourers build many of the roads and airstrips which are important today – Honiara built from a large American military base becomes the new capital after 1945

- Pro-American, anti-British radical religious movement or 'cargo cult' becomes very powerful on the most populous island of Malaita before being repressed with thousands of arrests. Eclipsed in early 1950s but only after it nullifies local divisions and becomes the basis for effective large-scale popular organizations on Malaita

- Since the early 1970s commercial fishing and, to a lesser extent, canning become major industries controlled by Japanese companies

- 1978 independence achieved – new constitution prevents people born outside the Solomons from owning land although leases are permitted

- 1984–86 Solomons government action against poaching by US tuna fleet results in major confrontation with the Reagan Administration which issues damaging sanctions but finally relents and signs an agreement

- 1989 riot of 5,000 unemployed Melanesian Malaitans in the capital of Honiara against alleged insults from Polynesians who originate from the outlier islands

- From 1992 relations with PNG become strained – allegations that the Solomons are giving support to rebels on the copper-rich secessionist island of Bougainville. PNG army incursions kill Solomon Islanders

- Increasing alarm about unsustainable logging practices prompted by government's special tax advantages – widespread reports of government corruption over issue of logging licences

- From 1991 Council of Trade Unions, opposition Labour Party and the Central Bank repeatedly warn about resource depletion, unrestrained deficit spending, high inflation, ever higher levels of foreign indebtedness and the imminent possibility of national bankruptcy

- 1995–96 paramilitary forces deployed to defend Malaysian logging interests against protesters – some inhabitants forcibly removed from their island so that it can be logged.

Political framework

- **Federal/local system.** Since 1993 nine provinces each have an elected premier and considerable powers over communications, rural health services and schools. Largely dependent on the central government for finance but provincial governments levy head taxes. Within each province various area councils deal with local or village matters. 1990 Honiara Town Council dissolved and is replaced with an authority comprising members of both the public and private sectors. Almost 40% of the paid work-force is employed by some level of government

- **Constitution – how democratic?** The Solomon Islands are a parliamentary democracy with the British Crown represented by a Governor General. A national parliament of 47 members elects the Prime Minister from its ranks

- **Which party controls?** Party discipline is very weak. There are a number of political parties with fluctuating membership. A very high turnover of MPs for whom re-election most often depends on clientelism and direct benefits for supporters rather than merit encouraging virtually uncontrolled deficit spending. As a result country close to insolvency

- **Ethnic politics?** Politics are not heavily ethnicized

- **Political control of the media?** Although the government owns the only radio station and a newspaper (there is no television station) these have not been particularly politicized. Nor has effective political pressure been applied to privately-owned newspapers despite threats to freedom of the press

- **How independent is the judiciary?** Judiciary appears to be fairly independent

- **Legislative and bureaucratic power?** Parties are quite weak allowing the executive and bureaucracy a fair degree of independence.

Further reading

Bennett, J.A. (1987) *Wealth of the Solomons: a History of a Pacific Archipelago*, Honolulu, University of Hawaii Press.

Stanley, D. (1996) *South Pacific Handbook*, Chico, Calif., Moon Publications.

Vanuatu

Historical background

- Earliest known settlement on northern islands dates from about 2000 BC

- Southern islands settled from distant Polynesia AD 1000–1500

- Vanuatu has the highest linguistic density in the world – one language for every 1,000 people

- 1606 island of Espiritu Santo the site of a small aborted Spanish settlement

- Early 1770s Captain Cook names islands as New Hebrides

- Archipelago does not enter into the global capitalist system until it becomes an important source of sandalwood for the British China trade 1825–65

- French and British settlers acquire large areas of land for plantations

- Significant land speculation leads eventually to confrontation and gunboat diplomacy between France and the UK before they establish a joint naval commission to control the archipelago in 1887

- 1906 naval commission formalized as the New Hebrides condominium government under joint French and UK control to thwart German colonial ambitions. Indigenous ni-Vanuatu divided on the basis of loyalties to English or French language, politics, culture and religion (Protestant or Catholic)

- 1863–1904 despite rapid depopulation due to disease, the islands become a major source of indentured (often coerced) labour for the development of plantations in Queensland (40,000 workers), Western Samoa and Fiji, and for the nickel mines of New Caledonia (another 10,000)

- Missionaries vigorously oppose the trade in people as it impedes their ability to convert and exploit the indigenous population for their local church-controlled projects. Missionaries establish many authoritarian denominational village communities by the 1890s when the labour trade virtually ends

- 1906 most migrants are deported under 'White Australia' policies

- 1920s thousands of indentured labourers admitted from Vietnam for French plantation owners form an important ethnic group

- Islands of Espiritu Santo and Éfaté become vast forward bases in the Second World War – half a million US troops pass through and hundreds of warships bring dollar prosperity. African-American soldiers bring new more egalitarian conceptions of race relations to indigenous people

- Later 1940s radical religious movements ('cargo cults') resist state and missionary authority

- 1950s after more than a century of population decline or stagnation the number of indigenous people begins to increase

- From the late 1960s the New Hebrides starts to develop as an important international tax haven – offshore financial centre becomes a major source of British governmental revenue and foreign exchange

- Starting in 1967 American and French business people develop an expensive suburb in Port Vila for tax haven professionals. Also sell 4,000 subdivided lots on vast tropical seaside plantations on Espiritu Santo to large numbers of American and Asian (especially Vietnamese) prospective migrants

- 1971 condominium government tightens immigration laws and imposes a special 50% value-added tax on developers when they register subdivided land they have sold. Promoters ordered to repay many millions of US dollars collected from overseas investors

- 1970s French settlers holding much of the land area (36%) alienated from the indigenous ni-Vanuatu become increasingly alarmed by the growing independence movement – especially as the anglophone leader Father Walter Lini calls for the return of all land to the indigenous people

- 1980 independent Republic of Vanuatu established but the elected socialist and non-aligned anglophone Vanua'aku Party government faces crisis. Powerful religious movements attempt to detach the northern and southern islands (most of the country) in a secessionist movement supported by the French government and rich American tax-haven and real-estate promoters

- PNG troops restore order on the northern secessionist island of Espiritu Santo – over 200 rebels imprisoned

- 1983 Vanua'aku Party re-elected after implementing its constitutional mandate to repossess land which has been alienated from the indigenous people

- 1980s the 'Melanesian Socialist' government centralizes power in the capital and works closely with tax-haven promoters and expatriate business interests. Seized lands are leased to them at low rents for up to 75 years – but government maintains an anti-nuclear and non-aligned foreign policy

- 1988 decision by President Lini's government to wind up a local land corporation (the powerbase of ambitious politician Barak Sope) leads to rioting in Port Vila. President dissolves parliament and names Sope, his nephew, as interim Prime Minister. Constitutional crisis leads to the arrest of the President, Sope and their allies

- 1991 elections result in an unstable right-wing francophone-led coalition government that later moves to outlaw trade unions and retrench a large proportion of public servants particularly those sympathetic to the opposition. Media censored amidst accusations of government interference in the judiciary

- 1995 Vanuatu government differs from regional neighbours in refusing to criticize French nuclear testing in Polynesia

- Mid 1996 scandal exposed after government officials (including PM) secretly sign letters guaranteeing US$100 million public debt. These could have bankrupted the country if they had not been seized in the UK and the fraudsters promoting them arrested.

Political framework

- **Federal/local system.** Provincial governments have limited power in what remains a relatively centralized polity

- **Constitution – how democratic?** Vanuatu has a single-chamber parliament. 46 MPs elected by universal suffrage for four-year terms then elect a Prime Minister who chooses a Cabinet from MPs. MPs and provincial leaders elect a President by secret ballot for a five-year term as ceremonial head of state

- **Which party controls?** Relatively stable political groupings after independence but the ruling Vanua'aku Party splits into two in 1991. Since then unstable, strained and fluid coalition in power, led by the conservative and mostly francophone Union of Moderate Parties. Vanuatu becomes increasingly like other Melanesian polities: constantly shifting alliances, intrigue, a large number of weak divided parties and corruption at high levels

- **Ethnic politics?** Politics are linguistic and 'islandized' – not particularly ethnicized except to the degree that indigenous people are loyal to either anglophone or francophone colonial traditions

- **Political control of the media?** High level of political control of the media. Particularly noticeable in the suppression of stories on Radio Vanuatu and in the *Vanuatu Weekly* newspaper both owned by the state. The ruling government also frequently acts to suppress private newspapers

- **How independent is the judiciary?** At times questions are raised about the independence of the judiciary. 1994 courts allow the Public Service Commission to retrench all 600 striking public servants. 1995 two Australian judges resign from Vanuatu's judiciary claiming unprofessional conduct by the expatriate Chief Justice who is sometimes seen as too close to the government in power

- **Legislative and bureaucratic power?** The bureaucracy is small and weak by Pacific Islands standards and politically motivated retrenchments erode morale and efficiency. From the 1980s mass retrenchments of public servants – especially those suspected of disloyalty to the dominant party. Although parties are not particularly stable this threat to the independence of the public service from party leaders is not decreasing.

Further reading

MacClancy, J. (1980) *To Kill a Bird with Two Stones: a Short History of Vanuatu*, Port Vila, Vanuatu Cultural Centre.

Premdas, R.R. and Steeves, J. (1989) *Politics and Government in Vanuatu from Colonial Unity to Post-Colonial Disunity*, Townsville, James Cook University of North Queensland.

Van Trease, H. (ed.) (1995) *Melanesian Politics: Stael Blong Vanuatu*, Suva, University of the South Pacific Press.

Micronesia

by Anthony van Fossen

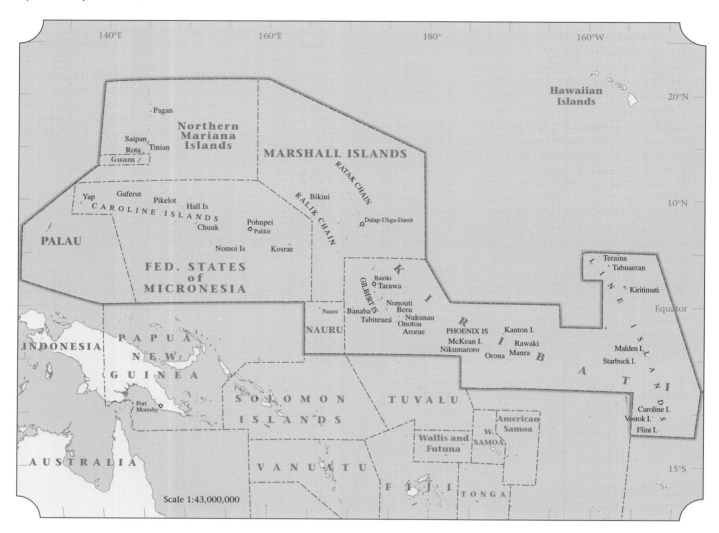

Federated States of Micronesia

Historical background

- Federated States of Micronesia (FSM) formed in 1978 by Chuuk (called Truk until 1990), Pohnpei, Yap, and Kosrae previously part of the US-administered Trust Territory of the Pacific Islands

- Original settlement occurs before 2000 BC

- Islands ruled by hereditary aristocracies which build great stone cities on Pohnpei and Kosrae. At one time Kosrae has the most hierarchical society in all of Micronesia and traditionally the high chief of Yap controls an extensive empire – all of Yap, western Chuuk, Guam and the Northern Marianas

- Traditional matrilineal principles still privileged – property is passed through women and masculine chiefs are selected through the mother's group. Numerous languages are spoken in FSM

- After 1526 Portuguese, Spanish, French, British, American and Russian explorers visit the group

- 19th C. whalers and traders in *bêche-de-mer*, copra and coconut oil bring diseases which reduce the indigenous population by about 50% within a few decades

- 1886 Spanish establish colonial control but a 1890 revolt of Pohnpeians against convict-like forced labour leaves the Governor and 1,500 Spanish troops dead

262

- 1899 Germany buys the group from Spain but their authoritarian administration and imposition of forced labour lead to another revolt in Pohnpei 1910–11. Four Germans killed, seventeen Pohnpeians executed and 426 exiled to Palau
- 1914 Japan occupies the islands and begins settler colonies which substantially outnumber indigenous Micronesians by 1941
- Chuuk (Truk) is the principal Japanese naval base in the central Pacific and an important battleground during the Second World War
- US Operation Hailstone in February 1944 is one of the classic examples of surgical bombing in history – 180,000 tons of Japanese shipping sunk in two days. 45,000 Japanese survivors are bypassed and left to starve with the Chuukese because of the effective US blockade
- 1947 islands absorbed into the Trust Territory of the Pacific Islands which the USA administers after pressuring the UN into creating the only trusteeship based on strategic factors
- 1978 FSM constitution lays foundation for democratic participation
- 1983 79% of voters approve a 50-year Compact of Free Association with the USA which gives the USA complete and exclusive military access to the FSM in return for over US$1.3 billion in aid by 2001. The security arrangement can be terminated only by mutual agreement with economic and defence provisions renewable after 1999 – the status of free association continues indefinitely
- 1980s–1990s health continues to deteriorate – serious cholera outbreak on Chuuk in 1982–83
- 1991 FSM admitted to the General Assembly of the UN
- FSM economy continues to be heavily dependent on US aid and imports with few signs of genuine self-reliant economic development. Numerous expensive government-funded projects assisted by the UN fail, for example large debt-financed fishing operations
- 1995 the Asian Development Bank replaces the UN as the principal adviser and source of assistance – recommends strong emphasis on tourism.

Political framework

- **Federal/local system.** FSM has strong state and municipal governments while the federal government is relatively weak. Some political leaders occasionally threaten state secession in a country where national identity is relatively weak. In Chuuk, Pohnpei and Yap traditional chiefs are powerful forces in local politics (often elected mayors) and greatly influence how commoners vote in elections
- **Constitution – how democratic?** 1979 federal constitution is based on democratic principles but the political system diverges in a number of important ways from the US model. The state constitutions of Chuuk, Pohnpei and Yap, while being formally democratic delegate certain powers over 'traditional' concerns to hereditary chiefs
- **Which party controls?** Political parties are unimportant relative to chiefs and clientelist networks
- **Political control of the media?** Despite some attempts at political control the press details many cases of government corruption in the mid 1990s
- **How independent is the judiciary?** The judiciary appears to be relatively independent
- **Legislative and bureaucratic power?** Clientelist networks and (outside Kosrae) chiefs are the centres of governmental power in the FSM. There appears to be a high level of corruption and it is difficult in many places to discover how large sums of aid are actually spent, although it appears that many politicians and senior bureaucrats have accumulated significant wealth.

Further reading

Hanlon, D. (1988) *Upon a Stone Altar: a History of the Island of Pohnpei until 1890*, Honolulu, University of Hawaii Press.

Peattie, M.R. (1988) *Nanyo: the Rise and Fall of the Japanese in Micronesia*, Honolulu, University of Hawaii Press.

Guam

Historical background

- Guam (the Southern Marianas) split from the closely related Northern Marianas in 1898 when Spain sold it to the USA. The division persists even though both are controlled by the Japanese during the Second World War and by the USA ever since
- Guam first settled from Malaysia or Indonesia at least as early as 1320 BC
- To 16th C. there is a hierarchical matrilineal system common to other parts of Micronesia but no unified polity so that chiefdoms often fight against each other

- 1521 Magellan lands in Guam during the first circumnavigation of the globe – claimed by Spain in 1565
- 1668–1815 Guam becomes a provisioning station in the Acapulco–Manila trade route along which Mexican silver is exchanged for spices and gems from the Philippines
- Imported unfamiliar diseases, devastating typhoons and Spanish aggression reduce the indigenous population by 95% from 1521 to 1741. Survivors become Catholics, intermarry with Spanish soldiers and Philippine settlers to make up the Chamorros of today. Chiefs are disempowered partly by Jesuit missionaries accepting converts of all ranks and the people are heavily hispanicized losing many Micronesian cultural traditions

Micronesia

- 1820s–1850s hundreds of US and British whaling ships become prominent visitors – Guam sufficiently significant to its Asia trade for the USA to establish a consulate

- 1898 USA buys Guam and the Philippines for US$20 million after winning the Spanish-American War. Run under naval jurisdiction with no trial by jury and the Captain making all laws

- 1941 Guam surrenders to Japanese forces

- 1944 US invasion – 11,000 Japanese and hundreds of Chamorros killed. By mid 1945 200,000 US soldiers on Guam preparing to invade Japan

- 1950 Guam transferred from the navy to the Department of the Interior – Guamanians become US citizens and pay income taxes. Guam becomes an important facility in the Korean and Vietnam Wars when the B-52s which bomb Indo-China take off from Andersen Airforce Base

- Guam remains very significant strategically and is one of the most militarized islands in the world – US Navy and Air Force bases or military reservations cover a third of the island

- 20% of the island's land confiscated from private owners by the US armed services during the Second World War becomes the property of the military after the war when these bases become permanent installations

- 1986 many displaced landowners and heirs not satisfied with the final out-of-court settlement and the later transfer of some expropriated land to the government of Guam rather than to them. US federal government still controls over 30% of the land with the government of Guam owning somewhat more – the remainder being in private hands

- 1970s onwards a period of dramatic and sustained growth in the tourism industry following establishment of commercial air links. Tourism oriented particularly toward Japanese vacationers and financed principally by Japanese capital which owns most of the hotels. Tourism is the largest civilian employer and at present draws 1.3 million visitors annually.

Political framework

- **Federal/local system.** The US federal government exercises considerable control over Guam and can revoke local government at any time. Local government has some resemblance to that of a US state controlling local taxation and expenditure. A common feature of local politics is attacking federal policies, decisions and regulations which are deemed inappropriate or against Guam's interests. Although there is some movement toward localization of power the goal of most elected local politicians and US President Clinton is to make Guam a commonwealth, with extensive powers of self-government.

In the mid 1990s this is blocked by a Congress reluctant to do anything which might lessen federal control over an island of great strategic importance

- **Constitution – how democratic?** Guam does not have full democracy – a proposed constitution is not ratified and the country is run according to the rather anachronistic Organic Act of 1950. Guam is an 'unincorporated' territory of the USA – 'unincorporated' because some provisions of the US constitution do not apply. An elected congressman represents Guam in Washington but cannot vote. Guamanians pay full federal income taxes but they are ineligible to vote in presidential elections. In other ways Guam's government resembles that of an American state with an elected governor and a bicameral legislature

- **Which party controls?** There are Republican and Democratic parties as on the US mainland with Democrats more often holding power in Guam. Personalities, families and ethnicity seem more important than parties

- **Ethnic politics?** Although they are a minority of eligible voters Chamorros dominate Guam's politics. They sometimes attempt to restrict the political participation of non-Chamorro residents and are more inclined to favour higher levels of autonomy from Washington. Stronger Chamorro nationalist movements, especially in the 1990s, demand repatriation of the large and growing Filipino immigrant population. In 1995 Chamorro nationalists engage in militant protests and begin to achieve some success in gaining leasehold rights to formerly federal lands for Chamorros who are landless

- **Political control of the media?** There is little direct political control over the media

- **How independent is the judiciary?** The judiciary tends to integrate Guam into mainstream US policies – the US President appoints the judge of the District Court of Guam to an eight-year term

- **Legislative and bureaucratic power?** The legislature and bureaucracy are somewhat independent of relatively weak parties but bureaucratic activities may be co-ordinated by party allegiances. Federal investigations in the late 1980s revealed widespread political corruption in Guam and 100 department heads (mostly Democrats) and the Democrat Governor Ricardo Bordallo were indicted. In 1990 Bordallo chained himself to a statue of a Micronesian chief and shot himself just before he was to be flown to serve a prison sentence for corruption on the US mainland.

Further reading

Rogers, R.F. (1995) *Destiny's Landfall: a History of Guam*, Honolulu, University of Hawaii Press.

Kiribati

Historical background

- British colonial administration creates one of the largest countries in the world. Kiribati (pronounced Kiri-bas) is over 3,870 km from east to west and 2,050 km from north to south, with 3.5 million km² of sea but only 817 km² of land

- Kiribati has a single culture and language although atolls north of the equator are more hierarchical in social organization than those to the south. Such differences persist today

- 14th C. Samoans, Tongans and Fijians invade but merge into older groups through intermarriage

- From 1537 Spanish, British, Russian and US explorers pass through

- 1820s–1850s Kiribati is a favourite whaling ground – the first white settlers are deserters from whaling ships

- From the 1850s resident Europeans become prosperous traders of *bêche-de-mer*, turtle shells, coconut oil and copra. Missionaries arrive later and convert the entire population to Christianity – conflicts between Protestants and Catholics continue to this day

- 1850s–1890s indigenous labour (known locally as I-Kiribati) is recruited or captured for whaling ships as well as plantations in Australia, New Caledonia, Fiji, Samoa, Tahiti, Hawaii, Peru, central America and Réunion in the Indian Ocean. Population decline ends only in about 1915

- 1892 British declare a protectorate over the Gilbert (later Kiribati) and Ellice (later Tuvalu) Islands to halt encroachment of US and German interests

- 1900 highly profitable phosphate deposits discovered on Banaba (Ocean) Island – crucial to producing fertilizers for agricultural development in Australia and New Zealand. Annexation quickly follows with capital moved from Tarawa to Banaba between 1908 and 1941. Periodic labour unrest during these years from Banabans protesting about environmental devastation and grossly inadequate compensation for mining their land

- 1915–16 colony extended to include the Line and Tokelau Islands, Christmas Island (now called Kiritimati) added in 1919 and the uninhabited Phoenix Islands in 1937. Sale of land by locals prohibited after 1917

- 1941 Japanese occupy significant northern islands including phosphate-rich Banaba – thousands of I-Kiribati and soldiers die in 1942–43 battles when USA retakes islands

- Islanders petitioning for US rule after 1945 are arrested by British colonial officials who later strengthen the co-operative movement making it less profitable for large trading companies to return

- 1956 Revenue Equalization Reserve Fund established to accumulate Banaban phosphate royalties and invest them in foreign stocks and bonds. By 1996 this is worth approximately US$300 million contributing more than US$5 million annually to government revenue

- 1957 British conduct their first tests of hydrogen bombs near Christmas Island (see Figure 24)

- 1975 Ellice Islands secede to form Tuvalu

- 1979 British grant independence to Kiribati as rich phosphate deposits on Banaba are mined out and Banaban secessionism cools. The USA renounces claims to the Phoenix and Line Islands the same year

- 1982 Kiribati government purchases extensive landholdings in the Line Islands from a subsidiary of Burns Philp the Australian trans-national corporation

- 1988 plans announced to move almost 7% of the national population from overpopulated Tarawa to the outlying Line and Phoenix Islands which are thinly inhabited

- 1990s economy becomes increasingly dependent on remittances (from 1,500 phosphate miners in Nauru and over 1,000 I-Kiribati seamen on foreign vessels), foreign aid, fishing royalties and the sale of unusual postage stamps

- 1992 Kiribati begins compensation claim on the USA and Japan for damage done to the country during the Second World War

- Kiribati is one of the countries which could completely disappear beneath the sea in the 21st C. as the greenhouse effect raises sea levels (see Figure 23).

Political framework

- **Federal/local system.** Government is centralized on Tarawa but the scattered nature of the country encourages considerable local autonomy

- **Constitution – how democratic?** New parliamentary constitution promulgated at independence in 1979. Voters elect a President from among three or four candidates nominated by the Assembly's 41 members – 95% of whom are elected through universal suffrage

- **Which party controls?** Political parties are loose groupings of people supporting similar policies rather than powerful organizations in their own right. Most of the 39 elected members of the House of Assembly formally present themselves for election as independent candidates. Principal political groupings reflect Protestant or Catholic religious affiliations. Although 54% of I-Kiribati are Catholic their representative party remains in opposition from independence in 1979 until it formed the government in 1994

- **Ethnic politics?** Politics are 'islandized' rather than ethnicized

- **Political control of the media?** Although the government owns the only radio station (there is no television broadcasting) political control of the media is weak

- **How independent is the judiciary?** The judiciary is independent and free from government influence – civil rights and civil liberties are respected in law and practice

Micronesia

- **Legislative and bureaucratic power?** Within a weak political party structure the legislature and bureaucracy are fairly independent.

Further reading

Macdonald, B. (1982) *Cinderellas of the Empire: Towards a History of Kiribati and Tuvalu*, Canberra, Australian National University.

Van Trease, H. (ed.) (1993) *Atoll Politics: the Republic of Kiribati*, Suva, University of the South Pacific Press.

Marshall Islands

Historical background

- The Marshalls exist as a single cultural and linguistic entity for thousands of years although Nauru is politically conflated with them under German colonial rule 1888–1914
- Settlement from about 2000 BC establishes a hierarchical, hereditary social system
- The Marshalls are never unified under a single leader but a single language connects them and one chief often controls several atolls – at times the whole western Ralik Chain. Chiefs and matrilineal principles of hereditary land transmission remain strong today despite pervasive American influence on social behaviour
- From 1526 Spanish, British and Russian explorers visit
- Whalers prominent in other areas of the Pacific in the first half of 19th C. successfully repelled by the islanders
- 1857 Protestant missionaries arrive during two decades when coconut plantations, copra trading stations and a coconut oil factory established
- 1886 Germany annexes the Marshalls
- 1914 the Japanese Navy seizes the islands and inaugurates a colony where Japanese eventually outnumber the Marshallese – powers of chiefs given to Japanese administrators and companies
- 1935 Japan starts fortifying large bases on many of the islands used for the invasion of Kiribati in 1941
- After the Japanese bombing of Pearl Harbor the US counter-attack in Micronesia begins with bloody battles in the Marshalls where artillery barrages are the fiercest of any in the war. Heavy aerial bombardment neutralizes Japanese bases so that the US Navy can move effectively into western Micronesia
- By 1946 almost all Japanese settlers are repatriated
- 1946–58 the USA conducts well over 67 atmospheric nuclear tests on atolls in the Marshalls including the first peacetime explosions of atomic and hydrogen bombs (see Figure 24)
- Many suspect that islanders are used as experimental subjects so that the long-term effects of radiation of humans can be assessed. In 1994–95 the US Department of Energy declassifies some documents which provide conclusive evidence that Marshall Islanders were deliberately exposed to high levels of radiation (including injections of tritium and chromium-51 as well as genetic and bone marrow transplant experiments)

so that effects on their health can be studied by US medical researchers. In 1995 Japanese scientists discover that 40% of the former inhabitants of one island have cancer. 40,000 US servicemen also exposed to radiation in Marshalls tests
- 1961 secretive base is established in Ralik Chain and becomes the world's most important missile testing site
- Numerous protests ever since from local (evicted) landowners sometimes result in 'sail-ins' and occupations which halt the testing programme
- US government insists on negotiating exclusively with the co-operative Marshall Islands central government which expects to receive about US$170 million in rental payments by 2001. In 1995 a lease for the expansion of the base signed
- 1978–79 new national government is formed by Marshall Islanders who split from the rest of the US Trust Territory of the Pacific Islands because of political, cultural and economic differences – thereby also not having to share revenues received from the US missile testing ranges
- 1986 Compact of Free Association with the USA implemented making Marshall Islands even more dependent on US funds. US$1 billion to be paid by 2001 on condition that about US$6 billion in current and pending lawsuits concerning damages resulting from nuclear testing are dropped
- 1991 the Marshalls become full members of the UN
- 1995 UN report suggests that the rise in the sea level resulting from the greenhouse effect may completely submerge the Marshall Islands within 35 years. No island is more than a few metres above sea level (see Figure 23).

Political framework

- **Federal/local system.** All legislative power is centralized in the parliament (*Nitijela*). No provinces or states exist although 24 municipalities do exist each with a mayor. Little aid filters from the capital to the outer islands but municipalities are empowered to raise revenue through local taxes
- **Constitution – how democratic?** The 1979 constitution combines features of British, American and Marshallese chiefly political systems. The unicameral 33-member *Nitijela* elects one of its members as President who selects a Cabinet from parliamentarians. The President must dissolve the *Nitijela*

after two parliamentary votes of no confidence in the Cabinet. Although the political model is formally democratic many commoners contend they are afraid to vote against the will of their local chief for fear of endangering their entitlements to land and other resources which chiefs control

- **Which party controls?** High chiefs particularly Amata Kabua (President 1979–96) and his presidential successor and cousin Imata Kabua have been supreme. The opposition is weak and comes from a handful of loosely organized politicians and parties

- **Ethnic politics?** Politics are not ethnicized to any significant degree

- **Political control of the media?** 1991 Cabinet places severe restrictions on opposition use of the single government-owned radio station – the most important source of news and information in the country. Attempts by the government to control the flow of information in the most important newspaper, the privately-owned *Marshall Islands Journal*, have been successfully resisted thus far

- **How independent is the judiciary?** There is some political pressure on the judiciary. 1996 parliamentary resolution led

to the resignation of the Supreme Court Chief Justice with other charges of unconstitutional pressure on Attorney General in that same year

- **Legislative and bureaucratic power?** There is strong disciplinary pressure on legislators and bureaucrats exerted by the Kabua high chiefs.

Further reading

Dibblin, J. (1990) *Day of Two Suns: US Nuclear Testing and the Pacific Islanders,* London, Virago.

Hezel, F. (1983) *The First Taint of Civilization: a History of the Caroline and Marshall Islands in Pre-Colonial days 1521–1885,* Honolulu, University of Hawaii Press.

Hezel, F. (1995) *Strangers in Their Own Land: a Century of Colonial Rule in the Caroline and Marshall Islands,* Honolulu, University of Hawaii Press.

Nauru

Historical background

- Nauru has been a single distinct entity except for a short period of incorporation into the Marshall Islands by Germany 1888–1914

- Original inhabitants castaways from the Marshall Islands and other Micronesian islands, the Solomon Islands and perhaps elsewhere making the language a very distinctive fusion of elements

- 1798 British whaling ship *Hunter* lands followed by other whalers during the 1830s

- Whaling ship deserters often become beachcombers and advisors to rival chiefs as well as traders eager to increase the demand for firearms and ammunition plunging the island into civil war between clans from 1878

- 1888 Germany occupies and incorporates Nauru into the Marshall Islands at the request of resident Germans associated with large German copra firms

- From 1907 mining of the world's highest grade phosphate begins using non-unionized migrant labourers from Kiribati, Tuvalu and China who are segregated and paid on racial criteria. Phosphate essential in making fertilizer that is virtually indispensable for the development and global pre-eminence of agriculture in Australia and forestry in New Zealand

- For some time phosphate mining makes Nauru the richest Pacific Island country but a 1910 epidemic of infantile paralysis kills over 10% of children

- 1914 Australia takes Nauru from the Germans in the early days of the First World War and is named sole administrator and

joint trustee (with New Zealand and the UK) by the League of Nations in 1918

- 1920s epidemics of influenza (killing over 15% of all Nauruans), leprosy (affecting about 25%) and tuberculosis

- 1940–41 German and Japanese bombing is prelude to invasion

- 1942 the Japanese occupy Nauru but their plan to export phosphate to Japan is thwarted by continual American bombing. Over 60% of Nauruans deported by the Japanese to their Micronesian colony of Truk/Chuuk – only two-thirds survive forced labour, brutality, disease and starvation

- 1946 those deportees left alive return to Nauru

- 1947 UN names Australia the administrator of the Nauru trust territory and phosphate exports recommence

- 1956 Hammer DeRobert, who earlier led a four-month civil service strike, elected head chief

- 1963 DeRobert rejects an Australian offer of citizenship for his people and resettlement on Curtis Island in Queensland – demands complete sovereignty

- 1968 Nauru becomes the smallest independent state in the world

- 1970 Nauru acquires ownership of its phosphate resources for A$21 million to be paid over three years to the British Phosphate Commissioners

- 1988 Commission of Inquiry condemns Australian, New Zealand and UK negligence between 1921 and 1968 when they were fiduciaries of the Nauru trust. Among other things they purchased phosphate at 30–50% of the world price which alone deprived Nauruans of accumulated revenues of US$404 million

Micronesia

- 1989 Nauru takes its case for restoring the environment damaged by mining before independence to the World Court
- 1990 exports of phosphate begin to decline sharply as reserves come close to exhaustion
- 1992 in a landmark decision about colonial accountability, sovereignty over natural resources and liability for environmental damage the World Court accepts Nauru's case for compensation
- 1993 Australia settles out-of-court for US$73 million rather than face a judgement which could have been ten times higher. New Zealand and the UK each agree to pay Australia about US$10 million toward this settlement
- 1990s the Nauru government and the affiliated phosphate royalty trust, which is supposed to invest hundreds of millions of dollars of royalties to provide security for Nauruans in the post-phosphate future, reveal substantial losses in dubious and fraudulent investments
- 1996–97 politics become extremely unstable with repeated changes of President – five changes occurring within one four-month period.

Political framework

- **Federal/local system.** Nauru Local Government Council controlled largely by chiefs and was very powerful but it was dissolved in 1992 after contracting debts reaching hundreds of millions of dollars. Its successor, the Nauru Island Council, has strictly limited functions and is clearly subordinated to the central government

- **Constitution – how democratic?** Despite a constitution which appears to guarantee democracy Hammer DeRobert ruled Nauru in an authoritarian, uncompromising manner during most years 1968–92
- **Which party controls?** Parties are not very strong and politics are largely personalized and clientelist
- **Ethnic politics?** Politics as such are not ethnicized but the 'guest worker' system does effectively deprive non-Nauruan minorities of citizenship rights
- **Political control of the media?** The media are underdeveloped and in the past the government-owned radio station was subject to some political control
- **How independent is the judiciary?** Judicial independence is in theory supported by the fact that cases may be appealed all the way to the High Court of Australia
- **Legislative and bureaucratic power?** The legislature and bureaucracy are known to be subject to discipline by the President.

Further reading

Macdonald, B. (1995) 'Nauruan phosphate and public policy', *Archifacts*, vol.22, pp.9–25.

Weeramantry, C. (1992) *Nauru: Environmental Damage under International Trusteeship*, Melbourne, Oxford University Press.

Williams, M. and Macdonald, B. (1985) *The Phosphateers*, Melbourne, Melbourne University Press

Northern Mariana Islands

Historical background

- The northern Marianas split from the closely related southern Marianas (Guam) when they were sold by Spain to Germany in 1898. The division persists even though both are controlled by the Japanese during the Second World War and by the USA ever since
- People from Indonesia or Malaysia settle the northern Marianas and cultivate rice at least as early as 1527 BC
- Indigenous peoples form a single shared cultural unit with hierarchical chiefdoms but no single polity
- 1565 Marshalls claimed by Spain
- Indigenous people marry Spanish, Filipino, Chinese, German, Japanese and American partners over the centuries to form the contemporary Chamorros who are similar to Guamians in the strength of Spanish and US influences
- 1698 after constant Chamorro revolts against colonial rule the Spanish resettle most indigenous inhabitants in Guam

- 19th C. when people begin returning as hispanicized Chamorros they find coastal settlements have been established by other Micronesians from the Caroline Islands. They coexist peacefully – the Chamorros farming and the Carolinians fishing
- 1899 Germany buys the Northern Marianas from Spain primarily to exploit copra
- 1914 Japan seizes the islands and quickly makes them into a highly profitable sugar-producing settler colony for Okinawans, Japanese and Koreans. Within 25 years settlers outnumber the Chamorros by more than 10:1 and the Northern Marianas become an important source of sugar and molasses-based alcoholic drinks
- 1944 127,000 US troops land from 600 ships – 2,000 aircraft use napalm for the first time against 80,000 Japanese troops. In one day the USA destroys 402 Japanese aircraft and out of 30,000 Japanese soldiers on Saipan only 2% survive – 419 Saipanese and 3,426 Americans also killed. Saipan then provides the forward bases for 200,000 US troops preparing to invade Japan

- 400 Americans and 8,000 Japanese lose their lives in the invasion of Tinian where the USA builds the longest and busiest runways in the world from which B-52s fly to bomb Japanese cities and drop the first atomic bombs in 1945

- 1947 Northern Marianas become part of the Trust Territory of the Pacific Islands under US Navy administration. 1948–62 the CIA takes over the northern half of Saipan to conduct secret military operations

- 1969 Guam voters reject persistent requests from the poorer islands of Saipan and Rota for integration with Guam. Ill-feeling caused by the collaboration of many Saipanese with the Japanese occupation forces during the Second World War contributes to this rejection

- 1975 over 78% of voters elect to split from the Trust Territory of the Pacific Islands and become a self-governing commonwealth in association with the USA

- 1986 islanders become US citizens bringing substantial amounts of foreign aid. In return the US military gain access to large tracts of land (including more than two-thirds of the island of Tinian) to be used for military purposes at will. Marianas part of a strategic arc extending to Guam and Palau as the USA retains full control of defence and foreign affairs

- Self-government and control over immigration allow the Northern Marianas to admit Asian labour particularly from the Philippines and China – migrants exceed the local population by more than 5:1 by 1990. Asian labour works in domestic service and in the booming tourism industry which is largely owned by and oriented toward Japanese visitors providing a tourist density higher than Hawaii's by 1990

- In addition migrant labour works in factories producing huge quantities of garments using 'made in USA' labels for wages lower than the mainland minimum even though the clothing is allowed duty-free entry into the US market. Reports of excessive exploitation, prostitution, non-payment of wages, forced confinement to barracks during non-working hours, rape and murder lead to a US congressional investigation in late 1994. A temporary Philippine government ban on its nationals accepting unskilled employment follows the next year

- Although the situation does not change substantially in subsequent years the first labour unions in the Northern Marianas begin to appear in the mid 1990s

- 1990s after a decade of spectacular growth the economy enters into a prolonged decline characterized by low investment, capital flight and declining incomes despite continuing growth in the tourism industry.

Political framework

- **Federal/local system.** There are constant disputes between Washington and the Northern Marianas government over the scope of the commonwealth's powers – particularly acute in the areas of immigration and taxation. Marianans do not vote in US national elections, do not pay US income taxes and a number of very wealthy American tax exiles reside on Saipan

- **Constitution – how democratic?** The 1978 constitution as amended in 1986 specifies a democratic model along US lines. The commonwealth's government resembles that of a US state with an elected Governor and a bicameral legislature

- **Which party controls?** Neither the Republicans nor Democrats consistently control the Northern Marianas polity but each party tends to mirror local family alliances more than the parties' national political agendas

- **Ethnic politics?** Politics are becoming increasingly ethnicized. Chamorros, now a minority as a result of immigration policies implemented by their leaders in the 1980s and 1990s, attempt to deny citizenship to Asian residents even to those born on the islands

- **Political control of the media?** There is little direct political control of the media

- **How independent is the judiciary?** The judiciary appears to be generally independent particularly at the level of the US District Court which is headed by a federal judge. Some questions are raised about the independence of the local Superior Court and Supreme Court

- **Legislative and bureaucratic power?** Corruption is rampant and the family clientelist alliances for which each of the major parties provide a label exercise considerable influence over the legislature and bureaucracy.

Further reading

Farrell, D.A. (1991) *History of the Northern Mariana Islands*, Saipan, Department of Education, Commonwealth of the Northern Mariana Islands.

Kluge, P.F. (1991) *The Edge of Paradise: America in Micronesia*, Honolulu, University of Hawaii Press.

Peattie, M.R. (1988) *Nanyo: the Rise and Fall of the Japanese in Micronesia*, Honolulu, University of Hawaii Press.

Palau

Historical background

- Palau (sometimes spelled Belau) has strategic significance as part of a US military arc especially after bases in the Philippines closed in 1992
- Evidence of human settlement from Indonesia at least as early as 1000 BC
- Abandoned terraces suggest intensive agriculture and more hierarchical social formations which peter out from about AD 1000
- Very close ties with Micronesian islands like Yap to which stone money (very important in traditional Yapese political economy) is exported – links with South-East Asia also maintained
- As elsewhere in Micronesia there are relatively inegalitarian chiefdoms with matrilineal descent – women inherit and divide land and older women choose a masculine chief. These practices continue today and chiefs are still powerful. Southern and northern Palauans speak different languages
- After 1543 Spanish, Portuguese and British ships arrive but the Spanish eventually claim Palau in 1686
- During Spanish rule epidemics of influenza and dysentery as well as increased casualties following the introduction of guns reduce the population – by 90% 1783–1882
- 1899 Germany buys the islands from Spain – begins exploiting the rich phosphate deposits and uses Palauan forced labour to establish coconut plantations
- 1914 Japan seizes Palau – quickly creates a settler colony for Japanese, Okinawans and Koreans establishing pineapple plantations and rice paddies. Phosphate mining operations expanded along with bauxite mines
- Palauans are marginalized, their lands sold or confiscated and Japanese bureaucrats replace chiefs. Palau becomes the centre of a vast Japanese empire in Micronesia and attains a population of 30,000 (80% Japanese) which is roughly twice the population of the entire Republic of Palau today
- 1941–42 Japanese launch attacks from Palau on the Philippines and the Netherlands East Indies (now Indonesia)
- 1944 two and a half months of fighting see 12,500 Japanese and 2,240 Americans die – continuous US bombing immobilizes other Japanese forces
- 1947 Palau becomes part of the Trust Territory of the Pacific Islands administered by the USA
- 1978–79 Palau votes to separate from the rest of the Trust Territory and acquires some self-governing power. But by approving the world's first anti-nuclear constitution Palau appears committed to policies unacceptable to the USA because it frustrates the Pentagon's insistence that it should have the option to build bases
- 1980s periodic government insolvency and political instability with death threats, fire bombings, bribery scandals, the assassination of the country's first President and the apparent suicide of his successor in 1988
- Instability intimately connected to the continuing failure of referenda to gain the 75% majority needed to overrule the constitution's anti-nuclear provisions so that Palau can gain US assent for independence. US government offers hundreds of millions of dollars after independence in exchange for a Compact of Free Association. This would allow the US to establish nuclear bases on Palau with the right of 'eminent domain' over virtually all of Palau although this is later modified to encompass one-third of the country
- 1993 pro-compact government amends the constitution so that the compact could be approved by a simple majority. 68% of voters later approve the 50-year compact and the Palau Supreme Court dismisses appeals. Compact promises US$450 million by 2009 with later payments to be negotiated
- 1994 Palau achieves independence and UN membership
- In the post-war period the economy of Palau becomes ever more dependent on US aid for viability although there are plans for major tourism developments. During the 1990s the number of easily exploited foreign workers (principally from the Philippines) grows dramatically to about 30% of the total population by 1996. Taiwan, which Palau recognizes, becomes a very significant source of investment in development projects.

Political framework

- **Federal/local system.** Local chiefs have considerable and growing power since self-government in 1981. Each of the sixteen states (which correspond to traditional chiefdoms) has a constitution, governor and legislature. Village government is largely controlled by hereditary chiefs
- **Constitution – how democratic?** At national level Palau is generally a US-style polity with a President, Vice-President and a bicameral legislature elected by universal adult suffrage. However, some states have undemocratic constitutions with officials chosen because of their traditional aristocratic status rather than being elected. This undemocratic chiefly style of governance is found in almost all villages. The national Council of Chiefs has greater influence than in other Micronesian polities
- **Which party controls?** The pro-compact *Ta Belau* (One Palau) Party generally rules with the Coalition for Open, Honest and Just Government being in opposition. But chiefs and their constituencies are far more important than parties
- **Ethnic politics?** The large and growing numbers of foreign workers from Asia, particularly the Philippines, are becoming an issue which is ethnicizing politics
- **Political control of the media?** Government attempts to control the rather undeveloped media have not been particularly effective
- **How independent is the judiciary?** Doubts are often expressed about the independence of Palau's judiciary
- **Legislative and bureaucratic power?** Chiefly influences over the legislature and bureaucracy are strong and to some degree are expressed under party labels.

Further reading

Liebowitz, A.H. (1996) *Embattled Island: Palau's Struggle for Independence*, Westport, Conn., Praeger.

Peattie, M.R. (1988) *Nanyo: the Rise and Fall of the Japanese in Micronesia*, Honolulu, University of Hawaii Press.

Polynesia

by Anthony van Fossen

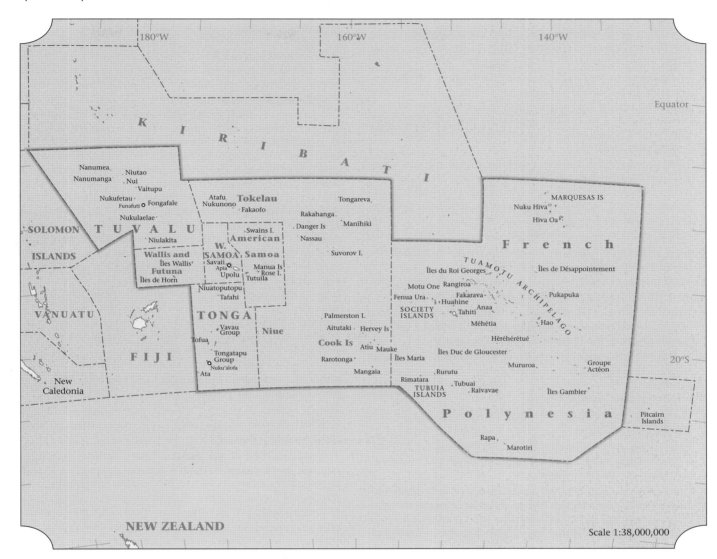

American Samoa

Historical background

- Samoa is culturally unified for millennia until the USA and Germany split eastern from western territories in 1900
- 800 BC Polynesians settle and about 900 years later Samoans in turn settle Tahiti, the Marquesas, Tokelau and Futuna
- Principal island of Tutuila is traditionally subordinated to Upolu in Western Samoa and is a place to which troublesome Upolu chiefs are banished

- Manua is largely independent of foreign influence
- Even today Samoan society continues to be organized around the clan or extended family (*aiga*) whose chief (*matai*) controls family land. A village may have one or many *matais* depending on the number of *aiga*
- The Samoas have a unified culture and language but are in constant contact with Tonga and Fiji
- 1722 Dutch, French and British navigators visit Samoa

271

Polynesia

- From 1803 runaway sailors and escaped convicts from Australia settle
- From 1830 mainly British missionaries become the most powerful religious figures as well as traders and implanters of capitalism. As in Western Samoa, and many other islands in the Pacific, ministers continue today to be accorded great status as well as political and economic influence
- The harbour in Tutuila becomes a popular port for whalers. US ships in particular are attracted to this natural cyclone shelter as a naval base and coaling station for ships *en route* to Australasia. USA reaches agreement with the local high chief which results in the transfer of harbourside lands for a coaling port in 1878
- 1900 Samoas colonized and partitioned into western (German) and eastern (US) sectors after chronic dynastic civil wars led by Samoan aristocrats throughout the later 19th C. Treaties signed with Samoan aristocrats preserving their political and land tenure systems which persist into the present-day regime of benevolent paternalism
- Early 1900s after falling to about half the level of 1839 the indigenous population begins to rise
- 1904 USA annexes the Manua group – makes Swains Island an administrative part of American Samoa in 1925
- Best-selling book *Coming of Age in Samoa* based on Margaret Mead's research in Manua during the 1920s brings a controversial image of the islands to a global audience
- 1920s–1930s the *Mau* independence movement is treated relatively sympathetically and adroitly by US military rulers avoiding the crisis which bedevils New Zealand colonial administrators in Western Samoa
- Thousands of US marines are trained in American Samoa during the Second World War and are favourably received
- Early 1950s twin economic pillars undermined as technological change make the naval base obsolete and copra exports face an uncertain future
- Later 1950s civilian colonial administration successfully encourages the development of two large tuna canneries with concessional tax rates and entry to the US market free of tariffs and quotas. Together they supply half the canned tuna consumed in the USA and make American Samoa today the second largest exporter of canned tuna in the world after Thailand
- 1960s cash-oriented economy begins to emerge strongly with a massive public works programme and a temporary boom in the tourism industry although copra prices continue to be depressed to the present day
- 1983 US sovereignty over Swains Island and New Zealand's possession of Tokelau are confirmed
- 1990s see massive retrenchment from the civil service substantially increasing unemployment. Further emigration of American Samoans to Hawaii and California – 60% more American Samoans live in the USA than in the territory itself
- Canneries become the main source of paid employment using mainly migrant labour from Western Samoa and Tonga. Despite agitation by mainland unions in the early 1990s labour is paid at about half the US minimum wage
- 1995 seven new diversified manufacturing projects for products such as watches, paper cartons and sausages announced. These are expected to provide about a quarter of paid employment in American Samoa in the near future.

Political framework

- **Federal/local system.** Local chiefs (*matais*) have considerable power though not as great as in Western Samoa. The Office of Samoan Affairs links federal, territorial and local systems and is controlled by *matais* from its paramount official to 14 county *matais* and 52 village mayors. Ultimate authority is held by the Secretary of the Interior in Washington but in practice considerable power is given to *matais* at local and territorial levels
- **Constitution – how democratic?** American Samoa is an unincorporated territory of the USA because some provisions of the US constitution and some other laws do not apply. The US Congress does not sanction the local constitution because it has many features violating American law including the power of chiefs (who select all eighteen members of the Senate from among themselves) and racial restrictions on land ownership. The constitution generally marginalizes commoners, women and people who are not of Samoan ancestry. The US Secretary of the Interior holds ultimate authority but in practice allows American Samoa to implement its own constitution and pass its own laws. The executive branch comes closest to the US model of a state with a Governor (who has the power to veto legislation) and a Lieutenant Governor selected since 1977 by popular election. The bicameral legislature (*Fono*) departs considerably from the American model – only the lower house is popularly elected. Since 1980 the territory bi-annually elects a representative to Washington who has considerable congressional privileges but is unable to vote
- **Which party controls?** Local political parties do not exist although candidates often identify themselves with US Republican or Democratic parties
- **Ethnic politics?** Politics are not particularly ethnicized although the constitution contains provisions which privilege those who are ethnically Samoan
- **Political control of the media?** There are few significant attempts by politicians to control the media directly. Although the television station is owned by the government, the radio station and two newspapers are privately owned – all are critical of numerous cases of corruption and fraud in the public sector
- **How independent is the judiciary?** The Secretary of the Interior appoints the Associate Justice and Chief Justice of the High Court who supervise and administer a judiciary which is reasonably independent of the executive and legislative branches and outside pressures
- **Legislative and bureaucratic power?** The legislature is largely independent of parties which do not formally exist. The bureaucracy is very politicized and extremely dependent on political favour. The executive branch department and office heads are appointed by the Governor with the approval of the legislature and are responsible to the Governor. These positions are filled by supporters of the government. The public service is further demoralized by frequent financial crises and periodic massive retrenchment. Corruption and fraud are endemic and inadequate action is taken against them.

Further reading

Stanley, D. (1996) *South Pacific Handbook*, Chico, Calif., Moon Publications.

Sutter, F.K. (1984) *Amerika Samoa*, Honolulu, University of Hawaii Press.

ook Islands

Historical background

- The islands have a common culture and language but current boundaries not firmly established until Nassau is finally annexed by the UK in 1892

- Today the Cooks have one of the largest territorial areas per capita in the world – 2.2 million km² of sea for less than 20,000 people

- Late 12th C. Polynesians from Samoa and Raiatea (French Polynesia) conquer earlier Polynesian settlers in the archipelago

- 14th C. Cook Islands Maoris settle New Zealand forming part of the Maori population there

- From 1595 Spanish, Russian and British navigators (including Cook, Bligh and the mutineers on the *Bounty*) sporadically explore the archipelago

- 1820s British missionaries establish control and together with Christianized chiefs coerce the scattered population into villages and act as a restraining influence on traders, visiting whaling ships and labour recruiters. But Peruvian slavers are active in the northern islands during the 1860s

- Disease contributes to the 65% decline in Maori population during the 19th C.

- 1888 UK declares a protectorate being concerned about French interest in the area – Cook Islands included in the boundaries of New Zealand in 1900

- Rule from New Zealand gradually erodes chiefly power, elevates a Euro-Polynesian bourgeoisie and emphasizes secular education considerably more than in most Polynesian societies

- After 1900 trade is redirected from French Tahiti to New Zealand de-emphasizing copra, the primary export, for which there is little demand in New Zealand. Growth of citrus fruits, particularly oranges, encouraged for export to New Zealand

- US airbases on several islands during the Second World War but there are no attacks on the islands

- 1965 Cooks enter into free association with New Zealand giving internal self-government but limited control over defence and foreign policies. Pattern of aid dependency and emigration initiated as Cook Islanders are given non-reciprocal New Zealand citizenship

- 1974 international airport is opened generating an important tourism industry but accentuating emigration as the crisis in the citrus industry becomes more intense. Currently in New Zealand there are more than twice as many Cook Islanders (and in Australia over half as many) as in the Cooks themselves

- 1978 Premier found guilty of using government funds to fly in voters from New Zealand to allow his Cook Islands Party a fifth consecutive election victory. He is removed from the premiership after a High Court decision removes his government

- Mid 1980s Cooks tax haven becomes an important contributor to the local economy and the source of considerable new influences on the government

- UN advisers encourage ambitious local politicians to borrow large amounts of money to build infrastructure and tourist attractions including a luxury hotel project which is left incomplete. Contractor, chief banker and principal insurer go bankrupt – later imprisoned in Italy for Mafia ties

- Early 1990s the government becomes increasingly optimistic about the potential to draw billions of dollars of revenue from the rich sea-bed deposits of manganese, cobalt and other minerals within the Cooks' vast territorial waters. Many claim that it may be as long as 100 years before exploitation is profitable

- Mid 1990s high-level official inquiry in Auckland into the effectiveness of New Zealand's tax and fraud offices in monitoring the use of the Cook Islands tax haven by New Zealand companies. This brings constant public criticism of the Cooks government for its uncooperative defence of the country's financial secrecy laws

- 1995 Prime Minister involved in a scandal when it is revealed that he secretly signed letters of government debt guarantee for sums equal to over ten times the country's GDP

- Scandal aggravates a crisis of confidence and capital flight which force the Cooks to withdraw its currency and revert to the NZ$

- 1996 the government, which is defaulting on its large debts to overseas interests and local banks and pension funds, announces neo-liberal reforms. Two-thirds of public service positions to be retrenched, wages sharply cut for those who remain, governmental departments, ministries and several diplomatic missions to be eliminated. Widespread privatization also proposed.

Political framework

- **Federal/local system.** Local government is not particularly strong and the politics of central government is oriented around the clientelist or 'pork barrel' interests of very small local electorates

- **Constitution – how democratic?** The 1965 constitution gives the Cook Islands self-government in free association with New Zealand. The Cooks increasingly control their foreign affairs and can unilaterally move to full independence at any time while New Zealand must gain the Cooks agreement for any alteration of the micro-state's international status. Internal government is on the Westminster model – an elected unicameral parliament from whose 25 MPs (including a unique parliamentarian who represents Cook Islanders *outside* the country) the Prime Minister, Deputy Prime Minister and Cabinet are chosen. The British monarch is the head of state represented locally by a Cook Islander Governor-General. The Hereditary House of Paramount Chiefs advises on indigenous custom and land matters but does not have legislative power nor does it seriously compromise the Cooks polity

Polynesia

- **Which party controls?** The Cook Islands Party rules for most of the period since the first general election in 1965. Despite the association of the Cook Islands Party with the current severe economic crisis the opposition remains feeble and divided
- **Ethnic politics?** Politics are not highly ethnicized although government members sometimes use chauvinistic rhetoric
- **Political control of the media?** Both main newspapers, the *Cook Islands News* and the *Cook Islands Press* are threatened by the government during the 1990s for being overly critical. The state-owned television station, public and private radio stations are tame. In 1995 the government begins requiring special visas for foreign journalists and media reporters after the Prime Minister takes advantage of parliamentary privilege to attack them. He accuses his critics on the *Cook Islands Press* and at TV New Zealand of being financed by the CIA to overthrow his government
- **How independent is the judiciary?** The judiciary is independent. In 1978 the Chief Justice removed the Premier and his Cook Islands Party from office – the first time in commonwealth history that a court ruling changed a government. In 1995 and 1996 some judicial decisions relating to the offshore financial centre indicate judicial independence
- **Legislative and bureaucratic power?** The dominant Cook Islands Party controls the legislature and is connected with extensive politicization, contract-based hiring, intimidation, corruption, theft, nepotism and weakening of bureaucratic independence during the 1990s.

Further reading

Crocombe, R. (1979) *Cook Islands Politics – the Inside Story*, Auckland, Polynesian Press.

Scott, D. (1991) *Years of the Pooh-Bah: a Cook Islands History*, Rarotonga, Cook Islands Trading Corp.

Stanley, D. (1996) *South Pacific Handbook*, Chico, Calif., Moon Publications.

French Polynesia

Historical background

- Islands unified as a French colony later 19th C. in a territorial area of 5 million km² of which about 0.07% is land
- Evidence of Polynesian occupation dates from AD 300. Tongans and Samoans settled the Marquesas and migrate onward to Easter Island, Hawaii, New Zealand and the Society Islands including Tahiti
- From 1521 Spanish, Dutch, British (including Cook, Bligh and the *Bounty*), French, American and Australian navigators explore the group. European influence re-centres the group on Tahiti away from the former centre of Raiatea
- 19th C. whalers, adventurers, merchants in pearls, pearl shells, *bêche-de-mer* and sandalwood then labour recruiters and slavers extend capitalist influences
- 1842–43 French annex the Marquesas and impose a protectorate over Tahiti. The repercussions and the anti-French Tahitian guerrilla movement bring France and Britain to the brink of war in 1844. French administrators progressively undermine indigenous chiefs
- 1860s cotton venture during US Civil War brings other Pacific Islands workers and 1,000 Chinese labourers whose descendants and more recent migrants form the significant Chinese minority of today
- 1887 France gives Britain an interest in the New Hebrides (Vanuatu) in exchange for the Leeward Islands of the Society group and formally annex Rapa in 1901
- Later 19th C. economy based on the export of citrus fruits and copra. Phosphate mining on Méhétia to fertilize Japanese and Australasian farms important from 1908 to the 1960s
- New European diseases, sales of arms and alcohol produce a massive decline in the Polynesian population during 19th C. which begins to increase only in the 1920s
- From his arrival in 1891 to his death there in 1903 the painter Gauguin builds powerful images of Tahiti, Polynesia and the Pacific Islands for the popular imagination in Europe and elsewhere in the world. Best-selling writers such as Michener consolidate these images especially as their work become the basis for films
- During the Second World War, although the USA establishes a naval base and the phosphate mines sustain Australasian agriculture, French Polynesia remains outside the Pacific War
- Immediate post-war period brings nationalism and a tremendous increase in labour union activity among Polynesians
- 1966 President de Gaulle moves French atomic testing from Algeria to Mururoa in the Tuamotu group – over 175 explosions occur in the next 30 years (see Figure 24). International protests force the tests underground in 1975
- Nuclear testing programme brings a dramatic increase in funds, infrastructure, French settlers and demand for local labour but traditional agricultural export economy collapses. Massive migration occurs from the outer islands to Tahiti for plentiful jobs at higher wages. Few Polynesians migrate to metropolitan France although several thousand migrate to New Caledonia
- From later 1960s tourism becomes prominent with the opening of an international airport and the filming of *Mutiny on the Bounty* on Tahiti. Setbacks from the late 1980s as indigenous people vote and demonstrate to stop large developments on Moorea and Tahiti. Polynesians retain over 85% of the territory's land although Chinese people lease a considerable proportion of it

- 1987 the capital of Papeete faces the worst rioting and violence in its history (US$70 million of damage) and a state of emergency is declared after French security forces try to break a union picket line
- 1990–95 winding-down then suspension of the nuclear testing programme bring recession, increased taxation, high and rising levels of unemployment and labour unrest
- 1995–96 temporary resumption of French nuclear testing sparks riots of mostly unemployed youths, calls for independence and the burning of dozens of Papeete buildings – US$40 million in damage
- 1996 after local opposition is refracted across Asia-Pacific France again suspends nuclear testing
- With tourism stagnant and few alternative goods or services of significance to export the economic future of the territory seems uncertain.

Political framework

- **Federal/local system.** Local and territorial governments are relatively weak – central government in Paris retains extensive powers. Paris selects a High Commissioner who controls the police, military, judiciary, foreign affairs, international trade, immigration, broadcasting, international communications, education and municipal councils. The High Commissioner can dissolve the Territorial Assembly and take personal control of the territorial budget – as he did in 1992. In 1962 General de Gaulle does not even bother to consult the Territorial Assembly before announcing plans to shift the nuclear testing programme to French Polynesia
- **Constitution – how democratic?** The Constitution of France is supreme, although since 1977 French Polynesia has limited internal self-government. The Territorial Assembly is gerrymandered to favour conservative outer islands. Like the municipal councils it can be effectively negated by the High Commissioner. The territory elects two representatives and a senator to Paris. The unification of Europe is perceived as further eroding direct democracy and almost 90% of voters boycott elec-

tions to the European Parliament in 1990 at the urging of all French Polynesian political parties

- **Which party controls?** From 1975 to 1982 most members of the Territorial Assembly favour independence but ever since neo-Gaullist anti-independence parties rule. In the mid 1990s the anti-nuclear pro-independence party has been gaining popularity
- **Ethnic politics?** Politics are not highly ethnicized. Territorial and local politics tend to be based on loyalties to individual politicians and clientelism
- **Political control of the media?** The principal TV and one of the radio stations are owned by the government and broadcast many programmes originating in France, although one of the smaller radio stations is pro-independence. Prominent newspapers are conservative and are not subject to direct political control
- **How independent is the judiciary?** The judiciary is controlled from Paris and is independent to the degree that it administers mostly metropolitan laws with a degree of impartiality
- **Legislative and bureaucratic power?** Political parties are not particularly powerful or stable influences over legislators. In the late 1980s and 1990s various conservative party government leaders are found guilty or accused of fraud (including electoral fraud) and corruption which involves using their influence over the bureaucracy for personal or familial benefit.

Further reading

Aldrich, R. (1990) *The French Presence in the South Pacific 1842–1940*, Honolulu, University of Hawaii Press.

Aldrich, R. (1993) *France and the South Pacific Since 1940*, Honolulu, University of Hawaii Press.

Henningham, S. (1991) *France and the South Pacific: a Contemporary History*, Honolulu, University of Hawaii Press.

Newbury, C. (1980) *Tahiti Nui: Change and Survival in French Polynesia*, Honolulu, University of Hawaii Press.

Niue

Historical background

- About AD 900 Niue settled by Samoans with a gerontocracy but without hereditary chiefs. Tongans invade 600 years later so the Niuean language is closely related to Samoan and Tongan

- Although Tongan hereditary chiefs assume control over the entire island in 16th C. today Niue is unusual in Polynesia in not having any remnants of a hierarchical or hereditary chiefly social system

- 1774 Captain Cook sights Niue but otherwise islanders prevent Europeans (including whalers) from visiting the island

- Samoan missionary Paulo converts the islanders to Christianity by 1861 and builds the foundation for a political and economic power structure which is still today significantly controlled by religious organizations

- 1860s Peruvian and US slavers kidnap a substantial number of Niueans – many later leave voluntarily to become phosphate miners in the eastern Pacific

- 1900 UK establishes protectorate over Niue and transfers administration to New Zealand the following year

- Economy based on copra exports but Niue is the earliest Polynesian economy to be based significantly on migrant remittances – from Tahiti and Samoa after the 1860s and New Zealand after 1900

- 1974 Niue becomes internally self-governing in free association with New Zealand who retains control over defence and foreign affairs. Niueans become New Zealand citizens but not *vice versa*

- Since land ownership is often difficult to determine agricultural development is difficult, shipping is unreliable and few other economic opportunities are available. Niue remains the most dependent on remittances and aid amongst Pacific Islands

- 1970s and 1980s population continuously lost – Niueans in New Zealand currently outnumber those on the island by about 7:1

- From 1991 New Zealand government reduces aid to Niue and attempts to encourage the development of the private sector at the expense of government employment and expenditure

- 1992 ambitious local development programme announced to reverse depopulation, economic stagnation and dependency. Most proposals soon frustrated but the tax haven and several agricultural enterprises are initially successful. Temporary reversal of population loss because of high Niuean unemployment rates and living costs in New Zealand

- 1994–96 one of the longest periods of parliamentary paralysis in commonwealth history – voting in Legislative Assembly deadlocked

- Election relieves deadlock but does not end the problems of isolation, dependency and underdevelopment.

Political framework

- **Federal/local system.** Local government is present in the form of elected village councils but these are overshadowed by the Niue Assembly where 30% of members are elected on the common roll and 70% by village constituencies

- **Constitution – how democratic?** Niue has a Westminster-style constitution with 20 Legislative Assembly members electing a Premier from its ranks – Premier chooses three other members to join the Cabinet. A Governor-General represents the British monarch. Although Niue's full independence is limited somewhat by New Zealand taking responsibility for its defence and some of its foreign affairs, Niue increasingly conducts its own external relations entering into numerous treaties, agreements, and international organizations such as the SPF. Niue expresses independence of New Zealand's anti-nuclear policies by allowing US Navy visits during the 1990s

- **Which party controls?** There is only one political party, the Niue People's Party, but it is in almost permanent opposition since its founding in 1986. The 1996 elections focus on Premier Lui's contention that political parties are unnecessary and divisive impediments to Niue's development. Loosely organized independents continue to hold power and he is re-elected Premier

- **Ethnic politics?** Politics are not very ethnicized

- **Political control of the media?** Robert Rex the Premier 1974–92 exercised authoritarian control over all aspects of government including the government-owned media. Although the opposition advertises on state-owned radio and TV in recent elections, the radio prayer programme of a Catholic priest who criticized the government for favouritism is terminated on the advice of the Premier in 1995. After the privately-owned *Niue Star* criticized the government in the mid 1990s the expatriate husband of the editor quickly faced a deportation order

- **How independent is the judiciary?** The High Court and Court of Appeal are relatively independent and there is a right of appeal to the New Zealand Supreme Court

- **Legislative and bureaucratic power?** The political party system is undeveloped and does not exercise great power over the legislature or bureaucracy but both are influenced by the personal favour of present and past Premiers.

Further reading

Douglas, N. and Douglas, N. (eds) (1994) *Pacific Islands Yearbook*, 17th edn, Suva, Fiji Times.

Stanley, D. (1996) *South Pacific Handbook*, Chico, Calif., Moon Publications.

Tokelau

Historical background

- Tokelauans are closely related to people of Tuvalu and Samoa and seem to originate from there as well as from Rarotonga in the Cook Islands. The three atolls unified in pre-European times under the chiefs of Fakaofo, the island with the largest population

- From 1765 British and US navigators explore Tokelau but Fakaofo appears unknown to Europeans until 1835 when sighted by whalers

- Late 1860s Protestant and Catholic missionaries from Britain achieve great political power after converting a population severely depleted by disease and labour recruiters – particularly Peruvian slavers who bring a dysentery epidemic in 1863

- From the 1860s copra-based export economy established initially by polyglot collection of European deserters from whaling ships

- 1877 British rule begins and is formalized into a protectorate in 1889

- 1916 Tokelau annexed to the Gilbert and Ellice Islands colony (now Kiribati and Tuvalu) – this is terminated in 1925 and jurisdiction transferred to New Zealand

- 1948 Tokelau archipelago becomes a territory of New Zealand along with citizenship for Tokelauans

- 1964 Tokelauans reject proposals to unite their islands with Western Samoa or the Cook Islands

- 1960s population peaks at nearly 2,000

- 1960s to mid 1970s New Zealand government operates the Tokelauan Resettlement Scheme to overcome serious problems of overcrowding the atolls. Many families migrate to North Island, New Zealand and in turn sponsor other migrants. Scheme suspended in 1976 when local population stabilizes and demand for labour from the Pacific Islands declines in New Zealand

- 1980 US government renounce claims on Tokelau dating from 1856. In return the three *faipule* (headmen) of Tokelau relinquish Swains Island traditionally part of Tokelau but currently belongs to American Samoa. Treaty ratified in 1983 but some Tokelauans continue to express dissatisfaction with Swains concession

- Continuing decline in copra prices so Tokelau becomes ever more dependent on income from aid, postage stamps, tuna fishing fees and remittances from Tokelauan emigrants in New Zealand – they outnumber the people remaining on the islands by 2:1

- From late 1980s Tokelau increasingly protests against practices producing environmental degradation such as drift-net fishing which is blamed for the severe deterioration in tuna stocks available to subsistence fishermen

- Cyclones, once rare, become more frequent and severe after 1987 and crystallize local fears about global climate change. Tokelau consists of three atolls with a maximum height of just 4 metres so is in dire danger of submergence by rising sea levels caused by the greenhouse effect (see Figure 23).

Political framework

- **Federal/local system.** Tokelau's polity is very localized with relatively little national sentiment or central governmental power although this is changing in the 1990s as the national government is strengthening. A New Zealand administrator has considerable influence and many formal, if increasingly nominal, powers. Mayors administer village affairs but their power is diminishing in relation to an ever stronger headman (*Faipule*). The headman deals with the New Zealand administrator, regulates the public service, presides over the island Council of Elders and the court. He also serves one year in three as Head of the National Council of *Faipule* created in 1992 to act on behalf of the national legislature (*Fono*) during most of the year when it is not in session. There is no national capital – the legislature meets on different islands on a rotating basis

- **Constitution – how democratic?** The Tokelau Islands Act 1948 has been extensively amended to give Tokelauans today a higher degree of internal self-government. This remains incomplete as the country is still administered by New Zealand although Tokelau's consent is required for any New Zealand law to be extended there. In 1995 legislative power formally transferred from the New Zealand parliament to Tokelau's legislature although the New Zealand administrator continues to have veto power. Despite these limitations on full democracy Tokelauans express satisfaction with their relationship to New Zealand on four UN De-colonization Commission visits 1976–94. However, the system of government tends to marginalize or exclude women and younger people and the 45 members of the national legislature are not popularly elected. On each of the atolls fifteen legislators are selected by the Council of Elders (family heads), the elected mayor and headman

- **Which party controls?** There are no parties or even campaigns – personality, family ties and village alignments are the most important determinants of who is elected headman or mayor

- **Ethnic politics?** Politics tend to be very 'islandized' but not particularly ethnicized

- **Political control of the media?** The national radio stations are not subject to overt political control

- **How independent is the judiciary?** Jurisdiction over serious civil and criminal cases is exercised by New Zealand's appointed commissioner and High Court. Most cases are over petty infractions (there is no gaol on Tokelau) and are judged by the elected headman

- **Legislative and bureaucratic power?** Neither are subject to untoward political control.

Further reading

Huntsman, J. and Hooper, A. (1996) *Tokelau: a Historical Ethnography*, Honolulu, University of Hawaii Press.

Tonga

Historical background

- Unified in its present boundaries in 1845 although it has cultural and linguistic unity for thousands of years
- Variety of evidence points to the possibility that Tonga is the earliest settled area in Polynesia – material traces of Polynesian settlement as early as 1140 BC
- Tonga is an intensely hierarchical society for many centuries and conquers Niue, Rotuma, Tokelau, and Wallis as well as significant areas of Samoa and eastern Fiji in prehistoric times. Its aristocracy forms close ties with indigenous ruling classes of these archipelagos which continue today. Tongan warriors also make incursions into the Solomon Islands and New Caledonia
- From 1616 visited by explorers from Holland, Spain, France and Britain (including Captain Cook as well as the mutinying crew of the *Bounty*)
- 1845 unified kingdom formally established after half century of civil and dynastic conflict
- By the 1870s a coconut- and copra-based export economy established
- The Wesleyan (Methodist) church allied with the monarchy becomes and remains a powerful political, economic, social and cultural actor
- 1875 constitution proclaimed closely modelled on the Kingdom of Hawaii – it continues to prevent any law being enacted without actual, not merely formal, royal assent
- Tonga maintains a high degree of independence until it becomes a British protectorate in 1900 losing power over its foreign affairs. Even after 1900 the unbroken rule of the Tongan monarchy has a high degree of sovereignty over internal affairs always maintaining formal independence (in the style of Siam/Thailand)
- During the Second World War the main island of Tongatapu becomes an important Allied shipping base and Tongan troops fight the Japanese in the Solomons
- Early 1960s the balance of trade deteriorates – economy becomes substantially dependent on foreign aid and remittances from an ever larger number of emigrants to New Zealand, Australia and the USA
- 1970 full independence restores complete control over all internal and foreign affairs. Since Tonga was never formally colonized its undemocratic constitution is not vetted by the UN which is unlikely to approve it if ever given the opportunity to do so
- 1972 Tonga claims the uninhabited Minerva Reefs to prevent libertarian adventurers from founding a new tax haven. If the adventurers had been successful it would allow widespread entrepreneurial state-creation in international waters especially in the Pacific
- 1986 neo-liberal economic policies implemented raising unpopular regressive taxation, sharply reducing company taxes, cutting personal income tax rates and banning labour unions

- 1980s–1990s commoners (99.9% of the population) intensify demands for democracy in opposition to a near absolute monarchy. They focus on the legality of the government sale of 6,600 Tongan passports (for as much as US$30,000 each) to foreigners including some dubious Hong Kong characters and Marcos, the ex-dictator of the Philippines, and his family. Questions are raised by commoner parliamentarians about the mysterious destination of the proceeds of these sales
- 1989 popularly elected commoner parliamentarians succeed in rejecting a government budget for the very first time. Deeper structural change, however, is slow. The Royal Family and 33 nobles retain extraordinary power over all realms of Tongan society including land allocation
- In the 1990s the Tongan government creates international controversy and conflict with the Indonesian government by claiming the last sixteen geostationary satellite slots over the Pacific. Members of the Royal Family have a majority interest in a new US$50 million company leasing the slots to other users
- New ventures in Tonga – growing squash for the Japanese market – prove to be lucrative but legal barriers to Tongan workers entering core countries around Asia-Pacific become even higher
- 1993–97 the King negotiates with the governments of Sarawak (Malaysia) and PNG to supply Tongan agricultural workers for plantations which are leased or jointly owned by the Tongan government in these countries
- About 2.5% of the population continue to emigrate annually to New Zealand, Australia and the USA – often illegally.

Political framework

- **Federal/local system.** The Tongan polity is centralized around the figure of the monarch in the capital of Nuku'alofa and there are no municipal councils. The only form of local government is through town and district officers who represent the central government locally. Nuku'alofa is administered directly by parliament. The electoral strength of the pro-democracy movement in 1993 and 1996 led the central government to provide more resources to local government in an attempt to influence popular opinion in favour of the King and nobles
- **Constitution – how democratic?** Tonga's 1875 constitution defines the country as a constitutional monarchy although the King has near absolute power. The King decides who are the 33 nobles that will select colleagues to serve in the Legislative Assembly. Every three years commoners elect nine representatives to sit in a parliament of 30 members where they are routinely outvoted by 21 appointed parliamentarians aligned with the monarch and aristocrats. Furthermore, the monarch can veto legislation, dismiss Cabinet members, dissolve parliament, suspend *habeas corpus* and declare martial law at will
- **Which party controls?** The pro-democracy movement won the commoners seats by a landslide in 1993 but internal divi-

278

sions led to the collapse of their People's Party formed a year later. Nevertheless, pro-democracy candidates still won seven out of the nine popularly elected parliamentary seats in 1996. The King is antagonistic toward the creation of political parties and denies that they can exist in Tonga until laws are passed to govern their operations. He opposes the creation of such laws. Personalities are often more important than policies among elected politicians who are structurally prevented from having much influence in parliament

- **Ethnic politics?** Politics are not generally ethnicized although ethnic issues are raised in relation to the sale of passports to Asians

- **Political control of the media?** The radio stations and the only regular newspaper are owned by the government. Formal criticism of the King is unlawful with high and recently increased penalties. Criticism of the powerful oligarchy is muzzled through legal action against critics in a country where libel is a criminal offence. Foreign journalists are frequently banned from entering the country. Nevertheless, magazines and dissident newsheets reach a growing proportion of the population and convey a more critical attitude toward the existing political system

- **How independent is the judiciary?** The judiciary is relatively independent with the highest court of appeal consisting of three judges from other commonwealth countries – like the current Chief Justice. In general the judiciary is constrained by laws which are made in a system dominated by the monarch and the oligarchy. Ultimate judicial appeal is to a Privy Council presided over by the King who appoints all judges

- **Legislative and bureaucratic power?** No political parties currently exist and the legislature is subservient. The bureaucracy is small even by Pacific Islands standards but there are reports of corruption though little action is taken against malefactors if they are aristocrats or their allies.

Further reading

Campbell, I.C. (1994) *Island Kingdom: Tonga Ancient and Modern*, Christchurch, University of Canterbury Press.

Tuvalu

Historical background

- 1976 Tuvalu established when nine of the Polynesian atolls of the Ellice Islands split from the Micronesian Gilbert Islands which later become Kiribati

- Population is basically Polynesian. About 2,000 years ago Samoans settle in the south and Tongans move to the northern atolls. Micronesians from Kiribati settle Nui island a few hundred years ago

- People from Tuvalu later move to create Polynesian outliers to the Solomons in Melanesia and what are now the Federated States of Micronesia

- From 1568 Spanish, English, Americans, Russian and Dutch explorers visit various islands in the archipelago

- 1821–70 whalers settle ashore and later become trading agents in coconut oil and copra which become basis of the local economy

- 1850–75 labour recruitment important: voluntary migration to plantations in Fiji, Samoa and Hawaii; involuntary slavery to Peruvian guano mines 1863–64. Emigration and disease reduce population from 20,000 to 3,000

- From 1861 Samoan missionaries quickly convert all islanders and establish puritanical rule – pastors become the economic and political elite

- 1892 to keep out US traders Britain declares Tuvalu a protectorate with the Gilbert Islands (now Kiribati) – they become a colony in 1916

- Tuvalu is never attacked in the Second World War even though a US base is established

- Many co-operatives are established after the Second World War giving Tuvaluans greater control over their export trade and limiting income inequalities

- 1978 Tuvalu becomes independent. Probably the smallest independent state in the world in terms of population and GDP depending heavily on foreign aid plus sales of postage stamps and tuna fishing licence fees. Also crucial are remittances from overseas workers especially phosphate miners in Nauru and sailors on foreign ships

- 1981 electoral defeat of the first Prime Minister attributed to his investing most of the government's funds with a California business. Money reportedly returned in 1984 with interest

- 1983 US formally renounce claims to four of Tuvalu's nine islands

- 1987 Tuvalu Trust Fund established by Australia, New Zealand and the UK – an overseas investment fund which produces substantial revenues for the government (quarter of recurrent budget in 1990). Capital value is over US$30 million by 1994

- 1991 parliament passes legislation establishing a State Church and banning all new religions

- 1991–95 relations with the UK strained when Tuvalu government prepares compensation claim for neglect of the economy and infrastructure during the colonial period. UK strongly attacks Tuvalu's financial policies while Tuvalu refuses any future British aid and removes the Union Jack from its flag

- 1994 unprecedented tidal waves strike low-elevation Tuvalu and intensify criticism of CO_2 emissions by industrialized countries that cause the greenhouse effect (see Figure 23)

- Popular fears aggravated of cultural and physical extinction with the projected disappearance of the entire country beneath the sea within a generation. Government's principal priority becomes resettlement but approval for relocation not secured from any other country by 1997.

Political framework

- **Federal/local system.** Since 1966 elected island councils provide local government on each outer island – they tend to resist central government control

- **Constitution – how democratic?** A democratic polity with an elected unicameral parliament of twelve members and a Prime Minister chosen from their ranks. The four Ministers and Speaker of the House are also elected parliamentarians. The Governor-General represents the British Crown

- **Which party controls?** Party politics are in their infancy with independents being in power. No political parties until 1992 when the Tuvalu United Party is formed by Prime Minister Paeniu

- **Ethnic politics?** Politics are not particularly ethnicized but tend to be 'islandized'

- **Political control of the media?** The state owns the radio station and two newspapers but they are not subject to direct political control – no TV station

- **How independent is the judiciary?** The judiciary is reasonably independent. Decisions of the High Court of Tuvalu may be appealed to the Fiji Court of Appeal and finally to the Privy Council in London

- **Legislative and bureaucratic power?** Both the legislature and bureaucracy are generally independent especially because party politics are weak.

Further reading

Banks, A.S., Day, A.J. and Muller, T.C. (1996) *Political Handbook of the World: 1995–1996*, Binghamton, NY, CSA Publications of the State University of New York at Binghamton.

Macdonald, B. (1982) *Cinderellas of the Empire: Towards a History of Kiribati and Tuvalu*, Canberra, Australian National University.

Wallis and Futuna

Historical background

- 15th and 16th C. Tongans settle Wallis (Uvea) but Samoans settled Futuna several thousand years before and resist attempted Tongan invasions

- Polynesians from this archipelago settle outlier islands in Melanesia. Wallisians (Uveans) settle in the Loyalty group of New Caledonia and Futunans settle in Vanuatu and the Solomon Islands

- Wallisians maintain frequent contact with Tonga in pre-European times. Both Wallis and Futuna have hierarchical societies but as befitting their respective Tongan and Samoan origins, Wallis tends to be more inegalitarian, unified and aggressively militaristic. The Wallisian language is closely related to Tongan while Futunan still shares many linguistic features of Samoan

- 1616 Dutch navigators explore Futuna but only in 1767 do Europeans visit Uvea – the new name coming from Captain Samuel Wallis who visits on his way from Tahiti

- Early 19th C. US whalers have a more sustained influence. Their introduction of guns allows a kingdom to be created on Wallis putting an end to the constant struggles between rival chiefs for supremacy over the entire island

- Catholic missionaries set the groundwork for French influence – one of them, Pierre Chanel, is martyred in 1841 and canonized to become Polynesia's only Catholic saint in 1954

- 1842 three kingdoms (one on Wallis and two on Futuna) solidify when the Kings petition France for protection at the same time as Tahiti is brought under French influence. A protectorate is formalized by 1888

- Wallis and Futuna are very unusual among Pacific Islands because they avoid extreme depopulation through disease. Even a serious epidemic of dysentery on Futuna (killing 3% of its population in 1932) does not prevent the population there from rising almost 20%, 1925–35

- From the mid 19th C. copra production emerges as the resource pillar but is not fully developed and the economy is never very dynamic

- Wallis and Futuna are the only French jurisdiction in the Pacific to be loyal to the Vichy collaborationists in France until Pearl Harbor attacked by Japan in 1941. Thereafter Wallis becomes an important US base although it is outside the area of active hostilities

- 1959 nearly 95% of the electorate vote to become an overseas territory of France a status granted two years later

- Aid from Paris and emigrant remittances from New Caledonia make most islanders strong supporters of French colonialism in the region as a whole. Emigrants to New Caledonia outnumber those remaining in Wallis and Futuna by the late 1980s and are a significant voting bloc in New Caledonian elections

- In the mid 1990s, with independence for New Caledonia appearing inevitable and repatriation of Wallisians and Futunans seen as undesirable or impossible (since it would more than double the population of the territory), migrants ally themselves with the indigenous Kanak independence movement

- Increasing emphasis recently on local economic development strategies for Wallis and Futuna. Some movement toward developing tourism, despite past resistance of local chiefs including the adamant and successful opposition to plans for a Club Med resort in the 1970s

- 1990s see the spectacular emergence of a new form of organization. Left-wing labour unionism attacks the Catholic Church and the traditional aristocratic hierarchy blaming them for stifling the political, economic and intellectual potential of the people

- Labourite mobilization in the 1992 and 1993 elections led to the first defeat for the conservatives in the Territorial Assembly since it was established in 1962

- 1994 general strike over the high cost of living and the absence of a system of secular primary education is the culmination of labour unrest since 1990.

Political framework

- **Federal/local system.** As a French overseas territory Wallis and Futuna have a senior administrator (appointed by the High Commissioner in New Caledonia) with extensive powers in the capital on Wallis. Although three district chiefs (*faipule*) and 20 village chiefs (*pule*) have great influence, bureaucratic administration is centralized in the French style. In 1983 the two Kings of Futuna contend that power is too concentrated on Wallis and request in vain that Futuna and Wallis become separate overseas territories of France

- **Constitution – how democratic?** The 1961 territorial statute, with amendments, operates under the constitution of the French Fifth Republic. The Territorial Assembly has limited legislative powers and the administrator can veto most decisions. The administrator also controls finance, education, law and order, defence and foreign affairs. He also presides over the Territorial Council, a proxy Cabinet consisting of the three Kings and three appointees of the administrator. Although the

territory elects one deputy and one senator to the French parliament and votes for a representative to the EU parliament direct democratic control over territorial affairs is not very extensive. Nevertheless, there is no movement in Wallis and Futuna supporting independence from France unlike New Caledonia and French Polynesia

- **Which party controls?** Conservative Gaullists control the Territorial Assembly 1964–92 when they are defeated in elections as the territory moves to the left. In 1993 a left-wing leader is elected president of the Territorial Assembly

- **Ethnic politics?** Ethnic politics are confined to locational, cultural and linguistic differences between the Tonga-descended Wallisians and the Futunans who are related to Samoans

- **Political control of the media?** Despite initial opposition from the Kings TV is introduced on Wallis in 1986 and Futuna in 1994 – radio began in 1979. All stations are heavily oriented toward direct broadcasts from Paris although part of the radio broadcasts are in Wallisian. Print journalism is very weak. There are few direct political attempts to censor the media

- **How independent is the judiciary?** Within the context of a judiciary controlled by the legal system of metropolitan France it is independent

- **Legislative and bureaucratic power?** The bureaucracy is not particularly dependent on political parties but like the legislature is largely subservient to the French senior administrator.

Further reading

Aldrich, R. (1990) *The French Presence in the South Pacific 1842–1940*, Honolulu, University of Hawaii Press.

Aldrich, R. (1993) *France and the South Pacific since 1940*, Honolulu, University of Hawaii Press.

Henningham, S. (1991) *France and the South Pacific: a Contemporary History*, Honolulu, University of Hawaii Press.

Western Samoa

Historical background

- Samoa is culturally unified for millennia until the USA and Germany split eastern from western territories in 1900
- Earliest evidence of Polynesian settlement dates from 1000 BC
- 14th–17th C. Samoans, Fijians and Tongans regularly intrude on each others territory
- From 1722 Dutch, French and British explorers pass through the islands but European settlement does not begin until after the British missionary John Williams lands in 1830
- 1838–39 British and US naval forces conclude commercial treaties with Samoan aristocrats followed by more white immigrant settlers
- 1869–73 civil war over an aristocratic title. Europeans, especially Germans, sell guns and ammunition to indigenous aristocrats in exchange for the best land in the islands – about 16% of all the land in Western Samoa
- Large coconut plantations are developed employing indentured Solomon Islands and Chinese workers who migrate in large numbers and soon constitute almost 10% of the population
- By the late 1890s cocoa, bananas and especially copra are established as the resource pillars of the Samoan export economy
- Germany, the USA and the UK support rival aristocratic factions in an intermittent civil war during the later 19th C.
- 1889 international naval confrontation between Germany, the USA and the UK in the principal port of Apia. German and US (but not British) warships refuse to leave Apia in the face of an advancing hurricane – all but one British warship sunk with 146 lives lost
- 1899 Samoas partitioned – Western Samoa becomes the principal German colony in the South Pacific; USA takes American Samoa; British withdraw in exchange for German concessions in the Solomon Islands, Tonga, and Niue
- 1914 New Zealand annex Western Samoa after the outbreak of the First World War – German plantations seized and almost all Chinese workers deported
- 1918 administrative errors allow a ship known to be carrying influenza into Apia – epidemic kills 22% of the population. The disease is never introduced into American Samoa because of tighter quarantine
- 1920s and 1930s hostility grows toward colonial rule in both Samoas. Strong non-violent independence movement (the *Mau*) active in civil disobedience between 1927 and 1936. The movement is accommodated and lightly repressed in American Samoa but is crushed by New Zealand in Western Samoa. Eleven Samoans killed by police machine-gun fire on unarmed demonstrators
- Large numbers of US marines stationed on Upolu during the Second World War build roads, the airport and have an extensive influence on the people
- 1946 UN continues New Zealand trusteeship over Western Samoa

- Early 1950s bring a boom in the export economy. But worsening balance of trade deficits produce chronic economic crisis by the early 1960s
- 1962 independence achieved and a constitution approved by universal adult suffrage. But future franchise and elected officials restricted to aristocratic *matais* (chiefs) for 47 of 49 Legislative Assembly seats – the other two being for non-Samoans
- From the 1960s Western Samoa emerges as a labour source for American Samoa's tuna canneries, factories and unskilled jobs in New Zealand, Australia and the USA. Migrant remittances and foreign aid become increasingly important to the domestic economy
- 1973–74 oil crisis reverses favourable attitudes toward Western Samoan migrants in the receiving countries especially New Zealand. New restrictions and arrests for overstaying are designed to diminish the labour flows and cool relations between the countries
- 1981 six-month public service strike and continuing inflation of over 20% contribute to constitutional crisis the following year. Three different Prime Ministers in one year. Also a legal challenge over the restriction of voting to aristocratic *matais* which is first supported but then overturned on appeal
- 1990 a qualified form of universal suffrage is adopted but with elected officials still limited to aristocratic *matais*
- 1990–91 two devastating cyclones kill eleven, leave more than 5% of the population homeless and destroy property, livestock, infrastructure and export crops
- Western Samoans in New Zealand (about half born there) and substantial communities of migrants in American Samoa, Hawaii, and California provide a large and ever increasing volume of remittances. Private remittances account for 29% of GDP and 47% of imports 1984–90
- 1990s substantial increase in exports from new tax-free manufacturing operations that take advantage of duty-free entry to New Zealand and especially Australian markets. Large number of low-wage, twelve-hour shift jobs created for non-union labour. With government support employers use draconian action against wildcat strikes protesting poor wages and working conditions
- 1994–95 widespread popular protests and demonstrations against a new regressive 10% sales tax sweep the country. Reports of government corruption, extravagance and financial crises (including spectacular losses by the state-owned Polynesian Airlines) lead to censorship and repression of critics.

Political framework

- **Federal/local system.** Local government has become increasingly powerful during the 1990s. In over 300 villages where about 90% of Western Samoans live, *matai*s and clerics perform many of the most important governmental functions

- **Constitution – how democratic?** There is a parliamentary system with a Prime Minister elected from Legislative Assembly members. But encoded in the constitution are very distinctive Samoan political principles particularly relating to the hereditary aristocracy. There is a ceremonial head of state with considerably more influence than in most commonwealth countries – it is expected that they will be drawn from the heads of the four royal houses. Before 1990 only chiefs could vote but since then all citizens over the age of 21 have been allowed to vote, but only chiefs may stand for the 47 Samoan parliamentary seats. In short a system without universal rights of candidacy is not very democratic

- **Which party controls?** The Human Rights Protection Party rules – the opposition Samoa National Development Party does not seriously challenge for control of government. Personalities and expediency rather than ideology or policies are significant and votes are often bought

- **Ethnic politics?** Politics are not very ethnicized although there are separate seats and electoral rolls for Samoans (47 seats) and non-Samoans (2 seats)

- **Political control of the media?** The government owns newspapers, two radio stations, the local TV station and is hostile toward the minority of the media which it does not own. It calls repeatedly for more restrictive controls over the privately-owned *Samoa Observer* and Magik radio station which tend to be critical of the government. In 1993 the government legislated that journalists disclose sources and also strengthened defamation laws. In 1994 the offices of the *Samoa Observer* were destroyed by fire after it exposed official corruption

- **How independent is the judiciary?** The judiciary is not independent. The current Chief Justice succeeded his brother-in-law in 1992 after *simultaneously* operating as Acting Chief Justice, Attorney-General and private practitioner. As Acting Chief Justice he fined the *Samoa Times* for suggesting that he disqualify himself from judging a murder case prosecuted by his Attorney-General's office against a person defended by his sister who is closely associated with his legal firm

- **Legislative and bureaucratic power?** There are relatively large numbers of independents in the legislature on which the ruling party often relies for support but this offers the bureaucracy little independence. Since 1990 the Prime Minister appoints all its chief executives. The Chief Auditor was suspended in 1995 for revealing widespread government corruption – the Deputy Prime Minister (re-elected 1996) prevented the auditing of government accounts from 1990 to 1993.

Further reading

Meleisea, M. (1987) *The Making of Modern Samoa*, Suva, University of the South Pacific.

Meleisea, M. and Meleisea, P.S. (eds) (1987) *Lagaga: a Short History of Western Samoa*, Suva, University of the South Pacific.

Stanley, D. (1996) *South Pacific Handbook*, Chico, Calif., Moon Publications.

Anglonesia

by Anthony van Fossen

Norfolk Island

Historical background

- Although Norfolk uninhabited when Captain Cook arrives in 1774 there is some evidence of earlier settlement
- 1788–1814 British prison colony established then abandoned
- 1825 alarm about the intentions of foreign powers sees the British prison colony re-established. The sadistic brutality displayed to prisoners who stage a number of revolts led to its stigmatization as 'Hell on Earth'
- 1856 as the last of the prisoners leave for Tasmania (Australia) all the inhabitants of Pitcairn settle on Norfolk Island as free farmers where they are joined later by more settlers from Australia, New Zealand and the UK
- 'Norfolk' – an evolved form of Pitcairnese combining Tahitian and 18th C. English – is spoken by islanders of Pitcairn background who also speak standard contemporary English
- Whaling becomes the primary export industry until 1962 with temporary booms in bananas (1930) and bean seed (1940s)
- 1914 Norfolk loses its position as a separate British colony and is placed under the authority of Australia. Islanders vigorously oppose both of these moves and initiate a long period of contesting Australian central governmental authority which continues to this day
- 1944 military airfield built – used later for tourism which becomes dominant in the 1960s and is the most significant industry today. Very large tourist numbers relative to the resident population but in a dispersed, relaxed and generally rural scene
- 1960s becomes the first significant Pacific Islands tax haven – company registrations shoot up from 36 to 1,571 between 1965 and 1971. But development into a full offshore financial centre is thwarted by the Australian government in the 1970s. Most of its clients move to Vanuatu although there is still a large number of companies registered on Norfolk at present
- No corporate or personal income taxation on the island today and millionaires, like the author Colleen McCollough, continue to be attracted to living on Norfolk
- 1976 proposal to integrate the island into the Australian commonwealth is vigorously opposed by all elected politicians eventuating in an appeal to the UN
- 1979 Norfolk begins to participate in Pacific Island regional organizations as an entity separate from Australia who then introduce new rules for the South Pacific Commission which eliminate Norfolk's ability to participate
- 1991 proposal to include Norfolk in the Australian federal electorate is rejected by a large majority in a local referendum and is abandoned by the Australian government the next year. Opponents claim that such proposals are attempts to deprive the island of sovereignty, local character, control over immigration and favoured tax status.

Political framework

- **Federal/local system.** There is a considerable and growing level of local control but Pitcairn-descended islanders and wealthy mainlanders are prominent critics of Australian government policies toward Norfolk. An Australian-appointed administrator and Governor General must assent to enactments of the Norfolk Island Legislative Assembly for these to become law. Many arrangements are peculiar to the territory like the absence of personal and corporate income taxation, Australian-style pensions, unemployment benefits and workers compensation as well as the presence of stricter immigration control. All Norfolk islanders are citizens of Australia with free non-reciprocal rights of entry to the mainland
- **Constitution – how democratic?** The Norfolk Island Act 1979 established an elected Legislative Assembly of nine members. Although this increased the level of local democracy many residents still claim it is insufficient but only a minority favour complete independence
- **Which party controls?** Parties *per se* do not exist
- **Ethnic politics?** Tight control over immigration to restrict the number of mainlanders who reside on the island is an important element in local ethnic politics in a polity dominated by islanders of Pitcairn descent. Few permits are issued allowing permanent residency and these go disproportionately to the wealthy
- **Political control of the media?** The media are not controlled by direct political means
- **How independent is the judiciary?** The judiciary is independent with the High Court of Australia empowered to decide on appeals against decisions of the Norfolk Island Supreme Court
- **Legislative and bureaucratic power?** The parties which exist on the Australian mainland do not play a part in Norfolk Island politics. Since 1985 the public service is controlled within the territory and there have been few cases of overt political interference.

Further reading

Clarke, P. (1986) *Hell and Paradise: the Norfolk–Bounty–Pitcairn Saga*, New York, Viking.

Hoare, M. (1988) *Norfolk Island: an Outline of its History 1774–1987*, St. Lucia, University of Queensland Press.

Treadgold, M.L. (1988) *Bounteous Bestowal: the Economic History of Norfolk Island*, Canberra, Australian National University.

Pitcairn Islands

Historical background

- The Pitcairn Islands encompass four islands annexed by Britain in 1902 and they remain the last British colony in the region. Only Pitcairn is inhabited
- Once occupied by Polynesians but these settlers disappear in prehistoric times
- 1767 discovered by the British Captain Carteret – 23 years later nine fugitive Englishmen from the 1789 mutiny on the *Bounty* and nineteen Polynesians (six men, twelve women and a child) arrive on Pitcairn. Children born on the island educated in accordance with puritanical British standards
- Islanders continue today to speak Pitcairnese – an amalgam of 18th C. English and Tahitian in addition to standard English
- 1838 Pitcairn becomes the first British colony in the Pacific Islands after six years under the virtual dictatorship of an ambitious English adventurer named Joshua Hill who arrives via Hawaii and Tahiti
- 1856 all Pitcairners migrate to Norfolk Island
- 1858 43 people in six families return – their descendants form most of the present population and are called Pitcairners
- Economy remains based on subsistence agriculture, handicrafts and small-scale trading as well as the sale of postage stamps, investment interest, remittances from overseas migrants and aid
- Highest population (233) recorded in 1937 – loss of population (mostly to New Zealand) accelerates after 1968 when the last regular passenger ship service ends
- 1983 US coal magnate makes bid for uninhabited Henderson Island, the largest in the group. Offers US$1 million for development projects in addition to building airfields on Pitcairn and Henderson and providing three small aeroplanes. British government reject his bid
- 1988 UN declares Henderson a World Heritage Site to protect it from further development initiatives
- 1992 discoveries of large sea-bed mineral deposits within Pitcairn's extensive exclusive economic zone containing manganese, gold, silver, copper, zinc and iron – believed to be formed by underwater volcanoes. These are seen as having the potential to dramatically alter the archipelago's economy at some (as yet indefinite) time in the future
- 1993 relations with the UK cool as islanders formally express dissatisfaction to the Governor over British policy toward Pitcairn and raise the issue of a transfer of sovereignty
- 1995 problems with Britain and France deepen as islanders (supported by Greenpeace) take the British government to court over its failure to oppose nuclear testing at French Polynesia's Mururoa atoll to which Pitcairn is the closest inhabited island (see Figure 24).

Political framework

- **Federal/local system.** Although a British territory local government has considerable *de facto* autonomy – the Island Council elected by universal adult suffrage has executive and judicial powers
- **Constitution – how democratic?** The 1940 constitution specifies a colonial arrangement which in principle provides for limited political democracy. The Governor, who is British High Commissioner in New Zealand, rarely exercises *de jure* power to alter decisions of the Island Council
- **Which party controls?** There are no political parties
- **Ethnic politics?** Politics are not highly ethnicized
- **Political control of the media?** There is little political control over the media
- **How independent is the judiciary?** The judicial system is relatively independent. The local Island Court has limited jurisdiction and restricted abilities to jail and fine – it is rarely required to sit
- **Legislative and bureaucratic power?** Parties do not exist and politicians exercise no influence over the small number of office holders.

Further reading

Birkett, D. (1997) *Serpent in Paradise*, London, Picador.

Clarke, P. (1986) *Hell and Paradise: the Norfolk–Bounty–Pitcairn Saga*, New York, Viking.

Appendix B: data for Brunei, Macau, the Russian Far East and the Pacific Islands

Demographic indicators

Table B.1 *Total population and population density*

	Total population				Population density (people per km²)			
	1970	*1994*	*1995*	*1996*	*1970*	*1994*	*1995*	*1996*
Brunei	130,000			301,000	23			52
Macau	226,000			435,000	11,300			22,523
Russian Far East	5,800,000			7,514,000	0.9			1.2
Melanesia								
Fiji	520,000			798,000	29			43
New Caledonia	108,000		185,000		6		10	
Solomon Is	161,000		378,000		6		13	
Vanuatu	87,000		173,600		7		14	
Micronesia								
FSM	56,600	104,700			81	150		
Guam	85,000		146,000		155		266	
Kiribati	50,000		80,800		61		100	
Marshall Is	22,080		54,000		122		299	
Nauru	6,900	10,200			327	481		
N. Mariana Is	11,300		57,900		25		127	
Palau	12,000		16,500		25		34	
Polynesia								
Am. Samoa	27,000			56,000	135			281
Cook Is	20,000		20,200		84		85	
Fr. Polynesia	112,300		216,200		32		61	
Niue	5,100	2,300			20	9		
Tokelau	1,550		1,500		158		149	
Tonga	83,000		97,700		119		140	
Tuvalu	5,800		10,000		168		289	
Wallis & Futuna	8,500		14,500		31		53	
W. Samoa	140,000		171,000		49		60	
Anglonesia								
Norfolk Is.	1,400	1,900			41	55		
Pitcairn Is.	85	60			3	2		

Source: *World Data* (1995) CD-ROM Social Indicators Stack, Washington DC, World Bank; *Asia-Pacific Population Data Sheet* (1996) Bangkok, UN; country sources.

Table B.2 *Infant mortality, life expectancy, and urban population*

	Infant mortality rate per 1,000 live births				Life expectancy at birth (years)			Urban population (% total)			
	1970	1993	1994	1995	1970	1993	1994	1970	1993	1994	1995
Brunei	54	8			68	75		62	58		
Macau	25	9				73		97	99		
Russian Far East	29		21				62	71			76
Melanesia											
Fiji	49	22			64	72		35		40	
New Caledonia	41		10		64		71	44	58		
Solomon Is	69	26			61	71		7		16	
Vanuatu	115		44		48		66	17			24
Micronesia											
FSM	28		49			71		30		26	
Guam	22	8					76	26	38		
Kiribati	105	54				57		26		35	
Marshall Is	79	60			58		63	52		65	
Nauru	52	38						100	100		
N. Mariana Is	37			10					53		
Palau	48	28				69			69		
Polynesia											
Am. Samoa	27			19		73		41	46		
Cook Is	34	20				71			25		
Fr. Polynesia	64			10			71	53	55		
Niue	26	11				63			30		
Tokelau											
Tonga	46			20	62		68	21		31	
Tuvalu				28			63			42	
Wallis & Futuna				25			72				
W. Samoa	67	33			61	67		20			21

Source: *World Data* (1995) CD-ROM Social Indicators Stack, Washington DC, World Bank; *Key Indicators of Developing Asian and Pacific Countries* (1996) Manila, Asian Development Bank; *Asia-Pacific in Figures* (1994) New York, UN; *Asia-Pacific Population Data Sheet* (1996) Bangkok, UN; country sources.

Economic indicators

Table B.3 *Gross national product per capita (US$)*

	1970	1971	1972	1973	1974	1975	1976	1977	1978	1979	1980	1981	1982	1983	1984	1985	1986	1987	1988	1989	1990	1991	1992	1993	1994	1995
Brunei							9,160	10,060	11,050	14,980	17,730	17,940	21,700	19,530	17,890	16,180	13,370	12,890	12,180	12,230	12,820	14,140				
Melanesia																										
Fiji	400	450	530	710	930	1,130	1,240	1,300	1,370	1,650	1,870	2,060	1,850	1,630	1,720	1,620	1,820	1,780	1,780	1,860	1,890	1,940	2,090	2,180	2,320	
N. Caledonia	3,617	3,656	3,727	3,361	4,377	5,049	5,960	6,414	6,133	7,540	8,461	6,967	6,226	5,563	5,264	5,547	7,656	9,300	12,698	13,100	14,911	15,305	16,559			
Solomon Is	195	222	232	298	310	320	290	310	330	460	440	530	560	530	590	510	600	630	670	740	730	680	710	740	800	
Vanuatu										614	564	607	651	766	916	920	940	870	980	1,070	1,150	1,060	1,110	1,150	1,150	
Micronesia																										
Kiribati															580	520	610	560	680	710	700	720	710	730		
Polynesia																										
Tonga	180										581					750	800	850	940	1,040	1,150	1,340	1,430	1,530	1,650	1,705
W. Samoa												709									749		960	960	970	

Source: *World Data* (1995) CD-ROM National Accounts Stack, Washington DC, World Bank; *Key Indicators of Developing Asian and Pacific Countries* (1995, 1996) Manila, Asian Development Bank; country sources.

Table B.4 Gross domestic product per capita (US$)

	1970	1971	1972	1973	1974	1975	1976	1977	1978	1979	1980	1981	1982	1983	1984	1985	1986	1987	1988	1989	1990	1991	1992	1993	1994	1995
Brunei	1,360	1,480	1,924	2,603	7,455	6,741	7,332	8,621	11,761	15,697	25,546	22,872	20,638	16,512	15,646	13,815	9,929	11,518	10,976	11,936	13,969	14,511	14,570	14,409	16,270	17,462
Macau																					10,410	11,417	13,516	14,972	15,891	17,165
Russian Far East																								1,196		
Melanesia																										
Solomon Is											821								1,038	996	1,030			1,243	1,295	1,395
Micronesia																										
FSM						725		701						1,182			1,318	1,368	1,563	1,575	1,539	1,655	1,699	1,885	1,962	2,036
Guam	2,353	2,539	2,926	3,422	3,904	4,071	4,151	5,144	5,951	5,780	5,388	5,641	5,913	6,087	6,244	7,084	8,563	8,832	13,678	14,680	17,501	19,580	20,823	20,456	20,958	
Kiribati	293	300	347	606	996	1,028	756	701	805	759	493	504	500	485	555	358	352	374	456	469	445	461	450			
Marshall Is						967	871	859				824	891	1,068	1,116	1,046	1,288	1,397	1,450	1,435	1,487	1,495	1,587	1,608	1,653	
Nauru	4,746					8,552	6,335	5,398	8,279	11,230	9,392	10,902	15,833	11,844	8,293	7,412	6,395	6,744	8,022	8,696	7,021	2,708	3,529	4,100		
N. Mariana Is						2,720										9,100			16,143	14,941	13,889	12,185	10,208	9,545	9,249	
Palau						1,097		1,295						2,038	2,496	2,418					5,085	5,545	5,477	5,935		
Polynesia																										
Am. Samoa				2,462	3,014	1,657							1,845			4,859						2,612				
Cook Is	465		485			940	754	864	999				1,400	1,370	1,495	1,583	2,051	2,550	3,297	3,425	3,468	3,655	3,670	3,858	4,457	5,111
Fr. Polynesia	1,973	2,075	2,125	2,354	3,305	3,677	4,941	5,326	6,314	7,630	8,448	7,693	7,465	7,348	7,552	8,053	11,937	13,091	13,019	12,639	15,478	14,799	15,781	15,358	15,467	17,083
Niue															1,040					926				1,045		
Tokelau											544			621					802					972		
Tonga	166	174	187	272	350	433	377	388	460	483	602	662	647	654	612	622	718	887	1,117	1,111	1,176	1,336	1,364	1,491		
Tuvalu						180						616	473	489	531	429	524	629	871	930	1,040	1,215	1,205	1,146	1,338	
Wal. & Fut.																484					547	1,507			1,979	
W. Samoa									654	643	748	632	673	604	523	520	571	651	708	666	676	666	651	673	784	
Anglonesia																										
Norfolk Is.						6,456	6,170	7,385																		

Source: *The Europa World Yearbook* (1970–96) London, Europa; *Far East and Australasia* (1997) London, Europa; *Key Indicators of Developing Asian and Pacific Countries* (1970–96) Manila, Asian Development Bank; *Statistical Yearbook for Asia and the Pacific* (1979, 1993) New York, UN; *UN Statistical Yearbook* (1985, 1994) New York, UN; *The World Factbook* (1995) Washington DC, Central Intelligence Agency; country sources.

Table B.5 *Gross domestic product distribution and employment distribution.*
Ag: agriculture; Ind: industry; Ser: services

		GDP distribution (%)				Employment distribution (%)		
		Ag	Ind	Ser		Ag	Ind	Ser
Brunei	1972	3	72	25	1972	3	46	51
	1992	3	48	51	1991	2	24	74
Macau					1989	0.6	46	53
					1994	0.2	32	67
Russian Far East					1994	9	24	67
Melanesia								
Fiji	1970	26	12	62	1966	56	14	30
	1995	23	23	54	1990	40	14	46
New Caledonia	1970	22	25	53	1969	43	20	37
	1990	13	15	72	1989	14	20	66
Solomon Is	1970	63	10	27	1970	23	12	65
	1991	48	9	43	1993	27	14	59
Vanuatu	1980	22	5	73	1967	82	3	15
	1995	23	13	64	1989	77	4	19
Micronesia								
FSM	1983	42	2	56				
	1990	48	13	39	1990	48	13	39
Guam	1973	1	31	68	1970	1	21	78
	1980	1	38	67	1994	1	16	83
Kiribati	1972	49	5	46	1968	75	7	18
	1992	24	9	67	1990	78	5	17
Marshall Is	1994	17	13	70	1988	21	21	58
N. Mariana Is					1970	7	14	79
	1994	1	21	78	1990	3	44	53
Palau					1970	17	20	63
	1992	29	13	58	1990	8	17	75
Polynesia								
Am. Samoa					1970	2	35	63
					1990	2	43	55
Cook Is	1970	27	22	51	1971	23	22	55
	1995	18	9	73	1991	13	14	73
Fr. Polynesia	1970	5	48	47	1970	6	31	63
	1993	4	15	81	1995	3	15	82
Niue					1981	20	26	54
					1991	6	9	85
Tonga	1970	53	2	45	1966	74	3	23
	1995	36	13	51	1994	39	21	40
Tuvalu					1968	71	8	21
	1994	28	7	65				
W. Samoa	1980	46	12	42	1971	67	7	26
	1993	43	22	35	1991	73	8	19
Anglonesia								
Norfolk Is.	1976	2	14	84	1978	5	16	79

Source: *The Europa World Yearbook* (1970–96) London, Europa; *Far East and Australasia* (1997) London, Europa; *Key Indicators of Developing Asian and Pacific Countries* (1996) Manila, Asian Development Bank; *Statistical Yearbook for Asia and the Pacific* (1979) New York, UN; *World Data* (1995) CD-ROM National Accounts and Social Indicators Stacks, Washington DC, World Bank; *Yearbook of Labour Statistics* (1996) Geneva, International Labour Office; country sources.

Table B.6 *Investment (I), saving (S) and government consumption*

		I	S			
		Investment and saving (% GDP)			*Government consumption (% GDP)*	
Brunei	1982	12			1970	16
	1994		35		1993	35
Macau	1994		28			
Melanesia						
Fiji	1970	22	19		1970	14
	1992	15	20		1994	17
New Caledonia	1990	35			1990	33
Solomon Is	1980	36	8		1970	19
	1991	28	−2		1991	31
Vanuatu					1980	32
	1990	40	28		1993	28
Micronesia						
FSM	1977	29	8			
	1989	31				
Kiribati	1972	8	16		1972	28
					1992	54
Marshall Is	1977	31	14			
	1991	43				
Palau	1977	23	14		1993	49
Polynesia						
Cook Is					1970	32
Fr. Polynesia	1980	25	25			
	1993	16	36			
Tonga	1970	26	15		1970	17
	1992	16	9		1992	19
Tuvalu					1994	31
W. Samoa	1980	33	−5		1980	18
	1992	42	−15		1992	23
Anglonesia						
Norfolk Is.	1978	19	38		1978	12

Source: *World Data* (1995) CD-ROM National Accounts Stack, Washington DC, World Bank; *Key Indicators of Developing Asian and Pacific Countries* (1970–96) Manila, Asian Development Bank; *Statistical Yearbook for Asia and the Pacific* (1979, 1993) New York, UN; *The World Factbook* (1995) Washington DC, Central Intelligence Agency; country sources.

Table B.7 *Long-term external debt (US$ million)*

	1970	1993	1994	1995
Melanesia				
Fiji	12	330		
Solomon Is	1		165	
Vanuatu	1		47	
Micronesia				
FSM			129	
Kiribati		16		
Marshall Is		169		
Polynesia				
Cook Is			124	
Tonga	1			89
W. Samoa	6			168

Source: *World Data* (1995) CD-ROM External Debt no.1 Stack, Washington DC, World Bank; *Key Indicators of Developing Asian and Pacific Countries* (1970–96) Manila, Asian Development Bank; *Statistical Yearbook for Asia and the Pacific* (1979, 1993) New York, UN; *The World Factbook* (1995) Washington DC, Central Intelligence Agency; country sources.

Table B.8 *Exports (X) and imports (M) (% GDP)*

		X	M
Brunei	1970	54	47
	1994	47	39
Macau	1990	49	45
	1995	31	32
Melanesia			
Fiji	1970	48	52
	1992	56	50
New Caledonia	1970	48	61
	1992	14	32
Solomon Is	1970	25	35
	1995	72	60
Vanuatu	1980	33	42
	1993	44	60
Micronesia			
FSM	1977	4	74
	1994	35	96
Guam	1970	3	48
	1991	3	20
Kiribati	1980	23	110
	1992	13	114
Marshall Is	1975	4	23
	1994	25	80
Nauru	1970	100	16
	1991	100	81
N. Mariana Is	1991	43	65
Palau	1977	51	112
	1993	32	46
Polynesia			
Am. Samoa	1973	93	50
	1991	243	291
Cook Is	1970	32	71
	1995	4	102
Fr. Polynesia	1970	13	63
	1995	5	27
Niue	1984	5	80
	1993	7	157
Tokelau	1983	10	32
Tonga	1975	42	71
	1992	21	51
Tuvalu	1994	1	109
W. Samoa	1980	25	63
	1992	31	88
Anglonesia			
Norfolk Is.	1978	87	88

Source: *World Data* (1995) CD-ROM National Accounts Stack, Washington DC, World Bank; *Key Indicators of Developing Asian and Pacific Countries* (1970–96) Manila, Asian Development Bank; *Far East and Australasia* (1997) London, Europa; *Statistical Yearbook for Asia and the Pacific* (1979) New York, UN; country sources; *The World Factbook* (1985–95) Washington DC, Central Intelligence Agency.

Table B.9 *Major trading partners: exports (% total)*

Brunei	1972	Japan 52	Malaysia 13	Singapore 8	Thailand 6	USA 8
	1995	Japan 57	UK 9	Singapore 10	Thailand 12	
Macau	1971	Germany 8	Hong Kong 16	Angola 13	France 12	Portugal 11
	1995	Germany 10	Hong Kong 10	USA 42	China 10	UK 7
Russian Far East	1992	Japan 47	China 27	S. Korea 7		
	1994	Japan 63	China 10	S. Korea 11		
Melanesia						
Fiji	1970	UK 32	USA 16	Canada 12	Australia 9	New Zealand 7
	1995	UK 20	USA 12	Japan 6	Australia 24	New Zealand 5
New Caledonia	1970	France 45	Japan 45	USA 5		
	1992	France 32	Japan 24	USA 4		
Solomon Is	1970	Japan 52	Australia 15			
	1995	Japan 60	Australia 3	UK 8		
Vanuatu	1970	France 44	USA 37	Japan 13	Australia 3	
	1995	Germany 20	Spain 12	Japan 27	Australia 13	
Micronesia						
FSM	1993	Japan 76	USA 23			
Guam	1970	USA 71	Hong Kong 8	Japan 7	Philippines 7	
	1994	FSM 15	S. Korea 8	Japan 44	Taiwan 7	
Kiribati	1970	Australia 55	New Zealand 35	UK 10		
	1995	Japan 24	France 20	USA 16	Hong Kong 9	
Marshall Is	1982	USA 93		Guam 4		
Nauru	1970	Australia 59	New Zealand 25	UK 16		
N. Mariana Is	1994	USA 99				
Palau	1984	Japan 59	Guam 16	N. Mariana Is 10	USA 8	
Polynesia						
Am. Samoa	1990	USA 97				
Cook Is	1987	New Zealand 87	Japan 10			
	1990	New Zealand 31	Japan 24	Hong Kong 33		
Fr. Polynesia	1970	France 83	Italy 8			
	1994	France 33	Japan 46	USA 9		
Niue	1970	New Zealand 66	Cook Is 30			
	1985	New Zealand 88	Cook Is 7			
Tonga	1970	Netherlands 38	New Zealand 30	UK 7	Australia 6	
	1995	Japan 53	New Zealand 6	USA 26	Australia 3	
Tuvalu	1995	S. Africa 64	Colombia 9	Belgium 9		
Wallis & Futuna	1980	New Caledonia 69	Vanuatu 31			
W. Samoa	1970	New Zealand 47	Netherlands 18	Germany 13	USA 7	
	1995	New Zealand 6	Australia 87			
Anglonesia						
Norfolk Is.	1966	Australia 66	New Zealand 66			
	1985	Australia 63	New Zealand 20	EU 16		

Source: *Direction of Trade Statistics* (1978, 1996) Washington DC, IMF; *The Europa World Yearbook* (1970–96) London, Europa; *Key Indicators of Developing Asian and Pacific Countries* (1980–96) Manila, Asian Development Bank; country sources.

Table B.10 *Major trading partners: imports (% total)*

Brunei	1972	Japan 20	USA 19	Singapore 1	UK 14	
	1995	Malaysia 9	USA 6	Singapore 45	UK 13	
Macau	1971	Hong Kong 64	Japan 2	USA 2	UK 2	
	1995	Hong Kong 29	Japan 3	USA 7	China 22	
Russian Far East	1992	China 48	Japan 19	S. Korea 12		
	1994	China 83	Japan 9	S. Korea 8		
Melanesia						
Fiji	1970	Australia 24	New Zealand 12	UK 17	Japan 15	
	1995	Australia 45	New Zealand 17	USA 11	Japan 6	Singapore 8
New Caledonia	1970	France 50	EEC 15	Australia 13	USA 7	
	1995	France 45	EEC 14	Australia 13	New Zealand 6	
Solomon Is	1970	Australia 45	UK 16	USA 10	Japan 7	
	1995	Australia 42	New Zealand 8	Singapore 12	Japan 10	
Vanuatu	1970	Australia 40	Japan 12	France 15		
	1995	Australia 24	Japan 45	Fiji 5	New Zealand 7	
Micronesia						
FSM	1975	USA 45	Japan 20			
	1993	USA 65	Japan 18			
Guam	1970	USA 63	Japan 18	Hong Kong 4		
Kiribati	1970	Australia 59	UK 12	Fiji 5	Japan 7	
	1995	Australia 17	France 50	Fiji 11		
Marshall Is	1975	USA 46	Japan 11			
	1994	USA 85	Japan 6			
Nauru	1968	Australia 81	New Zealand 9			
N. Mariana Is	1974	USA 66	Japan 8			
Palau	1975	USA 52	Japan 25			
Polynesia						
Am. Samoa	1970	USA 58	New Zealand 16	Australia 9	Japan 8	
	1991	USA 59	New Zealand 8	Australia 11	Japan 8	
Cook Is	1990	New Zealand 42	Italy 32	Australia 5		
Fr. Polynesia	1970	France 61	USA 15	New Zealand 4		
	1994	France 45	USA 14	New Zealand 7	Australia 7	
Niue	1970	New Zealand 79	Japan 4	Fiji 9		
	1993	New Zealand 86	Japan 5			
Tonga	1970	New Zealand 38	Australia 16	Fiji 16	UK 9	
	1995	New Zealand 42	Australia 27	Fiji 7	USA 9	
Tuvalu	1981	Fiji 36	Australia 33	New Zealand 26	UK 5	
	1995	Fiji 66	Australia 17	New Zealand 4	UK 3	
W. Samoa	1970	New Zealand 32	Australia 17	USA 14	Japan 11	Fiji 4
	1995	New Zealand 37	Australia 21	USA 12	Japan 11	Fiji 12
Anglonesia						
Norfolk Is.	1966	Australia 58	New Zealand 7	Asia 27	Europe 8	
	1985	Australia 52	New Zealand 21	Asia 16	Europe 11	

Source: *Direction of Trade Statistics* (1978, 1996) Washington DC, IMF; *The Europa World Yearbook* (1970–96) London, Europa; *Key Indicators of Developing Asian and Pacific Countries* (1980–96) Manila, Asian Development Bank; country sources.

Table B.11 *Major export commodities (% total)*

Brunei	1972	fuels 94			
	1994	petroleum 45	gas 47		
Macau	1983	manufactures 92	machinery 5		
	1995	textiles 78	toys 4	electronics 2	
Russian Far East	1980	timber 51	food and fish 25	raw materials 6	
	1992	timber 29	food and fish 29	raw materials 27	
Melanesia					
Fiji	1970	sugar 51	coconut oil 8	fish 7	
	1995	sugar 36	textiles 24	gold 8	
New Caledonia	1970	ferro-nickel 40	nickel ore 37	nickel products 22	
	1995	ferro-nickel 55	nickel ore 24	nickel products 14	
Solomon Is	1970	copra 51	timber 40		
	1994	copra 4	timber 54	fish 20	palm oil 8
Vanuatu	1970	copra 46	timber 7	cocoa 4	
	1995	copra 4	timber 8	cocoa 4	beef 14
Micronesia					
FSM	1977	copra 78	handicrafts 20		
	1993	fish 87	textiles 7		
Guam	1971	fuels 52	manufactures 19	machinery 16	raw materials 7
	1994	fuels 29	fish 40	vehicles 8	tobacco 5
Kiribati	1970	phosphate 86	copra 6		
	1993	fish 12	copra 39		
Marshall Is	1977	copra 98			
	1994	chilled fish 47	frozen fish 21	fuels 21	
Nauru	1970	phosphate 100			
	1993	phosphate 100			
Palau	1977	coconut oil 49	tuna 44	copra cake 6	
	1993	fish 99			
Polynesia					
Am. Samoa	1970	canned tuna 90	pet food 6	fresh fish 4	
	1990	canned tuna 97	pet food 3		
Cook Is	1970	fruit juice 48	bananas 13	other fruit 28	copra 10
	1995	manufactures 56	food products 32		
Fr. Polynesia	1970	copra oil 17	pearls 4		
	1995	pearls 55			
Niue	1971	passion fruit 27	copra 14	other fruit 14	
	1993	taro 83	yams 4		
Tokelau	1984	copra 86	handicrafts 14		
Tonga	1970	copra 49	bananas 17	coconut 17	other fruit 8
	1995	squash 47	fish 24	vanilla beans 16	
Tuvalu	1980	postage stamps 78	copra 9		
	1990	postage stamps 46		copra 9	
Wallis & Futuna	1980	trochus shell 100			
W. Samoa	1970	copra 40	cocoa 31	bananas 16	
	1995	vehicle parts 86	copra 2		

Source: *The Europa World Yearbook* (1970–96) London, Europa; *Far East and Australasia* (1997) London, Europa; *Key Indicators of Developing Asian and Pacific Countries* (1980–96) Manila, Asian Development Bank; *Statistical Yearbook for Asia and the Pacific* (1979) New York, UN; country sources.

Table B.12 *Major import commodities (% total)*

Brunei	1972	machinery 38	manufactures 26	food 17	chemicals 6
	1994	machinery 42	manufactures 35	food 12	chemicals 5
Macau	1983	manufactures 54	machinery 12	food 14	fuel 7
	1995	manufactures 55	machinery 19	food 14	fuel 5
Russian Far East	1989	machinery 34	food 37	manufactures 8	
	1992	machinery 24	food 27	manufactures 42	
Melanesia					
Fiji	1970	fuels 11	materials 9	machinery 8	manufactures 6
	1995	fuels 11	food 15	machinery 23	manufactures 39
New Caledonia	1970	machinery 45	food 7	materials 33	textiles 4
	1995	machinery 35	food 19	materials 37	textiles 4
Solomon Is	1970	machinery 18	food 11		
	1994	machinery 37	food 13	fuels 9	
Vanuatu	1970	food 18	machinery 10		
	1995	food 18	machinery 31	manufactures 30	fuels 8
Micronesia					
FSM	1984	food 45	machinery 19	materials 8	
	1993	food 35	machinery 20	fuels 10	manufactures 29
Guam	1971	manufactures 37	machinery 27	food 23	fuels 7
Kiribati	1970	food 42	manufactures 28	machinery 13	fuels 7
	1994	food 40	manufactures 23	machinery 17	fuels 9
Marshall Is	1976	food 51	fuels 21	manufactures 20	machinery 5
	1994	food 32	fuels 23	manufactures 9	materials 11
Nauru	1966	materials 35	food 15	machinery 20	
	1987	materials 6	food 23	machinery 8	
N. Mariana Is	1994	fuels 11	food 13	machinery 6	textiles 6
Palau	1975	materials 9	food 22		
	1992	fuels 37	food 15		
Polynesia					
Am. Samoa	1970	food 28	fuels 24	jewellery 17	machinery 7
	1991	food 12	fuels 33	materials 8	machinery 5
Cook Is	1970	manufactures 39	food 28	machinery 20	materials 8
	1995	manufactures 33	food 27	machinery 18	materials 21
Fr. Polynesia	1970	machinery 51	food 19	materials 20	textiles 6
	1995	machinery 18	food 8	materials 6	
Niue	1970	food 33	vehicles 16	materials 13	fuels 7
	1993	food 30	vehicles 10	machinery 12	raw materials 15
Tonga	1970	food 36	manufactures 31	raw materials 17	machinery 15
	1995	food 28	manufactures 27	machinery 21	fuels 12
Tuvalu	1980	food 38	manufactures 28	machinery 14	fuels 13
	1989	food 27	manufactures 23	machinery 10	fuels 10
Wallis & Futuna	1974	raw materials 34	food 21	fuels 19	machinery 15
W. Samoa	1970	food 22	textiles 6	timber 5	
	1995	food 32	machinery 34	raw materials 34	
Anglonesia					
Norfolk Is.	1977	manufactures 27	food 12	vehicles 8	fuels 7

Source: *The Europa World Yearbook* (1970–96) London, Europa; *Far East and Australasia* (1997) London, Europa; *Key Indicators of Developing Asian and Pacific Countries* (1980–96) Manila, Asian Development Bank; *Statistical Yearbook for Asia and the Pacific* (1979, 1985) New York, UN; country sources.

Social indicators

Table B.13 *Main ethnic groups (% total population)*

Brunei	1995	Malay 67	Chinese 16	Indigenous 6	
Macau	1995	Chinese 95	Portuguese 3		
Russian Far East	1989	Russian 80	Ukrainian 8	Yakut 4	

Melanesia

		Indo-Fijian	Indigenous Fijian		
Fiji	1970	51	43		
	1995	44	51		
		Melanesian	European	Polynesian	Indonesian
New Caledonia	1969	42	38	10	2
	1989	45	34	12	3
		Melanesian	Polynesian	Micronesian	
Solomon Is	1970	93	4	2	
	1986	94	4	1	
		Ni-Vanuatu	European		
Vanuatu	1970	93	2		
	1996	98	1		

Micronesia

		Chamorro	Caucasian	Filipino	Asian
Guam	1970	56	28	12	1
	1990	40	14	23	6
		Micronesian			
Kiribati	1978	98			
	1990	97			
		Marshallese			
Marshall Is	1980	97			
	1988	97			
Nauru	1967	Nauruan 50	Other Pacific Is 27	Chinese 15	Caucasian 8
N. Mariana Is	1990	Filipino 33	Chamorro 29	Micronesian 14	Asian 14
Palau	1990	Palauan 83	Filipino 10	Chinese 1	

Table B.13 *Main ethnic groups (% total population) (continued)*

Polynesia

		Samoan	Caucasian	Tongan
Am. Samoa	1974	93	3	2
	1990	89	2	4
Cook Is	1982	Polynesian 89	Euro-Polynesian 8	European 2
		Polynesian	European	
Fr. Polynesia	1977	83	12	Asian 5
	1991	84	10	Chinese 4
		Niuean		
Niue	1976	93		
	1991	88		
		Tokelauan	Part-Tokelauan	
Tokelau	1986	57	40	
	1991	59	39	
		Tongan		
Tonga	1966	98		
	1986	99		
Tuvalu	1979	Tuvaluan 97	Other Pacific Is 2	
		Wallisian	Futunan	European
Wallis & Futuna	1969	66	30	2
	1990	64	32	2
W. Samoa	1966	Samoan 90	Euronesian 10	

Anglonesia

		Pitcairner		
Pitcairn Is.	1976	89		
	1992	83		

Source: *Far East and Australasia* (1997) London, Europa; *Statesman's Yearbook* (1970–96) London, Macmillan; *The World Factbook* (1985–96) Washington DC, Central Intelligence Agency; country sources.

Table B.14 *Women's paid labour, population per physician, and government social security expenditure*

	Women's paid labour (% women aged 15–64)		Population per physician		Government social security expenditure (% total)	
Brunei	1980	51	1970	3,333		
	1995	48	1995	1,136		
Macau	1980	47	1982	820	1985	2.2
	1995	40	1995	518	1990	5.7
Russian Far East			1980	410		
			1995	490		
Melanesia						
Fiji	1970	5	1970	2,176	1970	0.1
	1995	23	1994	1,826	1995	0.2
New Caledonia	1976	24	1970	1,460	1981	7.1
	1990	38	1993	539		
Solomon Is	1970	2	1970	4,550	1973	2.8
	1995	51	1993	6,500	1988	4.9
Vanuatu	1980	51	1980	5,218	1980	0.2
	1995	55	1990	7,365		
Micronesia						
FSM	1973	27	1976	2,936	1991	1.0
	1995	33	1989	3,125	1994	1.9
Guam	1980	45	1975	1,364	1970	0.5
	1994	59	1986	823	1994	1.5
Kiribati	1990	14	1985	1,939		
Marshall Is	1970	1	1976	3,855	1990	1.9
	1995	30	1987	2,137	1993	0.2
Nauru			1971	693		
N. Mariana Is	1970	6	1976	1,259		
	1995	76				
Palau			1976	1,428		
	1990	45	1993	1,385	1993	2.1
Polynesia						
Am. Samoa	1970	37	1984	1,389		
	1995	44				
Cook Is	1981	27	1972	909		
			1991	931		
Fr. Polynesia	1980	33	1985	814	1980	7.6
	1995	37	1993	680		
Niue	1976	26	1980	1,500		
	1986	36	1993	767		
Tokelau			1979	394		
	1986	30	1986	513		
Tonga	1976	7	1970	3,955	1970	0.5
	1995	17	1992	2,195	1995	0.7
Tuvalu	1973	3	1980	1,750	1980	0.3
	1979	8	1986	2,767		
Wallis & Futuna			1981	2,750		
			1991	4,146		
W. Samoa			1970	2,960		
	1995	49	1992	4,818		

Source: *World Data* (1995) CD-ROM National Accounts and Social Indicators Stacks, Washington DC, World Bank; *The Europa World Yearbook* (1970–96) London, Europa; *Far East and Australasia* (1997) London, Europa; *Statistical Yearbook for Asia and the Pacific* (1993) New York, UN; *Asia-Pacific in Figures* (1994) New York, UN; *The World's Women* (1995) New York, UN; country sources.

Documents

compiled by Michael Dawson

Introduction

Part 3 is a collection of key documents which is intended to add to the picture of the Asia-Pacific provided by the maps and data in Parts 1 and 2. It also provides insights into the policies and practices of countries in the region. Cross-references to the maps in Part 1 and the historical background for each country in Part 2 will be provided where appropriate.

This part is divided into two main sections. The first groups together documents which reflect the contemporary state of Asia-Pacific relations and includes documents relating to the principal regional organizations in the spheres of economic development and security. Also included are documents relating to global organizations in which Asia-Pacific countries play a significant role. The second section is structured around important historical themes and relationships, especially those within and between the major players in the region over the last century. To provide a comprehensive documentary history of the Asia-Pacific over this period is beyond the scope of this book. However, it is hoped that this section will give a taste of the richness and complexity of the historical background of the region. From UN Security Council reso-

lutions and international treaties to important speeches and communiqués, the documents provide insights from a wide range of perspectives so adding to the picture of the Asia-Pacific.

Organizations, events, and processes are not necessarily marked by concise and self-explanatory documents, and a number of considerations have been taken into account when compiling this selection. Where an important intergovernmental organization is founded on, or committed to, a formal set of principles or objectives set out in a treaty or charter, then the appropriate sections of that document have been included. While the effectiveness of an organization and its motivation – or even the sincerity of its members – can be a matter of considerable debate, the very fact that public commitments are made says something about those making the commitments. In the case of transnational and informal organizations which do not have legal charters or their equivalent, documents such as public relations material have been included rather than a description by outside observers. Each document is preceded by an introductory note and followed by its source.

1 Contemporary relations

1.1 Regional collaboration

APEC: First Ministerial Meeting, 1989

Asia-Pacific Economic Co-operation (APEC) is one of the Asia-Pacific region's most prominent and important international forums (see Figure 10). The APEC initiative for closer economic co-operation was proposed by Australian Prime Minister Bob Hawke in January 1989. The first ministerial meeting was held in November of the same year. Reproduced below is the Joint Statement from that meeting, and also the Chairman's Summary Statement and a Work Programme developed at the meeting. The original members of APEC are listed in the opening paragraph of the Joint Statement. An important factor in the founding of APEC was concern over the implications for world trade at a time when there were major problems in developing a new General Agreement on Tariffs and Trade (GATT) at the Uruguay Round of negotiations (see WTO document, Section 1.3).

Ministerial Meeting, Canberra, 6–7 November 1989.

Joint Statement

Ministers from Australia, Brunei Darussalam, Canada, Indonesia, Japan, Republic of Korea [South], Malaysia, New Zealand, The Philippines, Singapore, Thailand, and the United States gathered in Canberra, Australia on 6–7 November 1989 to discuss how to advance the process of Asia Pacific Economic Co-operation. [...]

Discussions covered a variety of topics under four agenda items:

- World and Regional Economic Developments
- Global Trade Liberalization – The Role of the Asia Pacific Region
- Opportunity for Regional Co-operation in Specific Areas, and
- Future Steps for Asia Pacific Economic Co-operation

At the conclusion of this first meeting, Ministers expressed satisfaction with the discussions, which demonstrated the value of closer regional consultation and economic co-operation on matters of mutual interest.

Ministers also expressed their recognition of the important contribution ASEAN and its dialogue relationships have played in the development to date of APEC, and noted the significant role ASEAN institutional mechanisms can continue to play in supporting the present effort to broaden and strengthen regional economic co-operation.

Multilateral Trade Negotiations

The discussions on world and regional developments, and on global trade liberalization, focused particularly on the need to advance the present round of Multilateral Trade Negotiations [MTN]. Every economy represented in Canberra relies heavily on a strong and open multilateral trading system, and none believes that Asia Pacific Economic Co-operation should be directed to the formation of a trading bloc.

Ministers agreed that the further opening of the multilateral trading system was of substantial and common interest for all countries in the region, and that the Uruguay Round represents the most immediate and practical opportunity to pursue this objective on a broad basis. In particular, Ministers reaffirmed their commitment to open markets and to expand trade through the successful conclusion of the Round by December 1990.

Ministers agreed that continued close consultation within the region should be used wherever possible to promote a positive conclusion to the Round. In this respect, it was agreed that Ministers concerned with trade policy should meet in early September 1990 to discuss the emerging results and consider how to unblock any obstacles to a comprehensive and ambitious MTN result. Ministers would then meet again in Brussels in early December on the eve of the concluding session. In the meantime, senior officials should consult regularly in Geneva to exchange views on MTN progress.

Ministers expressed strong support for the timely and successful completion of the Uruguay Round. They noted that much remained to be done if the December 1990 conclusion was to be achieved. They called on all Contracting Parties to work with them more vigorously to that end.

Future Steps

Ministers agreed that it was premature at this stage to decide upon any particular structure either for a Ministerial-level forum or its necessary support mechanism, but that – while ideas were evolving – it was appropriate for further consultative meetings to take place and for work to be undertaken on matters of common interest and concern.

Accordingly, Ministers welcomed the invitation of Singapore to host a second Ministerial-level Consultative meeting in mid 1990, and they also welcomed the Republic of Korea's offer to host a third such meeting in Seoul during 1991.

Ministers asked their respective senior officials, together with representation from the ASEAN Secretariat, to meet early in 1990 to begin preparations for the next Ministerial-level consultative meeting.

They asked senior officials to undertake or set in train further work on a number of possible topics for regional economic co-operation, on the possible participation of other economies in future meetings, and on other issues related to the future of such co-operation, for consideration by Ministers at their next meeting.

Summary Statement

Attached to this joint statement is Chairman Evans's concluding summary statement which records the substance of discussions during this meeting.

Visiting participating Ministers and their Delegations expressed their deep appreciation to the Government and people of Australia for organizing the meeting and for the excellent arrangements made for it, as well as for the warm hospitality extended to them.

Chairman's Summary Statement

Introduction

1. This meeting has brought together in an unprecedented way key decisions makers from twelve dynamic economies in the Asia Pacific Region: Brunei Darussalam, Canada, Indonesia, Japan, the Republic of Korea, Malaysia, New Zealand, Philippines, Singapore, Thailand, the United States and Australia. The presence here of ministers from across this vast region, addressing constructively and with great goodwill and commitment our common economic concerns, has shown that the time is indeed right to advance the process of Asia Pacific Economic Co-operation.

2. The stimulus for this meeting was Australian Prime Minister Hawke's call, in January 1989, for more effective Asia Pacific Economic Co-operation. That proposal stemmed from a recognition that the increasingly interdependence of regional economies indicated a need for effective consultations among regional decision-makers to:

- help strengthen the multilateral trading system and enhance the prospects for success in the Uruguay round;
- provide an opportunity to assess prospects for, and obstacles to, increased trade and investment flows within the Asia Pacific region; and
- identify the range of practical common economic interests.

3. In making and following up this proposal Australia, working closely with ASEAN and other participants, sought to give a sense of direction to a range of earlier proposals for closer regional economic co-operation. The intense process of consultation which has taken place since January, and culminated in this meeting, has succeeded in those terms: for the first time we have had the opportunity to assess collectively, and in some depth, the economic prospect of the region, the factors which can

help us to maintain the impressive momentum of growth of recent years as well as the problems which, if not anticipated, could impede future development.

4. A key theme which has run through all our deliberations in the last two days is that the continuing economic success of the region, with all its implications for improved living standards for our people, depends on preserving and improving the multilateral trading system through progressive enhancement of, and adherence to, the GATT framework. By contributing to that effort through the Uruguay Round and beyond, this region can not only help assure its own economic future but improve economic prospects globally. We are all agreed that an open multilateral trading system has been, and remains, critical to rapid regional growth. None of us support the creation of trading blocs.

World and Regional Economic Developments

5. Our exchanges on world and regional economic developments have underlined the extent to which the economic prospects of regional economies are interconnected. Our discussions have highlighted the pace of structural change which has occurred in the region in recent years, and to the opportunities provided by emerging new patterns of regional and international specialization. They have also underlined the strong contribution which sound macro- and micro-economic policies and market oriented reforms have played in the region's growth, and provided a useful opportunity for us to compare experiences on these matters.

6. Participants noted the changing relative strengths and the growing interdependence of regional economies. Participants noted that the non-inflationary economic expansion of the United States, now nearly 7 years in duration, has played a key role in the economic performance of the region. They also welcomed the extent to which Japan and other Western Pacific economies are acting increasingly as engines of growth for the region as a whole. The increase in living standards in all parts of the region in recent decades was particularly welcome. It was agreed that an important aspect of Asia Pacific Economic Co-operation is to maintain conditions which will lead to accelerated development in the currently less developed parts of the region, including the Pacific Island countries, and that open access to developed country markets is essential for such development.

7. Ministers also noted some potential threats to further growth and to the further productive interdependence of Asia Pacific economies. The positive trends of recent years could be disrupted if, instead of continued willingness to undertake structural change, there were to be increased resort to protectionism and if instead of positive joint international action to further liberalize trade, there were to be increased resort to retaliatory or defensive measures.

First APEC Ministerial Meeting, Canberra, November 1989

Trade Liberalization and The Role of the Asia Pacific Region

8.   There was general recognition that the Uruguay Round represents the principal, and most immediate and practical, opportunity before us to strengthen and further liberalize the multilateral trading system. All Ministers emphasized the importance, both for the region and for the world economy, of a timely and successful outcome to the Uruguay Round. In this regard, Ministers agreed that continued close consultation, and where possible, support for each others' Uruguay Round objectives could contribute significantly to achieving such an outcome.

9.   In this respect, it was agreed that Ministers concerned with trade policy should meet in early September 1990 to discuss the emerging results and consider how to unblock any obstacles to a comprehensive and ambitious MTN result. Ministers would then meet again in Brussels in early December on the eve of the concluding session. In the meantime, senior officials should consult regularly in Geneva to exchange views on MTN progress.

10.   Ministers expressed strong support for the timely and successful completion of the GATT Round. Ministers noted that much remained to be done if the December 1990 conclusion was to be achieved. They called on all Contracting Parties to work with them more vigorously to that end.

11.   Ministers agreed that the Asia Pacific region has a long-term common interest in promoting world-wide trade liberalization. By working together, the region can inject positive views into a range of important international economic forums, including not only the GATT but the OECD, and sectoral bodies (e.g. the International Telecommunications Union). It was acknowledged that our regional economies would be better placed to show such leadership if we can continue the recent trend of reducing impediments to trade among ourselves, without discriminating against others. It was further agreed that the prospects for such further liberalization of trade in the region would need to be based on better information about emerging regional trade patterns and developments, as well as the economic impact of such developments.

Regional Co-operation in Specific Areas

12.   Rapid growth and increasingly interdependence in the Asia Pacific are giving rise to both challenges and opportunities at the sectoral level.

13.   It was agreed that it would be useful to focus further on the scope for co-operation in the area of investment, technology transfer and associated areas of human resources development. Areas which warrant consideration include:

- co-operative programmes for human resource development;
- the scope to enhance exchange of information on scientific, technological and industrial indicators, policies and developments;
- the scope to enhance the comparability of foreign direct investment statistics; and
- the scope for collaborative research and development projects.

14. In discussing the adequacy of regional infrastructure, Ministers concluded that there would be merit in seeking to develop techniques which might help countries in the region to better anticipate the kind of bottlenecks which might occur as a result of rapid growth. There was general support for work to explore further co-operation in specific areas relating to infrastructure, including telecommunications, maritime transport and aviation.

15. Ministers also noted the need to identify more clearly the scope to extend co-operation in other areas, including energy, resources, fisheries, the environment, trade promotion and tourism and it was agreed that officials should carry forward preliminary work in other areas for consideration at future meetings.

General Principles of Asia Pacific Economic Co-operation

16. The discussion of all these areas has served to underline the broad areas of economic interest participants have in common. In particular, a consensus emerged in the following principles of Asia Pacific Economic Co-operation:

- the objective of enhanced Asia Pacific Economic Co-operation is to sustain the growth and development of the region, and in this way, to contribute to the growth and development of the world economy;
- co-operation should recognize the diversity of the region, including differing social and economic systems and current levels of development;
- co-operation should involve a commitment to open dialogue and consensus, with equal respect for the views of all participants;
- co-operation should be based on non-formal consultative exchanges of views among Asia Pacific economies;
- co-operation should focus on those economic areas where there is scope to advance common interests and achieve mutual benefits;
- consistent with the interests of Asia Pacific economies, co-operation should be directed at strengthening the open multilateral trading system; it should not involve the formation of a trading bloc;
- co-operation should aim to strengthen the gains from interdependence, both for the region and the world economy, including by encouraging the flow of goods, services, capital and technology;

- co-operation should complement and draw upon, rather than detract from, existing organizations in the region, including formal intergovernmental bodies such as ASEAN and less formal consultative bodies like the Pacific Economic Co-operation Conference [subsequently Council] (PECC); and
- participation by Asia Pacific economies should be assessed in the light of the strength of economic linkages with the region, and may be extended in future on the basis of consensus on the part of all participants.

Carrying Forward Regional Economic Co-operation

17. Further Consultative Meetings. It is evident that there is a large range of significant issues confronting the region, and affecting each participant's fundamental economic interests. Ministers agreed that it was premature at this stage to decide upon any particular structure for a Ministerial-level forum (or its necessary support mechanism), but that while ideas were evolving it was both appropriate and valuable for further consultative meetings to take place and for work to be undertaken on matters of common interest and concern. Accordingly, Ministers welcomed the invitation of Singapore to host a second Ministerial-level Consultative meeting in mid 1990, and they also welcomed the Republic of Korea's offer to host a third such meeting during 1991. It was further agreed that it would be appropriate, in the case of any future such meetings, for at least every other such meeting to be held in an ASEAN member country.

18. Work Programme. Ministers agreed that if co-operation is to lead to increasingly tangible benefits, the process of co-operation needs to progress beyond agreements on general principles. This will involve the identification and implementation of specific projects as well as enhancing the capacity for objective professional analysis to allow a more systematic identification of our common interests. In this context, Ministers identified the following broad areas as the basis for the development of a work programme:

- Economic studies: including the review and analysis of the economic outlook for the region and its implications for policy, and the improvement of regional economic and trade data;
- Trade liberalization: with an initial focus on consultations among participants at Ministerial as well as official level to pursue a timely and comprehensive outcome for the Uruguay Round of multilateral trade negotiations;
- Investment, technology transfer and human resource development: including programmes for information exchange and training; and
- Sectoral co-operation: in fields such as tourism, energy, trade promotion, environment matters and infrastructure development.

19. Within these categories, Ministers further identified a wide range of specific activities or projects which has significant potential for enhancing the process of regional economic co-operation; these are listed in the Attachment to this Summary Statement. It was agreed that these subjects should be closely considered by senior officials, together with any other proposals that may be made by participants, with a view to setting in train a viable short- to medium-term work programme. Progress in the implementation of that work programme would be reviewed at the next Ministerial-level meeting.

20. Ministers agreed that two particular projects should proceed as soon as possible, viz.:

(a) Review of data on regional trade flows and developments (covering trade in goods and services) and on capital flows (including direct investment) in order to:
  • identify areas where there is a need to improve the comparability of regional data;
  • identify gaps in data and improve country and industry sector coverage; and
  • develop new data bases as necessary.

(b) Examination of mechanisms to facilitate the identification of trade, investment and technology transfer opportunities in regional countries, which might include:
  • the establishment of joint sectoral industry groups to identify specific projects, particularly the small and medium scale industry;
  • a data base on commercial opportunities;
  • the promotion of regional confederations of chambers of industry;
  • specific joint project investment studies; and
  • enterprise to enterprise linkages.

It was agreed that senior officials would settle the detailed arrangements for implementation of these projects at their next meeting.

21. Support Mechanism. While some Ministers expressed a preference for moving as soon as possible to servicing the future needs of the APEC process through specifically identified structural arrangements of one kind or another, it was agreed that consideration of the support mechanism would benefit from a further period of reflection and evolution of the co-operation process. Accordingly, Ministers agreed that arrangements for the next one or two Ministerial-level Meetings should be overseen by senior officials from participating economies, joined by representation from the ASEAN Secretariat.

22. It was agreed that this group of Senior Officials should convene at an early date, preferably no later than January 1990, in the first instance to advance a work programme in the way outlined above.

23. It was agreed that follow-up work should draw on existing resources for analysis in the Asia Pacific region, including the work of PECC task forces. The Chairman of the Standing Committee of PECC indicated PECC's willingness to assist in this regard.

24. Participation. Ministers have noted the importance of the People's Republic of China and the economies of Hong Kong and Taiwan to future prosperity of the Asia Pacific region. Taking into account the general principles of co-operation identified above, and recognizing that APEC is a non-formal forum for consultations among high-level representatives of significant economies in the Asia Pacific region, it has been agreed that it would be desirable to consider further the involvement of these three economies in the process of Asia Pacific Economic Co-operation.

25. It has been agreed that it would be appropriate for senior officials to undertake further consultations and consider issues related to future participation in the APEC process by these and other economies, including those of the Pacific Islands, and to report back to the next APEC Ministerial-level Meeting.

Conclusion

26. I believe we have made very worthwhile progress during our two days of discussions. We have been able to build on the efforts of those who have sought to promote Asia Pacific Economic Co-operation in the past and are able to look forward to a further positive process of evolution. Such evolution will take place on the basis of further careful consensus building, drawing constructively on existing mechanisms, such as the valuable institutions and processes of ASEAN as well as the analytical capacity of the PECC.

27. We have all been pleased with the way in which leaders from this diverse and dynamic region have been able to reach consensus on a range of important issues. There is good reason for confidence that, by sustaining the spirit of goodwill and flexibility which has been shown at this meeting, we can develop Asia Pacific Economic Co-operation to benefit not only the region, but to enhance world wide economic prospects.

Specific Elements of a Work Programme

(A) Economic Studies

• Convene regular consultations on the economic outlook for the region and factors influencing economic prospects, drawing on, for example, the work of the Pacific Economic Outlook work of the PECC.

• Review data on regional trade flows and developments (covering trade in goods and services) and on capital flows (including direct investment) in order to
  – identify areas where there is a need to improve the comparability of regional data
  – identify gaps in data and improve country and industry sector coverage
  – develop new data bases as necessary.

- Feasibility study as to what kind of analytical capacity might be desirable and affordable in order to project regional growth, investment patterns and trade flows, including for the purpose of anticipating potential infrastructure bottlenecks.

(B)   Trade

- Intensify regional consultations at appropriate levels (both Ministerial and official) to pursue a timely and comprehensive outcome to the Uruguay Round negotiations.

- This would be usefully complemented by a working group of regional officials to support these consultations and other trade matters of regional interest.

- Review the differences in regional customs, practices and procedures and the possibilities for harmonization, including the liberalization of business visa requirements.

- Form a regional association of trade promotion organizations to promote intra regional trade.

- Explore the scope for developing greater intra-industry trade including the establishment of a regional programme of sub-contracting and multi-sourcing for finished products and industrial intermediates.

(C)   Investment, Technology Transfer and Related Aspects of Human Resources Development

- Examine mechanisms to facilitate the identification of trade, investment and technology transfer opportunities in regional countries, which might include
  - the establishment of joint sectoral industry groups to identify specific projects; particularly the small and medium scale industry;
  - a data base on commercial opportunities;
  - the promotion of regional confederations of chambers of industry;
  - specific joint project investment studies; and
  - enterprise to enterprise linkages.

- Co-ordinate regional trade promotion events and regional business seminars including consideration of an Asia Pacific Fair to promote regional trade, investment flows, technology transfer and human resources development.

- Examine the feasibility of establishing a 'clearing house' mechanism (e.g. an Asia Pacific Information Centre for Science and Technology) for the exchange of information on scientific, technological and industrial indicators, policies and developments, including the implications for new skills in the region.

- Establish a comprehensive programme for Human Resources development including the identification of critical skills and gaps in know-how; and the establishment of a data base on education and human resources planning and an informal information exchange network to share the expertise of regional countries.
  - Consider programmes to establish networks among educational and related institutions, the exchange of managers, scientific and technical personnel throughout the region and the establishment of regional training programmes including fellowships and scholarships.
  - Particular attention might be given to the needs of small and medium scale enterprises.

- Consider the concept of industrial/technology parks (centres of technical excellence), their possible contribution to infrastructural development in the Asia Pacific region and associated training programmes.

- Undertake a survey of research and development activities and policies of each country in the region and assess the potential for regional R & D co-operation.

- Areas for co-operative R & D might include micro electronics, information technology, genetic engineering, biotechnology, resources, biosphere, ecology and the environment.

(D)   Sectoral Co-operation

- Formation of groups of experts in each of the major infrastructure sectors (electric power, tele-communications) to assess national needs in the region, including technical studies of existing facilities and their development needs, the nature and extent of current bilateral assistance programmes, the adequacy of bilateral and multilateral financing facilities to support infrastructure development and the scope for harmonizing telecommunications standards in the region.

- Consider co-operative efforts in regional transportation links, including consultations and improved data collection, designed to provide cost effective capacity to meet anticipated growth in demand.

- Examine how to manage fisheries resources in the region in a way which maintains their long term economic viability and ensures a proper economic return to the owners of the resource.
  - recognizing the scope for using existing organizations, such as the South Pacific Commission or the Forum

- Fisheries Agency, to build a framework for enhanced fisheries co-operation.

- Consider the scope for co-operative regional efforts to improve the long term economic viability of tropical forests, including research, and improved harvesting and management techniques.

- Examine the scope to improve regional exchanges in relation to the basic energy resource supply and demand outlook, and energy policies and priorities, including the environmental implications of growing energy use.

- Examine regional tourism trends and prospects, including the potential for co-operative measures to facilitate regional tourism.

- Improved remote sensing on a global scale, inter alia to provide early warnings of natural disasters and improved climatic change studies.

- Examine the interaction between environmental considerations and economic decision-making, initially in the area of ocean pollutants and other threats to the Pacific environment with a view to strengthening marine resource conservation.

Source: APEC Net Site, Singapore, APEC Secretariat. Available from: http://www.apecsec.org.s

APEC: Declaration, 1996

It was agreed at the first meeting that APEC should continue to evolve, through ministerial meetings, its work programme and other forms of consultation. While this evolution has certainly taken place APEC does not involve any legally binding commitments or sanctions. However, the ministerial meeting in Manila in 1996, building on earlier meetings on Blake Island near Seattle, USA (1993), in Bogor, Indonesia (1994) and, especially, the 1995 meeting in Osaka, Japan, made the following declaration on a 'Framework for Strengthening Economic Co-operation and Development'. By the end of 1996 membership had expanded to eighteen countries which are listed in the opening paragraph.

Declaration on an APEC Framework for Strengthening Economic Co-operation and Development

Manila, November 1996.
We, the Ministers of Australia, Brunei Darussalam, Canada, Chile, the People's Republic of China, Hong Kong, Indonesia, Japan, the Republic of Korea, Malaysia, Mexico, New Zealand, Papua New Guinea, the Republic of the Philippines, Singapore, Chinese Taipei, Thailand, and the United States of America, meeting in Manila from 22–23 November 1996.

1 **Recalling** the vision articulated by the Leaders on Blake Island of an Asia Pacific community built upon the growing interdependence and co-operation in the region;

2 **Heeding** the call made by the Leaders in Bogor for APEC to lead the way in intensifying development co-operation in the region;

3 **Building** on the essential elements of economic and technical co-operation contained in the Osaka Action Agenda, as one of the three pillars on which to deepen

the spirit of community in the Asia-Pacific;

4 **Acknowledging** that economic and technical co-operation and trade and investment liberalization and facilitation are mutually complementary and supportive;

5 **Recognizing** the need for a new framework of economic co-operation and development which will provide greater focus and coherence in the growing number of regional programmes and activities in the economic and technical co-operation areas;

6 **Conscious** of APEC's achievements in the area of economic and technical co-operation since its foundation;

To this end, Ministers jointly resolve to:

Adopt the following Framework for Strengthening Economic Co-operation and Development to guide member economies in the implementation of Part II of the Osaka Action Agenda, entitled Economic and Technical Co-operation.

I   Goals

We agree that the goals of economic and technical co-operation and development in APEC are:

- to attain sustainable growth and equitable development in the Asia-Pacific region;

- to reduce economic disparities among APEC economies;

- to improve the economic and social well-being of the people; and

- to deepen the spirit of community in the Asia Pacific.

II   Guiding Principles

1.   In line with APEC's fundamental principles, we will pursue economic co-operation and development in the region on the basis of:

- **mutual respect and equality** including respect for diversity and the different situations of members, focusing on members economies' strengths;

- **mutual benefit and assistance**, with a firm commitment to making genuine contributions toward the goals of sustainable growth and equitable development and reducing disparities in the region, based on the APEC member economies' diverse and complementary capabilities;

- **constructive and genuine partnership**, creating opportunities for mutually beneficial exchange between and among industrialized and developing economies, thus promoting the development and dynamism of the economies in the region. This will include a working partnership with the private/business sector, other pertinent institutions, and the community in general, to ensure that co-operation is consistent with market principles. This partnership will engender co-operative undertakings toward the efficient allocation of resources

Leaders from the member countries of APEC at Subic Bay, Philippines, November 1996

and reduction of economic disparities within an increasingly integrated Asia Pacific Community; and

• **consensus building**, in line with the consultative, consensual approach nurtured through the development of APEC, while respecting the autonomy of each economy through their voluntary participation.

2. We emphasize the need to jointly undertake economic and technical co-operation activities that will promote the full participation of all men and women in the benefits of economic growth. In pursuing these activities, we shall be guided by our responsibility in making economic growth consistent with environmental quality.

III Character of APEC Economic and Technical Co-operation

1. To achieve our goals, we agree that economic and technical co-operation in APEC must be goal-oriented with explicit objectives, milestones, and performance criteria.

2. Considering the increasing role of the private/business sectors in APEC, we encourage them not only to participate but also initiate economic and technical co-operation activities in line with APEC goals. Thus, economic and technical activities can combine government actions, private sector projects and joint public–private activities with the

public sector playing a direct or indirect role in creating an enabling environment for private sector initiative.

3. To help build a growing sense of community and promote a spirit of enterprise that leads our people to work with and learn from each other in a co-operative spirit, economic and technical co-operation activities should draw on voluntary contributions commensurate with member economies' capabilities and generate direct and broadly shared benefits among APEC member economies to reduce economic disparities in the region.

IV Organizing Themes and Priorities

1. To achieve sustainable growth and equitable development, and benefit from the move towards free and open trade and investment, and to promote the welfare of economies of the region, we give priority to joint co-operative activities which:

• **Develop Human Capital**, the region's main asset in economic development, to broaden the benefits of economic growth, deepen the basis for sustainable growth, and strengthen social cohesion domestically and regionally;

• **Develop Stable, Safe and Efficient Capital Markets** to promote capital flows that generate real economic returns, to mobilize domestic savings through broad, deep capital and financial markets, as discussed by the Finance Ministers Meeting and to enhance the environment for private investment in infrastructure;

- **Strengthen Economic Infrastructure** to eliminate bottlenecks to economic growth, especially in such areas as telecommunications, transportation, and energy in order to further integrate members into the regional economy, and the region into the global economy;

- **Harness Technologies for the Future** to ensure that APEC joint activities promote the flow and expand the capacities of its members to absorb existing industrial science and technology as well as develop new technologies for the future, thus promoting a free flow of information and technology;

- **Safeguard the Quality of Life Through Environmentally Sound Growth** by promoting sound policies and practices, taking into account concerns about sustainable development.

- **Develop and Strengthen the Dynamism of Small and Medium Enterprises** so that they may respond more efficiently and effectively to market developments in a more open and liberal economic development.

2.   We will support new themes that may emerge in the co-operation process that are consistent with the goals and guiding principles defined in this framework.

3.   In consonance with the goals, principles, and themes laid out in this Declaration, we hereby urge Working Groups and other relevant APEC fora to co-ordinate with each other and integrate their work on cross-cutting issues to achieve focused outcomes and demonstrate breakthroughs in advancing the goals of APEC in the light of Part II of the Osaka Action Agenda and the themes mentioned in paragraph 1 of this section.

4.   We are confident that, by giving further coherence and direction to our economic and technical co-operation, we will contribute substantially to the goal of a prosperous Asia Pacific community as we move towards the twenty-first century.

Source: APEC Net Site, Singapore, APEC Secretariat.
Available from: http://www.apecsec.org.s

The ASEAN Declaration (Bangkok Declaration), 1967

The Association of South-East Asian Nations (ASEAN) is an important and well-established international organization formed in 1967 (see Figure 10). The Bangkok Declaration, which established ASEAN, is reproduced below. The original five members (Brunei joined in 1984) have co-operated together in the face of changing external circumstances and perceived threats. They have sought to avoid conflict between

each other and promote a consensual approach to a range of issues. Important factors in the early development of ASEAN were the war in Vietnam and the eventual fall of South Vietnam, Laos and Cambodia to communist regimes. However, the post-Cold War era has seen Vietnam, Laos and Cambodia drawn into ASEAN. Vietnam joined in 1995 with Laos, Cambodia and Burma/Myanmar being admitted in 1997. The full members of ASEAN are augmented by Dialogue Partners, including China, the USA, Russia and Australia, and Observers (see also ASEAN Regional Forum document, Section 1.2).

Thailand, 8 August 1967.

The Presidium Minister for Political Affairs/Minister for Foreign Affairs of Indonesia, the Deputy Prime Minister of Malaysia, the Secretary of Foreign Affairs of the Philippines, the Minister for Foreign Affairs of Singapore and the Minister of Foreign Affairs of Thailand:

MINDFUL of the existence of mutual interests and common problems among countries of South-East Asia and convinced of the need to strengthen further the existing bonds of regional solidarity and co-operation;

DESIRING to establish a firm foundation for common action to promote regional co-operation in South-East Asia in the spirit of equality and partnership and thereby contribute towards peace, progress and prosperity in the region;

CONSCIOUS that in an increasingly interdependent world, the cherished ideals of peace, freedom, social justice and economic well-being are best attained by fostering good understanding, good neighbourliness and meaningful co-operation among the countries of the region already bound together by ties of history and culture;

CONSIDERING that the countries of South-East Asia share a primary responsibility for strengthening the economic and social stability of the region and ensuring their peaceful and progressive national development, and that they are determined to ensure their stability and security from external interference in any form or manifestation in order to preserve their national identities in accordance with the ideals and aspirations of their peoples;

AFFIRMING that all foreign bases are temporary and remain only with the expressed concurrence of the countries concerned and are not intended to be used directly or indirectly to subvert the national independence and freedom of States in the area or prejudice the orderly processes of their national development;

DO HEREBY DECLARE:

FIRST, the establishment of an Association for Regional Co-operation among the countries of South-East Asia to be known as the Association of South-East Asian Nations (ASEAN).

SECOND, that the aims and purposes of the Association shall be:

1   To accelerate the economic growth, social progress and

cultural development in the region through joint endeavours in the spirit of equality and partnership in order to strengthen the foundation for a prosperous and peaceful community of South-East Asian Nations;

2   To promote regional peace and stability through abiding respect for justice and the rule of law in the relationship among countries of the region and adherence to the principles of the United Nations Charter;

3   To promote active collaboration and mutual assistance on matters of economic, social, cultural, technical, scientific and administrative fields;

4   To provide assistance to each other in the form of training and research facilities in the educational, professional, technical and administrative spheres;

5   To collaborate more effectively for the greater utilization of their agriculture and industries, the expansion of their trade, including the study of the problems of international commodity trade, the improvement of their transportation and communications facilities and the raising of the living standards of their peoples;

6   To promote South-East Asian studies;

7   To maintain close and beneficial co-operation with existing international and regional organizations with similar aims and purposes, and explore all avenues for even closer co-operation among themselves.

THIRD, that to carry out these aims and purposes, the following machinery shall be established:

(a) Annual Meeting of Foreign Ministers, which shall be by rotation and referred to as ASEAN Ministerial Meeting. Special Meetings of Foreign Ministers may be convened as required.

(b) A Standing committee, under the chairmanship of the Foreign Minister of the host country or his representative and having as its members the accredited Ambassadors of the other member countries, to carry on the work of the Association in between Meetings of Foreign Ministers.

(c) Ad hoc Committees and Permanent Committees of specialists and officials on specific subjects.

(d) A National Secretariat in each member country to carry out the work of the Association on behalf of that country and to service the Annual or Special Meetings of Foreign Ministers, the Standing Committee and such other committees as may hereafter be established.

FOURTH, that the Association is open for participation to all States in the South-East Asian Region subscribing to the aforementioned aims, principles and purposes.

FIFTH, that the Association represents the collective will of the nations of South-East Asia to bind themselves together in friendship and co-operation and, through joint efforts and sacrifices, secure for their peoples and for posterity the blessings of peace, freedom and prosperity.

DONE in Bangkok on the Eighth Day of August in the Year One Thousand Nine Hundred and Sixty-Seven.

Source: ASEANWEB, Jakarta, ASEAN Secretariat. Available from: http://www.asean.or.id

ASEAN Free Trade Area, 1992

In 1992 the full members of ASEAN agreed to a scheme for preferential tariffs with the object of creating a free trade area. The Agreement, which is reproduced below, follows on from ASEAN's well-established style of consensus and dialogue with considerable discretion and flexibility on implementation being left to individual members.

Agreement on the Common Effective Preferential Tariff (CEPT) Scheme for the ASEAN Free Trade Area (AFTA)

The Governments of Brunei Darussalam, the Republic of Indonesia, Malaysia, the Republic of the Philippines, the Republic of Singapore and the Kingdom of Thailand, Member States of the Association of South-East Asian Nations (ASEAN):

MINDFUL of the Declaration of ASEAN Concord signed in Bali, Indonesia on 24 February 1976 which provides that Member States shall co-operate in the field of trade in order to promote development and growth of new production and trade;

RECALLING that the ASEAN Heads of Government, at their Third Summit Meeting held in Manila on 13–15 December 1987, declared that Member States shall strengthen intra-ASEAN economic co-operation to maximize the realization of the region's potential in trade and development;

NOTING that the Agreement on ASEAN Preferential Trading Arrangements (PTA) signed in Manila on 24 February 1977 provides for the adoption of various instruments on trade liberalization on a preferential basis;

ADHERING to the principles, concepts and ideals of the Framework Agreement on Enhancing ASEAN Economic Co-operation signed in Singapore on 28 January 1992;

CONVINCED that preferential trading arrangements among ASEAN Member States will act as a stimulus to the strengthening of national and ASEAN Economic resilience, and the development of the national economies of Member States by expanding investment and production opportunities, trade, and foreign exchange earnings;

DETERMINED to further co-operate in the economic growth of the region by accelerating the liberalization of intra-ASEAN trade and investment with the objective of creating the ASEAN Free Trade Area using the Common Effective Preferential Tariff (CEPT) Scheme;

DESIRING to effect improvements on the ASEAN PTA in consonance with ASEAN's international commitments;

Article 1: Definitions

For the purposes of this Agreement:

1. *'CEPT'* means the Common Effective Preferential Tariff, and it is an agreed effective tariff, preferential to ASEAN, to be applied to goods originating from ASEAN Member States, and which have been identified for inclusion in the CEPT Scheme in accordance with Articles 2 (5) and 3.

2. *'Non-Tariff Barriers'* mean measures other than tariffs which effectively prohibit or restrict import or export of products within Member States.

3. *'Quantitative restrictions'* mean prohibitions or restrictions on trade with other Member States, whether made effective through quotas, licenses or other measures with equivalent effect, including administrative measures and requirements which restrict trade.

4. *'Foreign exchange restrictions'* mean measures taken by Member States in the form of restrictions and other administrative procedures in foreign exchange which have the effect of restricting trade.

5. *'PTA'* means ASEAN Preferential Trading Arrangements stipulated in the Agreement on ASEAN Preferential Trading Arrangements, signed in Manila on 24 February 1977, and in the Protocol on Improvements on Extension of Tariff Preferences under the ASEAN Preferential Trading Arrangements (PTA), signed in manila on 15 December 1987.

6. *'Exclusion List'* means a list containing products that are excluded from the extension of tariff preferences under the CEPT Scheme.

7. *'Agricultural products'* mean:

- (a) agricultural raw materials/unprocessed products covered under Chapters 1–24 of the Harmonized System (HS), and similar agricultural raw materials/unprocessed products in other related HS Headings; and

- (b) products which have undergone simple processing with minimal change in form from the original products.

Article 2: General Provisions

1. All member States shall participate in the CEPT Scheme.

2. Identification of products to be included in the CEPT Scheme shall be on a sectoral basis, i.e. at HS 6-digit level.

3. Exclusions at the HS 8/9 digit level for specific products are permitted for those Member States, which are temporarily not ready to include such products in the CEPT Scheme. For specific products, which are sensitive to a Member State, pursuant to Article 1 (3) of the Framework Agreement on Enhancing ASEAN Economic Co-operation, a Member State may exclude products from the CEPT Scheme, subject to a waiver of any concession herein

provided for such products. A review of this Agreement shall be carried out in the eighth year to decide on the final Exclusion List or any amendment to this Agreement.

4. A product shall be deemed to be originating from ASEAN Member States, if at least 40% of its content originates from any Member State.

5. All manufactured products, including capital goods, processed agricultural products and those products falling outside the definition of agricultural products, as set out in this Agreement, shall be in the CEPT Scheme. These products shall automatically be subject to the schedule of tariff reduction, as set out in Article 4 of this Agreement. In respect of PTA items, the schedule of tariff reduction provided for in Article 4 of this Agreement shall be applied, taking into account the tariff rate after the application of the existing margin of preference (MOP) as at 31 December 1992.

6. All products under the PTA which are not transferred to the CEPT Scheme shall continue to enjoy the MOP existing as at 31 December 1992.

7. Member States, whose tariffs for the agreed products are reduced from 20% and below to 0%–5%, even though granted on an MFN basis, shall still enjoy concessions. Member States with tariff rates at MFN rates of 0%–5% shall be deemed to have satisfied the obligations under this Agreement and shall also enjoy the concessions.

Article 3: Product Coverage

This Agreement shall apply to all manufactured products – including capital goods, processed agricultural products, and those products falling outside the definition of agricultural products as set out in this Agreement. Agricultural products shall be excluded from the CEPT Scheme.

Article 4: Schedule of Tariff Reduction

1. Member States agree to the following schedule of effective preferential tariff reductions:

- (a) The reduction from existing tariff rates to 20% shall be done within a time frame of 5 years to 8 years, from 1 January 1993, subject to a programme of reduction to be decided by each Member State, which shall be announced at the start of the programme. Member States are encouraged to adopt an annual rate of reduction, which shall be $(X - 20)\%/5$ or 8, where X equals the existing tariff rates of individual Member States.

- (b) The subsequent reduction of tariff rates from 20% or below shall be done within a time frame of 7 years. The rate of reduction shall be at a minimum of 5% quantum per reduction. A programme of reduction to be decided by each Member State shall be announced at the start of the programme.

- (c) For products with existing tariff rates of 20% or below as at 1 January 1993, Member States shall decide upon a programme of tariff reductions, and announce at the start, the schedule of tariff reductions. Two or more Member States may enter into arrangements for tariff reduction to 0%–5% on specific products at an accelerated pace to be announced at the start of the programme.

2. Subject to Articles 4 (1) (b) and 4 (1) (c) of this Agreement, products which reach, or are at tariff rates of 20% or below, shall automatically enjoy the concessions.

3. The above schedules of tariff reduction shall not prevent Member States from immediately reducing their tariffs to 0%–5% or following an accelerated schedule of tariff reduction.

Article 5: Other Provisions

A. Quantitative Restrictions and Non-Tariff Barriers

1. Member States shall eliminate all quantitative restrictions in respect of products under the CEPT Scheme upon enjoyment of the concessions applicable to those products.

2. Member States shall eliminate other non-tariff barriers on a gradual basis within a period of five years after the enjoyment of concessions applicable to those products.

B. Foreign Exchange Restrictions

Member States shall make exceptions to their foreign exchange restrictions relating to payments for the products under the CEPT Scheme, as well as repatriation of such payments without prejudice to their rights under Article XVIII of the General Agreement on Tariffs and Trade (GATT) and relevant provisions of the Articles of Agreement of the International Monetary Fund (IMF).

C. Other Areas of Co-operation

Member States shall explore further measures on border and non-border areas of co-operation to supplement and complement the liberalization of trade. These may include, among others, the harmonization of standards, reciprocal recognition of tests and certification of products, removal of barriers to foreign investments, macroeconomic consultations, rules for fair competition, and promotion of venture capital.

D. Maintenance of Concessions

Member States shall not nullify or impair any of the concessions as agreed upon through the application of methods of customs valuation, any new charges or measures restricting trade, except in cases provided for in this Agreement.

Article 6: Emergency Measures

1. If, as a result of the implementation of this Agreement, import of a particular product eligible under the CEPT Scheme is increasing in such a manner as to cause or threaten to cause serious injury to sectors producing like or directly competitive products in the importing Member States, the importing Member States may, to the extent and for such time as may be necessary to prevent or to remedy such injury, suspend preferences provisionally and without discrimination, subject to Article 6 (3) of this Agreement. Such suspension of preferences shall be consistent with the GATT.

2. Without prejudice to existing international obligations, a Member State, which finds it necessary to create or intensify quantitative restrictions or other measures limiting imports with a view to forestalling the threat of or stopping a serious decline of its monetary reserves, shall endeavour to do so in a manner, which safeguards the value of the concessions agreed upon.

3. Where emergency measures are taken pursuant to this Article, immediate notice of such action shall be given to the Council referred to in Article 7 of this Agreement, and such action may be the subject of consultation as provided for in Article 8 of this Agreement.

Article 7: Institutional Arrangements

1. The ASEAN Economic Ministers (AEM) shall, for the purposes of this Agreement, establish a ministerial-level Council comprising one nominee from each Member State and the Secretary-General of the ASEAN Secretariat. The ASEAN Secretariat shall provide the support to the ministerial-level Council for supervising, co-ordinating and reviewing the implementation of this Agreement, and assisting the AEM in all matters relating thereto. In the performance of its functions, the ministerial-level Council shall also be supported by the Senior Economic Officials' Meeting (SEOM).

2. Member States which enter into bilateral arrangements on tariff reductions pursuant to Article 4 of this Agreement shall notify all other Member States and the ASEAN Secretariat of such arrangements.

3. The ASEAN Secretariat shall monitor and report to the SEOM on the implementation of the Agreement pursuant to the Article III (2) (8) of the Agreement on the Establishment of the ASEAN Secretariat. Member States shall co-operate with the ASEAN Secretariat in the performance of its duties.

Article 8: Consultations

1. Member States shall accord adequate opportunity for consultations regarding any representations made by other Member States with respect to any matter affecting the implementation of this Agreement. The Council referred

to in Article 7 of this Agreement, may seek guidance from the AEM in respect of any matter for which it has not been possible to find a satisfactory solution during previous consultations.

2. Member States, which consider that any other Member State has not carried out its obligations under this Agreement, resulting in the nullifications or impairment of any benefit accruing to them, may, with a view to achieving satisfactory adjustment of the matter, make representations or proposal to the other Member States concerned, which shall give due consideration to the representations or proposal made to it.

3. Any differences between the Member States concerning the interpretation or application of this Agreement shall, as far as possible, be settled amicably between the parties. If such differences cannot be settled amicably, it shall be submitted to the Council referred to in Article 7 of this Agreement, and if necessary, to the AEM.

Article 9: General Exceptions

Nothing in this Agreement shall prevent any Member State from taking action and adopting measures, which it considers necessary for the protection of its national security, the protection of public morals, the protection of human, animal or plant life and health, and the protection of articles of artistic, historic and archaeological value.

Article 10: Final Provisions

1. The respective Governments of Member States shall undertake the appropriate measures to fulfil the agreed obligations arising from this Agreement.

2. Any amendment to this Agreement shall be made by consensus and shall become effective upon acceptance by all Member States.

3. This Agreement shall be effective upon signing.

4. This Agreement shall be deposited with the Secretary-General of the ASEAN Secretariat, who shall likewise promptly furnish a certified copy thereof to each Member State.

5. No reservation shall be made with respect to any of the provisions of this Agreement. In witness Whereof, the undersigned, being duly authorized thereto by their respective Governments, have signed this Agreement on Common Effective Preferential Tariff (CEPT) Scheme for the Free Trade Area (AFTA).

Done at Singapore, this 28th day of January, 1992 in a single copy in the English Language.

Source: ASEANWEB, Jakarta, ASEAN Secretariat. Available from: http://www.asean.or.id

NAFTA, 1994

A very different approach from that of ASEAN's to establishing a free trade area is embodied in the North American Free Trade Agreement between the USA, Canada, and Mexico. NAFTA is a formal agreement with legally binding obligations on the member governments and firmly set in the context of their existing commitments. The Agreement is lengthy, detailed and rather legalistic, only the opening articles are included below.

Preamble

The Government of Canada, the Government of the United Mexican States and the Government of the United States of America, resolved to:

STRENGTHEN the special bonds of friendship and co-operation among their nations;

CONTRIBUTE to the harmonious development and expansion of world trade and provide a catalyst to broader international co-operation;

CREATE an expanded and secure market for the goods and services produced in their territories;

REDUCE distortions to trade;

ESTABLISH clear and mutually advantageous rules governing their trade;

ENSURE a predictable commercial framework for business planning and investment;

BUILD on their respective rights and obligations under the General Agreement on Tariffs and Trade and other multilateral and bilateral instruments of co-operation;

ENHANCE the competitiveness of their firms in global markets;

FOSTER creativity and innovation, and promote trade in goods and services that are the subject of intellectual property rights;

CREATE new employment opportunities and improve working conditions and living standards in their respective territories;

UNDERTAKE each of the preceding in a manner consistent with environmental protection and conservation;

PRESERVE their flexibility to safeguard the public welfare;

PROMOTE sustainable development;

STRENGTHEN the development and enforcement of environmental laws and regulations; and

PROTECT, enhance and enforce basic workers' rights;

US President Bill Clinton at the NAFTA signing ceremony in December 1993, it came into effect the following month

HAVE AGREED as follows:

Part One – General Part

Chapter One – Objectives

Article 101: Establishment of the Free Trade Area

The Parties to this Agreement, consistent with Article XXIV of the General Agreement on Tariffs and Trade, hereby establish a free trade area.

Article 102: Objectives

1.   The objectives of this Agreement, as elaborated more specifically through its principles and rules, including national treatment, most-favored-nation treatment and transparency are to:

(a) eliminate barriers to trade in, and facilitate the cross border movement of, goods and services between the territories of the Parties;

(b) promote conditions of fair competition in the free trade area;

(c) increase substantially investment opportunities in their territories;

(d) provide adequate and effective protection and enforcement of intellectual property rights in each Party's territory;

(e) create effective procedures for the implementation and application of this Agreement, and for its joint administration and the resolution of disputes; and

(f) establish a framework for further trilateral, regional and multilateral co-operation to expand and enhance the benefits of this Agreement.

2.   The Parties shall interpret and apply the provisions of this Agreement in the light of its objectives set out in paragraph 1 and in accordance with applicable rules of international law.

Article 103: Relation to Other Agreements

1.   The Parties affirm their existing rights and obligations with respect to each other under the General Agreement on Tariffs and Trade and other agreements to which such Parties are party.

2.   In the event of any inconsistency between the provisions of this Agreement and such other agreements, the provisions of this Agreement shall prevail to the extent of the inconsistency, except as otherwise provided in this Agreement.

Article 104: Relation to Environmental and Conservation Agreements

1. In the event of any inconsistency between this Agreement and the specific trade obligations set out in:

(a) Convention on the International Trade in Endangered Species of Wild Fauna and Flora, done at Washington, March 3, 1973;

(b) the Montreal Protocol on Substances that Deplete the Ozone Layer, done at Montreal, September 16, 1987, as amended June 29, 1990;

(c) Basel Convention on the Control of Transboundary Movements of Hazardous Wastes and Their Disposal, done at Basel, March 22, 1989, upon its entry into force for Canada, Mexico and the United States; or

(d) the agreements set out in Annex 104.1, such obligations shall prevail to the extent of the inconsistency, provided that where a Party has a choice among equally effective and reasonably available means of complying with such obligations, the Party chooses the alternative that is the least inconsistent with the other provisions of this Agreement.

2. The Parties may agree in writing to modify Annex 104.1 to include any amendment to the agreements listed in paragraph 1, and any other environmental or conservation agreement.

Article 105: Extent of Obligations

The Parties shall ensure that all necessary measures are taken in order to give effect to the provisions of this Agreement, including their observance, except as otherwise provided in this Agreement, by state and provincial governments.

[...]

Annex 104

Bilateral and Other Environmental and Conservation Agreements

1. The Agreement Between the Government of Canada and the Government of the United States of America Concerning the Transboundary Movement of Hazardous Waste, signed at Ottawa, October 28, 1986.

2. The Agreement between the United States of America and the United Mexican States on Co-operation for the Protection and Improvement of the Environment in the Border Area, signed at La Paz, Baja California Sur, August 14, 1983.

[...]

Source: NAFTANET, Austin, Tex., NAFTAnet, Inc. Available from: http://www.nafta.net

Charter of the Organization of American States, 1948

> The Organization of American States is one of the oldest extant regional organizations in the Asia-Pacific. The OAS encompasses all the independent countries in North, Central and South America and provides a forum for a range of issues. The Charter of the OAS (the first three articles of which are reproduced below) was first signed in 1948 and has been amended a number of times since, most notably for the addition of extra purposes such as the promoting of representative democracy and the limitation of conventional weapons. The legalistic nature of the principles in Article 3 of the Charter is in contrast to the consensual approach of Asian-based organizations.

Signed in Bogota in 1948 and amended by the Protocol of Buenos Aires in 1967, by the Protocol of Cartagena de Indias in 1985, and by the Protocol of Managua in 1993. In force as of January 29, 1996.

IN THE NAME OF THEIR PEOPLES, THE STATES REPRESENTED AT THE NINTH INTERNATIONAL CONFERENCE OF AMERICAN STATES,

Convinced that the historic mission of America is to offer to man a land of liberty and a favorable environment for the development of his personality and the realization of his just aspirations;

Conscious that that mission has already inspired numerous agreements, whose essential value lies in the desire of the American peoples to live together in peace and, through their mutual understanding and respect for the sovereignty of each one, to provide for the betterment of all, in independence, in equality and under law;

Convinced that representative democracy is an indispensable condition for the stability, peace and development of the region;

Confident that the true significance of American solidarity and good neighborliness can only mean the consolidation on this continent, within the framework of democratic institutions, of a system of individual liberty and social justice based on respect for the essential rights of man;

Persuaded that their welfare and their contribution to the progress and the civilization of the world will increasingly require intensive continental co-operation;

Resolved to persevere in the noble undertaking that humanity has conferred upon the United Nations, whose principles and purposes they solemnly reaffirm;

Convinced that juridical organization is a necessary condition for security and peace founded on moral order and on justice; and In accordance with Resolution IX of the Inter-American Conference on Problems of War and Peace, held in Mexico City,

HAVE AGREED upon the following

Part One

Chapter I: Nature and Purposes

Article 1

The American States establish by this Charter the international organization that they have developed to achieve an order of peace and justice, to promote their solidarity, to strengthen their collaboration, and to defend their sovereignty, their territorial integrity, and their independence. Within the United Nations, the Organization of American States is a regional agency.

The Organization of American States has no powers other than those expressly conferred upon it by this Charter, none of whose provisions authorizes it to intervene in matters that are within the internal jurisdiction of the Member States.

Article 2

The Organization of American States, in order to put into practice the principles on which it is founded and to fulfil its regional obligations under the Charter of the United Nations, proclaims the following essential purposes:

a. To strengthen the peace and security of the continent;

b. To promote and consolidate representative democracy, with due respect for the principle of non-intervention;

c. To prevent possible causes of difficulties and to ensure the pacific settlement of disputes that may arise among the Member States;

d. To provide for common action on the part of those States in the event of aggression;

e. To seek the solution of political, juridical, and economic problems that may arise among them;

f. To promote, by co-operative action, their economic, social, and cultural development; and

g. To achieve an effective limitation of conventional weapons that will make it possible to devote the largest amount of resources to the economic and social development of the Member States.

Chapter II: Principles

Article 3

The American States reaffirm the following principles:

a. International law is the standard of conduct of States in their reciprocal relations;

b. International order consists essentially of respect for the personality, sovereignty, and independence of States, and the faithful fulfilment of obligations derived from treaties and other sources of international law;

c. Good faith shall govern the relations between States;

d. The solidarity of the American States and the high aims which are sought through it require the political

organization of those States on the basis of the effective exercise of representative democracy;

e. Every State has the right to choose, without external interference, its political, economic, and social system and to organize itself in the way best suited to it, and has the duty to abstain from intervening in the affairs of another State. Subject to the foregoing, the American States shall co-operate fully among themselves, independently of the nature of their political, economic, and social systems;

f. The American States condemn war of aggression: victory does not give rights;

g. An act of aggression against one American State is an act of aggression against all the other American States;

h. Controversies of an international character arising between two or more American States shall be settled by peaceful procedures;

i. Social justice and social security are bases of lasting peace;

j. Economic co-operation is essential to the common welfare and prosperity of the peoples of the continent;

k. The American States proclaim the fundamental rights of the individual without distinction as to race, nationality, creed, or sex;

l. The spiritual unity of the continent is based on respect for the cultural values of the American countries and requires their close co-operation for the high purposes of civilization;

m. The education of peoples should be directed toward justice, freedom, and peace.

[...]

Source: OAS/Public Information Net Site, Washington DC. Available from: http://www.oas.org

PECC, 1980

> The Pacific Economic Co-operation Council, formed in 1980, is an informal transnational grouping of academics, business representatives and political figures. As the organization stresses its informality and flexibility, the document selected is rather different from others in this section. There is no formal charter or agreement and the document below is taken from the PECC internet web site. It is, therefore, PECC's public face, and includes a brief introduction and background to the organization. Note the relationship with APEC.

Introduction

The Pacific Economic Co-operation Council (PECC) is a tripartite, non-governmental organization committed to promoting economic co-operation in the Pacific Rim. It comprises representatives from 22 Asia-Pacific economies who meet regularly to work on practical government and business policy issues to increase trade, investment and economic development in the region.

It is the only organization in the region that brings business, government and researchers together on an equal footing to address key trade and investment issues. Though it has an independent agenda, PECC maintains direct links to governments in the region to enable its work to be channelled to Ministers and policy makers.

PECC anticipates emerging economic opportunities and problems for business and governments. In addition it establishes task groups to address issues in individual sectors on a regional level as well as the level of individual member economies. It has become a clearing house for policy and business research, serving as a catalyst for new initiatives in policy change.

Background: The Creation of an Independent Regional Institution

PECC was formed in 1980 at the initiative of the Prime Ministers of Japan and Australia. They called for the establishment of an independent, regional mechanism to advance economic co-operation and market-drive integration. A vital characteristic of the new body, they asserted, should be its independent, unofficial status which would permit it to address economic issues and measures free of the constraints of formal governmental policies and relationships. Hence, the need for an informal process involving business and independent research institutions alongside governments.

This remains PECC's strength and the basis for its continued regional role alongside the formal body of APEC which emerged in 1989. Drawing upon a broader-based constituency than APEC throughout the Asia-Pacific area, PECC reflects the region's great diversity in resource wealth, finance and capital, technology and labour. Recognizing that governments alone will not be able to bridge the great differences in culture, language, political processes and historical backgrounds within the region, PECC provides a flexible, informal, tripartite network in which business leaders, researchers, and officials can interact.

From the time of its creation, PECC advocated the need for a formal, inter-governmental organization in the Pacific. The regional Ministerial process of APEC has realized that goal and now provides PECC with a formal channel by which its practical recommendations can be implemented.

Structure
Standing Committee

The Standing Committee is PECC's governing body, which meets several times a year. It includes the Chairs of PECC Committees of the 22 member economies. The Pacific Basin Economic Court (PBEC), the regional business organization, and the Pacific Trade Development Conference (PAFTAD), the region-wide organization of academic economists, also have seats on the Standing Committee.

Member Committees

Each committee comprises senior business representatives, former Ministers and high level officials and some of the region's foremost academics.

> Australia, Brunei Darussalam, Canada, Chile, China, Colombia, Hong Kong, Indonesia, Japan, Korea, Malaysia, New Zealand, Pacific Island Nations, Mexico, Peru, Philippines, Russian Federation, Singapore, Chinese Taipei, Thailand, United States, Vietnam.

The Work Programme

PECC holds major working meetings each year when leaders of business, government and research and invited Ministers join to give their assessments of regional economic issues and begin identifying future issues.

PECC's substantive works programme is carried out by a range of forums, task forces and project groups. These cover trade policy, Pacific economic outlook, financial and capital markets, human resource development, small and medium enterprises, science and technology, minerals and energy, telecommunications, transport, tourism, fisheries, food and agriculture.

Many of these groups mirror those of APEC although the issues discussed may be different. This allows for direct interaction between PECC task forces and APEC working groups.

The agendas for the PECC task forces and projects are guided by tripartite international advisory groups and they are co-ordinated by representatives from different PECC Member Committees in the region. The Co-ordinators meet regularly to advise the Standing Committee and to co-ordinate the overall efforts of PECC's work programme. PECC actively seeks participation from the World Trade Organisation, the OECD, the Asian Development Bank, the World Bank and United Nations Agencies as well as APEC officials.

Source: PECC, Singapore, Point Publishing. Available from: http://www.pecc.net

1.2   Post-Cold War security

While the organizations and relationships covered in the documents in Section 1.1 differ, the main area for collaboration is clearly trade and economic development. The documents in this section relate to another of the Asia-Pacific's major preoccupations: security. As with other parts of the world in the 1990s, the countries of the Asia-Pacific have had to re-examine their security arrangements in the absence of Cold War certainties.

ASEAN Regional Forum: First Meeting, 1994

The ASEAN Regional Forum (ARF), as its name implies, was an initiative of ASEAN with support from its Dialogue Partners including the USA. The purpose of the ARF is to provide a forum where the majority of the states in the Asia-Pacific region can discuss security issues. The participants, as indicated in the second paragraph of the Chairman's Statement issued after the first meeting of the ARF, consisted of Foreign Ministers of those countries which would normally be represented at ASEAN meetings in one capacity or another. As with ASEAN and the ASEAN Free Trade Area, the approach of the ARF is one of encouraging dialogue and co-operation. In 1997 the membership of the ARF is: Australia, Brunei, Burma/Myanmar, Cambodia, Canada, China, India, Indonesia, Japan, South Korea, Laos, Malaysia, New Zealand, Papua New Guinea, Philippines, Russia, Singapore, Thailand, USA, Vietnam, and the European Union (35 countries including fifteen from the EU).

First Meeting of the ASEAN Regional Forum, Thailand, 25 July 1994

Chairman's statement

1.   The First Meeting of the ASEAN Regional Forum (ARF) was held in Bangkok on 25 July 1994 in accordance with the 1992 Singapore Declaration of the Fourth ASEAN Summit, whereby the ASEAN Heads of State and Government proclaimed their intent to intensify ASEAN's external dialogues in political and security matters as a means of building co-operative ties with states in the Asia-Pacific region.

2.   Attending the Meeting were the Foreign Ministers of ASEAN, ASEAN's Dialogue Partners, ASEAN's Consultative Partners, and ASEAN's Observers or their representatives. The Minister of Foreign Affairs of Thailand, served as Chairman of the Meeting.

3.   Being the first time ever that high-ranking representatives from the majority of states in the Asia-Pacific region came to specifically discuss political and security co-operation issues, the Meeting was considered a historic event for the region. More importantly, the Meeting signified the opening of a new chapter of peace, stability and co-operation for Southeast Asia.

4.   The participants of the Meeting held a productive exchange of views on the current political and security situation in the Asia-Pacific region, recognizing that developments in one part of the region could have an impact on the security of the region as a whole. It was agreed that, as a high-level consultative forum, the ARF had enabled the countries in the Asia-Pacific region to foster the habit of constructive dialogue and consultation on political and security issues of common interest and concern. In this respect, the ARF would be in a position to make significant contributions to efforts towards confidence-building and preventive diplomacy in the Asia-Pacific region.

5.   Bearing in mind the importance of non-proliferation of nuclear weapons in the maintenance of international peace and security, the Meeting welcomed the continuation of US–DPRK [North Korea] negotiation and endorsed the early resumption of inter-Korean dialogue.

6.   The Meeting agreed to:

(i)   convene the ARF on an annual basis and hold the second meeting in Brunei Darussalam in 1995; and

(ii)   endorse the purposes and principles of ASEAN's Treaty of Amity and Co-operation in South-East Asia, as a code of conduct governing relations between states and a unique diplomatic instrument for regional confidence-building, preventive diplomacy, and political and security co-operation.

7.   The Meeting also agreed to entrust the next Chairman of the ARF Brunei Darussalam, working in consultation with ARF participants as appropriate, to:

(i)   collate and study all papers and ideas raised during the ARF Senior Officials Meeting [SOM] and the ARF in Bangkok for submission to the second ARF through the second ARF-SOM, both of which to be held in Brunei Darussalam. Ideas which might be the subjects of such further study including confidence and security building, nuclear non-proliferation, peacekeeping co-operation including regional peacekeeping training centre, exchanges of non classified military information, maritime security issues, and preventive diplomacy;

(ii)   study the comprehensive concept of security, including its economic and social aspects, as it pertains to the Asia-Pacific region;

(iii)study other relevant internationally recognized norms and principles pertaining to international and regional political and security co-operation for their possible contribution to regional political and security co-operation;

(iv) promote the eventual participation of all ARF countries in the UN Conventional Arms Register; and

(v) convene, if necessary, informal meetings of officials to study all relevant papers and suggestions to move the ARF process forward.

8. Recognizing the need to develop a more predictable constructive pattern of relationships for the Asia-Pacific region, the Meeting expressed its firm conviction to continue to work towards the strengths and the enhancement of political and security co-operation within the region as a means of ensuring a lasting peace, stability, and prosperity for the region and its peoples.

Source: ASEANWEB, Jakarta, ASEAN Secretariat. Available from: http://www.asean.or.id

Establishment of CSCAP, 1993

The Council for Security Co-operation in the Asia Pacific is a non-governmental organization, its purpose is to provide structures and mechanisms to encourage confidence building and security co-operation in the region. CSCAP was founded by strategic studies centres from ten different countries. These founding institutions issued the Kuala Lumpur Statement in 1993 establishing CSCAP and adopted the CSCAP Charter later the same year. The Statement and the first six articles of the Charter are reproduced below. CSCAP was originally made up of broad-based committees from the countries of the founding institutions (listed in the Statement), they have since been joined by committees from New Zealand, Russia and North Korea.

Establishment of the Council for Security Co-operation in the Asia Pacific (CSCAP), 8 June 1993

The Kuala Lumpur Statement

The ending of the Cold War and the fundamental transformation ensuing from the elimination of superpower rivalry have provoked a far-reaching re-evaluation of security arrangements in the Asia Pacific region.

Four institutions in the region, namely the ASEAN Institutes of Strategic and International Studies (ASEAN ISIS), the Japan Institute of International Affairs (JIIA), Pacific Forum/CSIS (Honolulu), and the Seoul Forum for International Affairs, together with representatives of other research institutes from the region, have undertaken an in-depth examination of the security issues and challenges facing Asia Pacific today and in the future.

A series of conferences on Security Co-operation in the Asia Pacific (SCAP) have been held: first in Honolulu (October 29–30, 1991), second in Bali (April 17–19, 1992), and third in Seoul (November 1–3, 1992). Participants from seventeen countries, including scholars as well as officials acting in their private capacities, have taken part in these meetings.

The discussions at these meetings have clearly shown the need for more structured processes for regional confidence building and security co-operation. The meetings welcomed the initiatives at the official level to develop a formal or informal inter-governmental regional forum for dialogue on political-security issues.

In particular, the meetings noted the concrete steps that have been taken by the ASEAN Post Ministerial Conference (PMC) at which the six ASEAN foreign ministers (Brunei, Indonesia, Malaysia, the Philippines, Singapore and Thailand) meet annually with foreign ministers of other Asia Pacific countries (Australia, Canada, Japan, the Republic of Korea, New Zealand and the United States) and a representative of the European Community. The participants in the SCAP process believe that the PMC makes a significant contribution to the development of a multilateral political-security dialogue for the Asia Pacific region. The participants support the multilateralization of the ASEAN PMC process and the establishment of a Senior Officials Meeting (SOM). The participants in the SCAP process believe that the ASEAN PMC process should be inclusive and welcome the early inclusion of other countries in the region.

The participants also welcomed initiatives for the establishment of other regional processes, such as the North Pacific Co-operative Security Dialogue proposal. These initiatives can only strengthen the broader regional processes.

As representatives of non-governmental institutions concerned with the security, stability and peace of the region, we also feel that we have the responsibility to contribute to the efforts towards regional confidence building and enhancing regional security through dialogues, consultations and co-operation.

It is with this objective in mind that we are establishing a Council for Security Co-operation in the Asia Pacific (CSCAP). It will be open to all countries and territories in the region. The Council's activities will be guided by a Steering Committee consisting of representatives of non-governmental institutions in the region who are committed to the ideals of regional security co-operation.

Steering Committee members will seek to establish broadbased committees in each of their respective countries or territories. These committees should include government officials in their private capacities.

We also propose that CSCAP establish Working Groups that will be given the tasks of undertaking policy-oriented studies on specific regional political-security problems.

Initially the CSCAP Steering Committee will be co-chaired by Amos Jordan (Pacific Forum/CSIS) and Jusuf Wanandi (CSIS Jakarta). The Steering Committee will be served by a Secretariat. ISIS Malaysia has accepted this responsibility for the first two years.

The founding members of CSCAP are:

Strategic and Defence Studies Centre, Australian National University, Australia;

University of Toronto–York University Joint Center for Asia Pacific Studies, Canada;

Centre for Strategic and International Studies, Indonesia;

Japan Institute of International Affairs, Japan;

The Seoul Forum for International Affairs, Republic of Korea;

Institute of Strategic and International Studies, Malaysia;

Institute for Strategic and Development Studies, Philippines;

Singapore Institute of International Affairs, Singapore;

Institute for Security and International Studies, Thailand;

Pacific Forum/CSIS, United States of America.

Kuala Lumpur, 8 June 1993.

The CSCAP Charter

Article I: The Name of the Organization

The name of the organization shall be the Council for Security Co-operation in the Asia Pacific, henceforth to be referred to as CSCAP.

Article II: The Purpose and Functions of CSCAP

1 CSCAP is organized for the purpose of providing a structured process for regional confidence building and security co-operation among countries and territories in the Asia Pacific region.

2 The functions of CSCAP are as follows:
   a. to provide an informal mechanism by which political and security issues can be discussed by scholars, officials, and others in their private capacities;
   b. to encourage the participants of such individuals from countries and territories in the Asia Pacific on the basis of the principle of inclusiveness;
   c. to organize various working groups to address security issues and challenges facing the region;
   d. to provide policy recommendations to various intergovernmental bodies on political-security issues;
   e. to convene regional and international meetings and other co-operative activities for the purpose of discussing political-security issues;
   f. to establish linkages with institutions and organizations in other parts of the world to exchange information, insights and experiences in the area of regional political-security co-operation; and
   g. to produce and disseminate publications relevant to the other purposes of the organization.

Article III: Membership

1 Membership in CSCAP is on an institutional basis and consists of Member Committees. Admission of new members into CSCAP shall require the unanimous agreement of the Steering Committee.

2 When evaluating an application for membership, consideration shall be given to whether or not the applicant:
   a. endorses the Kuala Lumpur Statement on the Establishment of the Council for Security Co-operation in the Asia Pacific (CSCAP) of June 8, 1993;
   b. has co-operated with other CSCAP members on various projects related to regional security; and
   c. has established a broad-based Member Committee, with the capacity to participate actively in CSCAP.

3 a. Applicants not fully meeting all the requirements for full membership may be accepted as Candidate Members pending fulfilment of the requirements.
   b. Candidate Members are eligible to participate in all CSCAP activities except for membership of the Steering Committee.

Article IV: Associate Membership

1 Associate membership may be granted to institutions in a country or territory not represented in the Steering Committee and which have demonstrated interest and involvement in the stated objectives and activities of CSCAP.

2 a. Associate members may participate in CSCAP Working Group activities.
   b. Associate members may participate in the CSCAP General Meeting as observers.

Article V: Member Committees

1 A Member Committee shall be formed for each country or territory represented in CSCAP.

2 The Member Committee shall be broad-based, composed of non-governmental and government affiliated institutions in political-security studies and/ or individuals (including officials) in their private capacities.

Article VI: The Steering Committee

1 The Steering Committee shall be the highest decision-making body of CSCAP.

2 The Steering Committee shall be comprised of one formally designated representative from each Member Committee.

3 a. The Steering Committee normally shall be co-chaired by a member from an ASEAN Member Committee and a member from a non-ASEAN

b. The term of the Co-Chairs shall be two years.

4   The Steering Committee may establish Sub-committees on membership, finance, and working groups, and other Sub-committees as deemed necessary.

5   The Steering Committee shall meet at least twice a year.

6   a. The quorum for the Steering Committee shall be at least three quarters (3/4) of the total members.
    b. Except for questions of membership, decisions of the Steering Committee shall be made by at least eighty per cent (80%) of the quorum.

[...]

Source: Australian CSCAP, Strategic and Defence Studies Centre Net Site, Canberra, Research School of Pacific and Asian Studies, Australian National University. Available from: http://coombs.anu.edu/Depts/RSPAS/AUSCSCAP/Auscscap.html

US–Japan Joint Declaration on Security Alliance for the Twenty-first Century, 1996

One of the Asia-Pacific's pivotal relationships, in security as well as economic fields, between Japan and the USA, has had to be re-assessed in the absence of the Cold War framework which played such an important role in its development in the post-Second World War period (see Section 2.1). The Joint Declaration issued by US President Clinton and Japan's Prime Minister Hashimoto after their Tokyo meeting in April 1996, emphasizes the continued enhancement and development of their co-operation on security matters as an important factor in maintaining peace and economic prosperity in the region. The arrangements for security remain much the same and build on agreements of the Cold War period. What has changed is the context, with a move from the perceived communist threat to a period of uncertainty.

Tokyo, Japan, 17 April 1996

1.   Today, the President and the Prime Minster celebrated one of the most successful bilateral relationships in history. The leaders took pride in the profound and positive contribution this relationship has made to world peace and regional stability and prosperity. The strong Alliance between the United States and Japan helped ensure peace and security in the Asia-Pacific region during the Cold War. Our Alliance continues to underlie the dynamic economic growth in this region. The two leaders agreed that the future security and prosperity of both the United States and Japan are tied inextricably to the future of the Asia-Pacific region.

The benefits of peace and prosperity that spring from the Alliance are due not only to the commitments of the two governments, but also to the contributions of the Japanese and American people who have shared the burden of securing freedom and democracy. The President and the Prime Minister expressed their profound gratitude to those who sustain the Alliance, especially those Japanese communities that host US Forces, and those Americans who, far from home, devote themselves to the defence of peace and freedom.

2.   For more than a year, the two governments have conducted an intensive review of the evolving political and security environment of the Asia-Pacific region and of various aspects of the US–Japan security relationship. On the basis of this review, the President and the Prime Minister have seen expanded political and security dialogue among countries of the region. Respect for democratic principles is growing. Prosperity is more widespread than at any other time in history, and we are witnessing the emergence of an Asia-Pacific community. The Asia-Pacific region has become the most dynamic area of the globe.

At the same time, instability and uncertainty persist in the region. Tensions continue on the Korean Peninsula. There are still heavy concentrations of military force, including nuclear arsenals. Unresolved territorial disputes, potential regional conflicts, and the proliferation of weapons of mass destruction and their means of delivery all constitute sources of instability. [...]

The US–Japan alliance and the treaty of mutual co-operation and security

4.   The President and the Prime Minister underscored the importance of promoting stability in this region and dealing with the security challenges facing both countries.

In this regard, the President and the Prime Minister reiterated the significant value of the Alliance between the United States and Japan. They reaffirmed that the US–Japan security relationship, based on the Treaty of Mutual Co-operation and Security [of 1960, see Section 2.1] between the United States of American and Japan, remains the cornerstone for achieving common security objectives, and for maintaining a stable and prosperous environment for the Asia-Pacific region as we enter the twenty-first century.

(a) The Prime Minister confirmed Japan's fundamental defence policy as articulated in its new National Defense Program Outline adopted in November, 1995, which underscored that the Japanese defence capabilities should play appropriate roles in the security environment after the Cold War. The President and the Prime Minister agreed that the most effective framework for the defence of Japan is close defence co-operation between the two countries. The co-operation is based on a combination of appropriate defence capabilities for the Self-Defense Forces of Japan and the US–Japan security arrangements. The leaders again confirmed that US deterrence under the Treaty of

Mutual Co-operation and Security remains the guarantee for Japan's security.

(b) The President and the Prime Minister agreed that continued US military presence is also essential for preserving peace and stability in the Asia-Pacific region. The leaders shared the common recognition that the US–Japan security relationship forms an essential pillar which supports the positive regional engagement of the US.

The President emphasized the US commitment to the defence of Japan as well as to peace and stability in the Asia-Pacific region. He noted that there has been some adjustment of US forces in the Asia-Pacific region since the end of the Cold War. On the basis of a thorough assessment, the United States reaffirmed that meeting its commitments in the prevailing security environment requires the maintenance of its current force structure of about 100,000 forward deployed military personnel in the region, including about the current level in Japan.

(c) The Prime Minister welcomed the US determination to remain a stable and steadfast presence in the region. He reconfirmed that Japan would continue appropriate contributions for the maintenance of US forces in Japan, such as through the provision of facilities and areas in accordance with the Treaty of Mutual Co-operation and Security and Host Nation Support. The President expressed US appreciation for Japan's contributions, and welcomed the conclusion of the new Special Measures Agreement which provides financial support for US forces stationed in Japan.

Bilateral co-operation under the US–Japan security relationship

5. The President and the Prime Minister, with the objective of enhancing the credibility of this vital security relationship, agreed to undertake efforts to advance co-operation in the following areas.

(a) Recognizing that close bilateral defence co-operation is a central element of the US–Japan alliance, both governments agreed that continued close consultation is essential. Both governments will further enhance the exchange of information and views on the international situation, in particular the Asia-Pacific region. At the same time, in response to the changes which may arise in the international security environment, both governments will continue to consult closely on defence policies and military postures, including the US force structure in Japan, which will best meet their requirements.

(b) The President and the Prime Minister agreed to initiate a review of the 1978 Guidelines for US–Japan Defense Co-operation to build upon the close working relationship already established between the United States and Japan.

The two leaders agreed on the necessity to promote bilateral policy co-ordination, including studies on bilateral co-operation in dealing with situations that may emerge in the areas surrounding Japan and which will have an important influence on the peace and security of Japan.

(c) The President and the Prime Minister welcomed the April 15, 1996 signature of the Agreement Between the Government of the United States of America and the Government of Japan Concerning Reciprocal Provision of Logistic Support, Supplies and Services Between the Armed Forces of the United States of America and the Self-Defense Forces of Japan, and expressed their hope that this Agreement will further promote the bilateral co-operative relationship.

(d) Noting the importance of inter-operability in all facets of co-operation between the US forces and the Self-Defense Forces of Japan, the two governments will enhance mutual exchange in the areas of technology and equipment, including bilateral co-operative research and development of equipment such as the support fighter (F-2).

(e) The two governments recognized that the proliferation of weapons of mass destruction and their means of delivery has important implications for their common security. They will work together to prevent proliferation and will continue to co-operate in the ongoing study on ballistic missile defence.

6. The President and the Prime Minister recognized that the broad support and understanding of the Japanese people are indispensable for the smooth stationing of US forces in Japan, which is the core element of the US–Japan security arrangements. The two leaders agreed that both governments will make every effort to deal with various issues related to the presence and status of US forces. They also agreed to make further efforts to enhance mutual understanding between US forces and local Japanese communities.

In particular, with respect to Okinawa, where US facilities and areas are highly concentrated, the President and the Prime Minister reconfirm their determination to carry out steps to consolidate, realign, and reduce US facilities and areas consistent with the objectives of the Treaty of Mutual Co-operation and Security. In this respect, the two leaders took satisfaction in the significant progress which has been made so far through the Special Action Committee on Okinawa (SACO) and welcomed the far reaching measures outlined in the SACO Interim Report on April 15, 1996. They expressed their firm commitment to achieve a successful conclusion of the SACO process by November 1996.

Regional co-operation

7. The President and the Prime Minister agreed that the two governments will jointly and individually strive to

achieve a more peaceful and stable security environment in the Asia-Pacific region. In this regard, the two leaders recognized that the engagement of the United States in the region, supported by the US–Japan security relationship, constitutes the foundation for such efforts.

The two leaders stressed the importance of peaceful resolution of problems in the region. They emphasized that it is extremely important for the stability and prosperity of the region that China play a positive and constructive role, and, in this context, stressed the interest of both countries in furthering co-operation with China. Russia's ongoing process of reform contributes to regional and global stability, and merits continued encouragement and co-operation. The leaders also stated that full normalization of Japan–Russia relations based on the Tokyo Declaration is important to peace and stability in the Asia-Pacific region. They noted also that stability on the Korean Peninsula is vitally important to the United States and Japan and reaffirmed that both countries will continue to make every effort in this regard, in close co-operation with the Republic of Korea.

The President and the Prime Minister reaffirmed that the two governments will continue working jointly and with other countries in the region to further develop multilateral regional security dialogues and co-operation mechanisms such as the ASEAN Regional Forum, and eventually, security dialogues regarding North-East Asia.

Global co-operation

8. The President and the Prime Minister recognized that the Treaty of Mutual Co-operation and Security is the core of the US–Japan Alliance, and underlies the mutual confidence that constitutes the foundation for bilateral co-operation on global issues.

The President and the Prime Minister agreed that the two governments will strengthen their co-operation in support of the United Nations and other international organizations through activities such as peacekeeping and humanitarian relief operations.

Both governments will co-ordinate their policies and co-operate on issues such as arms control and disarmament, including acceleration of the Comprehensive Test Ban Treaty (CTBT) negotiations and the prevention of the proliferation of weapons of mass destruction and their means of delivery.

The two leaders agreed that co-operation in the United Nations and APEC, and on issues such as the North Korean nuclear problem, the Middle East peace process, and the peace implementation process in the former Yugoslavia, helps to build the kind of world that promotes our shared interests and values.

Conclusion

9. In concluding, the President and the Prime Minister agreed that the three legs of the US-Japan relationship – security, political and economic – are based on shared values and interests and rest on the mutual confidence embodied in the Treaty of Mutual Co-operation and Security. The President and the Prime Minister reaffirmed their strong determination, on the eve of the twenty-first century, to build on the successful history of security co-operation and to work hand-in-hand to secure peace and prosperity for future generations.

Prime Minister of Japan
President of the United States.

Source: US Department of State Net Site. Available from: http://www.state.gov

1.3 International organizations

The purpose of the selection of documents in this section is to provide some insights into major world-wide organizations in which a significant number of Asia-Pacific countries participate. Section 1.3 also looks at a new development which links a number of Asian and European countries, and the work of a non-governmental organization which scrutinizes every country's human rights record.

The United Nations

Set up by the victors of the Second World War the United Nations now includes most of the major countries of the world. The purposes and principles of the UN are clearly laid out in the Preamble and Articles 1 and 2 of the Charter below. The extent to which the organization has been able to act on those principles has been constrained by the Cold War relations of its founding and most powerful members. The post-Cold War era has seen action by the UN in a number of regions with varying degrees of success (see Section 2.3, 'Cambodia and the UN'). The extract from the UN Charter is followed by a list of members from the Asia-Pacific region and their date of admission. China was a founding member in 1945, however, it was represented by the Nationalist Kuomintang government until 1971 even though that government controlled only Taiwan after 1949. Since 1971 the government of the People's Republic has represented China.

Preamble to the Charter of the United Nations

WE THE PEOPLES OF THE UNITED NATIONS DETERMINED

to save succeeding generations from the scourge of war, which twice in our lifetime has brought untold sorrow to mankind, and

to reaffirm faith in fundamental human rights, in the dignity and worth of the human person, in the equal rights of men and women and of nations large and small, and

to establish conditions under which justice and respect for the obligations arising from treaties and other sources of international law can be maintained, and

to promote social progress and better standards of life in larger freedom,

AND FOR THESE ENDS

to practice tolerance and live together in peace with one another as good neighbours, and

to unite our strength to maintain international peace and security, and

to ensure, by the acceptance of principles and the institution of methods, that armed force shall not be used, save in the common interest, and

to employ international machinery for the promotion of the economic and social advancement of all peoples,

HAVE RESOLVED TO COMBINE OUR EFFORTS TO ACCOMPLISH THESE AIMS

Accordingly, our respective Governments, through representatives assembled in the city of San Francisco, who have exhibited their full powers found to be in good and due form, have agreed to the present Charter of the United Nations and do hereby establish an international organization to be known as the United Nations.

Chapter I

Purposes and Principles

Article 1

The Purposes of the United Nations are:

1. To maintain international peace and security, and to that end: to take effective collective measures for the prevention and removal of threats to the peace, and for the suppression of acts of aggression or other breaches of the peace, and to bring about by peaceful means, and in conformity with the principles of justice and international law, adjustment or settlement of international disputes or situations which might lead to a breach of the peace;

2. To develop friendly relations among nations based on respect for the principle of equal rights and self-determination of peoples, and to take other appropriate measures to strengthen universal peace;

3. To achieve international co-operation in solving international problems of an economic, social, cultural, or humanitarian character, and in promoting and encouraging respect for human rights and for fundamental freedoms for all without distinction as to race, sex, language, or religion; and

4. To be a centre for harmonizing the actions of nations in the attainment of these common ends.

Article 2

The Organization and its Members, in pursuit of the Purposes stated in Article 1, shall act in accordance with the following Principles.

1. The Organization is based on the principle of the sovereign equality of all its Members.

2. All Members, in order to ensure to all of them the rights and benefits resulting from membership, shall fulfil

326

in good faith the obligations assumed by them in accordance with the present Charter.

3. All Members shall settle their international disputes by peaceful means in such a manner that international peace and security, and justice, are not endangered.

4. All Members shall refrain in their international relations from the threat or use of force against the territorial integrity or political independence of any state, or in any other manner inconsistent with the Purposes of the United Nations.

5. All Members shall give the United Nations every assistance in any action it takes in accordance with the present Charter, and shall refrain from giving assistance to any state against which the United Nations is taking preventive or enforcement action.

6. The Organization shall ensure that states which are not Members of the United Nations act in accordance with these Principles so far as may be necessary for the maintenance of international peace and security.

7. Nothing contained in the present Charter shall authorize the United Nations to intervene in matters which are essentially within the domestic jurisdiction of any state or shall require the Members to submit such matters to settlement under the present Charter; but this principle shall not prejudice the application of enforcement measures under Chapter VII.

[...]

[Asia-Pacific members of the UN and date of admission]

With the admission of Palau, there are now 185 Member States of the United Nations. The Member States and the dates on which they joined the Organization are listed below:

Member (Date of Admission)

Australia (1 Nov. 1945)

Brunei Darussalam (21 Sept. 1984)

Cambodia (14 Dec. 1955)

Canada (9 Nov. 1945)

Chile (24 Oct. 1945)

China (24 Oct. 1945)

Colombia (5 Nov. 1945)

Costa Rica (2 Nov. 1945)

Democratic People's Republic of Korea (17 Sept. 1991)

Ecuador (21 Dec. 1945)

El Salvador (24 Oct. 1945)

Federated States of Micronesia (17 Sept. 1991)

Fiji (13 Oct. 1970)

Guatemala (21 Nov. 1945)

Honduras (17 Dec. 1945)

Indonesia (28 Sept. 1950)
By letter of 20 Jan. 1965, Indonesia announced its decision to withdraw from the United Nations 'at this stage and under the present circumstances'. By telegram of 19 Sept. 1966, it announced its decision 'to resume full co-operation with the United Nations and to resume participation in its activities'. On 28 Sept. 1966, the General Assembly took note of this decision and the President invited representatives of Indonesia to take seats in the Assembly.

Japan (18 Dec. 1956)

Lao People's Democratic Republic (14 Dec. 1955)

Malaysia (7 Sept. 1957)
The Federation of Malaya joined the United Nations on 17 Sept. 1957. On 16 Sept. 1963, its name was changed to Malaysia, following the admission to the new federation of Singapore, Sabah [...] and Sarawak. Singapore became an independent State on 9 August 1965 and a Member of the United Nations on 21 Sept. 1965.

Marshall Islands (17 Sept. 1991)

Mexico (7 Nov. 1945)

Myanmar [Burma] (19 Apr. 1948)

New Zealand (24 Oct. 1945)

Nicaragua (24 Oct. 1945)

Palau (15 Dec. 1994)

Panama (13 Nov. 1945)

Papua New Guinea (10 Oct. 1975)

Peru (31 Oct. 1945)

Philippines (24 Oct. 1945)

Republic of Korea (17 Sept. 1991)

Russian Federation (24 Oct. 1945)
The Union of Soviet Socialist Republics was an original Member of the United Nations from 24 Oct. 1945. In a letter dated 24 Dec. 1991, Boris Yeltsin, the President of the Russian Federation, informed the Secretary-General that the membership of the Soviet Union in the Security Council and all other United Nations organs was being continued by the Russian Federation with the support of the 11 member countries of the Commonwealth of Independent States.

Samoa (15 Dec. 1976)

Singapore (21 Sept. 1965)

Solomon Islands (19 Sept. 1978)

Thailand (16 Dec. 1946)

United States (24 Oct. 1945)

Vanuatu (15 Sept. 1981)

Viet Nam (20 Sept. 1977)

Source: UN Net Site, New York, UN Department of Public Information. Available from: http://www.un.org

The World Trade Organization Agreement, 1994

> In 1994 a new World Trade Organization emerged after a lengthy and difficult set of multilateral negotiations known as the 'Uruguay Round'. WTO provides the institutional framework for the conduct of international trade by its members. It incorporates the General Agreement on Tariffs and Trade made in 1994 which supersedes the earlier GATT agreement of 1947. The document below includes the preamble, Articles I–III and parts of Article IV of the agreement to establish the WTO. Around 120 of the world's nations are members of the WTO including the following covered within the scope of this book: Australia, Brunei, Burma/Myanmar, Canada, Chile, Colombia, Costa Rica, Ecuador, El Salvador, Fiji, Guatemala, Hong Kong, Indonesia, Japan, South Korea, Macau, Malaysia, Mexico, New Zealand, Nicaragua, Peru, Philippines, Singapore, Thailand, and the USA.

Marrakech agreement establishing the World Trade Organization

15 April 1994

The Parties to this Agreement,

Recognizing that their relations in the field of trade and economic endeavour should be conducted with a view to raising standards of living, ensuring full employment and a large and steadily growing volume of real income and effective demand, and expanding the production of and trade in goods and services, while allowing for the optimal use of the world's resources in accordance with the objective of sustainable development, seeking both to protect and preserve the environment and to enhance the means for doing so in a manner consistent with their respective needs and concerns at different levels of economic development,

Recognizing further that there is need for positive efforts designed to ensure that developing countries, and especially the least developed among them, secure a share in the growth in international trade commensurate with the needs of their economic development,

Being desirous of contributing to these objectives by entering into reciprocal and mutually advantageous arrangements directed to the substantial reduction of tariffs and other barriers to trade and to the elimination of discriminatory treatment in international trade relations,

Resolved, therefore, to develop an integrated, more viable and durable multilateral trading system encompassing the General Agreement on Tariffs and Trade, the results of past trade liberalization efforts, and all of the results of the Uruguay Round of Multilateral Trade Negotiations,

Determined to preserve the basic principles and to further the objectives underlying this multilateral trading system,

Agree as follows:

Article I: Establishment of the Organization

The World Trade Organization (hereinafter referred to as 'the WTO') is hereby established.

Article II: Scope of the WTO

1. The WTO shall provide the common institutional framework for the conduct of trade relations among its Members in matters related to the agreements and associated legal instruments included in the Annexes to this Agreement.

2. The agreements and associated legal instruments included in Annexes 1, 2 and 3 (hereinafter referred to as 'Multilateral Trade Agreements') are integral parts of this Agreement, binding on all Members.

3. The agreements and associated legal instruments included in Annex 4 (hereinafter referred to as 'Plurilateral Trade Agreements') are also part of this Agreement for those Members that have accepted them, and are binding on those Members. The Plurilateral Trade Agreements do not create either obligations or rights for Members that have not accepted them.

4. The General Agreement on Tariffs and Trade 1994 as specified in Annex 1A (hereinafter referred to as 'GATT 1994') is legally distinct from the General Agreement on Tariffs and Trade, dated 30 October 1947, annexed to the Final Act Adopted at the Conclusion of the Second Session of the Preparatory Committee of the United Nations Conference on Trade and Employment, as subsequently rectified, amended or modified (hereinafter referred to as 'GATT 1947').

Article III: Functions of the WTO

1. The WTO shall facilitate the implementation, administration and operation, and further the objectives, of this Agreement and of the Multilateral Trade Agreements, and shall also provide the framework for the implementation, administration and operation of the Plurilateral Trade Agreements.

2. The WTO shall provide the forum for negotiations among its Members concerning their multilateral trade relations in matters dealt with under the agreements in the Annexes to this Agreement. The WTO may also provide a forum for further negotiations among its Members concerning their multilateral trade relations, and a framework for the implementation of the results of such negotiations, as may be directed by the Ministerial Conference.

3. The WTO shall administer the Understanding on Rules and Procedures Governing the Settlement of Disputes

(hereinafter referred to as the 'Dispute Settlement Understanding' or 'DSU') in Annex 2 to this Agreement.

4. The WTO shall administer the Trade Policy Review Mechanism (hereinafter referred to as the 'TPRM') provided for in Annex 3 to this Agreement.

5. With a view to achieving greater coherence in global economic policy-making, the WTO shall co-operate, as appropriate, with the International Monetary Fund and with the International Bank for Reconstruction and Development and its affiliated agencies.

Article IV: Structure of the WTO

1. There shall be a Ministerial Conference composed of representatives of all the Members, which shall meet at least once every two years. The Ministerial Conference shall carry out the functions of the WTO and take actions necessary to this effect. The Ministerial Conference shall have the authority to take decisions on all matters under any of the Multilateral Trade Agreements, if so requested by a Member, in accordance with the specific requirements for decision-making in this Agreement and in the relevant Multilateral Trade Agreement.

2. There shall be a General Council composed of representatives of all the Members, which shall meet as appropriate. In the intervals between meetings of the Ministerial Conference, its functions shall be conducted by the General Council. The General Council shall also carry out the functions assigned to it by this Agreement. [...]

Source: International Trade Law Site/Monitor, Tromso, Law Faculty of the University of Tromso. Available from: http://itl.irv.uit.no/trade_law

The World Bank Group

> As outlined below in its own public relations material, the World Bank consists of a group of connected organizations established at different times since 1944. As with the UN and WTO countries of the Asia-Pacific are well represented, however, it should be noted that status within the group is usually dependant on economic strength.

The World Bank Group at a glance

The World Bank Group comprises five organizations: the International Bank for Reconstruction and Development (IBRD), the International Development Association (IDA), the International Finance Corporation (IFC), the Multilateral Investment Guarantee Agency (MIGA), and the International Centre for the Settlement of Investment Disputes (ICSID).

International Bank for Reconstruction and Development (IBRD)

The IBRD, founded in 1944, is the World Bank Group's main lending organization. It lends to developing countries with relatively high per capita incomes. The money the IBRD lends is used to pay for development projects, such as building highways, schools, and hospitals, and for programmes to help governments change the way they manage their economies.

*   *Interest rate charged on IBRD loans*: 6.98 per cent as of July 1, 1996. The rate is changed every six months.
*   *Maturity on loans*: 15 to 20 years, with a grace period of about five years.
*   *Source of funds*: The IBRD raises most of its money on the world's financial markets. It sells bonds and other debt securities to pension funds, insurance companies, corporations, other banks, and individuals around the world.
*   *Ownership*: IBRD is owned by its 180 member countries. Each of these countries has voting power in the institution. Voting power is based on a country's shareholding, which in turn is based on a country's economic strength.
*   *Lending*: During the past five years, the IBRD approved an annual average of $15.6 billion in loans for development projects.

International Development Association (IDA)

The IDA was established in 1960 to provide assistance on concessional terms to the poorest developing countries – those that cannot afford to borrow from the IBRD. IDA loans, known as 'credits', are provided mainly to countries with annual per capita incomes of about $865 or less.

*   *IDA credits are interest free*, but carry a small service charge.
*   *Terms on credits*: 35 or 40 years, with a 10-year grace period.
*   *Sources of funds*: IDA resources are derived from contributions from governments, IBRD profits, and repayments on earlier IDA credits.
*   *Ownership*: IDA has 159 member countries. A country must be a member of IBRD before it can join IDA.
*   *Lending*: During the past five years, IDA approved an annual average of $6.5 billion in credits to help pay for development projects.

International Finance Corporation (IFC)

The IFC was established in 1956 to help strengthen the private sector in developing countries. IFC lends directly to the private sector, while the IBRD and IDA lend to governments. IFC aids the private sector by providing long-term loans, equity investments, guarantees and 'standby financing', risk management and 'quasi-equity instruments', such as subordinated loans, preferred stock, and income notes.

- *Interest rate on IFC loans and financing*: Market rates, which vary between countries and projects. Maturity on loans: three to 13 years, with grace periods as long as eight years.
- *Source of funds*: About 80 per cent is borrowed in the international financial markets through public bond issues or private placements and 20 per cent is borrowed from the IBRD.
- *Ownership*: IFC is owned by 170 member countries.
- *Lending*: IFC investments have risen from about $4 billion in fiscal 1993 to more than $8 billion in fiscal 1996, including syndications and underwriting for private-sector projects in developing countries.

Multilateral Investment Guarantee Agency (MIGA)

MIGA was established in 1988 to help developing countries attract foreign investment. MIGA provides investors with investment guarantees against 'non-commercial risk', such as expropriation and war. It also provides governments with advice on improving the climate for foreign investment.

- *Coverage*: MIGA may insure up to 90 per cent of an investment, with a current limit of $50 million per project.
- *Membership*: 134 countries.
- *Guarantees*: In fiscal 1996, MIGA issued 68 guarantee contracts worth about $862 million.

International Centre for Settlement of Investment Disputes (ICSID)

ICSID was founded in 1966 to promote increased flows of international investment by providing facilities for the conciliation and arbitration of disputes between governments and foreign investors. ICSID also provides advice, carries out research, and produces publications in the area of foreign investment law.

- *Membership*: 126 countries as of June 30, 1996.
- *Cases*: Last year, five new requests for arbitration were registered and ten cases were pending before the Centre.
- *Research and publications*: ICSID's publications in the field of foreign investment law include multi-volume collections of investment laws and treaties and a semi-annual law journal.

Source: World Bank Net Site. Available from: http://www.worldbank.org/html/

Asia–Europe Meeting, 1996

In 1996 a new initiative for 'peace, global stability and prosperity' between the European Union and a number of East Asian nations was launched. ASEM is seen as a way of building on existing links such as the ASEAN Regional Forum. The Chairman's Statement outlines the wide range of political and economic topics discussed by the heads of state and government at the two-day meeting. The meeting agreed a number of follow-up measures and that the initiative should continue in an 'evolutionary' way. Further meetings are planned for 1998 and 2000. The Bangkok meeting involved the fifteen members of the European Union, with Brunei, China, Indonesia, Japan, South Korea, Malaysia, Philippines, Singapore, Thailand, and Vietnam. Countries expressing an interest in joining ASEM at the next meeting include Australia, India, New Zealand, Pakistan, and Russia.

Chairman's Statement of the Asia–Europe Meeting

Bangkok, 2 March 1996

Towards a common vision for Asia and Europe

1. The inaugural Asia–Europe Meeting (ASEM) was held in Bangkok on 1–2 March 1996 and attended by the Heads of State and Government from ten Asian nations and fifteen European nations with the Head of Government of Italy acting also as President of the Council of the European Union, and the President of the European Commission. The Heads were accompanied by their Foreign Ministers, Members of the Commission and other Ministers. This historic Meeting was chaired by the Prime Minister of Thailand.
[...]

3. The Meeting discussed a wide range of issues and provided the opportunity for the Heads to share their concerns and aspirations, and develop a common vision of the future. The Meeting recognized the need to strive for a common goal of maintaining and enhancing peace and stability, as well as creating conditions conducive for economic and social development. To this end, the Meeting forged a new comprehensive Asia–Europe Partnership for Greater Growth. This partnership aims at strengthening links between Asia and Europe thereby contributing to peace, global stability and prosperity. In this connection, the Meeting underscored the importance of both Asia and Europe maintaining dialogue with other regions.

4. The Meeting recognized that an important goal of this partnership is for both Asia and Europe to share the responsibilities in building greater understanding between the peoples of both regions. Strengthened dialogue on an

Leaders from Singapore, the UK, Vietnam, Germany, Ireland, Japan, the European Commission, Italy, and Thailand at the 25-nation Asia–Europe Meeting, Bangkok, March 1996

equal basis between Asia and Europe in a spirit of co-operation and through the sharing of perceptions on a wide range of issues would enhance mutual understanding and benefit both regions. The dialogue will, in view of the global implications of the major regional integrations, also help ensure that such integrations benefit the international community as a whole.

Fostering political dialogue

5. The Meeting of the Heads from Asia and Europe reflects their common desire to strengthen political dialogue between Asia and Europe. Counties of Asia and Europe should highlight and expand common ground, enhance understanding and friendship, and promote and deepen co-operation. The dialogue among the participating countries should be conducted on the basis of mutual respect, equality, promotion of fundamental rights and, in accordance with the rules of international law and obligations, non-intervention, whether direct or indirect, in each other's internal affairs. The Heads reviewed political and security situations in both regions and underlined the importance of support for international initiatives to solve outstanding problems. The Meeting also agreed to promote intellectual exchanges between the two regions in the context of fostering political dialogue.

6. The Meeting agreed on the importance of enhancing the already existing dialogues between Asia and Europe on general security issues and in particular on confidence-building. Many Asian countries have established regular dialogue with the European Union. The European Union and the Asian nations have also engaged in discussions on political matters at such fora as the ASEAN–EU Dialogue,

the ASEAN Regional Forum (ARF) and the ASEAN Post Ministerial Conferences (PMC).

7. The Meeting reaffirmed its strong commitment to the United Nations Charter, the Universal Declaration on Human Rights, to the 1986 Declaration on the Right to Development, the 1992 Rio Declaration on Environment and Development, the 1993 Declaration of Vienna and Programme of Action of the World Conference on Human Rights, the 1994 Cairo Programme of Action of the International Conference on Population and Development, the 1995 Copenhagen Declaration on Social Development and Programme of Action, and to the 1995 Beijing Declaration and Platform of Action for the Fourth World Conference on Women. The Meeting also agreed to co-operate in promoting the effective reform and greater democratization of the UN system, including inter alia the issues concerning the Security Council, the General Assembly, the Economic and Social Council and UN finances, with a view to reinforcing its pre-eminent role in maintaining and promoting international peace and security and sustainable development. In this connection, the Meeting agreed to the initiation of a dialogue between representatives of participating nations of the ASEM in New York to consider the vital question of the UN reform.

8. The Meeting agreed on the importance of strengthening global initiatives on arms control, disarmament and non-proliferation of weapons of mass destruction and reaffirmed that Asian and European countries will enhance co-operation in these fields. The Meeting therefore attached particular importance to the early conclusion of the Comprehensive Test Ban Treaty in 1996. The Meeting noted that, in their efforts to contribute to the Nuclear Non-Proliferation Treaty (NPT) regime, the

ten Southeast Asian countries have concluded the Southeast Asia Nuclear Weapon-Free Zone (SEANWFZ) Treaty in Bangkok in December 1995. The Leaders reiterated their determination to pursue systematic and progressive efforts to reduce nuclear weapons globally with the ultimate goal of eliminating those weapons and of general and complete disarmament under strict and effective international controls. The Meeting emphasized its commitment to the non-proliferation and prohibition of biological and chemical weapons, in particular to the early entry into force of the Chemical Weapons Convention. The Meeting supported efforts in the Conference on Disarmament to start negotiations on a fissile material cut-off on the basis of the agreed mandate.

Reinforcing economic co-operation

9.   The Meeting recognized the great potential for synergy between Asia and Europe on account of the economic dynamism and diversity of the two regions. Asia's emergence as an immense market has spawned great demand for consumer goods, capital equipment, financing and infrastructure. Europe, on the other hand, is a major market in the world for goods, investments and services, even more so since the completion of the Single Market. Opportunities thus exist for both regions to expand the market for goods, capital equipment and infrastructure development projects, and to increase the flows of capital, expertise and technology.

10. The Meeting recognized that the growing economic links between the two regions form the basis for a strong partnership between Asia and Europe. To further strengthen this partnership, the Meeting expressed its resolve to generate greater two-way trade and investment flows between Asia and Europe. Such a partnership should be based on the common commitment to market economy, open multilateral trading system, non-discriminatory liberalization and open regionalism. The Meeting stressed that any regional integration and co-operation should be WTO consistent and outward looking.

11. The Meeting agreed that the ASEM process should complement and reinforce efforts to strengthen the open and rules-based trading system embodied in the WTO. Full participation in the WTO by ASEM countries will strengthen the organization. Recognizing the importance of the first WTO Ministerial Conference to be held in Singapore in December 1996, the Meeting agreed that the participants from Asia and Europe will work closely together towards the success of the WTO. The Meeting agreed that a priority facing the WTO was how to ensure full implementation of commitments made in the Uruguay Round. Participants also underlined the urgent need to bring unfinished Uruguay Round negotiations to successful conclusions and to pursue the so called built-in-agenda, agreed to at Marrakech. Asian and European participants will consult closely on new issues for the WTO agenda.

12. To promote greater trade and investment between Asia and Europe, the Meeting agreed to undertake facilitation and liberalization measures involving the simplification and improvement of customs procedures, and standards conformance. ASEM will also aim for the reduction of trade barriers to avoid trade distortion and create better market access thus encouraging greater trade flows between Asia and Europe. The Meeting underscored the urgent need to increase European investments in Asia from their present low levels, as well as to encourage Asian investments in Europe.

13. The Meeting decided to ask senior officials to convene an informal meeting at an early opportunity on ways to promote economic co-operation and in particular liberalization and facilitation of trade and investment. Initial emphasis should be placed on the WTO issues indicated above, but officials should also try to identify other measures that could be taken by ASEM countries in order to facilitate trade and investment. Officials may also look into how training programmes, economic co-operation and technical assistance could be further intensified in order to facilitate trade and investment.

14. The Meeting agreed to encourage the business and private sectors, including small and medium sized enterprises of the two regions, to strengthen their co-operation with one another and contribute towards increasing trade and investment between Asia and Europe. For this purpose, the Meeting agreed to establish in due course an Asia–Europe Business Forum.

Promoting co-operation in other areas

15. The Meeting agreed that intensified science and technology cross-flows between Asia and Europe, especially in priority driving sectors such as agriculture, information and communication technology, energy and transport, are important for strengthening the economic links between the two regions. The Meeting expressed the view that co-operation in the field of human resources development constitutes an important component of the economic co-operation between Asia and Europe. The Meeting also supported the strengthening of co-operation on all levels of education and vocational and management training. The Meeting also stressed the need to improve development co-operation between the two regions, giving priority to poverty alleviation, promoting the role of women and co-operating in the public health sector, including the strengthening of global efforts to combat AIDS and to promote AIDS prevention. The Meeting further agreed that the two regions should promote a dialogue within the ASEM on development co-operation with other regions, where feasible, sharing their respective experiences in this area.

16. The Meeting acknowledged the importance of addressing environmental issues such as global warming, protection of water resources, deforestation and

desertification, biodiversity of species, marine environment protection and agreed that mutually beneficial co-operation should be undertaken in this field including the transfer of environmentally sound technology to promote sustainable development. The Meeting agreed to strengthen co-operation between the two regions to deal with the illicit drug trade, money laundering, terrorism and other international crimes, including exploitation of illegal immigration, both bilaterally and through existing multilateral initiatives.

17. The meeting called for the strengthening of cultural links between Asia and Europe, particularly the fostering of closer people-to-people contacts, which is indispensable to the promotion of greater awareness and understanding between the peoples of both regions. The Meeting emphasized that these new links between Asia and Europe should help overcome misperceptions that may exist between the two regions, and could be further reinforced through promoting cultural, artistic, educational activities and exchanges involving particularly youth and students, and tourism between the two sides. In this respect, the Meeting was informed about the results of the Europe–Asia Forum on culture, values and technology, recently held in Venice. The Meeting also encouraged co-operation in the preservation of cultural heritage.

Future course of ASEM

18. The Meeting regarded the ASEM as a useful process for promoting further co-operation between Asia and Europe. The Meeting recognized that the ASEM process needed to be open and evolutionary. The Meeting agreed that inter-sessional activities are necessary although they need not be institutionalized. The Meeting further agreed that follow-up actions to be undertaken jointly by the participants to the ASEM will be based on consensus. The Meeting also agreed to facilitate co-operation between Asian and European business leaders.

19. The Meeting agreed to the following follow-up measures:

- The Foreign Ministers and the Senior Officials' Meeting in charge of the First ASEM would co-ordinate and prepare for the Second ASEM on the basis of the result of the First ASEM. In this connection, a Foreign Ministers' Meeting would be held in 1997;

- An Economic Ministers' Meeting would be held in Japan in 1997 to discuss relevant economic issues;

- An informal Senior Officials' meeting would be held in Brussels in July 1996 on ways to promote economic co-operation between the two regions, and in particular liberalization and facilitation of trade and investments, with an initial emphasis on WTO issues;

- A Meeting of Government and Private Sector Working Group would be convened in Thailand to draw up within six months an Asia–Europe Investment Promotion Action Plan to promote greater cross-flows of investment between Asia and Europe. Such a group could also study the current status of and potentials for investment between Asia and Europe and recommend measures to be taken in this regard;

- An Asia–Europe Business Forum would hold its inaugural meeting in France in 1996 and the next meeting in Thailand. At this Forum, Senior Officials would consider the appropriate modalities for fostering greater co-operation between the business and private sectors of the two regions. In this connection, a business conference would be held in 1997;

- Malaysia would act as co-ordinator for the study of integrating a trans-Asian railway network (commencing initially with the railway project of the Mekong Basin Development) and also the study of the subsequent possible integration of this railway network with the trans-European railway network;

- The establishment in Thailand of an Asia–Europe Environmental Technology Centre to undertake research and development activities as well as provide policy guidance to both regions' governments and peoples;

- An Asia–Europe Foundation would be set up in Singapore with contributions from Asian and European countries, to promote exchanges between think-tanks, peoples and cultural groups. In this connection, Singapore has offered to contribute US$1 million to seed this foundation;

- An Asia–Europe University Programme would be started to foster exchanges of students and scholars with a view to developing better understanding of the cultures, histories and business practices of both regions;

- Intellectual exchanges between Asia and Europe through the holding of seminars and symposia on international and regional issues and the establishment of networks amongst the appropriate think-tanks from both regions;

- Objective studies on the economic synergy between Asia and Europe to provide future prospects and a solid basis for development effective policy measures;

- Youth exchange programmes of mini 'Davos-type' to strengthen cultural links and the mutual understanding between the two regions.

The Meeting also agreed to consider the following:

- A Meeting of Finance Ministers;

- An Asia–Europe Co-operation Framework which will spell out the principles and mechanisms for long-term Asia–Europe co-operation in political, economic, social and other areas;

- The establishment of a study group on enhancing technological exchanges and co-operation, particularly in the areas of agriculture, environmental protection, and technological upgrading and improvement of enterprises;

- The development of closer co-operation among customs authorities in Asia and Europe in the areas of customs procedure and prevention of illicit drug trade;
- Co-operation in the development of the Mekong River Basin.

20. The Meeting agreed to hold the Second ASEM in two years' time in the United Kingdom and the Third ASEM in the Republic of Korea in the year 2000.

Source: Official Home Page of the Asia–Europe Meeting, Bangkok '96, Thailand, Ministry of Foreign Affairs. Available from: http://asem.inter.net.th/index.html

Amnesty International's Annual Report, 1996

Most of the documents reproduced above represent, in one way or another, an official view. The aspirations of countries have been to the fore. Key words such as co-operation, peace and prosperity reoccur with notable regularity. Amnesty International is a non-governmental organization opposed to violations of human rights. With its origins in the early 1960s Amnesty has grown into a world-wide organization. Each year it produces a report on human rights violations. Reproduced below are extracts from the 1996 report on the Americas and Asia/Pacific. It makes depressing reading, and the contrast with sentiments expressed in the other documents is clear to see. Whole paragraphs dealing with countries outside of the scope of this book have been omitted from the two extracts.

The Americas

Human rights violations, January to December 1995

Extrajudicial executions

- Hundreds of people were victims of extrajudicial executions or possible extrajudicial executions by members of the security forces or their agents in at least 16 countries of the region, including Brazil, Colombia, and Guatemala.

Disappearances

- Disappearances took place in at least six countries of the region, including Colombia and Guatemala.
- The fate of thousands of people who disappeared in previous years remains unknown with more than 4,200 of such cases in Peru, more than 1,500 in Colombia, and more than 300 in Mexico.

Torture or ill-treatment

- Torture and ill-treatment, including rape, took place in at least 20 countries, including Colombia, Mexico, Peru, and Venezuela.

- Cases of detainees who died apparently as a result of torture while in police custody were reported in Brazil, Ecuador, Jamaica, and the USA.

Prisoners of conscience

- More than 1,000 prisoners of conscience or possible prisoners of conscience were held in seven countries. Peru and Cuba held at least 500 prisoners of conscience or possible prisoners of conscience each and Colombia at least 100.

Unfair trials

- At least 300 people were imprisoned after unfair trials in Colombia, and at least one in Cuba.

Detention without charge or trial

- Detentions without charge or trial took place at least in two countries of the region: Panama and Paraguay.

Death penalty

- At least 62 executions were carried out in four countries of the region: Cuba (2), Saint Lucia (1), Saint Vincent and the Grenadines (3), and the United States of America (56).
- More than 3,000 people were in death row in the USA. Seven other countries held prisoners under sentence of death, including Bahamas, Jamaica, and Trinidad and Tobago.

Human rights abuses by armed opposition groups

- Hundreds of abuses by armed opposition groups took place in Colombia and Peru.

Summary

The gap between what most governments of the region say and what they do to change the human rights situation widened. While the language of human rights has been almost universally adopted by the institutions of the states, human rights violations are still taking place throughout the region.

Different patterns of impunity for perpetrators of human rights violations were present throughout Latin-America. In Colombia, almost total impunity continued to prevail in judicial investigations into extrajudicial executions, disappearances, and torture by the armed forces. In Peru, thousands of unresolved cases of human rights violations perpetrated by members of the security forces and government officials over the past 15 years were definitely closed by law. In Mexico and Brazil the climate of impunity in which the security forces operate puts virtually all the population at risk.

In Chile, military and civilian courts continued to close investigations into past human rights violations, even though a number of officers had their prison sentences confirmed, while legislation that would contribute to further closing of such cases was discussed. In Argentina, new revelations by members of the armed forces regarding the fate of people who disappeared during the period of military government (1976–1983) failed to prompt judicial investigations to establish the circumstances of thousands of disappearances.

In Haiti, although President Jean-Bertrand Aristide expressed his commitment to ending impunity, little was achieved in practice, largely because of slow progress in the much needed reform of the justice system. In Honduras, positive steps were taken to bring to justice those responsible for some past human rights violations. The first charges against security officers on human rights violations took place, and judicial proceedings were continuing at the end of the year. However, in other cases little or no progress was made.

Extrajudicial executions and disappearances took place during 1995 in at least 16 countries of the region. In Colombia, at least 1,000 people were extrajudicially executed; in Brazil, victims numbered in the hundreds. In Guatemala, more than 150 extrajudicial executions by members of the security forces and government-backed armed groups were reported. Many extrajudicial executions also took place in Nicaragua and Venezuela. In Mexico, 17 unarmed peasants were massacred by the judicial police in a single incident in Guerrero State.

In Colombia, more than 150 people disappeared after detention by the armed forces, the police or paramilitary groups. Paramilitary forces operating in rural areas were also responsible for numerous disappearances of political and community activists. In Peru, nine people were reported to have disappeared in 1995 and the fate of at least 4,200 people who disappeared in previous years is still unknown.

Torture and ill-treatment were widespread in almost all countries of the region. In Mexico, extensive use of torture and ill-treatment by law enforcement agents continued to be reported, as in past years. Dozens of people were also tortured during and immediately after the operations in Chiapas State between 9 and 14 February, and as a result of police raids on suspected Zapatista National Liberation Army members in others parts of the country.

In Peru, complaints of torture by detainees suspected of terrorism continued to be received. In a single arrest in August in the Village of Chalhuayacu, 41 people were said to have been forced to sign a document in which they admitted to being subversive. In Brazil, evidence that torture was widespread and a common method of extracting information from criminal suspects was confirmed by the Chamber of Deputies Human Rights Commission. In Venezuela, widespread use of torture by the security forces was reported.

In the United States of America (USA), there were deaths in police custody in disputed circumstances and widespread allegations of torture and ill-treatment by police and prison officers. Chain-gangs were introduced in prisons in several states. In Jamaica, scores of prisoners on death row were reportedly ill-treated and at least two prisoners died in custody.

Prison conditions continued to be appalling in some of the countries of the region including Venezuela and Haiti and poor in many others, including Cuba, the Dominican Republic and Paraguay.

The death penalty continued to be used extensively in the USA, where 56 prisoners were executed in 1995, the highest number recorded since executions resumed in 1977. Two states – Pennsylvania and Montana – carried out executions for the first time in more than 30 and 50 years respectively. In Cuba, two men were executed and at least three others were sentenced to death.

[...]

Chile is one of the few countries in Latin America to retain the death penalty. While no executions were carried out in 1995, five political prisoners continued to face possible death sentences after a military prosecutor called for the death penalty in their cases. In Guatemala, the Congress passed a law extending the death penalty to the master minders and perpetrators of kidnapping or abduction, the perpetrators and those attempting to cover up such crimes. However, the law was neither ratified nor vetoed by President Ramiro de León Carpio within the legally specified period, leaving its status unclear.

[...]

In Peru, hundreds of prisoners of conscience and possible prisoners of conscience remained in prison at the end of the year. In addition, more than 5,000 people sentenced after unfair trials in previous years also remained in prison. Prisoners of conscience and political prisoners were also held in Colombia, Mexico, and Venezuela.

Human rights defenders were victims of persecution, intimidation and death threats in most of the countries of the region, including Argentina, Brazil, Colombia, Cuba, Guatemala, Honduras, Mexico, and Peru. In Mexico and Colombia, dozens of human rights defenders, including journalists, were threatened with death for criticizing the human rights situation in the country. Some of them were directly attacked for their activities.

[...]

In Guatemala, journalists, members of human rights groups and members of the judiciary were intimidated, threatened and, in some cases, victims of extrajudicial executions. Women human rights defenders appeared to be particularly targeted in Colombia and Mexico.

In addition to human rights violations carried out by the governments, armed opposition groups committed abuses in Colombia and Peru. In Colombia, armed opposition groups committed numerous grave human rights abuses, including scores of deliberate and arbitrary killings. At least 400 people were held hostage, principally by the Fuerzas Armadas Revolucionarias de Colombia (FARC), Revolutionary Armed Forces of Colombia and the Ejército de Liberación Nacional (ELN), National Liberation Army. Some were released while others were killed in captivity. In Peru, dozens of civilians were deliberately and arbitrarily killed by the Partido Comunista del Perú (Sendero Luminoso) (PCP), Communist Party of Peru (Shining Path).

Asia/Pacific

Human rights violations, January to December 1995

Extrajudicial executions

- Hundreds of extrajudicial executions or possible extrajudicial executions were reported in 12 countries, including Australia, Bangladesh, India, Indonesia and East Timor, Pakistan, Papua New Guinea, the Philippines and Sri Lanka.

Disappearances

- 'Disappearances' were reported in four countries in 1995 – India, Indonesia and East Timor, the Philippines and Sri Lanka.
- The fate of at least 3,000 people who disappeared in the region in recent years remains unknown.

Torture or ill-treatment

- Thousands of cases of torture or ill-treatment, including rape, were reported in 21 countries including Bangladesh, Cambodia, China, India, Indonesia and East Timor, Pakistan and the Philippines.
- At least 1,700 people died as a result of torture in custody or inhuman prison conditions in 11 countries, including India, Mongolia, Myanmar and Pakistan.

Prisoners of conscience

- At least 5,000 prisoners of conscience or possible prisoners of conscience were held in 18 countries. China held thousands and Afghanistan and India held more than 1,000 each. Other prisoners of conscience and political prisoners were held in Indonesia and East Timor, Myanmar, Nepal, the Republic of Korea and Sri Lanka.

Unfair trials

- At least 96 people were imprisoned after unfair trials reported in three countries – China, Indonesia and East Timor and Vietnam.
- Throughout the region more than 3,000 people remained in jail after unfair trials in previous years.

Detention without charge or trial

- Nine countries held a total of more than 4,000 people. China detained people in massive numbers and India held more than 3,000, while hundreds were held in Sri Lanka. Detentions without trial were also recorded in Pakistan, Malaysia and Bangladesh.

Death penalty

- 13 countries passed at least 3,305 death sentences in 1995.
- More than 2,291 executions were carried out in 12 of these countries. China executed 2,190. More than 50 people were executed in Singapore. Executions were also recorded in Indonesia and East Timor, Japan, Malaysia, Pakistan, the Republic of Korea, Taiwan and Viet Nam.
- A documented total of at least 168 prisoners remained under sentence of death in four countries – India, Indonesia and East Timor, Japan and the Republic of Korea. The true figure is believed to be much higher.

Human rights abuses by armed opposition groups

- Armed opposition groups committed abuses including torture, hostage taking and deliberate and arbitrary killings in six countries, including Afghanistan, Cambodia, India, the Philippines and Sri Lanka.

Summary

Behind the Asia/Pacific's image of economic dynamism, governments in the region were responsible in 1995 for torturing, extrajudicially executing, disappearing and executing their citizens, while thousands remained incarcerated after unfair trials. Women, children and the elderly were all victims, and the ease with which perpetrators of human rights violations were able to escape punishment contributed to the continuing climate of fear in many countries.

Torture and ill-treatment, often leading to deaths in custody, continued to be a major concern throughout the region, with thousands of victims including women, children and human rights defenders reported from Afghanistan to Australia.

As the civil war raged unabated in Afghanistan, hundreds of cases of torture including rape were reported. Victims were tortured solely because they belonged to a rival ethnic group, or to extract money from their families. In China, torture of political and criminal detainees remained widespread, often to force confessions or to intimidate and punish prisoners, with many victims tortured with electro-shock weapons.

In India, torture of detainees was endemic in every state, with many victims coming from underprivileged sections of society. Torture was also reported in Bangladesh, Cambodia, Indonesia and East Timor and the Philippines.

Many people died as a result of torture or ill-treatment in detention. In Myanmar, more than 1,300 prisoners died as a result of illness and ill-treatment when they were forced to work on road building projects. Many of these prisoners were made to labour long hours, breaking rocks while held in leg-irons and denied adequate food or sleep.

[...]

Twenty-one aboriginal people died in custody or during police operations in Australia – the highest number since records started being kept in 1980 – and police reportedly continued to harass relatives who were unwilling to accept official explanations and called for further investigations.

Many people were sent to prison in the Asia/Pacific region after unfair trials. China continued to jail political prisoners after blatantly unfair trials – operating a verdict first, trial second policy. Verdicts were often based on confessions extracted under torture, and some defendants facing the death penalty were denied the right to legal representation or to be given advance notice of their trial. In December, the prominent dissident Wei Jingsheng was sentenced to 14 years in prison after an unfair trial, despite international condemnation.

In Indonesia and East Timor, at least 20 prisoners of conscience were sentenced to prison terms after unfair trials and some 150 political prisoners continued to serve sentences of up to life imprisonment after unfair trials in previous years. In Viet Nam, members of religious groups were among those given prison sentences after unfair trials.

Amnesty International documented the cases of at least 5,000 prisoners of conscience or possible prisoners of conscience in 18 countries in the region, although the organization believes the real figure to be much higher. More than 2,200 of these are imprisoned in China and at least 1,000 in Afghanistan.

Sri Lanka held more than 300 prisoners of conscience, and hundreds of possible prisoners of conscience and political prisoners were held in the Republic of Korea (South Korea) and Myanmar. Citizens forcibly returned from other countries were among possible prisoners of conscience reported in the People's Democratic Republic of Korea (North Korea).

Prisoners of conscience were among thousands of people detained without charge or trial in the region. China continued to detain countless numbers of people without charging them with an offence or bringing them to trial. In some areas only 10 per cent of those detained under the shelter and investigation administrative procedure had actually committed an offence.

[...]

Region-wide governments continued to use the death penalty for a widening range of offences. China sentenced people to death in massive numbers, with a recorded 3,110 death sentences and 2,190 executions in 1995, although Amnesty International believes the real figure to be much higher. China executed more people than the known figures for the rest of the world put together, with the death penalty applicable for 68 crimes including re-selling value-added tax receipts, speculating and profiteering and causing damage to public property.

Singapore executed at least 50 people – the majority for non-violent drug-related offences. Despite the lack of official information, there were reliable indications that the real figures were much higher. In March, Flor Contemplacion, a Filipina domestic worker, was executed for murder despite international appeals for her sentence to be commuted.

The death penalty was also used in Taiwan, where at least 15 people were sentenced to death, some of them after unfair trials based on forced confessions. Executions also took place in Japan, Malaysia, the Republic of Korea, and Viet Nam.

As well as the high level of judicial executions, extrajudicial executions remained a major concern in the Asia/Pacific region. During the continuing violence in the Indian state of Jammu and Kashmir, scores of people were extrajudicially executed by security forces. Scores of arbitrary killings took place during the escalating violence in the Pakistani city of Karachi. Extrajudicial executions by police and security forces were also reported in Indonesia and East Timor and the Philippines.

[...]

Deliberate and arbitrary killings, torture including rape and hostage taking were just some of the abuses committed by armed opposition groups against civilians throughout the Asia/Pacific region.

[...]

Ongoing violence between the government and armed opposition groups in the Philippines resulted in further abuses. The Muslim armed group, Abu Sayyaf, killed more than 50 people in an attack on Ipil town in April, and were also responsible for kidnapping civilians for ransom. Armed opposition groups were also responsible for human rights abuses in Cambodia, India and Myanmar.

There were some positive human rights developments in the region. Daw Aung San Suu Kyi, leader of the National League for Democracy (NLD), was released after nearly six years of house arrest in July in Myanmar. However, other leaders of the NLD remain in detention. Political prisoners and prisoners of conscience were released in the Republic of Korea, Nepal and the Philippines. The Pakistan government announced the establishment of a Ministry for Human Rights and in a rare move in Malaysia, the King granted clemency to a taxi driver sentenced to death.

The work of non-governmental organizations (NGOs) throughout the region in 1995 continued to be vital in protecting humans rights. Hundreds of NGO members came together for regional summits, participating in the parallel NGO form of the Asia-Pacific Economic Co-operation (APEC) meeting in Osaka, Japan in November.

In August, nearly 30,000 women and men gathered in Beijing, China for the Fourth United Nations World Conference on Women. NGOs from almost every country in the world participated in the largest NGO Forum ever and welcomed the inclusion of human rights protection in the Beijing Declaration and Platform for Action. Amnesty International called on governments to ensure the commitments agreed in Beijing were followed up by concrete action.

Source: Amnesty International On-line. Available from: http://www.amnesty.org

2 Historical themes

2.1 The USA and Japan

When in 1996 the leaders of Japan and the USA made their Joint Declaration looking forward to the twenty-first century, they described the relationship between the two countries as 'one of the most successful bilateral relationships in history': they were clearly thinking of relatively recent history. The following documents provide examples of the relationship between the two countries over the course of the twentieth century. The importance of their relationship to the history of the Asia-Pacific is undeniable, its success is more problematic. (See also the Historical Background points for Japan and the USA in Part 2.)

The Root–Takahira Agreement, 1908

From the turn of the century the growing presence of the USA in the Pacific and the rise of Japanese nationalism and imperialism saw the two powers come into increasingly close but uneasy contact. The following note from Kogoro Takahira, Japanese Ambassador to the USA, and the reply from Elihu Root, US Secretary of State, in November 1908, has been seen as a diplomatic recognition of each others interests in the region in order to avoid increasing tension. Japanese interests included a growing presence in Manchuria, while the USA had acquired the Philippines in 1898 as a result of its war with Spain (see Figure 4).

The exchange of views between us, which has taken place at the several interviews which I have recently had the honor of holding with you, has shown that Japan and the United States holding important outlying insular possessions in the region of the Pacific Ocean, the Governments of the two countries are animated by a common aim, policy, and intention in that region.

Believing that a frank avowal of that aim, policy, and intention would not only tend to strengthen the relations of friendship and good neighborhood, which have immemorially existed between Japan and the United States, but would materially contribute to the preservation of the general peace, the Imperial Government have authorized me to present to you an outline of their understanding of that common aim, policy, and intention:

1 It is the wish of the two Governments to encourage the free and peaceful developments of their commerce on the Pacific Ocean.

2 The policy of both Governments, uninfluenced by any aggressive tendencies, is directed to the maintenance of the existing status quo in the region above mentioned and to the defense of the principle of equal opportunity for commerce and industry in China.

3 They are accordingly firmly resolved reciprocally to respect the territorial possessions belonging to each other in said region.

4 They are also determined to preserve the common interests of all powers in China by supporting by all pacific means at their disposal the independence and integrity of China and the principle of equal opportunity for commerce and industry of all nations in that Empire.

5 Should any event occur threatening the status quo as above described or the principle of equal opportunity as above defined, it remains for the two Governments to communicate with each other in order to arrive at an understanding as to what measures they may consider it useful to take.

If the foregoing outline accords with the view of the Government of the United States, I shall be gratified to receive your confirmation.

I take this opportunity to renew to your excellency the assurance of my highest consideration.

Root responded to Takahira's note as follows.

I have the honor to acknowledge the receipt of your note of today setting forth the result of the exchange of views between us in our recent interviews defining the understanding of the two Governments in regard to their policy in the region of the Pacific Ocean.

It is a pleasure to inform you that this expression of mutual understanding is welcome to the Government of the United States as appropriate to the happy relations of the two countries and as the occasion for a concise mutual affirmation of that accordant policy respecting the Far East which the two Governments have so frequently declared in the past.

[...]

Source: Ferrell, R.H. (ed.) (1971) *America as a World Power 1872–1945*, Columbia SC, University of South Carolina Press.

Breakdown of negotiations, 1941

The growing territorial and economic ambitions of Japan, especially in China in the 1930s, eventually resulted in the interests of Japan and the USA becoming irreconcilable. The following extract contains the propositions that were put to Japan's ambassadors on 26 November 1941 at the end of a long and fruitless round of negotiations. Given Japanese policy at the time, the terms, including a Japanese withdrawal from China, were bound to be unacceptable. On 7 December the

Japanese responded in writing to say that agreement through further negotiations seemed impossible, the US naval base at Pearl Harbor was attacked the same day.

Section II

Steps to be taken by the Government of the United States and by the Government of Japan

The Government of the United States and the Government of Japan propose to take steps as follows:

1 The Government of the United States and the Government of Japan will endeavor to conclude a multilateral non-aggression pact among the British Empire, China, Japan, the Netherlands, the Soviet Union, Thailand and the United States.

2 Both Governments will endeavor to conclude among the American, British, Chinese, Japanese, the Netherlands and Thai Governments an agreement whereunder each of the Governments would pledge itself to respect the territorial integrity of French Indochina and, in the event that there should develop a threat to the territorial integrity of Indochina, to enter into immediate consultation with a view to taking such measures as may be deemed necessary and advisable to meet the threat in question. Such agreement would provide also that each of the Governments party to the agreement would not seek or accept preferential treatment in its trade or economic relations with Indochina and would use its influence to obtain for each of the signatories equality of treatment in trade and commerce with French Indochina.

3 The Government of Japan will withdraw all military, naval, air and police forces from China and from Indochina.

4 The government of the United States and the Government of Japan will not support – militarily, politically, economically – any government or regime in China other than the National Government of the Republic of China with capital temporarily at Chungking.

5 Both Governments will give up all extraterritorial rights in China, including rights and interests in and with regard to international settlements and concessions, and rights under the Boxer Protocol of 1901.

Both Governments will endeavor to obtain the agreement of the British and other governments to give up extraterritorial rights in China, including rights in international settlements and in concessions and under the Boxer Protocol of 1901.

6 The Government of the United States and the Government of Japan will enter into negotiations for the conclusion between the United States and Japan of a trade agreement, based upon reciprocal most-favored-nation treatment and reduction of trade barriers by both countries, including an undertaking by the United States to bind raw silk on the free list.

7 The Government of the United States and the Government of Japan will, respectively, remove the freezing restrictions on Japanese funds in the United States and on American funds in Japan.

8 Both Governments will agree upon a plan for the stabilization of the dollar-yen rate, with the allocation of funds adequate for this purpose, half to be supplied by Japan and half by the United States.

9 Both governments will agree that no agreement which either has concluded with any third power or powers shall be interpreted by it in such a way as to conflict with the fundamental purpose of this agreement, the establishment and preservation of peace throughout the Pacific area.

10 Both governments will use their influence to cause other governments to adhere to and to give practical application to the basic political and economic principles set forth in this agreement.

Source: Ferrell, R.H. (ed.) (1971) *America as a World Power 1872–1945*, Columbia SC, University of South Carolina Press.

Declaration of war, 1941

The day after Pearl Harbor was attacked US President Roosevelt made the following announcement to Congress. Figure 7 gives a good indication of the scale of the conflict that followed. While most countries of the western Pacific and the possessions of the European colonial powers in the area were engulfed in the war, the decisive military struggle was between Japan and the USA. Indeed, Japan still held most of the territories it had conquered when the USA forced its unconditional surrender in August 1945.

Yesterday, December 7, 1941 – a date which will live in infamy – the United States of America was suddenly and deliberately attacked by naval and air forces of the Empire of Japan.

The United States was at peace with that Nation and, at the solicitation of Japan, was still in conversation with its Government and its Emperor looking toward the maintenance of peace in the Pacific. Indeed, one hour after Japanese air squadrons had commenced bombing in Oahu, the Japanese Ambassador to the United States and his colleague delivered to the Secretary of State a formal reply to a recent American message. While this reply stated that it seemed useless to continue the existing diplomatic negotiations, it contained no threat or hint of war or armed attack.

It will be recorded that the distance of Hawaii from Japan makes it obvious that the attack was deliberately planned many days or even weeks ago. During the intervening time the Japanese Government has deliberately sought to deceive the United States by false statements and expressions of hope for continued peace.

President Roosevelt asks for an immediate declaration of war before a joint session of Congress, 8 December 1941

The attack yesterday on the Hawaiian Islands has caused severe damage to American naval and military forces. Very many American lives have been lost. In addition American ships have been reported torpedoed on the high seas between San Francisco and Honolulu.

Yesterday the Japanese Government also launched an attack against Malaya.

Last night Japanese forces attacked Hong Kong.

Last night Japanese forces attacked Guam.

Last night Japanese forces attacked the Philippine Islands.

Last night the Japanese attacked Wake Island.

This morning the Japanese attacked Midway Island.

Japan has, therefore, undertaken a surprise offensive extending throughout the Pacific area. The facts of yesterday speak for themselves. The people of the United States have already formed their opinions and well understand the implications to the very life and safety of our Nation.

As Commander-in-Chief of the Army and Navy I have directed that all measures be taken for our defense.

Always will we remember the character of the onslaught against us.

No matter how long it may take us to overcome this premeditated invasion, the American people in their righteous might will win through to absolute victory.

I believe I interpret the will of the Congress and of the people when I assert that we will not only defend ourselves to the uttermost but will make very certain that this form of treachery shall never endanger us again.

Hostilities exist. There is no blinking at the fact that our people, our territory, and our interests are in grave danger.

With confidence in our armed forces – with the unbounded determination of our people – we will gain the inevitable triumph – so help us God.

I ask that the Congress declare that since the unprovoked and dastardly attack by Japan on Sunday, December seventh, a state of war has existed between the United States and the Japanese Empire.

Source: Ferrell, R.H. (ed.) (1971) *America as a World Power 1872–1945*, Columbia SC, University of South Carolina Press.

Peace Treaty, 1951

The unconditional surrender of Japan was followed by US military occupation, the objectives of the occupying forces under their Supreme Commander, General Douglas MacArthur, included the dismantling of Japan's military capacity, the discouragement of anything that might revive Japan's aggressive nationalism and the promotion of democratic institutions. Considerable and lasting progress towards achieving these objectives was made, but the advent of the Cold War was also an important factor in the normalizing of the relationship. The Peace Treaty, of which key articles are reproduced below, was signed in 1951 and went into force in April 1952. Article 6 deals with the withdrawal of occupying forces.

Article 1

(a) The state of war between Japan and each of the Allied Powers is terminated as from the date on which the present Treaty comes into force between Japan and the Allied Power concerned as provided for in Article 23.

(b) The Allied Powers recognize the full sovereignty of the Japanese people over Japan and its territorial waters.

Article 2

(a) Japan, recognizing the independence of Korea, renounces all right, title and claim to Korea, including the islands of Quelpart, Port Hamilton and Dagelet.

(b) Japan renounces all right, title and claim to Formosa and the Pescadores.

(c) Japan renounces all right, title and claim to the Kurile Islands, and to that portion of Sakhalin and the islands adjacent to it over which Japan acquired sovereignty as a consequence of the Treaty of Portsmouth of September 5, 1905.

(d) Japan renounces all right, title and claim in connection with the League of Nations Mandate System, and accepts the action of the United Nations Security Council of April 2, 1947, extending the trusteeship system to the Pacific Islands formerly under mandate to Japan.

(e) Japan renounces all claim to any right or title to or interest in connection with any part of the Antarctic area, whether deriving from the activities of Japanese nationals or otherwise.

(f) Japan renounces all right, title and claim to the Spratly Islands and to the Paracel Islands.

Article 3

Japan will concur in any proposal of the United States to the United Nations to place under its trusteeship system, with the United States as the sole administering authority, Nansei Shoto south of 29° north latitude (including the Ryukyu Islands and the Daito Islands), Nanpo Shoto south of Sofu Gan (including the Bonin Islands, Rosario Island and the Volcano Islands) and Parece Vela and Marcus Island. Pending the making of such a proposal and affirmative action thereon, the United States will have the right to exercise all and any powers of administration, legislation and jurisdiction over the territory and inhabitants of these islands, including their territorial waters. [...]

Article 5

[...]

(c) The Allied Powers for their part recognize that Japan as a sovereign nation possesses the inherent right of individual or collective self-defense referred to in Article 51 of the Charter of the United Nations and that Japan may voluntarily enter into collective security arrangements.

Article 6

(a) All occupation forces of the Allied Powers shall be withdrawn from Japan as soon as possible after the coming into force of the present Treaty, and in any case not later than 90 days thereafter. Nothing in this provision shall, however, prevent the stationing or retention of foreign armed forces in Japanese territory under or in consequence of any bilateral or multilateral agreements which have been or may be made between one or more of the Allied Powers, on the one hand, and Japan on the other.

(b) The provisions of Article 9 of the Potsdam Proclamation of July 26, 1945, dealing with the return of Japanese military forces to their homes, to the extent not already completed, will be carried out. [...]

Article 9

Japan will enter promptly into negotiations with the Allied Powers so desiring for the conclusion of bilateral and multilateral agreements providing for the regulation or limitation of fishing and the conservation and development of fisheries on the high seas.

Article 10

Japan renounces all special rights and interests in China, including all benefits and privileges resulting from the provisions of the final Protocol signed at Peking on September 7, 1901, and all annexes, notes and documents supplementary thereto, and agrees to the abrogation in respect to Japan of the said protocol, annexes, notes and documents.

Article 11

Japan accepts the judgments of the International Military Tribunal for the Far East and of other Allied War Crimes Courts both within and outside Japan, and will carry out the sentences imposed thereby upon Japanese nationals imprisoned in Japan. The power to grant clemency, to reduce sentences and to parole with respect to such prisoners may not be exercised except on the decision of the Government or Governments which imposed the sentence in each instance, and on the recommendation of Japan. In the case of persons sentenced by the International Military Tribunal for the Far East, such power may not be exercised except on the decision of a majority of the Governments represented on the Tribunal, and on the recommendation of Japan. [...]

Japan's Prime Minister Shigeru Yoshida signs the Peace Treaty, San Francisco, 8 September 1951

Article 14

(a) It is recognized that Japan should pay reparations to the Allied Powers for the damage and suffering caused by it during the war. Nevertheless it is also recognized that the resources of Japan are not presently sufficient, if it is to maintain a viable economy, to make complete reparation for all such damage and suffering and at the same time meet its other obligations. [...]

Article 23

(a) The present Treaty shall be ratified by the States which sign it, including Japan, and will come into force for all the States which have then ratified it, when instruments of ratification have been deposited by Japan and by a majority, including the United States of America as the principal occupying Power, of the following States, namely Australia, Canada, Ceylon, France, Indonesia, the Kingdom of the Netherlands, New Zealand, Pakistan, the Republic of the Philippines, the United Kingdom of Great Britain and Northern Ireland, and the United States of America. The present Treaty shall come into force for each State which subsequently ratifies it, on the date of the deposit of its instrument of ratification.

(b) If the Treaty has not come into force within nine months after the date of the deposit of Japan's ratification, any State which has ratified it may bring the Treaty into force between itself and Japan by the notification to that effect given to the Governments of Japan and the United States of America not later than three years after the date of deposit of Japan's ratification. [...]

Article 26

Japan will be prepared to conclude with any State which signed or adhered to the United Nations Declaration of January 1, 1942, and which is at war with Japan, or with any State which previously formed a part of the territory of a State named in Article 23, which is not a signatory of the present Treaty, a bilateral Treaty of Peace on the same or substantially the same terms as are provided for in the present Treaty, but this obligation on the part of Japan will expire three years after the first coming into force of the present Treaty. Should Japan make a peace settlement or war claims settlement with any State granting that State greater advantages than those provided by the present Treaty, those same advantages shall be extended to the parties to the present Treaty.

Source: Ferrell, R.H. (ed.) (1975) *America in a Divided World 1945–1972*, Columbia SC, University of South Carolina Press.

Treaty of Mutual Co-operation and Security, 1960

Cold War logic was to deepen the Japanese–US relationship still further, with the perceived communist threat in South-East Asia and the growing strength of the Japanese economy, it was important for the USA to tie Japan into its alliance system. John Foster Dulles, who had drawn up the Peace Treaty, arranged the first post-war alliance at the same time. A new Treaty of alliance was agreed in 1960 and extracts are reproduced below. As well as general security, much of which becomes the responsibility of the USA, the Treaty also seeks collaboration in economic matters, an increasingly important factor in the relationship. For a more recent view of Japanese–US relations see the Security Alliance document in Section 1.2.

The United States of America and Japan,

Desiring to strengthen the bonds of peace and friendship traditionally existing between them, and to uphold the principles of democracy, individual liberty, and the rule of law,

Desiring further to encourage closer economic cooperation between them and to promote conditions of economic stability and well-being in their countries,

Reaffirming their faith in the purposes and principles of the Charter of the United Nations, and their desire to live in peace with all peoples and all governments,

Recognizing that they have the inherent right of individual or collective self-defense as affirmed in the Charter of the United Nations,

Considering that they have a common concern in the maintenance of international peace and security in the Far East,

Having resolved to conclude a treaty of mutual cooperation and security,

Therefore agree as follows:

Article I

The Parties undertake, as set forth in the Charter of the United Nations, to settle any international disputes in which they may be involved by peaceful means in such a manner that international peace and security and justice are not endangered and to refrain in their international relations from the threat or use of force against the territorial integrity or political independence of any state, or in any other manner inconsistent with the purposes of the United Nations.

The Parties will endeavor in concert with other peace-loving countries to strengthen the United Nations so that its mission of maintaining international peace and security may be discharged more effectively.

Article II

The Parties will contribute toward the further development of peaceful and friendly international relations by strengthening their free institutions, by bringing about a better understanding of the principles upon which these institutions are founded, and by promoting conditions of stability and well-being. They will seek to eliminate conflict in their international economic policies and will encourage economic collaboration between them.

Article III

The Parties, individually and in cooperation with each other, by means of continuous and effective self-help and mutual aid will maintain and develop, subject to their constitutional provisions, their capacities to resist armed attack.

Article IV

The Parties will consult together from time to time regarding the implementation of this Treaty, and, at the request of either Party, whenever the security of Japan or international peace and security in the Far East is threatened.

Article V

Each Party recognizes that an armed attack against either Party in the territories under the administration of Japan would be dangerous to its own peace and safety and declares that it would act to meet the common danger in accordance with its constitutional provisions and processes.

Any such armed attack and all measures taken as a result thereof shall be immediately reported to the Security Council of the United Nations in accordance with the provisions of Article 51 of the Charter. Such measures shall be terminated when the Security Council has taken the measures necessary to restore and maintain international peace and security.

Article VI

For the purpose of contributing to the security of Japan and the maintenance of international peace and security in the Far East, the United States of America is granted the use by its land, air and naval forces of facilities and areas in Japan. [...]

Source: Ferrell, R.H. (ed.) (1975) *America in a Divided World 1945–1972*, Columbia SC, University of South Carolina Press.

2.2   The Cold War

With the 1949 communist victory in the Chinese Civil War, the Cold War framework became as important to the Asia-Pacific as it already had to Europe. The USA built an alliance system in the region to counter what it saw as a threat. Japan has already been mentioned in Section 2.1 and the ANZUS and SEATO alliances are included in this group of documents. In addition there are three documents relating to a conflict which was far from cold – the Korean War.

The Korean War and China, early 1950s

The division of Korea was originally a result of the process of 'liberation' by the victors of the Second World War. Russia had liberated the northern part of the country from the Japanese and their unconditional surrender delivered the south into the hands of the USA. Governments established in the two parts of the country reflected this. In June of 1950, only ten months after the communist victory in China had forced their nationalist opponents to retreat to Taiwan (then known as Formosa), the communist government in North Korea tried to reunite the country by force. The USA was not slow to link the two. US President Truman made the following announcement two days after the attack. Three years later, with the Chinese army fighting alongside the North Koreans, he made another announcement on the matter and the emphasis was changed.

The attack upon Korea makes it plain beyond all doubt that communism has passed beyond the use of subversion to conquer independent nations and will now use armed invasion and war. It has defied the orders of the Security Council of the United Nations issued to preserve international peace and security. In these circumstances, the occupation of Formosa by Communist forces would be a direct threat to the security of the Pacific area and to United States forces performing their lawful and necessary functions in that area.

Accordingly, I have ordered the Seventh Fleet to prevent any attack on Formosa. As a corollary of this action, I am calling upon the Chinese Government on Formosa to cease all air and sea operations against the mainland. The Seventh Fleet will see that this is done. The determination of the future status of Formosa must await the restoration of security in the Pacific, a peace settlement with Japan, or consideration by the United Nations.

President Truman's announcement three years later.

In June 1950, following the aggressive attack on the Republic of Korea, the United States Seventh Fleet was instructed both to prevent attack upon Formosa and also to insure that Formosa should not be used as base of operations against the Chinese Communist mainland.

This has meant, in effect, that the United States Navy was required to serve as a defensive arm of Communist China. Regardless of the situation of 1950, since the date of that order the Chinese Communists have invaded Korea to attack the United Nations forces there. They have consistently rejected the proposals of the United Nations Command for an armistice. They recently joined with Soviet Russia in rejecting the armistice proposal sponsored in the United Nations by the Government of India. This proposal had been accepted by the United States and 53 other nations.

Consequently there is no longer any logic or sense in a condition that required the United States Navy to assume defensive responsibilities on behalf of the Chinese Communists. This permitted those Communists, with greater impunity, to kill our soldiers and those of our United Nations allies in Korea.

I am, therefore, issuing instructions that the Seventh Fleet no longer be employed to shield Communist China. Permit me to make this crystal clear: This order implies no aggressive intent on our part. But we certainly have no obligation to protect a nation fighting us in Korea.

Source: Ferrell, R.H. (ed.) (1975) *America in a Divided World 1945–1972*, Columbia SC, University of South Carolina Press.

UN Resolutions on Korea, 1950

The attack by the forces of North Korea began on Sunday, 25 June 1950. Later that day the UN Security Council passed the first of the following resolutions. Russia was boycotting the council because the nationalists from Taiwan still held the council seat for China, so there was no veto. The second resolution was passed on 27 June and UN forces, the vast majority of which were from the USA and under US command, started the counter attack soon after.

Security Council Resolution 82 (1950)

Recalling the finding of the General Assembly in its resolution of 21 October 1949 that the Government of the Republic of Korea is a lawfully established government having effective control and jurisdiction over that part of Korea where the United Nations Temporary Commission on Korea was able to observe and consult and in which the great majority of the people of Korea reside; and that this Government is based on elections which were a valid expression of the free will of the electorate of that part of Korea and which were observed by the Temporary Commission; and that this is the only such government in Korea;

345

Mindful of the concern expressed by the General Assembly in its resolutions of 12 December 1948 and 21 October 1949 of the consequences which might follow unless member states refrained from acts derogatory to the results sought to be achieved by the United Nations in bringing about the complete independence and unity of Korea; and the concern expressed that the situation described by the United Nations Commission on Korea in its report menaces the safety and well being of the Republic of Korea and of the people of Korea and might lead to open military conflict there;

Noting with grave concern the armed attack on the Republic of Korea by forces from North Korea,

Determines that this action constitutes a breach of the peace,

I. *Calls for* the immediate cessation of hostilities; and

Calls upon the authorities in North Korea to withdraw forthwith their armed forces to the 38th parallel;

II. *Requests* the United Nations Commission on Korea
(a) To communicate its fully considered recommendations on the situation with the least possible delay,
(b) To observe the withdrawal of North Korean forces to the 38th parallel, and
(c) To keep the Security Council informed on the execution of this resolution;

III. *Calls upon* all Members to render every assistance to the United Nations in the execution of this resolution and to refrain from giving assistance to the North Korean authorities.

Security Council Resolution 83 (1950)

Having determined that the armed attack upon the Republic of Korea by forces from North Korea constitutes a breach of the peace;

Having called for an immediate cessation of hostilities; and

Having called upon the authorities of North Korea to withdraw forthwith their armed forces to the 38th parallel; and

Having noted from the report of the United Nations Commission for Korea that the authorities in North Korea have neither ceased hostilities nor withdrawn their armed forces to the 38th parallel, and that urgent military measures are required to restore international peace and security; and

Having noted the appeal from the Republic of Korea to the United Nations for immediate and effective steps to secure peace and security,

Recommends that the Members of the United Nations furnish such assistance to the Republic of Korea as may be necessary to repel the armed attack and to restore international peace and security in the area.

Source: Ferrell, R.H. (ed.) (1975) *America in a Divided World 1945–1972*, Columbia SC, University of South Carolina Press.

ANZUS, 1951

In 1951 at the Japanese peace conference in San Francisco, another piece of the US alliance system for the region was put in place. The experience of the Second World War had demonstrated to both Australia and New Zealand that Britain was no longer in a position to guarantee their security while America was. The treaty – known as 'ANZUS' from the initials of the signatories – is reproduced here.

The Parties to This Treaty,

Reaffirming their faith in the purposes and principles of the Charter of the United Nations and their desire to live in peace with all peoples and all Governments, and desiring to strengthen the fabric of peace in the Pacific Area,

Noting that the United States already has arrangements pursuant to which its armed forces are stationed in the Philippines, and has armed forces and administrative responsibilities in the Ryukyus, and upon the coming into force of the Japanese Peace Treaty may also station armed forces in and about Japan to assist in the preservation of peace and security in the Japan Area,

Recognizing that Australia and New Zealand as members of the British Commonwealth of Nations have military obligations outside as well as within the Pacific Area,

Desiring to declare publicly and formally their sense of unity, so that no potential aggressor could be under the illusion that any of them stand alone in the Pacific Area, and

Desiring further to coordinate their efforts for collective defense for the preservation of peace and security pending the development of a more comprehensive system of regional security in the Pacific Area,

Therefore declare and agree as follows:

Article I

The Parties undertake, as set forth in the Charter of the United Nations, to settle any international disputes in which they may be involved by peaceful means in such a manner that international peace and security and justice are not endangered and to refrain in their international relations from the threat or use of force in any manner inconsistent with the purposes of the United Nations.

Article II

In order more effectively to achieve the objective of this Treaty the Parties separately and jointly by means of continuous and effective self-help and mutual aid will maintain and develop their individual and collective capacity to resist armed attack.

Article III

The Parties will consult together whenever in the opinion of any of them the territorial integrity, political independence or security of any of the Parties is threatened in the Pacific.

Article IV

Each Party recognizes that an armed attack in the Pacific Area on any of the Parties would be dangerous to its own peace and safety and declares that it would act to meet the common danger in accordance with its constitutional processes.

Any such armed attack and all measures taken as a result thereof shall be immediately reported to the Security Council of the United Nations. Such measures shall be terminated when the Security Council has taken the measures necessary to restore and maintain international peace and security.

Article V

For the purpose of Article IV, an armed attack on any of the Parties is deemed to include an armed attack on the metropolitan territory of any of the Parties, or on the island territories under its jurisdiction in the Pacific or on its armed forces, public vessels or aircraft in the Pacific.

Article VI

This Treaty does not affect and shall not be interpreted as affecting in any way the rights and obligations of the Parties under the Charter of the United Nations or the responsibility of the United Nations for the maintenance of international peace and security.

Article VII

The Parties hereby establish a Council, consisting of their Foreign Ministers or their Deputies, to consider matters concerning the implementation of this Treaty. The Council should be so organized as to be able to meet at any time.

Article VIII

Pending the development of a more comprehensive system of regional security in the Pacific Area and the development by the United Nations of more effective means to maintain international peace and security, the Council, established by Article VII, is authorized to maintain a consultative relationship with States, Regional Organizations, Associations of States or other authorities in the Pacific Area in a position to further the purposes of this Treaty and to contribute to the security of that Area.

Source: Ferrell, R.H. (ed.) (1975) *America in a Divided World 1945–1972*, Columbia SC, University of South Carolina Press.

Korean War Armistice, 1953

In September 1950 the communist forces had taken most of South Korea. By November of the same year the UN forces had recovered all of the South and penetrated deep into the North. They in turn were thrown back with the intervention of the Chinese, but only as far as the region of the 38th parallel. This mobile warfare was over by the spring of 1951 but the war dragged on until July 1953 when the following Armistice agreement was signed. The agreement and the Demilitarized Zone exists to this day. Though the Cold War has disappeared elsewhere, in the late 1990s it still exists between the two Koreas.

The undersigned, the Commander-in-Chief, United Nations Command, on the one hand, and the Supreme Commander of the Korean People's Army and the Commander of the Chinese People's Volunteers, on the other hand, in the interest of stopping the Korean conflict, with its great toll of suffering and bloodshed on both sides, and with the objective of establishing an armistice which will insure a complete cessation of hostilities and of all acts of armed force in Korea until a final peaceful settlement is achieved, do individually, collectively, and mutually agree to accept and to be bound and governed by the conditions and terms of armistice set forth in the following Articles and Paragraphs, which said conditions and terms are intended to be purely military in character and to pertain solely to the belligerents in Korea.

Article I. Military Demarcation Line and Demilitarized Zone

1   A Military Demarcation Line shall be fixed and both sides shall withdraw two (2) kilometers from this line so as to establish a Demilitarized Zone between the opposing forces. A Demilitarized Zone shall be established as a buffer zone to prevent the occurrence of incidents which might lead to a resumption of hostilities. [...]

6   Neither side shall execute any hostile act within, from, or against the Demilitarized Zone.

7   No person, military or civilian, shall be permitted to cross the Military Demarcation Line unless specifically authorized to do so by the Military Armistice Commission.

8   No person, military or civilian, in the Demilitarized Zone shall be permitted to enter the territory under the military control of either side unless specifically authorized to do so by the Commander into whose territory entry is sought.

9   No person, military or civilian, shall be permitted to enter the Demilitarized Zone except persons concerned with the conduct of civil administration and relief and persons specifically authorized to enter by the Military Armistice Commission. [...]

The chief UN Armistice delegate and the North Korean Communist delegate sign Armistice documents, Panmunjom, Korea, 29 July 1953

Article II. Concrete Arrangements for Cease-fire and Armistice

A. General

12 The Commanders of the opposing sides shall order and enforce a complete cessation of all hostilities in Korea by all armed forces under their control, including all units and personnel of the ground, naval, and air forces, effective twelve (12) hours after this Armistice Agreement is signed. [...]

Article III. Arrangements Relating to Prisoners of War

51 The release and repatriation of all prisoners of war held in the custody of each side at the time this Armistice Agreement becomes effective shall be effected in conformity with the following provisions agreed upon by both sides prior to the signing of this Armistice Agreement.

(a) Within sixty (60) days after this Armistice Agreement becomes effective, each side shall, without offering any hindrance, directly repatriate and hand over in groups all those prisoners of war in its custody who insist on repatriation to the side to which they belonged at the time of capture. Repatriation shall be accomplished in accordance with the related provisions of this Article. In order to expedite the repatriation process of such personnel, each side shall, prior to the signing of the Armistice Agreement, exchange the total numbers, by nationalities, of personnel to be directly repatriated.

Each group of prisoners of war delivered to the other side shall be accompanied by rosters, prepared by nationality, to include name, rank (if any) and internment or military serial number.

(b) Each side shall release all those remaining prisoners of war, who are not directly repatriated, from its military control and from its custody and hand them over to the Neutral Nations Repatriation Commission for disposition in accordance with the provisions in the Annex hereto: 'Terms of Reference for Neutral Nations Repatriation Commission'. [...]

Source: Ferrell, R.H. (ed.) (1975) *America in a Divided World 1945–1972*, Columbia SC, University of South Carolina Press.

SEATO, 1954

The South-East Asia Collective Defence Treaty was signed in September 1954 shortly after the Geneva Conference (see Section 2.3). It pulled together a number of post-Second World War US alliances in the region and was intended to be a counterpart to NATO in Western Europe, indeed the parallels that were seen with NATO account for the 'O' in SEATO. The parties to the Treaty were the Philippines, Thailand, Japan, Pakistan, Australia, New Zealand, Britain, France and the USA. Key articles and the protocol relating to Cambodia, Laos, and South Vietnam (the 'free' territory) are reproduced below. SEATO did not prove as successful as NATO. Tensions and conflicts of interest, not least over the conduct of the war in Vietnam, seriously undermined SEATO by the early 1970s.

(1) The South-East Asia Collective Defence Treaty

Preamble

The parties to this treaty: recognizing the sovereign equality of all the parties; retaining their faith in the purposes and principles set forth in the UN Charter, and their desire to live in peace with all peoples and governments; reaffirming that, in accordance with the UN Charter, they uphold the principle of equal rights and self-determination of peoples; declaring that they will earnestly strive by every peaceful means to promote self-government and to secure the independence of all countries whose peoples desire and are able to undertake its responsibilities; intending to declare publicly and formally their sense of unity so that any potential aggressor will appreciate that the parties stand together in the area; and desiring further to co-ordinate their efforts for collective defence for the preservation of peace and security, have agreed as follows:

Articles

Art. 1. The parties undertake, as set forth in the UN Charter, to settle any international disputes in which they may be involved by peaceful means in such a manner that international peace, security and justice are not endangered, and to refrain in their international relations from the threat or use of force in any manner inconsistent with the purpose of the United Nations.

Art. 2. In order more effectively to achieve the objectives of this treaty, the parties, separately and jointly, by means of continuous and effective self-help and mutual aid, will maintain and develop their individual and collective capacity to resist armed attack and to prevent and counter subversive acts from without against their territorial integrity and political stability.

Art. 3. The parties undertake to strengthen their free institutions and to co-operate with one another in the further development of economic measures, including technical assistance, designed both to promote economic progress and social well-being and to further the individual and collective efforts of governments towards these ends.

Art. 4.

(1) Each party recognizes that aggression by means of armed attack in the treaty area against any of the parties, or against any state or territory which the parties by unanimous agreement may hereafter designate, would endanger its own peace and safety, and agrees that it will, in that event, act to meet the common danger in accordance with its constitutional processes. Measures taken under this paragraph shall be immediately reported to the UN Security Council.

(2) If, in the opinion of any of the parties, the inviolability or integrity of the territory or the sovereignty or political independence of any party in the treaty area, or of any other state or territory to which the provisions of Paragraph (1) of this article from time to time apply, is threatened in any way other than by armed attack, or is affected or threatened by any fact or situation which might endanger the peace of the area, the parties shall consult immediately in order to agree on the measures which should be taken for the common defence.

(3) It is understood that no action on the territory of any state designated by unanimous agreement under Paragraph (1) of this article, or on any territory so designated, shall be taken except at the invitation or with the consent of the government concerned.

Art. 5. The parties hereby establish a Council, on which each of them shall be represented, to consider matters concerning the implementation of this treaty. The Council shall provide for consultation with regard to military and any other planning as the situation obtaining in the treaty area may from time to time require. The Council shall be organized so as to be able to meet at any time.

Art. 6. This treaty does not affect, and shall not be interpreted as affecting in any way, the rights and obligations of any of the parties under the UN Charter or the responsibility of the United Nations for the maintenance of international peace and security. Each party declares that none of the international engagements now in force between it and any other of the parties, or any third party, is in conflict with the provisions of this treaty, and undertakes not to enter into any international engagement in conflict with the treaty.

Art. 7. Any other state in a position to further the objectives of this treaty and to contribute to the security of the area may, by unanimous agreement of the parties, be invited to accede to this treaty. Any state so invited may become a party to the treaty by depositing its instrument of accession with the Philippine Government.

Art. 8. The treaty area is the general area of South-East Asia, including also the entire territories of the Asian parties, and the general area of the South-West Pacific, not including the Pacific area north of 21 degrees 30 minutes North latitude. The parties may, by unanimous agreement, amend this article to include the territory of any state acceding to this treaty in accordance with Article 7, or otherwise to change the treaty area.

Art. 9.

(1) This treaty shall be deposited in the archives of the Philippine Government. Copies thereof shall be transmitted by that Government to the other signatories.

(2) The treaty shall be ratified and its provisions carried out by the parties in accordance with their respective constitutional processes. Instruments of ratification shall be deposited as soon as possible with the Philippine Government, which shall notify all the other signatories of such deposit.

(3) The treaty shall enter into force between the states which have ratified it as soon as the instruments of ratification of a majority of signatories shall have been

deposited, and shall come into effect with respect to each other state on the date of deposit of its instrument of ratification.

Art. 10. The treaty shall remain in force indefinitely, but any party may cease to be a party one year after notice of denunciation has been given to the Philippine Government, which shall inform the governments of the other parties of each notice of denunciation.

Art. 11. The English text of this treaty is binding on the parties, but when the parties have agreed to the French text thereof and have so notified the Philippine Government, the French text shall be equally authentic and binding.

(2) US 'Understanding'

The delegation of the United States of America, in signing the present treaty, does so with the understanding that its recognition of the effect of aggression and armed attack, and its agreement with reference thereto in Article 4, Paragraph (1), apply only to communist aggression, but affirms that in the event of other aggression or armed attack it will consult under the provisions of Article 4.

(3) Protocol on Indo-China

Designations of states and territory as to which the provisions of Articles 3 and 4 are to be applicable – The parties to the South-East Asia Collective Defence Treaty unanimously designate for the purposes of Article 4 of the treaty the States of Cambodia and Laos and the free territory under the jurisdiction of the State of Vietnam.

The parties further agree that the above-mentioned states and territory shall be eligible in respect of the economic measures contemplated by Article 3. This protocol shall come into force simultaneously with the coming into force of the treaty.

(4) The Pacific Charter

The delegates, desiring to establish a firm basis for common action to maintain peace and security in South-East Asia and the South-West Pacific, and convinced that common action to this end, in order to be worthy and effective, must be inspired by the highest principles of justice and liberty, do hereby proclaim:

(1) In accordance with the provisions of the UN Charter, they uphold the principle of equal rights and self-determination of peoples, and will earnestly strive by every peaceful means to promote self-government and to secure the independence of all countries whose peoples desire it and are able to undertake its responsibilities.

(2) They are each prepared to continue taking effective practical measures to ensure conditions favourable to the orderly achievement of the foregoing purposes in accordance with their constitutional procedures.

(3) They will continue to co-operate in the economic, social and cultural fields in order to promote higher living standards, economic progress and social well-being in this region.

(4) As decreed in the South-East Asia Collective Defence Treaty, they are determined to prevent or counter by appropriate means any attempt in the treaty area to subvert freedom or to destroy their sovereignty or territorial integrity.

Source: Degenhardt, H.W. (ed.) (1986) *Treaties and Alliances of the World*, 4th edn, Harlow, Longman.

2.3   Conflict in Indo-China

In this context 'Indo-China' is used to mean the territory which was formally a French colonial possession and currently comprises of Vietnam, Cambodia and Laos (see Figure 5). This relatively small area has been the scene of intense conflict for much of the twentieth century. The earliest document reproduced below is from 1945. Before that the area had been subjected to a long period of colonial domination and Japanese occupation (see Historical Backgrounds of the countries concerned in Part 2).

Vietnam's Declaration of Independence, 1945

The following Declaration of Independence was made at the end of the Second World War by the Viet Minh, a movement with strong communist and nationalist elements. Led by Ho Chi Minh it had been fighting against the Japanese occupation and controlled much of the country by the end of the war. US advisers supported its struggle against the Japanese and the Viet Minh hoped to gain American support in its bid for independence, hence the American style to the Declaration. The major threat to independence was France attempting to re-establish its colonial rule. The USA was placed in a difficult position as France was an ally.

'We hold truths that all men are created equal, that they are endowed by their Creator with certain unalienable Rights, among these are Life, Liberty and the pursuit of Happiness.'

This immortal statement is extracted from the Declaration of Independence of the United States of America in 1776. Understood in the broader sense, this means: 'All peoples on the earth are born equal; every person has the right to live to be happy and free.'

The Declaration of Human and Civic Rights proclaimed by the French Revolution in 1791 likewise propounds: 'Every man is born equal and enjoys free and equal rights.'

These are undeniable truths.

Yet, during and throughout the last eighty years, the French imperialists, abusing the principles of 'Freedom, equality and fraternity', have violated the integrity of our ancestral land and oppressed our countrymen. Their deeds run counter to the ideals of humanity and justice.

In the political field, they have denied us every freedom. They have enforced upon us inhuman laws. They have set up three different political regimes in Northern, Central and Southern Viet Nam (Tonkin, Annam, and Cochinchina) in an attempt to disrupt our national, historical and ethical unity.

They have built more prisons than schools. They have callously ill-treated our fellow-compatriots. They have drowned our revolutions in blood.

They have sought to stifle public opinion and pursued a policy of obscurantism on the largest scale; they have forced upon us alcohol and opium in order to weaken our race.

In the economic field, they have shamelessly exploited our people, driven them into the worst misery and mercilessly plundered our country.

They have ruthlessly appropriated our rice fields, mines, forests and raw materials. They have arrogated to themselves the privilege of issuing banknotes, and monopolised all our external commerce. They have imposed hundreds of unjustifiable taxes, and reduced our countrymen, especially the peasants and petty tradesmen, to extreme poverty.

They have prevented the development of native capital enterprises; they have exploited our workers in the most barbarous manner.

In the autumn of 1940, when the Japanese fascists, in order to fight the Allies, invaded Indochina and set up new bases of war, the French imperialists surrendered on bended knees and handed over our country to the invaders.

Subsequently, under the joint French and Japanese yoke, our people were literally bled white. The consequences were dire in the extreme. From Quang Tri up to the North, two millions of our countrymen died from starvation during the first months of this year.

On March 9th, 1945, the Japanese disarmed the French troops. Again the French either fled or surrendered unconditionally. Thus, in no way have they proved capable of 'protecting' us; on the contrary, within five years they have twice sold our country to the Japanese.

Before March 9th, many a time did the Viet Minh League invite the French to join in the fight against the Japanese. Instead of accepting this offer, the French, on the contrary, let loose a wild reign of terror with rigour worse than ever before against Viet Minh's partisans. They even slaughtered a great number of our '*condamnés politiques*' imprisoned at Yen Bay and Cao Bang.

Despite all that, our countrymen went on maintaining, vis-à-vis the French, a humane and even indulgent attitude. After the events of March 9th, the Viet Minh League helped many French to cross the borders, rescued others from Japanese prisons and, in general, protected the lives and properties of all the French in their territory.

In fact, since the autumn of 1940, our country ceased to be a French colony and became a Japanese possession.

After the Japanese surrender, our people, as a whole, rose up and proclaimed their sovereignty and founded the Democratic Republic of Viet Nam.

The truth is that we have wrung back our independence from Japanese hands and not from the French.

The French fled, the Japanese surrendered. Emperor Bao Dai abdicated, our people smashed the yoke which pressed hard upon us for nearly one hundred years, and finally made our Viet Nam an independent country. Our people at the same time overthrew the monarchical regime established tens of centuries ago, and founded the Republic.

For these reasons, we the members of the Provisional Government representing the entire people of Viet Nam, declare that we shall from now on have no more connections with imperialist France; we consider null and void all the treaties France has signed concerning Viet Nam, and we hereby cancel all the privileges that the French arrogated to themselves on our territory.

The Vietnamese people, animated by the same common resolve, are determined to fight to the death against all attempts at aggression by the French imperialists.

We are convinced that the Allies who have recognized the principles of equality of peoples at the Conferences of Teheran and San Francisco cannot but recognize the independence of Viet Nam.

A people which has so stubbornly opposed the French domination for more than 80 years, a people who, during these last years, so doggedly ranged itself and fought on the Allied side against Fascism, such a people has the right to be free, such a people must be independent.

For these reasons, we, the members of the Provisional Government of the Democratic Republic of Viet Nam, solemnly declare to the world:

'Viet Nam has the right to be free and independent and, in fact, has become free and independent. The people of Viet Nam decide to mobilise all their spiritual and material forces and to sacrifice their lives and property in order to safeguard their right of Liberty and Independence.'

Source: Griffith, R. (ed.) (1992) *Major Problems in American History Since 1945*, Lexington, Mass., D.C. Heath.

The Geneva Conference, 1954

The French attempt to re-establish their colonial rule resulted in the first phase of the Vietnam War (1946–54). France embarked on a long and difficult campaign against the Viet Minh. America became more involved when France joined them in the NATO alliance in 1949. The following year the USA recognized the newly proclaimed – but French dominated – governments of Vietnam, Cambodia, and Laos. However, the military situation did not go well for the French and, in 1954, a large French force was surrounded at Dien Bien Phu. The Geneva Conference, called mainly to discuss the situation in Korea, turned to Vietnam as Dien Bien Phu fell to the Viet Minh. The Final Declaration of the Conference is reproduced below. France had been defeated, the newly independent states of Cambodia and Laos remained and struggled to pursue neutral and non-communist policies in the face of strong opposition movements, and Vietnam was split with the Viet Minh holding the North. The USA had been present at the conference, but made its own declaration which is also reproduced below.

FINAL DECLARATION, dated the 21st July, 1954, of the Geneva Conference on the problem of restoring peace in Indo-China, in which the representatives of Cambodia, the Democratic Republic of Viet-Nam, France, Laos, the People's Republic of China, the State of Viet-Nam, the Union of Soviet Socialist Republics, the United Kingdom, and the United States of America took part.

1. The Conference takes note of the agreements ending hostilities in Cambodia, Laos and Viet-Nam and organizing international control and the supervision of the execution of the provisions of these agreements.

2. The Conference expresses satisfaction at the ending of hostilities in Cambodia, Laos and Viet-Nam; the Conference expresses its conviction that the execution of the provisions set out in the present declaration and in the agreements on the cessation of hostilities will permit Cambodia, Laos and Viet-Nam henceforth to play their part, in full independence and sovereignty, in the peaceful community of nations.

3. The Conference takes note of the declarations made by the Governments of Cambodia and of Laos of their intention to adopt measures permitting citizens to take their place in the national community, in particular by participating in the next general elections, which, in conformity with the constitution of each of these countries, shall take place in the course of the year 1955, by secret ballot and in conditions of respect for fundamental freedoms.

4. The Conference takes note of the clauses in the agreement on the cessation of hostilities in Viet-Nam prohibiting the introduction into Viet-Nam of foreign troops and military personnel as well as of all kinds of arms and munitions. The Conference also takes note of the declarations made by the Governments of Cambodia and Laos of their resolution not to request foreign aid, whether in war material, in personnel or in instructors except for the purpose of the effective defence of their territory and, in the case of Laos, to the extent defined by the agreements on the cessation of hostilities in Laos.

5. The Conference takes note of the clauses in the agreement on the cessation of hostilities in Viet-Nam to the effect that no military base under the control of a foreign State may be established in the regrouping zones of the two parties, the latter having the obligation to see that the zones allotted to them shall not constitute part of any military alliance and shall not be utilized for the resumption of hostilities or in the service of an aggressive policy. The Conference also takes note of the declarations of the Governments of Cambodia and Laos to the effect that they will not join in any agreement with other States if this agreement includes the obligation to participate in a military alliance not in conformity with the principles of the Charter of the United Nations or, in the case of Laos, with the principles of the agreement on the cessation of hostilities in Laos or, so long as their security is not threatened, the obligation to establish bases on Cambodian or Laotian territory for the military forces of foreign Powers.

Conference room of the Palais des Nations, Geneva, 21 July 1954. Seated lower left side are delegations from the USA and Cambodia; lower right, Vietnam, France, and Laos; upper left, the USSR and the UK; and upper right, China and the Viet Minh

6. The Conference recognizes that the essential purpose of the agreement relating to Viet-Nam is to settle military questions with a view to ending hostilities and that the military demarcation line is provisional and should not in any way be interpreted as constituting a political or territorial boundary. The Conference expresses its conviction that the execution of the provisions set out in the present declaration and in the agreement on the cessation of hostilities creates the necessary basis for the achievement in the near future of a political settlement in Viet-Nam.

7. The Conference declares that, so far as Viet-Nam is concerned, the settlement of political problems, effected on the basis of respect for the principles of independence, unity and territorial integrity, shall permit the Viet-Namese people to enjoy the fundamental freedoms, guaranteed by democratic institutions established as a result of free general elections by secret ballot. In order to ensure that sufficient progress in the restoration of peace has been made, and that all the necessary conditions obtain for free expression of the national will, general elections shall be held in July 1956, under the supervision of an international commission composed of representatives of the Member States of the International Supervisory Commission, referred to in the agreement on the cessation of hostilities. Consultations will be held on this subject between the competent representative authorities of the two zones from 20 July 1955 onwards.

8. The provisions of the agreements on the cessation of hostilities intended to ensure the protection of individuals and of property must be most strictly applied and must, in particular, allow everyone in Viet-Nam to decide freely in which zone he wishes to live.

9. The competent representative authorities of the Northern and Southern zones of Viet-Nam, as well as the authorities of Laos and Cambodia, must not permit any individual or collective reprisals against persons who have collaborated in any way with one of the parties during the war, or against members of such persons' families.

10. The Conference takes note of the declaration of the Government of the French Republic to the effect that it is ready to withdraw its troops from the territory of Cambodia, Laos and Viet-Nam, at the request of the governments concerned and within periods which shall be fixed by agreement between the parties except in the cases where, by agreement between the two parties, a certain number of French troops shall remain at specified points and for a specified time.

11. The Conference takes note of the declaration of the French Government to the effect that for the settlement of all the problems connected with the re-establishment and consolidation of peace in Cambodia, Laos and Viet-Nam, the French Government will proceed from the principle of respect for the independence and sovereignty, unity and territorial integrity of Cambodia, Laos and Viet-Nam.

12. In their relations with Cambodia, Laos and Viet-Nam, each member of the Geneva Conference undertakes to respect the sovereignty, the independence, the unity and the territorial integrity of the above mentioned states, and to refrain from any interference in their internal affairs.

13. The members of the Conference agree to consult one another on any question which may be referred to them by the International Supervisory Commission, in order to study such measures as may prove necessary to ensure that

the agreements on the cessation of hostilities in Cambodia, Laos and Viet-Nam are respected.

US Declaration

As I [US Under Secretary of State Walter Bedell Smith] stated on July 18, my Government is not prepared to join in a declaration by the Conference such as is submitted. However, the United States makes this unilateral declaration of its position in these matters:

Declaration

The Government of the United States being resolved to devote its efforts to the strengthening of peace in accordance with the principles and purposes of the United Nations takes note of the agreements concluded at Geneva on July 20 and 21, 1954 between (a) the Franco-Laotian Command and the Command of the People's Army of Viet-Nam; (b) the Royal Khmer Army Command and the Command of the People's Army of Viet-Nam; (c) Franco-Vietnamese Command and the Command of the People's Army of Viet-Nam and of paragraphs 1 to 12 inclusive of the declaration presented to the Geneva Conference on July 21, 1954 declares with regard to the aforesaid agreements and paragraphs that (i) it will refrain from the threat or the use of force to disturb them, in accordance with Article 2 (4) of the Charter of the United Nations dealing with the obligation of members to refrain in their international relations from the threat or use of force; and (ii) it would view any renewal of the aggression in violation of the aforesaid agreements with grave concern and as seriously threatening international peace and security.

In connection with the statement in the declaration concerning free elections in Viet-Nam my Government wishes to make clear its position which it has expressed in a declaration made in Washington on June 29, 1954, as follows:

> In the case of nations now divided against their will, we shall continue to seek to achieve unity through free elections supervised by the United Nations to insure that they are conducted fairly.

With respect to the statement made by the representative of the State of Viet-Nam, the United States reiterates its traditional position that peoples are entitled to determine their own future and that it will not join in an arrangement which would hinder this. Nothing in its declaration just made is intended to or does indicate any departure from this traditional position.

We share the hope that the agreements will permit Cambodia, Laos and Viet-Nam to play their part, in full independence and sovereignty, in the peaceful community of nations, and will enable the peoples of that area to determine their own future.

Source: Ferrell, R.H. (ed.) (1975) *America in a Divided World 1945–1972*, Columbia SC, University of South Carolina Press.

The Gulf of Tonkin Resolution, 1964

The all-Vietnam elections proposed at Geneva for 1956 never happened and fighting continued. America provided an increasing amount of aid for anti-communist forces in the area, especially the government of South Vietnam in its struggle against the communist Vietcong guerrillas who were supported by the North. The Gulf of Tonkin Resolution, passed by the US Congress in August 1964, followed an incident involving American destroyers off the coast of North Vietnam. The incident was used as a pretext to escalate the war by direct US naval and air attacks against the North. On the ground US military support finally rose to over half a million troops. The resolution, reproduced below, was passed, after which US President Johnson made a statement, also included below.

Whereas naval units of the Communist regime in Vietnam, in violation of the principles of the Charter of the United Nations and of international law, have deliberately and repeatedly attacked United States naval vessels lawfully present in international waters, and have thereby created a serious threat to international peace; and

Whereas these attacks are part of a deliberate and systematic campaign of aggression that the Communist regime in North Vietnam has been waging against its neighbors and the nations joined with them in the collective defense of their freedom; and

Whereas the United States is assisting the peoples of southeast Asia to protect their freedom and has no territorial, military or political ambitions in that area, but desires only that these peoples should be left in peace to work out their own destinies in their own way: Now, therefore, be it

Resolved by the Senate and House of Representatives of the United States of America in Congress assembled, That the Congress approves and supports the determination of the President, as Commander in Chief, to take all necessary measures to repel any armed attack against the forces of the United States and to prevent further aggression.

Sec. 2.   The United States regards as vital to its national interest and to world peace the maintenance of international peace and security in southeast Asia. Consonant with the Constitution of the United States and the Charter of the United Nations and in accordance with its obligations under the Southeast Asia Collective Defense Treaty, the United States is, therefore, prepared, as the President determines, to take all necessary steps, including the use of armed force, to assist any member of protocol state of the Southeast Asia Collective Defense Treaty requesting assistance in defense of its freedom.

Sec. 3.   This resolution shall expire when the President shall determine that the peace and security of the area is reasonably assured by international conditions created by action of the United Nations or otherwise, except that it may be terminated earlier by concurrent resolution of the Congress.

On signing the resolution President Johnson made the following statement.

My fellow Americans: One week ago, half a world away, our Nation was faced by the challenge of deliberate and unprovoked acts of aggression in southeast Asia.

The cause of peace clearly required that we respond with a prompt and unmistakable reply.

As Commander in Chief the responsibility was mine – and mine alone. I gave the orders for that reply, and it has been given.

But, as President, there rested upon me still another responsibility – the responsibility of submitting our course to the representatives of the people, for them to verify it or veto it.

I directed that to be done last Tuesday.

Within 24 hours the resolution before me now had been placed before each House of Congress. In each House the resolution was promptly examined in committee and reported for action.

In each House there followed free and serious debate.

In each House the resolution was passed on Friday last – with a total of 502 votes in support and 2 opposed.

Thus, today, our course is clearly known in every land.

There can be no mistake – no miscalculation – of where America stands or what this generation of Americans stand for.

The unanimity of the Congress reflects the unanimity of the country.

The resolution is short. It is straightforward. I hope that it will be read around the world.

The position of the United States is stated plainly. To any armed attack upon our forces, we shall reply.

To any in southeast Asia who ask our help in defending their freedom, we shall give it.

In that region there is nothing we covet, nothing we seek – no territory, no military position, no political ambition.

Our one desire – our one determination – is that the people of southeast Asia be left in peace to work out their own destinies in their own way.

This resolution stands squarely within the four corners of the Constitution of the United States. It is clearly consistent with the principles and purposes of the Charter of the United Nations.

This is another new page in the outstanding record of accomplishments the 88th Congress is writing.

Americans of all parties and philosophies can be justly proud – and justly grateful. Proud that democracy has once again demonstrated its capacity to act swiftly and decisively against aggressors. Grateful that there is in our National Government understanding, accord, and unity between the executive and legislative branches – without regard to partisanship.

This is a great strength that we must always preserve.

This resolution confirms and reinforces powers of the Presidency. I pledge to all Americans to use those powers with all the wisdom and judgment God grants to me.

It is everlastingly right that we should be resolute in reply to aggression and steadfast in support of our friends.

But it is everlastingly necessary that our actions should be careful and should be measured.

We are the most powerful of all nations – we must strive also to be the most responsible of nations.

So, in this spirit, and with this pledge, I now sign this resolution.

Source: Ferrell, R.H. (ed.) (1975) *America in a Divided World 1945–1972*, Columbia SC, University of South Carolina Press.

Cease-fire in Vietnam, 1973

The escalation in fighting by the USA did not result in any real military progress, and with growing domestic opposition to the war America began withdrawing its troops in 1969. Negotiations between North Vietnam and the USA began, though bitter fighting continued. A cease-fire was eventually agreed in Paris in January 1973. The parties involved were the USA, North and South Vietnam and the Vietcong. The key articles are reproduced below. The USA withdrew from the war, whilst the South fought on until 1975 when it fell to the communists. Cambodia and Laos also fell to their communist opponents.

Article 1

The United States and all other countries respect the independence, sovereignty, unity, and territorial integrity of Vietnam as recognized by the 1954 Geneva Agreements on Vietnam.

Article 2

A cease-fire shall be observed throughout South Vietnam as of 2400 hours G.M.T., on January 27, 1973.

At the same hour, the United States will stop all its military activities against the territory of the Democratic Republic of Vietnam by ground, air and naval forces, wherever they may be based, and end the mining of the territorial waters, ports, harbors, and waterways of the Democratic Republic of Vietnam. The United States will remove, permanently deactivate or destroy all the mines in the territorial waters, ports, harbors, and waterways of North Vietnam as soon as this Agreement goes into effect.

The complete cessation of hostilities mentioned in this Article shall be durable and without limit of time.

Article 3

The parties undertake to maintain the cease-fire and to ensure a lasting and stable peace.

As soon as the cease-fire goes into effect:

(a) The United States forces and those of the other foreign countries allied with the United States and the Republic of Vietnam shall remain in place pending the implementation of the plan of troop withdrawal. The Four-Party Joint Military Commission described in Article 16 shall determine the modalities.

(b) The armed forces of the two South Vietnamese parties shall remain in place. The Two-Party Joint Military Commission described in Article 17 shall determine the areas controlled by each party and the modalities of stationing.

(c) The regular forces of all services and arms and the irregular forces of the parties in South Vietnam shall stop all offensive activities against each other and shall strictly abide by the following stipulations:
   – All acts of force on the ground, in the air, and on the sea shall be prohibited;
   – All hostile acts, terrorism and reprisals by both sides will be banned.

Article 4

The United States will not continue its military involvement or intervene in the internal affairs of South Vietnam.

Article 5

Within sixty days of the signing of this Agreement, there will be a total withdrawal from South Vietnam of troops, military advisers, and military personnel, including technical military personnel and military personnel associated with the pacification program, armaments, munitions, and war material of the United States and those of the other foreign countries mentioned in Article 3 (a). Advisers from the above-mentioned countries to all paramilitary organizations and the police force will also be withdrawn within the same period of time.

Article 6

The dismantlement of all military bases in South Vietnam of the United States and of the other foreign countries mentioned in Article 3 (a) shall be completed within sixty days of the signing of this Agreement.

Article 7

From the enforcement of the cease-fire to the formation of the government provided for in Articles 9 (b) and 14 of this Agreement, the two South Vietnamese parties shall not accept the introduction of troops, military advisers, and military personnel including technical military personnel, armaments, munitions, and war material into South Vietnam.

The two South Vietnamese parties shall be permitted to make periodic replacement of armaments, munitions and war material which have been destroyed, damaged, worn out or used up after the cease-fire, on the basis of piece-for-piece, of the same characteristics and properties, under the supervision of the Joint Military Commission of the two South Vietnamese parties and of the International Commission of Control and Supervision.

Article 8

(a) The return of captured military personnel and foreign civilians of the parties shall be carried out simultaneously with and completed not later than the same day as the troop withdrawal mentioned in Article 5. The parties shall exchange complete lists of the above-mentioned captured military personnel and foreign civilians on the day of the signing of this Agreement.

(b) The parties shall help each other to get information about those military personnel and foreign civilians of the parties missing in action, to determine the location and take care of the graves of the dead so as to facilitate the exhumation and repatriation of the remains, and to take any such other measures as may be required to get information about those still considered missing in action.

(c) The question of the return of Vietnamese civilian personnel captured and detained in South Vietnam will be resolved by the two South Vietnamese parties on the basis of the principles of Article 21 (b) of the Agreement on the Cessation of Hostilities in Vietnam of July 20, 1954. The two South Vietnamese parties will do so in a spirit of national reconciliation and concord, with a view to ending hatred and enmity, in order to ease suffering and to reunite families. The two South Vietnamese parties will do their utmost to resolve this question within ninety days after the cease-fire comes into effect.

Article 9

The Government of the United States of America and the Government of the Democratic Republic of Vietnam undertake to respect the following principles for the exercise of the South Vietnamese people's right to self-determination:

(a) The South Vietnamese people's right to self-determination is sacred, inalienable, and shall be respected by all countries.

(b) The South Vietnamese people shall decide themselves the political future of South Vietnam through genuinely free and democratic general elections under international supervision.

(c) Foreign countries shall not impose any political tendency or personality on the South Vietnamese people. [...]

Article 14

South Vietnam will pursue a foreign policy of peace and independence. It will be prepared to establish relations with all countries irrespective of their political and social systems on the basis of mutual respect for independence and sovereignty and accept economic and technical aid from any country with no political conditions attached. The acceptance of military aid by South Vietnam in the future shall come under the authority of the government set up after the general elections in South Vietnam provided for in Article 9 (b). [...]

Article 18

(a) After the signing of this Agreement, an International Commission of Control and Supervision shall be established immediately. [...]

(d) The International Commission of Control and Supervision shall be composed of representatives of four countries: Canada, Hungary, Indonesia and Poland. The chairmanship of this Commission will rotate among the members for specific periods to be determined by the Commission. [...]

Article 19

The parties agree on the convening of an International Conference within thirty days of the signing of this Agreement to acknowledge the signed agreements; to guarantee the ending of the war, the maintenance of peace in Vietnam, the respect of the Vietnamese people's fundamental national rights, and the South Vietnamese people's right to self-determination; and to contribute to and guarantee peace in Indochina.

The United States and the Democratic Republic of Vietnam, on behalf of the parties participating in the Paris Conference on Vietnam, will propose to the following parties that they participate in this International Conference: the People's Republic of China, the Republic of France, the Union of Soviet Socialist Republics, the United Kingdom, the four countries of the International Commission of Control and Supervision, and the Secretary General of the United Nations, together with the parties participating in the Paris Conference on Vietnam. [...]

Article 21

The United States anticipates that this Agreement will usher in an era of reconciliation with the Democratic Republic of Vietnam as with all the peoples of Indochina. In pursuance of its traditional policy, the United States will contribute to healing the wounds of war and to postwar reconstruction of the Democratic Republic of Vietnam and throughout Indochina.

Source: Ferrell, R.H. (ed.) (1975) *America in a Divided World 1945–1972*, Columbia SC, University of South Carolina Press.

Cambodia and the UN, 1990–93

The end of the Vietnam War was not the end of conflict in the area. The genocidal excesses of the new Khmer Rouge regime in Cambodia were ended by a Vietnamese invasion in 1978 to oust their former allies (see Cambodia's Historical Background in Part 2). Guerrilla warfare continued. The eventual withdrawal of the Vietnamese army in 1988 left the country torn by factions including the Khmer Rouge. However, the end of the Cold War provided a much better context for a peaceful solution. Co-operation in the UN and pressure from countries in the region helped produce a viable peace process. The two UN Security Council Resolutions reproduced below were part of that process. The first, from September 1990, details some of the interim arrangements including UN-conducted elections which were to lead to a final settlement. The second, from August 1993, concludes the process, recognizes the creation of a new government and provides a timetable for withdrawal of the UN forces which had supported the process.

Security Council Resolution 668 (1990)

The Security Council,

Convinced of the need to find an early, just and lasting peaceful solution of the Cambodia conflict,

Noting that the Paris International Conference on Cambodia (PICC), which met from 30 July to 30 August 1989, made progress in elaborating a wide variety of elements necessary for reaching a comprehensive political settlement,

Taking note with appreciation of the continuing efforts of China, France, the Union of Soviet Socialist Republics, the United Kingdom of Great Britain and Northern Ireland and the United States of America which have resulted in the Framework for a comprehensive political settlement of the Cambodia conflict as contained in Security Council document S/21689,

Taking note with appreciation also the efforts of the ASEAN countries and other countries involved in promoting the search for a comprehensive political settlement,

Taking note further with appreciation the efforts of Indonesia and France as Co-Chairmen of the PICC and of all participants in this Conference to facilitate the restoration of peace to Cambodia,

Noting that these efforts are aimed at enabling the Cambodian people to exercise their inalienable right to self-determination through free and fair elections organized and conducted by the United Nations in a neutral political environment with full respect for the national sovereignty of Cambodia,

1 Endorses the Framework for a comprehensive political settlement of the Cambodia conflict (S/21689) and encourages the continuing efforts of China, France, the Union of Soviet Socialist Republics, the United Kingdom of Great Britain and Northern Ireland and

the United States of America in this regard;

2 Welcomes the acceptance of this framework in its entirety by all the Cambodian parties, as the basis for settling the Cambodia conflict, at the informal meeting of the Cambodian parties in Jakarta on 10 September 1990 and their commitment to it;

3 Further welcomes the commitment of the Cambodian parties, in full co-operation with all other participants in the PICC, to elaborating this Framework into a comprehensive political settlement through the processes of the PICC;

4 Welcomes, in particular, the agreement reached by all Cambodian parties in Jakarta (S/21732) forming a Supreme National Council as the unique legitimate body and source of authority in which, throughout the transitional period, the independence, national sovereignty and unity of Cambodia is embodied;

5 Urges the members of the Supreme National Council, in full accord with the framework document (S/21689), to elect the Chairman of the Council as soon as possible, so as to implement the agreement referred to in paragraph 4;

6 Notes that the Supreme National Council will therefore represent Cambodia externally and it is to designate its representatives to occupy the seat of Cambodia at the United Nations, in the United Nations specialized agencies, and in other international institutions and international conferences;

7 Urges all parties to the conflict to exercise maximum self-restraint so as to create the peaceful climate required to facilitate the achievement and the implementation of a comprehensive political settlement;

8 Calls upon the Co-Chairmen of the PICC to intensify their consultations with a view to reconvening the Conference, whose task will be to elaborate and adopt the comprehensive political settlement and draw up a detailed plan of implementation in accord with this framework;

9 Urges the Supreme National Council, all Cambodians as well as all parties to the conflict to co-operate fully in this process;

10 Encourages the Secretary-General to continue, within the context of preparations for reconvening the PICC and on the basis of the present resolution, preparatory studies to assess the resource implications, timing and other considerations relevant to the United Nations role;

11 Calls upon all States to support the achievement of a comprehensive political settlement as outlined in this framework.

Security Council Resolution 860 (1993)

The Security Council,

Reaffirming its resolutions 668 (1990) of 20 September 1990, 745 (1992) of 28 February 1992, 840 (1993) of 15 June 1993 and other relevant resolutions,

Taking note of the reports of the Secretary-General dated 16 July 1993 (S/26090) and 26 August 1993 (S/26360),

Paying tribute to the continuing role of His Royal Highness Prince Norodom Sihanouk in achieving peace, stability and genuine national reconciliation for all Cambodia,

Recalling that, according to the Paris Agreements, the transitional period shall terminate when the Constituent Assembly elected through free and fair elections, organized and certified by the United Nations, has approved the Constitution and transformed itself into legislative assembly, and thereafter a new Government has been created,

Also taking note of the expressed wish of the Cambodia interim joint administration to maintain the mandate of the United Nations Transition Authority in Cambodia (UNTAC) until the establishment of a new Government in Cambodia as conveyed by the Secretariat,

1 Welcomes the reports of the Secretary-General, dated 16 July 1993 (S/26090) and 26 August 1993 (S/26360), and approves the UNTAC withdrawal plan contained in S/26090;

2 Fully supports the Constituent Assembly in its work of drawing up and approving a constitution, and stresses the importance of completing this work in accordance with the Paris Agreements;

3 Confirms that UNTAC's functions under the Paris Agreements shall end upon the creation in September of a new government of Cambodia consistent with those Agreements;

4 Decides that, in order to ensure a safe and an orderly withdrawal of the military component of UNTAC, the period of such withdrawal shall end on 15 November 1993;

5 Decides to remain actively seized of the matter.

Source: UN Net Site, New York, UN Department of Public Information. Available from: http://www.un.org

2.4 Revolution and change in China

Proclamation of the Central People's Government of the People's Republic of China, 1949

The following proclamation made by Mao Zedong in Beijing on 1 October 1949 marked the beginning of a new era for China. The fragile anti-Japanese alliance between the nationalist Kuomintang government under Chiang Kai-shek and the communists soon broke down after the surrender of Japan. The civil war resumed in 1946 and after a bitter struggle the remnants of the defeated Kuomintang government and army fled to the island province of Taiwan. The proclamation was read by Mao from the Tiananmen Gate of the Forbidden City. Note Deng Xiaoping in the list of council members.

The people throughout China have been plunged into bitter suffering and tribulations since the Chiang Kai-shek Kuomintang reactionary government betrayed the fatherland, colluded with imperialists, and launched the counter-revolutionary war. Fortunately, our People's Liberation Army, backed by the whole nation, has been fighting heroically and selflessly to defend the territorial sovereignty of our homeland, to protect the people's lives and property, to relieve the people of their sufferings, and to struggle for their rights, and it eventually wiped out the reactionary troops and overthrew the reactionary rule of the Nationalist government. Now the People's War of Liberation has been basically won, and the majority of the people in the country have been liberated. On this foundation, the first session of the Chinese People's Political Consultative Conference, composed of delegates of all the democratic parties and people's organizations of China, the People's Liberation Army, the various regions and nationalities of the country, and the overseas Chinese and other patriotic elements, has been convened. Representing the will of the whole nation, [this session of the conference] has enacted the organic law of the Central People's Government of the People's Republic of China, elected Mao Zedong as chairman of the Central People's Government; and Zhu De, Liu Shaoqi, Song Qingling, Li Jishen, Zhang Lan, and Gao Gang as vice-chairmen; and Chen Yi, He Long, Li Lisan, Lin Boqu, Ye Jianying, He Xiangning, Lin Biao, Peng Dehuai, Liu Bocheng, Wu Yuzhang, Xu Xiangqian, Peng Zhen, Bo Yibo, Nie Rongzhen, Zhou Enlai, Dong Biwu, Seypidin, Rao Shushi, Tan Kah-kee, Luo Ronghuan, Deng Zihui, Ulanhu, Xu Deli, Cai Chang, Liu Geping, Ma Yinchu, Chen Yun, Kang Sheng, Lin Feng, Ma Xulun, Guo Moruo, Zhang Yunyi, Deng Xiaoping, Gao Chongmin, Shen Junru, Shen Yanbing, Chen Shutong, Szeto Mei-tong, Li Xijiu, Huang Yanpei, Cai Ting-kai, Xi Zhongxun, Peng Zemin, Zhang Zhizhong, Fu Zuoyi, Li Zhuchen, Li Zhangda, Zhang Bojun, Cheng Qian, Zhang Xiruo, Chen Mingshu, Tan Ping-shan,

Zhang Nanxian, Liu Yazi, Zhang Dongsun, and Long Yun as council members to form the Central People's Government Council, proclaimed the founding of the People's Republic of China and decided on Beijing as the capital of the People's Republic of China. The Central People's Government Council of the People's Republic of China took office today in the capital and unanimously made the following decisions: to proclaim the establishment of the Central People's Government of the People's Republic of China; to adopt the Common Program of the Chinese People's Political Consultative Conference as the policy of the government; to elect Lin Boqu from among the council members as secretary general of the Central People's Government Council; to appoint Zhou Enlai as premier of the Government Administration Council of the Central People's Government and concurrently minister of Foreign Affairs, Mao Zedong as chairman of the People's Revolutionary Military Commission of the Central People's Government, Zhu De as commander-in-chief of the People's Liberation Army, Shen Junru as president of the Supreme People's Court of the Central People's Government and Luo Rong-huan as procurator general of the Supreme People's Procuratorate

Chairman Mao Zedong proclaims the founding of the People's Republic of China, 1 October 1949

of the Central People's Government, and to charge them with the task of the speedy formation of the various organs of the government to carry out the work of the government. At the same time, the Central People's Government Council decided to declare to the governments of all other countries that this government is the sole legal government representing all the people of the People's Republic of China. This government is willing to establish diplomatic relations with any foreign government that is willing to observe the principles of equality, mutual benefit, and mutual respect of territorial integrity and sovereignty.

Mao Zedong
Chairman
The Central People's Government
The People's Republic of China

Source: Kau, M.Y.M. and Leung, J.K. (eds) (1986) *The Writings of Mao Zedong 1949–1976, Vol.1*, Armonk NY, M.E. Sharpe, pp.10–11.

The Great Leap Forward, 1958

The Great Leap Forward was a bold, but largely disastrous, attempt to modernize Chinese agriculture and industry between 1958 and 1960. The rapid and radical changes included some ill-conceived plans, such as the million backyard furnaces. The disruption caused by the Great Leap Forward was exacerbated by a number of natural disasters resulting in wide-spread famine. Reproduced below is an extract from the report given by leading Party figure Liu Shaoqi/Shao-ch'i on 5 May 1958 to the Second Session of the Eighth Party Congress, which endorsed the Great Leap. Subsequently, Liu replaced Mao Zedong/Tse-tung as President of the People's Republic from 1959 to 1966 and was to play an important role in stabilizing the country.

[...]

The broad masses of the working people have realized more fully that individual and immediate interests depend on and are bound up with collective and long-term interests and that the happiness of the individual lies in the realization of the lofty socialist ideals of all the people. That is why they have displayed a heroic Communist spirit of self-sacrifice in the work. Their slogan is: 'Hard work for a few years, happiness for a thousand'. This mighty torrent of Communist ideas has swept away many stumbling blocks – individualism, departmentalism, localism and nationalism. In city and countryside, people vie with each other in joining in all kinds of voluntary labour. In building irrigation works, the peasants in many places have thrown aside the age-old narrow-minded idea of only looking after their native places. In the nation-wide emulation drive, many advanced units and individuals have enthusiastically passed on their technical experience, inventions and creations to the backward units and individuals so that

the latter can catch up with them. Many enterprises, organizations, schools, army units and individuals have taken the initiative in co-ordinating their activities with those of others so as to promote the progress of all concerned. All this is, as Lenin said, 'The actual beginning of Communism', 'The beginning of a change which is of world historic significance'.

All the factors mentioned above have combined to form the great revolutionary drive for socialist construction. Comrade Mao Tse-tung has put forward the slogans 'Catch up with and outstrip Britain in 15 years', 'Build socialism by exerting our utmost efforts and pressing ahead consistently to achieve greater, faster, better and more economical results', 'To be promoters of progress not of retrogress', 'Build our country and run our households industriously and with frugality' and 'Battle hard for three years to bring about a basic change in the features of most areas' – all these calls have quickly gripped the imagination of the huge army of hundreds of millions of working people and have been transformed into an immense material force. There has emerged in physical and mental labour a high degree of socialist initiative, a surging, militant spirit, a keenness in learning and studying that will not rest short of its aims, a fearless creative spirit. An emulation drive in which the backward learn from and catch up and compete with the advanced has been launched between individuals, production teams, enterprises, cooperatives, counties and cities. Set norms are being constantly surpassed and new techniques invented. Time after time the masses outstrip the targets set by enterprises and administrative organs.

The spring of 1958 witnessed the beginning of a leap forward on every front in our socialist construction. Industry, agriculture and all other fields of activity are registering greater and more rapid growth.

To begin with industry. The total value of industrial output for the first four months of this year was 26 per cent higher than in the same period last year; the April increase was 42 per cent. According to estimates made on the basis of the present situation, China's steel output this year will be over 7.1 million tons, coal output will reach 180 million tons; 60,000 machine tools will be produced and irrigation machinery with more than 3.5 million horsepower; the output of chemical fertilizers will amount to 1.3 million tons. In view of this, the rate of growth of China's industrial production this year will be much higher than that set in the original plan and will surpass that of any year in the First Five-Year period.

The revolutionary energy of the workers has also found expression in the trail manufacture of new products, in technical renovation, in the improvement of quality and lowering of production costs. In the first four months of the year, many kinds of small-sized tractors were successfully produced on a trial basis. Several of them can be used equally well for the cultivation of paddy fields, dry fields, mountain areas and terraced fields or for transport, for operating irrigation machinery or generating power for the processing of agricultural products and other purposes. In the first four months of the year, Shanghai successfully produced more than 1,000 kinds of new products on a trial basis. By adopting the new technique of three-tapping troughs, the Taiyuan Steel Plant has raised productivity by nearly 50 per cent. As labour productivity is being raised and raw materials saved, production costs in industry can be reduced by about 10 per cent compared with last year. This will save the state about 1,400 million yuan.

An upsurge is shaping up in capital construction in industry this year. Nearly 1,000 above-norm projects will be under construction this year; this is more than the total number of such projects under construction in the First Five-Year Plan period. In addition, construction work has already started on thousands of medium and small-sized coal mines, power stations, oil refineries, iron and steel plants, non-ferrous mines, chemical fertilizer plants, cement plants, engineering works and agricultural and animal products processing plants.

The output of local industry this year will show a considerable increase as a result of wide-spread industrial capital construction undertaken by local authorities. Take iron and steel for example. The amount of iron to be produced by local enterprises this year will reach 1,730,000 tons (as against the 593,000 tons produced last year) and that of steel will reach 1,410,000 tons (as against the 790,000 tons of last year). The rapid growth of the local industries is one of the outstanding features of this year's industrial upswing.

As a result of the intensive drive against waste and conservatism, the costs of capital construction in industry this year will be greatly reduced. In many cases, the same amount of funds needed to build one factory in the past now suffices to build two. For example, in terms of the planned costs, where it would previously have cost about 1,000 million yuan to build an iron and steel plant with an annual capacity of one million tons, such a plant can now be built for little more than 400 million yuan; for 60 million yuan we can now build a nitrogenous fertilizer plant with an annual capacity of 50,000 tons of synthetic ammonium, in the past such a plant would have cost 130 million yuan. The time needed for building a capital construction project, too, is much shorter now than in the past.

The upsurge in agriculture last winter and this spring gave a vigorous push to the new industrial upsurge of this year. The rapid development of industry in turn has prompted an even swifter growth of agriculture.

In agriculture, the most striking leap took place in the campaign of the cooperative farmers to build irrigation works. From last October to April this year, the irrigated acreage throughout the country increased by 350 million *mow*, that is, 80 million *mow* more than the total added during the eight years since liberation and 110 million *mow* more than the total acreage brought under irrigation in the thousands of years before liberation. At the same time, more than 200 million *mow* of low-lying and easily waterlogged farmland was transformed and irrigation facilities were improved on another 140 million *mow* of land. The loss of water and soil was brought under control over an area of 160,000 square kilometres. This gives proof of the power to conquer nature which the masses of the people have demonstrated in the field of agriculture following the great socialist revolution on the economic, political and ideological fronts and the release on a tremendous scale of our social productive forces.

In the same period, the peasants all over the country accumulated about 310,000 million *tan* of manure (including all kinds of manure, mostly clay and mud manures). This averages over 18,000 catties to a *mow*, which, calculated according to the amount of plant nutrients, is more than three times the amount accumulated in 1956, one of the best of recent years. In many places, work was undertaken on a large scale to improve the soil and level the ground.

In the first four months of this year, over 290 million *mow* of land was afforested in the country, one and a half times the total acreage afforested in the past eight years. Big advance was also registered in the development of mountain areas, land reclamation, utilization of wild plants, etc.

The labour organization of our agricultural cooperatives has made further improvement. In most cooperatives, attendance by able-bodied members (men and women) in collective work was over 90 per cent last winter and this spring.

A mass movement to improve farm tools is now spreading throughout the country. Tens of millions of peasants have invented all sorts of improved and semi-mechanized farm implements, water lifts, means of transportation and equipment for processing farm produce. Thus the centuries-old tradition of primitive manual labour has begun to change and labour productivity has increased enormously. At the same time, the peasants in various places have made energetic efforts to improve systems and methods of cultivation in accordance with local conditions. This is the budding of a great technical revolution in the rural areas. Work is also going ahead by leaps and bounds in transport and communications, commerce and other branches of the national economy. New records and inventions are being made continuously.

Rapid developments are also taking place in the fields of culture, education and public health. Energetic efforts are being made in many villages throughout the country to eliminate illiteracy and establish large numbers of primary and secondary schools financed by the people. Cultural and artistic activities among the masses are advancing quickly. The public health campaign centred on the elimination of the four pests, has already spread to every urban and rural district and achieved notable results.

The fact is that the growth of the social productive forces calls for a socialist revolution and the spiritual emancipation of the people; the victory of this revolution and emancipation in turn induces a forward leap in the social productive forces; and this in turn impels a progressive change in the socialist relations of production and an advance in man's ideology. In their ceaseless struggle to transform nature, the people are continuously transforming society and themselves.

[...]

Source: Hinton, H.C. (ed.) (1980) *The People's Republic of China 1949–1979: a Documentary Survey, Vol.2*, Wilmington, Del., Scholarly Resources.

The Cultural Revolution, 1967

Launched in 1966 the Cultural Revolution aimed to remove perceived bourgeois influences from the Communist Party and Chinese society. It also involved a power struggle between Mao and his opponents in the Party. The following document is an extract from *The Dictatorship of the Proletariat and the Great Proletarian Cultural Revolution,* a 1967 publication by three Chinese radicals (Wang Li, Chia Yi-hsueh and Li Hsin) giving an explanation of the purpose of the Revolution. The Cultural Revolution resulted in another period of immense upheaval for China. People were encouraged to denounce those with bourgeois tendencies, while student Red Guards enforced the new conformity with terrorizing zeal. By 1968 Mao had won his struggle, Liu Shaoqi was expelled from the Party and imprisoned, many others including Deng Xiaoping were removed from office, and order was restored, though the Cultural Revolution was to continue until Mao's death in 1976.

We are now in a new era of the world revolution, one in which imperialism is heading for total collapse and socialism is advancing towards worldwide victory. Sharp class struggles in diverse forms are going on like raging fires in the international arena and within various countries, in both the capitalist and socialist worlds. The struggles between different classes and political forces are extremely complicated. In the final analysis, the central issue of these struggles is that of state power.

Lenin said that the basic question in any revolution is that of state power. He also said that those who recognize only class struggle are not yet Marxists. Only he is a Marxist who extends the recognition of the class struggle to the recognition of the dictatorship of the proletariat.

The dictatorship of the proletariat is the quintessence of Marxism-Leninism, the fundamental issue of the proletarian revolution, and the 'magic weapon' which guarantees that the proletariat will defeat the bourgeoisie and be victorious in its socialist cause. For the proletariat, to have state power means to have everything; to lose state power is to lose all. The touchstone for distinguishing Marxist-Leninists from revisionists of all stripes has always been whether one upholds the dictatorship of the proletariat throughout the historical period of transition from capitalism to communism.

The new historical experience of the dictatorship of the proletariat tells us that the question of state power is fundamental for the revolution in capitalist countries where the proletariat has not yet seized political power; it also remains the fundamental issue for the revolution in socialist countries where the proletariat is already in power. Before coming to power, the proletariat and other revolutionary people should adhere to the principle of making revolution by violence, smashing the old state machine, and seizing political power by armed force. Once in power, the proletariat should carry the socialist revolution through to the end, prevent the revisionists from usurping the leadership of the Party and the state, prevent the restoration of capitalism, and defend and consolidate the dictatorship of the proletariat.

It was generally thought that with the proletariat's seizure of power, the question of political power was solved and that the main task for the revolution would be to transform the old economy, organize a new one, and engage in construction and education. It was not realized that state power might be recaptured by the bourgeoisie, that the proletariat might lose political power, and that the dictatorship of the proletariat might be transformed back into the dictatorship of the bourgeoisie.

The betrayal of the Tito clique caused Yugoslavia long ago to degenerate from a socialist state into a capitalist one. Later, in the birthplace of Leninism, the Khrushchev revisionist clique usurped the leadership of the Party and the state, causing the Soviet Union, after several decades of socialist construction, to take the road of capitalist restoration.

It is imperative for Marxist-Leninists to pay the greatest attention to these harsh facts and seriously ponder over them.

Having constantly studied and summed up the experience and lessons of the socialist revolution and the dictatorship of the proletariat in China and in other parts of the world, Comrade Mao Tse-tung has put forward the theses on contradictions, classes and class struggle in socialist society, solved a series of new important problems, and developed the Marxist-Leninist theory on the dictatorship of the proletariat to a new height.

With genius, Comrade Mao Tse-tung has creatively applied Marxist-Leninist materialist dialectics to socialist society and made a scientific analysis of the nature of contradictions in socialist society and the law of their development.

Comrade Mao Tse-tung has pointed out that contradictions exist in socialist society, contradictions between ourselves and the enemy and those among the people. These two types of contradictions are different in nature, and in given conditions each can be transformed into the other. Only by recognizing their existence and correctly understanding and handling them is it possible continuously to consolidate the dictatorship of the proletariat and push forward the cause of socialist revolution and construction.

Comrade Mao Tse-tung has pointed out that socialist society is still built on the basis of class antagonism and that throughout the very long historical period of socialism there is struggle between the proletariat and the bourgeoisie, and between the socialist and capitalist roads. The struggle between the two classes and between the two roads is the principal contradiction in socialist society and the motive force for its advance.

Since this struggle exists in a socialist country, there is a danger – if we are not vigilant and fail to adopt the necessary measures – of the dictatorship of the proletariat degenerating into the dictatorship of the bourgeoisie and of the restoration of capitalism.

The Soviet revisionist leading clique deliberately ignores the fact that contradictions exist in socialist society, and categorically denies the existence of classes and class struggle in the Soviet Union. Khrushchev does and so do his disciples Brezhnev, Kosygin, and Shelepin.

Such nonsense as their 'socialist-society-without-contradictions' is aimed at protecting the interests of the revisionist leading clique and the privileged strata of the Soviet Union, and at maintaining their reactionary rule over the Soviet people. Their denial of the existence of classes and class struggle in the Soviet Union is precisely a weapon they wield in the class struggle. As a matter of fact, they plant themselves firmly on the side of the bourgeoisie, suppressing the proletariat, and carrying on ruthless class struggle against the Soviet people. They use the allegation that there are neither classes nor class struggle as grounds for 'the state of the whole people' and 'the Party of the entire people', in order to deceive the Soviet people and the people of the world and cover up their traitorous deeds in abolishing the dictatorship of the proletariat. They have completely betrayed the great Lenin and Stalin. What they fear most is for the Soviet people to rise in rebellion against revisionism and capitalist restoration, engage in class struggle against them, overthrow their rule, and re-establish the dictatorship of the proletariat.

Comrade Mao Tse-tung often quotes the saying – 'The tree may prefer calm, but the wind will not subside' – to tell people that class struggle is an objective fact, independent of people's subjective will. It cannot be avoided, much as you want to. If you don't struggle with the class enemy, he will struggle with you; if you don't eliminate him, he will eliminate you. Marxist-Leninists cannot in any way deny or avoid class struggle. Instead, they should lead the proletariat, guiding them properly in the given circumstances according to the laws of class struggle, in order to carry the socialist revolution through to the end on the political, economic, ideological, and cultural fronts, smash the bourgeois plot for restoration, and consolidate the dictatorship of the proletariat.

Our country is at present engaged in a Great Proletarian Cultural Revolution without parallel in history. This is to avoid capitalist restoration and to consolidate the dictatorship of the proletariat and the socialist system in our country still further.

This Great Proletarian Cultural Revolution was initiated and is being led by Comrade Mao Tse-tung personally. The proletarian revolutionary line represented by Comrade Mao Tse-tung has won great victories over the bourgeois reactionary line after sharp struggle.

The struggle between the two lines within the [Chinese Communist] Party in the Great Proletarian Cultural Revolution is a reflection in the Party of class struggle in society. The social basis of the bourgeois reactionary line is chiefly in the bourgeoisie. This reactionary line is in essence defending the bourgeoisie. It has a certain following within the Party, that is, those whose bourgeois world outlook either remains unchanged or has not yet been sufficiently transformed. The handful of people within the Party who are in authority and are taking the capitalist road and who are opposed to the Party, to socialism, and to Mao Tse-tung's thought, and the ghosts and monsters in society take this line as their protective talisman and seize the opportunity to stir up trouble.

The present Great Proletarian Cultural Revolution is the most profound class struggle history has ever witnessed. The struggle between the two lines, as it is reflected in the Party, is likewise the most profound struggle in the history of our Party. Through all channels, the very few people who stubbornly cling to the bourgeois reactionary line are shifting the struggle between the two lines within the Party on to society to be interwoven with class struggle there.

Every forward step taken in the Great Cultural Revolution is the result of sharp struggle and of efforts to overcome various forms of resistance in society as well as in the Party. In the last few months, the revolutionary masses have been penetratingly exposing and criticizing the bourgeois reactionary line. This is a great debate of the largest scale on the question of the two lines. As a result of this great debate, the broad masses and revolutionary cadres have raised their class consciousness and ideological level, and are still more conscientiously supporting and implementing the proletarian revolutionary line represented by Chairman Mao. Despite the fact that a handful of people who stubbornly cling to the bourgeois reactionary line constantly change their tactics and resort to new tricks to counter Chairman Mao's correct line, the bourgeois reactionary line constantly meets with bankruptcy and failure as the irresistible mass movement of the Great Proletarian Cultural Revolution forges ahead.

Within half a year, the turbulent stream of the revolutionary mass movement has been washing away the rubbish left by the old society, resulting in earth-shaking changes in China. This is a truly great revolution under the conditions of the dictatorship of the proletariat. It is bringing about great changes in class relations and touches people to their very soul. Countless new things have appeared on the horizon, which have puzzled some people. Nevertheless, if one takes the struggle between the two classes and the two roads in socialist society as the key link, one can see clearly the great significance and chief characteristics of the Great Proletarian Cultural Revolution in our country.

[...]

Source: Hinton, H.C. (ed.) (1980) *The People's Republic of China 1949–1979: a Documentary Survey, Vol.2*, Wilmington, Del., Scholarly Resources.

Nixon's visit to China, 1972

After years of hostility and conflict the relationship between the United States of America and the People's Republic of China underwent a dramatic change for the better with the 1972 visit to the PRC of US President Richard Nixon. The groundwork had been done in the previous year, and included the admission of the PRC into the UN and membership of the UN Security Council in place of the Taiwan-based Republic of China. The document below is the Joint Communiqué issued at the end of the visit. Diplomatic relations between the two countries were finally normalized in 1979.

President Richard Nixon of the United States of America visited the People's Republic of China at the invitation of Premier Chou En-lai [Zhou Enlai] of the People's Republic of China from February 21 to February 28, 1972. Accompanying the President were Mrs Nixon, US Secretary of State William Rogers, Assistant to the President Dr Henry Kissinger, and other American officials.

President Nixon met with Chairman Mao Tse-tung of the Communist Party of China on February 21. The two leaders had a serious and frank exchange of views on Sino-US relations and world affairs.

During the visit, extensive, earnest and frank discussions were held between President Nixon and Premier Chou En-lai on the normalization of relations between the United States of America and the People's Republic of China, as well as on other matters of interest to both sides. In addition, Secretary of State William Rogers and Foreign Minister Chi Peng-fei held talks in the same spirit.

President Nixon and his party visited Peking and viewed cultural, industrial and agricultural sites, and they also toured Hangchow and Shanghai where, continuing discussions with Chinese leaders, they viewed similar places of interest.

The leaders of the People's Republic of China and the United States of America found it beneficial to have this opportunity, after so many years without contact, to present candidly to one another their views on a variety of issues. They reviewed the international situation in which important changes and great upheavals are taking place and expounded their respective positions and attitudes.

The US side stated: Peace in Asia and peace in the world requires efforts both to reduce immediate tensions and to eliminate the basic causes of conflict. The United States will work for a just and secure peace: just, because it fulfils the aspirations of peoples and nations for freedom and progress; secure, because it removes the danger of foreign aggression. The United States supports individual freedom and social progress for all the peoples of the world, free of outside pressure or intervention. The United States believes that the effort to reduce tensions is served by improving communication between countries that have different ideologies so as to lessen the risks of confrontation through accident, miscalculation or misunderstanding. Countries should treat each other with mutual respect and be willing to compete peacefully, letting performance be the ultimate judge. No country should claim infallibility and each country should be prepared to re-examine its own attitudes for the common good. The United States stressed that the peoples of Indochina should be allowed to determine their destiny without outside intervention; its constant primary objective has been a negotiated solution; the eight-point proposal put forward by the Republic of Vietnam and the United States on January 27, 1972, represents a basis for the attainment of that objective; in the absence of a negotiated settlement the United States envisages the ultimate withdrawal of all US forces from the region consistent with the aim of self-determination for each country of Indochina. The United States will maintain its close ties with and support for the Republic of Korea; the United States will support efforts of the Republic of Korea to seek a relaxation of tension and increased communication in the Korean peninsula. The United States places the highest value on its friendly relations with Japan; it will continue to develop the existing close bonds. Consistent with the United Nations Security Council Resolution of December 21, 1971, the United States favors the continuation of the ceasefire between India and Pakistan and the withdrawal of all military forces to within their own territories and to their own sides of the ceasefire line in Jammu and Kashmir; the United States supports the right of the peoples of South Asia to shape their own future in peace, free of military threat, and without having the area become the subject of great power rivalry.

The Chinese side stated: Wherever there is oppression, there is resistance. Countries want independence, nations want liberation and the people want revolution – this has become the irresistible trend of history. All nations, big or small, should be equal; big nations should not bully the small and strong nations should not bully the weak. China will never be a superpower and it opposes hegemony and power politics of any kind. The Chinese side stated that it firmly supports the struggles of all the oppressed people and nations for freedom and liberation and that the people of all countries have the right to choose their social systems according to their own wishes and the right to safeguard the independence, sovereignty and territorial integrity of their own countries and oppose foreign aggression, interference, control and subversion. All foreign troops should be withdrawn to their own countries.

From left: Zhou Enlai and Richard Nixon, 27 February 1972

The Chinese side expressed its firm support to the peoples of Vietnam, Laos and Cambodia in their efforts for the attainment of their goal and its firm support to the seven-point proposal of the Provisional Revolutionary Government of the Republic of South Vietnam and the elaboration of February this year on the two key problems in the proposal, and to the Joint Declaration of the Summit Conference of the Indochinese Peoples. It firmly supports the eight-point program for the peaceful unification of Korea put forward by the Government of the Democratic People's Republic of Korea on April 12, 1971, and the stand for the abolition of the 'UN Commission for the Unification and Rehabilitation of Korea.' It firmly opposes the revival and outward expansion of Japanese militarism and firmly supports the Japanese people's desire to build an independent, democratic, peaceful and neutral Japan. It firmly maintains that India and Pakistan should, in accordance with the United Nations resolutions on the India–Pakistan question, immediately withdraw all their forces to their respective territories and to their own sides of the ceasefire line in Jammu and Kashmir and firmly supports the Pakistan Government and people in their struggle to preserve their independence and sovereignty and the people of Jammu and Kashmir in their struggle for the right of self-determination.

There are essential differences between China and the United States in their social systems and foreign policies. However, the two sides agreed that countries, regardless of their social systems, should conduct their relations on the principles of respect for the sovereignty and territorial integrity of all states, non-aggression against other states, non-interference in the internal affairs of other states, equality and mutual benefit, and peaceful coexistence. International disputes should be settled on this basis, without resorting to the use or threat of force. The United States and the People's Republic of China are prepared to apply these principles to their mutual relations.

With these principles of international relations in mind the two sides stated that:

– progress toward the normalization of relations between China and the United States is in the interests of all countries;
– both wish to reduce the danger of international military conflict;
– neither should seek hegemony in the Asia-Pacific region and each is opposed to efforts by any other country or group of countries to establish such hegemony; and
– neither is prepared to negotiate on behalf of any third party or to enter into agreements or understandings with the other directed at other states.

Both sides are of the view that it would be against the interests of the peoples of the world for any major country to collude with another against other countries, or for major countries to divide up the world into spheres of interest.

The two sides reviewed the long-standing serious disputes between China and the United States. The Chinese side reaffirmed its position: The Taiwan question is the crucial question obstructing the normalization of relations between China and the United States; the Government of the People's Republic of China is the sole legal government of China; Taiwan is a province of China which has long been returned to the motherland; the liberation of Taiwan is China's internal affair in which no country has the right to interfere; and all US forces and military installations must be withdrawn from Taiwan. The Chinese Government firmly opposes any activities which aim at the creation of 'one China, one Taiwan', 'one China, two governments', 'two Chinas', and 'independent Taiwan' or advocate that 'the status of Taiwan remains to be determined'.

The US side declared: The United States acknowledges that all Chinese on either side of the Taiwan Strait maintain there is but one China and that Taiwan is a part of China. The United States Government does not challenge that position. It reaffirms its interest in a peaceful settlement of the Taiwan question by the Chinese themselves. With this prospect in mind, it affirms the ultimate objective of the withdrawal of all US forces and military installations from Taiwan. In the meantime, it will progressively reduce its forces and military installations on Taiwan as the tension in the area diminishes.

The two sides agreed that it is desirable to broaden the understanding between the two peoples. To this end, they discussed specific areas in such fields as science, technology, culture, sports and journalism, in which people-to-people contacts and exchanges would be mutually beneficial. Each side undertakes to facilitate the further development of such contacts and exchanges.

Both sides view bilateral trade as another area from which mutual benefit can be derived, and agreed that economic relations based on equality and mutual benefit are in the interest of the peoples of the two countries. They agree to facilitate the progressive development of trade between their two countries.

The two sides agreed that they will stay in contact through various channels, including the sending of a senior US representative to Peking from time to time for concrete consultations to further the normalization of relations between the two countries and continue to exchange views on issues of common interest.

The two sides expressed the hope that the gains achieved during this visit would open up new prospects for the relations between the two countries. They believe that the normalization of relations between the two countries is not only in the interest of the Chinese and American peoples but also contributes to the relaxation of tension in Asia and the world.

President Nixon, Mrs Nixon and the American party expressed their appreciation for the gracious hospitality shown them by the Government and people of the People's Republic of China.

Source: Ferrell, R.H. (ed.) (1975) *America in a Divided World 1945–1972*, Columbia SC, University of South Carolina Press.

Joint Declaration on Hong Kong, 1984

The island of Hong Kong was occupied by the British in 1841 with the addition of other areas including Kowloon in 1860. In 1896 China was forced to relinquish the 'New Territories' which surrounded Hong Kong on a 99-year lease. With the expiration of this lease fast approaching the following Joint Declaration was agreed in 1984 and came into force the following year. It was agreed that the whole of Hong Kong would be handed over to the PRC at midnight on 30 June 1997. However, it was also agreed that Hong Kong would become a Special Administrative Region retaining its own capitalist economic and social system for at least 50 years. Tension in the transition period was considerably heightened by the events of 1989 in Tiananmen Square, Beijing (see next document below).

Joint declaration of the government of the United Kingdom of Great Britain and Northern Ireland and the government of the People's Republic of China on the question of Hong Kong

The Government of the United Kingdom of Great Britain and Northern Ireland and the Government of the People's Republic of China have reviewed with satisfaction the friendly relations existing between the two Governments and peoples in recent years and agreed that a proper negotiated settlement of the question of Hong Kong, which is left over from the past, is conducive to the maintenance of the prosperity and stability of Hong Kong and to the further strengthening and development of the relations between the two countries on a new basis. To this end, they have, after talks between the delegations of the two Governments, agreed to declare as follows:

1. The Government of the People's Republic of China declares that to recover the Hong Kong area (including Hong Kong Island, Kowloon and the New Territories, hereinafter referred to as Hong Kong) is the common aspiration of the entire Chinese people, and that it has decided to resume the exercise of sovereignty over Hong Kong with effect from 1 July 1997.

2. The Government of the United Kingdom declares that it will restore Hong Kong to the People's Republic of China with effect from 1 July 1997.

3. The Government of the People's Republic of China declares that the basic policies of the People's Republic of China regarding Hong Kong are as follows:

(1) Upholding national unity and territorial integrity and taking account of the history of Hong Kong and its realities, the People's Republic of China has decided

to establish, in accordance with the provisions of Article 31 of the Constitution of the People's Republic of China, a Hong Kong Special Administrative Region upon resuming the exercise of sovereignty over Hong Kong.

(2) The Hong Kong Special Administrative Region will be directly under the authority of the Central People's Government of the People's Republic of China. The Hong Kong Special Administrative Region will enjoy a high degree of autonomy, except in foreign and defence affairs which are the responsibilities of the Central People's Government.

(3) The Hong Kong Special Administrative Region will be vested with executive, legislative and independent judicial power, including that of final adjudication. The laws currently in force in Hong Kong will remain basically unchanged.

(4) The Government of the Hong Kong Special Administrative Region will be composed of local inhabitants. The chief executive will be appointed by the Central People's Government on the basis of the results of elections or consultations to be held locally. Principal officials will be nominated by the chief executive of the Hong Kong Special Administrative Region for appointment by the Central People's Government. Chinese and foreign nationals previously working in the public and police services in the government departments of Hong Kong may remain in employment. British and other foreign nationals may also be employed to serve as advisers or hold certain public posts in government departments of the Hong Kong Special Administrative Region.

(5) The current social and economic systems in Hong Kong will remain unchanged, and so will the life-style. Rights and freedoms, including those of the person, of speech, of the press, of assembly, of association, of travel, of movement, of correspondence, of strike, of choice of occupation, of academic research and of religious belief will be ensured by law in the Hong Kong Special Administrative Region. Private property, ownership of enterprises, legitimate right of inheritance and foreign investment will be protected by law.

(6) The Hong Kong Special Administrative Region will retain the status of a free port and a separate customs territory.

(7) The Hong Kong Special Administrative Region will retain the status of an international financial centre, and its markets for foreign exchange, gold, securities and futures will continue. There will be free flow of capital. The Hong Kong dollar will continue to circulate and remain freely convertible.

(8) The Hong Kong Special Administrative Region will have independent finances. The Central People's Government will not levy taxes on the Hong Kong Special Administrative Region.

(9) The Hong Kong Special Administrative Region may establish mutually beneficial economic relations with the United Kingdom and other countries, whose economic interests in Hong Kong will be given due regard.

(10) Using the name of 'Hong Kong, China', the Hong Kong Special Administrative Region may on its own maintain and develop economic and cultural relations and conclude relevant agreements with states, regions and relevant international organizations. The Government of the Hong Kong Special Administrative Region may on its own issue travel documents for entry into and exit from Hong Kong.

(11) The maintenance of public order in the Hong Kong Special Administrative Region will be the responsibility of the Government of the Hong Kong Special Administrative Region.

(12) The above-stated basic policies of the People's Republic of China regarding Hong Kong and the elaboration of them in Annex I to this Joint Declaration will be stipulated, in a Basic Law of the Hong Kong Special Administrative Region of the People's Republic of China, by the National People's Congress of the People's Republic of China, and they will remain unchanged for 50 years.

4. The Government of the United Kingdom and the Government of the People's Republic of China declare that, during the transitional period between the date of the entry into force of this Joint Declaration and 30 June 1997, the Government of the United Kingdom will be responsible for the administration of Hong Kong with the object of maintaining and preserving its economic prosperity and social stability; and that the Government of the People's Republic of China will give its co-operation in this connection.

5. The Government of the United Kingdom and the Government of the People's Republic of China declare that, in order to ensure a smooth transfer of government in 1997, and with a view to the effective implementation of this Joint Declaration, a Sino-British Joint Liaison Group will be set up when this Joint Declaration enters into force; and that it will be established and will function in accordance with the provisions of Annex II to this Joint Declaration.

6. The Government of the United Kingdom and the Government of the People's Republic of China declare that land leases in Hong Kong and other related matters will be dealt with in accordance with the provisions of Annex III to this Joint Declaration.

7. The Government of the United Kingdom and the Government of the People's Republic of China agree to implement the preceding declarations and the Annexes to this Joint Declaration.

8. This Joint Declaration is subject to ratification and shall enter into force on the date of the exchange of instruments of ratification, which shall take place in Beijing before 30

June 1985. This Joint Declaration and its Annexes shall be equally binding.

Done in duplicate at Beijing on 19 December 1984 in the English and Chinese languages, both texts being equally authentic.

Source: Hong Kong Government Information Centre Net Site, Hong Kong, Information Services Department. Available from: http://www.info.gov.hk

Demonstrations in Tiananmen Square, 1989

The following two documents provide sharply contrasting views of the events which culminated in the crushing of the student demonstrations in Beijing's Tiananmen Square on 4 June 1989. Deng Xiaoping, who assumed leadership in 1978, introduced a policy of economic liberalization, but allowed little in the way of corresponding liberalization in the political system. However, as was the case elsewhere in the communist world, there were growing calls for reform and more democracy.

The death in 1989 of Hu Yaobang, dismissed as General Secretary of the Communist Party in 1987 for going too far with reforms and for failing to control student protests, led to an even greater wave of dissatisfaction. The first document is an open declaration dated 16 May 1989 and signed by numerous Chinese intellectuals in support of the students and their call for more democracy. The 'May Sixteenth Directive' of 1966 referred to in the first line was something that launched the Cultural Revolution.

The second document is an extract from the report by Chen Xitong, Mayor of Beijing, to the National People's Congress on 'quelling the counter-revolutionary rebellion'. Zhao Ziyang had replaced Hu Yaobang in 1987, and took much of the blame for the crises, and was himself dismissed from office.

The May Sixteenth Declaration

The 'May Sixteenth Directive' of 1966 is universally acknowledged by the Chinese people as a symbol of autocracy and darkness. Today, twenty-three years later, we find democracy and enlightenment strongly appealing. History has finally reached a turning point. At present, a patriotic democracy movement led by young students is rising across the country. Over the short period of less than a month, in one wave after another, larger-scale demonstrations have swept through Beijing and other cities. Several hundred thousand students have taken to the streets protesting corruption and calling for democracy and the rule of law. They have expressed the common will of workers, peasants, soldiers, cadres, intellectuals, and all other classes of working people. This is a national awakening which not only draws on the spirit of May

Fourth, but also goes beyond it. It is a great historical moment that will determine the fate of China.

Since the Third Plenum of the Eleventh Party Congress, China has embarked on a course of national revitalization. But there are problems. The weakness of political reform has affected the economic reform, when the latter has only begun to show results. The problem of corruption is getting worse and the social contradictions are intensified. The reforms in which the people put so much hope face a grave crisis. At this crucial moment, a moment which will determine the fate of the people, the country, and the ruling party, we, the undersigned Chinese intellectuals at home and abroad, on May 16, 1989, do solemnly and openly declare allegiance to the following principles:

1 We believe that in dealing with the current student movement the party and the government have not been rational enough. This is especially clear in the recent use of pressure tactics and threats of force against the students. We should draw a lesson from history. The Beijing government in 1919, the Guomindang [Kuomintang] government in the 1930s and 1940s, the Gang of Four in the late 1970s all these dictatorial regimes used force against student movements and in each case it led to their disgrace in the eyes of history. History tells us, 'Whoever would crush the student movement is doomed.' Recently the party and the government have shown a welcome increase in the use of reason, and the tension has been alleviated somewhat. If we apply principles of modern democratic governance, respect the people's will and respond to changing times, then we will see a democratic and stable China. If we do not, then a very hopeful China will be pushed into an abyss of genuine turmoil.

2 If we want to solve the current political crisis democratically, the first step must be to recognize the legality of the autonomous student organization which consists of the democratically elected representatives of the students. Not to do so is to violate the constitutional right of freedom of assembly. To label the student organization as 'illegal' can only lead to intensification of conflict and further crisis.

3 The immediate cause of the current political crisis is the corruption these young students have rightly opposed with their patriotic movement. The greatest mistake of the past ten years of reform is not the failure of education but the neglect of political reform. Totally untouched, the 'official standard' and feudal privileges have infected the world of exchange, and that has led to rampant corruption. This has not only devoured the fruits of economic reform but also shaken the people's faith in the party and the government. The party and the government should take this lesson to heart and, in accordance with the people's will, immediately advance the political reform, abolish official privilege and profiteering and guarantee that corruption will be eliminated.

368

4 During the student movement, the press, represented by the *People's Daily* and the New China News Agency, have concealed the truth, depriving the people of their right to know. The Shanghai Party Committee dismissed Qin Benli from his position as editor-in-chief of the *World Economic Herald*. These totally wrong measures are greatly contemptuous of the Constitution. Freedom of the press is an effective tool for eliminating corruption, maintaining national stability, and promoting social development. Absolute power corrupts absolutely. If we do not implement freedom of the press, and do not allow unofficial publications, then all the promises of openness and reform are nothing but empty words.

5 It is a mistake to call the student movement antiparty, antisocialist political turmoil. To recognize and protect the right of citizens to express different political opinions is the basic meaning of freedom of speech. Since liberation the true purpose of all the political campaigns has been to suppress and attack different political opinions. A society with only one voice is not a stable society. The party and the government must review the lessons of the 'Anti-Hu Feng campaign', the 'Anti-Rightist campaign', the 'Cultural Revolution', the 'Anti-spiritual pollution campaign', and the 'Anti-bourgeois liberalization campaign'. They must allow a broad expression of opinions and engage in discussion with the young students, intellectuals, and the whole people about state policy. Only then will it be possible for a genuinely stable and unified political system to take shape.

6 It is a mistake to say that there is a 'small handful of long-bearded manipulators' behind the scenes. All the citizens of the People's Republic of China, regardless of their ages, are politically equal. All have the political right to participate in discussion about government. Freedom, democracy, and the rule of law are not things that will some day simply be granted to the people from above. All truth-seeking, freedom-loving people must strive to achieve what the constitution promises: freedom of thought, freedom of speech, freedom of the press, freedom of publication, freedom of association, freedom of assembly, and freedom of demonstration.

We have arrived at a historical turning point. We, the long-suffering people, cannot afford to miss this opportunity. There is no place to retreat to.

All patriotic and concerned Chinese intellectuals should realize their inescapable historical mission, step forward to advance the cause of democracy, and strive for a politically democratic, economically developed modern China.

Long live the people!

Long live a free, democratic socialist motherland!

Signed at Beijing
May 16, 1989

Liu Zaifu, Yan Jiaqi, Bao Zunxin, Fan Zeng, Su Shaozhi, Su Xiaokang, Xu Gang, Su Wei, Su Shunkang, Li Tuo, Lao Mu, Lao Gui, Ke Zhilu, Wang Luxiang, Feng Lisan, Chen Lizu, Xu Xing, Wang Runsheng, Gao Gao, Xie Xuanjun, Xia Jun, Shen Dade, Wu Tingjia, Yuan Zhiming, He Huaihong, Zhang Boquan, Chen Xuanliang, Wang Zhaojun, Zhao Yu, Cheng Yi, Liu Ying, Han Hong, Deng Zhenglai, Yazi, He Shaofa, Zhu Shaoping [...]

Report to the National People's Congress on quelling the counter-revolutionary rebellion

Chairman, vice-chairmen, and members of the Standing Committee,

During late spring and early summer, namely, from mid-April to early June of 1989, a tiny handful of people exploited student unrest to launch a planned, organized and premeditated political turmoil, which later developed into a counter-revolutionary rebellion in Beijing, the capital. Their purpose was to overthrow the leadership of the Chinese Communist Party and subvert the socialist People's Republic of China. The out-break and development of the turmoil and the counter-revolutionary rebellion had a profound international background and a social basis at home. As Comrade Deng Xiaoping put it, 'This storm was bound to happen sooner or later. As determined by the international and domestic climate, it was bound to happen and was independent of man's will'. In this struggle involving the life and death of the party and the state, Comrade Zhao Ziyang committed the serious mistake of supporting the turmoil and splitting the party, and had the unshirkable responsibility for the shaping up and development of the turmoil. In face of this very severe situation, the party Central Committee made correct decisions and took a series of resolute measures, winning the firm support of the whole party and people of all nationalities in the country. Represented by Comrade Deng Xiaoping, proletarian revolutionaries of the older generation played a very important role in winning the struggle. The Chinese People's Liberation Army, the armed police and the police made great contributions in checking the turmoil and quelling the counter-revolutionary rebellion. The vast numbers of workers, peasants and intellectuals firmly opposed the turmoil and the rebellion, rallied closely around the party Central Committee and displayed a very high political consciousness and the sense of responsibility as masters of the country. Now, entrusted by the State Council, I am making a report to the Standing Committee of the National People's Council on the turmoil and the counter-revolutionary rebellion, mainly the happenings in Beijing, and the work of checking the turmoil and quelling the counter-revolutionary rebellion.

[...]

Source: Oksenberg, M. *et al.* (eds) (1990) *Beijing Spring, 1989: Confrontation and Conflict*, Armonk NY, M.E. Sharpe.

2.5   The Pacific Islands

This final section looks at experiences of some Pacific Islands, from imperialism in the nineteenth century to trusteeship following the Pacific War. More recent expressions of self-governing and independent island states are found in the final document from the South Pacific Forum organization. (See also the Pacific Island sections in Part 2.)

continued to be a source of tension to the present day. The Waitangi Tribunal was set up in 1976 to consider disputes relating to the Treaty and there have been a number of Maori successes. Two versions of the Treaty are reproduced here, the original English text and a modern English translation of the original Maori text by Professor Sir Hugh Kawharu. His notes to the translation give a good indication of the problem.

The Treaty of Waitangi, 1840

The 1840 Treaty of Waitangi between the British Crown and the Maori Chiefs is regarded as the founding document of the New Zealand nation. It was intended to determine the relationship between the increasing number of British settlers and the Maoris. Though some Chiefs refused to sign the Treaty, British Sovereignty was proclaimed over all of New Zealand later the same year. However, the two parties came to the Treaty with very different conceptions, some of which were embedded in the two different versions – an English text and a Maori text. The resulting differences of interpretation have

English text of the Treaty of Waitangi

Her Majesty Victoria Queen of the United Kingdom of Great Britain and Ireland regarding with Her Royal Favour the Native Chiefs and Tribes of New Zealand and anxious to protect their just Rights and Property and to secure to them the enjoyment of Peace and Good Order has deemed it necessary in consequence of the great number of Her Majesty's Subjects who have already settled in New Zealand and the rapid extension of Emigration both from Europe and Australia which is still in progress to constitute and appoint a functionary properly authorized to treat with

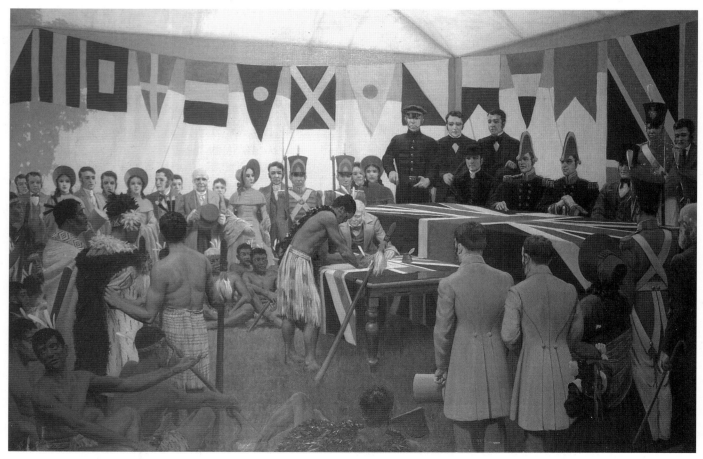

Marcus King, The Signing of the Treaty of Waitangi, February 6th, 1840, *1938, oil on canvas, 120.5 × 181 cm.*
Alexander Turnbull Library, Wellington, New Zealand

the Aborigines of New Zealand for the recognition of Her Majesty's Sovereign authority over the whole or any part of those islands.

Her Majesty therefore being desirous to establish a settled form of Civil Government with a view to avert the evil consequences which must result from the absence of the necessary Laws and Institutions alike to the native population and to Her subjects has been graciously pleased to empower and to authorize 'me William Hobson a Captain' in Her Majesty's Royal Navy Consul and Lieutenant Governor of such parts of New Zealand as may be or hereafter shall be ceded to Her Majesty to invite the confederated and independent Chiefs of New Zealand to concur in the following Articles and Conditions.

Article the first

The Chiefs of the Confederation of the United Tribes of New Zealand and the separate and independent Chiefs who have not become members of the Confederation cede to Her Majesty the Queen of England absolutely and without reservation all the rights and powers of Sovereignty which the said Confederation or Individual Chiefs respectively exercise or posses, or may be supposed to exercise or to possess, over their respective Territories as the sole Sovereigns thereof.

Article the second

Her Majesty the Queen of England confirms and guarantees to the Chiefs and Tribes of New Zealand and to the respective families and individuals thereof the full exclusive and undisturbed possession of their Lands and Estates Forests Fisheries and other properties which they may collectively or individually possess so long as it is their wish and desire to retain the same in their possession; but the Chiefs of the United Tribes and the individual Chiefs yield to Her Majesty the exclusive right of Preemption over such lands as the proprietors thereof may be disposed to alienate at such prices as may be agreed upon between the respective Proprietors and persons appointed by Her Majesty to treat with them in that behalf.

Article the third

In consideration thereof Her Majesty the Queen of England extends to the Natives of New Zealand Her royal protection and imparts to them all the Rights and Privileges of British Subjects.

[signed] W. Hobson Lieutenant Governor

Now therefore We the Chiefs of the Confederation of the United Tribes of New Zealand being assembled in Congress at Victoria in Waitangi and We the Separate and Independent Chiefs of New Zealand claiming authority over the Tribes and Territories which are specified after our respective names, having been made fully to

understand the Provisions of the foregoing Treaty, accept and enter into the same in the full spirit and meaning thereof in witness of which we have attached our signatures or marks at the places and the dates respectively specified.

Done at Waitangi this Sixth day of February in the year of Our Lord one thousand eight hundred and forty.

Translation of the Maori text of the Treaty of Waitangi

Victoria, the Queen of England, in her concern to protect the chiefs and the subtribes of New Zealand and in her desire to preserve their chieftainship[1] and their lands to them and to maintain peace[2] and good order considers it just to appoint an administrator[3] one who will negotiate with the people of New Zealand to the end that their chiefs will agree to the Queen's Government being established over all parts of this land and (adjoining) islands[4] and also because there are many of her subjects already living on this land and others yet to come. So the Queen desires to establish a government so that no evil will come to Maori and European living in a state of lawlessness. So the Queen has appointed 'me, William Hobson a Captain' in the Royal Navy to be Governor for all parts of New Zealand (both those) shortly to be received by the Queen and (those) to be received hereafter and presents[5] to the chiefs of the Confederation chiefs of the subtribes of New Zealand and other chiefs these laws set out here.

The first

The Chiefs of the Confederation and all the Chiefs who have not joined that Confederation give absolutely to the Queen of England for ever the complete government[6] over their land.

The second

The Queen of England agrees to protect the chiefs, the subtribes and all the people of New Zealand in the unqualified exercise[7] of their chieftainship over their lands, villages and all their treasures[8]. But on the other hand the Chiefs of Confederation and all the Chiefs will sell[9] land to the Queen at a price agreed to by the person owning it and by the person buying it (the latter being) appointed by the Queen as her purchase agent.

The third

For this agreed arrangement therefore concerning the Government of the Queen, the Queen of England will protect all the ordinary people of New Zealand and will give them the same rights and duties[10] of citizenship as the people of England[11].

[signed] William Hobson Consul and Lieut. Governor

So we, the Chiefs of the Confederation of the subtribes of New Zealand meeting here at Waitangi having seen the shape of these words which we accept and agree to record our names and our marks thus.

Was done at Waitangi on the sixth of February in the year of our Lord 1840.

Notes

[1] 'Chieftainship': this concept has to be understood in the context of Maori social and political organization as at 1840. The accepted approximation today is 'trusteeship'.

[2] 'Peace': Maori 'Rongo', seemingly a missionary usage (rongo – to hear, i.e. hear the 'Word' – the 'message' of peace and goodwill, etc.).

[3] Literally 'Chief' ('Rangatira') here is of course ambiguous. Clearly a European could not be a Maori, but the word could well have implied a trustee-like role rather than that of a mere 'functionary'. Maori speeches at Waitangi in 1840 refer to Hobson being or becoming a 'father' for the Maori people. Certainly this attitude has been held towards the person of the Crown down to the present day – hence the continued expectations and commitments entailed in the Treaty.

[4] 'Islands', i.e. coastal, not of the Pacific.

[5] Literally 'making', i.e. 'offering' or 'saying' – but not 'inviting to concur'.

[6] 'Government': 'kawanatanga'. There could be no possibility of the Maori signatories having any understanding of government in the sense of 'sovereignty', i.e. any understanding on the basis of experience or cultural precedent.

[7] 'Unqualified exercise' of the chieftainship – would emphasize to a chief the Queen's intention to give them complete control according to *their* customs. 'Tino' has the connotation of 'quintessential'.

A facsimile of the Maori text of the Treaty of Waitangi

A reflection on the signing of the Treaty of Waitangi from the 1980s

Source: *National Business Review* (February 1982)

8 'Treasures': 'taonga'. As submissions to the Waitangi Tribunal concerning the Maori language have made clear, 'taonga' refers to all dimensions of a tribal group's estate, material and non-material – heirlooms and wahi tapu (sacred places), ancestral lore and whakapapa (genealogies), etc.

9 Maori 'hokonga', literally 'sale and purchase'. Hoko means to buy or sell.

10 'Rights and duties': Maori 'tikanga'. While tika means right, correct (e.g. 'e tika hoke' means 'that is right'), 'tikanga' most commonly refers to custom(s), for example of the marae (ritual forum); and custom(s) clearly includes the notion of duty and obligation.

11 There is, however, a more profound problem about 'tikanga'. There is a real sense here of the Queen 'protecting' (i.e. allowing the preservation of) the Maori people's tikanga (i.e. customs) since no Maori could have had any understanding whatever of *British* tikanga (i.e. rights and duties of British subjects). This, then, reinforces the guarantees in Article 2.

Source: New Zealand Government Online, Wellington, IT Services, Department of Internal Affairs. Available from: http://www.govt.nz

A case for annexation of Hawaii, 1892

American missionaries first arrived in the Hawaiian Islands in 1820 and were soon followed by settlers. By 1840 there was pressure to produce a Western-style constitution for the Kingdom of Hawaii. Increasing American involvement and influence resulted in two treaties with Hawaii in 1875 and 1887. The first treaty was of considerable benefit to the growing US sugar interests on the islands, while the second allowed for the establishment of the US naval base at Pearl Harbor. In 1892 John L. Stevens, the US Minister in the islands, wrote to US Secretary of State John W. Foster arguing for outright US annexation of the Hawaiian Islands. An extract is reproduced below. Later the same year a coup involving US sugar interests overthrew the Hawaiian monarchy and established a republic. The new republic agreed to annexation in 1898. Hawaii was a US territory from 1900 until 1959 when it became the fiftieth state of the USA.

[...] One of two courses seems to me absolutely necessary to be followed, either bold and vigorous measures for annexation or a 'customs union', an ocean cable from the Californian coast to Honolulu, Pearl Harbor perpetually ceded to the United States, with an implied but not necessarily stipulated American protectorate over the islands. I believe the former to be the better, that which will prove much the more advantageous to the islands, and the cheapest and least embarrassing in the end for the United States. If it was wise for the United States, through Secretary Marcy, thirty-eight years ago, to offer to expend $100,000 to secure a treaty of annexation, it certainly can not be chimerical or unwise to expend $100,000 to secure annexation in the near future. To-day the United States has five times the wealth she possessed in 1854, and the reasons now existing for annexation are much stronger than they were then. I can not refrain from expressing the opinion with emphasis that the golden hour is near at hand. A perpetual customers union and the acquisition of Pearl Harbor, with an implied protectorate, must be regarded as the only allowable alternative. This would require the continual presence in the harbor of Honolulu of a United States vessel of war and the constant watchfulness of the United States minister while the present bungling, unsettled, and expensive political rule would go on, retarding the development of the islands, leaving at the end of twenty-five years more embarrassment to annexation than exists to-day, the property far less valuable, and the population less American than they would be if annexation were soon realized.

It may be said that annexation would involve the obligation of paying to the Hawaiian sugar-producers the same rate of bounties now paid to American producers, thus imposing too heavy a demand on the United States Treasury. It is a sufficient answer to this objection to say that it could be specifically provided in the terms of annexation that the United States Government should pay 6 mills per pound – $12 per ton – to the Hawaiian sugar-raisers, and this only so long as the present sugar-bounty system of the United States shall be maintained. Careful inquiry and investigation bring me to the conclusion that this small bounty would tide the Hawaiian sugar-planters over their present alarming condition and save the islands from general business depression and financial disaster. Could justice to American interests in the islands and care for their future welfare do less than this?

To give Hawaii a highly favorable treaty while she remains outside the American Union would necessarily give the same advantages to hostile foreigners, those who would continue to antagonize our commercial and political interests here, as well as those of American blood and sympathies. It is a well authenticated fact that the American sentiment here in 1890, the last year of the great prosperity under the sugar provisions of the reciprocity treaty, was much less manifest than before that treaty had gone into effect, and less pronounced than when Secretary Marcy authorized the negotiation of the annexation treaty in 1854. It is equally true that the desire here at this time for annexation is much stronger than in 1889. Besides, so long as the islands retain their own independent government there remains the possibility that England or the Canadian Dominion might secure one of the Hawaiian harbors for a coaling station. Annexation excludes all dangers of this kind.

Which of the two lines of policy and action shall be adopted our statesmen and our Government must decide. Certain it is that the interests of the United States and the welfare of these islands will not permit the continuance of the existing state and tendency of things. Having for so many years extended a helping hand to the islands and encouraged the American residents and their friends at home to the extent we have, we can not refrain now from aiding them with vigorous measures, without injury to ourselves and those of our 'kith and kin' and without neglecting American opportunities that never seemed so obvious and pressing as they do now. I have no doubt that the more thoroughly the bed rock and controlling facts touching the Hawaiian problem are understood by our Government and by the American public, the more readily they will be inclined to approve the views I have expressed so inadequately in this communication. [...]

Source: Ferrell, R.H. (ed.) (1971) *America as a World Power 1872–1945*, Columbia SC, University of South Carolina Press.

UN resolutions on Micronesia, 1947–91

The Allies victory in the Second World War left the USA in possession of numerous additional Pacific Islands previously controlled by Japan. The islands of Micronesia, over 2,000 of them, had been taken at some considerable cost, and while the USA was reluctant to annex them, it did not want to give them up. The solution was trusteeship. The first document reproduced below is United Nations Security Council Resolution 21, passed on 2 April 1947, making the USA the administrating authority for the islands. The USA conducted nuclear testing in the area from 1946 to 1963 (see Figure 24).

Negotiations towards ending the trusteeship began in 1969. A number of separate island groupings emerged in the transition to independence; the Federated States of Micronesia, the Marshall Islands and the Northern Mariana Islands. Autonomy was negotiated by 1979 and independence in 1986. The second resolution reproduced (Resolution 683), passed in 1990, recognizes their new status and formally terminates the trusteeship. The people of Palau, referred to in the resolution, gained independence in 1994. Also reproduced is the 1991 Resolution 703, admitting the Federated States of Micronesia to the UN as an independent member. Similar resolutions were also passed for the other new nations to emerge from the trusteeship.

Security Council Resolution 21 (1947)

Whereas Article 75 of the Charter of the United Nations provides for the establishment of an international trusteeship system for the administration and supervision of such territories as may be placed thereunder by subsequent agreements; and

Whereas under Article 77 of the said Charter the trusteeship system may be applied to territories now held under mandate; and

Whereas on 17 December 1920 the Council of the League of Nations confirmed a mandate for the former German islands north of the equator to Japan, to be administered in accordance with Article 22 of the Covenant of the League of Nations; and

Whereas Japan, as a result of the Second World War, has ceased to exercise any authority in these islands;

Now, therefore, the Security Council of the United Nations, having satisfied itself that the relevant articles of the Charter have been complied with, hereby resolves to approve the following terms of trusteeship for the Pacific Islands formerly under mandate to Japan.

Article 1

The Territory of the Pacific Islands, consisting of the islands formerly held by Japan under mandate in accordance with Article 22 of the Covenant of the League of Nations, is hereby designated as a strategic area and placed under the trusteeship system established in the Charter of the United Nations. The territory of the Pacific Islands is hereinafter referred to as the trust territory.

Article 2

The United States of America is designated as the administering authority of the trust territory.

Article 3

The administering authority shall have full powers of administration, legislation, and jurisdiction over the territory subject to the provisions of this agreement, and may apply to the trust territory, subject to the any modifications which the administering authority may consider desirable, such of the laws of the United States as it may deem appropriate to local conditions and requirements. [...]

Article 5

In discharging its obligations under Article 76 (a) and Article 84, of the Charter, the administering authority shall ensure that the trust territory shall play its part, in accordance with the Charter of the United Nations, in the maintenance of international peace and security. To this end the administering authority shall be entitled:

1 to establish naval, military and air bases and to erect fortifications in the trust territory;

2 to station and employ armed forces in the territory; and

3 to make use of volunteer forces, facilities and assistance from the trust territory in carrying out the obligations towards the Security Council undertaken in this regard by the administering authority, as well as for the local defense and the maintenance of law and order within the trust territory.

Article 6

In discharging its obligations under Article 76 (b) of the Charter, the administering authority shall:

1 Foster the development of such political institutions as are suited to the trust territory and shall promote the development of the inhabitants of the trust territory toward self-government or independence as may be appropriate to the particular circumstances of the trust territory and its peoples and the freely expressed wishes of the peoples concerned; and to this end shall give to the inhabitants of the trust territory a progressively increasing share in the administrative services in the territory; shall develop their participation in government; shall give due recognition to the customs of the inhabitants in providing a system of law for the territory; and shall take other appropriate measures toward these ends;

2 Promote the economic advancement and self-sufficiency of the inhabitants, and to this end shall regulate the use of natural resources; encourage the development of fisheries, agriculture, and industries; protect the inhabitants against the loss of their lands and resources; and improve the means of transportation and communication;

3 Promote the social advancement of the inhabitants and to this end shall protect the rights and fundamental freedoms of all elements of the population without discrimination; protect the health of the inhabitants; control the traffic in arms and ammunition, opium and other dangerous drugs, and alcohol and other spirituous beverages; and institute such other regulations as may be necessary to protect the inhabitants against social abuses; and

4 Promote the educational advancement of the inhabitants, and to this end shall take steps toward the establishment of a general system of elementary education; facilitate the vocational and cultural advancement of the population; and shall encourage qualified students to pursue higher education, including training on the professional level. [...]

Article 8

[...]

3. Nothing in this Article shall be so construed as to accord traffic rights to aircraft flying into and out of the trust territory. Such rights shall be subject to agreement between the administering authority and the state whose nationality such aircraft possesses. [...]

Article 13

The provisions of Articles 87 and 88 of the Charter shall be applicable to the trust territory, provided that the administering authority may determine the extent of their applicability to any areas which may from time to time be specified by it as closed for security reasons. [...]

Article 15

The terms of the present agreement shall not be altered, amended or terminated without the consent of the administering authority.

Security Council Resolution 683 (1990)

The Security Council,

Recalling Chapter XII of the Charter of the United Nations which established an international trusteeship system,

Conscious of its responsibility relating to strategic areas as set forth in Article 83, paragraph 1, of the Charter of the United Nations,

Recalling its resolution 21 (1947) of 2 April 1947, in which it approved the Trusteeship Agreement for the former Japanese Mandated Islands, since known as the Trust Territory of the Pacific Islands,

Noting that the Trusteeship Agreement designated the United States of America as Administering Authority of the Trust Territory,

Mindful that Article 6 of the Trusteeship Agreement, in conformity with Article 76 of the Charter, obligated the Administering Authority, inter alia, to promote the development of the inhabitants of the Trust Territory towards self-government or independence as may be appropriate to the particular circumstances of the Trust Territory and its peoples and the freely expressed wishes of the peoples concerned,

Aware that, towards this end, negotiations between the Administering Authority and representatives of the Trust Territory began in 1969 and resulted in the conclusion of a Compact of Free Association in the case of the Federated States of Micronesia and the Marshall Islands, and a Commonwealth Covenant in the case of the Northern Mariana Islands,

Satisfied that the peoples of the Federated States of Micronesia, the Marshall Islands and the Northern Mariana Islands have freely exercised their right to self-determination in approving their respective new status agreements in plebiscites observed by visiting missions of the Trusteeship Council and that, in addition to these plebiscites, the duly constituted legislatures of these entities have adopted resolutions approving the respective new status agreements, thereby freely expressing their wish to terminate the status of these entities as parts of the Trust Territory,

Hoping that the people of Palau will be able in due course to complete the process of freely exercising their right to self-determination,

Taking note of resolution 2183 (LIII) of the Trusteeship Council of 28 May 1986 and subsequent reports of the Trusteeship Council to the Security Council,

Determines, in the light of the entry into force of the new status agreements for the Federated States of Micronesia, the Marshall Islands and the Northern Mariana Islands, that the objectives of the Trusteeship Agreement have been fully attained, and that the applicability of the Trusteeship Agreement has terminated, with respect to those entities.

Security Council Resolution 703 (1991)

The Security Council,

Having examined the application of the Federated States of Micronesia for admission to the United Nations (S/22896),

Recommends to the General Assembly that the Federated States of Micronesia be admitted to membership in the United Nations.

Source: 1947 Resolution: Ferrell, R.H. (ed.) (1975) *America in a Divided World 1945–1972*, Columbia SC, University of South Carolina Press; others: UN Net Site, New York, UN Department of Public Information. Available from: http://www.un.org

The South Pacific Forum, from 1971

The South Pacific Forum is a rather informal international organization founded in New Zealand in 1971 and now links Australia and New Zealand with fourteen small island states. The Forum's aim is to promote co-operation between its members over a wide range of issues. The document reproduced below is an introductory description from the organization's internet site, and includes information on some of its activities and achievements. The sixteen participating states are listed in the document. The South Pacific Nuclear Free Zone Treaty, known as the Treaty of Rarotonga, which emerged from the Forum in 1985, was not recognized by France which has conducted several series of tests on Mururoa in French Polynesia since 1966. The 1995/96 series of tests were conducted in the face of considerable regional opposition.

The South Pacific Forum is the political grouping of independent and self-governing states in the South Pacific. Its secretariat, known as the South Pacific Forum Secretariat, has its headquarters in Suva, the capital of Fiji. Its sphere of political influence covers some 30 million square kilometres, stretching from the Republic of the

A meeting of the South Pacific Forum

Marshall Islands north of the equator and to New Zealand in the south.

The South Pacific Forum began with a meeting in Wellington, New Zealand in 1971 when its seven founding members Australia, the Cook Islands, Fiji, Nauru, New Zealand, Tongo and Western Samoa – met for the first time.

These member countries have since been joined by Niue, Papua New Guinea, Kiribati, Solomon Islands, Tuvalu, Federated States of Micronesia, the Republic of the Marshall Islands and Vanuatu [and Palau].

This grouping stemmed from a common desire by leaders to develop a collective response on a wide range of regional issues including trade, economic development, civil aviation and maritime, telecommunications, energy and political and security matters. In recent years, environmental issues have featured strongly in the annual summit of the Heads of Government.

Membership

Forum membership is open to only fully independent or self-governing (Pacific Island) countries (plus Australia and New Zealand), and the current membership stands at 15 [increased to 16 with Palau].

The Forum, chaired on a rotating basis by the Head of the host Government, is unique. Unlike similar international or regional organizations, there are no set rules governing the conduct of the Forum sessions – consensus and informality are the order of the day. No votes are taken on any issues even if there are disagreements. This unique feature rules out the possibility of leaders making conflicting statements on the Forum's stand on issues of common interests and concerns to the region. This, however, does not prevent Prime Ministers expressing views on matters outside the Forum consensus.

The South Pacific Forum has recorded some outstanding successes since its inception in 1971. The list below is by no means exhaustive, but gives an indication of achievement through regional co-operation.

Pacific Forum Line (PFL)

Ten member Governments of the South Pacific Forum took a significant step in 1977 in establishing this regional shipping venture as a means of providing adequate and reliable shipping services, thereby encouraging economic development in the region.

The PFL's main objective is to provide a viable shipping service to meet the special conditions of the region.

The PFL commenced trading in 1978 with three chartered conventional vessels. Now owned by 12 South Pacific Forum Governments, PFL operates three modern containerized vessels including two purpose-built roll-on, roll-off ships.

Forum Countries' Transport Ministers meet each year to discuss the broad objectives of the line while PFL's board of directors and management are responsible for policy and day-to-day operations.

Forum Fisheries Agency (FFA)

In 1979, the Forum Fisheries Agency (FFA) was established under a Convention signed by twelve Forum Members. The Convention reflects the common concern of member nations on matters of conservation, optimum use and coastal states' sovereign rights over the region's living marine resources.

FFA has its headquarters in Honiara, Solomon Islands. Its governing body is the Forum Fisheries Committee (FFC) which decides the FFA's annual budget and work programmes. The FFC also is responsible for the appointment of the FFA Director. After two years of negotiations, a multilateral Treaty on Fisheries with the United States was concluded and signed in Port Moresby, Papua New Guinea on 2 April 1987. This treaty was renewed in 1993.

The SPARTECA

Administered by the South Pacific Forum Secretariat through the Committee on Regional Economic Issues and Trade (CREIT), the South Pacific Regional Trade and Economic Co-operation Agreement aims, among other things, at enhancing the export capabilities of Forum Island Countries (FICs).

It guarantees duty-free and unrestricted access on a non-reciprocal basis for a wide range of FICs' products into the Australian and New Zealand markets.

SPARTECA was signed by Forum Heads of Governments at their 1980 summit in Tarawa, Kiribati.

Since it came into operation in 1981, exports from FICs to Australia and New Zealand have increased in several areas including timber and coconut products, canned fish and clothing – items which previously were subject to customs duty and/or import licensing.

The Treaty of Rarotonga

The South Pacific Nuclear Free Zone Treaty (SPNFZ), also known as the Treaty of Rarotonga is the manifestation of the South Pacific Forum's persistent stand against nuclear testing and the dumping of radioactive waste at sea within the region.

It represents firm support for the nuclear non-proliferation regime exemplified by the Non-Proliferation of Nuclear Weapons Treaty. The SPNFZ was adopted in the Cook Islands capital, Rarotonga (hence, the Treaty of Rarotonga) on 6 August 1985 and entered into force on 11 December 1986.

As of August 1993, eleven Forum members were party to the Treaty. The former USSR and the People's Republic of China have both signed and ratified Protocols 2 and 3 of the Treaty. Under Protocols 2 and 3, nuclear weapons states agree not to use or threaten to use nuclear explosive devices against any party to the Treaty, or territory in the

Rarotonga, Cook Islands, June 1995: a protest against French nuclear tests at Mururoa

zone for which a state party to Protocol 1 is responsible. They also undertake not to test nuclear explosive devices in the zone.

The USSR signed the Protocols on 15 December 1987 and ratified them on 21 April 1988. The People's Republic of China signed on 10 February 1987 and ratified them on 21 October 1988.

Assurances have been received from the United States and the United Kingdom that they are not acting inconsistently with the terms of the Treaty and its Protocols. [The USA, France and the UK signed the Protocols in March 1996.]

New Caledonia

Considerable attention has been devoted to the issue of decolonization in New Caledonia since it surfaced on the Forum's agenda in 1981. Two years later the 1983 Forum in Canberra called for a precise timetable for independence and asked the French Government to consider inviting a Forum Mission to New Caledonia to observe and assess progress towards decolonization.

Backed by the General Assembly of the United Nations, the Forum succeeded in the reinscription of New Caledonia on the UN List of Non-Self-Governing Territories in December 1986.

With the signing by the parties involved in New Caledonia of the Matignon and Oudinot Accords in 1988, which will lead to a referendum on independence in 1998, the South Pacific Forum has offered strong support for the process of economic and political development in the territory under the Accords. The Forum has established a Ministerial Committee to follow developments.

Source: South Pacific Forum Net Site, Suva, South Pacific Forum Secretariat. Available from: http://canl.cipac.nc/projhtml/forum.txt

Acknowledgements

Grateful acknowledgement is made to the following sources for permission to reproduce material in this book:

Text

Pages 334–7: courtesy of Amnesty International; Pages 351–2: Griffith, R. (1992) *Major Problems in American History Since 1945*, D.C. Heath and Company; Pages 359–60: Kau, M.Y.M. and Leung, J.K. (1986) *The Writings of Mao Zedong 1949–1976*, M.E. Sharpe, Inc.; Pages 360–4: Hinton, H.C. (1980) *The People's Republic of China 1949–1979*, Scholarly Resources, Inc.; Pages 368–9: Oskenberg, M., Sullivan, L.R. and Lambert, M. (1990) *Beijing Spring, 1989: Confrontation and Conflict – The Basic Documents*, M.E. Sharpe, Inc.

Figures

Figure 2: Winkleman, B. (1978) *Times Atlas of World History*, Times Books Ltd, by permission of HarperCollins Cartographic; Figure 4: Reproduced from *Oxford Atlas of Modern World History* (1989) by permission of Oxford University Press; Figure 5: Darby, H.C. and Fullard, H. (1970) *The New Cambridge Modern History Atlas*, Cambridge University Press, by permission of Reed Books; Figure 7: *World Book Encyclopaedia* (1992) 21, pp.397–400, World Book Publishing, a Scott Fetzer Company; Page 241: Miller, E. (1997) *Russian Far East Update*, VII(2), February 1997, Russian Far East Update.

Photographs

Cover: Hulton Getty; Page 305: Department of Foreign Affairs and Trade, Australia; Pages 310, 331, 353 and 365: Popperfoto; Page 316: Rex Features; Pages 341, 343 and 348: AP/Wide World Photos; Page 359: New China News Agency; Pages 370 and 373: Alexander Turnbull Library, Wellington, New Zealand; Page 372: The Department of Internal Affairs, National Archives/Te Whare Tohu Tuhituhinga O Aotearoa, New Zealand; Page 377: Eye Ubiquitous/Corbis; Page 378: © Greenpeace/Morgan.

Glossary

AFTA   ASEAN Free Trade Area; see Document, p.312

ANZAC   Australian and New Zealand Army Corps; an acronym also used for alliances between the countries

ANZUS   Australia, New Zealand and the United States; see Document, p.346

APEC   Asia-Pacific Economic Co-operation; see Documents, pp.303 and 309

ARF   ASEAN Regional Forum; see Document, p.320

ASEAN   Association of South-East Asian Nations; see Document, p.311

ASEM   Asia–Europe Meeting; see Document, p.330

CSCAP   Council for Security Co-operation in the Asia Pacific; see Document, p.321

FDI   foreign direct investment; defined on Figure 14, p.15

FSM   Federated States of Micronesia

GATT   General Agreement on Tariffs and Trade; precursor of the WTO, see Document, p.328

IMF   International Monetary Fund; see World Bank Group Document, p.329

NAFTA   North American Free Trade Agreement; see Document, p.315

NATO   North Atlantic Treaty Organization

NIC   newly-industrialized country

OAS   Organization of American States; see Document, p.317

OECD   Organization for Economic Co-operation and Development

OPEC   Organization of Petroleum-Exporting Countries

PECC   Pacific Economic Co-operation Council; see Document, p.318

PNG   Papua New Guinea

PRC   People's Republic of China

SAR   Special Administrative Region; handover status for Hong Kong and Macau, see Part 2 digest entries, pp.106 and 246

SEATO   South-East Asia Treaty Organization; see Document, p.348

SLORC   State Law and Order Restoration Council; official name for the military government of Burma/Myanmar, see Part 2 digest entry, p.40

SPF   South Pacific Forum; see Pacific Islands digest entry, p.248, and Document, p.376

WTO   World Trade Organization; see Document, p.328